Sustainable Prosperity in the Arab Gulf

Tracing the development journey of the Arabian Gulf region with a forward-looking perspective, this book describes how a combination of good fortune, creative experimentation, and determination has enabled the region to achieve prosperity. Today, the Arabian Gulf is well positioned to assume a pivotal role in the new global order.

Forced to balance an extreme climate and acute resource constraints, but also an exceptional location, the region's progress and prosperity have historically been precarious and vulnerable to external shocks. Efforts to transcend resource dependency have typically involved proactive attempts to enable other economic activities. This book argues that, while conventional economic diversification is making headway, the Gulf region is in fact amidst a far more holistic transformation that positions it for a pivotal role in the emerging multipolar global order. It now offers globally competitive regulations and world-class infrastructure at the heart of the Old World, flanked by two fast-growing continents. It has become the hub of choice for a growing share of inter-continental flows of people, trade, and capital, and has established strong economic ties in all directions. This book shows how, despite many risks and challenges, the region possesses the forward-looking vision and necessary resilience that can finally liberate it from its long-standing "resource curse" and a development paradigm that looks likely to provide the foundation for sustained well-being in the decades ahead.

The scope and rigor of the book make it suitable as a reference on the Arabian Gulf and for those interested in global affairs and economic development, as well as policymakers and the business community.

Jarmo T. Kotilaine has held several positions in the financial services sector and at government-related entities in the Gulf region and previously worked as an economic and financial consultant with a focus on financial sector development in emerging markets. He currently works at a fund supporting economic diversification in Bahrain. Dr Kotilaine studied economics and economic history at Oxford, Cambridge, and Harvard and has written widely in the regional media on economic financial market issues.

"A journey through history explained under the lens of sustainable prosperity, economic diversification and the evolution within the marketplace. Jarmo's storytelling takes you through the journey as an active listener. The storyline brings back fond memories and is quite nostalgic for the readers who have experienced and worked through the transitions within the regional marketplace over the past decades. The transition across the region has been quite exceptional, and the fact that the modern day GCC today holds the potential to be one of the fastest growing regions and to emerge as a powerhouse for influence is expertly expressed through Dr. Jarmo's wordsmithing."

Jamal Fakhro, *Managing Partner, KPMG Fakhro*

"When Jarmo speaks (or writes), I pay attention. I find his thoughts, analysis, and conclusions insightful and thought-provoking. I highly recommend this book for anyone who wants a better understanding of our region's past and wants to help build a better tomorrow for its future generations."

Suhail Algosaibi, *Founder and CEO, Falak Innovation*

"Dr Kotilaine has produced a compelling narrative of the economic history of the Arab Gulf from the earliest times to the 21st Century, including the extraordinary rags-to-riches story of the hydrocarbons era and describes with great clarity both the challenges and the potential opportunities that face these now-wealthy, but still largely hydrocarbon-dependent, states as they prepare for the post-oil age. This is a book that will fascinate the general reader, while also providing vital historical and cultural context to anyone who (like me) needs to understand the complex economic challenges that this region now faces."

Lord Philip Hammond of Runnymede

"Dr Kotilaine is considered a leading expert on the Gulf economies. His intimate knowledge of, not only economic issues, but also the underlying sociopolitical landscape and culture, make him uniquely qualified to shed the light on key aspects of the post oil transition. Recommended reading."

Hassan Jarrar, *Former CEO, Bahrain Islamic Bank*

"This work demonstrates how ongoing efforts to transform the economic models of the Gulf countries at the same time position them for a role of growing importance in the global economy. Among other things, the Gulf economies face a compelling opportunity to play a leading role in the global energy transition."

Abdulhussain Ali Mirza, *Former Minister of Electricity and Water Affairs, Former President, Sustainable Energy Authority, Kingdom of Bahrain*

"Jarmo Kotilaine's new book presents a lucid, coherent analysis and history of the transformation of the GCC countries from near empty, desert spaces into modern powerhouses of energy and finance. This is a fascinating story of energy resources being invested into productive infrastructure, of economic liberalisation through free zones, of freedom of movement of people and capital that transformed the economic geography of the Gulf. The GCC are now embarked on economic diversification 2.0, engaged in an energy transition to reduce their dependence on fossil fuels, develop their digital economies and move into higher value-added industries using modern tech."

Nasser Saidi, *President, Nasser Saidi & Associates*

"The Gulf countries are important actors in geopolitics and geo-economics thanks to their energy resources. This book will help readers, whatever their views on the local regimes, understand the history of the gulf economies and how they are preparing for a world less dependent on fossil fuels. Given fractures in the world order, an important read."

Sir Paul Tucker, *Author of* Global Discord

"Dr. Jarmo has a long experience in the region's economic affairs. The importance of this new book stems from its handling of a number of vital issues related to the future of sustainable development programs that Gulf governments are working to implement in accordance with their wise long-term visions, and then he seeks to develop solutions to them."

Adnan Ahmed Yousif, *Chairman, Bahrain Association of Banks*

Sustainable Prosperity in the Arab Gulf

From Miracle to Method

JARMO T. KOTILAINE

Routledge
Taylor & Francis Group
LONDON AND NEW YORK

Designed cover image: Getty Images/FrankRamspott

First published 2024
by Routledge
4 Park Square, Milton Park, Abingdon, Oxon OX14 4RN

and by Routledge
605 Third Avenue, New York, NY 10158

Routledge is an imprint of the Taylor & Francis Group, an informa business

British Library Cataloguing-in-Publication Data
A catalogue record for this book is available from the British Library

Library of Congress Cataloging-in-Publication Data
Names: Kotilaine, Jarmo, author.
Title: Sustainable prosperity in the Arab Gulf : from miracle to method / Jarmo T. Kotilaine.
Description: Abingdon, Oxon ; New York, NY : Routledge, 2023. | Includes bibliographical references and index.
Identifiers: LCCN 2023008075 (print) | LCCN 2023008076 (ebook) | ISBN 9781032437545 (hardback) | ISBN 9781032446783 (paperback) | ISBN 9781003373353 (ebook)
Subjects: LCSH: Persian Gulf Region—Economic conditions. | Persian Gulf Region—Economic policy.
Classification: LCC HC415.3 .K685 2023 (print) | LCC HC415.3 (ebook) | DDC 330.9536—dc23/eng/20230508
LC record available at https://lccn.loc.gov/2023008075
LC ebook record available at https://lccn.loc.gov/2023008076

ISBN: 978-1-032-43754-5 (hbk)
ISBN: 978-1-032-44678-3 (pbk)
ISBN: 978-1-003-37335-3 (ebk)

DOI: 10.4324/9781003373353

Typeset in Sabon
by Apex CoVantage, LLC

Contents

Preface

The Arabian Peninsula is a land of many paradoxes. It is an exceptionally strategically located landmass at the heart of the Old World but one characterized by some of the harshest climatic realities found anywhere on the planet. History dealt it an exceptionally poor hand for achieving prosperity. For millennia, a tiny population of Gulf Arabs was left to eke out a meager subsistence from rare patches of arable land, the surrounding seas, and the trade relations with other countries. Openness was critical for overcoming the extreme limitations of the local resource base. But it did not suffice to transcend the almost Hobbesian existence where, for the most part, life was, if not always "solitary, nasty" or "brutish," then all too often "short."[1]

Yet within a remarkably short period of time, an extraordinary economic miracle rose from the Arabian sands. By the 19th century, the region was discovered by the architects of the British empire, who recognized it as a strategic antechamber of their Indian possessions. Technological innovations such as the steam engine began to push up trade volumes and refashion travel. The first real opportunity to escape from almost universal penury was provided by the growing global popularity of Gulf pearls by the late 19th century. But the 20th century still dawned on a region on the periphery of the global economic order with minimal physical and social infrastructure. While much of the population on the Gulf coast were engaged in pearling, few could achieve more than a subsistence living in a business that was largely controlled by Indian merchants. Even this promising economic takeoff ultimately succumbed to the dual blows of the Great Depression and the rise of the much less costly cultured pearls in Japan.

Oil became the ultimate deus ex machina at this hour of need. The first regional find in Bahrain in 1932 was followed by the steady expansion of the industry into much of the Gulf littoral. A virtually unprecedented economic transformation by global standards swept across the peninsula during the ensuing decades. Today, Arabia is part of the global community and consciousness, envied and admired for the physical manifestations of its wealth and bold visions. This extraordinary ascent from penury to exceptional wealth took place in much less than a century. Today's Arabia is home to cities that dazzle the growing hordes of visitors with a constantly evolving panoply of innovative architecture. Its population lives in comfort their grandparents could scarcely dream of, with human development indicators that rival the advanced economies of the West. The Gulf continues to draw large numbers of people from all over the world, tourists and new residents alike. It is emerging as a hub of rapidly growing strategic weight in the 21st-century global economic order.

These impressive achievements nonetheless contrast with a sense of unease, an underlying anxiety about the potential fragility of this prosperity. Virtually since the onset of the oil era, the perceived need to prepare for a different kind of future has been an important part of regional policy debates. The various steps taken to this end have included sovereign saving along with proactive economic diversification. The often extreme vagaries of the oil market have done their part in continuously reshaping expectations between the extremes of complacency, on the one hand, and a heightened sense of urgency about economic re-engineering. Assumptions about the future of oil and the region's reserves alike have changed dramatically and repeatedly.

A new spirit of sober realism appears to have taken hold in recent years. The Saudi Vision 2030 embodies this ethos, underpinned by the recognition that future prosperity can no longer depend on the drivers and assumptions of the past. As much as the global energy market has kept confounding analysts over the years, there is a growing expectation that the twilight of the oil era now beckons. Moreover, the income generated by hydrocarbons is unlikely to sustainably match population growth, challenging the traditional posture of the government as the distributor-in-chief of resource windfalls. Economic diversification, despite impressive strides, is confronting obvious challenges. The "Great Arabian Infrastructure Boom" that reshaped and repositioned the Gulf region in the opening years of the new millennium is due for an overhaul. There is a need to shift to strategically anchored policy design and implementation to create a methodical foundation for future prosperity. Only thus can the Gulf ensure that the oil era does not become a short-lived moment of prosperity.

This book is intended as an overview of the Arab Gulf region's extraordinary development narrative. It traces key parameters of prosperity to pre-historic times and follows that narrative to the threshold of a new era when the region confronts an unprecedented opportunity to take charge of shaping its future in a way that is no longer primarily dictated by its resource endowments. This account is not intended as a conventional academic treatise but, rather, as an attempt to synthesize years of personal observation and involvement in the Gulf region's development journey. It builds on multiple perspectives and disciplines, reflecting the breadth and complexity of the topic. But the extraordinary race to modernity makes it particularly important to contextualize this narrative through the prism of history in recognition of the unique cultural and institutional contexts that heavily influence economic progress. The focus of this account is above all on economic factors, rather than culture, politics, or security, which to date have heavily dominated the literature about the region. But many aspects of this endeavor continue to be complicated by significant data limitations. While some of the observations can therefore not be treated as more than tentative, I hope they can help bring more attention to a region that both needs and deserves it.

As the Gulf charts out the way forward in a volatile world, it can draw much strength from its past achievements. This book concludes that a different way forward is not only possible but has the potential to engender prosperity that is more sustainable and inclusive than that seen to date. Getting there will require hard work, a remaking of many economic institutions, regulatory agility, and a major transformation of economic and business culture. But the region possesses compelling assets through its strategic location, infrastructure, regulations, and increasingly forward-looking culture of policy making. It has done much to put itself on the global map through effective reputation building. But the focus of policy will now have to change from building more to building better, making the existing infrastructure and systems operate with greater efficiency. Above all, the region will need dynamic and adaptable companies and an economically engaged workforce.

The opinions expressed in this book are entirely mine, unless explicitly attributed to others. They do not represent the official positions of any of the institutions I am or have been associated with. I thank late Abdullah J. Wallace for his patient counsel and editorial assistance with this project.

Note

1 Thomas Hobbes, *Leviathan*, chs. XIII–XIV.

1 Awaiting a miracle

The glittering skyscrapers that most people today associate with the Gulf metropoles offer precious little insight into Arabia's long history. A mere century ago, the region found itself on the verge of a major crisis. A spectacular pearling boom was collapsing under the dual blows of the Great Depression and the rise of perliculture in Japan. Even as Britain's Indian empire drove the growth of trade through the region, the Arabian Peninsula was still home to a modest population eking out a precarious living in extreme climatic conditions. There were next to no modern schools, and major epidemics were common. Yet, fast forward a century and the Gulf is one of the wealthiest parts of the world, profoundly integrated in the global economy. It is this extraordinary transformation that constitutes the subject of this book. It has been faster and more impressive than most economic paradigm shifts in human history and, despite its extraordinary accomplishments, it is far from over.

Extending over 3.2mn sq km, the Arabian Peninsula is the largest peninsula on the planet. It boasts an exceptional location at the heart of the Old World, flanked by Europe, Asia, and Africa, ideally positioned as a hub for inter-continental flows:

> *Commerce with neighboring countries was invited, to the west by long shores of Northeast Africa, to the northeast by those of Iran. ... [T]o the southwest, it was easy to cross to East Africa and coast along it in search of tropical products; to the east, the coast of Iran led on to India—and eventually the monsoon winds were to assist voyages both to Africa and India. Most important of all, the Red Sea and the Persian Gulf, supplemented by the Nile, the Euphrates, and the Tigris, are natural channels for through traffic between the Mediterranean basin and Eastern Asia; the Arabs were astride two of the world's great trade routes.*[1]

But Arabia also suffers some of the most forbidding climatic conditions known to man. Summer temperatures typically average 45°C and precipitation is minimal. There are practically no permanent bodies of surface water on the largely barren landmass. These extreme contrasts capture the challenge that nature has presented to the Gulf Arabs. Their abode offers a compelling platform for inter-continental traffic, while the hostile climate has never sustained a large population. An observation by Alexis

DOI: 10.4324/9781003373353-1

Wick has regionwide relevance: "At the core of the Red Sea ... lay a dense paradox: because of its strategic, commercial, and cultural importance, it had to have a certain population ..., yet it is thoroughly inhospitable; it absolutely had to be navigated, if only to sustain the population and foster commercial exchange."[2]

The historic circumstances of the Gulf offered a poor foundation for progress, as poignantly observed by 18th-century Dutch mechant Jan van Hulst: "They live in poverty on dates, salt and bread made of coarse corn. Their villages and houses too are wretched. They judge that the poor, infertile, soil they cultivate [is] not worthy of effort."[3] Henry Rooke, an English merchant in the 1780s described Jeddah as "an old and ill-built town, surrounded by a broken and ruinous wall. ... The people ... sit cross-legged on the ground on their meals, wash, pray, drink coffee, and smoke hookah five times in the day."[4] There was little in these accounts to suggest that the Gulf was about to unleash the exceptional potential of its geography without which it had little to fall back on.

Long antecedents

Inhabited for as much as 130,000 years and quite possibly much longer,[5] Arabia has seen a long succession of civilizations. Southern Arabia is believed to have welcomed the first human inhabitants of the peninsula from Africa and was home to several prosperous states, including that of the Sabaeans (roughly between 1200–800 BC and 275 AD) – often linked to the legendary Kingdom of Sheba. Between the mid-first millennium BC and the late sixth-century BC, the massive Ma'rib dam irrigated some 9,600 hectares of land and earned Qur'anic fame.[6] The ancient Greek geographer Ptolemy dubbed the region "Eudaimon Arabia" (Felix Arabia), a "happy" land that offered a sharp contrast to the vast expanse of sand further north. But even the desert was flanked by more verdant landscapes, whether the Fertile Crescent to the north, the Nile valley, or Persia.

As inhospitable as their domicile often appeared, seasonal wind patterns invited Gulf merchants out to the Arabian Sea, giving rise to regular interaction with East Africa and South Asia.[7] Similarly, in the Red Sea, the monsoon "permitted an enormous span of the world's inhabited spaces to be integrally connected."[8] By contrast, the known resource base of the Gulf region was historically modest. In the bronze age the Umm al Nar and Dalma cultures in the present-day UAE, as well as Ibri in Oman, were known for copper mining and smelting. Oman has seen copper extraction at least since the late third millennium BC and mines around Sohar were active around the fifth to sixth centuries AD. The legendary Mahd al Dhahab (Cradle of Gold) formation near Madinah saw active mining around 430–830 AD. Even the central Arabian Nejd region boasted some silver mining. Silver was also found in Yemen, notably the area of Radrad.

Particularly renowned among the ancient Arabian civilizations was Dilmun, centered on Bahrain, which in the Sumerian tradition enjoyed a mythical status as a sacred garden likened by some to Eden.[9] Bahrain's freshwater resources made it a rare haven of greenery on a long arid coastline. Dilmun prospered along the peninsular Gulf littoral along with other centers such as Megan in Oman and Failaka Island in Kuwait between the fourth and first millennia BC. At its peak, Dilmun controlled the shipping routes between Mesopotamia and the Indus Valley, but trade relations may have extended all the way to Southeast Asia. The area fell under first Assyrian and then Babylonian control before vanishing from the historical record after 538 BC. But extensive trade relations clearly continued. During the empire of Alexander the Great, Bahrain, known as Tylos, was renowned as a center of pearl trade but also boasted cotton plantations and handicrafts.[10] But Arabia remained contested terrain as invaders took an interest in the key trade routes. The ability of the local tribes to rebuff attacks by the more populous neighbors was always questionable, and especially "[c]oastal towns were prizes which too often changed hands."[11]

From the Golden Age to the threshold of modernity

In the seventh century, Arabia gave rise to one of the world's great religions, Islam. The call by Prophet Mohammed to spread the faith propelled the creation of a global power that eventually subjugated a land mass stretching from the Atlantic to India. The consequences were transformative: "In just over half a century from the rise of the Umayyads, much of western Asia and a great deal of the Mediterrranean were transformed from a scene of decaying political institutions and divisive social practices into an area ruled by a single authority, able to marshal its immense resources."[12] Even as the focal point of the Caliphate with time shifted away from the Hijaz, Makkah and Madinah established themslves as destinations for pilgrims from all over the Muslim world, with a remarkable 100,000 pilgrims recorded in the year 1279. In 1383, the Egyptian caravan consisted of 17,000, while the Damascus caravan of 1503 numbered 40,000.[13] Jeddah was designated as the port of Makkah in the seventh century.

The Caliphate began to disintegrate by the middle of the second millennium amid problems ranging from epidemics to the gunpowder revolution and the decline of the Mongol Empire. The rise of European territorial states, mercantilism, and the age of navigation challenged overland trade. The Portuguese arrived in the Arabian Sea in 1498, capturing Goa in 1510, and precipitated "the collapse of Indo-Arab commecial relations as they tried to monopolise the main supplying centres of the Asian goods."[14] The Portuguese imposed control over the Bab al Mandeb by capturing Aden and Socotra in 1505–1507. The Huwala principality of Hormuz was sacked in 1507 followed by several Omani coastal towns. The Comorão fort established in Hormuz in 1515 was described as one of the three "keys" of their empire, which soon expanded to Bahrain and Qatif. But the Portuguese ascendancy was never uncontested. Several European powers were active in India, and the 1550s saw almost continuous warfare with the Ottomans, who successfully defended the Red Sea. The Persians and the British challenged the Lusitanians in the Gulf. Bahrain fell in 1602, followed two decades later by Hormuz, where Bandar Abbas emerged as the main Persian port. The Portuguese based themselves in Muscat, ultimately abandoning it in 1650.[15]

Selim I's conquest of the two holy mosques in 1517 unleashed an era of Ottoman domination over the Hijaz, Asir, and Al Hasa. Following some subsequent reversals, Mohammad Ali Pasha of Egypt re-conquered much of the Gulf coast, notably Al Hasa and Qatar, for the Ottomans in 1830. But this was a fragile presence: "The relatively high rate of taxes, the manipulation of date prices, the customs and excise duties, the coinage restrictions, the failure to improve ports, the restrictions on trade with Najd, and the general corruption all caused discontent."[16] But the Ottoman footprint kept "the Al-Saud from imposing hegemonic control over the Gulf."[17]

Amid recurrent conflict, several precursors of future polities began to take shape. Independent states were headquartered in the central desert of the Nejd or Ha'il since the middle of the 18th century, although supremacy was disputed by the Al Sauds and the Al Rashids. In the Hijaz, the Hashemites oversaw a state from the 10th century, albeit eventually subject to Ottoman control. On the Gulf coast, above all, Kuwait and Bahrain operated a high degree of autonomy.[18] Oman stood out as "a virtual island, enclosed on three sides by the sea and on the fourth by the vast sand expanses of the Rub' al Khali."[19] The sea early on tied Oman to Africa and India, making the coast a harbinger of Arabia's future, hosting merchants from Persia, India, and East Africa.[20]

Economic progress was contiously challenged by piracy, which the shallow bodies of water surrounding the Arabian Peninsula lent themselves to: "Marine brigandage extended to the Gulf waters the Bedouin practice of raiding the property of those outside the protection of the tribal or regional shaikhs."[21] The Huwala *nakhila* of the Persian shores were particularly notorious sea rovers that haunted the Bahraini pearling fleets and suppliers to Basra alike. But many pirates enjoyed powerful backing, with sponsors ranging from the Portuguese to the Ottomans, who, apart from raising revenue, used these proxy conflicts to weaken their adversaries. In 1760, a British commentator claimed that "[t]he whole seacoast is a nest of rogues and hardened villains," even if "some of the best 'villains and rogues' ... enlisted with the Bombay navy."[22]

The growing British presence in Asia drove their interest in the Gulf.[23] Basra had since the 17th century been the main British base in the region. The post of the British political agent for the Lower Gulf was created in 1820, initially headquartered on Qishm Island but soon transferred to Bushehr. Jeddah emerged as the main Red Sea hub following the the 18th-century decline of Aden and Mokha (Mocha). Pilgrim numbers averaged some 45,000 a year toward the end of the century. They frequently brought goods to cover the costs of their trip while also constituting "the largest and richest market for products in the country."[24] An 1831 British report claimed a remarkable120,000 pilgrims, of whom 20,000 came "by sea from India, Malaya, the Arabian Gulf and the Red Sea ports of Suez, Qusair, Sawakin and elsewhere."[25]

Reclaiming center stage

The strategic importance of the Gulf in the 19th century pushed the British to formalize relations with the Arab principalities, typically by trading non-interference with their shipping for a commitment to protect the local rulers from external aggression. The General Treaty of Peace was signed in 1820 with the rulers from Bahrain to Umm al Qaiwain, while Aden was occupied in 1839. Reflecting Lord Curzon's forward policy, the 1853 Treaty of Maritime Peace in Perpetuity consolidated relations, rebranding the Pirate Coast as the Trucial Coast.[26] The agreements also reordered local politics by "stabiliz[ing] the identities of local political units. They forged the first link between political sovereignty (previously extended over tribes) and territory."[27]

The legendary "Great Game" further piqued British interest in the Gulf. Germany, Russia, and France were all eyeing Arabia by the early 20th century as reflected by the planned Baghdad railway. In order to contain their rivals, the British concluded another series of agreements starting in 1880. Kuwait followed suit in 1899, as eventually did Qatar following the departure of the Ottomans in 1916.[28] Oman, ruled by the Al Bu Sa'id family since 1749, saw its independence formally guaranteed by the 1862 Anglo-French agreement.

Pax Britannica altered the balance of power among the Arabian principalities. The Qawasim who had prospered as gatekeepers of the Straits of Hormuz were branded by the British as pirates. Ra's al Khaimah and Bandar Lengeh British were bombarded during the 1809 "Persian Gulf Campaign" and again a decade later, and the fragmentation of the Qawasim territory was encouraged. By contrast, the Bani Yas gained influence, supported by the discovery of fresh water on Abu Dhabi island and the rise of local pearling. Dubai, having emerged as a fishing village in the first half of the 18th century, formally broke away as the Al Maktoum family left Abu Dhabi to establish control there in 1833. Recognized by the British two years later, Dubai quickly moved to leverage its attractive location through lower duties that attracted merchants from established hubs such while safeguarding its autonomy by balancing the Al Nahyans off against the Qawasim.[29] After the imposition in 1887 of direct Persian administration on Lengeh delivered bureaucracy, higher duties, and an economic collapse, many more people crossed the straits, and "Persia's loss was Dubai's gain."[30] By 1902, Dubai was the "chief commercial emporium of the Trucial coast." By contrast, Abu Dhabi, whose population had reached 15,000 by the early 20th century, declined to a backwater as instability under Zayed bin Khalifa prompted many to leave.[31]

Notwithstanding occasionally quite blatant interventions, the British facilitated the emergence of the Arab Gulf principalities from the shadow of their more populous neighbors on the Persian–Mesopotamian coast. As opportunities in the "northern tier" dwindled "owing to the infirmity and Turkey and Persia,"[32] the politically fragmented Arab principalities presented an increasingly compelling alternative in which the British were keen to invest. Reflecting this shift, the British political agent moved from Bushehr to Bahrain in 1936–1946, making the island the center of their operations in the Gulf.[33]

The emergence of the modern Saudi Kingdom from its Nejd base proved another defining development. In 1913, future King Abdulaziz (Ibn Saud) defeated the Turkish forces in Al Hasa "with the explicit goal of gaining access to customs revenues from the ports of Jubayl, Qatif, and Ujayr."[34] They gained much more in the sedentary agricultural settlements. The 1915 Darin Pact with Britain explicitly recognized Ibn Saud and "had the unintended effect of legitimating Saudi control in contiguous areas."[35] The Ottoman decline prompted King Hussein to declare independence of the Hijaz in 1916. But the Hashemites struggled to consolidate their control, and growing resistance by the Bedouin tribes allowed Ibn Saud to capture the west by 1925. The gave them control over Jeddah's trade and the pilgrim traffic.[36] The regional *primus inter pares* had emerged.

Even amid its growing strategic significance, Arabia's economic base remained extremely narrow. Mohammed G. al Rumaihi put this succinctly: "Traditionally, the people of Bahrain have earned their livelihood from three main sources, pearl fishing, agriculture and trade."[37] These engendered ancillary activities ranging from shipbuilding to handicrafts. Even more extreme conditions obtained in areas such as Kuwait, which "had little fresh water and practically no agriculture. ... Until the discovery of oil, the only resources available to it were the acumen of its merchants and the skill of its pearl divers and boat builders."[38]

Tilling the land

Agriculture, serving everywhere as the initial impetus for sedentary settlements, is the most established economic sector in Arabia despite extreme geographic constraints. The economic potential of different parts of the region was historically determined by their access to fresh water.[39] In Bahrain, around 10 percent of the surface area was cultivated thanks to freshwater springs. But even there, a 17th-century observer noted that "[w]herever one digs, one finds water immediately but it is very unhealthy, which causes great epidemics."[40] In Qatar, arable land is still today estimated at no more than 3 percent of the surface area, and Lorimer observed that "agriculture hardly exists" there. In Kuwait, agriculture was effectively limited to the Al Jahra oasis and Failaka Island, which had freshwater wells.[41] A similar situation occurred along much of the Gulf coast with the notable exception of the Al Hasa region fed by the Dammam acquifer.

Some mountaneous areas benefited from sufficient precipitation, as in the southwestern Asir region of modern Saudi Arabia, or irrigation-based farming. The Hajar mountains sustain agriculture along the Hormuz coast, while the Tihamah coastal plain along the Red Sea benefits from irrigation thanks to the Hijaz and Asir mountains. Oases permit farming in several areas. Salient examples include the Al Hasa, Qatif, Al Qassim, Riyadh, and Ha'il oases in Saudi Arabia; the Liwa oasis in the southern Abu Dhabi desert; and the Buraimi oasis where the modern-day borders of the UAE, Oman, and Saudi Arabia converge. In particular, eastern Saudi Arabia benefited from a high water table and good farmland to support plantations: "far and away the largest concentration of ... agriculturalists lived in the extensive oasis of al-Hufuf with its seven enormous springs which have provided enough water for perhaps 27,000 acres of cultivated land and 2 million date palms."[42] In 1917 the holy city of Madinah was described as a " 'city of agriculturalists' producing dates, maize, and vegetables."[43]

Oman boasts the most established agricultural base among the modern GCC states. As late as 1967, the primary sector produced more than a third of the country's GDP. Distinct agricultural regions range from the northern mountains to occasional oases further south and the Dhofar coastal plain with its annual monsoon. Seasonal rains have made the Jabal al Akhdar ("Green Mountain") plateau an important farming hub for a range of fruit, including bananas, limes, sugar cane, and pomengranates, but also roses.[44] Through a network of wadis, this elevated area allows much of the coast access to shallow groundwater that is typically further distributed through the ancient system of irrigation canals: "most *aflāj* in all of Eastern Arabia were probably constructed in pre-Islamic times."[45]

The date palm (*Phoenix dactylifera*) holds an honored place in the Arabian culture and diet. Traditionally the main commercial crop of Arabia, dates historically accounted for roughly a quarter of the local minimum daily calorie intake, not least because they are "higher in calorific value than almost any other [fruit]."[46] They can be boiled and packed but also dried and preserved for extended periods, which makes them transportable. The palm provides a range of other useful materials: beams for house building, leaf mats for walls of houses, and *shashas* for fishing. The leaves were used for fans, baskets, bags, trays, and a range of other household implements. Fronds could be bound together and lined with pitch to make water tanks or small boats. The fibrous palm bark was turned into ropes and stuffing mattresses and saddles.[47]

Alfalfa (lucerne) was another important commercial crop, but grains such as wheat, barley, and millet were also grown on a small scale. Vegetable gardens were common in settled areas and produced water melons, sweet potatoes, beans, garlic, and onions, and later also tomatoes, cucumbers, carrots, pulses, etc. Similarly, fruit cultivation was common, with figs and limes being particularly popular. Mangoes, bananas, and other tropical fruits were also common. Al Hasa even produced cotton.[48] Animal husbandry was typically limited to camels, along with horses, goats, sheep, and donkeys, as well as poultry. Even the Bedouin engaged in animal husbandry, producing livestock, hides, wool, and milk, much of which was traded for other necessities.[49] Dishes based on camel milk have been an important component of the Gulf diet for centuries.

In general, however, agricultural production was not easily scalable in the arid climes and tradable surpluses consequently minimal. Moreover, production was vulnerable to extreme weather events. Dates were the main exception to localized subsistence farming and have at times been an important export product. For instance, Oman's batini dates that grew in the saline coastal air were considered inferior at home but boiled and dried for export to India on a large scale. In the 19th century, fardh date exports to the US became a mainstay of Oman's foreign trade.[50]

Local products of particular renown included aromatics from gum resins taken from the Burseraceae trees that only grow in southern Arabia and Somalia. Relatively easy to extract through incisions to the bark, the Greek historian Pliny the Elder described aromatics as the "chief products of Arabia." They enjoyed a legendary reputation across the ancient world: "Frankincense and myrrh were consumed in prodigious amounts for funerary, religious, and medicinal purposes in the Mediterranean world throughout antiquity, and in ever-increasing amounts in Roman times."[51] Their target markets ranged from the Mediterranean to India and China.

Arabian coffee is another regional product that gained global fame. The earliest documentary evidence of coffee drinking appears in the 15th-century writings of the Yemeni Ahmed al Ghaffar. Despite its rapidly growing popularity, it remained an "exclusively Red Sea commodity" for two centuries. It is grown in the hills of the Yemen and "for the most part, shipped off from any of the port cities of the Tihama coast, mainly Hudayda, Luhayya, and Mocha."[52] Much of the coffee made its way to other parts of the Ottoman empire. Muscat emerged as an important hub in this trade that ultimately extended far beyond the Gulf region. However, at least in the first half of the 18th century, "the volume of coffee exported for the Jidda–Suez market was roughly ten times greater than the volume exported, via the Gulf to Başra and Bandar Abbas."[53]

Scarce water resources have always severely constrained the primary sector, but rapid population growth in the 20th century made this an increasingly acute issue. Fiscal needs also became an important consideration: "One reason for the Saudis' preference for maintaining a healthy agricultural environment in the twentieth century is clear: they relied on it for tax revenue."[54] Major investments made in irrigation reflected the desire to boost government revenues while also encouraging the sedentarization of the Bedouin. Efforts to foster local food production, motivated by food security or rural employment considerations, took a devastating toll on the regional water resources. In the second half of the century, complaints about falling water tables and increasing salinity grew across the region. As the demand for food outstripped the potential for natural water extraction, the Gulf region developed an increasingly systemic dependency on imported food.

Fishing was another important primary sector activity along Arabia's long coastline. For many, fish was an important element of daily sustenance, often the only source of protein, but also used for cattle feed and as a fertilizer. Dried and salted fish was traded both regionally and over longer distances.[55] Many regions were known as centers of particular handicrafts. For instance, the Omani interior had many "pre-industrial" clusters with Nazwa renowned for its metalwork, notably copper containers, silver jewelry, and *khanjar* daggers. Bahla was a recognized center of pottery production. Weaving was common, but some towns established a reputation for specific products such as Bahla's goat hair cloaks and Sama'il's cotton cloth. Nazwa and Firq were known for indigo dying, and Nazwa even refined low-quality sugar.[56] In modern times, the inputs for these products are typically imported from elsewhere.

Tapping into trade flows

The extreme contrasts of geography have always given trade a prominent part in Arabian life: "The one historical gift geography gave the tribes of the Gulf before oil was a gift of default: an outward orientation. Regional subsistence has always depended on the vagaries of long-distance trade routes."[57] The Hijaz was systematically dependent on grain imports, mainly from the Nile delta. In the 18th century, the Gulf coast imported food from the Persian coast, while most rice, a key staple, came from northern India.[58] Intra-regional trade sustained above all the nomadic population of the Arabian interior, who financed their purchases through animal husbandry, handicrafts, and taxes or raids of passing caravans or even permanent settlements.[59] Trade profoundly shaped the region as "[m]aritime commerce constitutes an economic sphere linked to the fortunes of the Gulf and Indian Ocean rather than to those of Arabia. The ports were … removed from the tribal society of the villages and desert."[60]

But trade was not just about necessity as Arabia was centrally located and flanked by more populous and economically diverse regions. Of the three routes that linked Europe with the Far East, "Sindbad's 'middle way' through the Persian Gulf was the easiest, cheapest, and, not unexpectedly then, the most ancient and enduring. When it functioned well, this middle route through the Levant and Baghdad took precedence over all alternatives."[61] By contrast, the Red Sea route was shunned for its seasonal wind patterns.[62]

Trade necessitated investments in transportation. The domestication of the camel early on allowed the vast arid expanses of Arabia to be traversed. But these "ships of the desert" were slow and their capacity to carry especially bulkier wares was limited; hence the interest in maritime trade, which in turn further pushed up import dependency because Arabia possesses little timber suited for seaworthy vessels. While acacia wood was used to build smaller dhows, most vessels were acquired elsewhere or built from imported timber. Southern India was the main source of the much-prized teak wood and of coconut fiber for ropes.[63]

Arab efforts to leverage their geography for commerce could take the form of diret involvement by local merchants or trade facilitation. Gulf traders ventured out across the Arabian Sea and beyond. Persian merchants traded on both sides of the Gulf and, for instance, Oman had a Persian settlement by the second century AD.[64] Indian *bania* merchants were frequent visitors and built an enduring presence in Arabian ports early on. The Muscat community dates back to at least the 15th century, and in 1765 the Danish traveler Carsten Niebuhr claimed that it numbered "no fewer than twelve hundred."[65] A Manama community was documented in 1667. Sharjah had some 75 established Indian merchant families and Dubai 50 by the 1860s.[66]

The narrow range of Arabian exports made transit trade a compelling opportunity. This allowed Dilmun to trade in a diverse bundle of goods: timber, precious metals, gems, ivory, and luxuries such as pearls. Copper was widely available, and other metals included silver and tin. Agricultural products, such as grains and olive oil, and textiles were common.[67] Magan was said to supply "sissu and abba wood in large ships … strong powerful copper and various kinds of stones."[68] Arabian aromatics were widely traded, as were condiments, above all East Asian pepper, which seems to have appeared in the Mediterranean by the second millennium BC. But while these items offered the most lucrative profits, "the most common and cumulatively high-value merchandise consisted of the more banal items of everday necessity: cloth (linen, cotton, wool, silk), ceramics, grain, and the like."[69] Coffee became an important product, eventually involving growing imports particularly from the Dutch East Indies. Jeddah's annual coffee imports ranged from TL 14,000 to TL 271,000 in 1855–1910.[70] Southern Arabia was particularly heavily involved in the East African slave trade but also ivory and ostrich feathers.[71]

The early Islamic era was a period of rapid growth and innovation for Arabian commerce as a truly trans-continental trading system emerged. Merchants established banking institutions as well as promissory notes (*sakk*) that could be cashed against deposits across the Caliphate. A group of roughly 50 merchant families, known as *Karimis*, took over the Arabian Sea trade. Overland caravan routes, sometimes composed of as many as 5,000 camels, traversed Central Asia. Such networks were further facilitated by an Arab diaspora of settlements. Muslim pilgrimage further drove the growth of trade, elevating Jeddah to the hub for a large region between Egypt and the Arabian Sea.[72] The traditional trading patterns persisted well beyond the decline of the caliphates: "Before the Portuguese arrived, the Arabs of the Gulf, especially those of Oman and Yemen, were in full control of the East–West trade. ... Arab merchants and shipowners settled in Siam, Java, and Sumatra, marrying native women and introducing Arabic as the lingua franca in all the ports between Masqat and China."[73]

Following Vasco da Gama's pioneering 1497 expedition to India, the sea passage around the Cape of Good Hope challenged the long-standing supremacy of the Gulf route. While the Portuguese took pains to ensure their supremacy in the Arabian Sea, they also closely collaborated with the Indian community of Muscat, which transacted with the Sindh port of Thattha using Portuguese vessels.[74] Traditional trade patterns endured past the Lusitanian exit. A proposed British base in Dibba in 1648 promised to tap into a wide-ranging network: Caravan trade with Al Hasa delivered piececloth and horses, which were traded for Indian rice as well as fruit and cattle from Batinah. Slaves were sold to Basra, Kung, and Rig. In Muscat, the tally of foreign ships reached 92 in 1672. Most came from India but 16 were from Kung, whereas Mokha and the Maldives sent 2 ships each. Muscat actively worked to boost its competitiveness through low customs duties of 2.5–4 percent, while "many ships engaged in coastwise trade with the Gulf and from Sind paid no customs at all."[75] Mostly Jewish merchants from Leghorn, Venice, and Marseille traded with Bahrain and Qatif on the substantial scale of some 2–3mn guilders a year in the late 17th century. Greek merchants traded with Bahrain over the Caucasus while trade with India was largely controlled by *bania* merchants, who reportedly made a 30–40 percent profit on an annual turnover of some 3–4mn guilders.[76]

The Dutch became prominent in the Arabian Sea during the 17th century. The Vereenigde Oostindische Compagnie (VOC) was the largest foreign business in Persia until 1766. The Dutch also operated in Muscat and in 1756 were given a warehouse for their sugar and other goods.[77] Their operations extended to the Red Sea where protectionist practices and collusion by local and Indian merchants prompted them to abandon the Yemeni ports by the 1730s, while "[t]he sharifs of Mecca and the bashas of

Jeddah … did everything to attract European and Asian traffic to their cities."[78] However, Jeddah trade remained challenging due to security considerations, an extreme climate, and risks associated with navigation to the shallow port. Attempts to establish Dutch or English factories there failed. In 1783, 36 percent of all of Egypt's foreign trade passed through Jeddah. However, much of the Asian spice and other trade to Europe shifted to the Cape route. One contemporary estimated the cost of shipping coffee through the Red Sea at 86 percent of the price as compared to only 35 percent on the Cape route. In the case of textiles delivered to Marseille, the corresponding figures were 25 and 10 percent. The Red Sea pepper trade contracted by 80 percent by the first half of the 18th century.[79]

The English East India Company was incorporated on the last day of the year 1600 for the purpose of exporting English woolens in return for local products ranging from cotton to silk, rice, and spices.[80] The company was drawn to the Gulf as the shortest link between Europe and South Asia. The arrival in 1616 of the *James* in Jask was followed by the establishment of an EIC agency, which ultimately relocated to Bandar Abbas. The British took an interest in Persian silk as well as in Kerman (Carmenia) wool but made disappointing headway due to "the miserable condition" of the country. The role of the Gulf remained largely derivative – "a mere imperial conduit linking Britain to her Indian Empire."[81]

Even as the Bombay–Basra trade expanded, the British focus initially remained on what was known as the "northern tier;" that is, Mesopotamia and Persia. British merchants avoided the Arabian coast "because they perceived the threat of piracy to be too great and the commercial prospects to be too small."[82] Trade on the peninsular littoral followed established patterns, with shipping between the Gulf and India "entirely in the hands of local Arab, Persian, and Indian merchants with trading houses in both India and the Gulf shaikhdoms."[83] Muscat was the leading Arab port where even the EIC established a base in 1758, while Persia's onerous policies prompted Huwala traders from the Hormuz coast to relocate there.[84] Under Hamad bin Sa'id after 1785, customs duties at Muscat were cut to 6.5 percent and new commercial relations were established, for instance, with Afghanistan. The Al Bu Saids gained control over the gates of the Gulf, setting up a base in Gwadar in 1784, followed by Chahbar in 1793. They leased Bandar Abbas, along with some 100 km of the Persian coastline, in 1794–1868 and taxed passing ships. Muscat built pragmatic ties even with the British, who were keen to pre-empt French influence. In return for permitting an EIC factory in Bandar Abbas, the Muscatis were allowed to quintuple their salt exports to Calcutta. By 1802, this trade generated an annual income of MT$100,000, a third of the total received by the Sultan's Treasury.[85]

The Omanis stood out in the Gulf thanks to the diversity of their commercial networks. They secured the right to trade in Goa and Bombay while consolidating their presence in East Africa, where Zanzibar became their primary center. As "an entrepôt for the western Indian Ocean,"[86] Muscat supplied slaves to the Bombay Presidency and the French plantations in Ile de France (Mauritius) and Réunion. East African ivory and ambergris were shipped to India and even China, which in turn supplied "silk fabrics, camphor, musk, and spices." Arabia's exports to Asia and Africa were typically composed of "fabrics of linen, cotton, and wool, perhaps rugs, woodwork, metalwork, iron ore and bullion, and perhaps dates."[87] The French island colonies received wheat and other grains through the Omanis and in return supplied sugar, making Muscat "the only considerable outlet there is for the African coast, for the sugar of the Île de France and for other products."[88]

The upper Gulf ports eventually rose to challenge Muscat – an example of the kind of intra-regional rivalry that has continued to this day. After the Al Khalifas added Bahrain to the Utbi sphere around 1783, they set out to leverage the island's pearling strength to create a trading hub: "'Utbi merchants acquired ships that enabled them to sail directly to Surat and return with Indian goods that had been exchanged for pearls."[89] By assessing no tariffs, Bahrain was able undersell the Muscatis and others. By the end of the 1790s, Kuwaiti and Bahraini vessels had reportedly "engrossed the whole of the freight Trade carried on between Muscat and the Part of the Arabian shore, ... and a Principal Part of the freight Trade, carried on between Muscat and [Basra]."[90] Bahrain created a large network, shipping Mokha coffee from Muscat to Basra along with sugar, Indian spices, ghee, and rice. Other goods included pearls and dates, as well as gold and silver lace imported from Europe via Aleppo and copper from the Diyarbakir mines. Even as the Al Bu Saids repeatedly challenged Bahraini designs, the Al Khalifas responded with a pragmatic approach of negotiations and shifting alliances, not least with the Al Sauds, who threatened Oman on multiple fronts.[91] Sir John Malcolm described the Arabian Gulf trade with India as "prosperous," putting its annual value at Rs. 4mn in the 18th century. Three-quarters of this was reportedly for Basra and the remaining quarter for Bahrain and its neighbors.[92]

The rise of the Gulf emirates coincided with the collapse of Persia following the death of Karim Khan Zand in 1779. Basra was challenged by a major plague epidemic and a shortage of specie. By contrast, Kuwait leveraged its excellent port and large hinterland, reportedly drawing "caravans as large as 5000 camels and 1000 men."[93] Kuwait was the starting point of the advantageous "Great Desert Caravan Route" to Baghdad and Aleppo while also linking to important routes from the Nejd and Jabal Shammar. The Safavid siege of Basra in 1775–1779 prompted the EIC to establish direct relations with Kuwait and Zubarah. In 1793, the Basra factory was relocated to Kuwait for over two years. Kuwait further competed on customs duties, which were temporarily cut to just 2 percent by 1831. Kuwait's exports ranged from cloth and timber to foodstuffs such as rice, sugar, and spices, as well as tobacco and, increasingly, arms. Much of the merchandise was imported from India. In return, Kuwait supplied horses from Jabal Shammar – reportedly some 800 Arabian purebreds a year. Other exports included dates, wool, hides, and ghee.[94]

With the rise of the Gulf highway of trade, the Qawasim sought to replicate Muscat's success as gatekeepers. Their fleet by the turn of the 18th century consisted of 63 large vessels and 19,000 men in Ra's al Khaimah and Sharjah.[95] After the British challenged them in the early 19th century, the Qawasim focused their efforts on cultivating Bandar Lengeh as a transshipment port, capitalizing on the booming Indian rade whose volume quintupled between 1845 and 1865, tripling in 1861–1865 alone.[96]

The Utbi and Qawasim gained ground at Muscat's expense. Carsten Niebuhr estimated Ahmad bin Sai'd's receipts at some Rs. 100,000 (MT$50,000) per year. This quadrupled under Sultan bin Ahmad before falling back to MT$100,000 by 1820. A strategic rethink was needed as Muscat "was dependent on its status as an entrepot within profits coming from shipping charges and mark-ups."[97] Said bin Sultan set out to adapt by respositioning Muscat as a transshipment hub for East African goods instead. In 1820, the Omanis subjugated several ports on the Somalian coast before expelling the Mazari' from Pate and Pemba. African slave trade became an important revenue source thanks to a head tax of MT$5, and sometimes as much as MT$12. But the British resolve to combat slavery challenged the strategy, and in 1828 the Sayyid decided to leave Muscat for Zanzibar. He soon transformed local economy, shifting from slave trade to slave-driven plantation agriculture that produced gum copal and clove, albeit no longer for Muscat but Western markets, above all the US. Muscat's population reportedly collapsed from 55,000 to 8,000 between the 1850s and the 1870s as Omanis emigrated to Zanzibar, leaving commerce in the hands of the *bania* community. In 1862, the Canning Award split Zanzibar from Muscat and provided for an annual compensation of MT$40,000 to the Sayyid.[98]

Arabian foreign trade saw brisk growth by the middle of the 19th century. Lewis Pelly, the Political Resident in Bushehr, reported in 1866 that the total value of Gulf trade had risen from slightly less than £500,000 to more than £5mn two decades later, notwithstanding the disruptions created by the British decision to abolish slavery in 1833. The British government formally assumed control of the EIC's treaty obligations in 1858, but efforts by the Navy to curb the slave traffic between Arabia and East Africa reduced its presence in the Gulf, with the consequence of reviving the old scourge of piracy. While the European powers agreed to suppress slavery in their possessions in 1890, progress in the Gulf was retarded by the reliance of the pearling industry on imported labor and the continued social acceptance of slavery as it was practiced.

The 19th century saw transformative change also on the Red Sea, which served as "the primary channel for exchange between the Ottoman Empire and India, Indonesia, and other Indian Ocean ports."[99] Roughly a hundred established Indian merchant families in Jeddah were key players in this trade, their numbers having increased as Aden challenged Mokha. Jeddah's imports from India were dominated by raw silk, opium, indigo, and cotton. The range expanded around 1850 to include Burman rice from Calcutta, wheat, jute, tea, oil seeds such as sesame, and cotton textiles. Trade with Java was largely conducted via Singapore and was dominated by sugar, timber, and spices, above all pepper and ginger. Jeddah's exports to the region consisted above all of salt, which was monopolized through a competitive annual auction.[100]

The 1869 completion of the Suez Canal transformed the Red Sea axis, while the steam engine overcame the challenge of seasonal winds. The British initially resisted the canal, fearing interference with their India trade.

The French diplomat Ferdinand de Lesseps managed to leverage his relationship with Sa'id Pasha, the Khedive of Egypt and Sudan, to obtain a 99-year operating concession for the Compagnie universelle du canal maritime de Suez. But the canal was open to all ships. Despite a decade-long construction period with massive cost overruns, the new venture allowed the Red Sea to at times eclipse the Gulf trade. The British gained control of the canal in 1882, and the Convention of Constantinople six years later declared it a neutral zone under British protection.

The second half of the 19th century was a time of feverish innovation in a global economy reshaped by the Industrial Revolution. The British India Steam Navigation Company launched its Basra–Bombay route in 1862. The network came to include first Muscat and then Manama (1869), Qatif (1874), Kuwait (1874), Dubai (1904), and Sharjah (1932).[101] Ever larger steamboats reshaped commerce, making Bahrain, Bushehr, and Basra the leading nodes. Kuwait enjoyed a high reputation as it could accommodate all ships of the British fleet. Historic Red Sea ports such as Jeddah, Jizan, Massawa, and Aydhab were eclipsed by the end points of this new highway of commerce, namely, Aden and Suez.[102] The relative standing of Arabian ports continued to change as traders to responded to changes in regulations, politics, and economic forces.

Whereas the British gained virtually total control of the India trade by the 1920s, some local shipping continued. Bahrain had some 100 ships engaged in maritime transport in 1905, while Kuwait had had a 40,000 tn commercial fleet of 150 ships by the late 1920s. Such resources mattered when steamer traffic was disrupted during the two world wars. Local shipbuilding also continued, with Bahrain's total production reaching 119 vessels in 1926, 74 in 1927, and 89 in 1928. Kuwait even produced some European-style yachts. Indian traders gained ground also in the Gulf ports, although some Arab merchants remained important players, some even becoming EIC agents by the 1830s.[103]

By the 20th century, Bahrain's deepwater harbor and central location had made it the pre-eminent regional distribution center. Bahrain further benefited from the 1920–1942 Saudi embargo of Kuwait, which had refused to become a free port. Many Saudi merchants set up offices on the island, and in 1918–1919 Bahraini exports to Saudi Arabia made up 41.87 percent of the total of £1,317,811. Despite the rise of Ra's Tannurah as an alternative, the Saudi share of Bahrain's exports rose to 84.27 percent by 1931–1932 and remained over 50 percent until the end of the 1960s.[104] Kuwait also boasted an extensive network: In 1905–1906, 30.7 percent of its trade was with India, while the Ottoman Empire had a 26.7 percent share, Britain 14.6 percent, and Iran 9.21 percent.[105] The annual merchandise imports of Jeddah were estimated at £1.75mn, more than four times Bahrain's pearl exports around the turn of the century. Moreover, the 1893 total of 96,000 seaborne pilgrims remained the norm into the 1920s.[106] The 1930s depression hit trade, but many Gulf merchants resorted to smuggling, with, for instance, the Kuwaitis gaining renown for gold trading with India.

In 1865–1869, two telegraph lines connecting Britain with India were routed through the Gulf. In October 1932, the Gulf became "The Suez

Canal of the air" with the first landing of an Imperial Airways commercial flight in Bahrain, followed by regular traffic in 1934. By 1937, Imperial Airways operated five services a week for passengers and mail while adding a new stopover in Sharjah.[107] Dubai was added to the itinerary for an annual contribution of Rs. 5,000.[108]

Bahrain took pains to cement its pre-eminence. The 1950 Customs Ordinance capped duties at 5 percent, and in 1953 the government decided to build deep water anchorage in Manama, creating a Free Trade Area in 1957. The Mina Salman port was completed in 1962, and re-export tariffs were abolished in favor of a handling charge in 1964. Merchandise imports in the 1960s grew by 8–38 percent a year, and by 1966, the Gulf claimed nearly 81 percent of Bahrain's exports.[109] The value of Bahrain's imports rose from £1,350,000 in 1918–1919 to £22,841,506 in 1959 despite shocks such as the Great Depression that triggered a 43.67 percent drop in imports in 1930–1931 alone. Further challenges came from the 1957 devaluation of the Saudi riyal, the construction of the Dammam seaport, and new levies on imports from Bahrain.[110]

Dubai soon emerged as a serious contender in the lower Gulf, operating as a free port by the 20th century. It capitalized on increased government control in postwar India to corner the South Asian textile market and gold trade, eventually emerging as a key supplier of electronics and white goods to the subcontinent. Dubai proved remarkably astute in seizing opportunities: "When political and economic problems arose in India, Iran and its Arab neighbours, Dubai was well placed to benefit from influxes of skilled and experienced merchants."[111] Many of them were welcomed with land grants and later import licenses or other benefits. The initial wave of arrivals from the Hormuz was eventually joined by *ajami* Persians and even Iraqis. Abu Dhabi and Sharjah merchants voted with their feet in response to instability or economic stagnation. By 1948, Dubai's population was estimated to be four times that of the previously dominant Sharjah. South Asian immigration accelerated in the 1950s.[112]

Sheikh Rashid, watching the silting of creek in the 1950s, decided to invest in port infrastructure. The £400,000 cost estimate in 1954 was far beyond the means of the government. But the funding was raised through a £35,000 contribution by local merchants to the "Creek Bond" as well as loans by Kuwait, Qatar, and the BBME Bank. By 1960, the Sharjah Creek silted up almost completely, prompting even more business to shift to Dubai. Qatari funding was marshaled for road development. But Sheikh Rashid also understood that Dubai had to acquire an airport to draw visitors and business. Amid British skepticism due to the nearby Sharjah airport, Dubai chose to clear an area near Deira, which won British acquiescence because Sheikh Rashid promised to pay for the project himself.[113]

When the road to prosperity was paved with pearls

Pearling was the most profoundly transformative economic activity in pre-oil Arabia. The shallow waters of the Gulf coast are home to rich pearl banks inhabited by three species of pearl oyster – *Pinctada radiata*, *Pinctada margaritifera*, and *Pteria macroptera* – which supply both mother-of-pearl and actual pearls.[114] *Pinctada radiata* is also found in the Red Sea, along with other molluscs that produce nacre-bearing shells.[115] The history of Gulf pearling extends back millennia, with archeological evidence suggesting that pearls were used as adornments some 7,000 years ago. A 200 BC Assyrian inscription described "a parcel of fish eyes from Dilmun" – generally considered to be the first historical reference to Bahraini pearls. In 100 AD, the Roman historian Pliny similarly lauded Tylos (i.e., Bahrain) as being "famous for its vast numbers of pearls."[116]

The labor-intensive pearling business came to hold much of the Gulf population in its grip. But it also allowed much of the peninsular littoral to transcend its geographic limitations, extending permanent human habitation beyond areas that naturally benefited from access to fresh water. However, it gave rise to mono-commodity economies that effectively foreshadowed the oil era. Compact, highly valuable, and non-perishable, pearls were an ideal globalizing force. They were the oil before oil, a God-given resource available in abundance. But, like oil, they were a resource that was almost invariably exported with minimal value addition. An impressive local tradition of small-scale jewelry craftsmanship aside, most Gulf pearls left the region in an unprocessed form. The relative importance of pearling in the Red Sea was far less, but it played an important role in Hijazi trade.

Bahrain was the pre-eminent Gulf pearling center, boasting a fleet of some 1,000 pearling ships by late 15th century.[117] The pearl harvests of Al Hasa, Qatar, and Kuwait also tended to pass through Bahrain. The port of Julfar and Qays Island in modern-day Ra's al Khaimah was a secondary hub. Similarly, Dalma Island, some 42 km off the western Abu Dhabi coast, played an important role. Surat, Sindh, and Calcutta in India were among the main destinations of Gulf pearls, along with Bushehr in Persia, as well as Mokha in Yemen. Basra and Baghdad served as conduits to the Levantine, Turkish, and European markets. By the late 19th century, most of the pearl trade took place on the Bahrain–Bombay axis, while ports such as Bandar Lengeh and Dubai also emerged as important cogs in the system.[118]

The Gulf pearl banks were treated as communal property with no formal restrictions on access.[119] But the sector itself was highly regimented. The admirals of the pearling fleets were appointed annually by the local emirs. Expeditions were led by captains, who shared their profits with the crews, albeit with paltry allocations for the divers despite poor working conditions and high risks. Crew members almost invariably became chronically indebted to captains, who provided annual advances. Various middlemen and merchants were the main local beneficiaries of this system, but all of them were trumped by the mainly Indian buyers who visited the Gulf each year. The Gulf rulers taxed the pearl business.[120] Similar practices obtained in the Red Sea. For instance, the Farasan Islands boasted nine principal pearling beds, but many divers worked around the richer grounds of Eritrea's Dahlak Islands.[121]

Attempts by foreign companies to engage in Gulf pearling, starting with the Bombay-based Watson Company in 1857, were invariably rebutted by the British administrators committed to maintaining the established order.[122] However, formal regulation was introduced in the 1920s when the British Political Agent Major Clive Daly mandated licensing procedures, improved accounting and transparency in other areas, regulated lending practices, and insisted on the provision of a hospital ship. Disrupting the status quo, these reforms proved controversial and even triggered riots in Bahrain. Kuwait also began to regulate the sector in the late 1930s.[123]

The late 18th century constituted an important turning point for Gulf pearling when growing external demand coincided with the progressive depletion of the eastern Gulf pearling grounds. This was not without adverse consequences as "the resulting intensification of pearl-fishing led to overexploitation of the banks"[124] in Bahrain. The Gulf ports further entrenched their standing in the early 20th century as the Persian Hormuz ports declined with, for instance, Bandar Kung reportedly halving in size. Concurrently, the 19th and early 20th century witnessed "rising demand for pearls among the middle-class ladies of Europe and North America, as well as in the traditional customer groups of the European aristocracy."[125] The boom reached its apex between 1900 and 1912 when "the value of Bahrain's pearl exports increased sixfold, from around Rs 5,000,000 to over Rs 30,000,000. ... The 1912 value of Rs 30,500,000 represents the peak of the industry, equalling more than two million pound sterling's worth of pearls."[126]

The Hijazi coast was reportedly home to a fleet of 300 pearlers in 1886. A majority of them belonged to the Banu Zubayd who were active between Jeddah and Yanbu'. Jeddah itself boasted some 50 pearling vessels, mostly "small, eight to ten tons, with one sail, and crews of five to twelve men, many of whom were slaves."[127] By the 1870s, mother-of-pearl and shells were Jeddah's main exports, mainly destined for the Sudan, although a quarter was sent to Trieste. However, the industry declined rapidly toward the end of the 19th century because of overexploitation and customs policies, although the value of the business was still put at £82,135 in 1898. The number of Jeddah pearlers fell to a mere sixth by the early 20th century. A further 70 operated in other parts of the coast, mainly around Rabigh.[128]

Its secular rise notwithstanding, the pearling industry experienced endemic volatility that foreshadowed the oil era. For instance, in 1746, the number of pearling boats in Bahrain had dropped from the reported historical norm of around 1,000 to 300 but, within years, rebounded to 500–600 and eventually reached as many as 1,600 by 1820. Fluctuations within this range continued, with a fleet of 1,500 estimated in 1833, in contrast to a low of 400 in 1889. Samuel Zwemer of the American Mission in 1896 put the tally at 900. Each boat employed 8–20 men.[129]

Pearling profoundly reshaped the demographic realities of the Arab Gulf littoral as "from around the mid 18th century, pearling centres were no longer only located in those areas best able to provide manpower and staples from local sources (Bahrain and Julfar/Ras al-Khaimah), but in resource-poor zones lacking the subsistence base to support sizeable population centres."[130] Kuwait emerged as a town around 1710, became an independent sheikhdom in 1756, and boasted a fleet of 800 vessels by 1763. Abu Dhabi was founded 1761 following the discovery of some freshwater sources and counted 400 houses within two years. Zubarah was established in the north of the Qatari peninsula 1766, although it eventually faded into history as access to water failed altogether. Qatar began its rise despite extreme freshwater constraints thanks to some of the richest oyster banks in the region. But these "new towns" were inherently mono-commodity economies. In 1915, Lorimer described pearling as "the principal or only source of wealth among the residents of the Arabian side." In 1908, he commented on how "scrutiny of the trade statistics shows how artificial is the existence of the larger coast settlements of Trucial Oman and how entirely dependent they are on the proceeds of the pearl fishery for the means of purchasing the ordinary necessaries of life, which they do not themselves produce." In a prophetic statement, he estimated that: "Were the supply of pearls to fail, the trade of Kuwait would be severely crippled, while that of Bahrain might ... be reduced to about one-fifth of its present dimensions and the ports of Trucial 'Oman, which have no other resources, would practically cease to exist."[131] The ruler of Doha, Mohammed bin Thani, openly acknowledged in 1863: "We are all from the highest to the lowest slaves of one master, Pearl."[132] The rising wealth of the Gulf region thus came with an inherent vulnerability.

By the 19th century, pearling had unequivocally established itself as the dominant economic activity along the Arab Gulf coast. In 1810 Captain John Wainwright reported that "along its whole extent a valuable Pearl Fishery is carried on by the Arabs." In Bahrain alone, more than 20,000 men reportedly worked on pearling boats during the opening decades of the 20th century. Resident Arnold Burrowes Kemball's survey of the Trucial ports in 1844 put the local fleet at 2,530 – almost identical to Lorimer's subsequent estimate of 2,582. Dubai's pearling fleet almost quadrupled from 90 in 1844 to 335 in 1907, while Qatar boasted a total of 817 vessels by Lorimer's time. Around 1845, Abu Dhabi had over 300 boats and 2,500 crew. By 1909, over 400 boats supplied the ruler with an annual income of £60,000, when the emirate's population was estimated to have reached some 15,000. By the beginning of the 20th century, the industry in Kuwait employed approximately 15,000 men on 700 boats. Nonetheless, the region struggled to meet global demand. In 1878 Assistant Resident Captain Edward Law Durand noted that yields were growing scarcer and prices had doubled over the preceding quarter century. They more than doubled again by 1905.[133] By the beginning of the 20th century, close to half the male population of Bahrain was employed in pearling, and the country was home to some 30,000 divers in 1930. In Abu Dhabi, Dubai, Ajman, and Qatar, an astounding half or more of the entire population was engaged in pearling. In 1915, Lorimer in estimated the total region-wide headcount of the industry at 74,000, likely more than a quarter of the total population of the Gulf coast. Earlier estimates had put these figures at around 40,000 in 1818, 29,000 in the early 1830s, and 35,000 in 1878.[134]

Table 1.1 J.G. Lorimer's estimates of populations, their dependence on pearling, and pearl industry revenues in 1906–1907

Country	*Estimated population*	*Percentage employed in pearling, %*	*Pearl industry revenues, Rs.*
Bahrain	99,075	18	12,603,000
Trucial coast	72,000	31	8,000,000
Kuwait	37,000	20	8,000,000
Qatar	27,000	48	n/a

Source: Al-Maani and Alsharari, "Pearl Trade in the Persian Gulf," p. 50.

In terms of its financial significance, pearling on the Gulf littoral dwarfed all other activities. The Shah of Iran reportedly earned 50,000 ducats from Bahrain's pearling sector as early as 1689, while a further 100,000 went to his various representatives. A late 16th-century Portuguese account estimated 600,000 ducats per annum. Bahrain's pearls reportedly yielded Rs. 500,000 in 1790, while Persia imported Rs. 200,000 worth of Gulf pearls in 1800. In 1775, Abraham Parsons, a visiting merchant, claimed that Bahrain's fisheries could generate an income of £187,500 in a good year and seldom less than 112,500.[135]

In 1829, Resident Captain David Wilson claimed that the total value of the pearling business in Bahrain reached some £200,000–£240,000 a year, while an 1865 estimate put it at £400,000. By 1873–1874, the sector is said to have generated an income of Rs. 2.1mn. The aggregate pearl exports of Bahrain, the Trucial Coast ("Oman"), Muscat, Lengeh, Bushehr, and Bandar Abbas in 1873–1874 was estimated at £625,933. In 1896, Zwemer put the value of the business in Bahrain at £303,941. Lorimer estimated that Dubai's pearl exports rose from over Rs. 1mn in the 1870s to Rs. 10mn by the late 1890s. Region-wide figures as high as £400,000 to £500,000 were cited around the turn of the century, at which time pearls apparently accounted for three-quarters of the total value of Gulf exports.[136] An exceptional Gulf-wide total of £1,307,241 was recorded in 1902–1903. In 1926, Sir Charles Belgrave estimated the annual total at £1,500,000, which may have risen to 2mn by 1922. Available data on pearl exports to France reflect these trends, shooting up from Rs. 350,000 in 1907–1908 to Rs. 1,300,000 in 1908–1909 and to Rs. 4mn in 1909–1910.[137] Lorimer estimated that pearl trade generated two-thirds or more of all government income in the Gulf principalities.[138]

Having started to pave the road to economic modernization in the early 20th century, Gulf pearling was within a short period dealt a massive existential shock. The British biologist William Saville-Kent had developed a perliculture process in Australia in the 1890s. The innovation was patented in 1916 by Tokichi Nishikawa, whose father-in-law, Mikimoto Kokichi, had been experimenting with pearl oyster farming since 1888. The innovation was successfully commercialized by the late 1920s, and

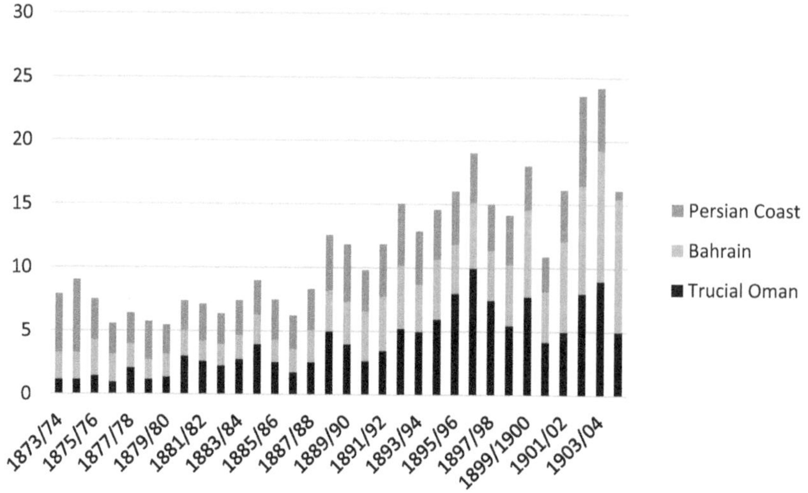

Figure 1.1 Total Gulf pearl exports per decade, million rupees. Total value of exports from Bahrain, the Trucial Ports, and the Persian coastal ports.

Source: Carter, "The History and Prehistory of Pearling," p. 200.

by 1935, Japan was home to 350 farms with an aggregate output of some 10mn pearls a year. With improving quality, they offered a cost-competitive alternative to natural pearls. This mattered even more when the Great Depression dramatically reduced the consumer demand for luxuries. Two of the main pillars of the Gulf economy, pearling and foreign trade, were both hard hit. The scale of devastation was captured by the British Political Agent in Kuwait, Colonel Harold Dickson, who reported in 1931 that "a few Bedouin pearl divers had died of starvation and in 1932 that the town now contained 'beggars' as well as 2,000 starving Persian refugees."[139]

The demise of the pearling industry was ruthless but not total: "Pearling continued, because low quality pearls and mother of pearl could be sold, and the rare high quality pearls kept their value, but overall profits were low."[140] Bahrain was still home to a total of 360 pearling boats in 1935 and boasted an overall workforce of 11,550 men. Strong sales were once again reported in 1936, but the improvement proved temporary. Two hundred seventy-one Bahraini pearling boats were licensed in 1937, seven more than the year before, but the number against lapsed to 252 in 1938. Rs. 756,000 worth of pearls were sold in 1938, down from Rs. 1,300,000 the year before.[141] By 1940, due to further disruptions caused by World War II, the industry contracted to only 191 boats and 7,500 men. The corresponding figures in 1945 were 121 and 5,100. At the end of the war, the government of India placed an embargo on pearl imports, although a concerted intervention by the Gulf rulers brought a reversal. Nonetheless, in 1946, Richard LeBaron Bowen, Jr. put the number of active pearling boats regionwide at just 530. Estimates of the aggregate value of the pearl harvest in the later 1940s hovered around $200,000–$250,000 (£54,300–£62,000).

Dubai's pearl trade in 1946 was estimated at one-tenth of the 1920s level at just £250,000.[142]

As late as 1950, 84 Bahraini boats took part in the diving season and generated an income of £850,000. However, the census no longer reported any pearl industry employees, suggesting a reliance on recruits from Iran and the Trucial Coast. By 1952, active Bahraini pearling boats numbered only 20 with 563 crew. By 1952–1953, a mere 12 dhows went out, and the industry was hit by the imposition of a pearl import tax by the government of India. The Bahraini Government's Annual Report in 1954 made the last reference to the pearl trade when its value was put at Rs. 378,000 (£27,400), generated by 11 boats and 500 men.[143] Yet some pearling took place even later: 4 boats in 1970 but "seldom ... more than two" in the mid-1970s.[144] In Kuwait, the last official departure of the pearling fleet was recorded in 1959. The twilight of the industry was more drawn out further south, and the Trucial Coast in the 1950s still attracted divers from the Batinah Coast. Their number apparently even increased in the early 1950s following a string of bad harvests on land. As a symbolic end of an era, Kuwait's pearl oyster market was closed in 2000. Bahrain, by contrast, has seen efforts to revive the sector in the 21st century.

Elusive modernity

Several forces converged by the 19th century to drive the integration of the Gulf in the global economy, but the 20th century nonetheless still dawned on a peninsula mired in poverty. The rulers of different emirates were at best consensual *primi inter pares* with limited revenues from pearling, fishing rights, the maintenance of irrigation channels, date cultivation, etc.[145] Modern infrastructure – administrative, social, or physical – was almost non-existent.

But signs of a different future were appearing. The emerging Saudi Kingdom capitalized on the infrastructure and institutions of the Hijaz, whose Shura Council had legislative and consultative fuctions that often transcended the province. In 1927, the general directorate of finance (*mudiriyah*) was established in Makkah and transformed into a ministry of finance in 1932. A general security board and the General Department of Health were set up in 1925. A proto-cabinet (*majlis al wukala'*) was introduced in 1931. A national fiscal system was formalized in 1925.[146] An 8 percent customs duty was levied after the incorporation of the Eastern Province, along with a 20 percent tobacco tax and a levy on religious minorities. Nonetheless, the total tax collection in 1927 only reached £1.5mn. Initial attempts to draft a national budget since 1929 only succeeded in 1934 with projected expenditures and revenues of around 14mn riyals. The government income came from the prilgrimage tax, concession payments by the oil companies, proceeds from the gold mines, and *zakat*. Public expenditure went on "defense, including the payment of grants to soldiers' widows and children, to the wounded and the sick. Other expenses ... included salaries for officials and the *ulama*, youth training and schools."[147]

While Bahrain may have prepared a state budget as early as 1919, the oldest surviving documentation dates from 1924. Roughly two-thirds of the Rs. 1,514,000 revenues came from customs receipts and other taxes, while expenditures totaled Rs. 1,523,000. The main spending category was Rs. 300,000 for the Manama and Muharraq water supply scheme. Education received Rs. 48,000 and public security Rs. 120,000.[148] Sheikh Mubarak the Great began the creation of Kuwait's administrative infrastructure. A customs administration was established in 1899. A rudimentary fiscal system with taxes on pearling and property was established but triggered a tax rebellion in 1909. Sheikh Salim created a security apparatus by the 1920s. But many administrative functions remained in private hands, until new agencies were created for health, education, finance, and municipal affairs in the 1930s. The public sector grew slowly until the 1950s, when ten departments were constituted under the Supreme Council.[149] Lorimer estimated the Kuwaiti sheikh's revenues at some $248,500. Sixty percent of this came from a maritime tax, 24 percent from a tax on pearl divers, and 8 percent from an import tax. Kuwait's state revenues in 1937 totaled Rs. 746,000, of which 78.9 percent went to the ruler's privy purse, another 10.5 percent to the family, 10.1 percent on the administration, and Rs. 2,000 for education. By 1945–19/46, revenues totaled Rs. 2.86mn, of which social services now claimed a third, the administration 21.2 percent, law and order 18.3 percent, and the municipality 5.8 percent. The ruling family's share was 21.7 percent.[150]

Qatar's national administrative infrastructure took shape after World War II. Only one customs official was employed by the government in 1943–1948. The public sector headcount stood at just 6 in 1949, 14 in 1951, and 42 in 1954. The first national budget was approved as late as 1953.[151] What administrative infrastructure existed in the Trucial States was fragmented and rudimentary. In 1908 Lorimer put the annual income of the governor of Abu Dhabi at £6,711, of which pearl trade generated 82 percent. The Dubai governor's income was about £4,569. The Sharjah governor earned £2,227 despite apparently widespread tax evasion. Nor did the money buy all that much: "[t]he [representative] shaykhdom's administrative infrastructure was so rudimentary as almost to be non-existant. The ruler had no civil service; no judges or law courts, except for the *mahkamah*; no army, apart from his personal guards; and no police force."[152]

Physical infrastructure became an early development priority. Bahrain's first power station project was launched in 1928 with a budget of Rs. 20,607. An Rs. 53,000 power station in Muharraq was completed in 1931. Elsewhere in the Gulf, comparable steps typically only materialized after World War II. Kuwait commissioned its first desalination plant in 1953. Power generation capacity stood at a mere 2.5 mW in the early 1950s,[153] but by 1954 an ambitious urban development plan was approved. Qatar's telephone exchange was launched in 1953, followed by a desalination plant in 1954 and a power plant in 1957, soon followed by the construction of an airfield and a dock. Abu Dhabi's Maqta bridge to the mainland was built in 1952, followed by a power station and two desalination plants a decade later. Progress was slow as Sheikh Shakhbut banned all new construction without his permission.[154]

Conclusion

The development journey of the Arabian Peninsula was characterized by remarkable continuity for centuries. A narrow resource base offered limited potential to generate wealth on a scale that exceeded local needs. Before oil, only pearls and some agricultural products were exported. Little was done to build other development drivers around these gifts of nature or with the financial resources they provided. The mono-commodity paradigm long predated oil.

These stark realities made it impossible to achieve sustainable well-being in the absence of openness. Trade had always been an absolute necessity for survival but also the sole means of transcending the acute constraints of the local economy. Participation in external commerce required the infrastructure and appropriate policies to receive foreign merchants or access to resources for shipbuilding. Beyond this, the prospects for trade revolved around what today would be termed political risk considerations. Commercial transactions were repeatedly challenged by external intruders and rent-seekers, above all piracy. This entailed profound fragilities: "When trade withered, routes shifted, or droughts deepened, the central regulation weakened, alliances changed, rivalries turned to war and tribes moved, with belongings and dependents, on camels and boats, up, down and across the Gulf."[155]

Regulation became a critical driver of prosperity early on. The rise of the Arabian ports frequently mirrored the relative failure of their neighbors, often thanks to proactive efforts to provide a superior business environment. Jeddah's 18th-century ascent capitalized on protectionist practices and corruption in Yemen. Bahrain marshaled a strategic vision to translate pearling profits into an infrastructure buildup, while Kuwait's rise reflected above all Basra's shortcomings. First Muscat and then Dubai benefited from the political chaos and protectionism of the Hormuz ports. Persia's recurrent instability cemented the appeal of the "Arabian alternative." But similar tactics shaped intra-Gulf competition as well. Few could match the creativity and persistence of Dubai, which put itself on the map despite its recent origins, the near-total lack of a hinterland, established neighbors, and a scant resource base. The city's proactive openness doubtless benefited from its virtually *ex nihilo* genesis, which reduced the number of vested interests and legacy challenges.

The growing British presence in south Asia proved instrumental in driving a renaissance of Arabian commerce. The evolving treaty relations with the Gulf rulers curbed intra-regional political instability and rent-seeking. By building reputations and better infrastructure, the Arab Gulf ports helped overcome the disadvantages that their small population and modest hinterlands otherwise represented. The progress of shipping technology further contributed to the rise of long-distance trade.

The 19th and early 20th centuries stand out as a period of accelerating economic change in Arabia. Progressive integration in expanding global commerce and the growing popularity of pearls allowed the settlement of much of the Gulf's arid littoral. On the Red Sea, the growth of trade and pilgrimage, enabled by technological progress and infrastructure investments – notably the Suez Canal – delivered similar advances. By the dawn of the 20th century, the Arabian Peninsula was very much part of the global system of exchange.

This cursory journey across time has identified factors of enduring importance in driving prosperity in the Gulf. In particular, the arid climatic conditions have historically endowed Arabia with a very modest population base. The realities of geography, climate, and sheer economics continue to place profound limitations on the attractiveness of the Gulf as a market in its own right. Similarly, the non-mineral resource base of the peninsula is very limited. Left purely to its own devices, Arabia is poorly positioned to achieve sustainable economic well-being. Openness is not optional but an absolute necessity and the most compelling development opportunity for a region with little else to fall back on.

The exceptional geographic location of the Arabian Peninsula has always positioned its exceptionally well for overseas commerce. By implication, the prosperity of the Gulf countries is critically linked to their ability to intermediate trade and other flows. This can only be achieved through a combination of cultural openness, political stability, security, business climate, and infrastructure. The lack of sizeable hinterlands for most Arabian ports means that trade facilitation must be underpinned by ongoing regulatory vigilance and a readiness for appropriate infrastructure upgrades. Similarly, the movements of people across the region have always translated into networks that had much the same effect on cementing economic interaction as regulations and infrastructure. The key drivers of prosperity in the pre-oil oil are surprisingly little different from the priorities of today.

Notes

1 Hourani, *Arab Seafaring*, pp. 4–5.
2 Wick, *The Red Sea*, p. 30.
3 Quoted in: Barendse, *Arabian Seas 1700–1763*/I, p. 243.
4 Quoted in: Barendse, *Arabian Seas 1700–1763*/I, p. 215.
5 A 2007 archeological expedition in Qatar found arrowheads dated back 700,000 years. Fromherz, *Qatar*, p. 42.
6 Hoyland, *Arabia and the Arabs*, p. 87.
7 Allen, *Sayyids, Shets and Sulṭāns*, p. 14.
8 Wick, *The Red Sea*, p. 35.
9 Niedercorn, "A Reconstruction of the Prehistory of Bahrain."
10 Niedercorn, "A Reconstruction," pp. 14–24.
11 Risso, *Oman & Muscat*, p. 8.
12 Chaudhuri, *Trade and Civilisation*, p. 44.
13 Facey, "The Queen of the India Trade," p. 11; Freitag, *Jeddah*, pp. 40–41.
14 Khan, "Arabian Sea Trade," p. 910.
15 Risso, *Oman & Muscat*, pp. 11–12; Allen, *Sayyids, Shets and Sulṭāns*, pp. 16–17.
16 Anscombe, *The Ottoman Gulf*, p. 168.
17 Crystal, *Oil and politics in the Gulf*, pp. 17–18.
18 Anscombe, *The Ottoman Gulf*, p. 14; Allen, *Sayyids, Shets and Sulṭāns*, pp. 20, 24.
19 Barendse, *Arabian Seas 1700–1763*/I, p. 259.
20 Risso, *Oman & Muscat*, pp. 4, 13; Allen, *Sayyids, Shets and Sulṭāns*, p. 70.
21 Anscombe, *The Ottoman Gulf*, p. 11.
22 Barendse, *Arabian Seas 1700–1763*/I, pp. 245, 249.
23 Al-Sabah, *Mubarak Al-Sabah*, pp. 108–109.

24 Ochsenwald, "The Commercial History of the Hijaz Vilayet," p. 53; Barendse, *Arabian Seas 1700–1763/I*, pp. 209, 219.
25 Facey, "The Queen of the India Trade," p. 11.
26 Zahlan, *The Making of the Modern Gulf States*, pp. 8. 13; Davidson, *Dubai*, p. 18.
27 Crystal, *Oil and Politics in the Gulf*, p. 17.
28 Zahlan, *The Making of the Modern Gulf States*, p. 9; Crystal, *Oil and Politics in the Gulf*, p. 30; Alghanim, *The Reign of Mubārak Al Ṣabāh*, pp. 256, 259, 262; Nuttall, *Shipping and Development in Dubai*, p. 29.
29 Davidson, *Dubai*, pp. 11–18; Allen, *Sayyids, Shets and Sulṭāns*, p. 54.
30 A "contemporary businessman" quoted in: Davidson, *Dubai*, p. 73.
31 Zahlan, *The Making of the Modern Gulf States*, p. 95; Nuttal, *Shipping and Development in Dubai*, pp. 21, 25–28; Davidson, *Abu Dhabi*, pp. 13–14, 24–26.
32 G. Dalyell of the Binns quoted in: Crystal, *Oil and Politics in the Gulf*, p. 17.
33 Zahlan, *The Making of the Modern Gulf States*, p. 15; Davidson, *Dubai*, pp. 24–29, 55–58.
34 Chaudhry, *The Price of Wealth*, p. 53.
35 Chaudhry, *The Price of Wealth*, p. 53; Peterson, *Saudi Arabia*, pp. 15–16.
36 Chaudhry, *The Price of Wealth*, p. 59.
37 Al-Rumaihi, *Social and Political Change*, p. 64.
38 Alghanim, *The Reign of Mubarak Al-Sabah*, p. 18.
39 Al-Rashed and Sherif, "Water Resources in the GCC Countries," pp. 62–64; Jones, *Desert Kingdom*, p. 26.
40 Barendse, *The Arabian Seas*, p. 45.
41 Al-Sabah, *Mubarak Al-Sabah*, p. 122.
42 Owen and Pamuk, *A History*, p. 78; Lancaster and Lancaster, *Honour Is in Contentment*, pp. 435–437.
43 Owen and Pamuk, *A History*, p. 78.
44 Allen, *Sayyids, Shets and Sulṭāns*, pp. 8–9.
45 Heard-Bey, *From Trucial States to United Arab Emirates*, p. 178.
46 Heard-Bey, *From Trucial States to United Arab Emirates*, p. 176.
47 Heard-Bey, *From Trucial States to United Arab Emirates*, p. 176.
48 Jones, *Desert Kingdom*, pp. 26–28; Risso, *Oman & Muscat*, p. 3; Heard-Bey, *From Trucial States to United Arab Emirates*, p. 180.
49 Jones, *Desert Kingdom*, p. 26.
50 Allen, *Sayyids, Shets and Sulṭāns*, pp. 11, 150–155.
51 Sidebotham, *Berenike*, p. 230; Hoyland, *Arabia and the Arabs*, pp. 103–107.
52 Wick, *The Red Sea*, p. 29.
53 Risso, *Oman & Muscat*, p. 77.
54 Jones, *Desert Kingdom*, p. 28.
55 Allen, *Sayyids, Shets and Sulṭāns*, pp. 13–14; Lancaster and Lancaster, *Honour Is in Contentment*, p. 60; Heard-Bey, *From Trucial States to United Arab Emirates*, p. 172.
56 Allen, *Sayyids, Shets and Sulṭāns*, pp. 9–10.
57 Crystal, *Oil and Politics in the Gulf*, p. 15.
58 Wick, *The Red Sea*, p. 28; Jones, *Desert Kingdom*, p. 26; Barendse, *Arabian Seas 1700–1763/I*, pp. 243–244; Risso, *Oman & Muscat*, p. 102.
59 Hoyland, *Arabia and the Arabs*, pp. 97–99, 109–110.
60 Risso, *Oman & Muscat*, p. 3; Allen, *Sayyids, Shets and Sulṭāns*, p. 7.
61 Abu-Lughod, *Before European Hegemoney*, p. 185.
62 Facey, "Queen of the India Trade," pp. 14–16.
63 Hoyland, *Arabia and the Arabs*, p. 90; Al-Otabi, *The Qawasim*, p. 118; Wick, *The Red Sea*, p. 36; Risso, *Oman & Muscat*, p. 3.
64 Risso, *Oman & Muscat*, p. 4.
65 Quoted in: Allen, *Sayyids, Shets and Sulṭāns*, p. 103.
66 Onley, "Indian Communities in the Persian Gulf," p. 232; Allen, *Sayyids, Shets and Sulṭāns*, p. 99; Davidson, *Dubai*, p. 89.

67 Niedercorn, "Reconstruction of the Prehistory of Bahrain," pp. 20–21; Crawford, *Dilmun and Its Gulf Neighbors*, p. 2; Allen, *Sayyids, Shets and Sulṭāns*, p. 99.
68 Quoted in: Hoyland, *Arabia and the Arabs*, p. 14.
69 Wick, *The Red Sea*, p. 35.
70 Ochsenwald, "Commercial History of the Hijaz Vilayet," p. 67.
71 Freitag, *Jeddah*, p. 43; Risso, *Oman & Muscat*, p. 4.
72 Shatzmiller, "Economic Performance," p. 136; Ashtor, "The Karimi Merchants"; Freitag, *Jeddah*, pp. 40–41.
73 Khuri, *Tribe and State*, pp. 15–16.
74 Risso, *Oman & Muscat*, p. 12.
75 Barendse, *The Arabian Seas*, pp. 48–50, 205.
76 Barendse, *The Arabian Seas*, p. 45.
77 Risso, *Oman & Muscat*, pp. 13–14, 55, 76.
78 Barendse, *Arabian Seas 1700–1763/I*, p. 210; Pankhurst, "Indian Trade," p. 454.
79 Freitag, *Jeddah*, pp. 43–47; Barendse, *Arabian Seas 1700–1763/I*, pp. 215–219.
80 Robins, *The Corporation That Changed the World*, pp. 64–69.
81 http://www.qdl.qa/en/1930s-gulf-%E2%80%98highway-between-east-and-west%E2%80%99
82 Onley, *The Arabian Frontier*, p. 33.
83 Onley, *The Arabian Frontier*, p. 33.
84 Barendse, *Arabian Seas 1700–1763/I*, p. 273.
85 Allen, *Sayyids, Shets and Sulṭāns*, pp. 35, 37, 40–42, 48.
86 Allen, *Sayyids, Shets and Sulṭāns*, pp. 1, 71–72.
87 Hourani, *Arab Seafaring*, p. 78; Toussaint, *History of the Indian Ocean*, p. 50; Khuri, *Tribe and State*, p. 15.
88 Risso, *Oman & Muscat*, pp. 4, 82, 119, 123.
89 Allen, *Sayyids, Shets and Sulṭāns*, p. 36; Abu-Hakima, *The Modern History of Kuwait*, p. 96.
90 Saldanha, *Selections from State Papers, Bombay regarding The East India Company's Connection with the Persian Gulf, with a Summary of Events, 1600–1800* (1908), quoted in: Abu-Hakima, p. 93.
91 Allen, *Sayyids, Shets and Sulṭāns*, pp. 36, 42, 44–46, 54–55, 59.
92 Abu-Hakima, *The Modern History of Kuwait*, p. 98.
93 Crystal, *Oil and Politics in the Gulf*, p. 19; Allen, *Sayyids, Shets and Sulṭāns*, pp. 33–34.
94 Alghanim, *The Reign of Mubarak Al-Sabah*, p. 30; Fattah, *The Politics of Regional Trade*, p. 159 ff.
95 Al-Otabi, *The Qawasim*, ch. 5; Allen, *Sayyids, Shets and Sulṭāns*, p. 53.
96 Nuttal, *Shipping and Development in Dubai*, p. 21.
97 Allen, *Sayyids, Shets and Sulṭāns*, pp. 55, 59, 74.
98 Allen, *Oman*, pp. 48–51; Allen, *Sayyids, Shets and Sulṭāns*, pp. 68, 73–76, 80–86, 89–92, 99; Allen, "The Indian Merchant Community," p. 39.
99 Pétriat, *Le négoce des lieux saints*, pp. 32–33.
100 Pétriat, *Le négoce des lieux saints*, pp. 34, 39.
101 Onley, *The Arabian Frontier* pp. 34–34.
102 Freitag, *A History of Jeddah*, p. 222.
103 Al-Kuwari, *Oil Revenues in the Gulf Emirates*, p. 9; Onley, *The Arabian Frontier*, p. 137; Barendse, *The Arabian Seas*, p. 21.
104 Al-Rumaihi, *Social and Political Change*, p. 114.
105 Al-Sabah, *Mubarak Al-Sabah*, pp. 108–109.
106 Owen and Pamuk, *A History*, p. 79; Facey, "Queen of the India Trade," p. 12.
107 http://www.qdl.qa/en/1930s-gulf-%E2%80%98highway-between-east-and-west%E2%80%99
108 Davidson, *Abu Dhabi*, p. 31; Davidson, *Dubai*, p. 25.
109 Al-Rumaihi, *Social and Political Change*, pp. 114–115.
110 Al-Rumaihi, *Social and Political Change*, pp. 110, 114.

111 Davidson, *Dubai*, pp. 67–72, 96–97.
112 Davidson, *Dubai*, pp. 68–91.
113 Nuttall, *Shipping and Development in Dubai*, pp. 32–34; Davidson, *Dubai*, pp. 68–95.
114 Carter, "The History and Prehistory of Pearling," p. 140.
115 Agius *et al.*, "Remembering the Sea," pp. 153, 158.
116 Datta and Nugent, "Bahrain's pearling industry," p. 25; Carter, *Sea of Pearls*, Ch. 1.
117 Carter, *Sea of Pearls*, p. 68.
118 Carter, *Sea of Pearls*, p. 233; Carter, "The History and Prehistory of Pearling," p. 146; Davidson, *Abu Dhabi*, p. 21; Al-Maani and Alsharari, "Pearl Trade in the Persian Gulf," pp. 46–48.
119 Al-Maani and Alsharari, "Pearl Trade in the Persian Gulf," p. 46.
120 Datta and Nugent, "Bahrain's Pearling Industry," pp. 26–38; Al-Maani and Alsharari, "Pearl Trade in the Persian Gulf," pp. 48–49.
121 Agius *et al.*, "Remembering the Sea," p. 153; Tareq Al-Thaqafi, "Rediscovering Saudi Heritage: Pearl Kings of Farasan Islands," *Arab News*, 3 January 2021, https://www.arabnews.com/node/1786421/saudi-arabia.
122 Al-Maani and Alsharari, "Pearl Trade in the Persian Gulf," pp. 46–47; Davidson, *Dubai*, p. 23.
123 Carter, *Sea of Pearls*, p. 271.
124 Carter, "The History and Prehistory of Pearling," p. 153.
125 Alghanim, *The Reign of Mubarak Al-Sabah*, p. 19.
126 Carter, *Sea of Pearls*, p. 157.
127 Ochsenwald, "Commercial History of the Hijaz Vilayet," p. 73.
128 Ochsenwald, "Commercial History of the Hijaz Vilayet," pp. 70, 73; Agius *et al.*, "Remembering the Sea," p. 158; Carter, *Sea of Pearls*, p. 177.
129 Barendse, *Arabian Seas 1700–1763*/I, p. 256.
130 Carter, "The History and Prehistory of Pearling," p. 181; Davidson, *Abu Dhabi*, p. 6.
131 J.G. Lorimer (1915), *Gazetteer of the Persian Gulf, Oman and Central Arabia: vol. 1. Historical, Calcutta*. Quoted in: Carter, "The History and Prehistory of Pearling," pp. 139–140.
132 Quoted in: Carter, *Sea of Pearls*, p. 164.
133 Carter, *Sea of Pearls*, p. 159; Davidson, *Abu Dhabi*, pp. 15, 24.
134 Quoted in: Carter, *Sea of Pearls*, p. 164.
135 Carter, "The History and Prehistory of Pearling," pp. 149, 152, 159.
136 Al-Maani and Alsharari, "Pearl Trade in the Persian Gulf," pp. 47, 49–50; Davidson, *Dubai*, pp. 22–23.
137 Carter, "The History and Prehistory of Pearling," p. 188.
138 Al-Maani and Alsharari, "Pearl Trade in the Persian Gulf," p. 49.
139 Owen and Pamuk, *A History*, p. 83.
140 Lancaster and Lancaster, *Honour Is in Contentment*, p. 56.
141 Al-Muraikhi, *Glimpses of Bahrain*, p. 84.
142 Davidson, *Dubai*, p. 31.
143 Al Muraikhi, *Glimpses of Bahrain*, pp. 84–85.
144 Anthony, *Arab States of the Lower Gulf*, p. 61.
145 Davidson, *Abu Dhabi*, p. 7.
146 Vassiliev, *The History of Saudi Arabia*, pp. 293, 296, 304; Peterson, *Saudi Arabia*, pp. 10–11, 16–25.
147 The expenditure equaled £1.75mn. Vassiliev, *The History of Saudi Arabia*, p. 305; Peterson, *Saudi Arabia*, pp. 18–19.
148 Al-Muraikhi, *Glimpses of Bahrain*, pp. 20–21.
149 Crystal, *Kuwait*, pp. 14–16; Al-Dekhayel, *Kuwait*, p. 83.
150 Al-Munais, *Social and Ethnic Differentiation in Kuwait*, p. 78; Al-Maani and Alsharari, "Pearl Trade in the Persian Gulf," p. 49; Al-Kuwari, *Oil Revenues in the Gulf Emirates*, pp. 15–17.

151 Al-Kuwari, *Oil Revenues in the Gulf Emirates*, p. 115.
152 Zahlan, *The Origins*, p. 57.
153 Khouja and Sadler, *The Economy of Kuwait*, p. 29.
154 Davidson, *Abu Dhabi*, p. 32.
155 Crystal, *Oil and Politics in the Gulf*, p. 15.

References

Abu Hakima and Ahmad Mustafa (1983), *The Modern History of Kuwait 1750–1965*, London: Luzac & Company Limited.

Abu-Lughod, Janet L. (1989), *Before European Hegemony: The World System A.D. 1250–1350*, Oxford: Oxford University Press.

Agius, Dionisius A., John P. Cooper, Lucy Semaan, Chiara Zazzaro, and Robert Carter (2016), "Remembering the Sea: Personal and Communal Recollections of Martime Life in Jizan and the Farasan Islands, Saudi Arabia," *Journal of Maritime Archeology*, vol. 11, pp. 127–177.

Alghanim, Salwa Muhammad Ahmad (1990), *The Reign of Mubārak Al Ṣabāh: Sheikh of Kuwait*, Thesis presented in fulfillment of requirements for the degree of Ph.D., Department of Economic and Political Studies, School of Oriental and African Studies, University of London, April 1990.

——— (1998), *The Reign of Mubarak Al-Sabah: Shaikh of Kuwait 1896–1915*, London: I.B. Tauris.

Allen, Calvin H., Jr. (1978), *Sayyids, Shets and Sulṭāns: Politics and Trade in Masqaṭ under the Āl Bū Sa'īd, 1785–1914*, Ph.D. dissertation, University of Washington, Seattle.

——— (1981), "The Indian Merchant Community of Masqat," *Bulletin of the School of Oriental and African Studies, University of London*, vol. 44, no. 1, pp. 39–53.

——— (1987), *Oman: The Modernization of the Sultanate* (*Profiles/Nations of the Contemporary Middle East*), Boulder, Colo.: Westview Press.

Anscombe, Frederick F. (1997), *The Ottoman Gulf: The Creation of Kuwait, Saudi Arabia, and Qatar, 1870–1914*, New York: Columbia University Press.

Anthony, John Duke (1975), *Arab States of the Lower Gulf: People, Politics, Petroleum* (The James Terry Duce Memorial Series, vol. III), Washington, D.C.: The Middle East Institute.

Ashtor, Eliyahu (1956), "The Karimi Merchants," *Journal of the Royal Asiatic Society*, vol. 1/2, pp. 45–56.

Barendse, Rene J. (2001), *The Arabian Seas: The Indian Ocean World in the Seventeenth Century*, vols. I and II, London: Routledge.

Carter, Robert A. (2005), "The History and Prehistory of Pearling in the Persian Gulf," *Journal of the Economic and Social History of the Orient*, vol. 48, no. 2, pp. 139–209.

——— (2012), *Sea of Pearls: Arabia, Persia, and the Industry That Shaped the Gulf*, London: Alfardan/Arabian Publishing.

Chaudhry, Kiren Aziz (1997), *The Price of Wealth: Economics and Institutions in the Middle East* (*Cornell Studies in Political Economy*), Ithaca, NY: Cornell University Press.

Chaudhuri, Kirti Narayan (1985), *Trade and Civilisation in the Indian Ocean: An Economic History from the Rise of Islam to 1750*, Cambridge: Cambridge University Press.

Crawford, Harriet E.W. (1998), *Dilmun and Its Gulf Neighbours*, Cambridge: Cambridge University Press.

Crystal, Jill (1992), *Kuwait: The Transformation of an Oil State*, Boulder, Colo.: Westview Press.

——— (1995), *Oil and Politics in the Gulf: Rulers and Merchants in Kuwait and Qatar* (*Cambridge Middle East Library*), Cambridge: Cambridge University Press.

Datta, Samar K. and Jeffrey B. Nugent (1985), "Bahrain's Pearling Industry: How It Was, Why It Was That Way and Its Implications," in: Nugent and Thomas, *op. cit.*, pp. 25–41.

Davidson, Christopher M. (2008), *Dubai: The Vulnerability of Success*, New York: Columbia University Press.

——— (2009), *Abu Dhabi: Oil and Beyond*, New York: Columbia University Press.

Al-Dekhayel, Abdulkarim (2000), *Kuwait: Oil, State and Political Legitimation*, Reading: Ithaca Press.

Facey, William (2005), "Queen of the India Trade," *Saudi Aramco World*, vol. 56, no. 6 (November/December), pp. 10–16.

Fattah, Hala (1996), *The Politics of Regional Trade in Iraq, Arabia, and the Gulf, 1745–1900*, Albany: State University of New York Press.

Freitag, Ulrike (2020), *A History of Jeddah: The Gate to Mecca in the Nineteenth and Twentieth Centuries*, Cambridge: Cambridge University Press.

Fromherz, Allen J. (2012), *Qatar: A Modern History*, London: I.B. Tauris.

Heard-Bey, Frauke (1982), *From Trucial States to United Arab Emirates*, London: Longman.

Hourani, George F. (1995), *Arab Seafaring in the Indian Ocean in Ancient and Early Medieval Times*, revised and expanded by John Carswell, Princeton, N.J.: Princeton University Press.

Hoyland, Robert G. (2001), *Arabia and the Arabs: From the Bronze Age to the Coming of Islam*, Abingdon: Routledge.

Jones, Toby Craig (2010), *Desert Kingdom: How Oil and Water Forged Modern Saudi Arabia*, Cambridge, Mass.: Harvard University Press.

Khan, I.A. (1978), "Arabian Sea Trade in the 15th and 16th Centuries," *Proceedings of the Indian History Congress*, vol. 39/II, pp. 907–914.

Khouja, M.W. and P.G. Sadler (1979), *The Economy of Kuwait: Development and Role in International Finance*, London: The Macmillan Press.

Khuri, Fuad I. (1980), *Tribe and State in Bahrain: The Transformation of Social and Political Authority in an Arab State*, Chicago: The University of Chicago Press.

Al-Kuwari, Ali Khalifa (1978), *Oil Revenues in the Gulf Emirates: Patterns of Allocation and Impact on Economic Development*, Boulder, Colo.: Westview Press.

Lancaster, William and Fidelity Lancaster (2011), *Honour Is in Contentment: Life before Oil in Ras al-Khaimah (UAE) and Some Neighbouring Regions* (*Studien zur Geschichte und Kultur des islamischen Orients*, XXV), Berlin: De Gruyter.

Al-Maani, Abed Al-Razzak and Saleh Alsharari (2014), "Pearl Trade in the Persian Gulf during the 19th Century," *Asian Culture and History*, vol. 6, no. 1, pp. 43–52.

Al-Munais, Waleed A.A. (1981), *Social and Ethnic Differentiation in Kuwait: A Social Geography of an Indigenous Society*, A thesis submitted for the degree of Doctor of Philosophy, School of Oriental and African Studies, University of London.

Al-Muraikhi, Khalil M. (1991), *Glimpses of Bahrain from Its Past*, Manama.

Niedercorn, John H. (1985), "A Reconstruction of the Prehistory of Bahrain, Landing Place of Noah," in: Nugent and Thomas, *op. cit.*, pp. 14–24.

Nugent, Jeffrey B. and Theodore H. Thomas, eds. (1985), *Bahrain and the Gulf: Past Perspectives and Alternative Futures*, London: Croom Helm.

Nuttall, Keith (2021), *Shipping and Development in Dubai: Infrastructure, Innovation and Institutions in the Gulf*, London: I.B. Tauris.

Ochsenwald, William L. (1982), "The Commercial History of the Hijaz Vilayet, 1840–1904," *Arabian Studies*, vol. 6, pp. 57–76.

Onley, James (2007), *The Arabian Frontier of the British Raj: Merchants, Rulers, and the British in the Nineteenth-Century Gulf*, Oxford: Oxford University Press.

——— (2014), "Indian Communities in the Persian Gulf, c. 1500–1947," in: Potter, *op. cit.*, pp. 231–266.

Al-Otabi, Mubarak (1989), *The Qawasim and British Control of the Arabian Gulf*, Ph.D. thesis, International Studies Unit, University of Salford.

Owen, E. Roger and Şevket Pamuk (1999), *A History of Middle East Economies in the Twentieth Century*, Cambridge, Mass.: Harvard University Press.

Pankhurst, Richard (1974), "Indian Trade with Ethiopia, the Gulf of Aden and the Horn of Africa in the Nineteenth and Early Twentieth Centuries," *Cahiers d'Études africaines*, vol. 55, pp. 453–497.

Peterson, John E. (2018), *Saudi Arabia under Ibn Saud: Economic and Financial Foundations of the State*, London: I.B. Tauris.

Pétriat, Philippe (2016), *Le négoces des lieux saints: Négociants hadramis de Djedda, 1850–1950* (*Bibliothèque historique des pays d'Islam*, vol. 9), Paris: Publications de la Sorbonne.

Potter, Lawrence G., ed. (2014), *The Persian Gulf in Modern Times: People, Ports, and History*, New York: Palgrave Macmillan.

Al-Rashed, Muhammad F. and Mohsen M. Sherif (2000), "Water Resources in the GCC Countries: An Overview," *Water Resources Management*, vol. 14, pp. 59–75.

Risso, Patricia (1986), *Oman & Muscat: An Early Modern History*, London: Croom Helm.

Robins, Nick (2012), *The Corporation That Changed the World: How the East India Company Shaped the Modern Multinational*, 2nd edition, London: Pluto Press.

Al-Rumaihi, Mohammed Ghanim (1973), *Social and Political Change in Bahrain since the First World War*, Ph.D. thesis, Durham University.

Al-Sabah, Souad M. (2014), *Mubarak Al-Sabah: The Foundation of Kuwait*, London: I.B. Tauris & Co.

Shatzmiller, Maya (2011), "Economic Performance and Economic Growth in the Early Islamic World," *Journal of the Economic and Social History of the Orient*, vol. 54, pp. 132–184.

Sidebotham, Steven E. (2011), *Berenike and the Ancient Maritime Spice Route*, Berkeley: University of California Press.

Toussaint, Auguste (1966), *History of the Indian Ocean*, London: Routledge & Kegan Paul.

Vassiliev, Alexei (2000), *The History of Saudi Arabia*, New York: New York University Press.

Wick, Alexis (2016), *The Red Sea: In Search of Lost Space*, Oakland: University of California Press.

Zahlan, Rosemarie Said (1989), *The Making of the Modern Gulf States: Kuwait, Bahrain, Qatar, the United Arab Emirates and Oman*, London: Unwin Hyman.

2 The double-edged sword

The 20th century brought unprecedented change to the Arabian Peninsula. The Great War shook the regional balance of power by triggering the disintegration of the Ottoman Empire and allowing the British to consolidate their hold over much of the Gulf littoral. Further inland, the Al Sauds established the dominant regional power. But the postwar era also delivered a serious economic crisis that dramatically weakened three principal sources of prosperity: trade, pearling, and pilgrimage. The same economic openness that had fueled the region's initial modernization now proved its greatest vulnerability, leaving the Gulf Arabs with precious little to fall back on.

But, unbeknownst to most, two important trends were colliding in ways that would ultimately revive Arabia's fortunes in a most spectacular fashion. Firstly, commercial oil drilling since the middle of the 19th century had made liquid hydrocarbons an increasingly important element of the global energy mix. Secondly, the invention of the internal combustion engine powered by petrol in the second half of the century unleashed one of the great economic leaps forward of the modern era. It pushed up the efficiency and scale of mechanized manufacturing but also spelled transformative growth for transportation.

The intense hunger for oil in the second half of the 19th century triggered a global search for deposits. Following pioneering operations around Europe by the early 1850s, the modern oil era truly took off in North America. West Virginia saw drilling in 1848, while Oil Springs in Ontario, Canada, were dug in 1858. Edwin Drake drilled his legendary "first well" near Titusville, Pennsylvania, in 1859. Further discoveries materialized in Peru in 1863 and the Dutch East Indies in 1885. The Russian Empire emerged as an oil giant, producing more than half of the world's output by 1900, although the Bolshevik revolution subsequently plunged the country into turmoil.[1]

The oil era dawns on the Middle East

The growing thirst for petrol soon enough brought prospectors to the Middle East as well, attracted by the region's multiple well-known signs of hydrocarbons deposits:

> *During all human history, and for millennia before, there have been in western Asia clear surface indications of the presence of petroleum. In*

DOI: 10.4324/9781003373353-2

> *places an oil-permeated rock-stratum outcrops on a hillside, elsewhere deposits of bitumen cover the ground, elsewhere gas or liquid oil seeps upwards through a crack or a weakening in the cover-rock of buried reservoir. Thus in Egypt the seepages at Jabal Zait earned that ridge its Roman name of Mons Petroleus, and other traces had long been noticed on the same coast, in the Sinai Peninsula, and in some of the Red Sea islands, notably the Farsan group. Oil-shales were known in the hinterland of Aden. In the Persian Gulf signs of oil or bitumen marked the crest of the ridge on Bahrain Island and were visible in the desert near Kuwait. Iraq contained the great bitumen deposits at Hit and elsewhere on the Euphrates, the lighted gas escape—the "burning fiery furnace"—near the future Kirkuk, traces of oil in the Upper Tigris, and abundant seepages at Qaiyara, Kirkuk, Tuz Khormatu, and in the Mandali district. In Persia traces of oil or bitumen were found in the north-west near Qasr-i-Shirin and conspicuously in ancient Edom.*[2]

Hydrocarbons had played a role in the Gulf economy for centuries. Bitumen had been used in the region as mortar, for water channel lining, and for caulking in shipbuilding, among other things. It was also collected for for lighting and as a fuel.

The emergence of the Middle Eastern petroleum industry was far from straightforward. Within the Ottoman Empire, regulations were a challenge: "the mining law was ill-drafted and largely inapplicable, its execution uncertain."[3] Deutsche Bank acquired priority rights for mining in connection with the concession given to the German-owned Ottoman Railway Company of Anatolia in 1888. The Zagros Basin of western Persia was seen as a high-potential prospect and the first concessions in the area were granted in the 1870s. The French geologist and archeologist Jacques de Morgan commented favorably on the exploration potential in 1892. Ultimately unsuccessful drilling took place also in Egypt in the late 1880s.

After several frustrations and a major corporate reorganization among the explorers, the oil era finally dawned on the Middle East in Masjed Soleyman in western Persia in May 1908. The project had been funded by William Knox D'Arcy, who had won a concession seven years earlier. In 1909, the Anglo–Persian Oil Company (APOC, future BP) was established as a subsidiary of the Scottish Burmah Oil Company. It went on to build its first refinery at Abadan near the Gulf coast in 1911.[4] After 1909, modest production began in Egypt's Read Sea coastal areas of Gemsa and Hurghada. Exploration in Mesopotamia was led by the Turkish Petroleum Company (TPC), established in 1912 by APOC (50 percent), Royal Dutch Shell (25 percent), and Deutsche Bank (25 percent). The legendary dealmaker Calouste Gulbenkian received a 5 percent beneficial interest. The company was due to receive a concession from the Ottoman Grand Vizier in 1914, but the war intervened.[5] But the sector's forward momentum now appeared irreversible. Global production, "which barely exceeded 4 million t/y in 1880 and 20 million in 1900, had in 1915 reached 59 million."[6]

In 1914, Winston Churchill, as First Lord of the Admiralty, made the Royal Navy an important APOC client in connection with his efforts to modernize the fleet by substituting petrol for coal. In a bid to cut Britain's reliance on foreign oil companies, the British government recapitalized APOC and acquired a 51 percent controlling stake in it that lasted for two decades. This provided an important financial lifeline for further exploration in the Middle East at a time when warfare was becoming increasingly mechanized. Lord Curzon memorably quipped that the Allies ultimately floated to victory on a wave of oil.

Echoing the post–World War I settlement, the 1920 San Remo Oil Agreement granted Deutsche Bank's share in TPC to the victorious French. In addition, the Americans, concerned about looming shortages in North America, began to militate for access to the Middle East, a position embodied in their 1921 Open Door policy. TPC ownership was ultimately split into four stakes of 23.75 percent each for APOC, Shell, Compagnie française des pétroles (CFP, later Total), and the Near East Development Company, which represented American oil firms. As of 1934, the American stake was equally split between Standard Oil of New Jersey and Socony-Vacuum. Important finds were made in 1927 at Baba Gurgur near Kirkuk in the province Mosul. The legendary Eternal Fire in the area turned out to sit atop the largest active oil field in the world. TPC was formally renamed as the Iraq Petroleum Company (IPC) in 1929. Along with APOC, it was to emerge as a key pioneer of oil exploration across the Gulf region.[7]

The Persian finds prompted British political agents in the Gulf to explore potential opportunities: "These investigations led them to the Naptha spring near Halul Island, the asphalt deposit at Bahrain, the seepage at Burqan, and other minor seepages." However, the 1904 survey by Guy Pilgrim of the Geological Survey of India (engaged by the British-controlled government of India) had given little encouragement. APOC "was not optimistic about finding commercial oil fields south of Basrah. This belief was based on the assumption that this area was in a region 'where sedimentary rocks were thinly developed and that folding, even if present, would be very gentle.'"[8] However, the Gulf rulers also took an interest in oil exploration. Having initially feared competition for labor on the part of the oil industry, amid the Great Depression they came to see "the oil industry as a remedy for the disastrous situation caused by the depression in the pearling industry."[9]

Gulf-bound

The 20th century belatedly arrived in the Gulf on 31 May 1932 when the region's first oil find was made near Jebel al Dukhan in the southern desert of Bahrain. This was a moment "of high significance for the whole of Arabia, whose oil prospects were thenceforth to be reconsidered with a new interest by companies."[10] The Awali find had been preceded by many reversals of fortune. Despite initial skepticism, especially the British were keen to hedge their bets and sought to rally the Gulf rulers behind their cause. For instance, in May 1911, Sheikh Isa bin Ali of Bahrain made a formal promise to the British political agent that any potential discoveries would not be developed without the consent of the British government.

The first attempt at oil exploration on modern Saudi territory was made on the Farasan Islands, far away from the current hydrocarbons heartland.

An early concession was held by Istanbul merchant Yusuf Assim, and a 1912 survey by the Eastern Petroleum Company led to the registration of the Farasan Island Oil Co. The capture of Farasan by the Idrisi in 1915 delayed exploration, however, and the company was ultimately closed in 1919. Aden merchant Hasan Ali produced kerosene in 1924–1926 until the Shell-controlled Red Sea Petroleum Company won a new concession in 1926. The move may have been more about containing Italian advances in the region than oil, which was valued at no more than 100,000 pounds.[11]

Following a lull during the Great War, efforts to locate oil on the Arabian mainland resumed in 1920 when British–New Zealander mining engineer and geologist Major Frank Holmes, known to the local Arabs as "Abu Naft" (Father of Oil), set up the Eastern and General Syndicate in London. Three years later, King Abdulaziz awarded Holmes a concession to prospect in the Al Hasa region, but the the geological assessments were disappointing and the venture was abandoned by 1927.[12] In late 1925, however, Holmes managed to win a concession in neighboring Bahrain as a reward for drilling water wells, although financial difficulties again frustrated his plans.

The British were not alone in eyeing opportunities in the Gulf. The 1920 San Remo Petroleum Agreement had excluded US oil companies from the postwar British and French protectorates in Mesopotamia, indirectly pushing them to focus their efforts on other parts of the Middle East. Such desings were complicated by the Red Line Agreement of 1928, which committed the TPC partners to refraining from unilaterally developing oil interests on the ex-Ottoman territory. The agreement applied to the entire Arabian Peninsula (as well as all to the Levant and Turkey) with the exception of Kuwait, which was recognized as a British dependency.

Even as investor interest in Arabian hydrocarbons intensified, the Great Depression significantly tightened financial market conditions and curbed the demand for oil. Moreover, it coincided with new oil finds in the US that confounded the earlier American anxiety about pending supply constraints. Of particular importance was the super-giant East Texas oil field discovered in September 1930.[13] By substantially boosting supply at a time when demand was contracting, this new resource pushed oil prices into a tailspin, not least because of the difficulties of controlling illegal production. The total output of the field at one point reached 900,000 b/d. Having stood at $1.88 per barrel in 1926, US crude prices plummeted to 82–87 cents in 1932 and further to 44–66 cents in 1933.[14]

Holmes' fundraising for Bahrain made minimal progress until November 1927, when the Eastern Gulf Oil Company, a subsidiary of the US-domiciled Gulf Oil Corporation, took an option to buy the rights of the syndicate and appointed Holmes their country manager. Soon thereafter, however, the 1928 Red Line agreement again intervened to prevent Gulf Oil from acting independently, while a lack of interest by the IPC consortium ultimately forced a sale of the concession.[15] Bahrain nonetheless received its first income from oil companies in 1926, followed by a total of £6,800 by 1934.[16]

In December 1928, the Standard Oil Company of California (SoCal) bought the Bahrain option but ran into immediate resistance from the

British Colonial Office. The stalemate was resolved in 1929 through the creation of the Bahrain Petroleum Company (Bapco) as a SoCal subsidiary. Formally incorporated in the British dominion of Canada, the company was required to have one British director and a British government-appointed local representative. Employment preference was to be given to British and Bahraini nationals. Bapco began drilling in October 1931. Ultimately, "oil in considerable quantities of 33–35 degree A.P.I. gravity was struck on 31 May 1932, its reservoir in porous limestone of Cretaceous age at a depth of 2,000–2,500 feet."[17] On 2 June 1932, Bapco went on to successfully complete the region's legendary first oil well, which reached an initial capacity of 400 b/d. Volumes grew rapidly from 31,000 barrels in 1933 to just over 285,000 in 1934. In December 1934, the first oil tanker left the island. Crude extraction passed the 1mn barrel mark the following year and jumped to more than 4.6mn in 1936. It fluctuated between 5 and 12mn barrels until 1957.

The difficulties of marketing Bahraini oil during the depression prompted Bapco to invest in local refining capacity in a pioneering instance of vertical integration. A 10,000 b/d facility in Sitrah was commissioned in 1937. SoCal simultaneously engaged Texas Corporation as a partner, seeking to leverage its global network for business development. The California–Texas Oil Company (Caltex) was incorporated in 1936, and the number of oil tankers calling in Bahrain rose from 50 in 1936–1937 to 84 in 1937–1938. There were periodic negotiations in 1934–1940 about expanding Bapco's concession to all of Bahrain, with IPC now also showing interest. Bapco ultimately prevailed in 1940, partly because of the government's reluctance to fragment a small market.[18] The total receipts of the Bahraini government between 1934 and 1970 reached BHD171.7mn.[19]

The Bapco refinery expanded its capacity to 25,000 b/d in 1937 and eventually to 33,000 b/d by the outbreak of World War II.[20] Following an attack by three Italian bombers in October 1940, new drilling was suspended for six years, leaving local production static at around 1mn tn/year. However, a pipeline from Dhahran more than doubled the crude supply to the refinery, and renewed expansion began in late 1943 with high-octane spirit as well as aviation and motor spirit added to the product mix. The throughput nearly doubled to 65,000 b/d in 1945.[21] As the capacity of the Saudi pipeline doubled between 1949 and 1952, Bapco added a 50,000 tn/year asphalt plant in 1948 and a 7,000 b/d reforming unit the following year. The output of oil products rose from 100,000 b/d in the middle of 1947 to 210,000 b/d in late 1951. Further expansion by 1969 took Bapco's refinery throughput to 239,385 b/d, while local crude extraction stood at only 76,201 b/d.

Endemic fiscal troubles in the young Saudi Kingdom drove the government's interest in replicating Bahrain's success. After a record flow of 132,109 in 1927, the flow of Muslim pilgrims plunged to 40,000 in 1931, 21,065 in 1932, and only 20,705 in 1933. This reversed an impressive rise in government income from just £50,000 a year in the first decade of the century to £5mn by the early 1930s. The broader economic impact was a little less devastating as "even the poorest pilgrim was estimated to spend at least £30 on local expenses."[22] Harry St John Bridger Philby, a

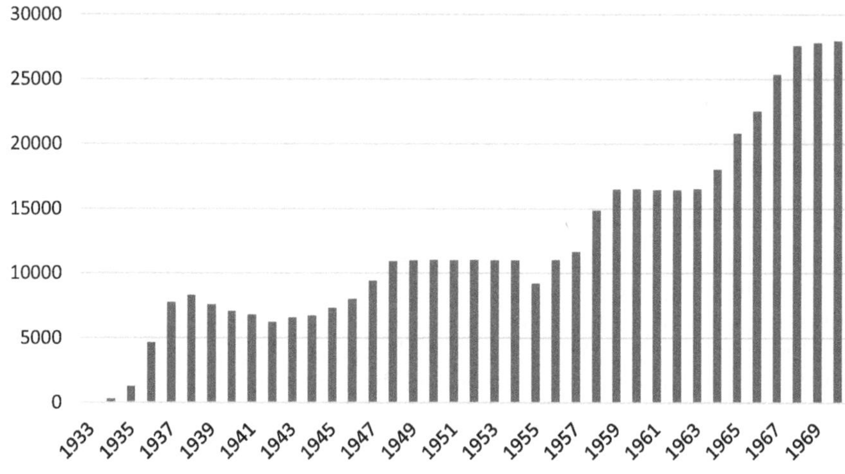

Figure 2.1 Bahrain's oil production, '000 US barrels.

Source: Al-Rumaihi, Social and Political Change in Bahrain, p. 124.

British Colonial Office intelligence officer who served as an advisor to King Abdulaziz, estimated that government revenues plummeted from roughly £1mn at the close of the 1920s to a quarter of that in 1933, while the public debt reached almost £220,000 in 1932. Expenditures rose further due to the 1933–1934 conflict with the Yemenis in Asir. Pilgrimage rebounded to almost 50,000 in 1937 but remained a far cry from the pre-crisis years.[23]

Philby used the financial crisis to win the sovereign's consent for oil exploration. A 1932 report identified promising oil seeps in Al Hasa. SoCal engaged Philby as an advisor, eventually beating the IPC to win a concession in May 1933: "When asked by the Saudi government for £100,000 gold, the IPC offered £10,000. SOCAL offered Abdel Aziz £50,000 gold, got the concession, and has been laughing all the way to the bank ever since."[24] Beyond an initial payment of 30,000 gold sovereigns, the agreement stipulated "an annual minimum payment of 5,000 sovereigns, two loans of 50,000 sovereigns each, when commercial oil should be discovered, and a royalty of 4 s. (gold) per ton."[25] While dramatically boosting government finances in an hour of need, the deal was extremely favorable to the Americans: "In an area of 350,000 square miles in eastern Arabia, ... the company was given the exclusive right to explore, prospect, drill for, extract, manufacture, transport and export all oil produced. ... The company agreed to build a refinery; supply the government with 200,000 gallons of gasoline and 100,000 gallons of kerosene yearly; and advance loans deductible from future royalties."[26] SoCal could expect to win a concession further to the West merely by matching competing bids.

A SoCal subsidiary, California–Arabian Standard Oil (Casoc), took over the Saudi concession. The pioneering Dammam No. 1 well was spudded at the end of April 1935 in an area deemed a geological replica of Bahrain.

After three fruitless years, Texaco joined the venture in 1936 as an equal partner. In July 1936, IPC-owned Petroleum Concession Ltd was granted a concession for the Hijaz for region. The cost was £32,000 in gold upon signing and an annual £7,500, which was to rise to £10,000 after four years along with small deliveries of refined products and 1 percent of the crude production. The Farasan Islands and Jizan also saw exploration in the late 1930s but to little avail. Casoc's concession expanded from 830,000 to 1.14mn sq km in 1939 to include the Saudi share of the neutral zone with Kuwait. The Saudi treasury received £140,000 (gold) upon signature, and the minimum annual dead rent was raised from £5,000 to £25,000.[27]

As the Casoc owners began to consider the thought of abandoning their Saudi venture, the oil era dramatically dawned on the Arabian mainland in 1938. Dammam No 7 on Jabal Dhahran was the first deep test well drilled by Casoc.[28] Having reached a depth of 1,440 meters, it delivered 1,585 barrels on 4 March and 3,810 barrels six days later, eventually churning out 32mn barrels during its exceptionally productive lifetime up until 1982. Two other wells were deepened to the same geological layer and commercial production began. By the end of 1939, Saudi Arabia was exporting 10,700 b/d. A 69-km pipeline was laid to the Ra's Tannurah port where a small 3,000 b/d refinery began operations in 1940.[29] The development of the new finds continued even during World War II: "Export of crude from al Khobar and Ras Tanura amounted to 510,000 tons in 1939 and in the four succeeding years to 665,000, 565,000, 590,000, and 640,000 the bulk of which was destined for the Bahrain refinery."[30] The operating company was renamed Arabian American Oil Company, or Aramco, in 1944.

Saudi public finances nonetheless remained strained as the war again hit revenues from pilgrimage and customs duties while "crop failures and increasing costs of imported supplies ... brought the government to the edge of bankruptcy."[31] Despite some \$38mn of British support by the end of 1943, King Abdulaziz approached the US concessionaires for a \$6mn advance on his future royalties.[32] Such payments reportedly totaled \$6.4mn in 1941 and a further 2.3mn in 1942. The US largesse was underpinned by strategic considerations. In 1941,

> *Secretary of the Interior Harold L. Ickes called to the attention of President Franklin D. Roosevelt a steady decline in the ratio of proven domestic reserves to annual production ... from an indicated twenty-two-years supply in 1930 to an indicated fifteen-years supply in 1940. ... An October study ... argued that "the United States must have extra-territorial reserves to guard against the day when our steadily increasing demand can no longer be met by our domestic supply."*[33]

This prompted Roosevelt to extend the US Lend-Lease program to Saudi Arabia in 1943. In 1944, Britain and the US contributed in equal proportion to an annual subsidy of £4–5mn, but by 1945, the US scaled up its support when "the British treasury ... insisted that the British subsidy be cut by 50 percent."[34]

These developments heralded a new balance of power in the postwar global energy markets. The growing interest in Saudi oil was matched by a readiness to invest in infrastructure that would more reliably deliver it to the end markets. The planned projects included an ambitious plan for a pipeline to the Mediterranean as well as a new refinery in Ra's Tannura, which began operations in late 1945 with an initial capacity of 50,000 b/d.[35] Saudi production kept rising to more than a million tons in 1944 and exceeded 2.5mn in 1945.

The American interest in Arabian oil deepened in the early Cold War years. The North American reserves were now seen as the last line of defense in an increasingly insecure world, which created a sense of urgency around developing new fields in parts of the Old World that were not under Soviet domination. Major field discoveries pushed up Saudi output from 2.5 to 41mn tons between 1945 and 1952. The Ra's Tanura refinery saw a capacity increase to 150,000 b/d in 1952, with a further boost to 200–210,000 b/d to follow.[36]

Despite the expanding output, the persistent fiscal challenges of the Saudi treasury triggered a search for revenue sources independent of the American oil majors. A particularly bold bid to turn the tables was made by King Saud, who set out to establish an independent Saudi Arabian Tankers Company in partnership with Aristotle Onassis in 1953. The plan was to establish a Saudi oil tanker fleet that would initially compete with and then eclipse Aramco, which would no longer be permitted to replace its aging vessels. This would have created the first Saudi-controlled element of the local petroleum industry. Although the subsequent drawn-out dispute was settled by the International Arbitration Tribunal in favor of Aramco in 1958, a similar initiative in Kuwait proved successful.[37]

Other oil companies also entered the Saudi market, led by the Pacific Western Oil Company (later Getty Oil), which signed 60-year deal in January 1949. The Saudis had the right to subscribe to a 25 percent stake and mandated the construction of a refinery whose products were to be delivered without cost. An initial contribution of $9.5mn was to be followed by annual payments of a million, as well as a royalty of 55 cents a barrel, one-eighth of the profits from production, and a quarter of refining profits. Drilling efforts succeeded in 1953. In 1957, the Japanese-owned Arabian Oil Company signed to conduct offshore exploration along the coast of the neutral zone. An license of at least 40 years was promised upon successful finds but on terms that heralded a new era in the relationship between oil companies and producer countries. In particular, "the government was to receive 56 instead of 50 percent of net income; the 56 percentage was to apply to all activities of an integrated company inside and outside of Saudi Arabia, including transport, refining, and sale of crude; the government was entitled to one-third of the seats on the company's board of directors."[38] This set a standard for subsequent exploration agreements involving the Red Sea littoral and the Rub' al Khali. It clearly signaled that the days of Arabia's natural resources being developed by the West on its own terms were coming to an end.

The desire to increase national control over oil led to the establishment of a new, fully Saudi-controlled entity. Established in 1962, the General Petroleum and Mineral Organization (Petromin) was put in charge of "oil and industrial development,"[39] partly because the Ministry of Petroleum

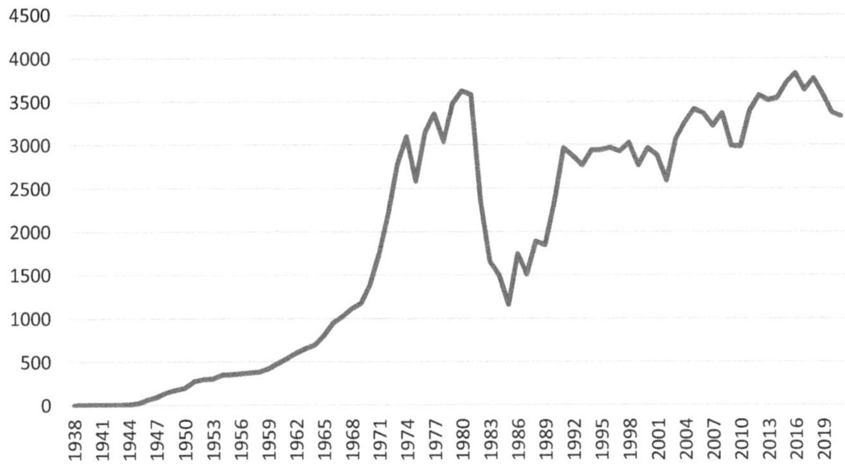

Figure 2.2 Saudi oil production, mn barrels.

Source: Knauerhase, The Saudi Arabian Economy, p. 94; Saudi Arabian Monetary Agency, Annual Reports, https://www.sama.gov.sa/en-us/EconomicReports/Pages/AnnualReport.aspx?&&p_SortBehavior=0&p_SAMAFAQSortOrder=45%2e0000000000000&&PageFirstRow=1&View=e672847e-173c-4344-be1f-66280d034f46.

and Mineral Resources was unable to engage in joint ventures with foreign companies as a government entity. Petromin was given a broad mandate to undertake exploration, refining, and distribution of all mineral resources outside of the Aramco concession. The plan addressed a wide range of activities: "refining, gathering and liquefication of gas, mining, petrochemicals, fertilizers, iron, steel, aluminium manufacture ..., as well as transport and distribution of various petroleum products."[40] The flagship projects were three, potentially four, large refineries and up to seven ethylene-based petrochemical plants.

Oil exploration in Kuwait moved more or less in tandem with Bahrain and Saudi Arabia. The nearby Persian finds had piqued the interest of the Geological Survey of India, and promising seeps were reported in 1912. Emir Sheikh Mubarak bin Sabah tried unsuccessfully to interest British companies in a concession. Frank Holmes' efforts to iniate exploration in the 1920s met with skepticism. When Holmes sold his concessions to Gulf Oil in 1927, APOC nonetheless decided to give Kuwait another look. Following years of parallel negotiations with the British and American contenders, the Kuwait Oil Company (KOC) was established in 1933 as a British–American partnership by APOC and Gulf Oil in an arrangement facilitated by the Mellon family. Andrew Mellon served as the US ambassador in London while his nephew William was chairman of Gulf. The new company was granted a concession for all of Kuwait in December 1934:

> *The area was of 6,000 square miles, the period seventy-five years, the initial payment Rs. 470,000, the annual dead-rent Rs. 95,000, and the royalty Rs. 3 per ton with an annual minimum of Rs. 250,000.*

> *All taxation was commuted to a payment of As. 4 per ton. These payments [were] trivial by comparison with those current in Iraq.*[41]

Drilling eventually began in 1936, and in February 1938 KOC hit the super-giant Burgan field. The oil flow soon reached 4,343 b/d, but commercial development was halted during World War II. KOC quickly made up for lost time thereafter, not least thanks to exceptionally low extraction costs. The first shipment of Burgan crude left Fahahil in June 1946. Total extraction shot up from 800,000 tn in 1946 to 6.3mn tn in 1948, while government income multiplied from $760,000 in 1946 to $5.95mn in 1948. By 1950, the new town of Ahmadi became the KOC operational hub and Mina al Ahmadi emerged as the main outlet of Kuwaiti oil to the world. A small refinery began operations in 1949 with an intake of 25,000 b/d that rose to 30,000 b/d within three years.[42]

Kuwait's rise was propelled forward by Iranian Prime Minister Mohammad Mosaddegh's May 1952 decision to nationalize the Anglo–Iranian Oil Company (previously APOC). In response, the British mobilized their navy to block Iranian oil from the world markets. The departure of British AIOC employees led to acute skill shortages and Iran's oil output plummeted from 241.4mn barrels in 1950 to just 10.6mn in 1952. The Western majors moved to double their production in Iraq, Kuwait, and Saudi Arabia to minimize market disruptions. Kuwait led the way thanks to its "enormous reserves which were close to the sea and very easy to produce."[43] Production rose by 63 percent in 1951 and 33.4 percent in 1952, to 37mn barrels.[44] Government receipts nearly tripled $18mn to $56mn in 1952. The following year, "Kuwait became the biggest oil producer in the Middle East and fourth biggest in the world, its income reached $168 million."[45] Kuwait's output remained on par with Saudi Arabia's until the early 1970s, while the government's oil revenues between 1946 and 1970–1971 totaled KWD3.48bn.[46]

The Kuwaiti authorities set out to boost their bargaining power vis-à-vis the Western majors early on. In 1948, Kuwait granted the American Independent Oil Company (Aminoil) the rights to its share of the Kuwaiti–Saudi neutral zone for a 60-year period. The emir retained rights in the operating and potential refining companies and claimed an eighth of the profits. The royalty of $2.50 a ton was "the highest, beyond compare, in the Middle East at the time."[47] An upfront payment of $7.5mn was followed by annual contributions of $625,000.

The Kuwait Oil Tanker Company was established as a private initiative in 1957, followed three years later by the Kuwait National Petroleum Company (KNPC) as an intended national champion. In 1962, KOC relinquished 60 percent of its concession to KNPC. Following abortive attempts by the government to persuade KOC to create downstream capacity, KNPC focused on refining, and exports from a new 200,000 b/d plant began in 1968. Initially set up by the government and private investors on a 60–40 basis, KNPC was fully nationalized in 1975, as was the tanker company four years later. In 1978 KNPC eventually took control of the Mina Abdulla refinery, which had been built by Aminoil in 1958 and nationalized in 1975. The Mina al Ahmadi refinery was added to the portfolio in 1980. A privately owned Petrochecmial Industries Company,

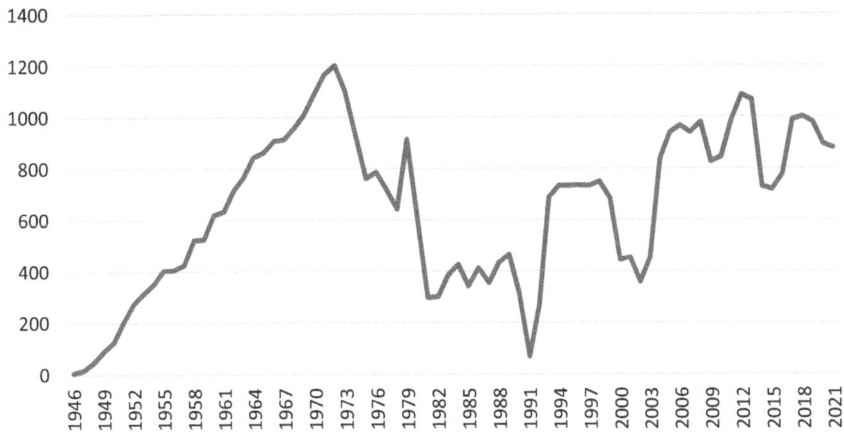

Figure 2.3 Kuwaiti oil production, mn barrels.

Source: OPEC, Kuwait Central Statistical Bureau.

established in 1963, also became part of the government-controlled cluster in 1976. In 1980, Kuwait Petroleum Company was configured as the national holding company responsible for all of these interests.[48]

Frank Holmes was the initial driving force for oil exploration in Qatar. Despite a disappointing 1926 oil survey, the Bahraini strike revived interest, not least because the Qatari peninsula shared many comparable geological features. An APOC mission identified a high-potential area in the Jebel Dukhan area, a curious echo of the Bahrain find. In order to overcome the limitations of the Red Line Agreement, IPC allowed APOC to act in Qatar on its behalf, and in May 1935 the company won a 75-year concession. Apart from a Rs. 3 royalty per ton, a payment of "Rs. 400,000 was to be made on signature, and annual sums of Rs. 150,000 (after five years, Rs. 300,000) were due in addition to royalty."[49] The concession was transferred to an IPC subsidiary named Petroleum Development (Qatar) Ltd.

Drilling of the Dukhan No 1 well began in October 1938 and the first strike materialized just over a year later. Completed in January 1940, the well produced 4,480 b/d. However, all existing wells and installations were destroyed in 1942, and work only resumed five years later. A 120-km pipeline was laid between the Dukhan field and the port of Umm Said (Mesaieed), allowing the first exports to leave Qatar in December 1949. Government income rose rapidly as oil royalties amounted to £400,000 in 1950; in 1951, "the tonnage royalty had been raised by the Company from Rs. 3 to Rs. 10, to £1.75 million. In August 1952 a retrospective arrangement for a half-and-half profit sharing ... was agreed."[50] However, the sudden prosperity also led to disputes within the ruling family and brought in a stronger British presence in return for the recognition of Ali bin Abdullah as ruler. Qatari production rose to 33,800 b/d by 1950 and to 169,000 b/d by 1959.[51]

The 1945 Truman declaration on the continental shelf paved the way for offshore oil exploration, a tantalizing step in view of the location of the known fields on the Gulf littoral. In 1949 Bahrain claimed all resources on its continental shelf subject to agreements with neighboring governments. A maritime border in Saudi Arabia was demarcated in February 1958 and an area designated to the northeast of Bahrain where the profits of all future oil discoveries were to be shared equally between the two neighbors. However, Saudi Arabia would exercise sovereignty and be responsible for field operations. In 1963, Aramco discovered the Abu Sa'fah oil field, where commercial production was launched in 1966.[52] Bahrain's 50 percent share has been the country's main source of oil revenue for since then.

In August 1949, Qatar granted an offshore concession to the International Marine Oil Company, a subsidiary of the Superior Oil Company and Investment Corporation. The concession was eventually transferred to Shell Overseas Exploration Company, whose subsidiary, the Shell Company of Qatar, gained a 75-year concession on the principle of equal profit sharing with the government in 1954. The first successful well was drilled at Idd al Sharqi in May 1960, and commercial production began in 1963, followed by the first exports from Halul Island in February 1964. By 1969, Idd al Sharqi production totaled 35,000 b/d, while another offshore field, Maydan Mahzam, turned out 100,000 b/d, figures that represented nearly half of the national total of 293,000 b/d.[53] Qatar as an oil producer remained in the shadow of Saudi Arabia and Kuwait, but government oil receipts nonetheless totaled QDR5.75bn in 1950–1970.[54]

The South joins in

While the upper Gulf countries transitioned to the oil era within a decade of Bahrain's pioneering find, progress further south proved far slower. Concerned about Holmes' Arabian ventures, APOC, through its D'Arcy Exploration subsidiary, managed to win a two-year exploration license for Oman as early as 1925. However, the work was challenged by tribal conflicts, prompting the geologist George Less to observe that: "Systematic exploration of the Arabian peninsula, or indeed its fringes, is greatly hampered by formidable natural barriers and by the still more serious obstacles caused by the independent spirit of its inhabitants."[55] Ultimately, the D'Arcy survey found little evidence of oil in Oman. Sultan Said bin Taimur nonetheless chose to grant a 75-year concession to an IPC subsidiary, Petroleum Development (Oman and Dhofar) Ltd, in 1937. Exploration was soon frustrated by a local sheikh.

Abu Dhabi's Sheikh Shakhbut bin Sultan Al Nahyan formally engaged IPC to undertake a water survey, but geologist Peter Cox, who arrived in 1935, was encouraged to prospect for oil as well. A two-year option was granted to the English adventurer William "Haji" Williamson in early 1936. A new IPC subsidiary, Petroleum Development (Trucial Coast, PDTC), was set up and more or less immediately focused its attention on the Buraimi Oasis area. PDTC was awarded a 75-year concession in 1939 for a sign-up fee of Rs. 300,000 and an annual rent of Rs. 115,000, just before the war halted all work. Other rulers along the Trucial Coast had entered into similar concession agreements in the 1930s, and payments were honored throughout the global conflict until surveys resumed in 1946. In 1950, Sheikh Shakhbut signed a deal with the Superior Oil Company of California, receiving Rs. 1.5mn up front and a further Rs. 1mn a year until oil was discovered. Drilling began at Ra's Sadr in 1950 and Jebel Ali in 1951 but proved unsuccessful while the Buraimi border dispute with Saudi Arabia halted further work there.[56]

Prospectors on the Trucial Coast took an early interest in offshore prospects. In 1953, a 65-year offshore concession was granted to D'Arcy Exploration, and Abu Dhabi Marine Areas Ltd (ADMA) was established as the operating company by BP and CFP. In 1958, ADMA struck oil at the Umm Shaif field near Das Island, some 160 km to the north of the Abu Dhabi mainland. This lucky strike turned out to have located yet another one of the Gulf region's super-giants. The well was completed in May 1960 and began producing at 3,674 b/d, with the first exports leaving Das Island in July 1962. Murban No. 3 well in the Bab field, located near the coast some 84 km to the southwest of Abu Dhabi, became PDTC's first onshore discovery in late 1959. Once completed in May 1960, it began producing at the rate of 3,674 b/d. Major subsequent discoveries included the Bu Hasa field in 1962 and the offshore Zakum field in 1965. In the first year of commercial oil production in 1962, Abu Dhabi extracted 14,200 b/d of crude, a figure that soon multiplied to 186,800 b/d in 1964. A 112-km pipeline and the Jebel Dhanna export terminal permitted commercial exports starting in December 1963.[57] Within years, Abu Dhabi joined Saudi Arabia and Kuwait in the top tier of Gulf oil producers. The impact on the public treasury was transformative, with oil typically delivering over 90 percent of public income.[58]

In 1937, the ruler of Dubai had secured a 25-year contract with the IPC subsidiary Petroleum Concessions Ltd, which gave him Rs. 60,000 upon signing, an annual rent of Rs. 30,000, an Rs. 200,000 discovery fee, and Rs. 3 per barrel extracted.[59] D'Arcy eventually obtained an offshore concession in Dubai in 1954, but development was delayed until Continental Oil Company bought a 50 percent stake and began drilling 12 years later. Dubai also drew attention as an oil logistics hub, with the British residency reporting in 1954 that "in the event that oil is found in the neighbouring Shaikhdoms, the port of Dubai would be the normal port of entry."[60] After the IPC concession expired in the 1960s, a new Dubai Petroleum Company was established, this time with the additional participation of partners from France, Germany, Spain, and the US.[61] Following the discovery of the offshore Fateh field in 1966, Dubai dispatched its first exports in 1969. Sharjah's protocol agreement with Iran over the disputed Abu Musa Island ensured that oil from the Mubarak field, discovered by the Buttes Gas and Oil Company operating through Crescent Petroleum in 1972, was shared equally with the northern neighbor. However, output levels began to decline quite quickly. Ra's al Khaimah's Saleh field was discovered in 1983 but is no longer active. The government of Abu Dhabi collected a total of BHD395.9mn from the oil companies active in the emirate between 1962 and 1970. Dubai's oil revenues in 1969–1970 totaled QDR154.3mn.[62]

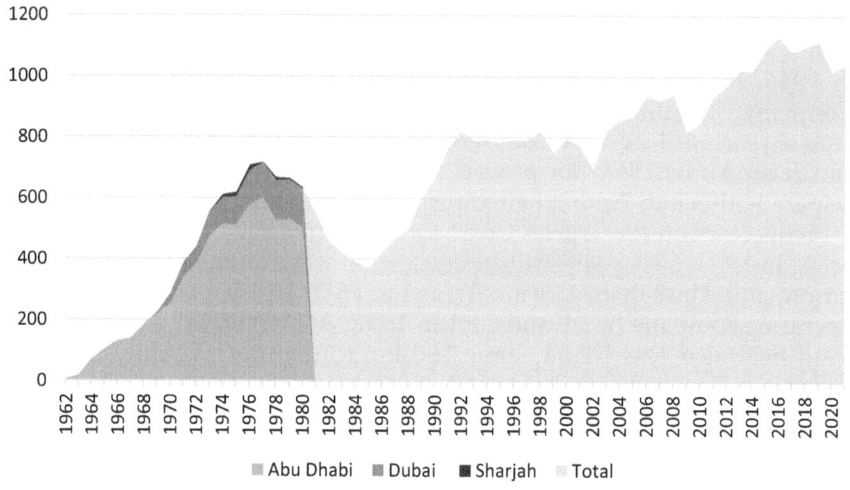

Figure 2.4 UAE oil extraction, mn barrels.

Note: The data series up to 1980 is broken down by emirate, starting in 1981 aggregate UAE national data.

The UAE set up its first refinery operations in 1976 – a 15,000 b/d facility at Umm al Nar. Its capacity was subsequently progressively increased to 90,000 b/d. The Ruwais refinery began operations in 1981 with an initial capacity of 27,000 b/d.

The development of the Omani oil sector lagged far behind the rest of the region. After World War II, Sultan Said bin Taimur asked Sir Cyril Fox of the Geological Survey of India to map out prospects in the southwestern region of Dhofar. A 1948 IPC mission delivered a negative conclusion, and the company relinquished its concession in 1950. In 1952, the concession was awarded to an American archeologist Wendell Phillips. Once again, tribal unrest disrupted work around Jebel Fahud of central Oman. The reconfigured Petroleum Development Oman (PDO) tried a new approach through Duqm in 1954, and drilling finally began in 1956. Shell launched a new drilling program in 1962, and the first successful well was eventually completed at Yibal in April 1962. Located near the Buraimi oasis, Yibal has remained Oman's largest field to this day, even though production has more than halved from the peak of 250,000 b/d. In subsequent years, a string of discoveries was made near Fahud and a 276-km pipeline was built to the coastal port of Saih al Maleh (renamed Mina al Fahal) near Muscat. Oman became the last Gulf country to join the club of oil exporters in July 1967. Oman made further significant discoveries in the 1970s and evenutally boosted its output to 400,000 b/d by the end of 1984.[63]

It took a full three decades for all of the GCC member states to establish themselves as oil producers. While all of them initially recorded substantial output gains, significant differences soon became apparent, effectively dividing the region into two groups. On the one hand, Saudi Arabia, Kuwait, and Abu Dhabi quickly established themselves as globally significant oil suppliers – and all of them eventually joined OPEC (Organization of the Petroleum Exporting Countries). All three countries are home to some of the largest super-giant fields in the world. By contrast, Bahrain, Qatar, and Oman made slower progress and eventually saw the momentum stall to varying degrees, although Qatar did join OPEC. In absolute terms, the largest oil reserves on the peninsula are found in Saudi Arabia, while Qatar leads the way in gas and can look forward to substantial gas surpluses for decades to come.

The variation in hydrocarbons endowments proved particularly pronounced when considered in per capita terms. The northern emirates of the UAE were the first ones to have to confront the end of the oil era in a federation where Abu Dhabi controls an estimated 94 percent of the total reserves. For instance, Dubai's production peaked at 410,000 b/d as early as 1992, before declining to 170,000 b/d by the end of the decade. It now stands at less than 70,000 b/d and the known reserves are expected to be exhausted within two decades. The onshore Margham field has been producing condensate at 25,000 b/d. Sharjah's production from the offshore Mubarak field in 1974 reached 60,000 b/d but had slumped to 5,900 b/d in 1985 before rebounding somewhat to 6,000 b/d in 2000. Ra's al Khaimah produced oil from at the modest rate of 11–12,000 b/d for awhile.

Comparable trends have been observed in Bahrain and Oman, although a combination of enhanced recovery techniques and further prospecting has successfully arrested and even reversed a the output declines. In Bahrain, production from the region's oldest oil field peaked at 79,000 b/d in 1970 before gradually declining to 32,000 b/d by 2009. It has since recovered to at times more than 50,000 b/d and continues to be supplemented by relatively steady 150,000 b/d production from Abu Sa'afah. In Oman, production declined from 972,0000 b/d in 2000 to 714,800 in 2012 but has subsequently rebounded to around 1mn b/d. Gas production has also expanded, most recently thanks to the Khazzan–Makarem tight gas deposit that was discovered in 2000. It began production in 2017, complemented by the nearby Ghazeer field starting in 2020. Qatar has recently seen a gradual decline in its modest oil production, albeit seemingly because of a strategic choice to prioritize the much more ample gas reserves, something that was reflected in the 2018 decision to leave OPEC.

However divergent the hydrocarbon endowments of the individual Gulf economies, they nonetheless invariably count as the most important natural resource of each country. Besides some mineral deposits, mainly in Saudi Arabia and Oman, the region has minimal other resource endowments to turn to. Even the region's smallest producer, Bahrain, has made significant strides in developing its hydrocarbons assets but also in terms of vertical integration. Now standing at clearly less than 20 percent of real GDP, the hydrocarbons sector is continuing to attract some substantial investments. The $4.2bn Bapco Modernization Program, which is creating one of the most complex refineries globally, is the largest single infrastructure project in the Kingdom's history. Similarly, the announcement of the Khalij al Bahrain offshore oil field and deep gas field discoveries in 2018 may herald a new lease on life for Bahrain's upstream sector. Exploration for new deposits has continued also in Dubai and the northern emirates.

Forging the "oil–government nexus"

Even if the penury of the 1930s drove the fiscal appetite for oil exploration, the actual windfalls far exceeded expectations. Whether the concession agreements were "fair" or not, they did promise both sides a marked improvement over the preceding status quo. The economic consequences of the oil strikes proved very similar across the Gulf. Oil created a revenue source that decisively dwarfed everything that had preceded it and quickly relegated the earlier fiscal constraints to memory. The most immediate beneficiary of this windfall was the "public treasury" – in practice, varying combinations of the government administration and the royal household. It was the "government" that, through the local rulers, had permitted oil exploration and could claim a legitimate status as the guardian of local natural resources. As oil showered the region, policymakers were left to figure out how to "channel this relatively sudden and unprecedented growth into stabilizing, orderly and self-sustaining development."[64]

Bahrain served as the pioneering example of the economic and fiscal transformation that oil delivered. The Bahraini lease agreement of 1930 had stipulated a minimal annual state revenue of Rs. 75,000 as well as an Rs. 3.5 royalty per ton. This translated into 14 percent of the value of the oil extracted, although Bapco also benefited from substantial tax and customs duty exemptions. By 1934, oil already delivered nearly a third of government income, and the revenue increase in 1935 alone was a remarkable Rs. 2,408,900.[65] In 1938–1939, Bahraini oil receipts were Rs. 3,544,283 compared to total government income of Rs. 7,404,325. By fueling imports, the oil sector also pushed up the income from customs duties. Nonetheless, oil decisively dwarfed customs receipts of Rs. 1,087,396 and even the budgeted expenditures, which reached Rs. 3,108,038.

A new agreement with Bapco in 1940 involved a lump-sum payment of Rs. 400,000 (30,000 pounds), followed by a minimum of 95,000 pounds in annual royalties during an initial 15-year period, to be further raised to 127,500 pounds in the event that new finds were made. By 1951, oil revenues were budgeted at Rs. 13,800,000, over two-thirds of the total budgeted revenues of Rs. 20,350,000, which now contrasted with expenditures of Rs. 5,200,000. The fiscal reliance on oil saw little change thereafter. As Bahrain's oil production rose from 65,000 b/d in 1966 to 70,000 b/d in 1967, government revenues reached BD12,399,184, of which 63 percent came from oil royalties at 20 percent from customs receipts.[66]

Developments elsewhere in the region were broadly comparable. Saudi oil revenues shot up from $10.4mn in 1946 to $333.7mn in 1960, $1,214mn in 1970, and $104.2bn in 1980. By 1970, some 88 percent of government revenues came from oil, a proportion that rose to 92 percent in 1973.[67] In Kuwait, the dependency was even greater. In Qatar, however, oil established itself as the main government revenue source only in the 1950s, reflecting the later start of commercial extraction.

The "oil–government nexus" consolidated itself at the core of the new conomic order in the Gulf with extraordinary speed. A clear ratchet effect was at play from the very beginning as the growing oil receipts drove new, increasingly ambitious development plans while simultaneously fueling the

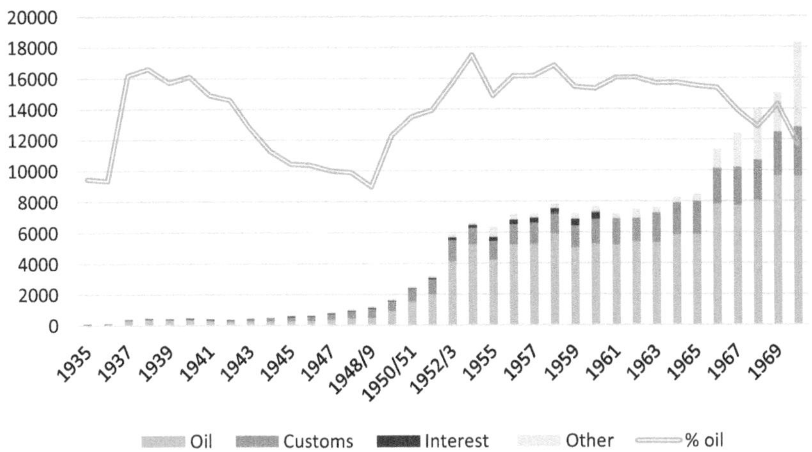

Figure 2.5 Composition of Bahrain's budget revenues, BHD '000.

Source: Al-Kuwari, Oil Revenues in the Gulf Emirates, p. 88.

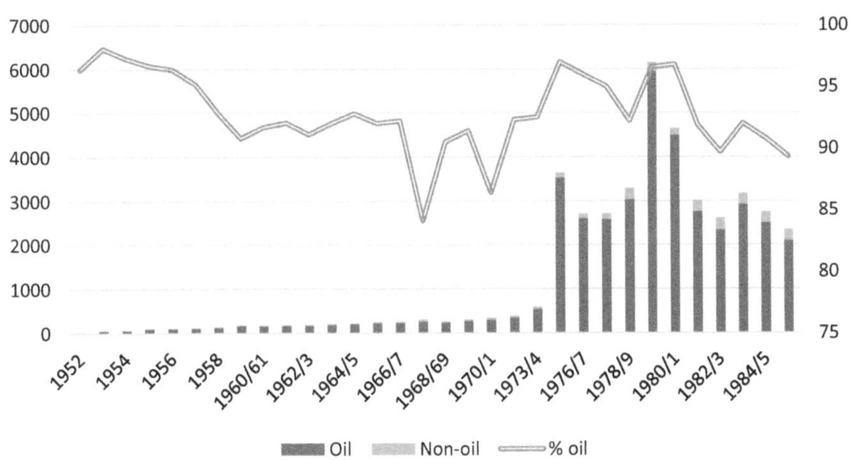

Figure 2.6 Composition of Kuwait's budget revenues, KWD million.

Source: Al-Kuwari, Oil Revenues in the Gulf Emirates, pp. 104, 110; Al-Dekhayel, Kuwait, p. 27.

expansion of the government sector. The relentless upward momentum of public spending soon made the concession agreements subject to scrutiny. After all, higher spending could only be funded in any one of three ways or a combination thereof: (i) increased oil production, which necessitated investment on the part of the foreign-controlled operating companies and could not thus be decided locally; (ii) increased prices, which were set by the international demand and supply conditions, although accounting practices could have some implications for Gulf government revenues; or (iii) a renegotiation of the revenue-sharing deal between the oil companies and the regionals governments. All three factors were at play, but the third option was seen to offer the greatest potential.

During the early oil era, increasing productive capacity was the main driver of revenue growth. In 1950, Aramco's $230mn pipeline from eastern Saudi Arabia to the Lebanese port of Sidon drove rapid growth. The Tapline's initial capacity of 300,000 b/d eventually rose to 500,000 b/d, and its massive capital requirements were met by turning Aramco into a four-way partnership in which Socal, Texaco, and Standard Oil of New Jersey (subsequently Exxon) each held 30 percent, along with Socony Vacuum's (subsequently Mobil) 10 percent stake.[68] This was connected with the American claim that the original Red Line Agreement had been rendered invalid during the war as CFP and Gulbenkian could be deemed enemy aliens due to the German occupation of France. A restructuring at IPC was used to push for the desired overhaul of Aramco's ownership structure.[69]

A sequence of economic challenges in the postwar years revealed the downside of agreements that linked government income to oil production volumes. Profit-sharing agreements presented an alternative pioneered by the Venezuelan government, which, frustrated by its revenues from oil field operators, in November 1948 "enacted an income-tax law that guaranteed a fifty-fifty division of profits. ... All existing taxes and royalties were left intact, but ... if oil income exceeded the aggregate of those taxes and royalties in a taxable year, the excess would be subject to an additional tax of 50 percent."[70] Saudi Arabia was quick to pay attention. The government's wartime financial difficulties had underscored the asymmetric relationship with Aramco, which pocketed a $1.10 profit per barrel while the Saudi treasury received a 21 cent royalty. King Abdulaziz, raising the prospect of nationalization, was able to win approval for profit sharing in 1950. The agreement was structured as an unusual win–win initiative whereby the Saudi government's revenues increase came at no loss for Aramco: "This miracle was achieved by calling the increased royalty an 'income tax' which, under the US tax code, could be deducted from tax payments at home."[71] Aramco's payments to the Saudi government nearly tripled from $39.2mn in 1949 to $111.7mn in 1950. The headquarters moved from New York to Dhahran.

The Venezuelan model quickly became the norm. The Kuwaiti authorities concluded a 50–50 agreement with KOC in 1950. The Bahraini royalty was more than tripled to Rs. 10 per ton following a devaluation in 1950, effectively making the Treasury's share 19 percent. Equal profit sharing was agreed in 1952 when Bapco's output reached 11mn barrels (30,000 b/d). This pushed up the Treasury receipts from around £400,000 a year until 1950 to some £2.25mn starting in 1952 thanks to a new fluctuating income tax.[72] In September 1952, PDQ committed to a 50–50 split, while Abu Dhabi conformed to the new regional norm in 1965.

Even as profit sharing improved the position of the Gulf treasuries, the upward momentum of government spending proved hard to restrain. A well-known case in point was a major financial crisis in Saudi Arabia in the late 1950s. A robust increase in government spending coincided with ineffective budgeting and production cuts by

Aramco. A fiscal system accustomed to passively channeling rising oil receipts soon cracked:

> *... contractors remained unpaid for completed projects while being asked to start work on new and equally costly ones, importers were not paid for goods delivered, and government employees were paid erratically, if at all. Gold and foreign currency reserves fell to their lowest ever, the rial's market value sunk to about half its official value, and the public debt rose by late 1957 to 1,800 million rials.*[73]

Stability was restored under the ensuing premiership of Prince – future King – Faisal with the support of an IMF–World Bank reform program. Gold and foreign currency reserves rebounded from $24mn to $186mn, and the government repaid its $180.7mn debt to SAMA. The riyal was devalued to 4.50 to the dollar and a budget surplus was once again achieved by 1961.[74] The crisis underscored the importance of good governance, especially as the rest of the region faced similar challenges. Bahrain recorded a budget deficit in 1961 and, with the exception of 1963, continue to post shorfalls until the 1970s. Even Kuwait saw deficits in 1959 and again in 1966–1967.[75]

A similar story played out in Oman during the first years of Sultan Qaboos' tenure, partly because of the costly Dhofar conflict. In 1972–1973 the government deficit reached OMR32mn ($124.7mn), further increasing to OMR42.6mn in 1974.[76] Loans from Saudi Arabia and Abu Dhabi helped bridge the shortfall but barely avoided a default in 1975. A World Bank technical assistance program led to the adoption of a more structured approach to economic and financial planning. The debt-to-GDP ratio, having peaked at 25.3 percent in 1976, nearly halved to 13.1 percent in 1979. Similar challenges emerged region-wide after the oil price corrections in the 1980s and 1990, as well as after 2008–2014.

Caught unawares

The onset of the oil era propelled a poor, sparsely populated part of the world to previously unfathomable prosperity. While the financial constraints on economic development were lifted almost instantaneously, the Gulf struggled to make effective use of the windfalls. The public administration was at best skeletal, the regional labor force small, the education system rudimentary at best, and the availability of specific skills extremely scarce. Those reared by a pre-modern economy were ill-prepared to serve as architects and engineers of modernization. This was to draw the region into an enduring dependence on external equipment, know-how, and manpower. Of course, the oil windfall did not all have to be spent. Saving offered many benefits, not least since it limited the distortionary impact on the broader economy. But in a region with no modern financial intermediaries to speak of, even saving created a dependency on external providers.

The oil windfall lent a potent impetus to the development of the public sector, as the Gulf governments by default assumed the role of distributors-in-chief. This gave rise to what has been referred to variously as the allocation, circulation, distribution, or (oil) rentier economies where "*the state becomes the main intermediary between the oil sector and the rest of the economy.*"[77] Under this model, "the creation of wealth is centred around [the state]; the rest of the society is only engaged in the distribution and utilisation of this wealth."[78] In short order, the ballooning oil–government nexus at the heart of the Gulf economy became the cuckoo chick that completely rearranged its abode and soon pushed out vestiges of the pre-hydrocarbons era.[79] While, for instance, Abu Dhabi's Sheikh Shakhbut at first sought to control the oil-funded modernization, his successor Sheikh Zayed put the emirate on a fast development trajectory after 1966.[80] A similar dynamic played out in Oman after the transition to Sultan Qaboos.

The early oil era saw substantial capital expenditure due to the need for broad-based modernization. In Bahrain, the share of capital expenditure was 19.4 percent between 1947–1948 and 1970 with a 1955 peak of 37.3 percent. Kuwait recoded an average of 18.8 percent in 1952 to 1970–1971. Having been as high as 70 percent in 1953, it touched a low of 8.6 percent in 1965–1966. Qatar allocated 17.1 percent of its budgets on capital expenditure in 1953–1970. With time, the share of government-funded investment declined in favor of recurrent spending, reflecting both the rising expectations of the population and the improving level of infrastructure.[81]

While the rapid development of the public sector stimulated new economic activities, it also made private businesses increasingly reliant on public expenditure. Importing consumables and capital goods, as well as contracting in connection with government infrastructure projects, became the backbone of the new Gulf corporate sector. New business elites were heavily shaped by personal relationships, reflecting government licensing practices: "The big trading houses, the family conglomerates that are involved in all business matters owe their wealth, one way or another, to some rent situation. Being a sales agent [is] the classical road to business and hence to wealth."[82] As a result, the failure of the pre-oil regional economy to build productive, rather than extractive or distributive, capacity carried over to the oil era. For instance, the 1980–1985 Saudi Third Development Plan explicitly recognized that "economic development is to a very large extent governmental activity" and "the private sector is dependent on government expenditure."[83]

The oil–government nexus made the public sector the ultimate underwriter of prosperity in the region. The hydrocarbons wealth came to be spread through an array of universal subsidies – effectively "negative taxation" – which drove up living standards but also meant that private companies could benefit from below-market and relatively static input costs.[84] Even economic downturns never fundamentally challenged the model but merely slowed down or paused its expansion. Consequently, as noted by Osama: "Economic activities have been oriented towards consumption rather than production, and 'symbols' of development have been imported such as advanced equipment and means of transportation. As a result, a gap has been created between people's aspirations and what they actually do to realise them."[85] The Gulf economic model gave rise to society of consumers, intermediaries, and distributors, not of creators or innovators.

The oil–government nexus had profound implications for the regional growth dynamics. On the positive side, oil reduced the need to seek other public sector funding sources and thus eased any potential fiscal burden on local businesses and individuals. But it also meant that the effects of oil price volatility would be amplified through variations in government spending and multiplier effects on the rest of the economy. Moreover, by reducing the perceived need for other kinds of funding mechanisms, the oil–government nexus delayed the development of the financial sector. The oil sector dynamics dictated banking sector liquidity, which meant that oil price variations would reverberate across the economy with often brute force.[86]

Shaping the global market

Oil became the fuel that defined the 20th century. Its share of commercial energy demand worldwide rose from 9 percent in 1920 to 55 percent by 1980, a period during which total energy consumption increased almost seven-fold.[87] During the decades of postwar reconstruction and rapid economic growth between 1950 and 1972, global energy consumption charged ahead by 179 percent. Oil met a lion's share of this increase and saw its share in global energy consumption shoot up from 29 percent to 46 percent. By 1973, oil accounted for 47 percent of all US energy use, but the dependency of other advanced economies was even greater: 64 percent in Western Europe and a remarkable 80 percent in Japan.[88]

This state of affairs put the Middle East in a pole position from the perspective of global energy security. Ensuring access to Gulf oil became a key goal of US foreign policy, starting with the February 1945 encounter between President Roosevelt and King Abdulaziz of Saudi Arabia. In a world torn into two competing blocks, the Gulf became the main repository of oil for the non-Communist countries. Its importance grew further with the rapidly rising US reliance on oil imports as domestic production began to drop in the early 1970s. Between 1948 and 1971, US reserves had risen from 21 to 38bn barrels while its total output nearly doubled fom 5.5 to 9.5mn b/d. But the global market share of the US shrank sharply from 64 percent to 22 percent. The situation was even more acute in Europe, where most of the known oil deposits had been left behind the Iron Curtain and the coal sector was suffering from critical shortages. The British government was particularly keen to protect its Gulf interests, which went far beyond just oil. For instance, an assessment of policy goals in Kuwait in 1953 sought to "ensure that Kuwait's investments would take place as much as possible in the sterling area" and "secure as much of Kuwait's trade as possible for British firms."[89]

This global context quickly turned oil into a highly politicized resource. For the Gulf economies, external demand trends offered the primary means of projecting their influence internationally. As global crude production rose from 8.7mn b/d to 42mn b/d between 1948 and 1972, the Middle Eastern output climbed from 1.1mn b/d to 18.2mn b/d. The global reserves moved up from 62 to 534bn barrels, while the Middle Eastern reserves posted a rise from 28 to 367bn barrels. Gulf oil production boomed ahead from some 350mn barrels in 1950 to exceed 1bn in 1960, 2.5bn in 1970, and nearly 5.5bn in 1980.[90] As of 1960, the Gulf Arab states accounted for 15 percent of global oil production, while a further 10 percent came from Iraq and Iran. By 1978, the Gulf states had nearly doubled their market share to a quarter of the global total.

Despite these shifts, the global oil market remained firmly in the hands of the leading Western oil majors that had shaped the industry: Standard Oil of New Jersey (Esso, Exxon), Standard Oil Company of New York (Socony, later Mobil), Standard Oil of California (Socal, Chevron), Gulf Oil, Texaco, Royal Dutch Shell, and British Petroleum (the successor of APOC/AIOC). Courtesy of Enrico Mattei, an Italian diplomat, the group came to be referred to as the Seven Sisters. CFP was another player of international stature. This market architecture represented a natural oligopoly and created obvious incentives for collusion; eight Western companies "controlled about 96 percent of Middle East production in 1959"[91] (including Iraq and Iran). A secret deal had been signed in 1928 between APOC, Shell, and Standard Oil of New Jersey at Achnacarry Castle in Scotland to establish output quotas in order to reduce competition and increase prices. This setup was appropriately branded by a 1952 US Federal Trade Commission report as the International Petroleum Cartel.[92]

As the geographic footprint of the upstream oil industry expanded, the unquestioned dominance by the majors generated controversy in many producer nations for which oil represented a critical source – often the only one – of export revenues. This resentment came to a head in the late 1950s when the Seven Sisters actively colluded to curb market prices. The immediate reason was the re-emergence of the Soviet Union as an oil exporter in 1955, accompanied by aggressive efforts to gain market share in Europe and Asia alike: "In these Cold War years, many in the West believed that the intensifying Soviet petroleum campaign represented not only a commercial venture, but also a political assault, the purpose of which was to create dependence in Western Europe, weaken the unity of NATO, and subvert the Western oil position in the Middle East."[93] In practice, while ideological factors doubtless played a role, so did the economic needs of the postwar Soviet Union for which "[o]il exports ... were one of the few things that they had to sell to the West"[94] in their desperate quest for hard currency. Coinciding with brisk output growth in the Middle East, these developments soon created a glut in the markets.

The Seven Sisters began a series of price cuts in February 1959. At the time, they controlled some 90 percent of the global market, a share that was to decline to 72 percent by 1972. By August 1960, Saudi oil prices had been brought down to $1.80 per barrel – a level last seen a full decade earlier. In contrast to the oil exporters, the cartel was relatively less sensitive to price fluctuations thanks to its developed downstream operations, whose margins invariably benefited from lower crude prices. Moreover, most downstream operations were located in the main consumer markets. Further tensions were created by a decision made by the Eisenhower administration to introduce a Mandatory Import Quota Program in order to protect US producers. This initially limited the imports of crude and refined products to less than 9 percent of domestic demand, a figure that was raised to 12.2 percent in 1962.[95]

These developments fundamentally threatened the ever more ambitious spending plans devised by the Gulf governments. An Arab Petroleum Congress held in Cairo in April 1959 called on the international oil majors to avoid unilateral decisions on output and prices while urging consultations with producer nations. A group of leading Middle Eastern producers informally met with Venezuelan representatives and agreed to seek their governments' backing for a consultative committee on oil with a view to boosting government revenues. The majors went ahead with a new round of price cuts, provoking the producers to call for an emergency meeting of Venezuela, Saudi Arabia, Iran, Iraq, and Kuwait in Baghdad in September 1960. The gathering formally established OPEC. The global oil market would never be the same again.[96]

OPEC was, from its inception, designed to be a power to reckon with as its five founding members accounted for more than 80 percent of global crude exports. The establishment of the organization represented "the first collective act of sovereignty on the part of the oil exporters," in the words of Fadhil al Chalabi, later an OPEC Deputy Secretary General, as well as "the first turning point," as he put it, "in the international economic relations towards the states' control over natural resources."[97] By contrast, the majors at first dismissed the organization, assuming that it could never work. After all, the global oil glut in the late 1950s had dramatically intensified the competition for market share. Moreover, in all of the member states, bar Iran, "the oil reserves in the ground actually belonged by contract to the concessionaires, the companies, thus limiting the countries' control."[98] Beyond this, the new organization faced some internal discord, not least the Iraqi threat toward Kuwait, which the government of Abdulkarim Qasim viewed as a renegade province. Saudi relations toward the West in fact improved markedly following the ascent to the throne of King Faisal and the departure of one of OPEC's main architects, Abdullah Tariki, from government.[99]

Despite these divergent reactions, unilateral price cuts by the majors soon became a thing of the past and major decisions were henceforth preceded by consultations with the producer nations. With time, OPEC's influence on output levels grew. A long period of relative price stability – or stagnation, depending on the perspective taken – ensued, with the price "being fixed at $1.75/barrel in August 1951 and ending up at just $1.80/barrel in February 1971."[100] This continuity helped fuel further rapid demand growth, partly because of the stimulus it imparted to downstream manufacturing, such as petrochemicals. Moreover, it entrenched the competitiveness of the Gulf producers, thanks to real production costs estimated at no more than $0.20 per barrel in their main fields.[101] As the global demand for oil grew, the Gulf economies could once again benefit from rising production to drive their domestic economic dynamics. For instance, Saudi Arabia saw average annual GDP growth of 10.5 percent in 1962–1967.

Despite this apparent Goldilocks scenario, growing fissures appeared in the global economy as the postwar expansion began to age. Mounting fiscal pressures created by the Cold War, most notably the protracted military conflict in Vietnam, challenged the postwar economic architecture. In a dramatic move, in August 1971 the Nixon administration took the US off the Bretton Woods gold exchange standard. The dollar floated and the US money supply began to expand. This quickly laid the groundwork for another conflict with OPEC as the dollar depreciation translated into lower oil revenues for the producer nations. In response, OPEC called on its members to push for price increases, which indeed materialized in 1972–1973.[102]

Amid growing economic turmoil, politics emerged as another important influence on the market. In September 1969, Muammar Qaddafi overthrew the Libyan monarchy on an openly nationalist agenda. His key demands included a more favorable deal with the 21 foreign oil companies active in the country. Libya at the time met a third of Europe's oil consumption. Following an initial agreement with Occidental, Qaddafi was able to secure his government a majority share (54–58 percent) of the profits generated by the all of the oil companies operating in Libya.[103] Other OPEC nations quickly followed suit. A December 1970 OPEC gathering in Caracas agreed to impose a 55 percent minimum tax rate on oil companies.

At the same time, the US saw its energy independence begin to slip away at an alarming pace. As of 1970, the US was the world's largest producer of oil, with peak production of 11.3mn b/d, but declining output amid booming demand soon thereafter forced President Richard M. Nixon to terminate the Mandatory Oil Import Quota Program. Imports of foreign crude shot up from 2.2mn b/d in 1967 to 6.2mn in 1973, pushing up US import dependency from 19 to 35 percent of total consumption. This further increased to 60 percent by the 1980s. In response, the US government looked to Saudi Arabia to hike its output from 8.5mn b/d in 1973 to 20mn b/d by 1980.[104] No less disconcerting, the global "reserve/production ratio was also steadily falling – from about 64 in 1960 to 52 in 1965 and 37 in 1970."[105]

In a major triumph for OPEC, the international majors approached the organization in January 1971 with a proposal for a new settlement. The Tehran agreement of February 1971 established a 55–45 profit-sharing model between six Middle Eastern producer nations and 22 global oil companies. It further increased the price of Arabian Light, the Saudi benchmark, from $1.80 to $2.18, which was due to be followed by annual inflation-adjusted increases of five cents a barrel.[106] In the case of Iran, the desire for higher prices was in no small measure driven by the government's ambitious development plans and unprecedented weapons purchases, facilitated in part by the US desire to position the country as the "policeman of the Gulf," which resulted in chronic fiscal challenges.[107] An April 1971 deal in Tripoli, involving Saudi Arabia, Iraq, Algeria, and the host nation itself, hiked the posted price in the Mediterranean to $3.45. The oil market began to tighten quite quickly in 1973. The price of Arabian Light rose form $2.59 per barrel in January to $2.95 by July.

Politics again intervened to complicate matters. On 6 October, the Egyptian and Syrian armed forces launched a surprise attack on Israel with the objective of expelling it from the Sinai Peninsula and the Golan Heights, which it had occupied in 1967. The operation had major implications for the oil market as the leaders of Egypt and Saudi Arabia had previously agreed to stop exports to Israel's allies. Ten days later, the so-called Gulf Six (Saudi Arabia, Kuwait, UAE, Qatar, Iraq, and Iran) agreed to hike the oil price from $3.01 per barrel to $5.12, while an embargo was instituted on the US, the Netherlands, Portugal, South Africa, and Rhodesia. Monthly production cuts were planned but ultimately not implemented. However, shipments to the US were completely halted following the announcement of a $2.2bn financial aid package to Israel by President Nixon on 19 October. The embargo was eventually lifted in March 1974.

Although producer compliance with the embargo was never total, the year 1973 marked a dramatic shift for the global economy as well as for the fiscal position of OPEC. The shock fundamentally shaped market expectations by underscoring the possibility of significant supply disruptions and revealing the sudden, sizeable impact these could have. Although a ceasefire materialized in the Arab–Israeli conflict on 25 October, a December 1973 OPEC meeting nonetheless proceeded to set a historically high oil price of $11.65 per barrel. With their pricing power reaching unprecedented heights, the OPEC members saw their oil revenues skyrocket from $7.7bn in 1970 to $88.8bn in 1974. For instance, Qatar's oil receipts of $1.9bn in 1974 compared to government expenditure of less than $150mn.[108]

More problematically, the seeming triumph of OPEC came with an increasingly bitter aftertaste. The extraordinary price rally delivered a major economic shock to Western consumer nations and put an abrupt end to decades of rapid demand growth as one consumer country after the other plunged into an economic crisis. In some cases, the situation became extremely precarious:

> *... over the summer of 1974 ... [t]he bottom was about to fall out of an Italian economy staggered by rising fuel costs, galloping inflation of 18.7 percent and 800,000 unemployed. ... [In Portugal, i]nflation was running at between 30 and 40 percent, tourism receipts were down 30 percent, and the breakdown of basic public services coincided with a deadly cholera epidemic.*[109]

Amid Cold War rivalry, right-wing governments collapsed across the Iberian Peninsula and in Greece, while the Soviets sensed an opportunity in France and Italy. A fundamental political reshaping of the Western world was viewed as a distinct possibility, with US Secretary of State Henry Kissinger observing that: "[t]he increasing costs of oil is prompting a significant number of Americans ... to consider the price of oil as the main reason for the collapse of the democratic regimes in Western Europe, which would make these countries ripe for Communist domination."[110]

But the crisis also began to reshape consumer behavior and policy, encouraging many countries to diversify their energy provision while also drawing attention to the importance of conservation. The US created the largest strategic petroleum reserve in the world, while alternative energy sources in time pushed oil off its pedestal as the main energy source for stationary uses. But the shock also encouraged exploration for new sources of oil. Among other things, the booming prices drew attention to the relatively costly North Sea and Alaskan oil reserves. With so many elements of the market now in flux, the year 1973 paved the way for exceptional market volatility.

For the Gulf economies, these new energy realities entailed significant complications. Attempts to stabilize prices required key producers to modify their output levels. But the profound structural shifts of the oil market also began to erode the ability of the OPEC producers to influence market dynamics as new sources of supply began to come online. Domestically, the oil boom firmly cemented the oil–government nexus, indeed to a point where the regional governments dismantled most remaining non-oil revenues sources while dramatically expanding the range of subsidies and benefits available to the citizenry. The fiscal and economic future of the Gulf region came to be ever more intimately tied to the black gold even as market fundamentals began to turn against the region.

Back to the drawing board

The 1970s marked a major milestone in the efforts of the Gulf governments to assert control over their national wealth. Not only had decades of rapid development strengthened the ability of the Gulf economies to assume a formal stake in managing their hydrocarbons assets but since late 1971, all of them were fully sovereign states. The concept of participation was seen as a way to fundamentally redraft the old concession agreements. Saudi-led negotiations on behalf of the Gulf countries ultimately culminated in an October 1972 agreement in New York, which "gave the producing states an initial 25 per cent ownership immediately, rising to 30 per cent in 1979, and thereafter by 5 per cent yearly until the magic figure of 51 per cent was reached in 1983."[111] However, control and management of the companies were still to be left in the hands of their Western founders. In practice, OPEC was not united behind the deal, and even Kuwait opted out.[112]

Political developments soon left these plans a dead letter. In response to US military support for Israel in 1973, the Saudi government took a 25 percent stake in Aramco and pushed this up to a controlling 60 percent in the following year. Riyadh eventually assumed full control of the company in 1980. In 1988, the national champion was formally renamed Saudi Arabian Oil Co (Saudi Aramco) and assumed full control of managing and operating all of the Kingdom's hydrocarbons assets. In 1972, the government of Qatar established the Qatar National Oil Company and the following year claimed 25 percent stakes in each of Qatar Petroleum Company and Shell Company of Qatar. 1974 saw the establishment of the General Petroleum Corporation, which took 60 percent holdings in the operating companies. In 1975, the government decreed full national ownership, which was implemented by early 1977 when the former concessionaries instead received service contracts. KOC became a fully government-owned entity in 1975 and placed under the umbrella of the Kuwait National Petroleum Company, which brought together all national hydrocabons assets in 1980. In 1976, the Bahraini government bought 60 percent of Bapco, and full government control was achieved in 1980.

Developments in the southern Gulf once again played out somewhat differently. The Abu Dhabi National Oil Company was established in 1971 and initially took a 25 percent stake in ADPC and ADMA. In December 1974, the interest in the operating companies rose to 60 percent. However, the 40 percent stake retained by the foreign owners was substantial compared to the new regional norm. The government has exercised ultimate oversight over the development of the hydrocarbons sector through the Supreme Petroleum Council since 1988 even as the individual emirates retain responsibility for managing their own hydrocarbons affairs. Dubai's energy policy is overseen by the Dubai Supreme Council of Energy, while Dubai Petroleum Establishment became fully government owned in 2007. Abu Dhabi relies on long-term production-sharing agreements between ADNOC and private companies, although the state holds a majority stake in all projects. In Oman, PDO established itself as the national champion, with roughly 70 percent of crude production but also virtually all of the natural gas output. The government took a 25 percent stake as of January 1974, increased to 60 percent halfway through the year. Shell was left with 34 percent of PDO, Total with 4 percent, and Partex with 2 percent.

As the Gulf countries imposed national control over their primary natural resource, they could align the development of the sector with their broader national strategies. Their ability to boost investment in exploration and productive capacity gave them greater strategic leverage as producers. They could also adopt a much more holistic approach to developing the hydrocarbons and related clusters, thereby potentially capturing much more of the relevant value chains.

Conclusions: A curious sense of déjà vu

Oil made the modern Gulf. It funded the region's broader modernization from extremely challenging initial conditions. The once cash-strapped Gulf governments evolved into the distributive heart of the economy, although a sizeable proportion of the wealth was also saved.[113] Oil funded everything from physical to social infrastructure, effectively rooting all development in the mounting hydrocarbons wealth. The expanding oil–government nexus crowded out other economic activities, consigning most of the pre-oil entrepreneurial traditions to history. The ability of local merchants to adapt to the new realities was constrained by foreign control of the oil cluster as well as financial constraints. Instead, the private sector came to be shaped by a rapidly deepening dependency on oil-funded imports and construction projects. This turned many Gulf merchants into residual claimants from a transformation made possible by others.

Despite its dramatic scale and speed, the oil-funded economic transformation shared numerous commonalities with the pre-oil era. Oil dramatically entrenched the long-standing role of openness as a guarantor of prosperity. The Gulf countries initially possessed neither the capital nor the know-how to develop the sector and thus had to depend on the international majors. As local energy demand in the Gulf was minimal, the hydrocarbons plenty could only be monetized through exports. This, in combination with the preferences of the foreign operating companies, meant that the regional resource base was developed with an almost exclusively upstream focus. This curbed the employment and broader economic development impulse the hydrocarbons sector delivered even if the initial impact on the small regional labor force could be quite profound: "In 1953, the oil industry provided employment for 50 per cent of Qatar's active population, and 19 per cent of Kuwait's in 1958."[114] Since the oil wealth rained on underdeveloped economies, much of the windfall was spent on a growing volume of imports. Even efforts to save a proportion of the rising income primarily benefited foreign service providers.

As profoundly transformative as oil proved, it also revealed itself to be a fickle friend. It integrated the Gulf economies in a global market and thereby exposed them to dynamics that they could not meaningfully influence. Nonetheless, the hydrocarbons cluster quickly dwarfed all other sectors, thereby firmly linking the dynamics of the non-oil economy to oil price and output variations. The growing import dependency, by effectively reducing incentives to develop local production capacity, meant that there was little to counter the Gulf economies' vulnerability to the vagaries of the oil market.

The rise of oil unleashed other structural trends that became increasingly challenging to manage. Public expenditure served as the primary tool for spreading the oil wealth. But while price variations made government revenues volatile, expenditures were subject to a ratchet effect. Moreover, the growing prosperity produced a substantial demographic dividend. This dynamic was further amplified by a massive influx of expatriates.

Herein lay the key vulnerability of the oil–government nexus. It was by no means guaranteed to generate wealth at a pace that matched the the mounting expectations of the expanding population. Under the circumstances, prosperity depended on either increased oil production or higher receipts for it. The desire to secure an appropriate funding base for socio-economic progress was an important consideration leading to the creation of a national oil industry in the Gulf.

The oil era echoed the static nature of the pre-oil order. Once established, the oil–government nexus continued to operate on a largely unaltered basis for decades even as it scaled up. Much like the pearling economy before it, this was not a model that involved inherent innovation or productivity gains beyond the steady technological progress of oil extraction. This was prosperity with few strings attached but, at the same time, prosperity that was doing precious little to perpetuate itself.

Much has been written about the problems of rapid oil-fueled development in the Gulf: problems of absorptive capacity, a culture of entitlement, and passive consumerism to the detriment of productive capacity. But while challenges were numerous, it is important to recognize that many things went right, perhaps surprisingly so. Poor, sparsely populated countries with rudimentary socio-economic structures transcended their challenging initial conditions and charted a surprisingly straight course to modernity. While this was the result of multiple factors, some seem to stand out as particularly significant. Firstly, policymaking in the region proved surprisingly technocratic. The leading economic sector was initially in the hands of the global oil majors, who operated much in the same way as they did elsewhere in the world. The Gulf was transformed by an industry that evolved in line with international best practices.

Secondly, the socio-political and administrative structures of the Gulf countries were very simple. The political establishment was invariably run by a ruler who typically governed in an inclusive, concensual manner while prioritizing stability and continuity. The way forward was charted in consultation with tribal leaders, merchants, advisors, and multilateral agencies. Even the basic rules for saving a proportion of the surpluses were established early on and fairly consistently adhered to.

The process of modernization was to a very large extent a greenfield modernization project. It was not a case of contested modernization debated among powerful institutions and powerbrokers with much to lose. Of course, the incentives or ability of people to resist change were minimal. But fundamentally, the process was fast and broad-based enough to leave virtually everyone better off. The inclusive culture of the Gulf region likely played an important part in delivering this success. It was agreed, or at least accepted, from early on that the oil wealth should benefit all. The massive windfalls brought the people schools and hospitals, as well as low-cost housing, financial assets, and other benefits. While this encouraged passive consumerism and disincentivized genuine economic participation, it also gave the people a meaningful stake in the new model and won their acquiescence through not just generosity but meaningful socio-economic progress.

Ultimately, oil equipped the Gulf countries with tools and resources that could be repurposed for other things as well. It developed human capital, put in place modern infrastructure, and made the Gulf an important repository of financial wealth. All of these factors would come to play an important role in the evolving development narrative of the region. While the track record of managing these assets was far from perfect, major mistakes, reversals, and discontinuities were avoided, whether by design, luck, or both. These assets, while they did not provide a sufficient foundation for sustained prosperity, now constitute important tools of the transtition toward a less oil-dependent future.

Notes

1 Yergin, *The Prize*, pp. 3–18.
2 Longrigg, *Oil in the Middle East*, p. 10.
3 Longrigg, *Oil in the Middle East*, p. 13.
4 Stocking, *Middle East Oil*, pp. 8–11.
5 Stocking, *Middle East Oil*, pp. 41–45.
6 Longrigg, *Oil in the Middle East*, p. 16.
7 Stocking, *Middle East Oil*, pp. 62–64.
8 Al-Kuwari, *Oil Revenues in the Gulf Emirates*, p. 23.
9 Al-Kuwari, *Oil Revenues in the Gulf Emirates*, p. 24.
10 Longrigg, *Oil in the Middle East*, p. 102.
11 Leatherdale, *Britain and Saudi Arabia*, pp. 206–207.
12 Stocking, *Middle East Oil*, pp. 70–72.

13 Smith, "The Great Black Giant."
14 https://tshaonline.org/handbook/online/articles/doe01; Wright, "The Dark Bounty of Texas Oil."
15 Archer, "Bahrain."
16 Al-Kuwari, *Oil Revenues in the Gulf Emirates*, p. 53.
17 Longrigg, *Oil in the Middle East*, p. 102.
18 Sorkhabi, "The Emergence of the Arabian Oil Industry."
19 Al-Kuwari, *Oil Revenues in the Gulf Emirates*, p. 53.
20 Longrigg, *Oil in the Middle East*, p. 103.
21 Longrigg, *Oil in the Middle East*, pp. 103, 135–136.
22 Owen and Pamuk, *A History*, p. 81; Lackner, *A House Built on Sand*, p. 30.
23 Owen and Pamuk, *A History*, p. 81.
24 Lackner, *A House Built on Sand*, p. 33.
25 Longrigg, *Oil in the Middle East*, p. 108.
26 Lackner, *A House Built on Sand*, p. 34.
27 Longrigg, *Oil in the Middle East*, pp. 110, 114–115.
28 Stegner, "Discovery!"
29 Sorkhabi, "The Emergence of the Arabian Oil Industry."
30 Longrigg, *Oil in the Middle East*, p. 132.
31 Anderson, *Aramco, the United States*, p. 29.
32 Stocking, *Middle East Oil*, p. 95.
33 Anderson, *Aramco, the United States*, pp. 36–37.
34 Owen and Pamuk, *A History*, p. 88.
35 Longrigg, *Oil in the Middle East*, p. 134.
36 Longrigg, *Oil in the Middle East*, pp. 205–206.
37 Lackner, *A House Built on Sand*, p. 39.
38 Knauerhase, *The Saudi Arabian Economy*, p. 184.
39 Stevens, "The Interaction," p. 29.
40 Hertog, "Petromin."
41 Longrigg, *Oil in the Middle East*, p. 111.
42 El Mallakh, "Planning in a Capital Surplus Economy," p. 426; Longrigg, *Oil in the Middle East*, p. 223; Zahlan, *The Making of the Modern Gulf States*, p. 30; Al-Kuwari, *Oil Revenues in the Gulf Emirates*, pp. 30, 145.
43 Field, *The Merchants*, p. 98.
44 Al-Kuwari, *Oil Revenues in the Gulf Emirates*, p. 64.
45 Field, *The Merchants*, p. 98.
46 Al-Kuwari, *Oil Revenues in the Gulf Emirates*, p. 54.
47 Longrigg, *Oil in the Middle East*, p. 215.
48 Al-Dekhayel, *Kuwait*, p. 26.
49 Longrigg, *Oil in the Middle East*, p. 106.
50 Longrigg, *Oil in the Middle East*, p. 231.
51 Sorkhabi, "The Qatar Oil Discoveries."
52 Simmons, *Twilight in the Desert*, p. 113; Zahlan, *The Making of the Modern Gulf States*, p. 124.
53 Sorkhabi, "The Qatar Oil Discoveries."
54 Al-Kuwari, *Oil Revenues in the Gulf Emirates*, p. 55.
55 Morton, "The Search for Oil."
56 Morton, "The Abu Dhabi Oil Discoveries"; Davidson, *Abu Dhabi*, p. 32.
57 Morton, "The Abu Dhabi Oil Discoveries."
58 Al-Kuwari, *Oil Revenues in the Gulf Emirates*, pp. 144–145.
59 Davidson, *Abu Dhabi*, p. 31; Davidson, *Dubai*, p. 27.
60 Quoted in: Nuttall, *Shipping and Development in Dubai*, p. 32.
61 Davidson, *Dubai*, pp. 100–101.
62 Al-Kuwari, *Oil Revenues in the Gulf Emirates*, p. 55.

63 Morton, "The Search for Oil."
64 El Mallakh, *Saudi Arabia*, p. 13.
65 Al-Rumaihi, *Social and Political Change*, pp. 123, 132.
66 Al-Rumaihi, *Social and Political Change*, p. 132.
67 Owen and Pamuk, *A History*, p. 210.
68 Peterson, *Saudi Arabia under Ibn Saud*, pp. 130–131; Stocking, *Middle East Oil*, pp. 101–102, 327–330.
69 Morton, "Once upon a Red Line."
70 Anderson, *Aramco, the United States*, p. 187.
71 Lackner, *A House Built on Sand*, p. 38.
72 Longrigg, *Oil in the Middle East*, p. 217.
73 Lackner, *A House Built on Sand*, p. 61.
74 Lackner, *A House Built on Sand*, p. 62.
75 Al-Kuwari, *Oil Revenues in the Gulf Emirates*, pp. 92, 112.
76 Allen and Rigsbee, *Oman under Qaboos*, p. 103.
77 Beblawi and Luciani, *The Rentier State*, p. 12.
78 Beblawi, "The Rentier State," pp. 51–52.
79 Beblawi, "The Rentier State," p. 56.
80 Zahlan, *The Making of the Modern Gulf States*, p. 93.
81 Al-Kuwari, *Oil Revenues in the Gulf Emirates*, pp. 80, 99–100, 126, 196.
82 Beblawi, "The Rentier State," p. 56.
83 Quoted in: Owen and Pamuk, *A History*, p. 210.
84 Owen, "One Hundred Years," p. 4.
85 Osama, *The Dilemma of Development*, p. 23.
86 Callen and Qu, "A Fiscal Framework," p. 20.
87 Al-Kuwari, *Oil Revenues in the Gulf Emirates*, p. 63.
88 US Energy Information Administration, *Annual Energy Review 2011*.
89 Zahlan, *The Making of the Modern Gulf States*, p. 33.
90 Owen and Pamuk, *A History*, p. 203.
91 Leeman, *The Price of Middle East Oil*, p. 15.
92 Sorkhabi, "The Road to OPEC."
93 Yergin, *The Prize*, p. 501.
94 Yergin, *The Prize*, p. 501.
95 Sorkhabi, "The Road to OPEC."
96 Sorkhabi, "The Road to OPEC."
97 Yergin, *The Prize*, p. 505.
98 Yergin, *The Prize*, p. 505.
99 Yergin, *The Prize*, pp. 505–506.
100 Owen and Pamuk, *A History*, p. 204.
101 Owen and Pamuk, *A History*, p. 204.
102 Bordo, "The Imbalances of the Bretton Woods System."
103 Lobban and Dalton, *Libya*, p. 58.
104 Cooper, *The Oil Kings*, pp. 90. 112.
105 Al-Kuwari, *Oil Revenues in the Gulf Emirates*, p. 67.
106 Al-Kuwari, *Oil Revenues in the Gulf Emirates*, p. 68.
107 Cooper, *The Oil Kings*, pp. 181–186.
108 Al-Kuwari, *Oil Revenues in the Gulf Emirates*, p. 70.
109 Cooper, *The Oil Kings*, pp. 194–195.
110 Quoted in Cooper, *The Oil Kings*, p. 196.
111 Lackner, *A House built on Sand*, p. 47.
112 Yergin, *The Prize*, p. 566.
113 Zahlan, *The Making of the Modern Gulf States*, p. 23.
114 Al-Kuwari, *Oil Revenues in the Gulf Emirates*, p. 50.

References

Allen, Calvin H., Jr. and W. Lynn Ringsbee II (2002), *Oman under Qaboos: From Coup to Constitution, 1970–1996*, London: Frank Cass.

Anderson, Irvine H. (1981), *Aramco, the United States, and Saudi Arabia: A Study of the Dynamics of Foreign Oil Policy, 1933–1950*, Princeton, N.J.: Princeton University Press.

Archer, Sinead (2012), "Bahrain: 80 Years and Still Producing," *GEO ExPro*, vol. IX, no. 4.

Beblawi, Hazem (1987), "The Rentier State in the Arab World," *Arab Studies Quarterly*, vol. 9, no. 4, pp. 383–398.

Beblawi, Hazem and Giacomo Luciani, eds. (1987), *The Rentier State*, London: Croom Helm.

Bordo, Michael D. (2018), "The Imbalances of the Bretton Woods System 1965 to 1973: U.S. Inflation, The Elephant in the Room," NBER Working Paper, No. 25409, Cambridge, Mass.: National Bureau of Economic Research.

Callen, Tim and Haonan Qu (2015), "A Fiscal Framework to Support Growth and Manage Dependence on Natural Resource Revenues," in: Al-Darwish *et al., op. cit.*, pp. 19–36.

Cooper, Andrew Scott (2011), *The Oil Kings: How the U.S., Iran, and Saudi Arabia Changed the Balance of Power in the Middle East*, New York: Simon & Schuster.

Al-Darwish, Ahmed, Naif Alghaith, Alberto Behar, Tim Callen, Pragyan Deb, Amgad Hegazy, Padamja Khandelwal, Malika Pant, and Haonan Qu (2015), *Saudi Arabia; Tackling Emerging Economic Challenges to Sustain Growth*, Washington, D.C.: International Monetary Fund.

Davidson, Christopher M. (2008), *Dubai: The Vulnerability of Success*, New York: Columbia University Press.

——— (2009), *Abu Dhabi: Oil and Beyond*, New York: Columbia University Press.

Al-Dekhayel, Abdulkarim (2000), *Kuwait: Oil, State and Political Legitimation*, Reading: Ithaca Press.

Field, Michael (1984), *The Merchants: Big Business Families of Arabia*, London: John Murray Publishers.

Hertog, Steffen (2008), "Petromin: the slow death of statist oil development in Saudi Arabia," *Business history*, vol. 50, no. 5, pp. 645–667.

Knauerhase, Ramon (1975), *The Saudi Arabian Economy*, New York: Prager.

Al-Kuwari, Ali Khalifa (1978), *Oil Revenues in the Gulf Emirates: Patterns of Allocation and Impact on Economic Development*, Boulder, Colo.: Westview Press.

Lackner, Helen (1978), *A House Built on Sand: A Political Economy of Saudi Arabia*, London: Ithaca Press.

Leatherdale, Clive (1983), *Britain and Saudi Arabia 1925–1939: The Imperial Oasis*, Abingdon: Frank Cass.

Leeman, Wayne E. (1962), *The Price of Middle East Oil: An Essay in Political Economy*, Ithaca, NY: Cornell University Press.

Lobban, Richard A., Jr. and Christopher H. Dalton (2014), *Libya: History and Revolution*, Santa Barbara, Calif.: Praeger.

Longrigg, Stephen Hemsley (1968), *Oil in the Middle East: Its Discovery and Development*, London: Royal Institute of International Affairs/Oxford University Press.

El Mallakh, Ragaei (1966), "Planning a Capital Surplus Economy: Kuwait," *Land Economics*, vol. 42, no. 4, pp. 425–440.

——— (1982), *Saudi Arabia: Rush to Development*, Baltimore, Md.: Johns Hopkins University Press.

El Mallakh, Ragaei and Dorothea H. El Mallakh, eds. (1982), *Saudi Arabia: Energy, Developmental Planning and Industrialization*, Lexington, Mass.: Lexington Books.
Morton, Michael Quentin (2011), "The Abu Dhabi Oil Discoveries," *GEO ExPro*, vol. 8, no. 3.
——— (2012), "The Search for Oil in Oman," *GEO ExPro*, vol. 9, no. 1.
——— (2013), "Once Upon a Red Line – The Iraq Petroleum Company Story," *GEO ExPro*, iPad app 6.
Nuttall, Keith (2021), *Shipping and Development in Dubai: Infrastructure, Innovation and Institutions in the Gulf*, London: I.B. Tauris.
Osama, Abdul Rahman (1987), *The Dilemma of Development in the Arabian Peninsula*, London: Croom Helm.
Owen, E. Roger (2008), "One Hundred Years of Middle Eastern Oil," Middle East Brief, No. 24, Brandeis University: Crown Center for Middle East Studies, January.
Owen, E. Roger and Şevket Pamuk (1999), *A History of Middle East Economies in the Twentieth Century*, Cambridge, Mass.: Harvard University Press.
Peterson, John E. (2018), *Saudi Arabia under Ibn Saud: Economic and Financial Foundations of the State*, London: I.B. Tauris.
Al-Rumaihi, Mohammed Ghanim (1973), *Social and Political Change in Bahrain since the First World War*, Ph.D. thesis, Durham University.
Simmons, Matthew R. (2005), *Twilight in the Desert: The Coming Saudi Oil Shock and the World Economy*, Hoboken, NJ: John Wiley & Sons, Inc.
Smith, Thomas (2015), "The Great Black Giant," *GEO ExPro*, vol. 12, no. 2.
Sorkhabi, Rasoul (2008), "The Emergence of the Arabian Oil Industry," *GEO ExPro*, vol. 5, no. 6.
——— (2010), "The Qatar Oil Discoveries," *GEO ExPro*, vol. 7, no. 1.
——— (2016), "The Road to OPEC 1960," *GEO ExPro*, vol. 7, no. 5.
Stegner, Wallace (1969), "Discovery! The Story of Aramco Then," *Aramco World*, vol. 20, no. 1 (January/February), pp. 12–21.
Stevens, Paul John (1982), "The Interaction between Oil Policy and Industrial Policy in Saudi Arabia," in El Mallakh and El Mallakh, *op. cit.*, pp. 27–45.
Stocking, George W. (1970), *Middle East Oil: A Study in Political and Economic Controversy*, Nashville, Tenn.: Vanderbilt University Press.
Wright, Lawrence (2017), "The Dark Bounty of Texas Oil: Will the Booms and Busts of the Energy Industry Always Dominate the State?," *The New Yorker*, 1 January 2018 issue (25 December 2017).
Yergin, Daniel (2008), *The Prize: The Epic Quest for Oil, Money & Power*, New York: Simon & Schuster, Inc.
Zahlan, Rosemarie Said (1989), *The Making of the Modern Gulf States: Kuwait, Bahrain, Qatar, the United Arab Emirates and Oman*, London: Unwin Hyman.

3 Determined to diversify

A generation into the oil era, more than half of Saudi Arabia's GDP came from the oil sector, which also generated a remarkable 85 percent of budgetary income came from oil.[1] Hazem Beblawi observed that "the Gulf states' drama is that [oil production] is not simply another economic activity added to the other existing productive sources within a viable and modern economy. ... In the Gulf, the oil sector dominates the economy; it is almost the unique source of wealth."[2] While alternatives to oil as a development driver were minimal, the petroleum-fueled road to modernity had to entail an acceptance of the unusually wide range of positives and negatives that the endemic oil dependency entailed.

It was recognized early on that the Gulf region's newfound prosperity stemmed from an exhaustible resource even if the full scale of the hydrocarbons endowments was only imperfectly understood. That the oil reserves would be depeleted within a generation was viewed as a real possibility. Early estimates in Bahrain suggested that the country's modest deposits might be exhausted within 15 years.[3] But even the expected remaining life span of the much more plentiful Saudi oil was thought by contemporaries to have fallen from 113.6 years in 1955 to the relatively modest 36.2 years by 1973.[4] Kuwait, by contrast, boasted the largest reserves globally in the mid-1960s and was expected to have another 80–100 years of production left.[5] But even this only translated into the equivalent of three to four generations – not a long time in a nation's history. Policymakers had to contemplate life without oil sooner or later. This in turn presented the far more pressing question of how the oil revenues could be best utilized in preparation for the post-oil future as "their main benefit to the economy lies in their proceeds, and their long-term impact lies in the purposes to which these proceeds have been directed."[6]

Thinking ahead

Economic diversification, a range of ideas around reducing the Gulf countries' economic reliance on oil, became part of the regional policy debates by the 1960s. But the overwhelming dominance and relative uniqueness of oil among Arabian resources in practice also meant that much attention had to focus on the ways in which oil itself was being extracted and used. Capturing the spirit of these discussions, in 1977 Saudi Arabia's Royal Commission for Jubail and Yanbu challenged old assumptions by

DOI: 10.4324/9781003373353-3

underscoring the stark implications of "business as usual": "To continue exporting our oil wealth in its crude form, to the point of total depletion, would have adverse economic effects in the not-too distant future. For then the Kingdom would find itself with no economic basis to rely on."[7]

As the idea of proactively developing non-oil economic activities began to gain currency, some progress materialized as the direct result of spending some of the windfall. But these activities tended to be derivative, not sustainable in the absence of such windfalls. With time, a far more strategic posture took shape with a focus on creating local productive capacity in areas such as manufacturing and various services. Channeling a proportion of the oil windfalls into savings, so-called financial diversification, was another logical option and held obvious appeal as an insurance policy in the face of the various oil-related risks: "by investing oil revenues in either local or international industries, the GCC countries could convert the volatile and exhaustible oil incomes into a more stable financial stream of wealth that could be used to develop their societies in the long run."[8] But not all Gulf economies were in a position to accumulate large savings.

Economic diversification was no simple exercise, designed as it was "to introduce fundamental structural change into an expanding economy rather than to simply enlarge the entity in existence."[9] Moreover, the Gulf economies appeared unlikely candidates for economic planning at a time it tended to be associated with the Soviet block or conditions of resource scarcity typically obtaining in poor developing countries. However, the approach had a compelling rationale, as noted by El Mallakh: "Capital ... tends to be underestimated when it is available. In [this] case, economic planning is required to minimize waste which could accompany a capital-surplus condition, especially when the surplus accumulation takes place rapidly and is unmatched by similar increases in other factors of production."[10]

Kuwait's Development Board was established in 1953 to plan capital investments, while the Investment Board handled the oil surpluses transferred to London. However, there was local resistance to these endeavors that were seen as being instigated by the British.[11] The Industrial Development Board, established in 1961, marked another attempt to draft long-term policies. It produced its first development plan for the period 1967–1968 to 1971–1972, motivated by the need to "reduce dependence on migrant labor and oil by policies of diversification and the expansion of the local educational system."[12] But the focus was relatively short-term, with an emphasis on boosting the role of the private sector in manufacturing and trade, which the government sought to support "via tariff protection, tax exemptions, cheap loans at low subsidised interest rates and the establishment of industrial estates."[13] Industrialization remained a key focus in the the second five-year plan spanning 1976–1981. But when the second oil boom in 1979 brought accelerating inflation and other bottlenecks, the government increasingly shifted its focus to "the investment of oil revenues overseas where higher returns were much more easily obtained."[14]

The Bretton Woods agencies advocated economic planning during the late 1950s fiscal crisis in Saudi Arabia. Anwar Ali, the head of the local IMF mission, who developed a fiscal reform plan, in 1958 proposed the creation of a economic development committee.[15] The International Bank for Reconstruction and Development in 1960 put forward a SAR400mn development program spanning the years 1961–1962. The diversification priorities centered on agricultural development, infrastructure investments, mining projects, and the expansion of the education sector. Reduced reliance on the state won early recognition with an emphasis on the "stimulation of private enterprise in power and industrial ventures."[16]

A dedicated Central Planning Organization was decreed in 1965 but was beset by numerous challenges, whether in terms of integration with other government departments or the practical complexities of execution. But substantial investments were made in capacity development, and the first Five-Year Development Plan was successfully prepared for 1970–1974.[17] A key objective of the plan was "[d]iversifying sources of national income and reducing dependence on oil through increasing the share of other productive sectors."[18] The plan also set out to support people "through training and small business projects ... and self-support for persons who have been dependent on social security payments."[19] Private enterprise was highlighted for "those activities that they can undertake more effectively than government agencies."[20] Power generation continued to be flagged as a particular opportunity for which capital was available through interest-free, long-term loans. The Bahraini government set up a Development Bureau in 1967 to explore opportunities for new industries.

Abu Dhabi's Council of Planning announced its first five-year development plan in 1968. Substantial investments were planned for social infrastructure, and BHD3mn was earmarked for the new Mina Zayed harbor. Overall, "299 million dinars were spent on putting in the necessary physical infrastructure for the new economy, including paved roads, bridges, and basic airport facilities, and 4 million dinars were spent on installing water pumps and a new sewerage system."[21] Social infrastructure was a logical priority but more generally "[m]indful of the need to keep the economy diverse and not entirely reliant on oil exports, the Council also ensured that the oil revenues were supporting the growth of pre-oil sectors, while also helping to establish a number of new ones."[22] In 1962 Qatar engaged the Arthur D. Little consultancy to review government ministries, and the findings "expressed concern over Qatar's overwhelming dependence on oil, which it projected would be exhausted by 1982. The report cautioned Qatar to develop other activities, especially its natural gas wealth. This created the basis for broad-based diversification into gas-based petrochemical industries.[23]

Oman joined in the regional trend with the "Word" of Sa'id bin Taimur in January 1968 along with a new development board.[24] Sultan Qaboos dramatically accelerated the pace of change, setting up a Supreme Council for Economic Planning and Development in 1972, supported by the new Center for Economic Planning and Development. While progress nonetheless proved slow, a deteriorating fiscal situation prompted the authorities to launch the first five-year plan in September 1976. Each plan was nested within a long-term development strategy, the first one covering the period 1970–1995 and the second, referred to as Vision 2020, extending from 1996 to 2020.

Easier said than done

Since the oil cluster had annihilated the old economic order in the Gulf, a new non-oil economy had to be created *ex nihilo*. But the limited resource base and the lack of alternative repositories of wealth meant that any attempt to reshape the economic model had to depend almost exclusively on oil revenues. Oil was forced into the somewhat paradoxical role of underwriting attempts to reduce the region's heavy economic reliance on oil. The Saudi authorities explicitly recognized this in 1970:

> *Dependence on oil is the obverse of the advantages derived from the abundance of oil. Rapid expansion of oil production has provided the Kingdom with both government revenues and foreign exchange to finance development. However, economic growth in Saudi Arabia has been primarily a product of this one sector. ... Moreover, it has led to the situation where further development of the economy over the coming decades is mainly dependent on growth in revenues and foreign exchange earnings from oil.*[25]

The benefit of hindsight led to the frustrating realization that the Gulf had done little to capture oil-related value chain. The first Saudi plan lamented the fact that three decades since the discovery of oil, manufacturing still only generated just under 2 percent of GDP and noted that "there is as yet nothing approaching an industrial complex."[26] The situation was little different in Kuwait, where industry made up 3.2 percent of GDP in 1965–1966 and only a slightly higher 4.9 percent in 1975–1976, compared to 63.4–70 percent for oil.[27]

This asymmetric development was in no small measure due to the fact that the Gulf region's leading economic sector remained in the hands of foreign capital. With the operating companies focusing squarely on the upstream segment, limited progress materialized further downstream. Refining and petrochemicals production tended to be located much closer to the ultimate consumers, with the heaviest concentrations in North America and Europe. After all, these were the main markets of the oil majors, not to mention regions where they could source talent and capital with relative ease. The regulatory environment in the West was known, tried and tested, not linked to specific contracts or concessions.

The lack of progress in diversification also reflected the simple fiscal models under which government revenues accrued almost entirely from crude. Saudi Arabia under King Faisal did put in place a fairly comprehensive system of domestic taxation, and "both direct and indirect taxes doubled between 1961 and 1968." However, "total domestic tax revenues never rose above 7 percent of all state revenues."[28] Since it was primarily oil export taxes that fed the public treasuries, the regional authorities had little reason to challenge the Western-controlled crude exporters. The ownership structure of the oil companies effectively trapped the Gulf governments in the role of residual claimants rather than drivers of the development of the most important sector in their economies.

The endemic interdependency between the oil–government nexus and the rest of the economy meant that progress in diversification tended to coincide with the continued growth of the hydrocarbons sector. Attempts to craft non-oil development drivers effectively further cemented the region's economic dependence on oil. Or, conversely, non-oil development efforts gathered momentum when the oil-generated resources for them increased. Oil was the horse that pulled the cart of non-oil development. In practice, the rapidly growing thirst of the advanced economies for hydrocarbons meant that, for instance, Saudi oil production was still expanding rapidly a full generation into the oil era: by a remarkable 18 percent in 1966, followed by 7.8 percent, 8.8 percent, and 5.3 percent, respectively, in each of the subsequent three years.[29]

But since such a momentum coud not be expected to continue indefinitely, new ideas around boosting government income gained growing attention. New resources for diversification could be most easily raised by increasing the share of government revenue from the oil companies. Hisham Nazer, who headed the Saudi CPO, noted: "The success of the (first five-year) plan depends on a number of factors, one of which was the oil companies' appreciation of the Government's need for greater financial capability, necessitating an increase in oil company payments to it, and called on them to 'redouble their efforts' in this regard."[30] If foreign capital had been necessary for driving the initial development of the oil sector, reapportioning the windfall was now seen as critical for funding diversification. In its absence, a substantial proportion of the wealth generated in Arabia flowed out almost instantaneously. In Saudi Arabia, net factor payments abroad had risen from SAR2.1bn, equal to some 24.6 percent of GDP, in 1962–1963 to just shy of SAR7bn, or 26.7 percent of GDP, in 1971–1972. The absolute increase was a remarkable 228.9 percent.[31] While the spectacular increase in government revenues had effectively concealed the massive outflow of capital, such win–win conditions were unlikely to apply indefinitely.

The diversification ambitions were complicated by the absence of many preconditions of successful non-oil development. Ragaei el Mallakh, commenting on Kuwait in the mid-1960s, observed that "the level of per capita income ... has allowed for the attainment of one of the highest savings rates in the world (45 per cent of the GNP). However, Kuwait is capable, thus far, of utilizing only 41 per cent of the total savings in domestic investments."[32] Factors referred to as "limitations of absorptive capacity" complicated local capital mobilization:

> *Skill shortages, scarcity of physical resources, inadequate infrastructure, and limited administrative and institutional machinery for monitoring and controlling the economy suddenly came into prominence, and the pace of growth ... fell far short of the potential.*[33]

The multiple structural limitations included:

- a very limited natural resource base beyond hydrocarbons;
- high transportation and associated costs of inputs that were not available locally;

- high local labor costs;
- small domestic markets which limited local effective demand;
- acute water scarcity, which complicated agricultural development but also mining and many types of manufacturing; and
- a systemic import dependency, which weakened the multiplier effects of domestic capital mobilization.[34]

From a purely financial perspective, it appeared difficult to justify a broad-based diversification agenda, especially outside of Saudi Arabia, whose sheer size made some of these constraints less binding. With the need to be selective and focused, diversification initiatives risked giving rise to an economic structure that was ultimately not very diverse.

Derivative diversification

The "new" non-oil private sector came into being as a "foster child" of the oil–government nexus. While the old pre-oil economy generally atrophied, some regional merchants proved adept at reorienting their businesses to capitalize on the emerging opportunities. For instance, in the Saudi case:

> *The burst of economic growth in the 1960s ... overwhelmingly favored a very small number of old, established Hijazi merchant houses, largely from the Jeddawi community ... while the traditional private sector shrank in numbers. ... The increase in the volume of imports and maritime transport benefited the few large firms and business families that enjoyed the overseas contacts and financial backing necessary to import large amounts of foodstuffs and consumer goods.*[35]

In the east, substantial investments by Aramco translated into contracting opportunities for local construction businesses.

Even as new private ventures sprung up, they tended to be modest in their scale and ambition, often constrained by the founders' resources and limited funding sources. For instance, Saudi Arabia saw a sharp rise in the numbers of new businesses a generation into the oil era, but most were very small: "Of the total 9,174 registered manufacturing businesses in 1967, 4,394 employed only one person and a comparable 3,769 had 2–4 employees. There were 26,870 businesses in the commercial sector and 20,838 only had one employee."[36]

Much of the new business creation tended to be opportunistic, rather than visionary, entrepreneurship, in an economy that offered attractive opportunities for people able to tap into the growing capital flows created by oil. In the words of Michel Chatelus: "*Getting access to the rent circuit is a greater preoccupation than reaching productive efficiency.*"[37] The growing volume of government contracts along with brisk population growth led many to view these rent opportunities as the fast ticket to wealth. The result over time was a frustrating paradox: "Even though the [Gulf states'] adopted economic policy encourages the private sector, the sector itself is so inefficient and excessively dependent on the oil revenues controlled by the government that the latter's dominance over the economy has been overwhelming."[38] This was derivative diversification, almost diversification by default, as the oil-generated surpluses had to be channeled into other economic activities, unless they were saved. A rising tide lifted all of the boats but remained a tide of oil.

With time, policy aspirations began to evolve beyond this reactive posture. One of the most logical diversification opportunities involved greater hydrocarbons value chain capture along with energy-intensive manufacturing. Bahrain's Bapco refinery marked the first step in this regard in the mid-1930s, although it was more the result of difficulties of marketing crude in the depressed 1930s than a deliberate strategic choice. Nonetheless, the refinery posted robust growth thanks to supply lines from Saudi Arabia that allowed it to expand far beyond the scale permitted by Bahrain's own endowments. Other small refinery projects sprung up in the wake of new oilfield discoveries, but more fundamental change only came more than a generation into the oil era. The Kuwaiti and Saudi governments took proactive steps to create national hydrocarbons-manufacturing clusters to parallel the Western-controlled majors.

The Kuwait National Petroleum Company, established in 1960 as a nationally controlled venture, drove the development of downstream capacity, amassing a portfolio of three major refineries through acquisitions and greenfield development: Mina al Ahmadi, Mina Abdullah, and Shuaiba. By 1983, refined oil product exports accounted for more than 40 percent of Kuwait's overall exports and 50 percent of their value. The aggregate refining capacity of the country reached some 700,000 b/d by 1989. Saudi Arabia's Petromin reflected similar ambitions. Established by the government in 1962, the company's key objectives included undertaking "in cooperation with private domestic and foreign companies, the advancement of the activities ... that are required to accelerate the growth of the oil and minerals sector." It was expected to establish "companies with the purpose of engaging in all phases of the industry of petroleum and minerals and their derivatives and by-products, including trade transactions, transportation, sales distribution and marketing."[39] In 1964, Petromin launched the Jeddah oil refinery, followed by the Luberef lubricants plant in partnership with Mobil. Collaboration with foreign companies provided the necessary technological know-how as well as market opportunities. By the mid-1980s, Saudi Arabia already boasted a refining capacity of 1.14mn b/d distributed across six refineries, including the 250,000 b/d Petromin–Mobil Refinery at Yanbu', now SAMREF. In 1985, Aramco and Shell launched the SASREF refinery in Jubail. Foreign majors thus re-entered the market as owner-operators but also delivered new technology and expertise, not to mention additional profit opportunities.

Whatever their limitations, these new ventures created more local capacity in the downstream segment as well as in energy-intensive and hydro carbons-based manufacturing. Such ambitions rapidly expanded in the 1970s, as observed by Paul Stevens: "One of the main reasons for the explosion in plans to locate refineries and petrochemical plants in the Arab world in 1974–1975 was the takeover of the operating oil companies by the governments."[40] Oil naturally assumed a central place in these designs through four particular compelling channels: "(a) moving downstream into refining and petrochemicals; (b) processing gas (either as an energy source or as a chemical feedstock); (c) developing energy-intensive industries such as metal smelting; and finally (d) developing ancillary industries to the oil sector that arise from forward and backward linkages."[41]

Better gas utilization offered a particularly compelling avenue for diversification. Natural gas was one of a narrow range of readily available local natural resources but had for years been treated as a low-value byproduct of oil, sometimes reinjected into oil reservoirs for pressure maintenance but typically merely flared. The costs of this neglect mounted with time, as observed by El Mallakh in 1966: "It has been estimated that the amount of natural gas being flared off in Gulf production … is also sufficient to supply two-thirds of the world's nitrogen needs and could be made into 20 million tons of nitrogen a year."[42] The imposition of national ownership of the sector quickly began to change matters with Saudi Arabia's $12bn master gas collection system, implemented starting in 1975, a particularly ambitious step.[43]

The establishment of the Saudi Ministry of Industry and Electricity in 1975 was followed by the incorporation in 1976 of Saudi Arabian Basic Industries Corporation (SABIC) "to provide capital and marketing of products in the basic industries using local hydrocarbon and mineral resources and other complementary and supporting industries."[44] While mainly tasked with converting associated gas into chemicals, polymers, and fertilizers, the 1982 creation of Hadeed expanded the remit to metals. Mirroring the Petromin model, SABIC served as an umbrella for 50–50 joint ventures with leading international manufacturing brands, including Exxon, Dow, Mobil, and Mitsubishi.[45] SABIC was an anchor tenant in the new industrial cities of Jubail and Yanbu. By the late 1980s, the company was targeting a 4–5 percent global market share in petrochemicals. The volume of SABIC's total production in 1985 reached 6.5mn tn, which doubled to 13mn within five years. It exceeded 35mn tons by 2001 and 60mn by 2012. While this new era for Saudi manufacturing was spearheaded by government initiatives, the booming sector also attracted more and more private investment: "The number of licensed factories was 207 in 1970. It increased to 3,252 in 1984. In the same period, operating plants rose from 207 to over 1,600. This number reached over 1,800 by 1986."[46]

Important forward strides notwithstanding, the manufacturing agenda was often held back by a heavy reliance on comparatively basic processes and limited value addition. Private ventures in particular frequently mirrored the Gulf region's long-standing trading traditions. In the words of Y.S.F. Al Sabah in 1980, "Most industry in Kuwait … is based on simple processing and largely depends on imports of primary capital, materials and intermediate goods."[47] Achieving efficient scale was a common challenge. Ramon Knauerhase observed in 1975 that in Saudi industry, "the 271 plants surveyed operated at only about 64 percent of capacity."[48] Henry Azzam reached a similar conclusion in 1988: "most of the basic industries … especially in petrochemicals, fertilizers and iron and steel, tend to operate much below design capacity. This … threaten[s] to wipe out most of the cost advantage arising from the domestic abundance of energy and raw materials."[49]

Successful diversification in capital-intensive sectors such as manufacturing depended on export opportunities for achieving scale. This necessitated costly investments in a global economic context over which the Gulf governments had limited control. The potential of greater hydrocarbons value chain capture depended on the Gulf producers' ability to serve the global market at a competitive cost. Problematically, the rest of the world was not always ready to accommodate such ambitions. An early, conspicuous achievement in the field of petrochemicals was the 600,000-ton per annum SABIC subsidiary Saudi Methanol Company's Al Razi complex which began production in February 1984. Within four months, the European Community imposed a 13.5 percent import duty on Saudi methanol after production had increased to 12 times the existing EC ceiling.[50]

The Europeans imposed further barriers on GCC petrochemical exports in 1986, placing a severe strain on relations between the two blocks. Nor were they alone, prompting the GCC Supreme Council in December 1987 to express "its worry regarding the protectionist policies, especially those which Japan is determined to apply, with regard to the imposition of duties and taxes on imports of crude oil and petroleum products."[51] Protectionism continued to cast a shadow on several GCC initiatives well into the 1990s. Eventually, however, the eroding the competitiveness of legacy technology in the West began to change the situation to the Gulf producers' advantage. Apart from access to cheap raw materials and a strategic location, the Gulf countries benefited from the progressive liberalization of global trade.[52]

Bahrain, motivated by a particular urgency about identifying non-oil growth drivers, became a regional trailblazer in diversification. The 1966 establishment of the Bahrain Fishing Company with the Ross Group of Grimsby, UK, marked a first step. A far more ambitious initiative was announced in 1968 – Aluminium Bahrain (ALBA), a $48mn mega aluminum smelter, one of the largest in the world. Following two years of construction, production started in May 1971 with an initial annual capacity of 120,000 metric tonnes. By using previously squandered natural gas as its key input, the project achieved a cost advantage that justified Australian alumina imports. ALBA also revealed the potential of clustering as new downstream businesses sprang up, including a facility to pulverize aluminum as well as $10mn extrusion plant. A $10mn privately funded cable factory was announced in 1977. Conversely, however, in 1975 the state acquired a majority stake in ALBA, extending it to 77.9 percent a year later. In 1972, plans were announced for a $60mn drydock complex. Concurrent with the large investments, smaller workshops and fabrication ventures mushroomed. In the 1960s, the number of industrial enterprises in Bahrain grew by an annual average rate of 13.6 percent.[53]

Food production commanded an important place in the Gulf diversification agenda. Both agriculture and fishing were recognized as key guarantors of food security but also offered ways to generate employment while reducing import reliance. This was a particularly compelling consideration in Saudi Arabia, which lagged behind its neighbors in urbanization. But also other Gulf countries were home to communities that had historically earned their livelihoods in the primary sector. While the extreme scarcity of arable land and fresh water had severely constrained agriculture in the past, the oil wealth now promised a way out. The most salient case of proactive agricultural diversification was the Saudi wheat policy, which was initiated in the 1970s through the introduction of generous guaranteed prices of SAR3,5000 per ton. It built on the 1968 Public Lands Distribution Ordinance under which the government had distributed 5–100 hectares of fallow land free of charge. Despite production costs that were five times the world price, generous government subsidies drove a four-fold increase in the wheat harvest during the 1970s. The forward momentum subsequently accelerated with annual output multiplying from 130,000 to 1.3mn tn in 1980–1985.[54] But the cost was daunting: "In three years of the early 1980s the government spent about $2.8 billion just to repurchase wheat that would have cost about $395 million on the international market."[55] In the early 1990s, the annual wheat output reached 2.5mn tn, which not only made the Kingdom fully self-reliant but also turned it into a leading grain exporter globally. However, the program relied on irrigation at a rate of some 1,300–1,500 cu m per ton, something that has led it to be described as "the most expensive fiasco in late twentieth-century agricultural history."[56] Saudi rural landscapes were profoundly reshaped as traditional farms yielded to large-scale agro-businesses. Asir's share of cultivated land fell from 80 percent in 1960 to 20 percent in 1984 while the Nejd expanded from 10 to 57 percent.[57] Mounting concern over depleting water reserves eventually led to the termination of the program in 2015–2016 after a 2007 decree had mandated annual quota reductions of 12.5 percent.

There were exceptions to the derivative diversification paradigm in the Gulf, but even initiatives without a direct connection to oil tended to depend on the wealth it had engendered. An important case in point were efforts to explore and develop the non-oil natural resources of Saudi Arabia and to expand its industrial base beyond the hydrocarbons value chain. The First Development Plan called for a structured program of prospecting for iron ore, phosphate, and natural gas deposits, and the Jeddah steel mill was built in 1976. Over time, important discoveries were made, especially in the Northern Province. Ma'aden ultimately emerged as a major champion of diversification and even took steps to revive the ancient gold mines of the Mahd al Dhahab, which had in fact seen some production between the 1930s and 1954.

On the Trucial Coast, development opportunities were particularly acutely constrained by a small population base. While Dubai managed to capitalize on its trading traditions, the oil windfalls made vertical integration and energy-intensive manufacturing logical opportunities for Abu Dhabi. The Abu Dhabi Gas Liquefaction Company began as a $105mn joint venture in the 1970s with a focus on the Japanese market. The Abu Dhabi Gas Industries Company (GASCO) was set up to supply gas to the Ruwais industrial complex. Benefiting from its own, albeit more modest, oil boom, Dubai began to focus on manufacturing opportunities, construction materials, petrochemicals, fertilizers, and metals. But similar opportunity sets region-wide led to comparable decisions. Within half a decade of the launch of ALBA in Bahrain, the Dubai Aluminium Company was incorporated in 1975 and began production four years later with an initial capacity of some 140,000 tn per annum.[58]

Diversification through distribution: The 1970s boom

The early diversification ambitions were dealt a major reality check by the 1970s oil price rally. While the previous strategies typically remained in place, the gradualist approach to economic development suddenly seemed like an unnecessary constraint. Saudi Arabia's First Development Plan still reflected the financial constraints created by the 1967 Middle East war. But the projected revenue of SAR33.8–37.4 compared to actual income of SAR80nm. The spending target of SAR41.3bn eventually nearly doubled to SAR78.2bn.[59]

The Gulf governments devised ambitious designs to put in place the physical attributes their new wealth seemingly entitled them to, especially as many viewed the higher oil prices as something of a "new normal." But diversification remained a game of moving goalposts. Even as non-oil investments were ramped up, the Saudi oil sector increased its GDP contribution from 51.3 percent in 1966–1967 to 64.8 percent in 1972–1973.[60] During the the first half of the 1970s, annual oil sector growth averaged 14.9 percent, while the non-oil private sector "only" managed 11 percent.[61]

Even as financial constraints were lifted, challenges around absorptive capacity persisted, "in the form of rapidly increasing inflation, a narrow base of domestic resources, an underdeveloped physical infrastructure, an inadequate manpower supply, and an overburdened administrative system."[62] With the scale of investments booming ahead, costs shot up: "One index of the expense involved in such a program is the calculation that in 1975 a particular public works project would cost up to three times as much in Saudi Arabia as it would in California."[63]

The increased project budgets proved far easier to spend in the infrastructure space than on creating new productive capacity. During the first plan, Saudi Arabia's investments in transport and communications more than doubled from the planned allocation to SAR11.4bn. Urban development saw an even faster increase to SAR8.3bn, whereas project spending in the agriculture and water sectors skyrocketed more than six-fold to SAR3.2bn. By contrast, industry and commerce managed just over a quarter of their project allocation of SAR228.4mn. The uphill struggle in manufacturing led the US Department of State to conclude that "the productive sectors, except petroleum-based industries, received little attention. ... On the whole, the First Plan's objectives were completely ignored."[64]

The Second Development Plan for the second half of the 1970s reflected the conditions of financial plenty and maintained an explicit commitment to diversification "based on the efficient utilization of human and natural resources of the Kingdom."[65] Investments in agriculture, industry, and mining finally began to develop traction. The planned 13.3 percent annual growth in the non-oil sector was now markedly ahead of the 9.7 percent pace projected for oil, which nonetheless continued to dwarf everything else at some three-quarters of GDP. The planned program expenditure of SAR498bn was nine times (in constant prices) the corresponding figure during the preceding plan. An impressive 63.9 percent of total spending was earmarked for development objectives, up from 58.3 percent in the first plan. Physical infrastructure remained a key priority, receiving SAR112.9bn as traffic on Saudi roads was forecast to rise by 15 percent a year and the number of vehicles projected to more than double from 200,000 to 500,000. More than 25,000 km of new roads were planned to connect all major population centers, while municipal infrastructure was seen as a way to make Saudi cities "healthier, more comfortable, more enjoyable, but less costly places in which to live, work and travel."[66]

In order to bring about the desired changes amid significant resource constraints, the second plan envisaged ambitious structural changes:

> *(a) additions to the foreign labour force to assist in development ...; (b) encouragement of rural–urban internal migration, thereby moving surplus manpower to areas of industrial employment opportunity; (c) all possible government assistance to the development of the productive sectors of private enterprise; and (d) technological advancement through prudent utilization of international co-operation agreements whereby access could be had to technical and managerial expertise as well as to skilled labour.*[67]

The flagship projects included the industrial cities of Jubail on the Gulf coast and Yanbu' on the Red Sea, both developed by a special Royal Commission set up in September 1975. The new foundations set out to attract new sources of domestic as well as foreign investment in an important departure from the heavily state-led development paradigm.

Even as the designs to reshape the Gulf economy developed momentum, absorptive capacity concerns persisted. With the Saudi money supply booming ahead by 62.6 and 83.2 percent in 1976 and 1977, respectively, inflation took off. But other indicators of progress told an encouraging story. During 1970–1985, Saudi Arabia's "generated electric power rose more than 38-fold; the length of paved road more than five-fold; and the volume of cargo handled in the ports some 30-fold."[68] Social infrastructure was profoundly transformed: "the number of boys' schools more than tripled, while the number of girls' schools ... increased some 15-fold. Educational enrollment rose sharply, by some five-fold at the primary level, 12-fold at the intermediate level, and 40-fold at the higher educational level. ... The number of hospital beds increased more than three-fold ..., and medical staff by some 15-fold.[69]

The boom years even alleviated the limitations posed by the small regional market. By dramatically pushing up aggregate demand, the oil plenty opened up a whole host of new profit-making opportunities amplified by novel initiatives to distribute the windfalls across the population. Capacity creation through diversification met its match in booming disposable incomes: "Social welfare programs and production subsidies were, in a fundamental way, mutually reinforcing, for they represented the state's intimate involvement in creating both supply and demand."[70]

As the coffers of the Gulf governments filled up, old policies were jettisoned with enduring implications for socio-economic development. The Saudi fisc morphed from a revenue collection agency to a wealth distribution mechanism. Domestic revenue collection came to contribute less than 1 percent of overall government income as the only direct tax that survived was "the *zakat* on Saudi business, at the rate of 1.5 percent of net profits."[71] Otherwise, subsidies replaced taxes: "[i]n industry, subsidies were given for machinery, raw materials, employee training, production costs, and finished goods."[72] While continuing with the old fiscal toolkit may have seemed anachronistic, its dismantling came at a cost: "With the decline of the tax bureaucracy the Saudi state lost not only a fundamental set of economic tools to govern the economy but also its main source of economic information."[73]

In a bid to proactively drive diversification, the Gulf governments set up dedicated funding vehicles. Much of this could be justified by the limitations of the banking system, which had done little to cater to smaller companies or to provide long-term credit. A decade after the pioneering creation of the Agricultural Development Bank in 1963, the Saudi government established the Saudi Industrial Development Fund, the Real Estate Development Fund, the Saudi Credit Bank, and the Saudi Contractors Fund, along with several other entities. The funds offered interest-free loans under the umbrella of sector programs that provided subsidies as well as fixed prices for new market entrants.[74]

The domestic investment environment changed dramatically as a small trickle of targeted financial incentives grew into a flood of cheap liquity that peaked at nearly SAR30bn a year in the early 1980s. In Kuwait, the

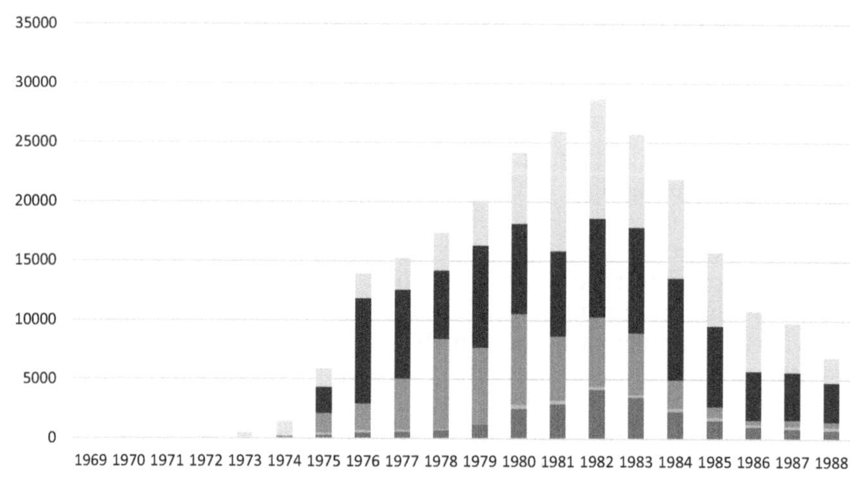

Figure 3.1 Loans provided by specialized Saudi government credit institutions and government subsidies, SAR mn.

Source: Chaudhry, The Price of Wealth, p. 152.

private sector focus expanded into areas such as manufacturing: "most notably following the establishment of the Shuaiba Industrial Area in 1964. The sector grew further in the 1970s and early 1980s, as a result of the state's protectionist and subsidisation policies."[75] The Kuwaiti model revolved heavily around state support through multiple channels:

> *(i) providing loans at a low interest rate; (ii) establishing industrial estates, including the construction of infrastructure in industrial areas; (iii) providing tariff protection against foreign goods, which are similar to those produced locally; and (iv) offering customs duty exemption on machines, equipment, spare parts and raw materials required by local manufacturing industries.*[76]

The first Kuwait plan (1967–1968 to 1971–1972) earmarked KWD88mn for the promotion of industrial development in the private and semi-private sectors. A further KWD18.5mn was allocated to the financial and commercial sectors with ambitions to establish Kuwait as a regional financial center. The second plan (1976–1977 to 1980–1981) dedicated a remarkable total of KWD140mn for industrial development, KWD20mn of it for private ventures. By the time the third plan began, the scale of support to private businesses had risen to KWD1,210mn, but an impressive KWD495mn of it was now destined for real estate and business services.

Comparable trends played out across the Gulf. While the number of corporate registrations shot up, numerous problems became evident. Government support created an enduring legacy of input price distortions and a culture of entitlement. Rising disposable incomes meant that the original aspirations for export-led diversification became less of a perceived necessity, while private investors found far less costly business opportunities at home. This deviation from capital-intensive export ventures undermined the economic impact of the new policies as an evolving GDP composition was not matched by export diversification. Moreover, the establishment of businesses with government backing meant that capital allocation was not driven by efficiency considerations. Even as entrepreneurs developed a domestic bias, openness remained the source of the export revenues that financed the distributive state.[77]

The public spending boom gave rise to a multitude of new projects and a massive influx of imports. Few Gulf businesses had the resources to participate in such activities, but the authorities were keen to spread the wealth. Regulatory changes enabled Gulf nationals to mediate commercial interaction with other countries: "It was by rewriting the rules governing foreign entry into the Saudi market that the government most radically reshaped domestic business. … It was possible for *any* Saudi to mediate foreign access to the Saudi market. Incorporation into the world economy … produced not one class of interlocutors, but a whole society of commission entrepreneurs."[78] Such practices opened up yet new opportunities for people to reap rents instead of engaging in genuine production. Champion speaks of Saudi nationals who act as "agents, brokers and middlemen between foreign business or industry and the Saudi state in the negotiations and award of contracts. The agents charge commissions, sometimes substantial, as a percentage of the total contract value in return for their services."[79] These practices coincided with the ascendancy of the Nejdi business elites over the once-dominant Hijazi establishment.[80] Inefficient as such intermediation may often have been, it commanded widespread social acceptance and also coincided with an explicit rejection of corruption. A 1956 Saudi law "prohibited, with severe penalties, private business engagements on the part of public servants and princes."[81] The tidal wave of oil wealth changed matters in the 1970s, but even then, the government passed a tender law to regulate procurement processes in 1977.

A whole new class of Gulf businessmen grew rich as gatekeepers between their domestic markets and the outside world. While rules varied somewhat across countries, they typically stipulated the need for local sponsors, whether for imports or bidding for government contracts. Gulf governments also introduced local content requirements such as the famous Saudi 30 Percent Rule in 1977. This gave rise to a whole new coterie of local subcontractors who worked with international construction firms undertaking government-funded projects, but "their sole purpose was to mediate between foreign firms and the state, acquiring contracts, permits, and labor import licenses."[82] Similarly, the Saudi Service Agency Regulations of 1978 required foreign businesses to appoint Saudi agents to channel bids for government contracts. A similar pattern obtained with labor imports "as no foreign individual or firm could enter the kingdom without a Saudi 'sponsor.'"[83]

The confluence of the diversification and distribution agendas in the heady 1970s gave rise to a tradition of state-sponsored private entrepreneurship, effectively a "corporate welfare state." Economic activity was undertaken by private businesses, but its scale and profitability were critically determined by government support. This dependency weakened the usual incentives and imperatives shaping private entrepreneurship. Ultimately, however, this was another instance of derivative diversification, with oil surpluses being channeled into non-oil activities but not necessarily in ways that would give these new ventures genuine sustainability beyond the life span of the oil boom itself.

With time, the region became much better at managing waves of hydrocarbons liquidity. The spectacular rise of Bahrain as a financial hub, while it constituted a reactive response to the rise of the petrodollar liquidity, also reflected a vision for proactively facilitating the rise of a new cluster. The oil boom began to draw international banks to the region, all the more after the Lebanese civil war pushed Beirut off its pedestal as the regional financial center.

Nothing lasts for ever

From the first oil shock in 1973–1974 to the second in 1979, oil consumers paid for a 15-fold rise in prices. Beginning in 1981, however, the tables were turned as a global glut triggered a violent price correction. The preceding price rally had substantially altered the dynamics of the global energy markets by curbing oil consumption, boosting energy efficiency, and fueling a broad-based search for alternatives. Nuclear energy experienced a renaissance, but new, costlier sources of oil could also now be developed in the North Sea, as well as in Asia, Africa, and Latin America. Their aggregate output roughly equaled Saudi Arabia's at 7.6mn b/d in 1973 but subsequently more than doubled to 15.6mn b/d in 1983, while Saudi Arabia was forced to reduce its production to 5.4mn b/d.[84] These "new" producers attained an aggregate output of 21.8mn b/d by 1993 – more than twice Saudi Arabia's 8.7mn b/d. Technological progress had halved the average cost of finding and developing new oil reserves from roughly $10 per barrel during the 1980s. The gradual normalization of the political risk landscape after the disruptions of the Iranian revolution and the onset of the Iran–Iraq war further contributed to the market reversal.

This economic reversal mirrored the extraordinary upturn that had preceded it. Total Gulf oil revenues "rose from some $5 billion in 1970 to just under $160 billion in 1980. Prices then began to drop again, bringing revenues down with them to a low of $37 billion in 1986."[85] The stark new market realities triggered the first ever OPEC output cut in March 1982 when the group's output was capped at 17.5mn b/d. A year later, OPEC reduced its target price from $35 to $29 per barrel but to little avail. Even as the GCC producers sought to stabilize the global market, some other OPEC members exceeded their quotas, while non-OPEC production continued to gather steam. Things eventually came to head in 1985 when Saudi Arabia, relinquishing its traditional swing producer role, flooded the markets, "selling its oil at a considerable discount, so precipitating a price collapse from $24 to $9/barrel during 1986."[86]

The Gulf region confronted the most profound economic shock since the collapse of pearling as the growth drivers that had delivered the fabulous boom went into reverse. A fiscal tailspin ensued as Saudi "[c]rude oil production declined from an average of 9.81 million barrels per day in 1981/1982 to an average of 3.2 million barrels in 1985. Oil prices dropped from peaks of $34 a barrel in 1981 to $11.5 a barrel in 1986. Government revenues fell drastically to around SR 50 billion in 1986 compared to nearly SR 400 billion in 1981."[87] By the autumn of 1986, the combined oil revenues of Saudi Arabia, Kuwait, and the UAE had plunged to a low of $27bn. By 1986, it proved impossible to formulate a government budget in Saudi Arabia. The government resorted to monthly fiscal plans and tried to manage cash flows by delaying projects.[88] A new quota agreement among the OPEC producers was ultimately reached in December 1986 to maintain a reference price of $18 per barrel. Collaboration was now achieved even with some non-OPEC nations, and prices were successfully stabilized in the range of $15–$18 per barrel during the remainder of the decade.

The oil–government nexus dramatically contracted as, for instance, Saudi budget spending nearly halved from SAR284.6bn in 1981 to SAR134.9bn in 1988. Major projects were mothballed or canceled altogether. Government construction contract awards more than halved between 1984 and 1985 to just over SAR14bn.[89] Saudi Arabia's cumulative fiscal deficits reached $141bn over the decade to 1992, while the deficit-to-GDP ratio

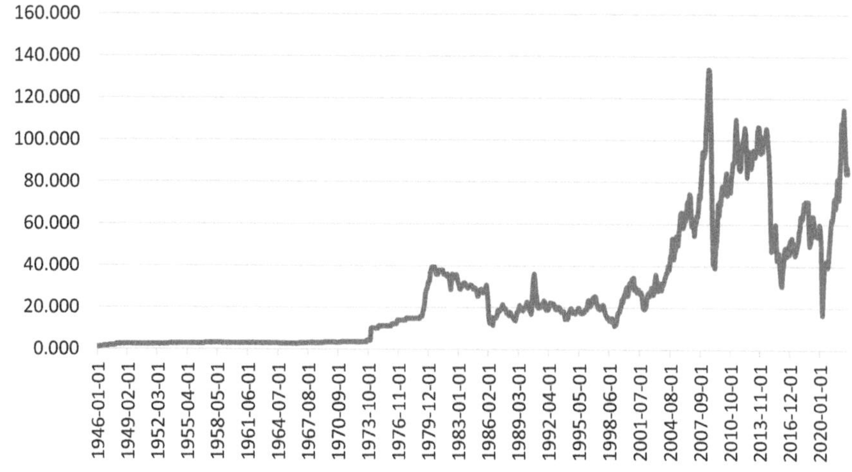

Figure 3.2 West Texas Intermediate (WTI) spot price since 1946, $/barrel.

Source: Federal Reserve Bank of St Louis, FRED Economic Data, https://fred.stlouisfed.org/series/DCOILWTICO.

peaked at 25.3 percent in 1987. By 1993, the ratio fell back to the single digits until a surplus was posted in 2000. The external position on the Kingdom was reversed from a $163bn cumulative surplus in 1973–1982 to a $138bn aggregate deficit between 1983 and 1992.[90] After an initial period of drawing down reserves, the government resorted to borrowing by 1987, tapping the international capital markets by the early 1990s. Saudi Arabia saw its domestic public debt rise from nothing in 1987 to $74bn by the end of 1993 (when the GDP was estimated at $121bn), while the external debt rose to $20bn. The debt-to-GDP ratio exceeded 100 percent by the end of the 1990s.[91] Saudi Arabia's nominal GDP nearly halved between 1981 and 1986 and only regained the 1981 level in 2000.[92] Per capita income fell from the neighborhood of $14,000 in the early 1980s to some $6,000 by 1994. Region-wide, the aggregate decline in per capita consumption from the early 1980s peak eventually exceeded 30 percent, a loss that was ultimately only recouped toward the end of the first decade of the new millennium. Regional per capita income fell from roughly four times the US level to just 1.5 times.[93]

While the extraordinary oil cycle underscored the urgency of economic reform, there was much less consensus on the way forward. This was partly due to the difficulties of estimating the scale and duration of the slump. Few could imagine that nearly two decades of reckoning would follow an era of seemingly limitless opportunities. One understandable response under the circumstance was to simply wait for things to revert "back to normal" and deal with the emergency through a combination of belt tightening and borrowing. With time, the initial wait-and-see approach began to give way to a more structured policy reaction. In Saudi Arabia, the new spirit of austerity was reflected in the fourth five-year plan (1985–1990), which stressed the importance of boosting productivity and the more rational use of resources. It underscored the strategic importance of diversification, in large part through the development of the manufacturing sector. A reduction in the number of unskilled foreign workers (by a minimum of 600,000) was highlighted. Key planks of the toolkit for dealing with adverse oil price swings were put in place. But the authorities also underscored the special role of oil:

> *... it would be misleading to expect that the multiple advantages which crude oil secures for the Kingdom can, in the foreseeable future, be substituted by another hitherto untapped natural resource. The Kingdom's development strategy has, therefore, taken the realistic course. Instead of turning from crude oil, the objectives have been to maximize the advantages of being the most efficient (in cost terms) and the most reliable (in terms of quantities of hydrocarbon reserves) among the leading oil producers in the world.*[94]

The plan underscored the importance of openness as a diversification driver, thereby reviving a strategic priority that had lost some of its perceived urgency in the 1970s. Agriculture, petrochemicals, and other manufacturing were all highlighted as activities that could generate foreign currency and reduce reliance on imports. But one sector outshone the others: "Because of its potential ability to be both a saver and producer of foreign exchange, manufacturing must take the central place in the economy's diversification."[95]

The stark fiscal realities of the 1980s forced the Gulf governments to identify new ways of mobilizing non-sovereign capital, whether private or foreign. This mattered all the more as new fiscal pressures emerged. For instance, while Saudi oil export revenues actually rose from $24bn in 1989 to $44bn in 1991, the government now also incurred military and "emergency" expenditures of $76bn in 1990–1992. Saudi Arabia and its allies shouldered much of the cost of liberating Kuwait from the Iraqi invaders. With revenues of $100bn over the same period, Saudi Arabia still ran deficits of $48bn over the three-year period, a figure that was higher than the $39bn recorded during the preceding three years despite a doubling of revenues.[96]

Other structural reform needs drew attention. The private sector had accounted for 85 percent of Saudi Arabia's GDP as late as 1970, but 54 percent of this came from oil companies. By 1985, the private sector share stood at 51.5 percent and in fact declined to a 1992 trough of 38.5 percent. In absolute numbers, the private sector began to rebound by 1988, and its GDP share gradually returned to 43 percent in 1999.[97] Efforts to encourage private investment involved regulatory and institutional reforms along with some infrastructure investments. The number of registered companies in Saudi Arabia rose from 1,181 in 1975 to nearly 7,000 in 1986, while their aggregate capital shot up from SAR2.2bn to SAR68.1bn. Particularly brisk change was observed in agriculture, with an increase in the national fruit and vegetable harvest from 706,000 tn in 1970 to 2,600,000 tn in 1989. Dairy production expanded from 156,000 to 500,000 tn, while poultry meat production rose from 7,000 to 226,000 tn.[98]

The government of Bahrain stimulated private entrepreneurship through measures including lower duties on imported raw materials and equipment, as well as reduced land rents in industrial zones. Export-oriented light industry was a priority. But Bahrain was also receptive to the idea of privatization, unveiling plans to sell some manufacturing companies in 1988, an option that was mooted even for Gulf Air. The new private businesses showed encouraging resilience in the conditions of austerity, whereas heavy industry typically struggled. Private additions to the corporate landscape by 1982 included "a plastics factory, an air-conditioner assembly plant, a boat repair facility, and an electrical equipment factory in addition to the Zayani cable factory."[99]

Elsewhere in the Gulf, the government assumed a more interventionist posture. The UAE tightened supervision over foreign companies while jettisoning the old partnership model. Limited liability companies became the only way foreign business could enter into joint ventures, and the Federal Companies Law of 1984 stipulated a 49 percent cap on foreign ownership.[100] Kuwait saw perhaps the sharpest policy reversal in the face of extraordinary stock market turbulence. Companies employing fewer than ten people made up 87 percent of all Kuwaiti industrial enterprises by 1965 and employed roughly a third of the workforce. The share of companies with fewer than five employees rose from 19 percent of the workforce in 1965 to more than a quarter by 1973. Since then, however, growth came to be led by large companies, while the share of smaller companies relapsed to the 1965 level.[101] The government became a major owner of leading Kuwaiti corporations following its takeover of the oil sector by 1980. By 1986, the state owned at least 57 percent of two insurers and two investment companies. Five of the 11 major industrial companies became majority government owned. The state controlled three banks in 1980 and took stakes in a total of eight by 1986.[102]

Despite the disruptions it delivered, the 1980s oil price correction probably also represented a necessary, even desirable rebalancing after the breakneck expansion of the 1970s. The onset of austerity forced Gulf policymakers to revisit some of the most generous policies introduced during the years of plenty. Not for the last time, subsidies were cut back and various government charges increased. Import duties on various products were hiked and the compensation of civil servants reviewed. The oil price gyrations also tested the Arabian welfare state model. While some steps were taken toward greater fiscal sustainability, cuts in recurrent expenditure often proved challenging to implement.

The economic rollercoaster of the late 20th century profoundly stress-tested the ability of the Gulf economy to manage exogenous shocks. While relative macroeconomic stability was ultimately restored, this relied heavily on short-term responses that did not morph into more strategic policy frameworks or institutional capacity that would build enduring resilience. Credible crisis management did not lead to transformative structural change, partly because the appetite for reform was diminished by exceptional political instability in the region, above all the 1979 revolution in Iran.

Nonetheless, elements of a new strategic posture began to gradually emerge. As noted by Peterson, "The decline in oil prices during the 1980s ...

hammered home a key lesson, namely, that prosperity and continued growth could not remain unhealthily dependent on oil income, reinforced by the fact that oil was a depletable resource – and was being depleted rapidly in some states."[103] No less important, while oil was the principal resource of the region, what mattered was not just the the scale of extraction and the price at which it was sold but, rather, what was done with it beyond the established practice of exporting crude. The fifth Saudi Development Plan for the first half of the 1990s explicitly recognized this: "While oil will be a vital part of the Saudi economy for a long time, the goal is to use petroleum as a resource for diversified industrial growth, rather than as a single export commodity."[104]

Raising the bar

As much of an uphill struggle as economic diversification proved in the late 20th century, some Gulf governments embraced new strategic objectives that transcended the oil–government nexus by focusing on competitiveness drivers beyond the regional resource endowments. A case in point was a renewed interest in the age-old Gulf traditions of long-distance trade and logistics. Such ventures saw diversification not as a primarily distributive exercise but as an opportunity to capitalize on the locational and regulatory advantages of Arabia in ways that would appeal to private investors.

Even as the range of potential diversification opportunities was essentially the same across the Gulf, policy options in some regional economies were acutely constrained by their extremely limited population base. However, it was arguably these population-scarce jurisdictions that witnessed the most transformative steps to redefine the diversification agenda. The idea of openness typically became central for such ventures, a calculus highlighted by El Mallakh in his early review of the UAE's economic development:

> *... the force of numbers, or more correctly the absence thereof, of native citizenry restricts to an inordinate degree the market upon which the nation can depend and develop. ... Clearly, the UAE must seek to augment the markets available to it either through more liberal immigration or export policies.*[105]

Historically, the UAE and Qatar faced the most extreme constraints in the Gulf in terms of their local market size. Diversification in these two economies thus critically hinged on their ability to tap the opportunities presented by the broader regional or global economy. While a more explicit export orientation offered an answer, it typically necessitated additional labor resources. In seeking to escape from these constraints, both countries had the good fortune of tapping and scaling up significant, monetizable resources that allowed them to stand against the adverse oil cycle. Oil production in the Emirates had only begun in the 1960s. Qatar began developing its massive North Dome gas deposits in the 1980s. Both countries benefited from substantial strategic investments at a time when most of the rest of the region was scaling back its project pipelines.

A similar situation occurred in Oman, which was able to counter the pressures of austerity by ramping up its oil production. Whereas all PDO output had come from 11 fields in 1967–1980, this total rose to 50 by 1988, eventually reaching nearly 100 by the end of the century. Oman's crude extraction increased from 23mn barrels in 1967 to 121.3mn in 1970, 103.2mn in 1980, and 182.6mn in 1985. In the 1990s, PDO also began to explore for gas and concluded an agreement to develop the central Oman gas fields supplying gas to an LNG plant in Qalhat, near Sur, in 1996. Oman's determination to swim against the current was largely driven by a pressing need for socio-economic development.[106]

The interest in proactive diversification in the Trucial States also reflected their rudimentary economic base which, however, entailed opportunities as well:

> *The result of this later start has been that the lower Gulf states are less economically diversified or socially evolved than their northern neighbours, but since development spending has got under way the rate of change has been more hectic. The states have had the advantage of being able to see what Kuwait and Bahrain have done and learn from some of their mistakes. This has enabled them to press ahead faster. Inevitably they have entered a race to catch up.*[107]

Dubai became the most salient example of this determination to innovate, having pursued progress for decades without resource revenues: "Dubai pulled itself up by its own bootstraps, without any oil revenues until 1969, to become the most dynamic trading centre in the Arabian peninsula."[108] The decline in local oil production by the early 1990s increased the sense of urgency. Gold trading had been central to Dubai's rise after the collapse of pearling and the city's rise to global prominence in this business. By the 1970s, 259 tn of the precious metal flowed through Dubai every year – over a fifth of the new gold supply of the non-Communist word and the equivalent of 5 kg for every resident of the emirate. Soon thereafter, however, global gold prices increased dramatically, leaving this preferred ornament beyond the reach of most consumers in India – the principal target market. Regulatory interventions by the Indian authorities further complicated matters. But Dubai proved quick to adapt as merchants moved into other products, thereby cementing the city's stature as a regional *entrepôt*.[109] The re-export trade had four main components:

> *There are capital goods, cars and foodstuffs which are imported through Dubai to be sold in other members of the UAE ...; there are ... re-exports of consumer goods of all types to the south Asian countries from Iran eastwards ...; and there are consumer durable exports to Mecca, Jeddah and Medina, where there is a big seasonal demand at the time of the Haj. By far the most unusual trade, however, involves more than \$100 million a year of consumer durable goods – watches, sound recorders, etc. – that are sold over the counters of shops within*

the UAE, and are taken out by the purchasers. It is reckoned that this trade accounts for three-quarters of all the consumer durable goods brought into Dubai.[110]

Beyond the nimbleness of its merchants, Dubai also benefited from a liberal ethos. Moreover, the emirate had never followed the regional trend of building a large government administration. This laissez-faire mentality became a powerful advantage:

Since he began to improve the creek in the 1950s, Shaikh Rashid has worked on the maxim that "what is good for my merchants is good for Dubai". Although he had to rely on the customs for his revenues before 1969, he imposed only very small duties. To encourage the business climate he issued liberal commercial regulations, which gave foreigners much more freedom to set up their own businesses than they enjoyed in other states. He also kept bureaucracy to an absolute minimum. Many of the activities which in other Gulf states are regarded as functions of government in Dubai are handled by private enterprise. This is the case with the airport, the port and the state's heavy industries.[111]

Although the UAE saw its GDP mirror the region-wide trend with a 4.5 percent decline in 1980–1989, Dubai stood ready to embrace new strategic aspirations around the idea of connectivity. In the mid-1980s when the Iran–Iraq war was pushing other Gulf governments to invest overseas, the Al Maktoum family made "a commitment to invest in their own domestic infrastructure so that Dubai would be able to support and enhance its existing re-export oriented commercial sector while also facilitating broader diversification."[112] By some estimates, Dubai spent a quarter of its GDP on seaports and roads in the 1980s and 1990s. The Jebel Ali deepwater port was a particularly bold departure, an entirely man-made facility nearly twice the size of Port Rashid. Dismissed by many contemporaries as a white elephant in the making, some speculated that its true purpose was to create the foundation for a planned federal capital. However, Sheikh Rashid had engaged consultants to plan a deepwater port as early as 1965, convinced that relying on the creek limited Dubai's expansion opportunities. Located 35 km to the southwest of Dubai, the new port was only some 110 km away from Abu Dhabi, and the expanding national highway system gave it good access to both cities. The port opened in 1979, following three years of construction, a massive facility with 15 km of quay and 67 berths. A greenfield investment, it possessed ample space for expansion. Port Rashid also established berths for containers starting in 1980. This significantly enhanced Dubai's appeal at a time when other Gulf ports were grappling with congestion following rapid growth in imports during the oil boom.[113]

Jebel Ali was initially managed by the US-based logistics business, Sealand Shipping Company, established in 1960 as a pioneer of container shipping. Sealand's decision to establish its global container business in the new port marked an ambitious attempt to put Dubai on the global logistics map despite its small domestic market and location off the main deep-sea shipping lanes. Problematically, Sealand's status ended up deterring other shippining companies, which prompted the Dubai authorities to establish the Jebel Ali Free Zone in 1985. This became a dramatic turning point for the entire region. The new venture explicitly targeted foreign companies on their own terms with a promise of a regulatory environment matching global standards. Apart from easy registration procedures and administrative support, the zone offered purpose-built office space and warehouses. As a free zone, it could operate outside of the Dubai/UAE fiscal systems, offering minimal taxation and free transfers of profits. A separate jurisdiction was ideal for businesses hoping to service other geographies through the Gulf, echoing the region's reputation for transhipment. Jurisdictional fragmentation also appealed to Gulf-based investors who enthusiastically embraced the chance to establish businesses with far less cost and bureaucratic red tape than they were accustomed to.

Marketing efforts at first focused heavily on Japan; Sony and Aiwa were among the first companies to set up their global distributions hubs in Jebel Ali. The logistics needs created by the Gulf War in the early 1990s provided another major impetus, as shipping lines shunned the upper Gulf. By moving faster than many other jurisdictions, Jebel Ali was able to acquire a competitive advantage as shipping lines began to use it "as a hub from the early 1990s, with 'spokes' extending not only to the Gulf but also to India and Pakistan."[114]

In 1990, Jebel Ali's remit was expanded to include light industry, and plans were developed for a broader cluster that would ultimately include the planned new Dubai International Airport. The same year, the free zone came under the control of the newly established Dubai Ports Authority, a fully Dubai government–owned company, which ran it as a joint offering with Port Rashid. New entrants included Mercedes Benz and Swarovski – global brand names that significantly enhanced its appeal.

The returns to Sheikh Rashid's bold gambit exceeded the most optimistic expectations of its architects and decisively confounded its initial naysayers: "The zone expanded from a modest 298 companies in 1990 to cover over 2,000 by 2001, [was in 2005] home to nearly 37,000 workers, and [had] attracted about $4 billion in investments.[115] Jebel Ali established itself as a regional trade facilitation center par excellence benefiting from the space, infrastructure, and regulations to respond flexibly to new opportunities. The value of Dubai's non-oil trade in constant 1995 prices skyrocketed from AED7.7bn in 1975 to AED40.5bn in 1990 and AED111.7bn by 2001, remarkable progress amid a region-wide depression. Growth proved particularly brisk in the area of re-exports, which shot up from AED0.6bn in 1975 to AED22.6bn by 2001. Their share of overall trade rose from 7.3 to 20.1 percent.[116]

The 1985 establishment of Emirates Airlines became another major game-changer in the diversification narrative. Originally launched with two aircraft leased from Pakistan International Airlines, Emirates became a key enabler and embodiment of Dubai's transformation. The company received an early impetus from the traffic created by the development of

Dubai's oil resources. The government consistently resisted direct financial subsidies or any retreat from the established open skies policy.[117] The lack of preferential treatment did not prevent the new carrier from becoming a key beneficiary and driver of the rapidly growing popularity of global travel:

> *By 1990, Emirates was flying to major hubs like London, Frankfurt and Singapore, taking advantage of the fact that most of the world's population lives within a reasonable flying time of the city-state. As Emirates grew, it became a kind of octopus, grabbing ever more far-flung parts of the world and drawing them to Dubai.*[118]

Dubai simultaneously continued to develop its international airport – itself an early diversification initiative from 1960.[119] It grew into a popular fueling station for the intercontinental flights of many foreign carriers. Annual passenger traffic exceeded 3mn by 1981 and topped 4.5mn by the end of the 1980s. Dubai's reach was by then expanding far beyond the Gulf–Arabian Sea region just when the emerging markets boom was about to take off. The number of passengers reached 12.3mn in 2000.

The successful creation of an international aviation hub created an opportunity to invite some transit passengers for longer stopovers, thereby laying the foundation for Dubai's tourism aspirations. While part of the appeal came from the Arabian mystique of a region that had not previously been a major player on the global tourism map, the subsequent progress rested on a strategic vision to create a purpose-built destination, initially positioned as a shopping hub known for mega-malls. Dubai effectively leveraged the synergetic relationship between connectivity and reputation-building that tied it into an expanding network the world over.

Forward thinking in Qatar was made possible by the progressive development of its massive North Field gas deposits. Shell's North West Dome-1 well had marked the discovery of the world's largest natural gas reserves in 1971. The infrastructure buildup around the find started in the 1980s and production, at the rate of 800mn cu ft per day, was initiated in 1989. Phase 1 of the field development went online in 1991. The gas was at first primarily used for domestic needs, not least because of modest progress with foreign sales and the disruptions caused by the Gulf War. Gas-based manufacturing became as a key plank of Qatar's diversification strategy. The Ras Laffan Industrial City and Mesaieed Industrial Area emerged as two key development clusters. New avenues for exports soon opened up thanks to the "the widespread use of combined cycle gas turbined in the 1990s in power generation"[120] along with substantial cost reductions across the LNG value chain. Exports finally began at the end of 1997, and within a decade, Qatar overtook Indonesia to become the world's leading producer.[121] The growth of the sector was rapid, and in 2009, "for the first time in the country's history, natural gas share of the economy surpassed the oil sector."[122]

The first generation of diversification

The "first wave" of strategic diversification in the Gulf opened up new investment opportunities in five main areas which all retained a link to oil, whether as a source of capital, energy, or a direct input:

1. Investments in social infrastructure, above all health care and education, were at first driven by a desire to transcend the modest initial conditions and subsequently by the growing population base.
2. The growing size and prosperity of the regional economies created a need for physical infrastructure, with demographics and urbanization fueling residential real estate demand.
3. The dramatic rise in imports called forth new trade facilitation services. Retail trade opportunities multiplied as, for instance, Saudi real per capita private consumption quadrupled between 1973 and 1982.
4. Hydrocarbons could be leveraged through greater value chain capture and as inputs for other energy-intensive activities.
5. The oil windfalls opened up new avenues for financial services, an opportunity that was proactively embraced by Kuwait and Bahrain.

Despite their continued links to oil, these developments significantly reshaped the Gulf economies. Human development indicators improved dramatically. Manufacturing growth extracted more value out of the regional natural resources, while downstream investments reduced sensitivity to oil price variations. Increased natural gas use turned a previously wasted resource into a driver of growth and jobs. Manufacturing (including refining) reached 33.1 percent of Saudi Arabia's real GDP by 1989.[123]

In financial services, the need to recycle petrodollars was initially derivative, but the sector soon expanded and diversified its remit. With a growing population and expanding transit trade volumes, some of these drivers became progressively less dependent on oil over time. Moreover, Bahrain's successes in the 1970s underscored the potential of the locational advantages of the Gulf as well as the benefits of regulatory innovation – factors altogether independent of oil.

Investment in connective infrastructure created new value but also promised substantial future potential by enabling the Gulf to capture global flows, whether in trade or tourism. Such capacity creation also increasingly differentiated the Gulf from its neighbors, which in principle shared some of the same locational advantages. Jebel Ali and the Dubai aviation cluster proved particularly far-sighted and ushered in a new era for the regional development narrative. In an echo of the pre-oil past, they pointed to a future where the Gulf would compete on its location, infrastructure, and regulatory innovation.

The different aspects of the regional diversification journey fed off each other. A growing population pushed up trade volumes, which necessitated new financial and infrastructure facilities. Improving human development created growing cadres of qualified professionals. Perhaps most significant, the Gulf established itself as an investment destination in a dramatic reversal for a region that had embarked on the oil era as a substantial capital net exporter.

The first decades of proactive diversification focused heavily on the sectoral composition of the Gulf economies. The main goal was to enable new economic activities in the hopes of establishing sustainable growth drivers as an insurance policy for an eventual post-oil future. But even as the "superstructure" of the modern GCC economy did evolve, its twin "founding" sectors maintained their special status at its core; this was diversification underwritten by oil and almost entirely funded by the regional sovereigns.

The policies of the 1970s and 1980s left the different aspects, or "axes," of diversification misaligned and this imbalance increased further over time. Even as the GDP composition slowly evolved away from oil, the Gulf fiscal system remained almost entirely reliant on oil revenues. The First Saudi Plan noted that over 85 percent of government revenue had historically come from oil exports. Although the need to identify new sources of government revenue was explicitly acknowledged, little meaningful change materialized.[124] The state of affairs by the 21st century was little different:

> *Because of the large income from ... exports of oil, gas or other "rents", the state is not forced to tax the local economy to finance its activities. ... the state ... is not under pressure to develop an efficient economic foundation for the society. Rather, it can see its role as that of distributing the revenues which flow into the country.*[125]

The lack of of alternative revenue sources meant that oil price corrections were dealt with through expenditure cuts, above all in the area of capital projects, which were typically easier to modify than recurrent expenditures. For instance, the Fifth Development Plan in Saudi Arabia, adopted in 1990, noted that "[t]his stage of infrastructural development in the Kingdom is largely ended."[126] This practice of pro-cyclical public spending dynamics amplified the oil price variations but also meant that "[e]xpenditure was being reduced most sharply in areas critical to economic development"; that is, capital projects.[127] The most effective aspect of fiscal re-engineering involved financial diversification. Accumulated sovereign savings helped reduce volatility in public spending while also addressing the issue of intergenerational equality. But while financial diversification generally advanced, it did not fundamentally transform the Gulf fiscal models, not least because reserves were run down during periods of lower oil prices. As accessible rainy-day funds, they furthermore disincentivized structural reforms.

The export bundle of the Gulf economies similarly did not fundamentally change during the closing decades of the century. In Saudi Arabia, oil made up 83.5 percent of all merchandise and service exports in 1985 and this proportion rose marginally to 90.8 percent in 2000.[128] The modest progress of the desired structural transformation reflected the limited productive capacity of the non-oil economy as well as its domestic bias. Moreover, the scale of oil exports was typically more than sufficient to achieve a substantial external surplus, which allowed the endemic import dependency to be financed with ease. But this state of affairs came at a cost, above all a disproportionate allocation of resources to relatively low-productivity activities.

With the main exception of industrial investments, the Gulf went against the global norm under which "[d]iversification in output and exports are closely linked to one another and are considered to be the outcome of structural transformation—the dynamic reallocation of resources from less productive to more productive sectors and activities."[129] Manufacturing tends to be of particular importance in this regard given its potential for innovation, productivity, and ongoing quality improvements.

The Gulf labor market dynamics quickly became sharply dichotomous, with the end result of a national workforce that relied almost entirely on "on-demand" public sector employment. This state of affairs did little to contribute to the development of the private sector and meant that many nationals did not not derive any direct benefit from its growth. The main exceptions to this tended to involve regional entrepreneurs and various rentiers but also a significant proportion of employees in the less oil-rich regional countries such as Bahrain.

This misalignment of the axes of diversification remained the most important hurdle to the economic re-engineering envisaged by Gulf planners. Even as the political determination to transcend the oil–government nexus grew stronger, implementation was thwarted by the institutional structures layered on top of it that in practice perpetuated it. One key consequence was the relative lack of substantial pools of private capital (with the exception of wealthy business families). The regional financial sector did little to compensate for this, being largely composed of commercial banks that effectively pumped oil-fueled liquidity into the economy through simple credit products. Alternatives were limited with the capital markets "still underdeveloped and ... not able to offer companies good alternative financing possibilities or to channel foreign portfolio capital into the private sector."[130]

Why did more fundamental change fail to transpire? Most immediately, of course, the oil price dynamics of the last three decades of the 20th century were extreme in comparison to the preceding decades. During this rollercoaster ride, it was no easy task to maintain a long-term strategic focus. The rudimentary fiscal system offered minimal fiscal stabilizers or other policy levers to counter the fluctuations. While foreign capital began to grow in importance, it remained relatively rare, not least due to regulatory restrictions.

After this checkered progress, was the proverbial glass half full or half empty? Edmund O'Sullivan's 1996 assessment reflected a common perception:

> *... more than two decades after Saudi Arabia committed itself to a strategy of diversifying away from dependence on oil, the energy market continues to determine the health of its economy. Despite expensive efforts to promote industrial development with cheap energy, low-cost finance, protectionism and central planning, the kingdom today remains ... essentially an oil-based economy.*[131]

Most non-oil activities reflected, and often amplified, the volatility inherent in the oil–government nexus. The widespread use of subsidies and social benefits further entrenched these patterns. The fact that the Gulf economies were able to achieve relative economic continuity through large-scale government borrowing in the 1980s and 1990s meant that many boom-time practices persisted long past the oil price correction. It also explains why the progress of diversification suffered from a persistent bias in favor of the non-tradable sector, which was underwritten by remarkably persistent government largesse even amid falling oil prices.

The oil–government nexus continued to cast a long shadow in other ways as well. While the larger manufacturing ventures in particular did allow the Gulf economies to carve a globally significant foothold in certain markets, economic policy was heavily influenced by the infant industry ideology popular at the time. Heavily subsidized input prices shaped the non-oil sector, for instance, selling gas to manufacturing concerns at well below the global market prices. Similarly, more intensive water use for agriculture could be justified by a desire to boost food security and socio-economic inclusion. Such practices meant that many of the initial achievements of diversification came at a dynamic cost, frequently with negative externalities such as waste and pollution. Unsustainable water use resulted in enduring damage to the regional underground aquifers. Low gas prices disincentivized exploration, which eventually began to constrain the growth of gas-based manufacturing ventures.

The heavy hand of the government had profound implications on the evolution of the Gulf corporate sector. The persistence of wide-ranging input subsidies, along with the systemic reliance on low-cost foreign labor, left most companies in a rentierist posture. Low and static input costs delivered often substantial rents when outputs commanded market prices. These margins were seldom eroded by significant taxation or government levies, which minimized pressures for ongoing productivity gains. Such distortions deepened over time because of policy continuity, which meant that real prices underwent a secular decline. In sectors such as heavy industry, technologically embodied productivity gains did materialize when production was scaled up. But new facilities often co-existed with progressively more outdated legacy technology. This sclerotic development pattern translated into an extensive growth model where GDP growth came almost exclusively through input accumulation: more capital and labor delivered more GDP. Yet by discouraging dynamic efficiency, these practices made it more difficult to deliver higher living standards.

The exceptional vagaries of the global oil markets in the 1980s and 1990s significantly tested the first-generation diversification, shaped as it had been by boom-era assumptions.[132] But the era of austerity also revealed that the diversification effort had developed some genuine momentum. Perhaps the most important legacy of these lean years was the growing conviction that sustained prosperity in the Gulf did indeed depend on economic re-engineering and openness. By challenging the limits of the state-led development model, the crisis years underscored the importance of identifying new sources of investment capital, which in turn required policy innovation. The established practice of joint ventures came with some assurances when it involved reliable local partners, but the appeal of the new free zone model pioneered by Dubai was an altogether different level.

Economic diversification, by reactivating many of the competitiveness drivers that predated oil, further underscore the strategic importance of openness for the Gulf economies. Most of the new diversification themes had an explicit link to the global economy. The regional logistics infrastructure once again began to be used to facilitate trade flows beyond the oil-financed imports. Financial services showed some signs of escaping from their oil-era orbit through more explicit links to global capital and trading opportunities but also by facilitating the local mobilization of previously exported capital. Large-scale manufacturing could transcend the demographic limitations of the Gulf economy only by ensuring their competitiveness in the global market. Their initial limitations notwithstanding, many of the first-generation diversification initiatives laid a credible foundation for further progress.

Notes

1 Knauerhase, *The Saudi Arabian Economy*, pp. 285, 336.
2 Beblawi, "Gulf Industrialization," p. 188.
3 Owen and Pamuk, *A History*, p. 86.
4 Knauerhause, *The Saudi Arabian Economy*, p. 191.
5 El Mallakh, "Planning in a Capital Surplus Economy," p. 428.
6 Al-Kuwari, *Oil Revenues in the Gulf Emirates*, p. 175.
7 Quoted in: El Mallakh, *Saudi Arabia*, p. 14.
8 El-Kharouf *et al.*, "The Gulf Cooperation Council," p. 133.
9 El Mallakh, *Saudi Arabia*, p. 193.
10 El Mallakh, *Economic Development and Regional Cooperation*, p. 74.
11 Owen and Pamuk, *A History*, p. 214.
12 Owen and Pamuk, *A History*, p. 215.
13 Braunstein, *Domestic Sources*, p. 8; Al-Dekhayel, *Kuwait*, pp. 164–165.
14 Owen and Pamuk, *A History*, p. 215.
15 Knauerhase, *The Saudi Arabian Economy*, p. 319.
16 Quoted in: Knauerhase, *The Saudi Arabian Economy*, p. 319.
17 Wilson, *Economic Development in Saudi Arabia*, pp. 22–23.
18 CPO, *Development Plan, 1390 A.H.*, p. 23.
19 CPO, *Development Plan, 1390 A.H.*, p. 25.
20 CPO, *Development Plan, 1390 A.H.*, p. 21.
21 Davidson, *Abu Dhabi*, pp. 50–51.
22 Davidson, *Abu Dhabi*, p. 50.
23 Dargin, "Qatar's Gas Revolution," p. 313.
24 Allen and Rigsbee, *Oman under Qaboos*, p. 100.
25 CPO, *Development Plan, 1390 A.H.*, p. 21.
26 CPO, *Development Plan, 1390 A.H.*, p. 34.
27 Al-Sabah, *The Oil Economy of Kuwait*, p. 85.
28 Chaudhry, *The Price of Wealth*, p. 83.
29 Knauerhase, *The Saudi Arabian Economy*, p. 194.
30 Quoted in: Knauerhase, *The Saudi Arabian Economy*, p. 171.
31 Knauerhase, *The Saudi Arabian Economy*, p. 74.
32 El Mallakh, "Planning in a Capital Surplus Economy," p. 432.
33 Al Makhawi, *The Gulf Cooperation Council*, p. 43.
34 El Mallakh, "Planning in a Capital Surplus Economy," p. 432.
35 Chaudhry, *The Price of Wealth*, p. 90.
36 Niblock, *The Political Economy*, p. 48.
37 Chatelus, "Policies for Development," p. 111.
38 Osama, *The Dilemma of Development*, p. 21.
39 Knauerhase, *The Saudi Arabian Economy*, p. 144.

40 Stevens, "The Interaction," p. 39.
41 Stevens, "The Interaction," p. 39.
42 El Mallakh, "Planning in a Capital Surplus Economy," pp. 433–434.
43 Shammas, *Saudi Arabia*, pp. 7–8.
44 Looney, *The Economic Development*, p. 69; Lackner, *A House Built on Sand*, p. 54.
45 Stevens, "The Interaction," p. 29; Rashid and Shaheen, *King Fahd*, p. 212.
46 Rashid and Shaheen, *King Fahd*, p. 212.
47 Al-Sabah, *The Oil Economy of Kuwait*, p. 85; Al-Kandari, *Industrial Development*, p. 40.
48 Knauerhase, *The Saudi Arabian Economy*, p. 142.
49 Azzam, *The Gulf Economies in Transition*, p. 125.
50 Ramazani, *The Gulf Cooperation Council*, p. 102.
51 Quoted in: Al Makhawi, *The Gulf Cooperation Council*, p. 69.
52 Wilson, "The Economic Relations," p. 275.
53 Lawson, "Managing Economic Crises," pp. 46–47.
54 Owen and Pamuk, *A History*, p. 213.
55 Chaudhry, *The Price of Wealth*, p. 183.
56 Chaudhry, *The Price of Wealth*, p. 183.
57 Chaudhry, *The Price of Wealth*, p. 179.
58 Peck, *The United Arab Emirates*, p. 98.
59 El Mallakh, *Saudi Arabia*, p. 152.
60 Knauerhase, *The Saudi Arabia Economy*, p. 84.
61 Saudi Arabian Monetary Agency, *Annual Report 1977*, p. 47.
62 El Mallakh, *Saudi Arabia*, p. 193.
63 Owen, "The Arab Economies."
64 El Mallakh, *Saudi Arabia*, pp. 154–155.
65 El Mallakh, *Saudi Arabia*, p. 164.
66 El Mallakh, *Saudi Arabia*, pp. 189, 191.
67 El Mallakh, *Saudi Arabia*, p. 194.
68 Niblock, *The Political Economy*, pp. 77, 82.
69 Niblock, *The Political Economy*, p. 82.
70 Chaudhry, *The Price of Wealth*, p. 152.
71 Chaudhry, *The Price of Wealth*, pp. 164, 166.
72 Chaudhry, *The Price of Wealth*, p. 151.
73 Chaudhry, *The Price of Wealth*, p. 165.
74 Chaudhry, *The Price of Wealth*, pp. 150–151.
75 Al-Dekhayel, *Kuwait*, p. 158.
76 Al-Dekhayel, *Kuwait*, p. 165.
77 Chaudhry, *The Price of Wealth*, p. 141.
78 Chaudhry, *The Price of Wealth*, p. 153.
79 Champion, *The Paradoxical Kingdom*, p. 11.
80 Champion, *The Paradoxical Kingdom*, pp. 93–95.
81 Champion, *The Paradoxical Kingdom*, p. 98.
82 Chaudhry, *The Price of Wealth*, p. 154.
83 Chaudhry, *The Price of Wealth*, p. 154.
84 Gately, "Lessons from the 1986 Oil Price Collapse," pp. 238–240.
85 Owen and Pamuk, *A History*, p. 203.
86 Owen and Pamuk, *A History*, p. 205.
87 Ramady, *The Saudi Arabian Economy*, p. 28; Hunter, "The Gulf Economic Crisis," p. 593.
88 Vasiliev, *The History of Saudi Arabia*, p. 453.
89 Vasiliev, *The History of Saudi Arabia*, p. 454.
90 Champion, *The Paradoxical Kingdom*, pp. 148, 156; Niblock, *The Political Economy of Saudi Arabia*, pp. 80, 126; SAMA Annual Reports.

91 Champion, *The Paradoxical Kingdom*, p. 165; Wilson, *Economic Development in Saudi Arabia*, pp. 31–32; IMF, *Saudi Arabia: Financial System Stability Assessment*, 2006, p. 9.
92 Niblock, *The Political Economy of Saudi Arabia*, p. 116.
93 Hvidt, *Economic Diversification*, pp. 15, 30; Gray, *The Economy of the Gulf States*, p. 52.
94 Ministry of Planning, *Fourth Development Plan*, p. 44.
95 Ministry of Planning, *Fourth Development Plan*, p. 45.
96 Champion, *The Paradoxical Kingdom*, p. 147; Niblock, *The Political Economy of Saudi Arabia*, pp. 116, 120, 125.
97 Niblock, *The Political Economy of Saudi Arabia*, p. 129.
98 Vassiliev, *A History*, pp. 455–456.
99 Lawson, "Managing Economic Crises," p. 47.
100 Peck, *The United Arab Emirates*, p. 110.
101 Lawson, "Managing Economic Crises," p. 49.
102 Al-Dekhayel, *Kuwait*, pp. 6–7; Azzam, *The Emerging Arab Capital Markets*, pp. 183–185.
103 Peterson, "Life after Oil," p. 1.
104 Ministry of Planning, *Fifth Development Plan*, p. 12.
105 El Mallakh, *The Economic Development of the United Arab Emirates*, p. 61.
106 Allen, *Oman*, pp. 94–95.
107 Field, *The Merchants*, p. 58.
108 Field, *The Merchants*, p. 60.
109 Field, *The Merchants*, p. 61; Davidson, *Dubai*, pp. 69–71, 105.
110 Field, *The Merchants*, p. 63.
111 Field, *The Merchants*, p. 64.
112 Davidson, *Dubai*, p. 106; Owen and Pamuk, *A History*, p. 219.
113 Nuttal, *Shipping and Development in Dubai*, pp. 51, 76–77; Davidson, *Dubai*, pp. 106–107.
114 Nuttal, *Shipping and Development in Dubai*, pp. 80, 89.
115 Davidson, *The United Arab Emirates*, p. 139.
116 Davidson, *The United Arab Emirates*, pp. 133–134.
117 Nuttal, *Shipping and Development in Dubai*, pp. 86–87.
118 Brook, *A History of Future Cities*, p. 354.
119 Nuttal, *Shipping and Development in Dubai*, p. 85.
120 Dargin, "Qatar's Gas Revolution," pp. 308–309, 314; 322–329.
121 Flower, "LNG in Qatar," p. 341.
122 Dargin, "Qatar's Gas Revolution," p. 315.
123 Beutel, *Saudi Arabien in den neunziger Jahren*, p. 14.
124 Chaudhry, *The Price of Wealth*, p. 34.
125 Hvidt, *Economic Diversification*, p. 3.
126 Quoted in: Niblock, *The Political Economy*, p. 104.
127 Niblock, *The Political Economy of Saudi Arabia*, p. 116.
128 Niblock, *The Political Economy of Saudi Arabia*, p. 126; Hvidt, *Economic Diversification in the GCC Countries*, p. 13.
129 Callen *et al.*, *Economic Diversification*, p. 7.
130 Azzam, *The Emerging Arab Capital Markets*, p. 12.
131 Quoted in: Champion, *The Paradoxical Kingdom*, p. 144.
132 Ramazani, *The Gulf Cooperation Council*, p. 100.

References

Allen, Calvin H., Jr. (1987), *Oman: The Modernization of the Sultanate (Profiles/ Nations of the Contemporary Middle East)*, Boulder, Colo.: Westview Press.

Allen, Calvin H., Jr. and W. Lynn Rigsbee II (2000), *Oman under Qaboos: From Coup to Constitution, 1970–1996*, London: Frank Cass.

Azzam, Henry T. (1988), *The Gulf Economies in Transition*, London: Macmillan.
——— (1997), *The Emerging Arab Capital Markets: Investment Opportunities in Relatively Underplayed Markets*, London: Kegan Paul International.
Beblawi, Hazem (2010), "Gulf Industrialization in Perspective," in: Seznec and Kirk, *op. cit.*, pp. 185–197.
Beblawi, Hazem and Giacomo Luciani, eds. (1987), *The Rentier State*, London: Croom Helm.
Beutel, Jörg (1990), *Saudi Arabien in den neunziger Jahren*, Sonderdruck aus Ifo-Schnelldienst Nr 20, Munich: Ifo-Institut für Wirtschaftsforschung, July 1990.
Braunstein, Juergen (2018), "Domestic Sources of Twenty-First-Century Geopolitics: Domestic Politics and Sovereign Wealth Funds in GCC Economies," *New Political Economy*, DOI: 10.1080/13563467.2018.1431619.
Brook, Daniel (2013), *A History of Future Cities*, New York: W.W. Norton & Company.
Callen, Tim, Reda Cherif, Fuad Hasanov, Amgad Hegazy, and Padamja Khandelwal (2014), *Economic Diversification in the GCC: Past, Present, and Future*, IMF Staff Discussion Note SDN/14/12, Washington, D.C.: International Monetary Fund.
Central Planning Organization (1970), *Development Plan, 1390 A.H.*, Riyadh.
Champion, Daryl (2005), *The Paradoxical Kingdom: Saudi Arabia and the Momentum of Reform*, New York: Columbia University Press.
Chatelus, Michel (1987), "Policies for Development: Attitudes Toward Industry and Services," in: Beblawi and Luciani, *op. cit.*
Chaudhry, Kiren Aziz (1997), *The Price of Wealth: Economics and Institutions in the Middle East (Cornell Studies in Political Economy)*, Ithaca, NY: Cornell University Press.
Dargin, Justin (2011), "Qatar's Gas Revolution," in: Fattouh and Stern, *op. cit.*, pp. 306–342.
Davidson, Christopher M. (2005), *The United Arab Emirates: A Study in Survival*, Boulder, Colo.: Lynne Rienner Publishers.
——— (2008), *Dubai: The Vulnerability of Success*, New York: Columbia University Press.
——— (2009), *Abu Dhabi: Oil and Beyond*, New York: Columbia University Press.
Al-Dekhayel, Abdulkarim (2000), *Kuwait: Oil, State and Political Legitimation*, Reading: Ithaca Press.
Fattouh, Bassam and Jonathan Stern, eds. (2011), *Natural Gas Markets in the Middle East and North Africa*, Oxford: Oxford Institute for Energy Studies.
Field, Michael (1984), *The Merchants: Big Business Families of Arabia*, London: John Murray Publishers.
Flower, Andy (2011), "LNG in Qatar," in: Fattouh and Stern, *op. cit.*, pp. 343–385.
Gately, Dermot (1986), "Lessons from the 1986 Oil Price Collapse," *Brookings Papers on Economic Activity*, vol. 2, pp. 237–284.
Gray, Matthew (2019), *The Economy of the Gulf States (World Economies)*, Newcastle upon Tyne: agenda publishing.
Hunter, Shireen T. (1986), "The Gulf Economic Crisis and Its Social and Political Consequences," *Middle East Journal*, vol. 40 (Autumn), pp. 593–613.
Hvidt, Martin (2013), *Economic Diversification in GCC Countries: Past Record and Future Trends*, Kuwait Programme on Development, Governance and Globalisation in the Gulf States, No. 27, January.
International Monetary Fund (2006), *Saudi Arabia: Financial System Stability Assessment, including Reports on the Observation of Standards and Codes on the Following Topics, Monetary and Financial Policy Transparency, Banking Supervision, and Payment Systems*, IMF Country Report No. 06/199, Washington, D.C.: International Monetary Fund, June 2006.

Al-Kandari, Abdullah Ramadan A. (1982), *Industrial Development; A Case Study of Kuwait: Problems, Plans, Prospect and Strategy*, Thesis presented to the University of Glasgow for the degree of Doctor of Philosophy.

Knauerhase, Ramon (1975), *The Saudi Arabian Economy*, New York: Prager.

Al-Kuwari, Ali Khalifa (1978), *Oil Revenues in the Gulf Emirates: Patterns of Allocation and Impact on Economic Development*, Boulder, Colo.: Westview Press.

Lackner, Helen (1978), *A House Built on Sand: A Political Economy of Saudi Arabia*, London: Ithaca Press.

Lawson, Fred H. (1991), "Managing Economic Crises: The Role of the State in Bahrain and Kuwait," *Studies in Comparative International Development*, vol. 26, no. 1 (Spring), pp. 43–67.

Looney, Robert E. (1990), *Economic Development in Saudi Arabia: Consequences of the Oil Price Decline*, Greenwich, Conn.: JAI Press.

Al Makhawi, Rashid A. (1990), *The Gulf Cooperation Council: A Study in Integration*, Thesis Submitted for the degree of Doctor of Philosophy, International Studies Unit, University of Salford.

El Mallakh, Ragaei (1966), "Planning a Capital Surplus Economy: Kuwait," *Land Economics*, vol. 42, no. 4, pp. 425–440.

——— (1968), *Economic Development and Regional Cooperation: Kuwait*, Chicago: The University of Chicago Press.

——— (1981), *The Economic Development of the United Arab Emirates*, London: Croom Helm.

——— (1982), *Saudi Arabia: Rush to Development*, Baltimore, Md.: Johns Hopkins University Press.

El Mallakh, Ragaei and Dorothea H. El Mallakh, eds. (1982), *Saudi Arabia: Energy, Developmental Planning and Industrialization*, Lexington, Mass.: Lexington Books.

Ministry of Planning (1985), *Fourth Development Plan, 1405–1410 A.H. [1985–1990 A.D.]*, Riyadh.

——— (1990), *Fifth Development Plan*, Riyadh.

Niblock, Tim with Monica Malik (2007), *The Political Economy of Saudi Arabia*, Abingdon: Routledge.

Nuttall, Keith (2021), *Shipping and Development in Dubai: Infrastructure, Innovation and Institutions in the Gulf*, London: I.B. Tauris.

Osama, Abdul Rahman (1987), *The Dilemma of Development in the Arabian Peninsula*, London: Croom Helm.

Owen, E. Roger (1981), "The Arab Economies in the 1970s," *Middle East Report*, vol. 100, October–December.

Owen, E. Roger and Şevket Pamuk (1999), *A History of Middle East Economies in the Twentieth Century*, Cambridge, Mass.: Harvard University Press.

Peck, Malcolm C. (1986), *The United Arab Emirates: A Venture in Unity (Profiles/Nations of the Contemporary Middle East)*, Boulder, Colo.: Westview Press.

Peterson, John E. (2009), "Life after Oil: Economic Alternatives for the Arab Gulf States," *Mediterranean Quarterly*, vol. 20, no. 3, pp. 1–18.

Ramady, Mohamed A. (2010), *The Saudi Arabian Economy: Policies, Achievements, and Challenges*, 2nd edition, New York: Springer.

Ramazani, Rouhollah K. (1988), *The Gulf Cooperation Council: Record and Analysis*, Charlottesville: University of Virginia Press.

Rashid, Nasser Ibrahim and Esber Ibrahim Shaheen (1987), *King Fahd and Saudi Arabia's Great Evolution*, Joplin, Mo.: International Institute of Technology.

Al Sabah, Yusuf S.T. (1980), *Oil Economy of Kuwait*, London: Keegan Paul International.

Seznec, Jean-François and Mimi Kirk, eds. (2010), *Industrialization in the Gulf: A Socioeconomic Revolution*, London: Routledge.

Shammas, Pierre (2000), *Saudi Arabia: Petroleum Industry Review*, https://journals.sagepub.com/doi/pdf/10.1260/0144598001491888.

Stevens, Paul John (1982), "The Interaction between Oil Policy and Industrial Policy in Saudi Arabia," in El Mallakh and El Mallakh, *op. cit.*, pp. 27–45.

Vassiliev, Alexei (2000), *The History of Saudi Arabia*, New York: New York University Press.

Wilson, Rodney (1994), "The Economic Relations of the Middle East: Toward Europe of within the Region?," *The Middle East Journal*, vol. 48, no. 2 (Spring), pp. 268–287.

Wilson, Rodney, with Abdullah Al-Salamah, Monica Malik, and Ahmed Al-Rajhi (2004), *Economic Development in Saudi Arabia*, London: RoutledgeCurzon.

4 Reaping the demographic dividend

This chapter marks a diversion from the pre-21st-century chronology that precedes it by reviewing the profound socio-economic transformation that oil delivered. From a modest starting point, the Gulf region saw its population multiply at least 15-fold over the past century to a point where it rivals the erstwhile regional hegemons – nearly 70 percent of that of Iran and 1.5 times that of Iraq. Driven in large part by a massive influx of expatriate labor, this change has left Gulf Arabs a narrow majority in their home region.

The composition of the Gulf region's wealth does not match this demographic boom. Measured as the value of a person's lifetime earnings, human capital accounts for two-thirds of national wealth in the advanced economies and 41 percent in low-income countries. In the Gulf, it is eclipsed by produced capital, natural resources, and financial assets – ranging from just 24 percent in Kuwait to 58 percent in Bahrain.[1] Boosting this share is a pressing imperative; while the average age of Gulf residents remains below 30, old-age dependency ratios are set to rise from less than 5 percent in 2015 to more than 20 by 2050. In Saudi Arabia alone, at least 10mn people will be 65 or older by 2050.[2] Reaping the demographic dividend is only possible through better education and increased economic participation. But these productivity gains must be achieved without compromising openness as the demographic challenges, while daunting, are temporary in nature.

Overcoming historical constraints

The historically paltry population base of the Gulf countries could only sustainably expand once sufficient economic surpluses liberated the region from the centuries-long "subsistence trap." Saudi Arabia's population in the early 1930s was just over 2mn, while the overall regional total is unlikely to have been much above 2.5mn, compared to over 10mn in Iran and some 4mn in Iraq. But by the late 1960s, some 46 percent of the Saudi population was below 15 years of age and the annual population growth rate had reached 2.8 percent. Elsewhere in the region, the crude birth rates per 1000 citizens ranged from 39.8 in Bahrain to 50.7 in Qatar in 1980.[3] Mortality converged with the advanced economy norm and by 2016, the GCC average life expectancy at birth had reached 76 years – a 46 percent increase over five decades.[4]

DOI: 10.4324/9781003373353-4

Truly exceptional growth occurred at times. Large-scale labor imports pushed up Kuwait's population at a compound annual rate of more than 8 percent during the three postwar decades, with a peak of some 16 percent in the late 1950s. Even the citizenry expanded by an annual 6.5 percent thanks to a program of naturalizing tribesmen.[5] Qatar's population shot up by 17.5 percent in 2007 alone, concurrent with a 15.2 percent gain in the UAE. Both countries today have overwhelming majorities of non-national residents. In Kuwait, expatriates make up over two-thirds of the total. Saudi Arabia has the largest majority of nationals, while Oman has seen some reversal from near-parity in recent years. Also, the balance in Bahrain remains relatively even.

The Gulf region's demographic transformation was exceptional in its speed and impact. Yemen, with an estimated population of 4.3mn in 1950, was the sole relative exception to extremely low population densities. Saudi Arabia's first demographic survey in 1963 estimated only 3.3mn inhabitants. The first Saudi census in 1974 counted 7mn residents,[6] but by 2019 the Kingdom was home to 34.2mn people and Yemen to 28.5mn. Oman saw its population double from approximately half a million in 1950 to 1mn by the late 1970s. The 2019 census recorded almost 5mn residents.

The pace of change proved particularly striking on the Gulf coast. A 1892 census in Qatar had counted only 9,830 inhabitants. This had shot up to 111,133 by 1970 and to 2,545,000 by 2016 – just 12 percent of them Qatari citizens. Bahrain's population in 1941 was 89,970–82.3 percent citizens. This had more than doubled to 216,303 by 1971. As of 2018, the Bahraini resident population numbered just over 1.6mn, with the share of nationals now standing at 46 percent. Kuwait's pioneering 1957 census recorded 206,473 people, which had multiplied to 4.6mn by 2018, with just over 30 percent of them Kuwaiti.[7] The seven Trucial emirates counted a mere 72,000 inhabitants in 1950. The pioneering 1968 census recorded 180,226 people.[8] The UAE total had risen to 9.5mn by 2018, which marked a hundred-fold increase in half a century but left the Emiratis at less than 12 percent of the total.

A region of pearl divers, Bedouins, farmers, and fishermen turned into one of urbanites within a generation. In 1963, some 72 percent of the Saudi workforce were "agricultural workers and bedouin." By 1974, the share of agriculture had fallen to 51.4 percent.[9] The share of city dwellers rose from 30 percent in 1960 to 84 percent by 1997. The nomadic population had dwindled to 5.25 percent by 1993. Urbanization proved even faster in Kuwait, with a jump from 60 to 98.2 percent between 1950 and 1980. Qatar saw an increase from 30 to almost 100 percent, Bahrain from 55 to 80.7 percent, and the UAE from 26 to 81 percent. Even Oman posted a jump from less than 5 to 22 percent.[10]

Such rapid change was no simple matter in a region with scarce arable land and water. Even as the urban population shot up 14-fold between 1950 and 1980, the number of cities hardly increased. Riyadh expanded 12-fold over the four decades to the late 1960s. Kuwait City and Doha more than tripled in size between 1968 and 1980, while Dubai grew by over 400 percent.[11]

Laying the foundation for formal education

It is almost impossible to fathom today that the Gulf had virtually no modern schools a mere century ago. Mosque-affiliated *kuttab*s taught reading and writing through a curriculum that revolved around memorizing the Qur'an. Past the age of 12, training was exclusively religious and only available to boys.[12] The first exception to this norm came when the Arabian Mission of the Dutch Reformed Church of the United States opened a small girls' school in Bahrain in 1892, followed by a boys' school by 1905.[13] The Ottomans set up some schools in the Hijaz, while Mohammed Ali of the Alireza merchant family established his pioneering Fallah School of Jeddah in 1903, followed by another in Makkah two years later.[14] Kuwait's first non-religious educational establishment, Al Mubarikiya School, opened its doors in 1912. Funded by local merchants, it trained clerks, with an emphasis on arithmetics and drafting. Al Ahmadia School opened by 1921, teaching, among other things, English.[15]

Government involvement began with an Rs. 1,000 monthly contribution to Bahrain's pioneering Al Hidayah al Khalifiyah School, set up in 1919. Full state administration soon followed, and the first state schools were established in the mid-1920s. A girls' school opened in 1928, and the 1929–1930 state budget even provided for a student mission to the American University of Beirut. By 1930, there were eight government schools in Bahrain, with a total of 500 boys and 100 girls. A secondary school opened in Manama in 1940, and some private schools began to spring up around the same time.[16]

Both government and private schools were established in the Hijaz. Makkah even boasted a military college and an agricultural training institute. Private schools also operated in Al Hasa. In 1926, King Abdulaziz established a Directorate of Education along with 12 schools in and around Riyadh. State schools soon opened in the leading provincial towns. However, religious studies made up 79 percent of the primary school curriculum and 25 percent at the secondary level. Some 705 Saudis were sent abroad to study as early as 1935. The oil industry sponsored schools while also offering vocational training.[17]

Kuwait imposed government oversight in 1936 when boys' education became free. The first government schools for boys and girls opened in 1937, followed by secondary schools in 1942–1946. Reforms in 1956 introduced three four-year cycles from the primary to the secondary level, preceded by a two-year kindergarten.[18] The 1962 Kuwaiti constitution formally tasked the state with education provision. Bahrain by 1966 had 82 schools, with 37,607 pupils and 1,654 teachers, as well as several specialized institutions.[19] The creation of a national system of education within a generation of the discovery of oil gave Bahrain an important first-mover advantage on its development journey.

The lower Gulf took years to catch up. Following Qur'anic schools since 1890, Qatar's Sheikh Abdullah bin Qassim Al Thani established the Heritage School in 1913 with a more diverse curriculum. However, the first modern boys' school opened its doors as late as 1952. The initial enrollment of 240 expanded a hundred-fold to 25,475 by 1973–1974. The first girls' school began in 1955 with only 50 pupils, but by 1982 girls made up 49 percent of the total school enrollment of 42,610.[20]

The Trucial Coast had individual private schools starting with Abu Dhabi's Ibn Khalaf school in 1903, Sharjah's Al Taimiah al Mahmoudiah School in 1907, and Dubai's Al Ahmediyah School in 1910. In 1930, Al Qasimiyah School of Sharjah blazed the trail of modern education. First the British and, after 1958, the Kuwaitis built schools in the main cities. Nonetheless, Abu Dhabi had only 5 schools and 528 students in 1965, figures that shot up to 21 and 4,900, respectively, by 1968.[21]

The Sa'idiyah Schools of Muscat (1935) and Salalah (1936) were the first secular schools in Oman. The American Mission ran an elementary school in Matrah, while Indian schools operated in Muscat and Matrah. A school was built in Sur in 1956 to serve the Omani interior, while PDO set up the Oman Technical and Trade school in 1967. By 1969, the three Sa'idiyah schools still only had a total of 900 students, and nearly two-thirds of adults were illiterate. Education was among the first four ministries created by Sultan Qaboos in 1970, and the government immediately funded 13 new primary schools, while some 700 students were sent abroad to study.[22]

The uneven progress of the Gulf education systems meant that the oil windfalls rained on economies marked by an extreme scarcity of qualified human capital. For decades, the expanding public administrations had no difficulty absorbing the growing numbers of local graduates, while private businesses were left to source their manpower through imports.

The emergence of modern healthcare

Challenges in the area of public health were even more extreme than in education. Well into the 20th century, "[h]arsh climatic conditions along with extreme poverty contributed to the high incidence of ... diseases, such as malaria, tuberculosis, dysentery, and trachoma."[23] Bronchitis and tonsilitis were common on the Gulf coast, which experienced a smallpox epidemic in the early 20th century, as well as numerous outbreaks of malaria, pneumonia, diphtheria, and even bubonic plague.[24]

The American missionaries blazed a trail in health care much as they had in schooling. In 1893, Samuel Zwemer opened a medical dispensary in Bahrain, followed a decade later by the 21-bed Mason Memorial Hospital. A 12-bed Victoria Memorial Hospital opened its doors in 1905. Government provision began with a clinic in Muharraq in 1925. A temporary public hospital launched in 1929 was replaced by Al Naim hospital by 1942. A Department of Health was constituted in 1938.[25]

In 1909, Kuwait's Sheikh Mubarak invited American Mission doctors from Basra to establish clinics. The first hospital – with two doctors – was set up at the amir's palace in 1911. The Olcott Memorial Hospital began operations in 1939, and health care was put under government control when the Amiri Hospital opened its doors in 1949 with four doctors. Following further expansion, Kuwait introduced free national health care in the 1950s.[26]

Saudi Arabia's pioneering medical facilities were primary care centers in Taif and Makkah, established in 1926 simultaneously with the Health Directorate in Makkah. As late as 1949, the Kingdom had only 11 doctors and fewer than 100 hospital beds. The Jeddah Eye Hospital opened its doors in 1950, followed by the Isolation Hospital in 1952 and the Riyadh Central Hospital in 1954. Aramco was at the forefront of preventive medicine, joining forces with WHO and the Ministry of Health to combat malaria, while other ventures tackled endemic diseases such as bilharziasis, leishmaniasis, trachoma, and tuberculosis. A nationwide health care system was in place by the late 1960s.[27]

In the lower Gulf, the first British dispensary, with one Indian doctor, was established in Dubai in 1939. The construction of Al Maktoum Hospital began in 1949, and within two decades it had become a 106-bed facility. In 1952 the American Mission set up a hospital in Sharjah and a maternity clinic in Ra's al Khaimah, followed by the 1960 establishment of a small clinic in Al Ain, which became the Oasis Hospital in 1963. In the late 1950s, the Trucial States Development Fund and the Kuwaiti government funded a national network. By 1968, hospitals operated in Abu Dhabi and Al Ain, with a total of 102 beds and 20 doctors. Qatar had only a single clinic with a single physician as late as 1945.[28]

The American Mission's Knox Memorial Hospital was established in Matrah, Oman, in 1935, followed by the British-run Sharon Thomas Memorial Hospital in Muscat in 1948. Medical dispensaries opened in Nizwa and Sur in 1956. But only 13 physicians were active in the Sultanate by 1958. Sultan Sa'id opened a 22-bed hospital in Salalah in 1966.[29] A comprehensive national health care system quickly took shape under Sultan Qaboos.

Developing human capital

Social infrastructure became a central preoccupation of Gulf policymakers in the postwar decades, recognized as a precondition for translating the oil wealth into sustained modernization. Following a massive building program by the Saudi government, 41,678 Saudi boys attended government schools by 1952, a figure that multiplied to 244,431 by 1965. By the late 1950s, education accounted for a tenth of government expenditure, with another 5 percent going to health.[30] The 1960 establishment of the Directorate General of Girls' Schools coincided with a first cohort of 5,224 pupils, which skyrocketed to 200,786 in 1973. In the first half of the 1970s, primary school enrollment expanded nearly three-fold; intermediate education grew by 375 percent and secondary schooling by 712 percent.[31] The number of hospitals rose from 29 in 1958 to 54 in 1973, while the tally of rural clinics went up from 45 to 206 and health centers from 37 to 360.[32]

Education claimed more than 20 percent of the Bahraini budget in the 1960s, with transformative impact. The literacy rate shot up from 10.5 percent in 1941 to 40.2 percent in 1971. Seventy-three percent of school-aged children attended government schools in 1971, nearly half continuing to secondary education. The corresponding figure in Qatar was only 20 percent, and in Saudi Arabia 5 percent.[33] Kuwait's student population increased from 3,600 in 1945 to some 250,000 in 1975, while the share of girls expanded from 5 percent in 1945 to more than 45 percent in 1975.[34] The race to modernity proved particularly dramatic in Oman, where the number of schools reached 42 in 1971, with 15,000 students. However, school construction proved much easier than genuine modernization, and in 1974 the World Bank described the system as being "of poor quality and with little relevance to the national needs."[35] A subsequent overhaul led to the establishment of a primary teacher training institute and two "accelerated" schools. By 1990, the number of schools reached 780 and students numbered over 300,000.[36]

Brisk economic development drove a growing interest in vocational training. Bapco's Bahraini Development Program, launched in 1948, trained 2,467 employees by 1957.[37] Kuwait's Secondary School for Commerce was founded in 1952, followed two years later by the Technical College. Oman ran secondary schools for industry, commerce, and agriculture. The government took over PDO's Technical Institute in 1970 and subsequently opened ten regional institutes. The Saudi government set up four vocational training centers in 1970. By the mid-1970s, the capacity had reached 2,500 but graduates only totaled 4,371. In a foretaste of what was to prove a region-wide uphill struggle, the new foundations were: "never able to find enough students to fill the available places."[38]

Tertiary education initially relied on foreign missions, with Bahrain receiving two graduates from the American University of Beirut in 1950 but as many as 302 by 1971. Riyadh University became a regional pioneer in 1957. The College of Petroleum and Minerals in Dhahran began operations in 1965, while the initially private King Abdulaziz University of Jeddah opened its doors in 1967. The total Saudi tertiary enrollment reached 3,886 in 1968, while 1,740 Saudis participated in an Overseas Program in 1970. But nearly half the students pursued degrees in Arabic or Islamic studies, with only 10 percent studying the sciences and 11 percent studying engineering.[39] The gross tertiary enrollment ratio jumped from 9 percent in 1985 to 68 percent in 2018.

Kuwait University opened its doors in 1966, with the enrollment rising from 418 to 40,000 to date. The Gulf Polytechnic was established in Bahrain in 1968, followed by the University College of Arts, Science and Education in 1979. The two merged in 1986 into the University of Bahrain, which now has more than 20,000 students. Bahrain is also home to Arabian Gulf University, created by the GCC governments in 1980. The Bahrain Polytechnic was set up in 2008 to cater to the needs of the industry. Qatar's Teacher's College opened its doors in 1973 with an initial enrollment of 1,000 and three years later became the University of Qatar.[40] The UAE University in Al Ain was the country's higher education pioneer in 1976. Higher colleges of technology were opened in Abu Dhabi and Al Ain in 1988, expanding to 17 campuses by 2015. American University in Dubai began operations in 1995, followed by its Sharjah counterpart two years later. Zayed University Gulf and Medical University were set up in 1998. Oman's first tertiary institution, Sultan Qaboos University, was launched in 1986 with an initial class of 580, while some 2,000 Omanis studied abroad. The student population reached 3,600 by 1993, 65 percent of them female. The Higher College of Technology has six branches, and there are six colleges of applied science.

The tertiary sector has been robust growth, but the physical infrastructure buildup still contrasts with very traditional learning processes and a modest scale of research.[41] Moreover, the humanities and business degrees dominate, reflecting the credentialist traditions of the public sector. The share of students in STEM disciplines varies from around 15 percent in Bahrain to 25 percent in the UAE, with only Oman managing some 45 percent. The share of business, law, social sciences, and humanities is around 70 percent in Bahrain and 50 percent even in Oman.[42] These realities have spawned ambitious initiatives such as King Abdullah University of Science and Technology and the Education City in Doha. Dubai has sought to boost higher education provision and tourism through free zones such as the Dubai International Academic City and Dubai Knowledge Village. Partnerships with foreign educational establishments have made the Gulf "the largest recipients of transnational higher education globally."[43]

The massive social infrastructure investments made by the Gulf governments stand out in global comparison. Since the 1980s, Saudi Arabia and Kuwait have channeled 6.0 and 5.5 percent per year of their GDP into education – well ahead of the advanced economy average of 4.9 percent. In 2016, the budget allocations for education ranged from 9.2 percent in Bahrain to 22.7 percent in Saudi Arabia. These figures compared to 15.2 percent in the US and 5.2 percent in Germany. Spending on health has been comparable, albeit somewhat behind the advanced economy norm.[44] This capital mobilization has pushed up the standing of the Gulf economies in the United Nations

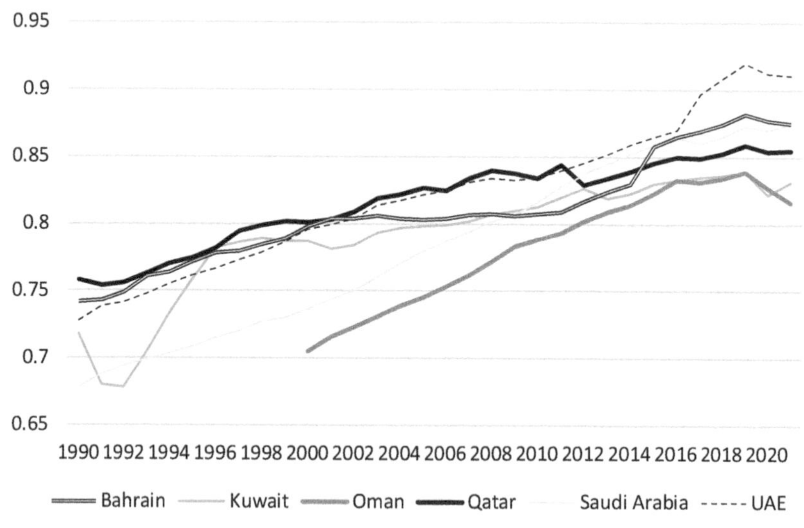

Figure 4.1 United Nations Human Development Index. N.B. Data for Oman only available as of the year 2000.

Source: United Nations Development Programme, Human Development Reports.

Human Development Index (HDI) from 0.725 (excluding Oman) in 1990 to 0.861 in 2021, compared to a rise in the global average from 0.601 to 0.732.[45]

Despite the impressive advances, the economic returns to these massive investments have been compromised by a frequent emphasis on quantity over quality. The average schooling of 12.4–13.3 years is estimated to deliver only 7.6–9.6 years of actual learning, with Kuwait and Bahrain at the two ends of the range. In some countries, more than half of all children "fail to attain minimum proficiency in basic foundational skills, such as reading and math."[46] The many reasons include limited pre-school education, a frequent lack of school autonomy and even teacher absenteeism. Formal credentials tend to trump skills, whereas "[m]odern methods of teaching and learning, which emphasize critical thinking and inquiry, and the development of key 21st century skills (such as problem solving, collaborative teamwork, socio-emotional, and digital skills) remain out of favor in many schools."[47]

The impressive health care infrastructure coincides with persistent public health challenges. Adult mortality is internationally high, roughly 2.17 per thousand, and "for every 100,000 people, almost 19 years are lost due to ill health, disability, or early death."[48] This is above all due to noncommunicable "lifestyle" diseases, such as cardiovascular conditions, diabetes, and cancer, where the region tends to top global league tables because of widespread obesity and sedentary lifestyles. These conditions account for 71.5 percent of deaths, followed by transport injuries. Consequently, Gulf human capital falls short of its promise, and the region is unable to fully reap the exceptional economic dividend potentially available to it. According to recent estimates: "a child born today in the GCC will only attain between 58 percent and 67 percent of his/her full health, learning, and potential productivity."[49]

Reshaping regional demographics

The dramatic postwar modernization of the Gulf social infrastructure struggled to eradicate the legacy of underdevelopment. Only 650 of the 30,000 Qatar inhabitants were literate in 1949. Kuwait's 1957 census counted only two native doctors and eight accountants.[50] Such extreme disparities drove a growing reliance on imported labor, building on the long tradition of openness.[51] The oil era dramatically reordered Gulf demographics.[52] Aramco opened recruitment centers in Asmara, Khartoum, Aden, Beirut, and Palestine in 1944–1949. Gulf-wide, skilled professionals and managers tended to come from the UK and the US, while artisans and clerical staff hailed overwhelmingly from India in an echo of the indentured labor system that had survived in the British Empire until 1916. Unskilled workers were initially recruited locally or from other Arab countries.[53]

The dependency on labor imports was most acute in Kuwait, where their share rose to 45 percent of the population in 1945 to 53.1 percent of an overall population of 468,000 within two decades. This total had itself risen by a remarkable 127 percent in eight years. The share of Kuwaitis in the country's workforce fell to 30 percent by 1975, while labor force participation declined from some 40 percent in the 1960s to less than

30 percent.[54] Saudi Arabia's larger population made it less reliant on labor imports. In 1952, Saudi nationals made up 61.7 percent of the labor force, although more than two-thirds of them were unskilled. By 1963, expatriate workers numbered ca. 60,000 – less than 10 percent of the workforce of 772,050. Remarkably, only 5,000 Saudis worked in government service. But within seven years, the number of expatriates shot up to 240,400 – almost a quarter of the workforce of just over a million – and "toward the end of the 1960s more than 80 percent of all workers hired by private businesses were non-Saudi."[55] During the first half of the 1970s, the natural increase of the Saudi labor force was estimated at 210,800, while the First Development Plan put overall manpower needs at 365,400. The labor market challenges went far beyond sheer numbers and included the "negative impact of social customs and traditions on the productive capacity of the labor force."[56] The government tried to engage the private sector in developing Saudi skills. Companies with more than 100 employees were mandated to train Saudis equalling at least 5 percent of their headcount for technical jobs. Foreign professionals were expected to transfer their skills to nationals, an endeavor that was soon found to have "not produced results of any significance."[57]

Gulf-wide, the number of expatriates had risen to 800,000–1.25mn by 1970. The oil boom pushed up the total to almost 2.8mn by 1975.[58] The social composition and face of the region's cities had changed fundamentally by the end of the 1980s:

> *In most of the Gulf states the indigenous population is outnumbered by immigrants – Egyptians, Palestinians, Yemenis, Iranians, Philippinos and other Far East Asians, as well as Indians and Pakistanis. The proportions vary from a high of 80 per cent in Abu Dhabi and Dubai, to 55–60 per cent in Kuwait and Qatar, down to about 20–30 per cent Saudi Arabia, Oman and Bahrain. Immigrants ... fill the manual laboring, technical and industrial jobs. They provide nearly all the labour in the service industries, where they work as porters, clerks, telegraph operators and hotel staff, and they account for most of the professional classes – doctors, teachers and engineers.*[59]

The expatriate population grew increasingly cosmopolitan due to "de-Arabization" in response to concerns over Arab nationalism and Marxism but also cost factors. The share of Arabs in the Gulf expatriate population fell from 72 percent in 1975 to 32 percent in 2004.[60] Southeast Asians in particular gained popularity in the austere 1980s. As of 1980, non-nationals made up 77.7 percent of the population of the UAE, 73.1 percent in Qatar, and 58.6 percent in Kuwait. Bahrain and Oman had lower proportions at 32 and 18.1 percent, respectively.[61] But foreign dominance in the labor force had become systemic everywhere outside of Saudi Arabia. By 1982, expatriates were estimated at 46 percent of the overall Gulf population. They constituted 85 percent of the UAE labor force, 82 percent in Qatar, and 77 percent in Kuwait. Even in Oman, their share reached 70 percent, and in Bahrain 58 percent. Only in Saudi Arabia did they fall narrowly short of parity at 46 percent. While the exact numbers were in some question as estimates of the Gulf foreign population ranged from 5.54mn to 7.2mn, the trend was unmistakeable.[62] During the decade following 1975, the Gulf labor force grew by 7.7 percent a year, and in Bahrain by 10.5 percent. The expatriate labor force boomed ahead at an annual 13 percent, led by 17 percent in Saudi Arabia and 15 percent in Bahrain. The foreign share of the regional workforce shot up from 39 to 65 percent.[63] Nowhere was this transformation quite as profound as in Dubai, where the share of nationals dropped from 62 percent in 1968 to less than 40 percent in 1976 and 17 percent in 1998, and reportedly as little as 4 percent by 2006.[64]

Within a generation, foreign labor overwhelmed the population-poor Gulf region. Even expanding social infrastructure provision for the purpose of developing national talent drew armies of foreign educators and health care providers. Moreover, results often failed to impress. The first Saudi Development Plan noted that 42,000 boys had completed less than four years of primary education. Efforts to train Saudi nurses had delivered only 33 graduates by 1970.[65] Girls' education presented a particular paradox. Their numbers in elementary schools had skyrocketed from 32,000 in 1965 to 115,000 in 1971 – roughly 30 percent of the total enrollment. However, options for secondary education remained woefully limited, with only one general academic secondary school for girls in the whole Kingdom, along with five small teacher training institutes.[66]

On the law of unintended consequences

As transformative as the foreign influx proved, these *Gastarbeiter* were viewed as temporary recruits needed to fill market gaps until local talent could replace them. Such considerations were used to justify restrictive regulatory practices, "a model of migration management anchored in the paradigm of 'temporary labour import', promoting short-term contracts and the turnover of migrants, preventing family reunification and naturalisation, limiting socio-economic rights and implementing deportation programmes for irregular migrants."[67] This caution stemmed from socioeconomic concerns. The foreign influx pushed up the demand for scarce resources while also challenging the cultural homogeneity of the region and distorting the gender balance due to the dominance of single men. There were persistent fears that the oil boom would prove temporary. In fairness, the practices were not fundamentally different from many European practices during the postwar boom.[68]

Regulations explicitly differentiated foreign labor from Gulf nationals amid recurrent calls for more national recruitment.[69] The Qatar Labor Law of 1962 called on foreign work visa applicants to demonstrate that they "possess skills beneficial to Qatar and have a Qatari national as a sponsor."[70] Similar practices were instituted by the Saudi Labor and Work Regulations of 1947, the Bahraini Labor Law of 1958, as well as the Kuwaiti Public Sector Labor Law of 1960 and Private Sector Law of 1964.[71] Work visas were seldom issued for more than two years, although they were typically renewable. Non-nationals could not change jobs and were required to return home once their employment contract ended. Foreigners were not allowed to acquire immovable property, and entrepreneurship was only possible as a minority partner. Full control of immigration proved impossible, and the Trucial emirates saw a steady influx of illegal arrivals from South Asia supported by transnational networks of middlemen. Wooden "VC-9" dhows transported people form Bombay and Karachi to the Gulf of Oman port of Khawr Fakkan, from where many went on to other emirates. Sharjah reportedly even encouraged immigration to counter the erosion in its influence vis-à-vis Dubai and Abu Dhabi.[72]

Even as foreign hands and brains largely built the modern Gulf, they were left in a curious existence incisively described as "permanent temporary residence."[73] Despite the desire to control immigration, the law of unintended consequences quickly manifested itself with brute force as the policies adopted drove an increasingly systemic dependency on foreign labor. Expatriate manpower offered properties that appealed to entrepreneurs. Labor imports from the main source markets tended to be less costly than domestic talent. As businesses faced "an almost perfectly elastic supply of cheap foreign labor,"[74] the bargaining power of expatriate workers was minimal, all the more because experienced workers could easily be replaced with new ones. Moreover, the widespread use of "recruitment commissions" left many arrivals in debt to various middlemen, while there was little formal regulation around working conditions and salaries.[75] Foreign labor was easy to recruit and lay off, and this optionality effectively translated into on-demand human capital – an effective insurance policy for managing oil-induced economic volatility. Because they could be screened and were keen to ensure contract renewal, foreign laborers were seen as more productive and malleable.

These labor market practices ossified into entrenched cultural attitudes; for instance, perceptions that certain activities were "for foreigners only." In Saudi Arabia, this built on the long-standing view that manual work was "associated with the less well respected tribes and artisans."[76] Champion speaks of the "'*mudir* syndrome' – a concept of honour in employment which dictates that nothing less than a position of authority, status and respect is acceptable."[77] Such attitudes undervalued vocational training, annihilating long-standing craftsmanship traditions.

These realities interwove the Gulf private sector and foreign labor into an intricate interdependency that has defied policy interventions. It challenged productivity and sustainable diversification on three levels. Firstly, private companies became more labor-intensive than the region's limited indigenous labor resources and plentiful financial capital would have suggested. Secondly, the combination of rapid population growth and the appeal of business activities with low setup costs drew a growing proportion of capital into domestically focused low-productivity businesses, thereby watering down economic diversification. Thirdly, the appeal of low-cost labor disincentivized investment in labor-saving technologies, with the pernicious consequence of dynamic inefficiency. Companies became stuck in a static low-productivity equilibrium where incentives to pursue innovation grew ever weaker, while the domestic focus concealed the erosion of competitiveness.

The flexible regulations notwithstanding, foreign labor has proven remarkably sticky. Even with substantial churn, the expanding foreign communities grew ever deeper roots, perpetuated through recruitment practices and efforts to bring in relatives and friends.[78] The 2005 UAE census found that "nearly a third (28.5 per cent) of immigrants resided in the UAE for more than ten years."[79] When the Saudi government set out to "consolidate rather than expand the foreign labor force"[80] in the 1980s, government agencies proved reluctant to comply, partly in abeyance to ambitions to drive private sector development but also because of personal interests.[81] Kuwait saw the proportion of foreigners in the labor force rise from 65 percent in 1970 to 72 percent in 1980 and 85 percent in 1990.[82]

These patterns became even more dramatically entrenched during the third oil boom when "the number of migrant workers trebled in Qatar and more than doubled in Bahrain and the UAE."[83] Earlier reform initiatives largely stalled, creating a situation where "available cheap labor might contribute to what is known in labor economics as the race to the bottom. The worsening labor conditions would encourage the private sector to employ the cheapest labor available worldwide rather than investing in human capital of the GCC national work force."[84] The labor market dichtomy further deepened. The proportion of nationals employed by Omani private firms fell from 48 to 16 percent. The share dropped from 46 to 20 percent in Saudi Arabia and from 30 to 19 percent in Bahrain. Kuwait remained static at a mere 3 percent, while Qatar saw a decline to just 1 percent. Foreigners came to account for more than 90 percent of the total labor force in Qatar and the UAE by 2011. Their share rose to 77 percent in Bahrain (2010) and stood at 50 percent even in Saudi Arabia (2009). By 2010, "the GCC was the third region of immigration in the world after North America and the EU."[85]

Accommodating the aliens

Beyond multiple challenges, the expatriate influx also spelled opportunity as Gulf citizens as owners, sponsors, builders, or investors stood to benefit from rapidly escalating demand for various services and products. Sponsors of foreign workers could charge a fee for their services. Trading in visas has persisted past initiatives to liberalize sponsorship regulations, a case in point being so-called letterbox companies set up for the sole purpose of obtaining and selling visas.[86]

Expatriate housing was invariably rented, often provided through purpose-built facilities; for example, compounds that offered security as well as a lifestyle not available elsewhere. Until recently, the costs of accommodation were almost invariably borne by employers, which incentivized Gulf nationals to invest in rental properties. Even when restrictions on foreign property ownership began to be relaxed, the underdeveloped mortgage markets and the preponderance of short-term employment contracts curtailed the pace of change. In the 2010s, real estate assets of nationals in some GCC countries generated over 20 percent of their total income.[87]

Private schools offering foreign curricula sprung up across Arabia along with cultural amenities (e.g., clubs). Entire city districts came to be reshaped by foreigners and a growing array of Indian, Far Eastern, and other markets, restaurants, and travel agencies. Shadow entrepreneurship (*tasattur*) gained popularity as local businessmen farmed out their companies to foreigners in return for a rent. De-regulation eventually challenged this model, but old habits die hard. Private health care has grown in importance, especially after health insurance was mandated for non-nationals. With time, these opportunities created powerful vested interests in the business community. Paradoxically, "members of the local population appeared, collectively, to resent the presence of so many foreigners as a threat to their culture and way of life, while as individuals they clearly benefited from their ability to import increasing numbers of migrants without control."[88]

Even as expatriate labor reshaped the Gulf economies, regulations often diluted the benefits. El Mallakh commented on the anxieties and uncertainties resulting from the fact "[a]liens work under contracts of short duration even in government jobs which might be more profitably conducted if a stronger element of continuity were present."[89] Sometimes, the regulations mattered less than the long-standing informal practices, which further contributed to "the permanent state of insecurity in which most migrant workers were forced to live, unsure of the regulations, easily exploited by their patrons, and subject, always, to the threat of instant deportation if they stepped out of line."[90]

One of the earliest criticisms of the growing dependency on foreign labor had to do with the outflow of remittances, although they also helped contain upward pressures on exchange rates at times of high oil prices.[91] By 2006–2010, remittances were estimated to exceed $269bn. Saudi Arabia accounted for $112.2bn of this total, followed by Kuwait at $50.7bn, the UAE at $49.3bn, and Qatar at $29.5bn. Remittances have been often viewed as a loss of capital, although absorption challenges in fact drove a substantial outflow of capital more generally. Local savings and investment opportunities were historically limited. Even higher income earners were motivated by the expectation that their sojourns in the Gulf would be of finite duration, almost never past retirement age. Even though GCC labor laws provided for end-of-service benefits, these were typically run by companies as unfunded liabilities. Turning these provisions into more formally regulated pension schemes would have enabled more of the funds to be invested locally. The idea of reforming the system has attracted increasing attention in recent years, including a World Bank proposal of mobility savings accounts. In 2020, the Dubai International Financial Center introduced the Employee Workplace Savings Plan.[92] A failure to retain more of this capital in the region has been a growing missed opportunity for the Gulf economy.

Into government service

The booming public sector in the early hydrocarbons era easily absorbed national job seekers. Government jobs soon became a mechanism for "spreading the wealth," with the Kuwaiti public sector in 1966 employing 73,779 people, ten times the number employed in oil industry.[93] This compared to an estimated 220,000 Kuwaiti citizens in 1965! Salaries already claimed 40 percent of the budget. A 1973 report by the Kuwaiti Planning Board openly admitted that "the employment policy depended on social and local political considerations more than the actual needs of the administration."[94] Salaries rose from KWD48mn in 1962–1963 to KWD164mn a decade later as the headcount expanded from 73,000 in 1964–1965 to 101,000 in 1971–1972. The public sector claimed nearly 40 percent of the total labor force by the mid-1970s.[95] Fifty-four percent of the public sector workforce were Kuwaiti nationals, while 52 percent of the Kuwaiti national labor force was in government service. This figure was not even higher only because of opportunities in a private sector riding the 1970s boom.

In Saudi Arabia, the number of civil servants multiplied from 35,700 in 1962 to 81,800 in 1969. This figure was projected to further increase to 210,800 by 1975, by which time the non-cadre headcount of the public sector was expected to reach 63,700. This rise was above all driven by the buildup of the education system, whose headcount was expected to almost double to 62,150 during the plan period.[96] The swelling government payrolls thus brought substantial benefits as well. A similar dynamic was observed in health care provision, and new resources were also legitimately needed to oversee and regulate an increasingly complex economy. The public sector accounted for more than a quarter of the Gulf labor force – in Kuwait as much as 55.9 percent – by the mid-1980s.[97]

The idea of public sector employment as a government responsibility became a key plank of the perceived social contract, albeit with challenging consequences: "employment in the public sector was not geared to real needs, but was instead used the solve the problem of the lack of competitive employment opportunities in the private sector."[98] As neither training nor career choices were driven by strategic objectives, much local human capital was misallocated, with early estimates of productivity delivering shocking results. By the mid-1970s, observers were commenting that "overstaffing of government departments is common. ... In addition, a feeling of indifference, apathy and the lack of sufficient incentives have afflicted a significant part of the civil service."[99] Many distortions became deeply entrenched:

> *waste of resources; shunning responsibility; weakness of professional ethics; limited competence; unnecessary centralisation; numerous unnecessary committees; inadequate communication; absence of demarcation lines for authority and responsibility; absence of clearly defined tasks for each job; prevalence of task dualism and repetition; and absence of co-ordination among agencies of administration and even within agencies.*[100]

The early 21st century nonetheless delivered another public sector employment boom. Bahrain, Kuwait, and Oman channeled 59, 74, and 64 percent, respectively, of all new national labor market entrants into government employ between 2009 and 2013. The Kuwaiti public sector payroll increased from 11 percent of GDP in 2000–2009 to 14 percent in 2010–2018.[101] By 2011, 919,108 Saudi nationals supplied 92.0 percent of public sector employment. By contrast, 724,655 Saudis made up only 10.4 percent of the private sector labor force. In the UAE, nationals occupied only 43,000 of the 2.2mn private sector jobs, whereas the public sector employed 495,000 Emiratis. In 2010, Qatar's private sector labor force numbered 952,653 but employed only 6,279 Qataris, who, by contrast, held 55,170 of the 101,565 government jobs. Kuwaiti nationals claimed 73.1 perecnt of the 313,500 public sector jobs of as of June 2011, while only 31,700 nationals worked in private businesses as of 2008.[102] Following decades of government-led job creation, roughly 35 percent of all employment in Saudi Arabia is in the public sector. The corresponding figure in Kuwait is more than a quarter, while it stands at approximately 20 percent in the UAE and Qatar. These proportions compared to 18 percent in the OECD and 12 percent in Turkey. In Saudi Arabia, Qatar, Bahrain, and Kuwait, public sector wages stand at at 180–250 percent of private sector compensation. By 2013, the average GCC public sector wage bill (excluding the United Arab Emirates) was 9.4 percent of GDP, almost twice that (5.2 percent) of other oil exporters.[103]

The Arabian welfare state

Spreading the wealth became a central plank of economic policy in the Gulf after Sheikh Abdullah Al Salim of Kuwait made "the fundamental decision that he (the state) should share part of the oil rent with the population."[104] The modest initial conditions made such largesse an effective way of boosting welfare. But it also built on long-standing traditions, whether of sovereign grants and favors or an inclusive culture built around family and tribal structures that sought to avoid marginalization.

Kuwait blazed a trail toward holistic welfare provision. Financial aid to families was introduced in 1955, and a contemporary British report commented of the notion that the Kuwaitis, "while paying no taxes, [were] entitled to free or state-subsidized education, health, water, electricity, telephone and other services."[105] Transfer payments rose sharply from 1.3 percent of budget expenditure in 1963–1964 to 21 percent in 1967–1968 to 1970–1971. Roughly a quarter of Kuwait's population benefited from social security by the end of the 1970s. Such programs cost some KWD130mn by 1972 – around a fifth of total government spending – an average per citizen of KWD275 ($960).[106]

Government land purchases became another important tool for wealth distribution. Kuwait launched a land acquisition program in 1952, and 22.3 percent of public spending was allocated to land purchases in the 1950s and 1960s. Over KWD2.2bn was disbursed in 1951–1981 – roughly 11 percent of total government expenditure. Land prices rose from KWD4 per square meter in 1952 to KWD129 in 1960, yet unneeded land was often resold to the private sector at minimal cost. The program was criticized for being wasteful and encouraging speculation.[107] However, it "not only succeeded in spreading the new wealth ... but also helped in stimulating economic activity particularly in such sectors as housing, trade and small scale industry."[108] More than 70 percent of Kuwaiti families were able to become landlords, and in 1953 the government also unveiled a low-income housing scheme that provided housing to some 15 percent of Kuwaitis by 1975.[109] The Savings and Credit Bank offered soft loans for land purchases and home construction. A Social Security Authority was established in 1976.

Few governments could match the generosity of Kuwait or did so much later. Qatar introduced a social allowance scheme in 1962 while also allocating 6.6 percent of government expenditure to land purchases in 1953–1970. Sheikh Zayed began a policy of land grants in Al Ain in the 1960s, while Abu Dhabi's social spending shot up from BHD23,000 in 1967 to BHD275,000 in 1970. In 1970, 30.9 percent of the Bahraini budget went toward social services, as compared to 11.6 percent in 1947. The allocation in Kuwait was 18.2 percent – up from 12.7 percent in 1952. Qatar saw the share rise from 11.5 to 16 percent in 1965–1970.[110] In Saudi Arabia, the 1962 Social Security Law provided means-tested support, while Social Insurance Regulations were adopted in 1969. An anti-inflationary subsidy program was unveiled in the mid-1970s, including "water (sold at 7 percent [of] cost), electricity, basic foodstuffs such as wheat, sugar, and rice, as well as free education, free medical care in government hospitals, interest-free loans for housing, and welfare support for the poor."[111] Concurrently, taxes were largely eliminated. Between 1970 and 1985, social security spending rose 50-fold and the cost of pensions some 30-fold. The coverage of social insurance expanded from 145,400 to 3.3mn and also included the private sector. While these steps brought increased economic security, they also gave rise to a dependency culture.[112] Region-wide, labor market participation declined from a range of 20–23 percent in 1975 to 16–27 percent in 1997.[113]

Bahrain and Kuwait established pension schemes for government officials as early as 1955, while the Kuwaiti pension law was adopted in 1960. Saudi Arabia launched its pension system in 1962, followed by Oman in 1975. Pensions were invariably provided through defined benefit pay-as-you-go schemes with high replacement ratios, typically calculated from peak earnings during a couple of years preceding retirement. Maximum benefits were often reached within a quarter of a century, which incentivized early retirement. Beyond this, survivors' pensions were offered to multiple dependents, leading to a "fundamental misalignment between the contribution rate and benefits."[114]

The Arabian welfare state ultimately matched Northern Europe in its scope and far outdid it in generosity. At its core, this was a wealth distribution mechanism, profoundly unlike the redistributive West European social insurance models. The default norm of universal provision made the system regressive. As income and wealth differentials grew, the biggest consumers were disproportionately favored. In Bahrain, only a third of the subsidies benefited low-income groups in the early 21st century.[115] These shortcomings were recognized relatively early on with, for instance, the Kuwaiti Ministry of Finance and Industry observing in 1965 that it was time "to transfer us gradually from the path of giving aids and allowances to the path of offering opportunities of productive work to every able-bodied citizen."[116] This proved a tall order when the 1970s oil windfall rushed in.

The Gulf entitlement culture rested on three main pillars. Firstly, citizens had universal access to key services, notably free public education and health care. Secondly, some key products, above all ones deriving from the nationally owned hydrocarbons assets, were provided at a heavily subsidized cost, typically with minimal differentiation between users. Finally, national assets were distributed in order to create private wealth. Land was often donated or sold cheaply along with support for housing. Efforts to develop the regional capital markets involved underpriced privatizations with a view to attracting broad-based participation.

Entrenched dualities

The GCC labor markets are characterized by deeply entrenched dualities. The dichotomy between a public sector staffed by nationals and private business addicted to low-cost foreign labor has proven extremely resistant to change. Marked differences persist in economic participation between women and men. The wealthiest Gulf economies – the UAE, Qatar, and Kuwait – stand out by having the resources to accommodate their citizenry within the public sector. The rest of the region has higher levels of private sector participation by nationals. These dualities have been assimilated in cultural attitudeds and resulted in endemic labor market fragmentation.

The pre-2009 decade vividly revealed the practical impact of these rigidities when a robust boom failed to deliver substantial increases in national employment. Roughly 4.3mn of the 5.1mn jobs created in the Gulf (excluding the UAE) in 2006–2012 were in the private sector. Nearly 88 percent of these were filled by foreign workers, whereas Gulf nationals claimed almost 85 percent of all new public sector jobs.[117] It became obvious that market forces alone were unlikely to ever ensure full national employment. For instance, Saudi Arabia would have needed 7.5 percent annual growth – much above the historical norm – to halve unemployment over five years. While foreign labor could be sourced almost instantaneously, a 1 percent increase in non-oil GDP pushed up national employment by less than half that rate, and by only 0.6 percent even after four years.[118]

Expatriates today make up over 80 percent of the Gulf labor force and nearly 90 percent of private sector employment. Non-nationals account for almost 95 percent of the labor force in Qatar and the UAE, but even in Saudi Arabia their share is roughly half.[119] Moreover, a large proportion of *khaliji* private sector employment has become derivative, dependent on increasing expatriate employment that engendered administrative and management positions that appeal to Gulf nationals. The retail sector has become an important employer of locals.

At the core of this state of affairs is the legacy of underpricing manual labor, "a development model that has employed low-wage and less-educated foreign workers without prioritizing productivity."[120] As a result, "over the past two decades, capital investment and labor force growth have been the main drivers of growth in the non-oil sector, while total factor productivity ... has generally declined."[121] An overwhelming majority of foreign workers have low educational attainment, with only 15 percent boasting at least some tertiary education. The UAE is an exception, with a

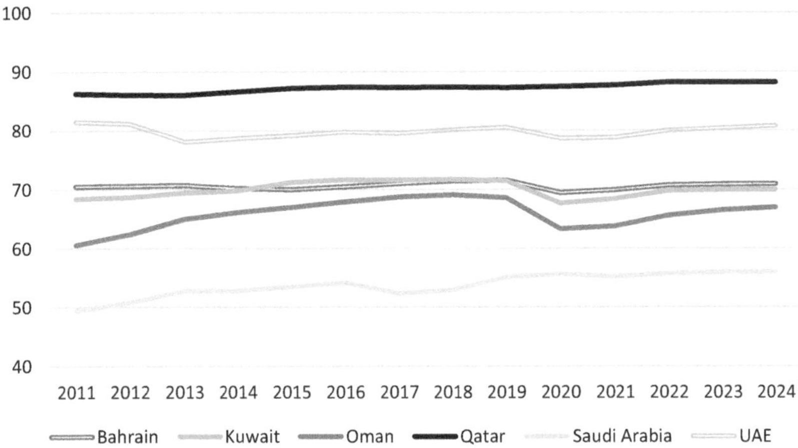

Figure 4.2 Total employment rate, ages 15+, percent.

Source: Modeled International Labor Organization estimates, World Bank World Development Indicators, https://hdr.undp.org/data-center/human-development-index#/indicies/HDI.

35 percent share that has been rising steadily.[122] Any attempt to challenge this model would obviously involve significant disruptions, which are frequently taken as an argument against policy changes.

The labor market structure and generous welfare provision have discouraged economic participation. Overall employment levels in the GCC range widely, with Saudi Arabia consistently at the low end of the spectrum and Qatar and the UAE – reflecting the numerical dominance of working-age expatriates in their populations – at the opposite extreme. Even as Gulf nationals have become more economically active, it was the case until recently that "most Saudi citizens aged 15 to 64 do not hold a job."[123] Economic participation barely exceeded 40 percent in the mid-2010s but temporarily passed 50 percent in late 2020 and again in late 2021, 66.8 percent for men but only 35.6 percent for women. Male unemployment was 5.2 percent, whereas the corresponding figure for women stood at 22.5 percent.[124]

Due to cultural reasons and large families, labor force participation by Gulf women still lags far behind men even as it has been trending up. Cost-effective childcare facilities, while improving, remain inadequate. Female employment has also been held back by minimal flexibility, as full-time on-site employment remains the norm. Limited public transportation options constrain mobility, a fact that triggered Saudi Arabia's historic 2018 decision to allow women to drive. Female employment has to date relied heavily on public sector jobs, above all in education and health care. However, the situation is far from uniform, and there are pronounced generational differences. The Saudi female labor force participation rate has increased dramatically from only 5.2 percent in 1992: the MasterCard Worldwide Index of Women's Advancement in 2012 found that only 24.9 Saudi women were active in the labor force for every 100 men, while Kuwait

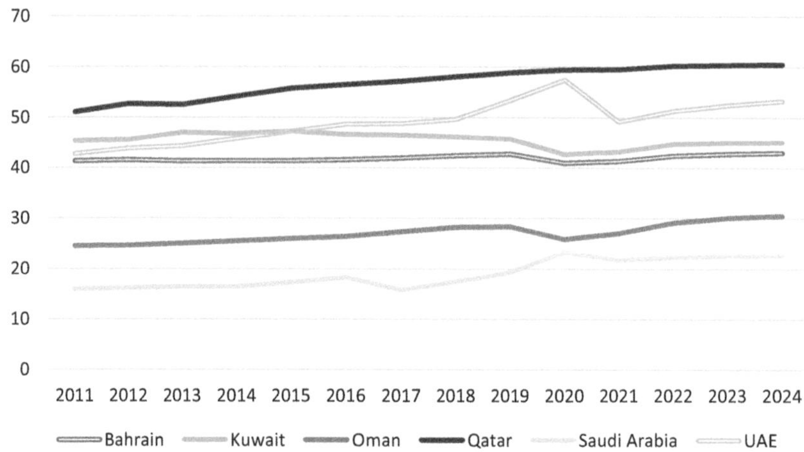

Figure 4.3 Female employment rate, ages 15+, percent.

Source: Modeled International Labor Organization estimates, World Bank World Development Indicators, https://hdr.undp.org/data-center/human-development-index#/indicies/HDI.

and Qatar achieved 52.7 and 54.3 percent, respectively, largely because of public sector jobs.[125]

Low female employment stands in stark contrast to Gulf women's superior educational attainment levels. Women tend to consistently study somewhat longer and with better outcomes than men.[126] They decisively outnumber men at advanced educational institutions, in some countries several-fold. In 2010, more than nine in ten working Saudi women had a secondary qualification or a university degree, while the corresponding figure for men was 60 percent. In Kuwait, 61 percent of women over 25 had a diploma or a higher degree, as compared to 39 percent for men.[127]

Even though the headline unemployment rates in the GCC are not exceptional by global standards, involuntary under- or unemployment is a persistent problem. Such joblessness is to a large extent structural and has not responded meaningfully to economic growth. For instance, in 2009 the UAE still had 14 percent unemployment among its nationals. Saudi national unemployment has persisted with remarkable consistency in the low double digits, and long-term unemployment is fairly common.[128] Moreover, there is large pool of informal employment, defined as "lacking social security contributions," which in Saudi Arabia was recently estimated at 27 percent and in Bahrain at 16 percent.[129]

Searching for solutions

The petroleum century has left the Gulf states with unusual demographic profiles. With the exception of the 1980s–1990s, relatively rapid growth made it possible to deliver higher living standards without having to address these anomalies. But this is a fragile status quo. Even as GDP growth has plateaued since 2014, natural population growth remains brisk despite gradually declining fertility rates. Some 4.5mn GCC nationals entered the labor force in 2010–2015, while the aggregate employment of nationals in 2010 was only some 5mn. With labor force growth running at 3–4 percent a year, around 1.2–1.6mn GCC nationals were added to these totals by 2019.[130] Saudi Arabia alone saw 200,000–450,000 new annual entrants, of whom the private sector absorbed less than 100,000 each year since 2015.[131]

By disincentivizing investments in productivity, the established labor market structures challenge the quest of higher living standards. By perpetuating rentierist business models, this status quo has distorted economic diversification: "Through large-scale imports of cheap labour ... GCC businesses have been locked into a low-productivity pattern of growth: substituting cheap foreign labor for process and technology upgrades that would make employment for more expensive and better-trained national employees feasible."[132] Breaking out of this vicious cycle is needed not just for inclusive prosperity but also for competitiveness as technological progress pushes out the global efficient frontier.

Policy efforts to address labor market challenges have for decades focused on three key aspects: the demand for labor, the supply of human capital, and the regulatory framework. In practice, the toolkit has traditionally revolved around "global and sectoral nationalization quotas, bans on expatriate hire in specific professions and temporary subsidization of national wages."[133] A more novel method has been proactive support for businesses formation. While effective in popularizing the idea of entrepreneurship, the economic impact of such programs has been compromised by the common preference for low-productivity activities. Job creation beyond family members has primarily involved low-cost expatriate labor.

Initiatives on the demand side have typically focused on creating private sector job opportunities for nationals. Saudi Arabia first introduced its Saudiization policy under the Fourth Development Plan (1985–1989) when the government set out to cut foreign manpower by nearly a quarter to 2.06mn.[134] In practice, the number of foreign workers more than doubled to some 5.5mn by 2000, concurrently with an estimated 45 percent drop in labor productivity. The numbers of low-skilled Asian laborers rose as businesses sought to manage costs, thereby boosting labor intensity and depressing wages. While the Saudiization minimum for some sectors was reduced to 10 percent during the third oil boom, the official Saudiization targets for companies with 20 or more workers rose from 5 percent in 1995 to 25 percent in 2000 and 75 percent in 2005.[135] Quotas became the regional norm by the mid-1990s.

The practical implementation of the nationalization programs proved far from straightforward as quotas engendered a multitude of abuses. It was common for businesses to "create sub-companies registered in sectors which demand lower Saudization ratios, import workers under false job descriptions ..., buy workers from other companies on an informal 'free visa' market, put Saudis on the payroll who do not actually do anywork, etc."[136] Pricing was distorted as companies had to "replace migrants with lesser-endowed local workers who have higher reservation wages."[137]

There have been multiple attempts to address the substantial wage gap between foreigners and locals. These have ranged from charges designed to push up the cost of labor imports to subsidies to bring down the cost of domestic labor at least temporarily. While the former has reduced the appeal of low-productivity labor, the latter has proven an uphill climb, partly because of the magnitude of the challenge: "In Qatar, expatriates earn about 13 percent of the wages received by nationals on average; in Kuwait, they earn 20 percent of national's [*sic*] wages. The gap is lowest in Saudi Arabia, with expatriates receiving nearly 40 percent of nationals' wages."[138] Morevover, while national salaries have tended to increase, expatriate wages have typically been much more static. While subsidies can deliver numbers in the short term, the longer-term impact is often limited. Moreover, with business models shaped by low-cost labor, direct substitution is in many cases neither realistic or desirable, "as it will increase the cost of production for private sector firms, and reduce their profitability and competitiveness."[139]

The revenues raised from levies on foreign labor have often been channeled into training Gulf nationals. Oman's *Sanad* program has achieved this since 1994 with a 7 percent wage levy, which may have helped the number of Omanis in the private sector surpass the public sector headcount in 2008. The Human Resources Development Fund (Hadaf) in Saudi Arabia adopted a similar approach in 2000.[140] Bahrain, in connection with a holistic labor market reform in 2006, mandated a BHD10 monthly fee on each foreign employee. Most of the revenue is spent on training programs and entrepreneurship support with the ambition of making the Bahraini the employee of choice. In practice, the fees have remained lower than initially planned, with various exemptions.[141]

Supply-side interventions have involved substantial investments in human capital, typically through training programs designed to address skill gaps. But national employment continues to be challenged by the poor alignment of the education system with the needs of the economy, while the private sector tends to have limited involvement in designing labor market policies.

Expatriate employment for specific skilled positions remains common. Market requirements are often not limited to precise technical qualifications but include various soft skills, experience, and the ability to transmit international practices and standards. This reflects a regional shortage of highly skilled employees, confirmed by the fact that, for instance, in Saudi Arabia, university degree holders made up only 0.2 percent of the total number of job seekers in 2010. The Saudi higher education system today is estimated to produce only roughly a fifth of the engineers demanded by the market, while some 70 percent of science jobs go to foreigners. Such shortages are reported in areas ranging from health and agriculture to information technology.[142]

In general, high-productivity sectors do not struggle to employ qualified Gulf nationals. Over two-thirds of the financial services sector in Bahrain is staffed by locals in the complete absence of national quotas. Moreover, while it is easier to replace people with higher salaries, this risks incurring a greater opportunity cost. The market for many specific skills is international, and full nationalization is hardly a desirable goal. Moreover, jobs at the top end of the labor market are limited in number, and transformative change is only possible through "mid-skills, mid-wage sectors, where enough jobs can be generated to make a difference to aggregate national employment, nationals are most likely to be competitive on skills, and the expatriate–local wage gap is the narrowest."[143] This is likely a market segment where "upskilling of nationals on the one hand and the restructuring of the private sector to adopt technology-intensive techniques that reduce its current excessive dependence on cheap and unskilled labor on the other hand"[144] will likely create the best chance of a broader paradigm shift.

Numerous factors influence the ability of GCC nationals to meet the needs of the labor market. Beyond considerations of prestige, religious and cultural factors often mean that certain activities are viewed as inappropriate. For instance, many Gulf nationals are reluctant to work at hotels or restaurants that serve alcohol. A 2010 study in the UAE found that only some 1.2mn of the 2.2mn private sector jobs in the country were unequivocally open to nationals.[145] Gulf nationals continue to shun many lower-income jobs for cultural reasons but also because very low wages cannot support a family, whereas much expatriate involvement involves singles or people whose families remain in their home countries.[146] Significant progress in many market segments is only possible once they have been transformed through technology and occupational standards to overcome their traditional labor bias. Beyond this, nationals are frequently disadvantaged by the perception that they "are more difficult to recruit, leave jobs more easily, and are harder to fire than foreigners."[147] Even if regulations have been modified, perceptions are sticky. In the eyes of many employers, national employees still entail risks that they can avoid by importing the desired numbers and qualifications without the need for further investment. The perceived docility of expatriates has enhanced this value proposition.

The inherent inefficiency of labor markets remains another challenge. Market information has historically been very limited, and job searches still often rely on informal networks, leading to accusations of *wasta* and preferential treatment. Western-style unemployment benefit systems are very recent. The pioneering national unemployment insurance system of Bahrain was put in place in 2007, while the Saudis followed with their *Hafiz* program in 2011. The UAE is launching its Involuntary Loss of Employment scheme for nationals and expatriates alike in 2023. Apart from offering financial benefits to qualifying candidates, these schemes maintain job centers and vacancy banks while also funding training. In practice, much of the labor market inefficiency is attributable to inadequate human resource functions at companies. Because of the small size of most businesses, HR departments tend to be rudimentary, frequently purely focused on routine tasks such as payroll. Minimal resources are devoted to talent development or to anticipating future recruitment needs. Few established service solutions are readily available through business process outsourcing companies.

Information technology now promises transformative change in overcoming informational asymmetries, as shown by the success of platforms such as LinkedIn. Global experience suggests that transparency brings efficiency. Apart from new digital clearing mechanisms, technology can help in skills verification and testing. Interviews can be conducted remotely at lower cost, often without additional middlemen.[148] Documentation can be standardized for easier comparability. National market intelligence tools, such as Labor Market Observatories, have increased in popularity. These track key indicators to identify trends and to develop timely responses to them. The Saudi National Manpower Tracking System operates a database of job seekers and universities. The Emirates Nationals Development Program was set up in 2005 to enable UAE nationals to find private sector jobs. The National Human Resource Development and Employment Authority (*Tanmia*) facilitates the process through specialized training and assistance with job placements.

The most ambitious labor market policy intervention in recent years has been the Saudi government's *Nitaqat* program, launched in 2011 with the objective of boosting Saudi private sector participation from 10 to 50 percent. Instead of rigid quotas, the program set out to compare companies in terms of their Saudiization record.[149] *Nitaqat* rewards businesses with a strong history of Saudi recruitment and penalizes laggards. The worst performers were not allowed to renew visas, while the best performers could recruit expatriates from non-compliant companies.

Nitaqat engendered considerable controversy, with many fearing that it would result in bankruptcies and token employment, and the work discipline of program beneficiaries was questioned. The program design sought to manage these risks by, for instance, exempting the smallest companies. Saudiization quotas were calculated over 13 weeks to discourage manipulation through temporary employment. A wage protection system sought to control wage payments. Within two years, by 2013, the transportation and communications sector saw job localization more than double from 9 to 20 percent. Manufacturing witnessed an increase from 13 to 19.3 percent as compared to a jump from 12.9 to 18.4 percent in retail and from 7.2 to 10.3 percent in construction. The changes were driven by increased Saudi recruitment: by 59 percent in transportation, 34 percent in construction, and 25 percent in manufacturing and trade. But many businesses struggled to adapt, and over 212,000 companies shut down by 2014.[150]

By 2018, the Saudi national private sector workforce had doubled to almost 2mn, but many jobs were found to be unproductive.[151] The share of Saudis earning the statutory minimum of SAR3,000 a month rose sharply. Such distortions triggered several revisions. In 2017, even the smallest companies were required to hire at least one Saudi national, while businesses with more than 25 employees had to offer *Saifi* internships to students. Only the most compliant companies could apply for new visas, with others limited to sponsorship transfers of resident expatriates. Higher quotas were introduced for particular market segments; for example, sales jobs.[152]

Despite attempts at proactive nationalization, the reliance on foreign labor remains heavy across the Gulf. While the COVID-19 disruptions drove substantial expatriate departures, traditional hiring practices soon resumed during the recovery period. In Saudi Arabia, just under 3.3mn economically active Saudi nationals made up 24.1 percent of all employment in the third quarter of 2020, down marginally from 24.4 percent a year earlier.[153] In Kuwait, as of June 2019, locals made up 73.8 percent of public sector employment, an increase from 68.1 percent in 2014. However, the private sector still accounted for a remarkable 84 percent of all jobs in the country. Only 3.9 percent of these jobs were held by Kuwaitis in June 2019, as compared to 4.7 percent in 2014.

Where do we go from here?

Despite numerous policy interventions over the years, the Gulf workforce "remains predominantly foreign, low skilled, and male, a consequence of the still relatively shallow national labor pools, labor-intensive jobs, and the prevalent sociocultural challenges that obstruct female participation."[154] To amplify the challenge, in recent years, "diversification to sectors that do not enhance productivity has only intensified, leading to further degradation of productivity at the aggregate level."[155] Overall labor productivity declined by some 2 percent a year in 2000–2018.[156] Today, a minority of Gulf nationals are engaged in genuinely productive work, a tiny fraction of them in anything innovative. But these realities also suggest key elements of the solution: a more efficient public sector, targeted welfare support, and further liberalization toward genuinely contested, efficient markets.[157]

Countering past trends is urgent from the perspective of the projected demographic dynamics but also essential for long-term prosperity. A failure risks leaving the Gulf short of realizing its economic potential, while serving as a source of social discord manifested in persistent un- or underemployment along with growing disparities of wealth. Even businesses that may have benefited from past practices now risk seeing their competitiveness erode. But addressing these risks requires a multifaceted, integrated overhaul of key aspects of the broader economic model in the Gulf. Partial solutions are unlikely to deliver much.

A departure from the traditional role of the government as the default employer of nationals is long overdue, while technology adoption is a pressing priority. The goal should be a leaner, much more meritocratic civil service that attracts people through development opportunities rather than just financial remuneration and working conditions. Achieving this is likely to prove much easier through a program of privatizing, corporatizing, mutualizing, or farming out functions that can be undertaken by private businesses.

Closing the sharp bifurcation of the GCC labor markets is as much a precondition as it is a desired outcome of a successful economic overhaul. The "current segmentation of the Gulf labor market makes large-scale job creation for nationals unrealistic,"[158] as they are shunned by employers because of their cost or (perceived) regulatory inflexibility. Reduced arbitrage opportunities between the market segments has already delivered some results: "increases in the price of foreign labor, together with the creation of an internally liberalized labour market, have produced the most convincing national employment results thus far."[159] Pushing up the lower end of the wage scale is essential since it will alter the relative pricing of labor and technology in favor of the latter, paving the way for more productive jobs. This is a key precondition for boosting local employment as "[t]here is a 'floor' or a minimum threshold that nationals are willing to accept, in terms of wages and benefits, working conditions, judgment of family and peers, etc."[160] In March 2021, Qatar set a floor for expatriate salaries through a pioneering QAR1,000 monthly minimum wage. Further allowances of QAR300 and 500, respectively, were mandated for food and housing when not provided in kind.[161] Establishing more robust occupational standards is another way of boosting productivity. Professionalization of jobs along with some further requirements – for example, knowledge of the local language and culture in the care sector – can help counter purely cost-driven recruitment practices.[162] Labor market liberalization helps bridge wage differentials. Lifting sponsorship regulations and permitting mobility by expatriate labor boosts its bargaining power. It allows people to seek better working conditions and reduces the ability of employers to take unfair advantage of workers, taking away "the incentive for employers to hire foreigners because they are more easily controllable."[163]

All Gulf governments have addressed the cost of foreign labor through a mix of visa and others fees. Beyond this, recent fiscal consolidation measures have pushed up the indirect costs through higher living expenses – for example, increased utility tariffs – although many individuals have responded by downsizing their homes or leaving families in their home countries. Increasing the costs of expatriate recruitment, quite apart from reducing labor market segmentation, can also bring other benefits, as shown by Dubai, which has "embraced expatriates and turned them into a source of revenue for the government rather than a burden on its resources."[164]

The impact of the widespread government subsidies ecurit Gulf nationals is typically compromised by their finite duration or generic nature. International experience shows that the cost of wage subsidies as a job creation tool "can be a multiple of the wages paid to the new employees,"[165] although still potentially less than GCC public sector employment. A more targeted approach is likely to be more effective as it it recognizes the needs of different market segments and creates incentives for compliance through *ex post* rewards. There may be a particular opportunity to subsidize transitions of public sector employees to the private sector.[166]

Financial incentives alone cannot rectify long-standing cultural patterns. More private companies must change their default modus operandi from "import the employer you need" to "develop the talent you require." Employees need to be seen as partners and recognized as such. Survey data fairly consistently suggest that the most important hurdle to national employment remains a lack of appropriate skills, including soft skills. Commitment is a widely reported challenge. Addressing these isues is likely to require explicit conditionality of training and employment support. Policy may also have to address the financial and human resource limitations of many businesses through more government-funded advice and support.

Reforms that address the cost gap in isolation risk undermining the business models of local companies and eroding the appeal of the Gulf in the eyes of foreign investors. Reduced labor market fragmentation has to go hand in hand with a broader commitment to productivity. Encouragingly, the behavioral flexibility during COVID-19 along with increased availability of cost-effective digital solutions is now pushing more GCC companies toward such business model overhauls. Immigration policy must more explicitly recognize the heterogeneity of the expatriate labor market. In terms of its broader economic impact, low-cost labor comes with negative externalities as it delays technological progress, while skilled professionals can deliver positive externalities: "targeting the hiring of high-skilled foreign workers could support a shift towards higher-productivity economic activities."[167]

The one-size-fits-all labor migration policy of the GCC countries is ill-suited for a productive economy since it "provides employers with limited flexibility to attract top talent."[168] Change could be facilitated through visa and employment charges that are either flat or explicitly regressive, thereby increasing the relative cost of unskilled labor. Such a shift would entail far fewer migrants in absolute numbers, but "there would be an expectation of better wages and working conditions, and greater job mobility within the countries of destination."[169] By breaking the historical dominance of low-productivity labor, such a move would mark a major step toward the strategic ambition of building knowledge-based economies.

The economic engagement of women has begun to make considerable headway. This should be coupled with efforts to increase market flexibility, since less rigid modes of participation are a powerful tool for inclusion. Since many women are expected to manage various family responsibilities, they are well positioned for part-time jobs but also to spearhead the rise of the "gig economy," which can help transcend the traditional binary choice between domestic responsibilities and a career. New low-cost options for entrepreneurship, such as Bahrain's virtual corporate registration (*sijilli*), which requires no capital or physical premises, can accelerate the process. COVID-19 may have accelerated change by increasing receptiveness to hybrid work.

Making local talent available on a more flexible basis can help create new alternatives to foreign labor, especially when facilitated by market intermediaries, such as manpower agencies and business process outsourcing firms. Under the traditional paradigm of full-time employment, cost considerations and regulatory flexibility made foreign labor the default choice for businesses looking to manage costs. Increased flexibility, by contrast, will allow businesses to meet their manpower needs with far greater optionality and scalability. But careful policy design is required to prevent the devaluation of full-time employment.

The debate about nationalization in the Gulf has often been presented as a zero-sum game. Yet a strong commitment to national employment need not – and should not – come at the expense of openness. This would be altogether unrealistic in a part of the world that still lacks the numbers to replace more than a fraction of the jobs currently held by non-nationals. Moreover, developed labor markets the world over are open to varying degrees, and most advanced economies boast substantial populations of expatriate professionals, craftsmen, and unskilled laborers alike.

Successful labor market reform in the Gulf requires a multipronged effort focused on the dual goals of economic activation and skill development. Regulatory rigidity must not be allowed to become an obstacle for willing individuals to participate in economic activity on terms that work for them. Human capital development hinges on a holistic education reform but also a substantial increase in availability of flexible, cost-effective solutions for lifelong learning.

The most logical way to overcome the bifurcation of the labor market is by eliminating the nationality-based regulatory differentiation that gave rise to it. This can only be a gradual process as it involves unwinding decades of economic incentives and cultural perceptions, and it does not entail regulatory uniformity. There is every reason to accept different types of employment contracts and modalities, but these should not be based, in the first instance, on nationality. The ultimate goal should be a market where the recruitment of foreign labor is driven purely by the need for skills. Individuals with a positive contribution to the economy must be recognized as assets worth investing in, rather than as a short-term fix.

It is only fair to expect the economic costs of foreign labor to be neutralized where possible. One source of resentment among Gulf nationals has been the perception that foreigners benefit from generous subsidies while remitting most of their income abroad. The former will cease to be an issue when welfare provision switches from indiscriminate universal subsidies to targeted benefits for needy citizens. Health care costs are increasingly borne through insurance. Remittances will become less of an issue when more expatriates transition to a long-term residency. Converting end-of-service benefits into a defined contribution pension scheme will boost the capital available for local investment.

Appropriately future-proofing the Gulf labor market is growing in urgency because of the evolving nature of work globally. The real challenge is no longer merely that of gainfully employing more citizens but doing so sustainably. While there is much debate about the impact of technological innovation on jobs, it is widely agreed that transformative change is underway, "and human workers will have to be increasingly flexible, adaptable and focused on managerial and social skills as machines and computers take over an increasing share of repetitive and routine tasks, be they physical or administrative."[170] An estimated half of the activities undertaken by paid labor could be automated, which could prove particularly disruptive for low-cost expatriate labor. In the UAE, over 93 percent of automation potential is found with jobs that currently rely on expatriate labor.[171] The risk, in the face of these realities, is that a combination of inertia, vested interests, and relative costs will be allowed to make low-cost expatriate labor a force that retards technological progress. This would entail mounting opportunity costs as it would deprive Gulf businesses from an opportunity to ride wave that is redefining productivity the world over. And it would dilute the demographic dividend available to the Gulf.

Notes

1 World Bank, "Building the Foundations," pp. 37, 48; Lange *et al.*, *The Changing Wealth of Nations*.
2 World Bank, "Deepening Reforms," p. 33; Malit and Naufal, "Labour Migration," p. 8.
3 El-Arifi, "The Nature of Urbanization," p. 229.
4 World Bank, "Building a Foundation," p. 42.
5 Khouja and Sadler, *The Economy of Kuwait*, p. 37.
6 An earlier government estimate had been a much lower 5.9mn while an independent assessment suggested only 4.3mn. Owen and Pamuk, *A History*, p. 211.
7 Al Sabah, *The Oil Economy of Kuwait*, p. 10; El Mallakh, "Planning in a Capital Surplus Economy," p. 426.
8 Davidson, *Abu Dhabi*, p. 39.
9 Niblock, *The Political Economy*, p. 51; Chaudhry, *The Price of Wealth*, p. 184.
10 Champion, *The Paradoxical Kingdom*, p. 111; El-Arifi, "The Nature of Urbanization," p. 227; Chaudhry, *The Price of Wealth*, p. 184; Al-Rumaihi, *Social and Economic Change*, p. 86.
11 El-Arifi, "The Nature of Urbanization," pp. 227, 229; CPO, *Development Plan*, p. 65.
12 Al-Dekhayel, *Kuwait*, p. 57; Allen and Rigsbee, *Oman under Qaboos*, pp. 10–11.
13 Al-Rumaihi, *Social and Political Change*, p. 187.
14 Field, *The Merchants*, p. 23.
15 Vassiliev, *The History of Saudi Arabia*, p. 309.
16 Al-Rumaihi, *Social and Political Change*, pp. 190–215.
17 Field, *The Merchants*, p. 31; Vassiliev, *The History of Saudi Arabia*, p. 310; Longrigg, *Oil in the Middle East*, p. 133; Peterson, *Saudi Arabia under Ibn Saud*, p. 175.
18 Al-Dekhayel, *Kuwait*, p. 58.
19 Al-Rumaihi, *Social and Political Change*, pp. 190–215.
20 El Mallakh, *Qatar: Energy*, p. 102.
21 Davidson, *Abu Dhabi*, pp. 35, 46; Al-Kuwari, *Oil Revenues in the Gulf Emirates*, p. 135.
22 Allen and Rigsbee, *Oman under Qaboos*, pp. 24, 166.
23 El Mallakh, *Qatar: Development*, p. 113.
24 Hawley, *The Trucial States*, p. 231; Al Muraikhi, *Glimpses of Bahrain*, pp. 180–185.
25 Al Muraikhi, *Glimpses of Bahrain*, pp. 180–185; Clarke, *Through the Changing Scenes of Life*.
26 Crystal, *Kuwait*, pp. 14, 59; Longrigg, *Oil in the Middle East*, p. 226.
27 Sebai *et al.*, "Health Care Services," pp. 19–20; Al-Rabeeah, "The History of Health Care," pp. S9–S10; CPO, *Development Plan*, p. 145.
28 Alhebshi *et al.*, "A History of Education"; Hawley, *The Trucial States*, pp. 231–233; El Mallakh, *The Economic Development*, pp. 21, 60; El Mallakh, *Qatar: Development*, p. 113; Davidson, *Abu Dhabi*, pp. 36, 46.
29 Alshishtawy, "Four Decades of Progress," p. 12; Allen and Rigsbee, *Oman under Qaboos*, pp. 11, 17, 24–25.
30 Vassiliev, *The History of Saudi Arabia*, p. 310. These figures appear to rely on secondary estimates and may contain a margin of error.
31 Allahmorad and Zreik, "Education in Saudi Arabia."
32 Lackner, *A House Built on Sand*, pp. 79, 82.
33 Al-Rumaihi, *Social and Political Change*, pp. 215–221.
34 Khouja and Sadler, *The Economy of Kuwait*, p. 33.
35 Allen and Rigsbee, *Oman under Qaboos*, p. 167.
36 Allen and Rigsbee, *Oman under Qaboos*, pp. 167–168.
37 Al-Rumaihi, *Social and Political Change*, pp. 223–224.
38 Lackner, *A House Built on Sand*, p. 80.

39 CPO, *Development Plan*, pp. 96–97, 123.
40 El Mallakh, *Qatar: Energy*, p. 103.
41 Shah, "Teaching–Learning Outcomes," pp. 2–3.
42 The Conference Board, *GCC Job Nationalization Policies*, pp. 22, 75, 104; PwC, *Understanding Middle East Education*, p. 16; Knight Frank, *Saudi Arabia Education Report 2021*.
43 Wilkins, "Who Benefits," p. 74.
44 The Conference Board, *GCC Job Nationalization Policies*, p. 88; World Bank, "Paving the Way," p. 12; World Bank, "Shaping Healthier Societies," p. 13.
45 http://hdr.undp.org/en/content/human-development-index-hdi
46 World Bank, "Building the Foundations," pp. 39–40, 42.
47 World Bank, "Building the Foundations," pp. 42, 45.
48 World Bank, "Building the Foundations," p. 42; Khoja *et al.*, "Health Care," https://www.ncbi.nlm.nih.gov/pmc/articles/PMC5650259.
49 World Bank, "Building the Foundations," p. 38.
50 Owen and Pamuk, *A History*, p. 208.
51 Risso, *Oman & Muscat*, p. 3.
52 Al-Kuwari, *Oil Revenues in the Gulf Emirates*, p. 50.
53 Seccombe and Lawless, *Work Camps and Company Towns*, p. 10; Seccombe and Lawless, "The Gulf Labour Market and the Early Oil Industry"; Thiollet, "Managing Migrant Labour in the Gulf," p. 8; Errichiello, "Foreign Workforce in the Arab Gulf States."
54 Field, *The Merchants*, p. 98; Khouja and Sadler, *The Economy of Kuwait*, pp. 39–41; El Mallakh, "Planning in Capital Surplus Economy," p. 426.
55 Knauerhause, *The Saudi Arabian Economy*, p. 322; Niblock, *The Political Economy*, p. 51.
56 CPO, *Development Plan*, p. 91.
57 CPO *Development Plan*, pp. 70, 90.
58 Baldwin-Edwards, *Labour Immigration and Labour Markets*, p. 8; Winckler, *Arab Political Demography*, p. 135.
59 Field, *The Merchants*, pp. 70–71.
60 Burke and Bazoobandi, "The Gulf Takes Charge," p. 33.
61 El-Arifi, "The Nature of Urbanization," pp. 230–231.
62 Azzam, *The Gulf Economies*, p. 48; Owen and Pamuk, *A History*, p. 209.
63 Baldwin-Edwards, *Labour Immigration and Labour Markets*, p. 8; World Bank, *Unlocking the Employment Potential*, p. 58.
64 Davidson, *Dubai*, pp. 190–191.
65 CPO, *Development Plan*, p. 72.
66 CPO, *Development Plan*, pp. 72, 96.
67 Thiollet, "Managing Migrant Labour in the Gulf," p. 4.
68 See, for instance: Knortz, *Diplomatische Tauschgeschäfte*.
69 Zahlan, *The Making of the Modern Gulf States*, pp. 35, 52.
70 El Mallakh, *Qatar: Development*, p. 21.
71 Owen and Pamuk, *A History*, p. 209.
72 Anthony, *Arab States of the Lower Gulf*, pp. 181, 183–184.
73 Espinoza *et al.*, *The Macroeconomics*, p. 55.
74 Espinoza *et al.*, *The Macroeconomics*, pp. 42–43, 49.
75 Espinoza *et al.*, *The Macroeconomics*, pp. 42–43, 49.
76 Lackner, *A House Built on Sand*, p. 80.
77 Champion, *The Paradoxical Kingdom*, p. 200.
78 Nagy, "Families and Bachelors," p. 59; Baldwin-Edwards, *Labour Immigration and Labour Markets*, p. 33.
79 Baldwin-Edwards, *Labour Immigration and Labour Markets*, p. 32.
80 Ministry of Planning, *Third Development Plan*, quoted in: Niblock, *The Political Economy*, p. 64.
81 Niblock, *The Political Economy*, p. 99.

82 Owen and Pamuk, *A History*, p. 216.
83 Baldwin-Edwards, *Labour Immigration and Labour Markets*, p. 8.
84 Saif, *The Oil Boom*, p. 17.
85 Espinoza *et al.*, *The Macroeconomics*, p. 40; Baldwin-Edwards, *Labour Immigration and Labour Markets*, p. 46.
86 Hertog, "A Comparative Assessment," p. 96.
87 AlShehabi, "Rootless Hubs," p. 113.
88 Owen and Pamuk, *A History*, p. 210.
89 El Mallakh, "Planning in a Capital Surplus Economy," p. 432.
90 Owen and Pamuk, *A History*, p. 210.
91 Espinoza *et al.*, *The Macroeconomics*, p. 61; El Mallakh, "Planning in a Capital Surplus Economy," pp. 432–433.
92 Attia and Price, *Arab Pension Systems*, pp. 50–51.
93 El Mallakh, "Planning in a Capital Surplus Economy," p. 430.
94 Al-Kuwari, *Oil Revenues in the Gulf Emirates*, pp. 152–153.
95 Khouja and Sadler, *The Economy of Kuwait*, p. 41.
96 CPO, *Development Plan*, pp. 78–79.
97 Zahlan, *The Making of the Modern Gulf States*, p. 71.
98 Al-Kuwari, *Oil Revenues in the Gulf Emirates*, p. 152.
99 Khouja and Sadler, *The Economy of Kuwait*, p. 34.
100 Osama, *The Dilemma of Development*, p. 59.
101 The Conference Board, *GCC Job Nationalization Policies*, p. 18; IMF, *Kuwait: 2020 Article IV Consultation*, pp. 6, 20–21.
102 NCB, "Empowering Human Capital," p. 10.
103 IMF, *Labor Market Reforms – Update*, p. 16; S&P Global Ratings, "Expat Exodus," p. 12; World Bank, "Building a Foundation," p. 44.
104 Beblawi, "The Rentier State," p. 52.
105 Crystal, *Oil and Politics*, p. 79.
106 Al-Kuwari, *Oil Revenues in the Gulf Emirates*, p. 153; Khouja and Sadler, *The Economy of Kuwait*, p. 35.
107 Owen and Pamuk, *A History*, p. 215; Al-Kuwari, *Oil Revenues in the Gulf Emirates*, pp. 80, 99–100, 126, 161; Al-Sabah,*The Oil Economy*, p. 55.
108 Khouja and Sadler, *The Economy of Kuwait*, p. 45.
109 Field, *The Merchants*, p. 56.
110 Al-Kuwari, *Oil Revenues in the Gulf Emirates*, pp. 80, 99–100, 120, 122, 126, 153–154, 160.
111 Owen and Pamuk, *A History*, p. 214.
112 Niblock, *The Political Economy*, pp. 47, 82.
113 Kapiszewski, *Nationals and Expatriates*, p. 75; Field, *The Merchants*, p. 56.
114 Attia and Price, *Arab Pension Systems*, p. 18.
115 Bahrain EDB, "Bahrain's Universal Subsidy Program," p. 22.
116 Quoted in: Al-Kuwari, *Oil Revenues in the Gulf Emirates*, p. 172.
117 IMF, *Labor Market Reforms – Update*, p. 10.
118 IMF, *Labor Market Reforms*, p. 8; IMF, *Labor Market Reforms – Update*, p. 26; Behar, "Comparing the Employment-Output Elasticities," p. 15.
119 S&P Global Ratings, "Expat Exodus," p. 10; Buttorff *et al.*, "Measuring Female Labor Force Participation," pp. 3–4.
120 Behar, "Comparing the Employment-Output Elasticities," p. 22.
121 IMF, *Labor Market Reforms – Update*, pp. 11, 21.
122 Al Faris and Soto, *The Economy of Dubai*, p. 248.
123 Hertog, *Can We Saudize the Labor Market*, p. 5.
124 Jadwa Investment, *Saudi Chartbook*, April 2021, p. 10; Jadwa Investment, "Unemployment Declines in Q3 2020," *Saudi Labor Market Update*, February 2021; General Authority for Statistics, *Labor Market Statistics Q4 2021*.
125 NCB, "Empowering Human Capital," p. 7.
126 World Bank, "Building the Foundations," pp. 40–41.

127 NCB, "Empowering Human Capital," p. 7.
128 Jadwa Investment, "Unemployment Continues to Drop," *Saudi Labor Market Update*, October 2021; NCB, "Empowering Human Capital," pp. 7–10.
129 Islam *et al.*, *Jobs Undone*, pp. 9–10.
130 IMF, *Labor Market Reforms – Update*, p. 7.
131 Hertog, *Can We Saudize the Labor Market*, p. 5.
132 Hertog, " A Comparative Assessment," p. 66.
133 Hertog, " A Comparative Assessment," p. 96.
134 Niblock, *The Political Economy*, p. 139; *Fourth Development Plan*, pp. 50–51.
135 Baldwin-Edwards, *Labour Immigration and Labour Markets*, pp. 24, 43; Hertog, "A Comparative Assesment," pp. 91–92.
136 Hertog, "A Comparative Assessment," p. 96.
137 Alfarhan and Al-Busaidi, "A 'Catch-22,'" p. 651.
138 The Conference Board, *GCC Job Nationalization Policies*, p. 41.
139 The Conference Board, *GCC Job Nationalization Policies*, p. 12.
140 Hertog, "A Comparative Assessment," p. 98.
141 Hertog, "A Comparative Assessment," p 100.
142 ICF Monitor, https://monitor.icef.com/2018/07/saudi-arabias-expanding-higher-education-capacity/
143 Hertog, "A Comparative Assessment," p 103.
144 The Conference Board, *GCC Job Nationalization Policies*, p. 86.
145 NCB, "Empowering Human Capital," p. 13.
146 The Conference Board, *GCC Job Nationalization Policies*, p. 103.
147 Hertog, *Can We Saudize the Labor Market*, p. 10.
148 Hertog, "The Future of Migrant Work," p. 4.
149 The Conference Board, *GCC Job Nationalization Policies*, p. 74.
150 The Conference Board, *GCC Job Nationalization Policies*, pp. 74–75.
151 Hertog, *Can We Saudize the Labor Market*, pp. 11–12.
152 The Conference Board, *GCC Job Nationalization Policies*, p. 74.
153 General Authority for Statistics, *Labor Market Statistics Q3 2020*.
154 The Conference Board, *GCC Job Nationalization Policies*, p. 23.
155 The Conference Board, *Prioritizing Productivity in The Gulf Region*, p. 6.
156 The Conference Board, *Prioritizing Productivity in The Gulf Region*, p. 3.
157 Islam *et al.*, *Jobs Undone*, pp. 87–99.
158 The Conference Board, *GCC Job Nationalization Policies*, p. 12.
159 Hertog, "A Comparative Assessment," p. 66.
160 Malit and Naufal, "Labour Migration," p. 6.
161 https://www.ilo.org/beirut/projects/qatar-office/WCMS_775981/lang--en/index.htm.
162 Malit and Naufal, "Labour Migration," p. 9.
163 Hertog, *Can We Saudize the Labor Market*, p. 17.
164 Kinnimont, *Future Trends*, p. 23; Malit and Naufal, "Labour Migration," pp. 10–11.
165 IMF, *Labor Market Reforms – Update*, p. 32.
166 Hertog, *Can We Saudize the Labor Market*.
167 IMF, *Labor Market Reforms – Update*, p. 30.
168 Callen *et al.*, *Economic Diversification*, p. 24; Malit and Naufal, "Labour Migration," p. 10.
169 Malit and Naufal, "Labour Migration," p. 11.
170 Hertog, "The Future of Migrant Work," p. 1.
171 Hertog, "The Future of Migrant Work," p. 1.

References

Allahmorad, Sidiqa and Sahel Zreik (2020), "Education in Saudi Arabia," *Education System Profiles, World Education News & Reviews*, 9 April 2020, https://wenr.wes.org/2020/04/education-in-saudi-arabia.

Allen, Calvin H., Jr. and W. Lynn Rigsbee II (2000), *Oman under Qaboos: From Coup to Constitution, 1970–1996*, London: Frank Cass Publishers.

Anthony, John Duke (1975), *Arab States of the Lower Gulf: People, Politics, Petroleum* (The James Terry Duce Memorial Series, vol. III), Washington, D.C.: The Middle East Institute.

El-Arifi, Salih A. (1986), "The Nature of Urbanization in the Gulf Countries," *GeoJournal*, vol. 13, no. 3, pp. 223–235.

Attia, Habib and William Price (2017), *Arab Pension Systems: Trends, challenges and options for reforms*, Abu Dhabi: Arab Monetary Fund, Washington, D.C.: World Bank Group.

Azzam, Henry T. (1988), *The Gulf Economies in Transition*, London: Macmillan Press.

Bahrain Economic Development Board (2010), "Bahrain's Universal Subsidy Program: Budgetary and Welfare Effects," *Bahrain Economic Quarterly*, Second and Third Quarter, pp. 21–23.

Baldwin-Edwards, Martin (2011), *Labour Immigration and Labour Markets in the GCC Countries: National Patterns and Trends*, Kuwait Programme on Development, Governance and Globalisation in the Gulf States, Research Paper no. 15, London: London School of Economics and Political Science.

Beblawi, Hazem (1987), "The Rentier State in the Arab World," *Arab Studies Quarterly*, vol. 9, no. 4, pp. 383–398.

Behar, Alberto (2018), "Comparing the Employment-Output Elasticities of Expatriates and Nationals in the Gulf Cooperation Council," IMF Working Paper, WP/15/191, Washington, D.C.: International Monetary Fund.

Burke, Edward and Sara Bazoobandi (2012), "The Gulf Takes Charge: The GCC in the MENA Region," in: Youngs, *op. cit.*, pp. 23–44.

Callen, Tim, Reda Cherif, Fuad Hasanov, Amgad Hegazy, and Padamja Khandelwal (2014), *Economic Diversification in the GCC: Past, Present, and Future*, IMF Staff Discussion Note SDN/14/12, Washington, D.C.: International Monetary Fund.

Central Planning Organization (1970), *Development Plan, 1390 A.H.*, Riyadh.

Champion, Daryl (2005), *The Paradoxical Kingdom: Saudi Arabia and the Momentum of Reform*, New York, Columbia University Press.

Chaudhry, Kiren Aziz (1997), *The Price of Wealth: Economics and Institutions in the Middle East* (*Cornell Studies in Political Economy*), Ithaca, NY: Cornell University Press.

Clarke, Angela (1993), *Through the Changing Scenes of Life, 1893–1993*, Manama: The American Mission Hospital in Bahrain.

The Conference Board (2019), *Pioritizing Productivity in the Gulf Region: A Path toward Sustained Growth through Smart Diversification*, Kuwait City: Gulf Center for Economics and Business Research.

——— (2021), *GCC Job Nationalization Policies: A Trade-Off between Productivity and Employment*, Kuwait City: Gulf Center for Economics and Business Research.

Crystal, Jill (1992), *Kuwait: The Transformation of an Oil State*, Boulder, Col.: Westview Press.

——— (1995), *Oil and Politics in the Gulf: Rulers and Merchants in Kuwait and Qatar* (*Cambridge Middle East Library*), Cambridge: Cambridge University Press.

Davidson, Christopher M. (2008), *Dubai: The Vulnerability of Success*, New York: Columbia University Press.

——— (2009), *Abu Dhabi: Oil and beyond*, New York: Columbia University Press.

Al-Dekhayel, Abdulkarim (2000), *Kuwait: Oil, State and Political Legitimation*, Reading: Ithaca Press.

Errichiello, Gennaro (2012), "Forcign Workforce in the Arab Gulf States (1930–1950): Migration Patterns and Nationality Clause," *The International Migration Review*, vol. 46, no. 2 (Summer 2012), pp. 389–413.

Espinoza, Raphael, Ghada Fayad, and Ananthakrishnan Prasad (2013), *The Macroeconomics of the Arab States of the Gulf*, Oxford: Oxford University Press.

Alfarhan, Usamah F. and Samir Al-Busaidi (2018), "A "Catch-22": Self-Inflicted Failure of GCC Nationalization Policies," *International Journal of Manpower*, vol. 39, no. 4, pp. 637–655.

Al Faris, Abdulrazak and Raimundo Soto, eds. (2016), *The Economy of Dubai*, Oxford: Oxford University Press.

Field, Michael (1984), *The Merchants: Big Business Families of Arabia*, London: John Murray Publishers.

General Authority for Statistics (2020), *Labor Market Statistics Q3 2020*, Riyadh.

——— (2021), *Labor Market Statistics Q4 2021*, Riyadh.

Hawley, Sir Donald (1971), *The Trucial States*, London: George Allen & Unwin.

Alhebsi, Ali, Lincoln D. Pettaway, and Lee "Rusty" Waller (2015), "A History of Education in the United Arab Emirates and Trucial Sheikdoms," *The Global eLearning Journal*, vol. 4, no. 1.

Hertog, Steffen (2012), "A Comparative Assessment of Labour Market Nationalization Policies in the GCC," in: Hertog, *National Employment, op. cit.*, pp. 65–106.

———, ed. (2012), *National Employment, Migration and Education in the GCC (The Gulf Region: Economic Development and Diversification*, vol. 2), Berlin: Gerlach Press.

——— (2018), *Can We Saudize the Labor Market without Damaging the Private Sector?*, Riyadh: King Faisal Center for Research and Islamic Studies.

——— (2019), "The Future of Migrant Work in the GCC: Literature Review and a Research and Policy Agenda," in: *Fifth Abu Dhabi Dialogue Ministerial Consultation*, 16–17 October 2019, Abu Dhabi Dialogue among the Asian Labor Sending and Receiving Countries, http://eprints.lse.ac.uk/102382/

International Monetary Fund (2013), *Labor Market Reforms to Boost Employment and Productivity in the GCC*, Gulf Cooperation Council/IMF Policy Paper, Annual Meeting of Ministers of Finance and Central Bank Governors, October 5, 2013, Riyadh, Saudi Arabia, Washington, D.C.: International Monetary Fund.

——— (2014), *Labor Market Reforms to Boost Employment and Productivity in the GCC—An Update*, Gulf Cooperation Council/IMF Policy Paper, Annual Meeting of Ministers of Finance and Central Bank Governors, October 25, 2014, Kuwait City, Kuwait, Washington, D.C.: International Monetary Fund.

Islam, Asif M., Dalal Moosa, and Federica Saliola (2022), *Jobs Undone: Reshaping the Role of Governments toward Markets and Workers in the Middle East and North Africa*, Washington, D.C.: World Bank Group.

Jadwa Investment (2021), "Unemployment Declines in Q3 2020," *Saudi Labor Market Update*, February 2021.

——— (2021), *Saudi Chartbook*, April 2021.

Kapiszewski, Andrzej (2001), *Nationals and Expatriates: Population and Labour Dilemmas of the Gulf Cooperation Council States*, Reading: Ithaca Press.

Khalaf, Abdulhadi, Omar AlShehabi, and Adam Hanieh, eds. (2015), *Transit States: Labour, Migration and Citizenship in the Gulf*, London: PlutoPress.

Khoja, Tawfiq, Salman Rawaf, Waris Qidwai, David Rawaf, Kashmira Nanji, and Aisha Hamad (2017), "Health Care in Gulf Cooperation Council Countries: A Review of Challenges and Opportunities," *Cureus*, vol. 9(8), e1587, https://www.ncbi.nlm.nih.gov/pmc/articles/PMC5650259/.

Khouja, M.W. and P.G. Sadler (1979), *The Economy of Kuwait: Development and Role in International Finance*, London: The Macmillan Press.

Kinnimont, Jane (2015), *Future Trends in the Gulf*, Chatham House Report, London: The Royal Institute of International Affairs.

Knauerhase, Ramon (1975), *The Saudi Arabian Economy*, New York: Prager.
Knight Frank (2021), *Saudi Arabia Education Report 2021*, Riyadh: Knight Frank.
Knortz, Heike (2008), *Diplomatische Tauschgeschäfte: "Gastarbeiter" in der westdeutschen Diplomatie und Beschäftigungspolitik 1953–1973*, Cologne: Böhlau Verlag.
Al-Kuwari, Ali Khalifa (1978), *Oil Revenues in the Gulf Emirates: Patterns of Allocation and Impact on Economic Development*, Boulder, Colo.: Westview Press.
Lackner, Helen (1978), *A House Built on Sand: A Political Economy of Saudi Arabia*, London: Ithaca Press.
Lange, Glenn-Marie, Quentin Wodon, and Kevin Carey, eds. (2018), *The Changing Wealth of Nations 2018: Building a Sustainable Future*, Washington, D.C.: World Bank Group.
Lawless, Richard I., ed. (1986), *The Gulf in the Early 20th Century: Foreign Institutions and Local Responses*, Occasional Papers Series, No. 31, Centre for Middle Eastern and Islamic Studies, University of Durham.
Longrigg, Stephen Hemsley (1968), *Oil in the Middle East: Its Discovery and Development*, London: Royal Institute of International Affairs/Oxford University Press.
Malit, Froilan, Jr. and George Naufal (2017), "Labour Migration, Skills Development and the Future of Work in the Gulf Cooperation Council (GCC) Countries," Working Paper, International Labour Organization, December 2017.
El Mallakh, Ragaei (1966), "Planning a Capital Surplus Economy: Kuwait," *Land Economics*, vol. 42, no. 4, pp. 425–440.
——— (1979), *Qatar: The Development of an Oil Industry*, Boulder, Colo.: International Research Center for Energy and Economic Development.
——— (1985), *Qatar: Energy & Development*, London: Croom Helm.
The Middle East Institute (2010), *Migration and the Gulf (Viewpoints)*, Washington, D.C.: The Middle East Institute, February 2010.
Ministry of Planning (1980), *Third Development Plan, 1400–1405 A.H.–1980–1985 A.D.*, Riyadh.
——— (1990), *Fifth Development Plan*, Riyadh.
Al-Muraikhi, Khalil M. (1991), *Glimpses of Bahrain from Its Past*, Manama.
Nagy, Sharon (2010), "Families and Bachelor: Visa States, Family Lives, and Community Structure among Bahrain's Foreign Residents," in: The Middle East Institute, *op. cit.*, pp. 58–62.
National Commercial Bank (2012), "Empowering Human Capital," *GCC Economic Review*, July 2012.
Niblock, Tim, with Monica Malik (2007), *The Political Economy of Saudi Arabia*, Abingdon: Routledge.
Osama, Abdul Rahman (1987), *The Dilemma of Development in the Arabian Peninsula*, London: Croom Helm.
Owen, E. Roger and Şevket Pamuk (1999), *A History of Middle East Economies in the Twentieth Century*, Cambridge, Mass.: Harvard University Press.
Peterson, John E. (2018), *Saudi Arabia under Ibn Saud: Economic and Financial Foundations of the State*, London: I.B. Tauris.
PwC (2018), *Understanding Middle East Education: UAE Country Profile*, 2nd edition 2018/2019, PwC Education and Skills Practice.
Al-Rabeeah, Abdullah (2003), "The History of Health Care in the Kingdom of Saudi Arabia with Emphasis on Pediatric Surgery," *Saudi Medical Journal*, vol. 24, supplement 1, pp. S9–S10.
Risso, Patricia (1986), *Oman & Muscat: An Early Modern History*, London: Croom Helm.

Al-Rumaihi, Mohammed Ghanim (1973), *Social and Political Change in Bahrain since the First World War*, Ph.D. thesis, Durham University.
S&P Global Ratings (2021), "Expat Exodus Adds to Gulf Region's Economic Diversification Challenges," *Comments/EMEA*, 15 February 2021.
Al Sabah, Yusuf S.T. (1980), *Oil Economy of Kuwait*, London: Keegan Paul International.
Saif, Ibrahim (2009), *The Oil Boom in the GCC Countries, 2002–2008: Old Challenges, Changing Dynamics*, Carnegie Papers 15, Washington, D.C.: Carnegie Endowment for International Peace.
Sebai, Zohair A., Waleed A. Milaat, and Abdulmohsen A. Al-Zulaibani (2001), "Health Care Services in Saudi Arabia: Past, Present and Future," *Journal of Family and Community Medicine*, vol. 8, no. 3, pp. 19–23.
Seccombe, Ian and Richard I. Lawless (1986), "The Gulf Labour Market and the Early Oil Industry: Traditional Structures and New Forms of Organization," in: Lawless, *op. cit.*, pp. 91–124.
——— (1987), *Work Camps and Company Towns: Settlement Patterns and the Gulf Oil Industry*, Occasional Papers Series, No. 36, Centre for Middle Eastern and Islamic Studies, University of Durham.
Shah, Iqtidar Ali (2017), "Teaching–Learning Challenges of Higher Education in the Gulf Cooperation Council Countries," *Afro Asian Journal of Social Sciences*, vol. VIII, no. 1, pp. 1–18.
AlShehabi, Omar (2015), "Rootless Hubs: Migration, Urban Commodification and the 'Right to the City' in the GCC," in Khalaf *et al.*, *op. cit.*, pp. 101–131.
Alshishtawy, Moeness M. (2010), "Four Decades of Progress: Evolution of the Health System in Oman," *Sultan Qaboos University Medical Journal*, vol. 10, no. 1, pp. 12–22.
Thiollet, Hélène (2016), "Managing Migrant Labour in the Gulf: Transnational Dynamics of Migration Politics since the 1930s," IMI Working Papers, No. 131, International Migration Institute, University of Oxford, July 2016.
Vassiliev, Alexei (2000), *The History of Saudi Arabia*, New York: New York University Press.
Wilkins, Stephen (2011), "Who Benefits from Foreign Universities in the Arab Gulf States?," *Australian Universities Review*, vol. 53, no. 1, pp. 73–83.
Winckler, Onn (2009), *Arab Political Demography: Population Growth, Labor Migration and Natalist Policies*, 2nd edition, Brighton: Sussex Academic Press.
World Bank (2004), *Unlocking the Employment Potential in the Middle East and North Africa*, Washington, D.C.: The World Bank.
——— (2015), *Shaping Healthier Societies and Building Higher Performing Health Systems in the GCC Countries, The Health, Nutrition, Population (HNP) Global Practice*, Washington, D.C.: The World Bank.
——— (2016), "Paving the Way for Women's Economic Inclusion in the Gulf Cooperation Council (GCC)," GCC Engagement Note, No. 3, Washington, D.C.: World Bank Group.
——— (2018), "Deepening Reforms – In Focus: Pension Systems in the Gulf," *Gulf Economic Monitor*, No. 2, Washington, D.C.: World Bank Group.
——— (2019), "Building the Foundations for Economic Sustainability: Human Capital and Growth in the GCC," *Gulf Economic Monitor*, No. 4, Washington, D.C.: World Bank Group.
Youngs, Richard, ed. (2012), *The GCC in the Global Economy* (*The Gulf Region: Economic Development and Diversification*, vol. 1), Berlin: Gerlach Press.
Zahlan, Rosemarie Said (1989), *The Making of the Modern Gulf States: Kuwait, Bahrain, Qatar, the United Arab Emirates and Oman*, London: Unwin Hyman.

5 Greasing the wheels of exchange

The development of the Gulf region's financial markets is an often overlooked story of rapidly growing importance. Having initially emerged as a by-product of the oil–government nexus, the sector's role in pooling and allocating capital is becoming increasingly critical for shaping the Gulf countries' future progress.

Within decades, oil made the Gulf one of the most plentiful repositories of financial assets in the world, which presented fundamental strategic choices. Saving minimized macro-economic distortions created a cushion for future contingencies and promised inter-generational equality. But saving alone was unrealistic in the face of cryingly obvious economic development needs. However, local investment was complicated by financial underdevelopment, which tended to "lead to the inefficient utilization of savings, suppress entrepreneurial development, accentuate speculation, increase inflationary pressure on real assets (e.g. real estate), and ... influence adversely the real rate of growth of the economy."[1]

Oil initially left the capital value chain largely in the hands of the state, something that subsequently proved remarkably resistant to change. As observed by Azzam in 1988: "Governments' expenditures in the region accounted for 90% of all domestic liquidity creation, more than half of all gross capital formation and nearly half of all consumptions spending."[2] But moving beyond the state-led development paradigm has been a long-standing ambition that has given the Gulf a sizable financial sector that is increasingly anchored in the global financial system.

Laying the foundations

The Gulf region embarked on the 20th century with no modern financial infrastructure. Foreign currency circulated widely, notably Ottoman coin and the Indian rupee. Maria Theresa thalers from the Habsburg Empire were not just a currency but also a measure of weight and a popular adornment. In the emerging Saudi Kingdom, individual regions had their preferred currencies until the word *Nejd* began to be counterstamped on foreign coinage in 1922 followed by a similar practice in the Hijaz. Local minting started in 1925.[3] A silver riyal was introduced in 1927 but suffered from fluctuations in the value of silver. Even as foreign coin was banned, the British gold sovereign remained in use until 1953. In 1954, the authorities began to issue so-called pilgrim receipts, an early form of paper currency

DOI: 10.4324/9781003373353-5

until formal banknotes were introduced in June 1961.[4] Saudi Arabia linked its currency to the US dollar at the rate of 3.75 riyals in 1960.

Elsewhere in the region, the Indian/Gulf rupee dominated until the introduction of the Kuwaiti dinar by the Kuwaiti Currency Board in 1960. The Indian devaluation in 1966 fractured the remaining rupee zone. The Bahrain Currency Board was set up in 1965, and the Bahrain dinar was initially used by Abu Dhabi as well. A joint currency board of Qatar and Dubai introduced the riyal in 1966. Oman's Saidi riyal was adopted in 1970, although some locally minted coin had circulated since 1940. All of the Gulf coast countries launched national currencies in 1971.

Financial intermediation in the Gulf historically revolved around credit mechanisms for pearling and trade. Individual merchants stored valuables and processed promissory notes for international trade transactions. Haji Yusuf Kanoo, having acquired a large safe in 1910, gained a reputation as the "Banker of Bahrain," mainly financing the pearling business while also operating an office in Bombay.[5] The Hijaz was home to a large community of money exchangers catering to pilgrims and merchants alike, a business described in a 1916 British report as "the most important and lucrative profession" in the region.[6]

Modern financial intermediation was brought to the Gulf by foreign banks. The Imperial Bank of Persia set up in Bahrain in 1900 but retreated in the face of local resistance. Many, not least in the ruling circles, worried about violations of the Shariah ban on *riba*. But as foreign economic relations expanded, so did the range of financing needs. The British Eastern Bank Ltd applied to set up in Manama in 1916, a plan that met with a lukewarm response by the the Foreign Office in Simla. The branch finally opened in July 1920, opening a new chapter in Gulf finance.[7] Nederlandsche Handel-Maatschappij, the trading arm of the Dutch Algemene Bank Nederland, blazed a trail in Jeddah in 1926, although some financial solutions were also available through "Gellatly, Hankey (Gellatly's), and, occasionally, International Agencies (Limited) and Haji Abdullah Alireza and Company."[8] By the outbreak of World War II, the region was home to just two Western-style banking institutions.

The discovery of oil brought rapid change. The British Bank of the Middle East (BBME) opened a branch in Kuwait in 1942, followed by Bahrain and Dubai within four years. The French-owned Banque de l'Indochine and Arab Bank opened offices in Jeddah in 1948. BBME expanded its network to Oman the same year, followed by branches in Sharjah, Qatar, and Abu Dhabi by 1959.[9] BBME, National Bank of Pakistan, and Bank Misr of Egypt set up in Saudi Arabia in 1950.1954 saw the entry of Banque du Caire, Banque du Liban et d'Outre Mer, and First National City Bank of New York. Qatar saw the entry of Eastern Bank, BBME, Arab Bank, Intra Bank of Lebanon, and Ottoman Bank (Grindlays Bank) between 1950 and 1965. The Eastern Bank opened its Sharjah office in 1958.[10] By the 1950s, all of the Gulf economies thus hosted at least some modern banking institutions.

After 1943, the financial cluster in newly independent Lebanon became an important complement to Gulf-based banks. The young republic embraced a liberal ethos, capitalizing on a global network of Lebanese businessmen as well as its good connectivity and advantageous location.

The number of Beirut banks shot up from 11 in 1945 to 90 within two decades. Lebanon further benefited from a safe haven status at a time when political risk cast a shadow on many other Arab countries. Liberal rules on client confidentiality helped Beirut attract a great deal of anonymous capital until the crash of Intra Bank in 1966 forced the authorities to step in. Gulf capital financed institutions such as Beirut–Riyad Bank (1959), Crédit Libanais (1962), Bank Audi (1962), and Byblos Bank (1962).[11]

By the 1950s, Gulf merchants began to eye opportunities in financial services, and in 1952 the National Bank (of Kuwait) became the first locally domiciled bank. Commercial Bank of Kuwait and Gulf Bank opened their doors in 1960, followed by Al Ahli Bank in 1967.[12] Saudi Arabia's National Commercial Bank was incorporated in Jeddah in 1953 following the merger of two leading local money changers into the Saleh and Abdulaziz al Ka'ki and Salem bin Mahfouz Company. Riyad Bank began operations in 1957 and Bank al Watany a year later, soon merging after the Kingdom's first banking crisis in 1960. The National Bank of Bahrain was incorporated in 1957. National Bank of Dubai led the way on the Trucial Coast in 1960, followed by National Bank of Abu Dhabi in 1968. The 50 percent government-owned Qatar National Bank began operations in 1965 and National Bank of Oman opened in 1973.[13] But local institutions continued to be far outnumbered by their foreign rivals, making up only 2 of the 12 Qatari banks in 1971. In 1974, the Saudi government set out to convert all commercial banks into publicly traded companies with at least 60 percent Saudi ownership. This bid to proactively develop the banking sector and the stock market left only 3 of the Kingdom's 12 banks under foreign control by 1979.[14]

Even as the Gulf banking sector expanded, its remit was limited, as noted by Y.S.F. Al Sabah in 1980: "The commercial banks in Kuwait are very conservative and are mainly concerned with two objectives: accumulation of domestic savings for outside short-term investment, and the financing of imports (which is very profitable)."[15] Gulf banks were not classic financial intermediaries seeking to allocate customer deposits into productive uses.[16] Instead of driving the transformation of the regional economies, they effectively merely mirrored the oil–government nexus.

Saving for the future

Creating buffers for the proverbial rainy was a logical choice for all Gulf economies. Effectively safeguarding national wealth meant that "funds derived from the sale of high-grade resources should be converted into other forms of capital, which are of equal or greater value."[17] Concerns about distortions created by oil-financed investments emerged early on. But while the need for structured saving was accepted, implementation was far from straightforward in the absence of proper financial infrastructure. As a result, the first formal mechanisms for managing oil revenues tended to be foreign inspired and operated. The Gulf emirates

> *had British bank accounts or created investment boards, through which they channelled their oil/gas royalties. Bahrain had the Government Reserve Fund, which allocated half of its assets into British*

> *stocks and half in fixed deposits with the Eastern Bank and the British Bank of the Middle East. Under British influence, Abu Dhabi created the Abu Dhabi Investment Board in 1967 and Kuwait created in 1953 the Kuwait Investment Board.*[18]

Bahrain's Public Reserve Fund was set up as early as 1935, partly in response to the Great Depression. By 1959, the fund was 89.5 percent invested in British securities and deposits and the rest in government of India loans. Kuwait saved an estimated quarter of its oil revenue in the 1950s, and the state reserve fund saw its assets climb from KWD4.4mn in 1952 to KWD475.3mn by 1964–1965. Qatar allocated 20.6 percent of its government income to a reserve fund in 1953–1970.[19]

Even in the absence of alternatives, these practices triggered considerable controversy. The Kuwait Investment Board was resented as a British-influenced institution and the widespread perception that it generated low returns. After several restructurings, the General Reserve Fund (GRF) was set up in 1960, operating effectively as the national treasury. Soon thereafter, an investment committee was established under the auspices of the Department of Finance and the Kuwait Investment Office opened in London. The composition of savings evolved from an exclusive focus on foreign deposits and securities in 1961 to 47.4 percent being invested or lent locally and a further 19.7 percent lent to Arab governments as of 1971.[20] In the mid-1970s, a Future Generations Fund took over half the GRF assets and received a tenth of all government income. The Kuwait Investment Authority was constituted in its current form in 1982. It began by investing in the largest New York–listed companies but eventually built a global portfolio. The investments proved hugely successful. By 1978, foreign investments earned the government KWD1.265bn as compared to oil revenues of KWD2.584bn; "by 1980 these had risen to KD 3.1 billion and KD 5.277 billion respectively."[21]

The first Gulf monetary authority, the Saudi Arabian Monetary Agency (SAMA), was established in October 1952 after government revenues had risen from an annual average of $13–16mn in 1938–1946 to $53.6mn in 1948 and more than $100mn by 1953.[22] The need for stronger governance extended SAMA's remit to the government's banking needs and the management of the foreign reserves. The 1966 Banking Control Law equipped SAMA with extensive powers to regulate the emerging sector with strict rules imposed for capital adequacy, lending ratios, and reserve requirements. The law helped cement the role of commercial banks by allowing them to offer a range of other services as well.[23] SAMA operated as the de facto sovereign wealth fund (SWF) of Saudi Arabia for years. By the early 1970s, it had deposits in 35 leading international banks, but the scope subsequently expanded to listed companies, starting with oil majors. In the mid-1980s, the foreign currency distribution was diversified to 60 percent US dollar and 40 percent deutschmark and Japanese yen.[24]

Abu Dhabi's entry into the hydrocarbons era was followed within years by the creation of the Abu Dhabi Investment Board, initially under British management. A parallel Abu Dhabi Investment Administration was established in 1971 as a more national vehicle and put in charge of managing all oil wealth three years later. Renamed as the Abu Dhabi Investment Authority in 1976, it has subsequently evolved into one of the largest sovereign wealth funds globally. ADIA invests the vast majority of its assets overseas – currently some 70 percent. In 1984 the Abu Dhabi Investment Council created the International Petroleum Investment Corporation (IPIC) as a joint venture between ADIA and ADNOC with the mandate to secure end markets for Abu Dhabi crude. Mubadala was established in 2002 as a vehicle for facilitating economic diversification and merged with IPIC in 2017. The Qatar Investment Board was established on a similar model in 1972.[25] The Qatar Monetary Authority, formed in 1973, transferred its reserves to the Board for management. The Board eventually morphed into the Qatar Investment Authority in 2005.

The financial standing of the Gulf was profoundly transformed by the 1970s oil boom, when the region's hydrocarbon rents rose from $5.2bn in 1970 to $158bn in 1980, equal to some $500bn in 2018 money. Having invested heavily in Sterling-denominated assets in the 1960s, to a point where they reportedly held a quarter of the UK's total gold and foreign currency assets, the Gulf states switched their focus to the US dollar after the 1967 devaluation of the pound. Between 1970 and 1982, the Gulf countries' collective holdings of US Treasuries shot up from $2.2bn to $42bn (or $107bn in 2018 dollars). Their share of the foreign-held Treasury securities rose from 2 percent to almost 30 percent before falling back to $22bn and less than 5 percent by 1987.[26]

Over time, the Gulf SWFs have evolved into globally significant investors, even if their international ambitions have not always been welcomed. In an early landmark case, the UK government stopped the purchase of a 22 percent stake in British Petroleum by the Kuwait Investment Authority in 1988 on "public interest" concerns. The resistance to Gulf funds has often been linked to a perceived lack of transparency and suspicions of political motivations. A 2006 attempt by Dubai's DP World to take over the management of six US ports was eventually dropped in the face of legislative opposition.[27] By contrast, Gulf SWFs played a critical role in supporting leading global financial institutions during the 2008 financial crisis, now often at the behest of Western governments. Between March 2007 and April 2008, Gulf funds took stakes of up to 10 percent in banks including Citigroup (ADIA and KIA), UBS (SAMA), Merrill Lynch (KIA), and Barclays (QIA). The aggregate value was some $35bn. While not devoid of controversy, these investments provided "a source of liquidity that was important in addressing market concerns about the capitalization of … financial institutions."[28] Following its elevation to the Saudi SWF in 2015, the Public Investment Fund (PIF) began to make salient foreign acquisitions such as a $3.5bn stake in Uber. In 2016, it entered into a high-profile partnership with SoftBank of Japan, setting up the Vision Fund for high-tech investments globally. While perceptions of Gulf SWFs have improved, renewed Western concerns about their activities resurfaced during the COVID-19 pandemic, with many claiming that important assets were being acquired at depressed prices. Yet, Gulf capital again proved central to shoring up Crédit Suisse in 2022, although market turbulence ultimately necessitated a takeover by UBS in early 2023.[29]

Following another wave of windfalls in the early 21st century, the combined assets of the Gulf SWFs quadrupled up to 2008 to reach $883bn.[30] By 2017, they were estimated at as much as $3trn, a remarkable 40 percent of the global SWF assets. A late 2022 estimate put the total at just under $3.8trn. The strategic posture of some of these funds has evolved beyond purely financial objectives. Many of them have invested in companies that have served as a source of knowledge and new technology: "linking their higher-return investments to the GCC's goals of economic diversification and socioeconomic development."[31]

Connecting with global finance

The 1960s brough a growing interest in alternatives to commercial banking. Kuwait pioneered institutions with an explicitly international focus. The Kuwait Investment Company was incorporated in 1961 with 50 percent state participation. The Kuwait Foreign Trade, Contracting, and Investment Company came into being three years later with an 80 percent government stake. In 1966 these two vehicles joined forces with local commercial banks to set up the United Bank of Kuwait in London – the first Gulf institution in a global financial center. Three years later, Banque Franco–Arabe d'Investissements Internationaux was formed with Société Générale in Paris. By 1970, this group of institutions had placed an estimated $5.2bn of Kuwaiti funds internationally, some $4bn of them sovereign assets. New consortium banks continued to spring up and were instrumental in allowing Western financiers to tap the petrodollar plenty while exposing Gulf institutions to international banking practices. Union des Banques Arabes et Françaises opened its doors in 1970, followed by European Arab Bank in 1972 and Banque Arabe International d'Investissements in 1973. The Kuwaitis soon expanded their interests to the developing world. By 1974 the Kuwait Fund for Arab Economic Development, established in 1961, had expanded its remit to all developing countries. Its capital rose from KWD50mn to KWD2bn by 1979. In 1964 the Kuwaiti Ministry of Finance collaborated with Egypt's Central Bank to establish Arab–African Bank with four other Arab governments as stakeholders.[32]

Kuwait blazed a trail, but it was Bahrain that truly put the Gulf on the map of global finance. The rising tide of petrodollars provided the trigger as Saudi Arabia's oil income shot up more than 120-fold from the 1960s average by the turn of the 1980s.[33] In October 1975 the Bahraini government took the far-sighted decision to permit the establishment of offshore banking units (OBUs), which created the mechanism for global financial institutions to set up on a basis comparable to other financial centers. The new regulations also offered a solution to the dislocations caused by the incipient Lebanese civil war that was undermining Beirut's pre-eminence in regional finance, leaving its bankers looking for alternatives.[34]

Bahrain's rise proved spectacular. Within a mere four months of the new OBU regulations being announced, a remarkable 32 international banks submitted licensing applications, led by Citibank, Algemene Bank Nederland, Lloyds Bank International, NatWest, and Société Générale. Bahrain's banking assets shot up from just under $500mn – held by 11 institutions –

to $1.7bn by the end of 1975. A mere year later, Bahrain counted 29 OBUs and by 1977 a total of 36 with aggregate assets of $15.7bn. By the end of 1979, these numbers had reached 53 OBUs and $27.8bn, respectively.[35]

The booming Bahraini financial cluster grew increasingly diverse. In 1976, new licenses were introduced for representative offices and investment banking. By 1981, OBUs alone contributed 8.5 percent of Bahrain's GDP and employed 3,596 Bahrainis by 1982 – the third-largest sector tally.[36] By 1983, the country was home to a total of 21 commercial banks, 63 representative offices, 16 investment companies, six foreign exchange brokers, and 77 offshore banking units (two more licenses waiting to be activated). By the tail end of the great oil boom in 1983, OBU assets stood at $62.7bn. Bahrain had arrived on a scale that rivaled centers such as Singapore, Hong Kong, and Luxembourg. But the ensuing lean years would reveal that this was not a proposition with an indefinite upside. Bahrain acquired an increasingly regional flavor as Arab countries provided 50 percent of new funds in 1978 and two-thirds by 1983. Growth stalled due to the receding tide of oil liquidity and the Iran–Iraq war.

Beyond the opportune circumstances, Bahrain's rise built on "the government's need to diversify the domestic economic base, the adoption of flexible policies to achieve the diversification strategy and the country's special locational advantages."[37] The importance of quality regulations was recognized early on. The Bahrain Monetary Agency, established in 1973, was immediately tasked with regulating commercial banks. It became a full-fledged central bank by 1975 and mandated monthly reporting for all banks. Prudential data were collected quarterly and accounts were audited annually, a system that proved instrumental in building Bahrain's reputation. Bahrain also represented a new kind of openness as Saudi Arabia capped foreign ownership at 40 permits, while Kuwait did not permit it at all.[38]

Bahrain filled a gap in the global financial architecture as its time zone gave it "the distinct advantage of operating in currency dealings and foreign exchange business after Singapore closes, but before the European centres open."[39] The new hub also radiated positive externalities on Bahrain's own economy as it increased "the sophistication of the marketplace by introducing new products, techniques and areas of business. … In 1977 the first Government of Bahrain Development Bond was issued and a Bahraini Dinar Eurobond market was authorised to open."[40] However, early on the Saudi authorities exhibited concern over the emergence of an offshore Riyal market, which they sought to address through the introduction of fixed income instruments for domestic liquidity management.[41]

The consortium bank model continued to scale up, with the Saudis joining in through Banco Arab–Español (Arebank) and Banco Saudi–Español (Saudesbank) in 1975 and 1979, respectively. London was home to Saudi International Bank, established in 1975 as a joint venture between SAMA and Morgan Guaranty. The Arab–Turkish Bank was opened in Istanbul in 1977, while Arab–Hellenic Bank began operations in Athens in 1979. Arab–Latin American Bank (Arlabank), incorporated in Lima in 1977, was dedicated to developing ties between South America and the Arab world.[42]

Capital for development

During the oil boom, Saudi commercial banks saw their assets climb almost ten-fold from SAR2.7bn to SAR119bn between the beginning of the 1970s and 1982. The share of foreign assets expanded from 19 to 40 percent in 1972–1980. The money changers re-emerged as a major force, having consolidated from 700–800 entities in the 1920s to a mere 50 by 1972. Their expansion benefited from an expatriate influx but also exploited regulatory lacunae. While SAMA closely regulated commercial banks, it paid minimal attention to the 224 exchange houses, of which "128 were not licensed by the Ministry of Commerce, and 91 of those had no commercial registration."[43] Many money changers began to offer overdraft facilities, effectively turning themselves into shadow banks, while commercial banks only served an estimated 30–40 percent of the population. In 1977, licensed bank branches numbered only 98, whereas the Al Rajhi Company for Foreign Exchange and Commerce boasted a national network of 230 offices.

Skepticism mounted about the ability of commercial banks to enable the ever more ambitious economic diversification plans. Apart from their limited product range and branch networks, their predominantly short-term deposit base made it difficult to finance longer-term strategic projects. Yet the age of plenty offered limited incentives to move beyond this posture: "Efficient utilization of savings was not perceived as a prime policy goal at times when countries of the region were facing problems of limited absorptive capacity and excess financial resources."[44] Even on the demand side, the prospect of easy money trumped innovation: "by investing in real estate and private shareholding companies, Kuwait's nouveaux riches gave the ruling coalition a strong disincentive to invest in productive enterprises. ... As speculation drove up the prices of urban property, state financial officers turned to overseas investments."[45]

State development banking institutions began to gain favor as an alternative to commercial banks. In 1960 the Kuwaiti Credit Bank (Savings and Credit Bank) was the pioneer, offering home loans, real estate–backed secured lending, farming credit, and personal loans for civil servants. The promotion of savings was added to the mandate in 1965. The Industrial Bank of Kuwait was incorporated in 1973, with private corporations holding 51 percent of its KWD10mn capital. [46] In 1980, the government established the Industrial Promotion Committee and the Kuwait Finance House to offer soft loans for manufacturing ventures, notably in the new industrial cities of Fintas and Subiyyah.

Saudi Arabia's Agricultural Development Bank (ADB) was chartered in 1965. The first development plan established an industrial bank while boosting the capital of ADB and calling for studies about a housing and real estate development bank. Ultimately, five government lending institutions saw the light under the auspices of the Ministry of Finance: the Saudi Credit Bank, the PIF, the Saudi Arabian Industrial Development Fund (SIDF), and the Real Estate Development Fund (REDF). PIF was tasked with funding flagship projects with tenors of up to 15 years, often jointly with regular banks. It also invested directly and held government stakes in leading corporations. SIDF, established in 1974, sought to promote the expansion of private industry through non-profit consultancy and interest-free loans. It was initially run by a team brought in from Chase Manhattan Bank, which built credibility and allowed the country to become "more or less self-sufficient in building materials"[47] by 1980. In 1979–1983, the fund financed 87 percent of the 723 new factories built in the Kingdom. Similar institutions sprung up across the Gulf region. The Omani Development Bank and the Oman Housing Bank began operations in 1977, followed by the Oman Bank for Agriculture and Fisheries in 1981.

State lending institutions morphed into a parallel financial system that soon outshone the traditional banking sector even as they struggled to meet market demand. By 1984, the Saudi government lenders had provided an impressive SAR168bn of loans. Unlike retail banks, they did not mandate "customary project design, disclosure, and accounting requirements,"[48] which pushed commercial lenders into "specialty market niches, [while] lending functions significant to long-term development were performed almost exclusively by the Saudi state banks and by Bahraini OBUs."[49]

The ascendancy of the state lenders gave rise to new risks beyond central bank oversight. For instance, the REDF typically made cash payments, and "approval of home building loans was virtually automatic."[50] Much funding went into into non-strategic ventures. These shortcomings quickly surfaced once the oil cycle turned: "by 1985 there was an excess capacity of 60 and 40 percent in commercial and residential buildings, respectively."[51] By the late 1970s, SIDF stopped participating in project evaluation while expanding its client base to first-time entrepreneurs. More than a third of its portfolio reportedly defaulted in the 1980s.

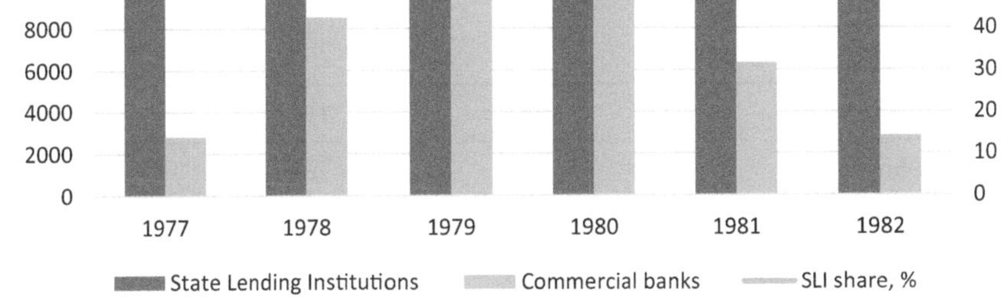

Figure 5.1 Loans for fixed capital investment in Saudi Arabia, SAR mn.

Source: Chaudhry, The Price of Wealth, p. 236.

The credit boom experienced a hard landing in the 1980s. In Saudi Arabia, "credit to the private sector, which had increased over 500% during the period 1976–81, grew only at an annual rate of less than 4% per year over the next five years."[52] Non-performing loans shot up to 20 percent of bank portfolios by 1986, and seven Saudi banks saw their profits drop from SAR1.8bn in 1982 to SAR535mn within four years.[53] Some protection came from the substantial net foreign assets of Gulf commercial banks that "exceeded $45 billion by the end of 1985."[54] But SAMA was forced to intervene in response to a crisis at Saudi Cairo Bank in 1982 and soon began to push for consolidation. The three remaining foreign banks were merged into the United Saudi Commercial Bank in 1983. The money changers were regulated in 1986. Many shut down, while the four largest applied for banking licenses.[55] The Al Rajhi Banking and Investment Corporation evolved into a leading Islamic retail institution.

SAMA unveiled an ambitious strategy of re-capitalizing and boosting the governance of Saudi banks. This allowed the sector to achieve remarkable expansion against an adverse economic tide. The number of bank branches rose from 247 to 1,036 during the 1980s, while manpower more than doubled from 11,000 to 25,000. In 1988–1993, seven banks increased their capital through share flotations, and the capital and reserves of the sector doubled from SAR15bn at the end of 1988 to SAR30bn by five years later.[56] Even the business community, having initially sued for leniency, accepted the need for proper regulation after banks had begun to scale back lending. In 1997, United Saudi Commercial Bank and Saudi Cairo Bank merged into United Saudi Bank, which joined Saudi American two years later. Domestic bank lending expanded by 90 percent in 1990–1995, and "three Saudi banks went to the market during 1993–97."[57]

Regulation was prioritized region-wide. The 1980 Union Law No. 10 established the Central Bank of the UAE as the regulator of the country's 21 banks.[58] As the new millennium dawned, retail banks overwhelmingly dominated the Gulf financial sector. In all markets, the largest five banks were local and accounted for 50–80 percent of all banking assets. Bahrain and the UAE had the largest proportion of foreign bank assets in the Gulf at 57 and 21 percent, respectively.[59]

Table 5.1 Saudi banking system

	1980	*1990*	*1998*
Assets, $ bn	21	69	109
Number of banks	10	12	11
Share of top five banks	80	76	75
Staff, '000	11	25	22
Branches	247	1.011	1,236
Return on assets, %	1.9	1.4	1.7
Simple capital ratio	6.1	7.2	10.4

Source: Al-Suhaimi, "Consolidation, Competition," p. 129.

The GCC banking sector entered the 21st century in good health and soon embarked on unprecedented growth. In 2003–2008, the UAE and Qatar saw annual private sector credit growth of some 35 and 45 percent, respectively. Oman held the rear but still managed around 20 percent. As a proportion of non-oil GDP, private sector credit in the Gulf exceeded all other emerging economies, with the inevitable consequence of new vulnerabilities. Even as domestic deposits funded most of the growth, external capital inflows expanded, fueled by expectations of currency appreciation. Banks developed heavy exposures to the region's property boom. Construction and real estate accounted for 50 percent of retail bank portfolios in Kuwait, 33 percent in Bahrain, and 25 percent in the UAE, which, moreover, also had important non-bank lenders.[60]

New risks stemmed from the rise of non-bank financial institutions, notably in Kuwait, where 95 investment companies held assets under management in excess of the country's GDP in 2008. This compared to banking assets at 84 percent. Loans to investment houses made up some 12 percent of commercial bank portfolios. Less stringent regulation along with substantial foreign and real estate exposures made the investment companies a particular weak link during the global financial crisis. Kuwait's Global Investment House failed to service much of its $3bn in leverage and in December 2008 defaulted on a $200mn *sukuk*. Investment Dar defaulted on a $100mn facility. In Bahrain, two offshore banks, The International Banking Corporation (TIBC) and Awal Bank, imploded. TIBC, owned by the Algosaibi Group, defaulted on a $2.2bn debt. Awal Bank, owned by the Al-Saad Group, sought to renegotiate. The UAE federal government pushed for an ultimately abortive merger of Dubai's leading mortgage companies.[61] Otherwise, however, the Gulf financial sector weathered the turbulence of the era with remarkably few disruptions, something that reflected the maturity of regulation and generally conservative banking practices.

Sovereign investment vehicles regrouped and the assets of the Saudi sovereign lending institutions equaled roughly 34 percent of GDP, "close to half that of the banking sector," in 2008.[62] Formally reconstituted as the national SWF under the auspices of the Council of Economic and Development Affairs in 2015, PIF plays a key role in pursuing the goals of Saudi Vision 2030. The 2021–2025 strategy of the fund envisages annual local investments of at least SAR150bn and a total asset portfolio of SAR4trn by 2025.[63] Around the turn of the millennium, Qatar created a number of development institutions under the auspices of QIA. Qatar Holding was set up in 2006 as a direct investment vehicle, while Qatari Diar undertakes real estate and infrastructure investments. In 2006, the government of Bahrain incorporated Mumtalakat and Nogaholding. Region-wide, most notably in Dubai, sovereign vehicles have been active players in real estate development.

Thinking beyond banks

Forward-thinking planners recognized the strategic importance of financial sector diversification early on. With the exception of the 1935 incorporation of the Arabian Automobile Company of Saudi Arabia, the Gulf capital markets date back to the early 1950s.[64] In 1952, Kuwait incorporated the National Bank as a local joint-stock company, but share trading remained minimal.[65] Joint-stock companies increased in popularity after the adoption of the Commercial Companies Law in 1960. Stock market regulations were approved in 1962. But it was only in 1971 that regulated share trading began under the oversight of the Ministry of Commerce and Industry amid exceptional liquidity: "Because the market has vast sums of capital chasing relatively few securities, shares can rise to ridiculous prices. ... New issues can be oversubscribed up to a hundred times."[66] These realities also gave rise to an informal market known as Souq al Manakh in the 1970s. It listed up to 46 Kuwaiti companies and 38 businesses incorporated elsewhere in the Gulf. Even firms banned from the official market could be traded. In its heyday, Manakh accounted for 80 percent of the overall equity trading volume in Kuwait, fueled by a speculative frenzy: "Students stopped attending classes and employees gave up their jobs – many mortgaging their homes – in order to play the extraordinary market which was producing unheard-of profits."[67]

But this was not smooth sailing. Following a major rally, reduced liquidity and rumors caused the main index to drop by 18.7 percent in late 1976, while volumes plunged by two-thirds. The government stepped in through share purchases and stricter rules on forward transactions, but renewed wobbles ensued in the summer of 1977. IPOs and rights issues were banned, while the Kuwait Foreign Trading, Contracting, and Investment Company invested KWD150mn to stabilize the market. The Central Bank set up a facility to resolve bad debts. The national obsession returned with a vengeance once regulations were again relaxed. One hundred twenty Kuwaiti and 23 Gulf businesses were incorporated by 1982, many of them offshore entities. Nearly KWD30bn of new liquidity flushed into the market as oil prices rebounded. The widespread use of postdated checks drove leverage, making Manakh the third largest market globally by capitalization, after New York and Japan.[68]

In August 1982, Souq al Manakh experienced one of the most spectacular crashes in the history of modern equity trading. The collapse was triggered by a bouncing check but fundamentally reflected tighter liquidity and anxiety about the Iran–Iraq war. The index plummeted from 240 in March 1982 to 110 in August when a major broker defaulted. Volumes fell from 602 to 72mn shares within a month and valuations ultimately shed 60–90 percent. By September, the total value of outstanding postdated checks was estimated at $94bn. The official market, having declined by only 6.5 percent in March–August, went on to fall by 53 percent between the end of 1982 and 1984.[69]

The Manakh crisis prompted yet another government rescue through low-interest loans to banks. Paradoxically, an attempt to empower the private sector through stronger capital markets paved the way for increased government ownership. Kuwait spent an estimated $2bn by May 1983 to stabilize the market, acquiring 48–50 percent of the equity of all traded companies in the process, a majority in nearly half of them.[70]

The Difficult Credit Facilities Resettlement Program covered almost all market participants, and the debts of smaller investors were eventually written off altogether. The episode served as a major warning to capital market advocates but also underscored the importance of regulation and investor protection.

The Kuwait Stock Exchange (KSE) was reconstituted in 1983 as an independent authority under the chairmanship of the Minister of Commerce. As a self-regulatory organization (SRO), it established trading procedures, registered brokers, and drove market development. Regular reporting and disclosure requirements were mandated for listed companies. Clearing and settlement were organized under the auspices of the Kuwait Clearing Company in 1986. The first modern Gulf bourse was born.

Gulf-wide, fiscal austerity fueled interest in new mechanisms for mobilizing capital. Saudi Arabia had seen gradual growth in the number of joint-stock companies since 1954, starting with the Arabian Cement Company, three electricity companies, and the National Printing and Publishing Company. Eleven new joint-stock companies were incorporated in 1955–1964, including Riyad Bank, three electric companies, two cement producers, and three petroleum service companies.[71] The 1965 Law of Companies formalized primary market issuance. The number of companies reached 14 by 1975, with a total capital of SAR2bn. The Saudiization of banks gave the market a further boost, with 48 new listings capitalized at some $20bn in 1976–1986.[72]

A secondary market with some 80 unlicensed brokers emerged in the late 1970s. Rules for trading through banks were adopted in 1984, while supervision was entrusted to a committee composed of the ministries of finance and commerce as well as SAMA. 1984 saw a landmark flotation of 30 percent of the industrial giant SABIC with a valuation of SAR3bn. By 1985, 44 joint-stock companies boasted a total capital of SAR67.2bn. However, trading remained minimal, at most SAR30mn a month, and deals could take weeks to conclude.[73] In 1985, the Saudi Share Registration Company, owned by the commercial banks, was established, while clearing was conducted by SAMA. An Electronic Share Information System was launched in 1990, offering de-materialization and a T+0 settlement cycle. A fully regulated Saudi Arabian Stock Exchange was finally established under the 2003 Capital Market Law, which designated the Capital Market Authority as the regulator.

Similar developments unfolded Gulf-wide, partly because of the popular notion that capital market development permitted wealth distribution without government expenditure. In 1979, Bahrain's Ministry of Trade allocated BHD10mn for the creation of the Bahrain Company for Light Industry, whose shares were offered at BHD2 each to attract retail investors. The Bahrain Stock Exchange (BSE) began trading with 34 listed companies in 1989. The Muscat Securities Market was established in 1988 and saw the number of listings rise from 68 to 145 between 1989 and 1996.[74] The Doha Securities Market opened in 1995, but organized trading in the UAE only began in 2000, through separate exchanges in Abu Dhabi and Dubai. The bourses invariably grew out of broker or bank-based trading systems.

By the close of the 20th century, the Gulf financial sector stood on two legs. Equity market capitalization varied from roughly a quarter of GDP in Oman and Qatar to around 40 percent in the UAE and Saudi Arabia, with only Bahrain and Kuwait in the 90–100 percent bracket as of 1996.[75] These markets did not derive their funding primarily from the oil–government nexus even if they inevitably mirrored the oil-linked liquidity dynamics. The bourses were conduits for private capital despite substantial government stakes. Retail investors typically set the tone in trading, while the governments drove market growth through privatizations and IPOs. The distributive ethos of the 1970s acquired a Thatcherite flavor as private investors were given a stake in the productive assets of the economy.

Perhaps the most striking differentiator of the Gulf stock markets from banks was their decidedly parochial ethos. While modeled on international practices, the exchanges constituted the first truly "home-grown" element of Gulf finance. They fell short of best practices at the close of the 20th century: "there is a lack of brokers and market makers; foreign access to the markets is generally restricted to GCC nationals; a number of large corporations remain under government control; and there is a general weakness in transparency requirements and the provision of information."[76] The Saudi market remained a purely domestic/GCC platform, until foreign participation in mutual funds was permitted in 1997, quickly followed by the London listing of the Saudi–American Bank's Saudi Arabian Investment Fund. BSE, by contrast, tried to establish links with other regional trading platforms early on – Muscat in 1995 and Amman a year later. KSE signed cross-listing agreements with Egypt and Beirut in 1996, having permitted foreign investment through mutual funds in 1994.[77]

A rollercoaster ride toward maturity

The 21st century opened with a bang. Saudi Arabia's TASI benchmark index, having stood at just 2,518.1 at the end of 2002, shot up to an all-time high of 20,634.86 on 25 February 2006. A gain of 84 percent was recorded in 2004 and 103.7 percent in 2005. Saudi Arabia accounted for approximately half of the Gulf market capitalization and as much as 80 percent of the value of trading. The aggregate GCC market capitalization skyrocketed from $117.0bn in 2000 to $1,135.5bn in 2005. The value of trading jumped from $23mn to $1.4bn. Market capitalization quadrupled from 50 percent to a remarkable 200 percent of GDP. A total of 59 IPOs – worth $15.5bn – were seen across the Gulf between 2001 and the first half of 2006. They benefited from substantial repatriation of Gulf investments in the aftermath of 9/11. Regional governments paid down their debt, which boosted bank liquidity and accelerated lending. More and more retail investors borrowed for trading. Saudi loans for "other purposes," which included margin lending, increased from $7.8bn in 2002 to $36bn by 2005.[78] Many sold assets and liquidated savings in order to buy into the boom.

A scarcity of alternatives was a major driver of the stock market mania. The 2002 listing of a 30 percent stake in Saudi Telecommunications

Company involved the sale of 60mn shares to Saudi citizens. The number of 40,000 portfolios in the country reportedly doubled and continued to rise with subsequent offerings that included leading petrochemicals companies. IPOs typically sold stocks at par with participation limited to nationals. Prices were usually below actual value, and allocations were fixed across all subscruptions. Prices almost invariably shot up upon listing, creating a situation where "rational citizens would have been irrational to remain out of the market."[79]

Echoing earlier bubbles such as Nasdaq, the extraordinary rally ended with a brutal crash. From a peak of 20,634.86 on 23 February, TASI plunged to a nadir of 7,500 by December. SAMA intervened by investing in mutual funds overwhelmed by redemption requests. But the absence of short-selling regulations and a shortage of sophisticated institutional investors entailed minimal obstacles on the downward slide.[80] While painful, the correction bred awareness of the risks of equity trading and of the need for market research. It also underscored the importance of robust regulation and technological development.

A range of measures were adopted to revive the market. Expatriate residents of Saudi Arabia were permitted to trade on Tadawul. The regulators recognized the importance of a more institutional investor base while trying to attract more listings. Tadawul had 86 listed companies in 2006, up from 77 in 2005, but the small free float of some equities made it relatively easy to influence prices. Important steps were taken to boost transparency and beef up the CMA's enforcement powers.[81]

Despite substantial positive progress, the Gulf equity markets have proven slow to reach their pre-2008 highs. Apart from Saudi Arabia since the Aramco listing, the only one to match the advanced economy average capitalization of around 80 percent of GDP is Qatar, whose General Retirement and Social Insurance Organisation is mandated to invest in domestic equities. Elsewhere in the Gulf, the proportion varies between just over 40 percent in Oman and more than 60 percent in Kuwait. Market liquidity is below 30 percent outside of Saudi Arabia, which exceeds the advanced economy average with a nearly 100 percent turnover ratio.[82] Despite diversification in listings, the product range is narrow. Even short-selling is a very recent phenomenon, pioneered by Tadawul in early 2017 and soon matched by Abu Dhabi and Dubai. Tadawul and Dubai launched derivatives trading in 2020 and Abu Dhabi in 2021.

The number of listed companies tends to lag behind comparator countries. Following an impressive buildup before the global financial crisis, new listing activity has remained below 2007 levels. Saudi Arabia is the only regional economy to have seen IPOs every year, thanks to mandatory listing requirements in certain sectors and the landmark offerings of the National Commercial Bank and Saudi Aramco. 2017 saw a recent peak of 27 IPOs but only $2.7bn raised in new capital.[83] Financial service providers make up one-third of capitalization in Saudi Arabia and more than two-thirds in Bahrain. Government ownership remains substantial, in the Saudi case some 40 percent of total capitalization before the Aramco listing.[84]

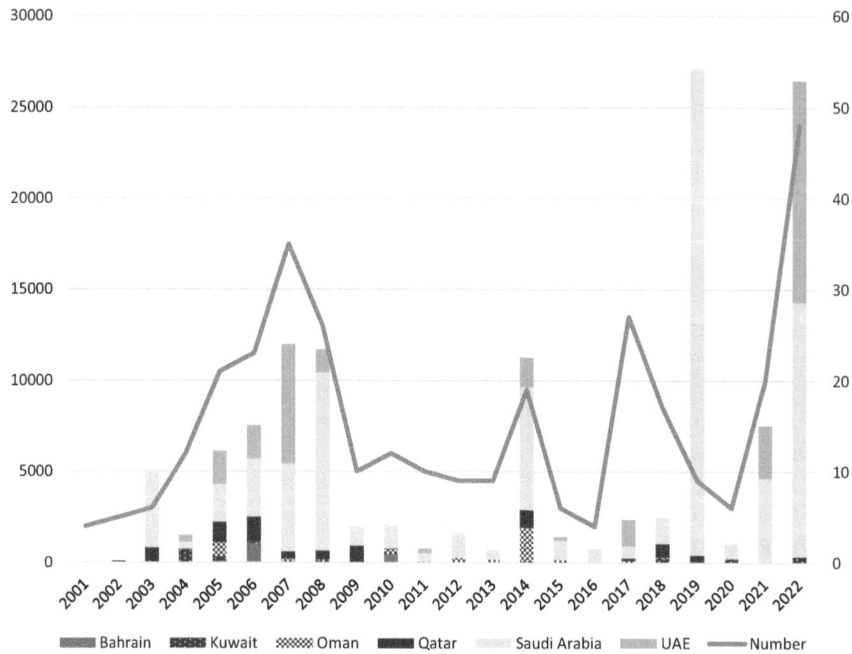

Figure 5.2 Capital raised through IPOs, $ mn.

Source: pwc; EY; KAMCO Invest; Zein and Grigorievna, "IPO in the Countries of the Gulf Cooperation Council," p. 3; regional exchanges.

The Gulf equity markets mirror and may have further cemented the structure of the regional corporate sector. Large companies, usually former SOEs, dominate, while genuinely private businesses, including family groups, are rare. Monetizing (quasi-)public assets re-emerged as a major IPO driver in 2021. The impact on the broader business landscape and the economy has been much less transformative.[85] Dedicated "SME" platforms have sought to address this issue. Saudi Arabia's Nomu was launched in 2017. Modeled on Nasdaq and London's AIM, it set out to create a less onerous regulatory environment for growth companies. Trading is limited to qualified investors, including experienced retail investors. Similar platforms include the Bahrain Investment Market and the Nasdaq Dubai Growth Market. In 2021, Qatar Exchange launched a Venture Market.

The Gulf markets have seen significant regulatory and institutional convergence with the advanced economies. Kuwait established an independent Capital Markets Authority in 2017. Most exchanges have adopted world-class technology, some through formal alliances with foreign operators. In 2008 Nasdaq OMX acquired a 30 percent stake in the Dubai International Financial Exchange. Since 2010, ownership of its successor, Nasdaq Dubai, has been split between Dubai Financial Market and Borse Dubai. Qatar Exchange partnered with NYSE Euronext in 2009. Dubai Financial Market (since 2006) and Boursa Kuwait (2019) are now listed companies. Tadawul IPOed in 2021.

Despite substantial improvement, corporate governance remains work in progress. Historically, foreign investors were deterred by low liquidity and a lack of hedging instruments. Caps on foreign participation were common but have now been relaxed. Saudi regulators have deliberately prioritized foreign institutions as a source of market stability.[86] Following the introduction of swap-based foreign access in 2008, qualified foreign investors (QFIs) were permitted in 2015. By late 2016, institutions were responsible for nearly 29 percent of the traded value of Tadawul, more than double the 13 percent average during the preceding six years. Institutions accounted for 27.15 percent and foreigners 13.8 percent of buying in December 2021. Foreigners held 3.05 percent of total Saudi market capitalization.[87] Most GCC markets are now included in the global benchmark indices. The MSCI Emerging Markets index includes equities from the UAE and Qatar as of 2014, as well as Saudi Arabia and Kuwait as of 2019–2020. FTSE Russell ranked the UAE as a secondary emerging market in 2010, followed by Qatar in 2016 and Saudi Arabia and Kuwait in 2018.

Market fragmentation remains a challenge, with eight active exchanges in the GCC. Integration ambitions have made limited progress. Initiatives, above all Nasdaq Dubai, to create regional trading platforms have failed to challenge the established exchanges or the national bias of regulators. While it is likely that technological progess and regulatory development will reduce hurdles on intra-regional trading, the lack of integration is widely recognized as a missed opportunity to drive market development.

The bumpy road toward fixed income markets

There was little need of a fixed income market before the fiscal challenges of the 1980s, although Bahrain issued five- to seven-year Government Development Bonds (GDBs) in 1977. But the plunging oil prices in the 1980s forced the Gulf governments to consider alternatives. Kuwait raised close to $5bn of debt through Treasury bonds in 1987 after its foreign assets had fallen from KWD320bn in 1980 to just KWD73bn in 1983. Saudi Arabia introduced the bond-type Bankers Special Deposit Accounts in 1986.[88] Two- to five-year GDBs were launched in 1988, and Treasury bills followed in 1991. Bahrain introduced weekly T-bill auctions in 1991. Oman launched three-month T-bills in 1987 and three- to seven-year development bonds in 1991 while floating a $225mn Eurobond in 1997. A UAE certificate of deposit program began in 1994. Bahrain saw the value of its outstanding issues rise from $186mn in 1987 to $787mn in 1992. Kuwait's total rose from $2.1bn in 1987 to $9.5bn in 1995. Saudi Arabia's outstanding GDBs climbed to $8bn in 1988 and eventually to $100bn in 1996.[89]

Issuance quickly dried up once the record deficits began to close. Governments retired debt, while central bank liquidity management through T-bills typically continued. Corporate fixed income issuance in the Gulf emerged very late, held back by regulatory limitations and a lack of institutional capacity. Bahrain's ALBA issued popular promissory notes in the 1970s. Corporate bonds were offered in the 1990s by Bahrain Commercial Facilities Company, ALBA, Bahrain International Bank, Kuwait's Commercial Facilities Company, and Kuwait Real Estate Bank. In an early landmark development, Qatar's Ras Laffan Liquefied Natural Gas

Company (Rasgas) managed to raise almost half of its initial financing through a \$1.2bn international private placement in December 1996.[90] Saudi Arabia saw occasional domestic issuance in the 1970s and dollar notes in the 1980s. Dubai led the way in developing asset-backed securities using mortgages issued for the Palm Jumeirah project in 2005. But region-wide corporate bond issuance in 2007 equaled only 3.2 percent of GDP, as compared to 10 percent in China and 112 percent in the US.[91]

Sovereign issuance revived after the 2008 crisis, facilitated by new Shari'ah-compliant *sukuk* structures.[92] Some leading corporations began to seek alternatives to bank finance led by a SAR3bn five-year corporate *sukuk* offering by SABIC in 2006.[93] Other leading names such as Saudi Electricity as well as the Islamic Development Bank (IsDB) initiated *sukuk* programs. Bank capital requirements under Basel III became another driver. But little happened below the top tier of companies. In Saudi Arabia, outstanding private sector domestic fixed income issuance reached some 5 percent of GDP in 2017. The small local markets pushed many toward external funding sources: "In 2017, private sector total external debt securities ranged from 21 percent of GDP in Saudi Arabia to around 77 percent of GDP in UAE."[94]

Issuance accelerated dramatically following the 2014 oil price drop, with all Gulf sovereigns repeatedly placing benchmark-size international issues. Despite some ratings erosion, most remain investment grade. Tenors have extended to 30-year and even perpetual issues. The outstanding GCC issuance stands at close to half a trillion US dollars following a climb from annual offerings of less than \$10bn until 2004 to \$151.1bn in 2020. The mounting government offerings, while risking some crowding out, have also helped put in place yield curves. As of 2019, the sovereign and quasi-sovereign names from the region are part of the JP Morgan Emerging Market Bond Index, which has brought institutional inflows into the Gulf. By contrast, retail investor participation remains rare due to high minimum ticket sizes.

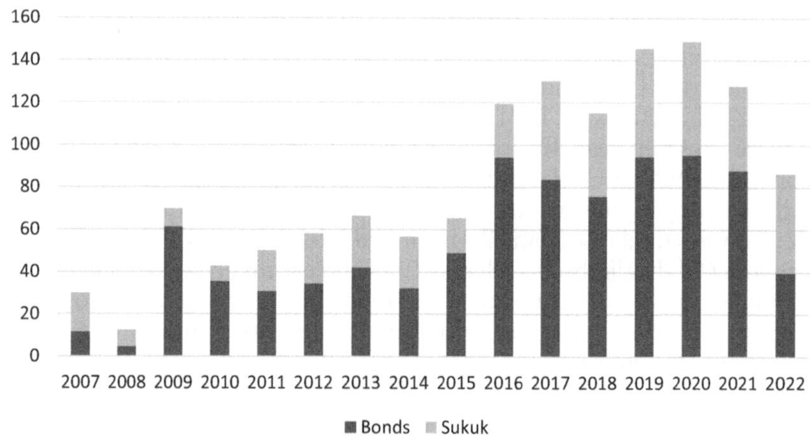

Figure 5.3 GCC primary bond and *sukuk* issuance, \$ bn. Issues with tenors of more than one year.

Source: Bloomberg, KAMCO Invest.

The slow rise of Gulf insurance

Insurance remains a marginal element of the GCC financial sector architecture. This reflects long-standing challenges of reconciling it with Shari'ah jurisprudence. Life insurance has faced strong cultural resistance and been disadvantaged be generous public welfare provision. Moreover, the insurance sector emerged in a largely unregulated environment, with the consequence of some unethical practices that undermined confidence.

Modern insurance provision in the Gulf began with the entry of the Lebanese Arabia Insurance Co. to Kuwait in 1949. Zurich Insurance, Libano Suisse Insurance, the New India Assurance Co., the Oriental Insurance Co., ALICO, Jordan Insurance, and Egypt Insurance followed during the 1950s. Norwich Union of the UK established an office in Bahrain in 1950 with Yusuf bin Ahmed Kanoo as its agent. A local venture, branded as the Co-operative Compensation Society in 1955, was formed by Bahraini taxi drivers for vehicle and accident insurance. Further entrants in the 1950s included the New Indian Assurance Co., Ltd, the Zayani Group, and Abdulla Yousif Fakhro & Sons – acting as agents for General Accident Insurance. Kuwait saw the creation of the locally controlled Kuwait Insurance Co. in 1960, soon followed by the Al Ahleia Insurance Co. and Gulf Insurance. Life insurance was introduced to the Gulf in 1961 by the Bahrain office of American Life Insurance Co. Qatar Insurance Co. was set up in 1964. The first public insurance company in the Gulf was Bahrain Insurance Co., established in 1969, which eventually morphed into the Bahrain National Holding Co.[95]

Indian insurers created the Trucial Coast market starting with the Oriental Insurance Co. in 1959 and the New Indian Assurance Company in 1962. ALICO, the Arabia Insurance Co., and the Qatar Insurance Co. entered in 1963–1964. British Insurance and Northern Insurance set up in the late 1960s. The first local players were Sharjah Insurance Co. and Dubai Insurance Co. in 1970. Abu Dhabi National Insurance Co. and Compagnie Libanaise d'Assurances began operations in 1972. Formal insurance provision in Oman began with American Life Insurance Co. in 1971, followed by Royal & Sun Alliance in 1972. Al-Ahlia Insurance Co. became the first national insurer in 1985.[96]

Kuwait was the first Gulf country to introduce formal insurance regulation through Law No. 24 of 1961, which designated the Ministry of Commerce as the supervisor. The UAE introduced its Federal Law No. 9 for the sector in 1984. The Higher Committee for Insurance began operations in 1993 with a brief to draft the general policies, becoming the Insurance Authority in 2007. Bahrain adopted its Insurance Law in 1987. Regulation was typically in the hands of ministries of commerce, although many subsequently transferred the responsibility to the central bank (Bahrain in 2002, Qatar in 2012) or the capital markets regulator (Oman in 2004).[97]

The development of modern insurance proved particularly challenging in Saudi Arabia. Since its inception in the 1950s, the sector remained in the hands of foreign agents until the Red Sea Insurance Co. was incorporated in 1974, followed by the Saudi United Insurance Co. in 1976. The lack of acceptable Shari'ah-compliant structures held back progress until a cooperative model based on *tabbru'* contracts won approval in 1977. The National Company for Cooperative Insurance – known as Tawuniya – was incorporated in 1986, initially with full PIF ownership and a mandate to proactively develop the sector. The Cooperative Insurance Companies Control Law of 2004 created a regulatory framework tasking SAMA with supervision. At the time, Saudi Arabia was home to some 75 companies or brokers, as well as 25 insurance agents. All insurers were required to obtain a licence within three years. NCCI, which controlled 40 percent of the market, did this in 2004 simultaneously with a 70 percent privatization. In 2018, Saudi Arabia accounted for half the global Shari'ah-compliant insurance market and 89.6 percent of the regional total.[98]

Re-insurance provision was pioneered by the Kuwait Reinsurance Co. in 1972. Arab Insurance Group (Arig) was incorporated in Bahrain in 1980 as a regional venture owned by the governments of Kuwait, Libya, and the UAE. The Oman Reinsurance Co. was set up in 2009. In 2005, Arig established Takaful Re, the pioneering Shariah-compliant reinsurer. More recently, new markets entrants have coincided with some departures and consolidation. In addition, 42.5 percent of Gulf insurance premiums were ceded to re-insurers in 2018 as compared to a global average of 5.0 percent. Saudi Arabia mandated a 30 percent total ceded premium requirement to reduce reliance on foreign reinsurers.[99]

The Gulf insurance market recorded annual growth of 8.9 percent in 2013–2018. The UAE accounted for 44.3 percent of the regional gross written premiums of $28.2bn and Saudi Arabia for 33.6 percent. Despite impressive progress, Gulf insurance remains an emerging industry. Insurance penetration in Saudi Arabia stood at just 0.5 percent as recently as 2003, with per capita spending of $45.5. Penetration tripled to 1.5 percent by 2020 but remained far behind the 3.3 percent reading in the UAE, let alone the global average of 7.4 percent. Saudi insurance density reached $281, but only $8 of this was on life insurance. The UAE total was $1,291 – $251 of it life. The global average was $809, of which $360 was claimed by life insurance. The UAE in 2018 made up 77.8 percent of the GCC life insurance market, but penetration in the segment was only 0.7 percent, as compared to 2.3 percent for non-life, and growth trailed the industry average.[100]

Government regulation has been instrumental in shaping Gulf insurance. Expanding car ownership became a key growth driver through mandatory vehicle and accident insurance. Bahrain's United Insurance Company was set up in 1986 to cater to vehicles crossing the newly built King Fahad Causeway to Saudi Arabia.[101] Recently, health insurance has become an important segment, with compulsory coverage for expatriates now the regional norm and with more market-based solutions applied to nationals as well. Saudi Arabia began the phased implementation of mandatory health insurance for private companies in 2005. The UAE required health insurance for foreigners in 2017, followed by Oman a year later. Bahrain, having established a similar policy, is now implementing a comprehensive National Health Insurance Program.

Regulation was also instrumental for shaping the Shariah-compliant *takaful* segment, which was pioneered by Bahrain Islamic Insurance Co.

in 1989 (subsequently Takaful International Co), Qatar Islamic Insurance Co. in 1995, and Kuwait's Wethaq Takaful and First Takaful in 2000. In 2003, the National Takaful Insurance Co. was set up, followed by Ritaj, Al-Khalijiyah, and Safat in 2006. Al Madina Takaful and Takaful Oman were incorporated in the Sultanate in 2014.[102] Following Bahrain, the UAE, and Qatar, Oman adopted a special regulatory framework for *takaful* in 2016. Having reached a market share of 22 percent in Bahrain as early as 2012, *takaful* expanded by an impressive 18 percent a year region-wide in 2012–2015. The momentum has since stalled, but *takaful*'s market share reached 37.6 percent in 2018. Shari'ah-compliant solutions attracted new customer segments; for instance, through life-type products such as family *takaful*. The GCC had nearly 40 *takaful* operators in 2018. Their $10.6bn total made up more than three-quarters of the global *takaful* gross written premiums.[103]

The Gulf insurance sector is fragmented, although the top five players control more than half of most national markets. The top 20 listed GCC insurers had a market share of 57.7 percent in 2018. In 2016 the Saudi insurance market had 34 licensed operators and a turnover of $9.8bn. Bahrain, despite being the smallest regional market, had 24 local insurance companies, 12 foreign insurers, 32 insurance brokers, and 29 actuaries in 2019. The UAE, which in 2016 accounted for 39 percent of GCC insurance contributions, had 61 companies, of which 22 were foreign. Kuwait is home to 35 insurers and Oman to 22.[104]

Some countries have mandated stock exchange listing to boost capitalization and transparency. Oman requires a minimum free float of 40 percent – even higher than Saudi Arabia's 30 percent. With some of the established market segments becoming intensely competitive, consolidation is growing in importance. Mergers and acquisitions numbered more than 20 in 2017–2019, involving also some non-GCC companies. They are likely to continue as technology reshapes the sector.[105]

The "missing" pillar: The relative absence of institutional investors

Despite significant convergence, major structural differences still set the GCC financial markets apart from their more mature peers. The role of institutional investors is a particular anomaly. While collective savings vehicles such as pension funds, insurance funds, and asset managers dominate capital markets in the West, GCC institutions are largely made up of various sovereign funds, some financial corporations, state-owned enterprises, and family offices. Many are substantial entities, but their weight and market behavior differ from Western institutions.[106]

Globally, institutions are important financial intermediaries. By pooling capital, they can both reduce its cost and boost management from the risk–revenue perspective. Because of their scale, resources, and fiduciary mandates, institutions tend to increase the efficiency of capital allocation. Their typically long-term liabilities allow them to offer funding with longer tenors than banks. They tend to be a source of stability and continuity in capital markets.

The role of collective savings vehicles is likely to remain a major differentiator between the GCC capital markets and their Western counterparts for years. Formal pension provision is relatively recent by historical standards and remains almost exclusively a government responsibility. After SWFs, public pension/social insurance funds are the second largest category of GCC institutional investors, with total assets of roughly $600bn as of 2020. They currently contribute roughly 5 percent of Gulf stock market capitalization. Problematically, the government pension systems are underfunded, with substantial actuarial deficits.[107] A 2015 survey by EY found that GCC pension fund holdings equaled a quarter of the region's GDP, with average holdings of some $15,000 per citizen. The UK had average holdings of more than four times this.[108] There is currently little formal regulation around occupational and voluntary retirement schemes. Company thrift schemes, where they exist, are often run in-house, with modest returns.

A holistic regulatory framework for encouraging long-term savings must be a key medium-term policy priority. Such a system has to be build on comprehensive regulation, including "prudential investment guidelines to ensure safety and liquidity of investments."[109] In the meantime, governments continue to address actuarial deficits almost exclusively through parametric reforms designed to extend the lifespan of the current funds. Sustainable change will also require investor education coupled with a public commitment to promote private savings.[110] Some regional pension funds have set up dedicated asset management companies; for example, Hassana in Saudi Arabia and Osool in Bahrain.

A new beginning?: Islamic finance

During the closing decades of the 20th century, Islamic finance appeared on the GCC financial landscape, catalyzed by the Organisation of the Islamic Conference, which advocated "specific economic and financial products and services that enabled Muslims to better adhere to their religious beliefs and principles in ways that they were unable to do with conventional banking."[111] The Islamic Development Bank was set up in Jeddah in 1975 as a multilateral entity to drive the development of the sector. The Gulf pioneers of Shari'ah-compliant banking were Dubai Islamic Bank (established in 1975), Kuwait Finance House (1978), and Bahrain Islamic Bank (1978). However, initial progress was slow, with a 1979 review observing: "Largely engaged in trade finance, [Islamic banks] have so far found it difficult to develop profit-sharing provision in the form of *Modaraba* and *Musharaka* arrangements as an alternative to interest-based loan portfolios."[112]

In the early 21st century, Islamic finance became the most dynamic element of the Gulf financial sector, achieving some 25 percent annual growth. International banks set up Islamic windows to expand their Gulf business. Bahrain's central bank adopted a proactive regulatory posture: "Separate consolidated figures for the Islamic banks in Bahrain were first introduced in 1998, in which year their total assets amounted to US$1,348 million.

Over the ensuing seven years the sector saw uninterrupted growth with assets at the end of June 2005 having risen to US$6,700 million, evidencing overall growth of 397%."[113] Al Rajhi, Al Bilad, and Al Jazira were the first Saudi banks to position themselves as fully Shariah-compliant, but all of their peers also began to offer Islamic products relatively early. Oman explicitly recognized Islamic finance through bespoke legislation and separate licensing processes in 2012.

Total assets of GCC Islamic banks grew at annual average rate of some 11 percent during the decade to 2018, far ahead around 6 percent for conventional banks.[114] The systemic significance of the Shariah-compliant market segment is greatest in Kuwait, where (as of 2016) they accounted for just under 40 percent of all bank assets, up from a quarter a decade earlier. In most of the region, Oman being the main exception, Islamic finance now makes up around a quarter of total bank assets. Saudi Arabia and the UAE are the largest Islamic financial markets in the Gulf, accounting for 29 and 28 percent of the regional total, respectively.[115]

Islamic finance has helped bring new customer groups under formal financial intermediation. Far beyond reshaping the banking sector, it has also helped enable broader financial sector development through innovations such as *takaful* and *sukuk*. But there is a growing perception that Islamic finance has fallen short of the expectations created during its early 21st-century rally. The gradual growth deceleration suggests that most of the "low-hanging fruit" has now been picked. While Islamic finance weathered the global financial crisis well thanks to its principles-based approach and lower reliance on leverage, it was not altogether unscathed. The heavy exposure of many IFIs to real estate – partly because of the limited range of other Shariah-compliant assets – left them vulnerable to the regional property market downturn. Globally, the annual growth of Islamic assets has decelerated to around 5 percent.

Shariah-compliant finance continues to be disadvantaged by a financial market infrastructure that was largely developed by and for conventional financial institutions. IFIs have often struggled to compete on product diversity and cost, not least because of the complexity of many structures. Attempts to expand the repertoire have frequently brought accusations of "Shariah wrappers" or thinly disguised conventional products.[116] The sector has struggled with multiple growing pains, including disputes about the Shariah compliance of structures used in the past. The Accounting and Auditing Organization for Islamic Financial Institutions (AAOIFI) shocked the industry in 2008 when it suggested that up to 85 percent of the *sukuk* issued in the Gulf were not truly in line with Islamic law. In particular, AAOIFI scholars attacked the widespread practice of repurchase agreements designed to ensure repayment at face value. They argued that the price of a *sukuk* should be determined by the value of underlying asset and could thus be more volatile.[117]

The industry has also been rattled by some high-profile failures, including the 2009 near-default of the Dubai property developer Nakheel on its $3.5bn *sukuk*. The absence of precedents triggered a major wave of market anxiety. Kuwait saw Investment Dar default on a $100mn *sukuk* and International Investment Group on a $200mn issuance. In 2011,

Investment Dar converted the offering into equity, while IIG restructured its sukuk. The UAE-based Dana Gas reached a restructuring deal with its creditors in 2018, having previously claimed that its $700mn *sukuk* was no longer repayable because it had become Shariah non-compliant.[118]

The fragmentation of the Islamic financial marketplace has been an source of inefficiency and cost. The Shariah compliance of each product must be affirmed by a Shariah advisory board. Historically, such boards have tended to be institution-specific and not bound by *fatwas* issued by others. This self-regulatory model has struggled to achieve meaningful standardization or even consistency. There were also concerns that independence could be compromised by the fact that each board reported to a given institution. A shortage of suitably qualified Shariah scholars has been an issue, while multiple board memberships of prominent scholars have generated controversy.

There have been various attempts to streamline standards; for instance, through IsDB-supported infrastructure institutions, including the following[119]:

- AAOIFI, set up in Bahrain in 1991 to establish and promote Shari'ah standards. Today, AAOIFI standards are adopted in seven jurisdictions and several others base their regulations on them.
- The General Council for Islamic Banks and Financial Institutions (CIBAFI), established in Bahrain in 2001, promotes sector development and fosters and supports research, innovation, and training.
- The International Islamic Financial Market, set up in Bahrain in 2002, focuses on harmonizing the trading infrastructure through formal standards and guidelines.
- The Islamic Financial Services Board (IFSB), established in Kuala Lumpur, Malaysia, in 2003, sets standards and provides guidance for regulators with a view to identifying, managing, and disclosing risks associated with Islamic financial products.[120]

Several regulators have sought to drive standardization by establishing national Shariah advisory boards. The first one of these, the Shariah Advisory Council of Bank Negara Malaysia, was set up as early as 1997, and in 2009 it became the "sole authoritative body" for shariah standards in the country. Similar entities now operate in jurisdictions such as Indonesia and Pakistan. Oman established a centralized advisory board as early as 2014 but with a relatively narrow remit. The Central Bank of Kuwait published its instruction of Shariah Supervisory Governance for Kuwaiti Islamic Banks in 2016. The UAE Cabinet approved a central advisory board in 2016, while the Central Bank of Bahrain adopted new rules of independent external Sharia compliance audit in 2018, further requiring that rulings be made public. The CBB has also established a national Shariah Advisory Board.

Financial centers for all

The early 21st-century golden era for global finance prompted several countries to proactively develop the sector. The 1986 Big Bang helped transform the City of London into one of the most dynamic financial centers in the world. Ireland used a strategic approach to create the International Financial Services Center. Similar initiatives unfolded in Hong Kong and Singapore. The Gulf economies were quick to join in, attracted by the prospect of new avenues for economic diversification and jobs, not to mention innovative ways of financing their ambitious development plans. Bahrain was determined to consolidate its role as the Gulf financial hub and reconstituted the CBB as a unified regulator for the entire financial sector in 2006 while adopting a proactive approach to enabling the development of new market segments. But the country's successes did not go unnoticed.

Dubai found itself in a situation not dissimilar to that confronting Bahraini policymakers in the 1970s. Its modest oil reserves dwindling, future prosperity was seen to hinge on new growth drivers. The Dubai International Financial Center was set up in 2004 on the basis of jurisdictional fragmentation. The new development was built on a 110-acre site centered on its iconic Gate building as the first regional greenfield cluster for financial services. It was viewed as a credible proposition, not least because its free zone status freed it from the legacy challenges of existing laws.[121] The DIFC put in place its own independent regulator and a judicial system capitalizing on the popularity of English law for financial contracts. It permitted 100 percent foreign ownership and offered a 50-year no tax guarantee. A lack of local talent has been a constraint that tied Dubai even more firmly to international networks. The DIFC's rise was not a foregone conclusion, but impressive progress did materialize despite the global financial crisis. Dubai also cemented its position as a regional commodity trading hub. The Dubai Multi Commodities Centre was established in 2002 as another free zone. Its subsidiaries include the Dubai Diamond Exchange, the Dubai Pearl Exchanges, and the Dubai Gold & Commodity Exchange established in November 2005. A fully electronic platform, it initially focused on gold futures but also offers contracts in commodities such as oil and copper as well as Indian rupees, along with other currencies.

The Qatar Financial Center, chartered in 2005, drew on the free zone approach, albeit one based on a separate licensing process rather than a physical location. The QFC Regulatory Authority uses English common law, with dispute resolution carried out through the Qatar International Court and Dispute Resolution Center.[122] QFC prioritized infrastructure investment and project finance in a bid to empower local economic development. In 2007 the government announced a plan to use the QFC standards as the basis for merging the QFC Regulatory Authority, Qatar Central Bank, and the Qatar Financial Markets Authority into a single regulator by 2009. Progress proved thorny, however, until the new 2012 Central Bank Law established the QCB as the "high competent authority" responsible for the licensing, supervision, and regulation of "all financial services."[123] As a center, Doha has remained in the shadow of its regional rivals.

In 2008, Saudi Arabia initiated an ambitious project for the King Abdullah Financial District (KAFD), a massive purpose-built real estate development in the Al Aqeeq area in the north of Riyadh. Pojected costs have shot up from $7.5bn to something close to $20bn. The district covers 1.6mn sq m and includes 59 tower blocks with more than 3mn sq m of space. KAFD is ultimately expected to house a population of 50,000 residents whose movement is facilitated by a monorail and over 11 km of air-conditioned tubes. Concern has been expressed regarding the ability of the market to absorb the substantial capacity increase, and new incentives have been mooted in the form of tax breaks, easier visa rules, and separate regulations.

Abu Dhabi Global Market (ADGM) is the most recent entrant on the GCC financial landscape. Designated as a free zone in 2013, it opened for business on the 114-hectare Al Maryah Island in late 2015. ADGM has three independent authorities: the Registration Authority, the Financial Services Regulatory Authority, and the ADGM Courts. The free zone also has an arbitration center, and ADGM Academy is a local provider of financial education. Hub71, launched in March 2019, marks a diversification play designed to attract innovative technology start-ups to ADGM. Financial center rankings point to significant progress in recent years, and ADGM had nearly 3,000 registered entities in late 2020.[124]

Embracing technological change

The 2008 financial crisis unleashed a wave of innovation in global finance. An industry burdened by a plethora of economic challenges, reputational damage, and mounting regulatory pressures was spurred to seek efficiency gains and new development opportunities through technology. FinTech landed in the Gulf relatively late, doubtless partly because infrastructure spending and population growth delivered resilient credit growth dynamics, which reduced the urgency of innovation. However, governments region-wide now actively support FinTech, which also enjoys growing popularity as an avenue for entrepreneurship.

FinTech offers many attractive opportunities, such as improved access to finance, by reducing the cost of delivery and compliance, thereby increasing inclusion. Mobile payments can leverage the know-your-customer as well as the risk and security frameworks of telecommunications operators. The lower infrastructure needs allow services to be delivered at a fraction of the cost of traditional banking. FinTech opens up new opportunities with respect to the under- and unbanked in the Gulf, above all low-wage expatriate laborers but also groups such as women, youth, and new entrepreneurs.[125]

By better connecting sources of capital with its users, FinTech can stimulate entrepreneurship and economic diversification while also fostering financial education and literacy. Through increased transparency, it can help SMEs build credit profiles more quickly. Crowdfunding promises new channels for capital mobilization, although GCC regulations still significantly restrict access. Digitization can re-energize social financing by facilitating the collection of *zakah* and other payments while also simplifying charity fundraising. FinTech can enable Gulf-based businesses and entrepreneurs to gain access to other markets at a competitive cost.

FinTech presents fundamentally new opportunities for Islamic finance. Improved access to information can boost efficiency by permitting easier comparability and incentivizing standardization. It can facilitate the filtering out of practices and structures deemed objectionable. By boosting transparency while reducing costs, FinTech can potentially put Islamic finance on a more level playing field with conventional finance. Apart from better customer interface and a responsive service delivery mechanism, FinTech can better harness market data and behavior analytics to further enhance the customer experience. IFIs can also create customer interfaces that go beyond the narrow remit of financial products; for instance, by linking financial choices to the broader *halal* economy.

FinTech, specifically RegTech, also promises to transform financial regulation by using increased transparency to reduce reliance on costly compliance burdens. After all, a key goal of regulation is to reduce informational asymmetries that entail risks. This can, in principle, be done through increased data capture and analytics empowered by technology. For instance, the BlockChain distributive ledger technology can create an unalterable digital record of transactions, which effectively eliminates the risk of errors from deliberate data/record manipulation. Greater transparency becomes achievable without institutional centralization or aggressive compliance burdens. We may be nearing a point where market transparency and reliability are more likely to be achieved through technology than through costly disclosure and reporting requirements.

Conclusion: Work in progress

Despite decades of growth and diversification, the GCC financial sector remains lop-sided, dominated by banks that, moreover, lag behind their OECD peers in terms of their asset base and lending. Azzam's 35-year-old verdict still rings true: "To attract private capital into the development process, a more sophisticated financial market need[s] to be developed, including the creation of new financial intermediaries, new investment instruments, ... efficient stock markets, investment funds and venture capital companies."[126] A recent IMF assessment reached astonishingly similar conclusions, noting that the overall "level of financial development ..., other than for Saudi Arabia, appears to be lower than would be expected given economic fundamentals."[127] Moreover, "institutionalization ... is proceeding within the financial sector in many ways as a result of economic growth, rather than as a precursor or foundation of economic growth."[128] The sector is yet to fully transcend its traditional reactive posture.

The continued dominance of retail banks entails limitations on the availability of capital – and appropriate financial solutions – for the development of the corporate sector and, ultimately, for economic diversification. Despite its substantial scale, corporate lending is very heavily tilted toward trade, services, and property, reflecting a long-standing cultural tendency to privilege "real estate and tangible assets as equity."[129] By contrast, the progress of credit bureaus and alternative collateralization mechanisms (e.g., through movables) remains modest. These factors deter entrepreneurs from innovative, higher risk ventures and help explain the declining returns to investments.[130]

Table 5.2 Assets of GCC financial institutions vs. comparators, 2017

	GCC	*US*	*Japan*	*Large emerging markets**
$ bn				
Financial institutions	2,855	50,886	24,391	38,687
Commercial banks	2,282	22,106	17,694	32,138
Non-bank financial institutions	573	28,781	6,697	6,549
Percent of total assets of financial institutions				
Commercial banks	80	43	73	83
Non-bank financial institutions	20	57	27	17
Percent of GDP				
Financial institutions	196	273	494	184
Commercial banks	156	119	358	141
Non-bank financial institutions	39	155	135	44
Private sector credit	72	53	100	52

*The grouping includes Brazil, China, India, Russia, and South Africa. The figures given are averages for the group.

Source: IMF, How Developed and Inclusive, p. 5.

Relatively weak competitive pressures in the Gulf banking sector, partly because of substantial government stakes and historical limitations on foreign ownership, curb inclusion and innovation. Thanks to strong margins made possible by good ratings and a low-cost deposit base, GCC banks have traditionally felt less pressure to embrace riskier activities such as SME lending, which makes up only some 4.5 percent of bank portfolios. Rejection rates of SME loan applications are multiples of advanced economy levels. The product range is often limited and collateral requirements excessive and almost invariably linked to immovable assets. While recent reforms on insolvency regulations will likely reduce the potential losses associated with SME loans, the room for improvement is considerable, "with banks recovering only 30 to 40 percent on defaulted loans compared to an average of 72 percent for advanced economies."[131]

Despite its shortcomings, financial sector development in the Gulf has created an increasingly diverse range of funding solutions. Saudi Arabia now boasts a globally substantial stock exchange that, especially since the Aramco listing in December 2019, is well diversified, with some 200 equities along with other instruments. The Gulf markets have opened up to foreign investors, which is attracting substantial amounts of institutional capital but also increasing analyst attention on regional corporations. While progress in the fixed income space is recent, new structures and increased sovereign issuance have delivered transformative change. But local currency markets are lagging, behind while only the top tier of the corporate sector participates. The underdevelopment of institutional investors has adverse implications for liquidity, market stability, governance, and transparency.

Completing the structural transformation of the Gulf financial sector from a passive distributor of oil windfalls to an effective driver of capital pooling and allocation will be critical for the economic future of the region.

To date, the regional financial institutions have been better at upholding the status quo than at channeling capital into new areas, a role that still tends to fall disproportionately on public funding vehicles. The regional venture capital and private equity industry, initially hard hit by the global financial crisis, is growing again but remains small and retains a significant real estate bias.

The further diversification of the Gulf financial sector constitutes an important priority going forward. The potential benefits of such a transformation are compelling, with the IMF estimating that "further financial development could be associated with higher annual per capita income growth of 0.4–0.7 percentage points in some GCC countries and increased financial inclusion could be associated with higher growth of some 0.3–0.7 percentage points."[132] But sustainable progress will hinge on continued regulatory and institutional reform, including the willingness of governments to overhaul their pension systems and more proactively develop the market for collective savings instruments. Gradual though progress may prove, it should benefit from fiscal consolidation and the aging of the population.

Notes

1 Azzam, *The Gulf Economies*, p. 67.
2 Azzam, *The Gulf Economies*, p. 33; Callen and Qu, "A Fiscal Framework," p. 19.
3 Chaudhry, The Price of Wealth, p. 65; http://www.sama.gov.sa/en-US/Currency/Pages/HistoricalInfo.aspx; Peterson, *Saudi Arabia*, pp. 19–21.
4 Ramady, *The Saudi Arabian Economy*, p. 80.
5 Sherbiny, *Oil and the Internationalization*, p. 5; Wilson, "Financial Development in the Arab Gulf," pp. 179–180; Dew, *History of Banking in Bahrain*, pp. 19–20.
6 Quoted in: Chaudhry, *The Price of Wealth*, p. 228.
7 Wilson, "Financial Development in the Arab Gulf," pp. 181–190.
8 Peterson, *Saudi Arabia under Ibn Saud*, p. 66.
9 Presley and Wilson, *Banking in the Arab Gulf*, pp. 18–19, 47–49, 69–70, 91–92, 112–113.
10 Peterson, *Saudi Arabia under Ibn Saud*, p. 117; Al-Suhaimi, "Consolidation, Competition, Foreign Presence," p. 128; Presley and Wilson, *Banking in the Arab Gulf*, pp. 92–94.
11 Sherbiny, *Oil and the Internationalization*, p. 9.
12 Presley and Wilson, *Banking in the Arab Gulf*, pp. 49–50.
13 Presley and Wilson, *Banking in the Arab Gulf*, pp. 70, 93–95, 112.
14 Presley and Wilson, *Banking in the Arab Gulf*, p. 19; Seznec and Mosis, *The Financial Markets*, p. 94.
15 Al-Sabah, *The Oil Economy of Kuwait*, p. 65.
16 Al-Sabah, *The Oil Economy of Kuwait*, p. 65; Chaudhry, *The Price of Wealth*, pp. 231–232.
17 Quoted in: Al-Kuwari, *Oil Revenues in the Gulf Emirates*, p. 174.
18 Braunstein, "Domestic Sources," pp. 4–5.
19 Al-Kuwari, *Oil Revenues in the Gulf Emirates*, pp. 80–81, 100–101.
20 Al-Kuwari, *Oil Revenues in the Gulf Emirates*, p. 102.
21 Owen and Pamuk, *A History*, p. 216.
22 Niblock, *The Political Economy*, p. 36.
23 Presley and Wilson, *Banking in the Arab Gulf*, pp. 18–21; Knauerhase, *The Saudi Arabian Economy*, pp. 250–256; Al-Suhaimi, "Consolidation, Competition, Foreign Presence," p. 128.

24 Knauerhase, *The Saudi Arabian Economy*, p. 238; El Mallakh, *Saudi Arabia*, p. 296.
25 El Mallakh, *Qatar: The Development*, p. 131.
26 Seznec and Mosis, *The Financial Markets*, pp. 155–157.
27 Braunstein, "Domestic Sources," p. 1; Amar *et al.*, *GCC Sovereign Wealth Funds*, p. 2; https://en.wikipedia.org/wiki/Dubai_Ports_World_controversy.
28 Asutay, "GCC Sovereign Wealth Funds," p. 7 (in an online version); Seznec and Mosis, *The Financial Markets*, p. 162; https://www.researchgate.net/publication/228122916_GCC_Sovereign_Wealth_Funds_and_Their_Role_in_the_European_and_American_Markets; Greene and Yeager, "Sovereign Wealth Funds," p. 258.
29 Andrew England and Simeon Kerr, "Cash-Rich Gulf Funds Hunt for Bargains as Asset Prices Plunge," *Financial Times*, 16 April 2020.
30 Seznec and Mosis, *The Financial Markets*, p. 159.
31 Naser, "The Role," p. 1660.
32 Sherbiny, *Oil and the Internationalization*, p. 12.
33 Sherbiny, *Oil and the Internationalization*, p. 16.
34 Gerakis and Roncesvalles, "Bahrain's Offshore Banking Center," pp. 271–273.
35 Ghantus, "The Financial Center," p. 135; Dew, *History of Banking in Bahrain*, p. 61.
36 Mogielnicki, *A Political Economy of Free Zones*, p. 111; Ghantus, "The Financial Center," p. 137.
37 Sherbiny, *Oil and the Internationalization*, p. 31.
38 Sherbiny, *Oil and the Internationalization*, p. 33.
39 Sherbiny, *Oil and the Internationalization*, p. 31.
40 Dew, *History of Banking in Bahrain*, p. 64.
41 Gerakis and Roncesvalles, "Bahrain's Offshore Banking Center," pp. 281–287.
42 Sherbiny, *Oil and the Internationalization*, pp. 23–24.
43 Chaudhry, *The Price of Wealth*, p. 233; Abdeen and Shook, *Saudi Financial System*, p. 69.
44 Azzam, *The Gulf Economies*, p. 67.
45 Lawson, "Managing Economic Crises," p. 52.
46 Al-Sabah, *The Oil Economy of Kuwait*, p. 73.
47 Owen and Pamuk, *A History*, p. 213.
48 Chaudhry, *The Price of Wealth*, p. 236.
49 Chaudhry, *The Price of Wealth*, p. 232.
50 Chaudhry, *The Price of Wealth*, p. 238.
51 Chaudhry, *The Price of Wealth*, p. 238.
52 Al-Suhaimi, "Consolidation, Competition," p. 129.
53 Chaudhry, *The Price of Wealth*, p. 277.
54 Azzam, *The Gulf Economies*, p. 4.
55 Chaudhry, *The Price of Wealth*, p. 281.
56 Al-Suhaimi, "Consolidation, Competition," p. 129.
57 Al-Suhaimi, "Consolidation, Competition," p. 129.
58 Presley and Wilson, *Banking in the Arab Gulf*, p. 119.
59 Al-Hassan *et al.*, "The GCC Banking Sector," p. 5.
60 Al-Hassan *et al.*, "The GCC Banking Sector," pp. 4, 9.
61 Espinoza *et al.*, *The Macroeconomics*, p. 10.
62 Setser and Ziemba, *GCC Sovereign Funds*, p. 20; Al-Hassan *et al.*, "The GCC Banking Sector," p. 6.
63 *Public Investment Fund Program 2021–2025*, https://www.pif.gov.sa/VRP%202025%20Downloadables%20EN/PIFStrategy2021-2025-EN.pdf.
64 Alkhaldi, *Saudi Capital Market*, p. 16.
65 Azzam, *The Emerging Arabic Capital Markets*, p. 183.
66 Field, *The Merchants*, pp. 309–310.
67 Zahlan, *The Making of the Modern Gulf States*, p. 74.

68 Crystal, *Kuwait*, p. 107.
69 Marmore, *Souq Al-Manakh*, p. 8.
70 Azzam, *The Emerging Arabic Capital Markets*, p. 184.
71 Alkhaldi, *Saudi Capital Market*, p. 16.
72 Azzam, *The Emerging Arab Capital Markets*, p. 141.
73 Azzam, *The Gulf Economies*, p. 78.
74 Lawson, "Managing Economic Crises," pp. 47–48; Azzam, *The Emerging Arab Capital Markets*, p. 169.
75 Jbili *et al.*, *Financial Systems*, p. 14.
76 Jbili *et al.*, *Financial Systems*, p. 16.
77 Jbili *et al.*, *Financial Systems*, p. 15; Azzam, *The Emerging Arab Capital Markets*, pp. 264–265.
78 Al-Hassan *et al.*, "IPO Behavior in GCC Countries," p. 22; Lerner *et al.*, *The CMA*, p. 3.
79 Lerner *et al.*, *The CMA*, pp. 2, 5.
80 Lerner *et al.*, *The CMA*, p. 5.
81 Lerner *et al.*, *The CMA*, pp. 7–8.
82 IMF, *How Developed and Inclusive*, p. 8.
83 pwc Middle East, *GCC Capital Markets Watch*, https://www.pwc.com/m1/en/publications/capital-markets-watch.html.
84 IMF, *How Developed and Inclusive*, p. 12.
85 Azzam, *The Emerging Middle East Financial Markets*, p. 15.
86 https://cma.org.sa/en/Market/QFI/Pages/default.aspx
87 https://www.saudiexchange.sa/wps/wcm/connect/24dfec23-8229-4668-92a3-a8679ddbfa7d/Monthly+Trading+and+Ownership+By+Nationality+Report+30-12-2021.pdf?MOD=AJPERES&CONVERT_TO=url&CACHEID=ROOTWORKSPACE-24dfec23–8229–4668–92a3-a8679ddbfa7d-nUqoxmK
88 Ramady, *The Saudi Arabian Economy*, p. 92.
89 Azzam, *The Emerging Arab Capital Markets*, pp. 80–83, 85.
90 Azzam, *The Emerging Arab Capital Markets*, pp. 76, 87.
91 Woertz, *GCC Bond Markets*, p. 4.
92 Iqbal and Molyneux, *Thirty Years of Islamic Banking*, pp. 7–12, 134–140.
93 Al-Saeed, *Sukuk Issuance in Saudi Arabia*, p. 27.
94 IMF, *How Developed and Inclusive*, p. 8.
95 Alshammri *et al.*, *A Comparative Study*; Alshammri *et al.*, "A Comparative Study," pp. 359–361.
96 Alshammri *et al.*, "A comparative study," pp. 360–361.
97 Alshammri *et al.*, *A Comparative Study*; Alshammri *et al.*, "A Comparative Study," p. 360.
98 Alshammri *et al.*, *A Comparative Study*; Alshammri *et al.*, "A Comparative Study," p. 358; Alpen Capital, *GCC Insurance Industry*, p. 14.
99 Alshammri *et al.*, *A Comparative Study*; Alshammri *et al.*, "A Comparative Study," p. 359; Alpen Capital, *GCC Insurance Industry*, pp. 15–16.
100 Alpen Capital, *GCC Insurance Industry*, pp. 10–12, 21, Swiss Re.
101 Alshammri *et al.*, "A Comparative Study," p. 358.
102 Alshammri *et al.*, "A Comparative Study," pp. 359–261.
103 Alpen Capital, *GCC Insurance Industry*, p. 13.
104 Alpen Capital, *GCC Insurance Industry*, p. 53; regional regulators.
105 Alpen Capital, *GCC Insurance Industry*, pp. 8, 30, 57; Jarmo T. Kotilaine, "Insurance, the Way It Is Meant to Be Is Just Getting Started," *Arab News*, 17 July 2022.
106 World Bank, "Deepening Reforms," pp. 33–34.
107 World Bank, "Deepening Reforms," p. 33.
108 EY, *Fast Growth, Divergent Paths*, pp. 10–12.
109 Attia and Price, *Arab Pension Systems*, p. 63.

110 Attia and Price, *Arab Pension Systems*, pp. 37, 63.
111 Dew, *History of Banking*, p. 92.
112 Presley and Wilson, *Banking in the Arab Gulf*, pp. 14, 146–147.
113 Dew, *History of Banking*, p. 95.
114 IMF, *How Developed and Inclusive*, p. 6.
115 IMF, *How Developed and Inclusive*, p. 7.
116 Iqbal and Molyneux, *Thirty Years of Islamic Banking*, pp. 107–122.
117 "Most sukuk 'not Islamic', body claims," Reuters, 21 November 2007, https://www.arabianbusiness.com/markets/equities/sukuk/most-sukuk-not-islamic-body-claims-197156; International Islamic Financial Market, *Sukuk Report*, pp. 18–19.
118 Zaheer and van Wijnbergen, "Sukuk Defaults."
119 Iqbal and Molyneux, *Thirty Years of Islamic Banking*, p. 109.
120 Iqbal and Molyneux, *Thirty Years of Islamic Banking*, pp. 59–65.
121 Mogielnicki, *A Political Economy of Free Zones*, p. 137.
122 Mogielnicki, *A Political Economy of Free Zones*, p. 117.
123 The Law of the QCB and the Regulation of Financial Institutions (Law no. (13) of 2012), qcb.gov.qa.
124 Mogielnicki, *A Political Economy of Free Zones*, pp. 62–64.
125 World Bank, *The Global Findex Database*; CGAP, "Islamic Microfinance: An Emerging Market Niche," p. 1.
126 Azzam, *The Gulf Economies*, p. 43.
127 IMF, *How Developed and Inclusive*, p. 3.
128 Young, *Markets Serving States*, p. 4.
129 Young, *Markets Serving States*, p. 5; IMF, *How Developed and Inclusive*, p. 6.
130 IMF, *How Developed and Inclusive*, p. 3.
131 IMF, *How Developed and Inclusive*, p. 19; Young, *Markets Serving States*, p. 17.
132 IMF, *How Developed and Inclusive*, p. 26.

References

Abdeen, Adnan M. and Dale N. Shook (1984), *The Saudi Financial System: In the Context of Western and Islamic Finance*, Chichester: John Wiley & Sons.

Alpen Capital (2019), *GCC Insurance Industry*, November 29, 2019.

Amar, Jeanne, Jean-François Carpantier, and Christelle Lecourt (2018). *GCC Sovereign Wealth Funds: Why Do They Take Control?*, Ecole d'éonomie d'Aix-Marseille Working Papers, No. 35.

Asutay, Mehmet (2011), "GCC Sovereign Wealth Funds and Their Role in the European and American Markets," *Equilibri*, vol. 12, no. 3 (December), pp. 335–354.

Attia, Habib and William Price (2017), *Arab Pension Systems: Trends, Challenges and Options for Reforms*, Washington, D.C.: World Bank Group.

Azzam, Henry T. (1988), *The Gulf Economies in Transition*, London: Macmillan Press.

——— (1997), *The Emerging Arab Capital Markets: Investment Opportunities in Relatively Underplayed Markets*, London: Kegan Paul International.

——— (2015), *The Emerging Middle East Financial Markets*, Bloomington, Ind.: AuthorHouse.

Braunstein, Juergen (2018), "Domestic Sources of Twenty-First-Century Geopolitics: Domestic Politics and Sovereign Wealth Funds in GCC Economies," *New Political Economy*, DOI: 10.1080/13563467.2018.1431619.

Callen, Tim and Haonan Qu (2015), "A Fiscal Framework to Support Growth and Manage Dependence on Natural Resource Revenues," in: Al-Darwish *et al.*, *op. cit.*, pp. 19–36.

CGAP (2008), "Islamic Microfinance: An Emerging Market Niche," *Focus Note*, no. 49 (August).

Chaudhry, Kiren Aziz (1997), *The Price of Wealth: Economics and Institutions in the Middle East* (*Cornell Studies in Political Economy*), Ithaca, NY: Cornell University Press.

Al-Darwish, Ahmed, Naif Alghaith, Alberto Behar, Tim Callen, Pragyan Deb, Amgad Hegazy, Padamja Khandelwal, Malika Pant, and Haonan Qu (2015), *Saudi Arabia; Tackling Emerging Economic Challenges to Sustain Growth*, Washington, D.C.: International Monetary Fund.

Dew, Philip (2011), *History of Banking in Bahrain*, Manama: Metro Graphics.

Espinoza, Raphael, Ghada Fayad, and Ananthakrishnan Prasad (2013), *The Macroeconomics of the Arab States of the Gulf*, Oxford: Oxford University Press.

EY (2015), *Fast Growth, Divergent Paths: The EY GCC Wealth and Asset Management Report 2015*, ey.com/mena.

Gerakis, A.S. and O. Roncesvalles (1983), "Bahrain's Offshore Banking Center," *Economic Development and Cultural Change*, vol. 31, no. 2 (January), pp. 271–293.

Ghantus, Elias T. (1985), "The Financial Center and Its Future," in: Nugent and Thomas, *op. cit.*, pp. 132–142.

Al-Hassan, Abdullah, Fernando Delgado, and Mohammed Omran (2007), "IPO Behavior in GCC Countries: Goody-Two-Shoes or Bad-to-the-Bone?," IMF Working Paper, WP/07/149, Washington, D.C.: International Monetary Fund.

Al-Hassan, Abdullah, May Khamis, and Nada Oulidi (2010), "The GCC Banking Sector: Topography and Analysis," IMF Working Paper, WP/10/87, Washington, D.C.: International Monetary Fund.

International Islamic Financial Market (2010), *Sukuk Report*, 1st edition, Manama.

International Monetary Fund (2018), *How Developed and Inclusive Are Financial Systems in the GCC?*, Gulf Cooperation Council/IMF Policy Paper, Washington, D.C.: International Monetary Fund.

Iqbal, Munawar and Philip Molyneux (2005), *Thirty Years of Islamic Banking: History, Performance and Prospects*, Basingstoke: Palgrave Macmillan.

Jbili, Abdelali, Vicente Galbis, Amer Bisat, and Cyrus Sassanpour (1997), *Financial Systems and Labor Markets in the Gulf Cooperation Council Countries*, Washington, D.C.: Middle Eastern Department, International Monetary Fund.

KAMCO Invest (2023), "GCC Fixed Income Market: 2022 – The Year That Was ...," *Investment Strategy & Research*, January 2023.

——— (2023), "GCC IPOs: 2022 – The Year That Was ...," *Investment Strategy & Research*, January 2023.

Knauerhase, Ramon (1975), *The Saudi Arabian Economy*, New York: Prager.

Al-Kuwari, Ali Khalifa (1978), *Oil Revenues in the Gulf Emirates: Patterns of Allocation and Impact on Economic Development*, Boulder, Colo.: Westview Press.

Lawson, Fred H. (1991), "Managing Economic Crises: The Role of the State in Bahrain and Kuwait," *Studies in Comparative International Development*, vol. 26, no. 1 (Spring), pp. 43–67.

Lerner, Josh, Ann Leamon, and Steve Dew (2017), *The CMA and the Saudi Stock Market Crash of 2006*, Riyadh: Bella Research Group, Capital Market Authority.

El Mallakh, Ragaei (1979), *Qatar: The Development of an Oil Industry*, Boulder, Colo.: International Research Center for Energy and Economic Development.

Marmore MENA Intelligence (2019), *Souq Al-Manakh & Five Other GCC Crises: 6 Lessons for our Economic Sustainability*, Kuwait: Markaz/Kuwait Financial Center K.P.S.C.

Mogielnicki, Robert (2021), *A Political Economy of Free Zones in Gulf Arab States* (*International Political Economy Series*), London: Palgrave Macmillan.

Naser, Hanan (2016), "The Role of the Gulf Cooperation Council's Sovereign Wealth Funds in the New Era of Oil," *International Journal of Economics and Financial Issues*, vol. 6, no. 4, pp. 1657–1664.

Niblock, Tim, with Monica Malik (2007), *The Political Economy of Saudi Arabia*, Abingdon: Routledge.

Nugent, Jeffrey B. and Theodore H. Thomas, eds. (1985), *Bahrain and the Gulf: Past Perspectives and Alternative Futures*, London: Croom Helm.

Owen, E. Roger and Şevket Pamuk (1999), *A History of Middle East Economies in the Twentieth Century*, Cambridge, Mass.: Harvard University Press.

Peterson, John E. (2018), *Saudi Arabia under Ibn Saud: Economic and Financial Foundations of the State*, London: I.B. Tauris.

Presley, John R. and Rodney Wilson (1991), *Banking in the Arab Gulf*, Basingstoke: Macmillan.

Ramady, Mohamed A. (2010), *The Saudi Arabian Economy: Policies, Achievements, and Challenges*, 2nd edition, New York: Springer.

Al Sabah, Yusuf S.T. (1980), *Oil Economy of Kuwait*, London: Keegan Paul International.

Al-Saeed, Khalid Sulaiman (2012), *Sukuk Issuance in Saudi Arabia: Recent Trends and Positive Expectations*, Ph.D. dissertation, School of Government and International Affairs, Durham University.

Setser, Brad and Rachel Ziemba (2009), *GCC Sovereign Funds: Reversal of Fortune*, Working Paper, New York: Council on Foreign Relations, Center for Geoeconomic Studies.

Seznec, Jean-François and Samer Mosis (2018), *The Financial Markets of the Arab Gulf: Power, Politics and Money* (*Routledge International Studies in Money and Banking*), New York: Routledge.

Alshammri, Ahmad Alrazni, Syed Musa Alhabshi, and Buerhan Saiti (2016), *A Comparative Study of the Historical and Current Development of the GCC Insurance and Takaful Industry*, The 18th Malaysian Finance Association Annual Conference (MFAC), Malacca, Malaysia, 29 May 2016.

Alshammri, Ahmad Alrazni, Syed Musa Syed Jaafar Alhabshi, and Buerhan Saiti (2018), "A Comparative Study of the Historical and Current Development of the GCC Insurance and Takaful Industry," *Journal of Islamic Marketing*, vol. 9, no. 2, pp. 356–369.

Sherbiny, Naiem A. (1985), *Oil and the Internationalization of Arab Banks*, Oxford: Oxford Institute for Energy Studies.

Al-Suhaimi, Jammaz (2001), "Consolidation, Competition, Foreign Presence and Systemic Stability in the Saudi Banking Industry," *BIS Papers*, vol. 4, pp. 128–132.

Wilson, Rodney (1987), "Financial Development in the Arab Gulf: The Eastern Bank Experience, 1917–1950," *Business History*, vol. 29, no. 2, pp. 178–198.

Woertz, Eckart (2008), *GCC Bond Markets*, Gulf Research Center, December.

World Bank (2018), "Deepening Reforms – In Focus: Pension Systems in the Gulf," *Gulf Economic Monitor*, No. 2, Washington, D.C.: World Bank Group.

Young, Karen E. (2015), *Markets Serving States: The Institutional Bases of Financial Governance in the Gulf Cooperation Council States*, LSE Kuwait Programme, No. 38, London: London School of Economics, September 2015.

Zaheer, Sajjad and Sweder J.G. van Wijnbergen (2013), "*Sukuk* Defaults: On Distress Resolution in Islamic Finance," Tinbergen Institute Discussion Paper, TI 2013–087/VI, first draft, July 2013.

Zahlan, Rosemarie Said (1989), *The Making of the Modern Gulf States: Kuwait, Bahrain, Qatar, the United Arab Emirates and Oman*, London: Unwin Hyman.

Zein, Aidrous Irina Ahmed and Sofya Glavina Grigorievna (2016), "IPO in the Countries of the Gulf Cooperation Council," *Miscellanea Geographica – Regional Studies on Development*, vol. 20, no. 3.

6 Build it and they will come

Infrastructure was a central plank of the Arabian development narrative in the 1970s. Amid the sudden financial plenty, modern high-rise blocks pushed aside old mudbrick houses while multilane expressways reshaped the region's cities and wove them into national networks. Governments commissioned prestige projects unseen in the region. Although this momentum came to be tested by the austerity of the 1980s and 1990s, the passion for infrastructure never disappeared thanks to demographics and diversification. In the lower Gulf it in fact gathered steam.

The infrastructure narrative returned with redoubled force at the dawn of the third millennium when several potent drivers coalesced to produce a fundamental shift in economic policy. Some of these were structural trends that had been in the making for years but were disrupted by temporary challenges. Others were more ad hoc in nature, but the Gulf governments proved remarkably astute in harnessing them. But it was above all the onset of the "third oil boom" by 2003 that ushered in this era of feverish development by once again casting aside capital constraints.

Even as the return of large infrastructure projects on the development agenda marked a déjà vu, the strategic context began to shift in important ways. Following the extreme economic rollercoaster ride of the preceding three decades, project investment was recognized as something much more than just a way of absorbing the hydrocarbons windfall. The traditional role of the government as the ultimate underwriter gave way to a more mixed model. Perhaps most significant, this Great Arabian Infrastructure Boom was not driven by sheer necessity but, rather, rested on a new, ambitious vision for the future of the Arabian peninsula in the post–Cold War global order. After a period of quiet, the Gulf now was catapulted into global consciousness even more forcefully, and also quite differently, than in the 1970s.

Building the road to modernity

Infrastructure has always been instrumental in putting the Arabian Peninsula on the global map. In the 19th century, steamships pushed up traffic volumes while reshuffling the hierarchy of Arabian ports. In the 1930s, airports added another important mode of global connectivity. Physical infrastructure became a salient concomitant of oil wealth, which financed everything from power generation to transportation and communications, not to mention education and health care.

DOI: 10.4324/9781003373353-6

The 1962 Ten-Point Program of the future Saudi Arabian King Faisal, published during his tenure as prime minister, expressly placed the immediate development emphasis on physical infrastructure and industry. Investments in roads and water were highlighted as areas of particular importance for the economic unification and integration of the Kingdom.[1] Similar developments unfolded region-wide until the meager 1980s forced the Gulf governments to aggressively pare back their project budgets. This was not an altogether negative phenomenon after a period of breakneck development that had fueled inflation and created excess capacity. It was also possible to argue that "the big projects are almost completed, the basic infrastructure is in place; a slowdown was inevitable."[2] Some of the more ambitious ventures conceived in the boom days continued, albeit sometimes scaled back or implemented with delays. But the oil price correction proved much more disruptive in the upper Gulf than in the lower Gulf. Dubai benefited from rising revenues as its hydrocarbons sectors was still in a buildup phase. Investments in the massive North Field in the 1990s allowed Qatar to sail against the wind. Oman's Sultan Qaboos put in place an ambitious modernization program funded through capacity increases in the oil sector. The lower Gulf economies were able to accelerate progress by adopting practices trialed by their northern neighbors. While the potential competitiveness drivers in the lower Gulf were not dramatically different from the rest of the peninsula, the later start pushed these countries to innovate in ways that would ultimately dramatically reshape the regional development narrative.

A new world order

If the twilight of the 20th century profoundly challenged the Arabian development ambitions, the after-tremors of the 1970s crisis worked their way through the entire global economy in transformative ways. The West experienced macroeconomic turbulence unseen in the post–World War II era, with persistent inflation and record unemployment that unleashed a potent yearning for change. Margaret Thatcher in the UK and Ronald Reagan and George Bush in the US ushered in a profound shift in economic thinking that soon went global. The postwar dirigisme and welfare state caved to a new political consensus underpinned by free market liberalism. A wave of deregulation transformed finance, trade, and business.

The economic rebound of the West dealt a mortal blow to the Cold War division of the world as the increasingly costly arms race proved beyond the capabilities of the Soviet-led Eastern Block. Efforts to reform the sclerotic system of central planning through Mikhail Gorbachev's perestroika program proved too little, too late and ultimately brought down the Soviet regime. A new era also beckoned for China. The reforms of Deng Xiaoping in the late 1970s unleashed a growth champion that would in time fundamentally reshape the global balance of power. The awakening giant developed a growing dependency on imported raw materials: "China became a net oil importer in 1993 and a net natural gas importer in 2007. It moved from depending on iron ore imports for only 3 percent of consumption in 1981 to more than half by 2003, while similar trends prevailed for other mineral resources."[3]

The triumphant free market opinion came to be enshrined in the so-called Washington Consensus that gave rise to a new ethos of globalization. Economic liberalization began to challenge the old First World–Third World division much as it had brought down the Berlin Wall. International trade boomed, expanding at roughly twice the rate of global GDP growth between 1985 and 2007, further facilitated by technological innovation. The rise of containerization in the 1970s had created an efficient multimodal structure and dramatically increased the size of ships and ports alike.[4]

A new era of "emerging markets" dawned. Acronyms like BRICs captured the minds of investors, while lower trade barriers, improving access to capital, and infrastructure upgrades transformed the dynamics of global commerce. Western companies outsourced production to emerging economies such as China that became a globally leading manufacturing powerhouse. The Chinese appetite for raw materials pushed global commodity prices up nearly four-fold in 2002–mid-2008 while crude prices rose eight times – only years after low oil prices had come to be viewed as the norm.[5] These realities dramatically boosted the value of the Arabian Peninsula as a supplier of commodities but also as an attractive hub in the evolving global economic order. Echoing centuries-old patterns, the location of the Gulf became its most powerful trump card.

Other factors further sped up this transformation. The tragic events of 11 September 2001 drew increased scrutiny to global capital flows, prompting many Gulf institutions and individuals to explore new opportunities for capital mobilization at home. Concurrently, the oil windfalls pushed up the gross official GCC reserves from $71.9bn in 2002 to $514.6bn in 2008.[6] This confluence of powerful economic forces meant that reversing the stagnation of the 1980s and 1990s proved far more dramatic than anyone could have anticipated, with the heady optimism driving Gulf policymakers to devise plans that grew more ambitious by the day.

Nowhere did these trends collide with a more transformative impact than in Dubai, which, contemplating the twilight of its short history as a minor oil producer, was desperate for new sources of prosperity. Feverish innovation during the closing decades of the 20th century had allowed Dubai to introduce important new elements to its development narrative. Above all, this strategic refocusing sought to capitalize on the region's unique geography through world-class connective infrastructure. Of course, what made sense for Dubai also made sense for virtually the entire Gulf region, which now embarked on the most massive infrastructure boom in its history. After two decades of austerity with the demographic drivers and diversification needs largely intact, many of the projects proved easy to justify. The growing tidal wave of oil wealth, as well as the era of the "Great Moderation" in global economic policy, removed many financial constraints.

Dubai dreaming

Dubai took on the mantle of the leading regional innovator in economic policy at the dawn of the new millennium.[7] Within a remarkably short period of time, the city has refashioned itself and continues to morph with a cosmopolitan flavor matched by few. This rise capitalized on the emirate's history as a haven for free trade and enterprise. Never a truly local settlement, Dubai early on "progressed beyond the too-many-foreigners complex."[8] It was not a typical outlet for a local hinterland but rather an *entrepôt* serving the maritime traders passing through it. Dubai's hinterland was the Gulf.[9] Having emerged as the *primus inter pares* among the Trucial ports, Dubai leveraged the 1971 establishment of the UAE to amplify its ambitions. The city was receptive to experimentation in a laissez-faire environment where "ideas crackled like fireworks."[10] Such creativity was recognized as critical for securing the city's regional standing and created a unique backdrop for its development designs.

The first major success of Dubai's global ambitions was the Jebel Ali Free Zone, which many had dismissed in the 1980s as a fanciful venture. But it rested on an underappreciated strategic vision at an opportune time: "For Dubai, the onset of containerization at a time when the emirate was in a process of building up its infrastructure was an opportunity – albeit a risky one – to invest in a new technology to ensure its place as a focal-point trading centre and to outpace and outflank potential rivals, by being more efficient in handling cargo."[11] In the end, the region's largest harbor gained traction remarkably quickly, and a combination of new infrastructure investment and regulatory innovation soon allowed it to expand far beyond the original designs. Jebel Ali proved a game-changer on multiple fronts. It confirmed the attractiveness of the locational advantages of the Gulf while demonstrating that ambitious local infrastructure investments could yield attractive returns. Emerging as the regional port of choice, Jebel Ali pushed up Dubai's share of GCC container volumes from 32 percent in 1985 to 47 percent by 1995 and 50 percent in 2015. During these three decades, the region-wide container trade volume climbed 20-fold to 31.1mn TEUs. Jebel Ali continued to grow and innovate, ready to accommodate the evolving needs of an expanding shipping industry.[12] In recent years, the Jebel Ali Free Zone is estimated to have accounted for close to third the foreign direct investment coming into Dubai. In 2018, it generated more than a third of Dubai's GDP and 10.7 percent of the UAE GDP. It delivered 70 percent of the value generated by Dubai's free zones. Jebel Ali further accounted for 16.2 percent of total employment in Dubai and 7.5 percent in the UAE.[13]

Other bold innovations contributed to Dubai's take-off. Within a relatively period of short time, Emirates airline transformed itself into a global "super-connector." Thanks to concomitant investments in the Dubai International Airport, Dubai saw an exponential rise in passenger numbers to 12.3mn in 2000, 27.4mn in 2008, and 88.2mn in 2017. In 2018, some 120 airlines operated from Dubai International, servicing more than 260 destinations. Linked in multiple ways to the city's rise as a tourism hub, just before the onset of the COVID-19 pandemic DBX reached the status of the busiest airport in the world, with its passenger traffic exceeding 90mn a year.

The expanding reach of Emirates fed Dubai's tourism designs, for which it served as an effective advertisement. The Dubai Commerce and Tourism Promotion Board was established as early as 1989 to promote the city as an up-market destination for business and leisure travelers. 2013 saw the launch of the Dubai Tourism Strategy 2020, which set the ambitious target of attracting 20mn annual visitors to the city, little different from the 19mn flocking to London in 2016. This was projected to rise further to 23–25mn by 2025. Dubai grabbed the attention of the world with increasingly fantastic ventures such as the Burj al Arab hotel, which set a new standard in luxury but also became the tallest hotel building on the planet, not to mention an iconic symbol. Reclamation projects such as the Palm Island and the World Islands reshaped the emirate's coastline to create more beaches and seafront properties. The opening years of the new millennium saw a growing tally of ambitious designs for new attractions, ever larger shopping malls, and hotels. In the words of Daniel Brook, "The instant global metropolis ... captivated the world with record-setting skyscrapers, indoor ski slopes and a stunningly diverse population."[14] The number of hotels stood at 48, with 4,764 keys in 1988. By 2017, the city had 681 hotels or serviced apartments with 107,400 rooms. Overseas tourists numbered 630,000 in 1990 and reached 8.4mn in 2010. This figure nearly doubled to 15.9mn in 2018. As a potent testament to the city's ambitions, Burj Khalifa remains at the time of writing the tallest building in the world.

Building on the success of a growing number of free zone ventures, the city planners kept pushing the limits ever further. The Dubai Strategic Plan 2015, presented in 2007, set the bold objective of transforming Dubai into a global financial, business, and leisure center. It attached particular importance to human capital, productivity, lifestyle, and regulatory factors as enablers of growth.[15] The readiness to keep reinventing the formula for success was unprecedented in the regional context, and the agility it represented became a key competitiveness driver.

In an effort to tap new sources of capital, Dubai began to look for ways to circumvent the legal restrictions on foreign ownership of property, much as it had used free zones to get around foreign ownership limits in the corporate sector. The pioneering move in this direction was the 1997 announcement of the Emirates Hills project developed by the government-owned Emaar Properties: "for the first time in the UAE's history, residential plots were being marketed not only to Emirati and GCC citizens, but also to "those 'others' that can either buy fully built-up villas or plots."[16] Emaar's subsequent Westside Marina project explicitly set out to "accommodate the expected growth of Dubai for tourists, international expatriates, and UAE and GCC citizens."[17] Foreign ownership was made possible through 100-year leases.

In 2002, Sheikh Mohammed issued a decree explicitly permitting foreign real estate ownership in Dubai – an unprecedented move in the Gulf context. By 2006, the government declared that no distinction would be made any longer between nationals and foreigners in the property market. This began to pull growing numbers of investor-residents to the city from all directions. Dubai became "an opportunity with particular appeal to wealthy families in unstable countries nearby. Loaded Lebanese afraid of another civil war back home, Indian nouveaux riches seeking respite from the poverty at their doorsteps, and Russian oligarchs banking assets stripped from operations in their decaying motherland all poured cash into Dubai properties."[18]

These trends brought international recognition to Dubai but also wove it into increasingly diverse networks cutting across continents. The city's population doubled between 2002 and 2008, and its physical footprint quadrupled. At one point, nearly a quarter of all construction cranes in the world were estimated to be operating in Dubai. During 2000–2004, the construction sector expanded by some 5 percent a year, while the number of completed buildings increased at an annual pace of 11 percent.[19] Dubai managed to achieve a novel synthesis described as "an incubator of cosmopolitan lifestyles in Arabian culture and as a model for entrepreneurial development."[20] This frantic development pushed Dubai to its pre-oil modus operandi. Having accounted for 46 percent of Dubai's GDP in 1975, the share of oil dropped to 3 percent by 2007.

Dubai's rise went hand in hand with proactive publicity that was unprecedented in the Gulf in its sophistication, reach, and incessant innovation. The ever-expanding Emirates airline not only created awareness but also delivered more and more travelers to the city. The free zone ventures built their reputations through well-known anchor clients such as Microsoft in the Internet City. The Media City proved particularly important for publicity: "Bringing major bureaus to the city helped make Dubai a global household name."[21] Soon enough, "Mohammed declared that Dubai should elevate itself to 'a par with the world's most prestigious financial centers, including London and New York.'"[22] In anticipation of future progress, the Al Maktoum International Airport was opened in 2010. Expected to be completed in the late 2020s, its passenger capacity is projected at 260mn. Another venture that met with widespread skepticism, the airport has at least so far remained in the shadow of DBX. The COVID-19 pandemic raised further questions about its viability.

This frantic pace of development transformed a small emirate into a global metropolis. Dubai's 1968 population of some 59,000 had risen to around 370,000 by 1985. It reached 910,000 by 2001, 1.9mn in 2010, and more than 3mn at the time of writing. By the year 2000, an estimated 53 percent of Dubai's population was born in a foreign country, and more kept flocking in: "For many in the developing world ..., the ability to move to a wealthy country without the pressure to change or conform is precisely Dubai's appeal."[23] As summed up by Daniel Brook: "Mohammed dreamed Dubai into a pinnacle of modernity: the entire world in one city."[24] However, this "full-on embrace of globalization has rendered Dubai demographically less Arab than Dearborn, Michigan, or Marseilles, France."[25] It is as if Dubai is in Arabia but no longer of Arabia. In essence, Dubai seems to have opted for globalization and openness with a gusto that redefined it to a point that now seems to offer no way back.

When the sky was the limit: The Great Arabian Infrastructure Boom

Dubai fundamentally reinvented the economic diversification agenda for the Gulf region. The new strategic posture was no longer about reallocating parts of the oil windfall into other economic activities but rather about combining regulatory reform, financial innovation, openness, and public relations in novel ways to craft an inherently dynamic and adaptable development narrative. Infrastructure held a place of pride in this new approach, something that echoed a broader global story with countries such as China successfully using large investment projects as a potent engine of economic progress.

The "Dubai model" soon enough became a powerful archetype envied and emulated in equal measure, while economic fundamentals of all of the Gulf countries pushed them in a similar direction. The meager 1980s and 1990s had forced all of the GCC governments to embrace diversification as an overriding policy priority. For a region with a modest population base but an advantageous geographic location, infrastructure development promised multiple advantages. It helped overcome the kinds of constraints – notably on population, local market size, and various trans-national flows – that had held back progress in the past. The substantial capital resources of the Gulf countries, even after the sharp drawdowns of the 1980s and 1990s, further contributed to this opportunity. Moreover, they were now once again growing at a brisk pace, which many expected to continue.[26] In an increasingly integrated world economy with rapidly growing trans-national flows of goods, people, and capital, infrastructure was an important anchoring and routing mechanism that often also generated opportunities for localized value addition. By developing the logistics sector, the Gulf economies could further cement their locational advantages by offering trade facilitation services that would induce companies to channel their business through Gulf-based assets as opposed to alternative infrastructure located elsewhere.

The Gulf infrastructure boom received a major boost from the accelerating forward march of globalization. Crumbling trade and investment barriers gave rise to increasingly numerous and complex trans-national value chains. The Gulf, partly thanks to its dollar pegs and absence of capital controls, was further advantaged by a financial market environment where the cost of capital fell to historically low levels following extraordinary monetary loosening in the US, whether in response to the imploding dot-com bubble or 9/11. The GCC business cycle proved highly uncorrelated with developments in the US, with the consequence of ample low-cost credit amid an oil boom. While this state of affairs quickly manifested itself in inflationary pressures as well as a growing tally of speculative projects, it also helped the region position itself as a globally recognized investment destination. This brought about a major shift in the way the region viewed itself and was in turn seen by the outside world.

As diversification regained momentum in the early 21st century, regulation began to receive unprecedented attention as a critical development driver. Its goal was to make it easy, safe, and cost-effective for companies to do business through or in the Gulf region. A similar logic applied to tourist visitors and new residents. Reflecting the necessity of scaling through openness, the Gulf economies are ardent advocates of the multilateral trading system. A November 2001 landmark meeting in Qatar was followed by the so-called Doha Round of trade talks that set out to reduce trade barriers with a more explicit recognition of the needs of developing countries. In December 2005, Saudi Arabia became the last Arab Gulf state to join the World Trade Organization. The Kingdom had effectively used its 1996 membership application to precommit to a broader structural overhaul. In an emblematic reflection of the new priorities, the 2012 World Bank Doing Business index – in the face of some controversy – rated Saudi Arabia the 12th easiest place in the world to do business. The GCC countries are signatories to the Greater Arab Free Trade Agreement, originally created in 1997, but also a large number of bilateral deals. Bahrain and Oman belong to a small group of nations with full free trade agreements with the US, since 2006 and 2009, respectively.

Other factors also pushed the Gulf countries to recalibrate their development strategies. The general economic malaise of the late 20th century had underscored the importance of policy innovation in several areas. Saudi Arabia in particular had witnessed a steady deterioration in its economic conditions that became particularly evident toward the late 1990s:

> *Among the dimensions and effects of this crisis were the relatively low level of foreign assets and reserves, the rise of unemployment, the continuing and substantial deficit in the balance of payments, the inadequate facilities available for the population as a result of too little public investment in the social and economic infrastructure, and the worsening of the poverty which still characterised life for some parts of the population.*[27]

While this created an appetite for change, the simultaneous increased influence of Crown Prince Abdullah made such efforts much more focused.

Even as the third oil boom dramatically boosted the ability of the Gulf countries to turn their strategic aspirations into reality, they no longer fully underwrote the investment plans as they had in the 1970s. The growing windfall was administered much more carefully than in the past, not least in order to restore macro-economic stability after years of persistent deficits. The region managed to bring down its aggregate public debt from 66 percent of GDP in 2002 to 12 percent by the end of 2008. According to estimates by the IMF, the Gulf governments only spent approximately 30 percent of their additional oil income in 2002–2005, which compared to a 75 percent share observed in the 1970s and the early 1980s.[28] But the tidal wave of oil liquidity still dramatically lifted the broader economy: "The region-wide budget contribution to aggregate demand – measured as the non-oil primary deficit – jumped by 10 percentage points from its average in the pre-boom years, to 51 percent of non-oil GDP at end-2008."[29]

Among the many factors that allowed the early 21st-century infrastructure narrative to take off so quickly was the existence of increasingly numerous mechanisms for channeling capital into productive ventures.

The financial sector assumed a critical role in bankrolling the infrastructure pipeline as the annual rate of real average credit growth in the region was close to 23 percent during 2003–2008. This nearly doubled the ratio of private sector credit to non-oil GDP to 122 percent by the end of 2008.[30] UAE domestic bank credit expanded by an annual average rate of 40 percent in 2004–2008 to nearly 100 percent of GDP, having stood at less than 25 percent as recently as 2004. This liquidity funded real estate projects but increasingly also mortgage loans that helped create the purchasing power for selling them in an environment of "[n]egative real interest rates and loan-to-value rates of up to 95 percent."[31] With the taps of credit opened to capacity, a growing range of ever more ambitious projects proved easy to finance. Dubai led the way with ambitious ventures, such as the three planned "Palms" of Jumeirah ($5bn), Jebel Ali ($7.5bn), and Deira ($12.5bn).[32] Foreign capital found new channels into the Gulf market whose appeal peaked in the run-up to 2008 as more and more investors took speculative bets on the revaluation of the GCC currencies. In 2005–2007, the foreign liabilities of the UAE banks alone expanded by 90 percent a year.[33] Similarly, the total outstanding foreign borrowing of UAE corporations shot up from some $40bn in 2005 to a peak of over $140bn by the middle of 2008.[34] In another important institutional innovation, a multitude of government-related entities, above all for property development, sprung up across the region, once again led by Dubai. Many of them tapped the market directly and took on substantial leverage, pushing up all government-related debt to 100–200 percent of GDP by 2010.[35]

The opening decade of the 21st century was a period of feverish policy innovation across the Gulf region. The Saudi government, keen to mobilize new sources of capital, approved numerous initiatives to this end, not least privatization. In 2001, the Supreme Economic Council set up a Privatization Committee that drove the partial divestment of several state assets. This agenda progressed hand in hand with much better regulation and infrastructure upgrades around the national capital markets, notably the establishment of a proper national stock exchange. One of the objectives of the authorities was to tap the estimated $1trn of Saudi money that was rumored to be held outside of the Kingdom. The ambitions around privatization were no longer just fiscal; it "was not being regarded primarily as an easy way for the government to meet its budget deficit, but as a process involving structural transformation."[36] Among other things, erstwhile state champions such as SABIC, Saudi Electricity Company, and Ma'aden became popular stocks but also regular fixed income issuers.

This confluence of factors quickly unleashed one of the most spectacular investment sprees in human history. According to MEED estimates, a total of $720bn was spent on capital projects in the Gulf during the 2000–2008 period. At its peak in March 2009, the GCC project pipeline was valued at $2.6 trn, of which an estimated $514bn worth was put on hold in 2008–2012 due to the global financial crisis.[37] Not surprising in view of its first-mover advantage, Dubai fairly consistently led the way in project volumes, thanks largely to the strong emphasis given to real estate development amid a potent property market rally.[38] But the boom quickly morphed into a region-wide story. The expanding project pipeline included connective infrastructure from municipal development to roads, airports, and seaports, as well as power generation, water desalination, manufacturing, and – of course – housing. Bahrain permitted foreign property ownership in 2001, followed by Qatar and Oman in 2004–2006, moves that began to pull substantial external capital into these countries. The massive capital mobilization moved the needle on diversification but perhaps less dramatically than might have been expected from all of the fanfare surrounding it, "with the ratio of real non-oil GDP to overall real GDP increasing by 3 percentage points during 2003–2008, to 64 percent."[39]

Dubai may have grabbed the limelight, but the boom years also proved profoundly transformative in Qatar. The 25.5trn cu m proven reserves of the North Field turned out to be the third largest in the world, with projected production potential for more than a century. The 1980s oil glut had drawn the government's attention to natural gas amid plummeting oil receipts.[40] Following an innovative joint venture agreement with BP and Total, an ambitious development plan was drafted, including a pan-GCC distribution network. The $1.5bn first phase of the North Field was completed in 1991. Qatargas launched its first liquefied natural gas (LNG) plant, a 7.7mn tn a year facility, in early 1997, with the first exports going to Japan. LNG production climbed to an annual 53.6mn tn within 12 years. The financial boon funded ambitious investments in gas-based manufacturing led by Industries Qatar, which produces petrochemicals, fertilizers, and steel on a scale only dwarfed by SABIC in the region. The production of construction materials emerged as another key growth driver. Qatar mirrored elements of the Dubai model with its own Qatar Financial Center and an ambitious tourism strategy that turned Qatar Airways into a global super-connector. A growing array of real estate developments explicitly targeted foreign buyers. The gas boom allowed Qatar to tap financial resources that supported the country amid the global financial crisis, even if concerns over reserve sustainability prompted the suspension of the North Field development for several years. The early 2021 investment decision on the $28.75bn North Field East project should push up Qatar LNG production capacity from 77mn to 110mn tn a year by late 2025.

Across the Gulf region, the annual pace of headline real economic growth reached 6.6 percent in 2003–2008, which was a full three percentage points above the pre-oil boom average for 1997–2002. Non-oil growth accelerated from 4.8 to 7.3 percent.[41] Massive fortunes were made as demand often outpaced even the unprecedented supply growth, pushing up rentals at a speed that forced the regional governments to intervene. The strong yields drew in speculative investors, some of them operating with less than savory motivations. The booming banking sector pumped unprecedented liquidity into the market, letting the property boom survive even the violent stock market crashes of 2006. The GCC markets "posted 22–60 percent gains in 2007, before declining by 29–73 percent in 2008 with the intensification of the global crisis."[42] For a region with a history of grappling with bubbles, the events in 2006–2008 delivered awkward echoes of the past even as the façade of modernity grew more imposing.

Duplication of effort across the Gulf region became a growing concern during the boom. The similar policy prescriptions across the region reflected similar circumstances. Apart from drafting diversification initiatives around broadly comparable competitiveness drivers, national or even sub-national initiatives were often motivated by an opportunitic desire to establish a competitive edge through a first-mover advantage. Successful pioneers invariably prompted others to emulate them, sometimes scaling up the concepts with superior resources. A growing army of consultants was ready to recycle successful initiatives among other buyers, which cast a lengthening shadow over the efficiency of capital utilization: "Many of the diversification efforts were duplicated across the region, thus raising the risk of oversupply. Most countries offer the same services and similar attractions (shopping, tourism, business conferences) and demand must come from abroad if these investments are to achieve a high return on the equity invested. This is the case in the financial sector with four countries competing to become the regional financial hub."[43] Such factors mattered little during the boom but returned to the forefront when the cycle turned.

Greenfield modernity

The concept of economic modernization *ex nihilo* moved to center stage during the Great Arabian Infrastructure Boom. Creating elements of a new non-oil economy from scratch converted large chunks of a complex brownfield economic re-engineering exercise to a string of much simpler greenfield ventures. The concept was seductively simple: build new clusters of modernity, "islands of excellence" with the most up-to-date technology, infrastructure – even regulation. In the Gerschenkronian spirit, this promised to leapfrog years of evolution by moving instantaneously to the desired end-state, albeit only in pockets of the economy. This practice translated into massive infrastructure investments that drove fast growth in their own right. But it also put in place a parallel economic structure that could attract people from the old economy and eventually promised to bring about broader modernization by rebalancing the two sub-economies in favor of the greenfield variant. Conceptually, this was little different from the transformative processes unleashed by the Industrial Revolution in the 19th century – a new economy superimposed on the old, which it eventually eclipsed.

The Saudi industrial cities of Jubail and Yanbu' were among the vanguards of this model. Built from scratch, they benefited from "lighter bureaucracies and better infrastructures, including extensive maritime loading terminals."[44] They became purpose-built platforms for massive manufacturing investments, leveraging regulatory reform for more effective capital mobilization. It was widely agreed that "[t]he legal flexibility surrounding the two cities was the singly most important spur for their growth."[45] To further facilitate their progress, the authorities redirected transshipment traffic from the established ports to them.

Dubai applied a similar approach to the Jebel Ali project and the aviation cluster, followed by the growing tally of other free zone initiatives. Dubai was quick to scale up the Jebel Ali formula through a combination of purpose-built infrastructure and jurisdictional fragmentation. This model allowed the emirate to quickly respond to investor needs but also reflected a pragmatic recognition of the thorny challenges of reforming the national legal system. Free zones allowed new ideas to be explored without upsetting the established order. Moreover, these jurisdictional bubbles were contained, which mitigated risks of potential failure. But they were also scalable in the event of success. The free zones typically exempted resident companies of taxation while permitting full repatriation of profits. New developments soon mushroomed across the city, including the the Dubai Airport Free Zone (1996); the Dubai Internet City, established in 1999; the Technology, ECommerce and Media Free Zone (TECOM, 2000); the Dubai Media City (2000); the Dubai Healthcare City (2002); and the Dubai International Financial Center (2002).[46] The number of such clusters eventually exceeded 30. In the early 21st century, this dual-track approach to modernization – "fixing the old and creating a new"[47] – went regional.

The Saudi government again jumped on board in 2005 when it unveiled a plan for six purpose-built economic cities. The new foundations were expected to account for some 20 percent of the Kingdom's GDP by 2020 while housing nearly 4.5mn residents and creating 1.3mn jobs in addition to the 7.5mn that existed in the country at the time of the announcement. The initial phase consisted of King Abdullah Economic City (KAEC) in Rabigh on the Red Sea coast (a planned budget of $27bn and a target population of 2mn), Prince Abdulaziz bin Musaid Economic City in Ha'il ($8bn, 80,000 people), Knowledge Economic City in Madinah ($7bn, 200,000), and Jazan Economic City in the southwest ($27bn, 250,000). Leveraging the idea of selective modernization, each city was to have its own specialized focus, and all were developed with separate, bespoke regulations.[48] By deliberately decentralizing economic activity, the new cities also set out to reduce the traditional dominance of Jeddah, Riyadh, and the Eastern Province while helping to escape urban sprawl and congestion. The economic cities were intended as harbingers of an economy that relied much less on the central government.

Immediately attacked by many as while elephants, the massive ventures have struggle to make headway amid recurrent economic volatility. The most advanced of new cities is KAEC, a development that covers an area of 173 sq km and boasts an industrial zone of 63 sq km as well as the largest port in the region. The first stage was completed in 2010, to be followed by a decade-long second phase. The city is now becoming a hub for electric vehicle production. Jazan, despite the shadow of the Yemeni war only 60 km from the border, has also made headway. The flagship project – Aramco's 400,000 b/d refinery – began operations in 2021, and an industrial city is now being planned.[49] The King Abdullah Financial District in Riyadh reflects the same spirit and is now a central plank in the broader growth and transformation of the capital.

An even more ambitious undertaking, Neom, was announced in 2017, and since 2019 the 25,500 sq km site has been developed by a

PIF subsidiary. Located in Saudi Arabia's northwestern Tabuk Province and bordering on Jordan and the Red Sea, the development was described by Crown Prince Mohammed bin Salman as "a world hub for everyone in the whole world."[50] Echoing some of Dubai's traditional trump cards, it is deliberately designed as an open cross-border city and a smart urban center expected to serve as a hub for innovation. In keeping with earlier practices, the city is due to be run autonomously.

Laudable as the ambition of driving diversification through targeted initiatives is, these ventures tend to be underpinned by the familiar theme of infrastructure investment. While the initial growth impetus of such can be potent, their long-term economic impact depends on much more than mere capacity creation. An indisputable success story, the first Saudi industrial cities are now mature projects with a combined population of a million people. Both are home to a number of large refineries and petrochemicals factories. Their leading anchor tenant, SABIC, reportedly contributed 9 percent of private sector value added in the kingdom 2011.[51] Starting with a clean slate has resulted in a growing number of other impressive success stories. But there are many other projects that have struggled to develop traction or been slow to do so.

Re-embracing openness

As the Gulf development journey has consistently demonstrated over the centuries, the limited resource base, small population, and strategic location of the region entail a strong connection between openness and prosperity. The link to openness became ever more central to the regional development strategies during the post-2000 boom, which coincided with an extraordinary rally in international trade. Higher oil prices quickly pushed up export values, while the boom at home sucked in more and more imports. Between 2000 and 2017, "the GCC's trade in goods and services grew at an average real rate of 7.5 percent, almost twice that of real GDP growth, compared with the global averages of 4.8 percent and 3.8 percent, respectively."[52] Since little was done to curb the region's endemic import dependency, "GCC countries' non-oil trade balance has been in constant deficit (about 11 percent of non-oil GDP in 2017)."[53] These trends further entrenched the position of the Gulf as one of the most trade-dependent geographies globally. The combined value of exports and imports of goods and services as a percentage of GDP exceeded 100 percent in 2017. This was "well above the average of 50 percent for emerging economies."[54] As a result, the GCC's weight in global trade has grown sharply, from 1.3 percent of global merchandise impots in 2000 to 2.9 percent in 2015. The change in services was even faster: from 2.2 percent of commercial service imports in 2005 to 4.0 percent in 2015. Transport services jumped from 3.2 to 7.7 percent over the same period.[55] Trade has thus been a critical driver of growth as well as prosperity through the substantial current account surpluses it has generated. With the commitment to export diversification, these trends possess obvious potential for further growth.[56]

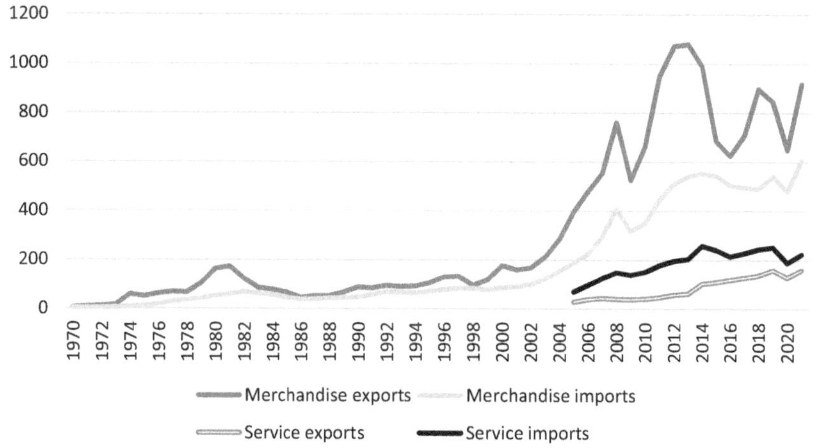

Figure 6.1 GCC foreign trade in goods and services, $ bn in current prices.

Source: United Nations Conference on Trade and Development, https://unctadstat.unctad.org/wds/ReportFolders/reportFolders.aspx?sCS_ChosenLang=en.

The growing strategic interest in export diversification in the Gulf combined with ambitions to attract more foreign capital, not least for creating more export-oriented productive capacity. After its pioneering role in the oil sector, foreign capital assumed an instrumental role in the emergence and expansion of financial services. Similarly, the large refinery and manufacturing joint ventures starting in the 1970s explicitly targeted international partners. By the new millennium, FDI was elevated to a central strategic priority in recognition of its potential for driving growth and diversification. By attracting established foreign businesses, the Gulf governments could also expect to create more private sector employment opportunities, a goal that had proven frustratingly elusive in the case of the low-productivity local ventures. Moreover, the late 20th-century austerity had revealed the inherent cyclicality and limitations of government funding and underscored the strategic importance of identifying alternatives to it. High hopes were attached to FDI as a source of new types of businesses and know-how. These new market entrants were expected to raise the bar on competition and productivity in a boost to longer-term growth prospects.

The Gulf economies set out to proactively court foreign capital through dedicated institutional capacity, various incentives, and regulatory reforms. Building on the initial successes of the free zone ideas, the Saudi Arabian General Investment Authority (SAGIA) was set up in 2000 when the new Law on Foreign Direct Investment in principle permitted full foreign ownership of businesses. The corporate tax on foreign investors dropped from 45 to 20 percent. The Bahrain Economic Development Board, also established in 2000, helped push up the inward FDI stock to parity with GDP. The Gulf governments offered a growing range of "sweeteners" that invariably included assistance with setting up but also

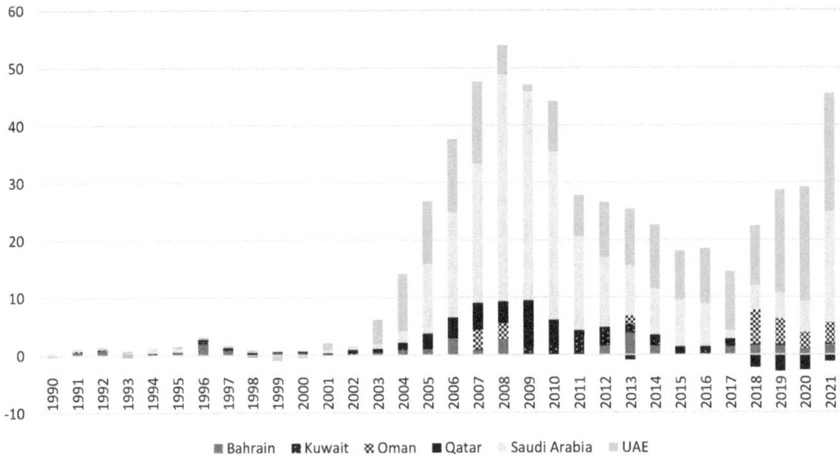

Figure 6.2 Inward foreign direct investment inflows, $ bn.

Source: United Nations Conference on Trade and Development, https://unctadstat.unctad.org/wds/ReportFolders/reportFolders.aspx?sCS_ChosenLang=en.

purely financial incentives; for example, exemptions from import duties on inputs, subsidies, or tax holidays. They could even comprise subsidies on land or real estate. Given the importance of job creation, it was common to offer assistance with recruitment and training, but many countries also relaxed their visa regimes to make it easier to recruit talent form abroad.[57] The country-specific initiatives have occasionally encouraged foreign companies to shop around for the best deal while leveraging the competition among investment promoters to extract benefits with little economic justification. This has sometimes brought in projects that ultimately did not have a sustainable rationale in their absence, thereby watering down the desired transformative impact of FDI.

In the new millennium, the combination of an exceptional economic upswing and proactive marketing dramatically fueled foreign investor interest in the Gulf. Having stagnated at minimal levels for years, the total FDI inflows shot up starting in 2003 and rallied until a peak in 2008. During this half-decade, the annual total increased almost ten-fold from $6.1bn to $53.9bn, which equaled some 5 percent of the region's aggregate GDP and perhaps as much as a quarter of all investment. Thereafter, however, a fairly consistent decline ensued, taking the tally to less than $20bn year, or less than 2 percent of the regional GDP. A renewed upswing began in 2018, reflecting a new generation of mega-projects but also structured policy initiatives such as Saudi Arabia's Ministry of Investment. The 2021 regional total of $44.4bn was the highest since 2010.

Logically, in view of their size, Saudi Arabia and the UAE have been the main targets of foreign investors, routinely accounting for some 80 percent of the Gulf total. Three sectors have dominated, with a roughly 60 percent aggregate share: real estate, petroleum, and chemicals. FDI has overwhelmingly involved greenfield projects rather than the acquisition of existing assets. This partly reflects the complications of investing in local businesses and the relative underdevelopment of private capital markets but likely also a limited range of attractive opportunities. In recent years, the US and India have been the leading sources of FDI, but the UAE has also served as an important conduit of capital into the rest of the region. Bahrain has maintained its position as the most open Gulf economy where, in the peak years before the global economic crisis, FDI could account for almost a third of all fixed capital formation. While traditionally Saudi Arabia and Kuwait had been the primary sources of FDI to Bahrain, the range of investors has become significantly more diverse in recent years.

Contemporaneously with the FDI rally, Gulf capital went on a global shopping spree, much as it had in the 1970s. The GCC sovereign wealth funds reportedly saw their total assets rise to $600mn–$1trn by the end of 2008, which roughly equaled half of all global SWF assets.[58] Many Gulf funds made salient acquisitions, including iconic properties and blue chip companies. But substantial amounts of capital also flowed into the rest of the Middle East–North Africa region. GCC investors participated in privatizations but also undertook infrastructure and equity investments. Some $60bn of Gulf sovereign money was placed in the rest of the Middle East–North Africa region in 2002–2006 – approximately 11 percent of the total estimated GCC capital outflows at the time.[59] The Gulf SWFs once again returned to the limelight during the COVID-19 pandemic. For instance, Saudi Arabia's PIF made high-profile global acquisitions, supported by the transfer of some $40bn of foreign reserves to its coffers in May 2020. Key new holdings included stakes in Boeing, BP, Carnival, Citigroup, Disney, Facebook, Jio Platforms, Royal Dutch Shell, and Total.

A new kind of openness also applied to people. Dubai's pioneering steps toward permitting foreign ownership of real estate proved extremely popular among local non-national residents and foreign property investors alike. Most Gulf governments soon began to overhaul their regulations around property development and foreign ownership. A growing number of prestige developments explicitly targeted foreign buyers. In turn, the expanding project pipeline brought in new people, from developers to construction workers, which drove up demand and supply in tandem. For instance, the UAE recorded 6 percent annual population growth in the 2000s.[60] Riyadh, boasting the largest population of locals among the Gulf cities, did not to fully jump on this bandwagon. But this did not stop an impressive transformation of the skyline, with re-zoning of the city center and ambitious developments starting with the Faisaliyah and the Kingdom Tower.

The Gulf countries succesfully tapped into the growing popularity of cross-border travel. In 2012, the number of travelers globally topped one billion for the first time, and all of the GCC governments were keen to seize this opportunity. Locational advantages made this a particularly attractive gambit, since close to 2bn people were estimated to be living within a 2.5-hour radius of the Gulf. The UAE and Qatar made massive investments in "super-connector" airlines and airport facilities. The extraordinary rise of Emirates now began to face competition from efforts to scale up Qatar Airways (originally established in 1993) and the incorporation of Etihad

Airways by Abu Dhabi in 2003. Despite charges of unsustainable duplication, one industry estimate in 2012 put the annual real growth potential of GCC aviation at 6.3 percent until the early 2030s, something that promised a prospective 294,000 jobs. Between 2000 and 2015, Dubai, along with Turkey and China, accounted for nearly 30 percent of emerging market air travel growth. However, new realities were already making themselves felt even before COVID-19, with a slowdown in 2018 and a small capacity reduction in 2019.[61]

Improving connectivity fed the rise of the Gulf tourism sector. Oman made its exceptional tourism potential a central plank of its development early on, quickly establishing a global reputation as a diverse destination. By 2018, the Sultanate welcomed 4.2mn tourists, almost equal to its population and up sharply from 2.1mn in 2017. As home to the most sacred shrines in Islam, Saudi Arabia was exceptionally well positioned to benefit from the growing prosperity of many Muslim nations, something that it moved to further embrace by lengthening the *Umrah* season to cover most of the year while also improving and scaling up the infrastructure around the sacred sites. The annual total of pilgrims rose from 5.7mn during the 2012 season to 7.5mn by 2017, with some estimates putting their contribution at as much as 7 percent of the Kingdom's GDP. Saudi Vision 2030 hopes to push up pilgrim numbers to an annual 30mn by 2030.[62] But Saudi Arabia's ambitions have progressed far beyond religious tourism to efforts to develop destinations and events tourism. Saudi Arabia has had five World Heritage sites inscribed on the UNESCO list, and recent years have seen a dramatic increase in the number of events and festivals. By 2018, tourism's GDP contribution was already estimated at 9 percent, and in a new impetus for growth, tourist visas were introduced in 2019.

By the late 2010s, the Gulf had truly arrived as a global tourism destination. In 2018, overnight visitors in Dubai spent $30.8bn, the highest figure globally. Makkah came in second with $20.1bn. The World Travel and Tourism Council estimated that the travel and tourism sector contributed some 8.6 percent of the regional GDP and nearly 7mn jobs in 2019. All of the Gulf economies have continued to reinvent their tourism narrative. The initial focus on infrastructure and brand-building has gradually morphed into a more events-led approach. Perhaps the most striking examples include an interest in large-scale international events that can drive investment but also further heighten the global profile of the region. In 2004, Bahrain became the first Gulf country to host the Formula 1 Grand Prix. Particularly high hopes were attached to Dubai Expo 2020 as well as the FIFA World Cup in Qatar in 2022. In 2014 the IMF observed that Dubai was expected to spend up to $18bn for the Expo 2020.[63] The Dubai Expo Committee originally projected 25mn visitors between October 2020 and April 2021, which promised to give rise to 277,000 jobs. Roughly 40 percent were expected to be in the tourism sector, with a further 30 percent in transport and logistics, retail, and business services. The rest were primarily in construction.[64] COVID-19 forced a one-year delay but also helped build publicity around the UAE's effective approach to managing the pandemic. While the post-COVID normalization is not yet complete, the Gulf region is remarkably well positioned to adapt and innovate as a recognized global leader in this area. The policy focus in this area appears undiminished even after the pandemic.

Plus ça change …

Quite possibly the most challenging structural aspect of the third oil boom was the persistent dominance of labor-intensive economic activities and the extensive growth model this entailed. The quick wins of the era revolved heavily around construction and the kinds of activities that the growing physical infrastructure made possible, above all retail trade – palpably embodied in a growing number of ever more impressive shopping malls – and hospitality. The deepening labor market dichotomy coincided with a regional productivity crisis that the oil windfalls effectively concealed for some time. Some of the successes of the third oil boom have been challenged by the new economic realities, technological innovation, and the COVID-19 pandemic. Increasingly, the Gulf development narrative has moved beyond the priorities of the boom years to explicitly prioritize productivity, talent, and innovation.

The Great Arabian Infrastructure Boom achieved a great deal. It helped broaden the foundation for non-oil economic activities. It drove and, in turn, benefited from increasingly effective reputation building as the Gulf economies established a name as some of the most appealing and trusted parts of the new emerging markets universe. It appeared to offer Western-style modernity and prosperity along with compelling competitive advantages, not least the strategic location. And it helped facilitate the growth and diversification of new financing mechanisms along with a much more diverse and versatile regulatory framework that could match global standards.

The GCC governments were much less directly involved in delivering economic growth in the early 21st century than they had been three decades earlier. This reflected the increased range of tools they were able to apply to the economic re-engineering exercise. Notably, a large number of different investment vehicles were set up thanks to regulatory reform, sometimes but by no means always, with direct or indirect government involvement. This reflected the faith of policymakers and investors alike in the growing range of domestic investment opportunities. Many of the new institutions devised and enabled new funding solutions. Once again, Dubai blazed a trail with a cluster of para-statals collectively referred to as "Dubai Inc." Established by the government of Dubai, various government funds, and the ruling Al Maktoum family, Dubai Inc came to encompass a multitude of often interrelated entities, including Emirates airline, Dubai Holding (est. 2004), Investment Corporation of Dubai (est. 2006), and Dubai World (est. 2006).[65] All of these umbrella organizations possessed a large number of subsidiaries; for example, Jebel Ali Free Zone, Dubai Ports World, Nakheel, and Limitless under Dubai World. These entities controlled most key assets of the emirate and drove Dubai's intended transformation by investing in strategic projects. They all built up their corporate brands and credit profiles, tapping a diversity of funding solutions. The model soon went regional. While upending traditional assumptions about Gulf goverments, these institutions also reflect the continued importance of sovereign capital in the development narrative.

The massive local capital mobilization during the early 21st-century boom marked a profound shift from the absorptive capacity concerns of the 1970s. More problematic, much of this activity involved was "easy money" in the spirit of the rent circuit with a decidedly local focus. As observed by the IMF:

> *The GCC economic model rewards firms ... in the nontradables sector. Producing in the tradables sector is typically more challenging and riskier because firms have to continually invest in new technologies to be internationally competitive. ... Producing goods and services to meet the consumption and investment needs of the domestic market has so far been a reliable income source, made possible by recycled oil revenues. This has provided incentives for economic activity to shift into mostly low-skilled sectors, contributing to declining labor and total factor productivity. In fact, large infrastructure projects may exacerbate the crowding out of the tradables sector as they increase risk-adjusted returns in the nontradables sector.*[66]

Amid a tidal wave of liquidity, this dynamically inefficient model kept getting scaled up. The long-standing labor market realities allowed this momentum to feed on low-cost manual labor. The poor working conditions of many of the expatriate laborers helped create a paradoxical perception – and often reality – where the region could offer first-world living conditions and third-world labor costs: "No minimum wage, liberal immigration laws, and a large pool of foreign labor freed companies from health-care and pension costs and meant that needs for temporary staff could easily be met."[67] The financial sector had a strong bias for balance sheet–based lending, which further muted the incentives to innovate or seek alternative focus areas for business activity.

Dramatic economic transformations often reshape economies faster than regulations are able to respond. Even as it was clear that new economic imbalances, overheating, and risks were emerging during the Great Arabian Infrastructure Boom, the regulatory responses were often reactive and piecemeal. There were attempts to impose greater transparency on property development practices while curbing real estate exposures in the financial sector. In practice, however, the extraordinary forward momentum of the boom was never properly matched by innovative measures to address the new risks it created. Many investors chose to indulge in the wishful notion that rapid growth would ultimately render any short-term challenges irrelevant.

Everything comes at a price

The onset of the global financial crisis in 2008 delivered a painful reckoning. A sharp oil price correction and a sudden dearth of global liquidity delivered a synchronized shock to the Gulf economy, one amplified by the sharp reversal of the speculative inflows of the pre-crisis days. The regional asset market collapsed as, in an uncomfortable echo of 2006, "[t]he region's stock market capitalization fell ... by 41 percent ($400 billion) between the collapse of Lehman Brothers in September and end 2008."[68] The real estate bubbles popped just as loudly.

The regional epicenter of the crisis was Dubai, which had previously seen the most spectacular bull run and buildup of leverage. Construction and property-related activities had risen to make up an estimated quarter of Dubai's GDP, reflecting the strategic emphasis on infrastructure but also the speculative froth topping an ebullient market.[69] Dubai saw the number of property transactions plummet to a quarter of their peak while prices rudely halved by early 2009. These vulnerabilities were exacerbated by an estimated 30 percent excess stock of residential real estate, with another 15 percent on track for completion within two years. Lenders pulled back on mortgages, further exacerbating the downward spiral.[70]

The greatest shock delivered by this market implosion was the Dubai World request for a six-month debt moratorium on 25 November 2009. Also involving the two subsidiaries Nakheel and Limitless, the plea pertained to a total of $26bn worth of facilities. Following a bout of extraordinary market turbulence with global repercussions, Abu Dhabi came to the rescue with a $10bn package. Just over $4bn of this was used to repay a maturing Nakheel *sukuk*. The developer subsequently underwent restructuring, and an agreement in principle with most lenders was announced in May 2010.[71] While these steps, followed by other government interventions, diffused the crisis, it continued to cast a long shadow. The crash eventually slashed Dubai property prices by a cumulative 60 percent, one of the sharpest corrections anywhere in the world, and laid bare the structural imbalances that euphoric projections before the crisis had given rise to. Similar reversals were observed region-wide, but none of them matched Dubai's rollercoaster ride as the regional bellweather market.

The crisis also disrupted the financial sector, which had underwritten the boom. This time Kuwait became the epicenter of the implosion because its cluster of investment companies had amassed total assets estimated at more than 100 percent of GDP, some 40 percent of it in proprietary trading.[72] The booming Islamic finance industry tended to have a particularly substantial exposure to the wobbly property sector. Several institutions were forced to restructure, and a sequence of high-profile defaults rattled regional investors.

This rude shock to the system revealed uncomfortable truths about the Gulf economies. The financial sector had developed a deepening real estate bias while failing to develop alternative investments. Somewhat paradoxically, this was the result of conservatives lending practices whereby "banks preferred to extend loans in seemingly secure markets, such as real estate where they were guaranteed with strong collateral. This resulted in an overexposure to the real estate market, and thus correcting this market was made more difficult since banks' portfolios were not adequately diversified."[73] While some of these excesses were subsequently corrected through tighter regulation, increased corporate transparency, and stricter financial sector supervision, much less progress materialized in product diversification. The growing supply of real estate also created other problems, most notably a steady decline in the return to capital as supply outpaced demand.[74]

Another fallacy exposed by the crisis was the notion that structural reforms could be deprioritized by growing the pie for all. Since the ever-growing project pipeline had delivered Chinese-style growth rates, the urgency of structural reform had waned: "the oil boom delayed some of the economic reform measures that the GCC countries had contemplated prior to 2002: increasing the level of domestic taxation, opening up some sectors, and implementing policies aimed at increasing nationals' employment in the private sector."[75] Infrastructure became the perceived quick win that engendered prosperity without the need for potentially contested policy compromises. But this also meant that the region had few alternative growth drivers to fall back on when the property bubble imploded. By channeling funds above all to large government projects and to well-established business elites, the financial sector had left new, entrepreneurial growth drivers too weak to compensate for the infrastructure slowdown.[76] While new company formation had accelerated during the boom, precious few of these businesses had achieved substantial grow, and many were washed away by economic volatility.

The events of 2008 at first seemed to sound a death knell to the Great Arabian Infrastructure Boom. Mutually reinforcing disruptions in the property markets and the financial sector proved devastating for many businesses and projects. But as potent as these setbacks were, the Gulf infrastructure narrative proved surprisingly resilient. The immediate catalyst for the rebound was the V-shaped recovery posted by oil prices in a global economy kept afloat by quantitative easing and ultra-low interest rates. This soon retriggered the traditional regional growth drivers of bank liquidity and government surpluses, further amplified by years of public stimulus spending.

While many of the ventures conceived during the boom remained on the agenda, the Gulf region proved remarkably adept at pruning off some of the excesses of the past. The travails of 2007–2009, followed by renewed regional challenges in 2011, led to a cull of the massive infrastructure pipeline but also resulted in a healthier focus of projects underpinned by genuine economic fundamentals. Most of the castles in the air that came down or incurred delays were prestige ventures and luxury real estate developments. By contrast, affordable housing enjoyed strong demand. And a growing population created a powerful case for pushing ahead with a number of public transportation developments in cities suffering from urban sprawl and congestion.

Dubai Metro was one of the landmark projects of the time. Ten Red Line stations were formally inaugurated in September 2009 after four years of development. The first two lines cost an estimated $7.8bn. In 2009, the Qatari government signed an agreement with Deutsche Bahn to create the Doha Metro and a national rail network, which began operations a decade later. Riyadh has been constructing a metro since 2014. Other land transportation projects include the GCC Railway, which, however, has faced several complications despite good progress on segments of it.

Strong growth also continued to be observed in the area of social infrastructure, with regulatory reform and demographic dynamics driving massive investments in new schools, universities, and hospitals. A preponderance of private university projects has coincided with some large public ventures. Notably, the Princess Noora bint Abdulrahman University in Riyadh brought together several women's colleges on a new, purpose-built campus that was developed in 2008–2011.

Proactive regulatory reform re-stabilized the Gulf property markets shaken up by the crisis. Dubai made a head start through the Real Estate Regulatory Agency established under its Land Department in 2007. Its remit was expanded from encouraging foreign investment to registering all market participants, including brokers. Mortgage lending became much more tightly controlled, while real estate transfer fees were doubled to 4 percent in a bid to discourage speculation. Rental increases were formally regulated. Al Etihad Credit Bureau was established in 2012 and, in a bid to boost market transparency, was followed in 2013 by a government online portal for real estate transactions and information. In practice, the effectiveness of these interventions was challenged by the use of cash for some 70–80 percent of local real estate transactions.[77]

The GDP share of the UAE real estate sector rebounded to 10.3 percent in 2015, and another 9 percent came from construction. Construction had generated 14 percent of Dubai's GDP in 2008.[78] Saudi Arabia's long-awaited Registered Real Estate Mortgage Law was adopted in 2012 in a deliberate bid to boost property ownership. A regulated secured lending structure allowed a borrower to retain the title to his or her property while also putting in place a system for dispute resolution. A simultaneous Finance Companies Control Law permitted Shariah-compliant companies to offer real estate financing.

For a while it looked like the Gulf real estate markets had overcome their challenges, but the recovery soon began to lose momentum, suggesting that some structural fault lines still persisted. Renewed oil market volatility dampened UAE sale price increases by the end of 2014. Sales began to decline by the spring of 2015 as developers continued to add new supply, while demand was eroded by tighter liquidity, a stronger dollar, more rigorous mortgage regulation, and higher transaction fees.[79] The inward capital flows of earlier years began to dry up. This was partly due to a challenging global economic backdrop but also slower job creation and reduced government spending growth, along with perceived risks in the broader Middle East region. Since 2014, many UAE properties shed nearly half of their value. Only in connection with the delayed Expo amid a robust post-COVID rebound in 2021 did the market show renewed growth.

Despite these challenges, the GCC remains one of the most important construction markets globally. In 2019, MEED estimated that there are over 6,700 projects with an aggregate value of $3.1trn at various stages of implementation or being planned. This includes mega-ventures ranging from Saudi Arabia's Neom to other new cities such as the Duqm development in Oman and Silk City in Kuwait. But while the totals are still impressive, a new sense of realism seems to have set in. According to MEED Projects, the GCC-wide project awards, which peaked at more than $160bn in 2006, subsequently declined to just over $120bn in 2012. A quick rebound ensued to around $180bn in 2014–2015. Since then, the annual aggregate fell back to about $100bn and less.

Taking stock of diversification 2.0

Economic diversification loomed large as an inspiration for the early 21st-century infrastructure ambitions. But it differed markedly from the 1970s boom that had channeled the unexpected oil windfall into new economic activities in a largely reactive manner. While supported by strategic planning, decisions came to be increasingly determined by the availability of capital and the "investment readiness" of various parts of the economy. Partly as a result, diversification "remained largely ineffective"[80] until the late 1990s.

While another oil price rally triggered the early 21st-century diversification drive, decision making proved far more strategic, partly in reflection of the very different initial conditions. Openness emerged as the overriding focus as regional competitiveness was seen to center around location and connectivity. This offered a major contrast to the focus on cheap energy and sudden financial wealth three decades earlier. While openness had always been a precondition for monetizing the hydrocarbons resources, the early 21st century saw it redefined in a much more holistic manner. This posture was logical during the high summer of globalization, a time of liberalization, financial deregulation, and economic integration.

Most of the second-generation diversification efforts fell into three main categories:

- Capitalize on the attractive location of the Arabian peninsula on a global scale. This new paradigm was no longer merely about intermediating trade and traffic flows between Arabia and other parts of the world but about positioning the peninsula as a preferred global hub whose infrastructure assets were used by other geographies to interact with each other. Proactive investments in quality connective infrastructure eventually far outshone options available elsewhere in the neigborhood. All of this was supported by an increasingly competitive regulatory framework.
- Position Arabia as a platform for location-agnostic activities. The 21st century has seen many services become less location-specific as digital technology allows them to be undertaken almost anywhere and delivered globally. The globalization of value chains has driven specialization across countries. A conducive regulatory environment, appropriate infrastructure, and attractive lifestyle increasingly outshine traditional resource endowment and cost arguments in driving investment decisions.

- Grow the local market through immigration. This has helped expand the available talent pool but also pushed up the domestic demand for various goods and services. These changes have enhanced the appeal of the platform idea but also created a larger local anchor for some infrastructure investments while pulling capital into the closed sector of the economy.

Reflecting the shift from comparative to competitive advantage, as well as the rise of globalization, the Gulf governments recognized the strategic value of regulatory reform. There was a strong emphasis on improving the business climate as well as fostering entrepreneurship in order to accelerate the transition to more private sector–led development.

In practice, it is impossible to identify an unequivocal cutoff between the two "generations" of diversification. Some early ventures, such as Bahrain's financial center, linked to locational advantages, infrastructure, and regulations. Localizing more downstream hydrocarbons activity from the traditional default choice of end markets marked another paradigm shift. Moreover, diversification was an evolutionary process whose early decades were inevitably shaped by the economic, demographic, and geographic realities of the time. The initial conditions in many cases forced policymaking into a largely reactive posture. But early developments often created the basis for continuous process re-engineering that in time allowed non-oil growth to increasingly decouple from its initial drivers.

While significant progress did materialize during the second generation of diversification, it can legitimately be argued that the oil–government nexus morphed instead of retreating. Sovereign capital frequently played a role in corporate entities designed to drive diversification. The involvement was often indirect through various funds and other vehicles. The experience of Bahrain, which was a regional leader in transitioning toward a post-oil future, also reflects the limitations of diversification. Despite some continued growth in hydrocarbons production, this founding sector of modern Bahrain saw its GDP share more than halve from nearly 45 percent to less than 20 during the first decade of the 21st century. However, oil and government services consistently jointly accounted for more than 30 percent the country's GDP.

Region-wide, the Great Arabian Infrastructure Boom did not dramatically accelerate the gradual progress seen since the early 1990s toward reducing the dominance of the oil sector. The GCC non-oil GDP as a proportion of total GDP stood at 58 percent in 1990, troughed at under 56 percent in 1992, and then continued to grow fairly steadily. It reached some 60 percent in 2000, rising further to 65 percent in 2008.[81] However, the misalignment between the different axes of diversification remained much more immutable. While oil averaged only 42 percent of the regional GDP in 2000–2017, oil revenues made up nearly 80 percent of all government income and oil sales nearly two-thirds (65 percent) of total merchandise exports.[82]

The lack of meaningful merchandise export diversification was the most profound limitation of the boom. This was partly because rising

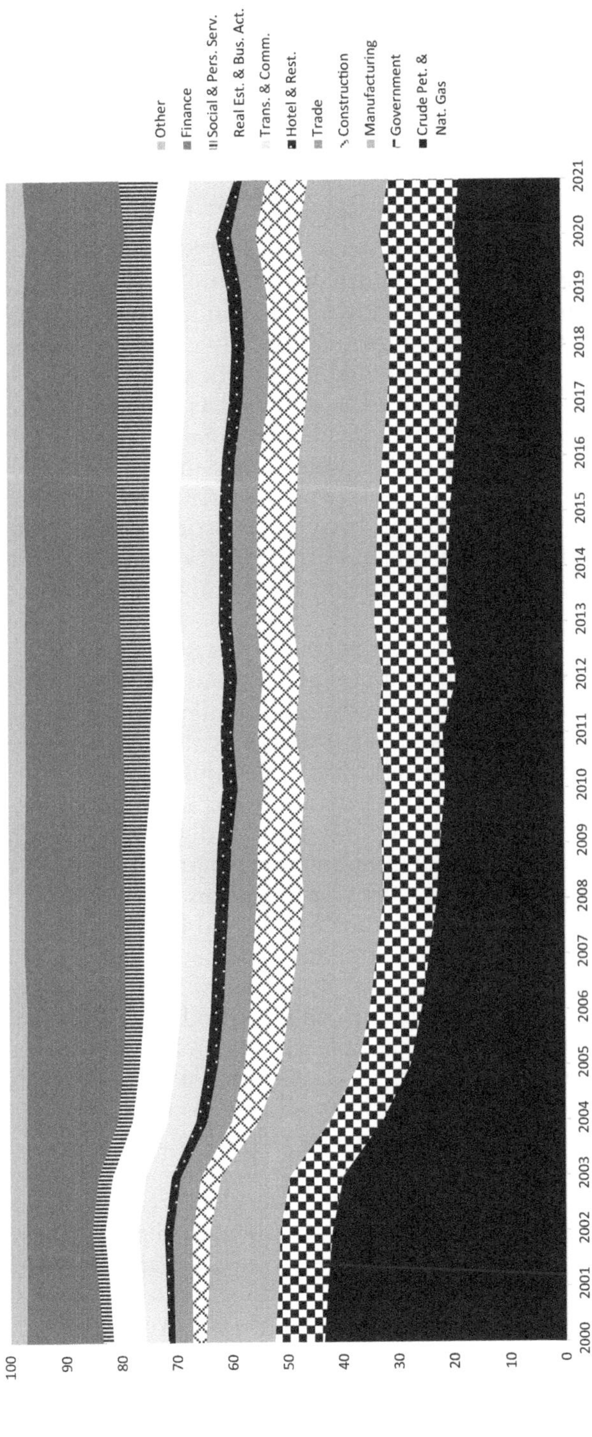

Figure 6.3 Composition of Bahrain's real GDP by sector, percent.

Source: Bahrain Information & eGovernment Authority, Bahrain Open Data Portal. https://www.data.gov.bh/en/ResourceCenter.

government spending drove consumer demand, which in turn fed the low-productivity non-tradables sector and thereby imports rather than exports.[83] Nonetheless, non-oil exports (including re-exports) rose from 16 of 32 percent of the regional non-oil GDP between 2000 and 2017, largely thanks to manufacturing. Change proved even more transformative in services that saw exports increase "from around 5 percent of non-oil GDP in 2000 to 12 percent in 2017,"[84] their growth outpacing that of imports. Tourism accounted for roughly half of this total, while the share of transportation was around 35 percent.

The growth of goods exports was not matched by gains in export quality. The extensive growth model tended to scale up well-established activities, notably "capital-intensive downstream industries—petrochemicals, refined hydrocarbons, aluminum—that directly capitalize on the region's competitive advantage in abundant hydrocarbons and subsidized energy."[85] A long history of subsidized inputs has delivered solid margins, reducing the urgency of pursuing productivity gains. The Gulf economies have carved out significant competitive niches in these areas while also building globally significant corporate names such as SABIC of Saudi Arabia and ALBA of Bahrain. Oman became the world's leading exporter of gypsum in 2017. But the flip side has been a heavy reliance on a fairly limited range of metals, minerals, and petrochemical products in the regional export bundle.

The GCC export diversification narrative has not yet become meaningfully self-perpetuating. Important new clusters have emerged through typically state-sponsored flagship investments. While many have performed well, they have spawned few related activities through further progressive value addition. GCC non-oil exports are unusually concentrated even when compared to other emerging markets. Export complexity, as measured by the Theil index, suggests only modest diversification since 1990, while the value added lags behind emerging market averages. The past 15 years have seen minimal export diversification outside of the UAE and Oman and actual reductions in Saudi Arabia and Kuwait.

For example, substantial investments have been made in mid-stream processing in the aluminium sector. By contrast, much less progress has been seen in the area of finished, specialized products. While the GCC is an important aluminum exporter, it has "relatively small direct involvement in the global value chains."[86] The new fiscal and economic realities now entail stronger incentives for increased value chain capture. Growing export sophistication and a commitment to quality are likely to drive productivity and create better jobs.

Government revenue diversification is another area where change has proven frustratingly elusive. This reflects a tenuous link between between non-oil growth dynamics and government income, although recent fiscal consolidation initiatives, including the introduction of VAT, are beginning to change this. Moreover, some Gulf countries have continued to make good progress with financial diversification. During the third oil boom in 2003–2008, gross official reserves increased ten-fold to $515bn, equal to more than a year's worth of mports.[87] The GCC gross international reserves topped $906bn by the middle of 2014. This equaled roughly 55 percent of the regional GDP, a sharp increase from 20 percent ($75bn) in 2000. The combined assets of the Gulf sovereign wealth funds are estimated at more than $3trn, while the range and scale of semi-sovereign funds more generally have expanded. Dividends paid by state-owned enterprises represent revenue diversification, something that at times been used as an argument against privatization.

Some progress materialized on the expenditure side where regulatory reform has reduced reliance on government spending. Private provision at one point rose to account for roughly half of Bahrain's gross value added in education and health care. The increasing reliance on health insurance has reduced the pressure on government budgets. The growing popularity of public–private partnerships has curbed the reliance on government capital expenditure in many areas. Pioneered through independent power and water projects, these practices were subsequently also applied to sewage treatment, social housing, and even transportation; for example, some Saudi airport projects.

Still looking for a way forward

The Great Arabian Infrastructure Boom was an important turning point for the Gulf region. At first, the ever more ambitious project announcements elicited criticism, often dismissed as incompatible with objective economic analysis. With time, however, the development agenda gained stronger strategic coherence and growing acceptance, all the more so after some of the initial "irrational exuberance" was shaved off by the 2008 slump.

It is still premature to evaluate the ultimate impact of the infrastructure buildup of recent decades. An element of it was unequivocally a bubble. Many of the initiatives to attract new residents through real estate investments or FDI through targeted investment promotion subsequently lost some of their momentum. Nonetheless, the infrastructure boom represented the first time a key growth driver in the Gulf was – in both its inspiration and execution – essentially divorced from the hydrocarbons narrative. While hydrocarbons-based manufacturing and power generation constituted an important element of the project pipeline, the overall thrust of the Great Arabian Infrastructure Boom was primarily about connectivity and demographics.

The boom helped connect the Gulf region – at all levels – with the outside world as well as within the region itself. According to the Global Connectedness Index, most GCC countries are among the top 50 connected countries in the world. Saudi Arabia alone boasts around 20mn Internet users, more than two-thirds of the total population, up from less than 500,000 in 2000. The Kingdom has more Facebook users than all other Arab countries except the much more populous Egypt. Saudi Arabia also has reached a global record of YouTube views per Internet user along with the highest Twitter penetration. Saudi Arabia and the UAE have more smartphones per capita than any other Middle Eastern country and the highest fiber broadband penetration globally. The UAE ranks third in the world in terms of connected devices owned by citizens.[88]

The rise of connective infrastructure engendered broader initiatives to integrate Arabia in the global economy. Some Gulf economies began to systematically attract foreign residents, with property ownership often held up as the ticket to long-term residency. This tied the region into multiple networks the world over. The idea of attracting new skills and capital now commands growing acceptance, and long-term residency is increasingly available to foreign professionals and investors. Not only will this attract more brains to the region but it will also reduce the cyclicality in resident numbers that reflected oil market dynamics and labor regulations.

The combination of infrastructure investment and openness has allowed the GCC countries to up their game as platforms for new kinds of businesses. For years the region has targeted foreign investors hoping to capitalize on the broader Gulf and other nearby markets. But the popularity of free zones has expanded the remit to global businesses that are not dependent on a particular location for their operations. The appeal of the Gulf stems from its combination of regulation, infrastructure, and lifestyle. The rise of digitalization has triggered numerous initiatives to attract start-ups and creative industries. Globalization means that the scale of the Gulf markets no longer constitutes a meaningful ceiling on the scale of investments. The Gulf is beginning to mirror the experiences of global hub destinations such as Silicon Valley, London, and Singapore that draw people and businesses from all over the world. The region is well positioned to take this narrative much further.

Regulatory innovation has established itself as an important concomitant of infrastructure development. This was traditionally a challenging area because of sometimes thorny legacy constraints. Influenced by factors ranging from Shari'ah law to some Middle Eastern secular legal practices and English common law, the regulatory framework was often heterogeneous, uneven, and sometimes outdated. The dispute resolution frameworks were almost invariably seen as slow and ineffective. Efforts to attract foreign capital at times run into resistance by local vested interests, many of which had amassed great wealth as brokers between the Gulf and the rest of the world.

Regulatory reform involved multiple, often country-specific solutions. Bahrain typically insisted on the integrity of its jurisdiction, with the stated ambition of "turning the whole country into a free zone." Proactive reform gained the country recognition as a business-friendly jurisdiction. Elsewhere, efforts to tackle regulatory challenges tended to involve some deliberate jurisdictional fragmentation. This was sometimes sector or activity specific but usually geographic. The advantage of this approach was the carte blanche it gave to regulatory innovation and bespoke institution building that could match global best practices in response to investor demands. "Starting from scratch" avoided the cumbersome process of trying to reconcile existing legal practices and traditions with international standards. Free zones also offered an opportunity to put in place first-class physical infrastructure, which in turn became a key draw in the eyes of investors. The downside of these ventures was their limited footprint, which pushed up costs but also entailed hurdles vis-à-vis the local market through additional licenses and fees.

Regulatory and institutional reform has gained growing recognition in the economic policy toolkit in the Gulf. Efforts in this area have typically intensified whenever the more established growth drivers have weakened. While most Gulf economies have maintained a differentiation between the free zones and national jurisidictions, the idea of eventual convergence is beginning to gain currency. This seems like a logical direction of travel going forward: "While SEZs can attract FDI by offering better infrastructure and regulatory environment, they should not be viewed as the end goal, but rather as a second-best and temporary solution before more business-friendly regulatory framework and practices are extended throughout the country."[89]

The Gulf region is now more open than ever. However, while formal hurdles on trade and investment have been dramatically scaled back to internationally low levels, non-tariff barriers abound. Administrative procedures and practices can be complicated and time-consuming. As a result, the IMF recently estimated that the only GCC countries that export at least in line with their economic potential are the UAE and Bahrain. The UAE does so across the board, perhaps reflecting the success of its free zones, whereas Bahrain does so only in services. Comparable limitations hamper FDI despite progressive reforms.[90]

However, if openness is to be a critical competitiveness driver, it is only logical to allow its full potential to be unleashed by lifting unnecessary, outdated restrictions. Economic diversification underpinned by increased openness promises to "support higher, sustained, and more inclusive growth by improving the allocation of resourcs across sectors and producers, creating jobs, triggering technology spillovers, promoting knowledge, creating a more competitive business environment, and enhancing productivity."[91] By liberalizing the regulatory framework around trade and FDI, the Gulf region could reap substantial benefits. Closing the FDI gap could push up non-oil per capital GDP growth by up to one percentage point. Unleashing the export potential "could provide an additional growth dividend in the range of 0.2–0.5 percentage point."[92]

Much debate in the GCC has focused on the role of exchange rates as a diversification tool. Lower real exchange rates would ordinarily boost export volumes through improved competitiveness. These arguments can be countered by "the still-low degree of economic diversification and the fact that fixed exchange rate regimes have delivered monetary policy credibility as well as low and stable inflation, costs of a change in the nominal values of GCC currencies will most likely outweigh the benefits. Competitiveness gains can instead be achieved by lowering unt labor costs by increasing productivity and containing relatively high average wages."[93] This underscores the urgency of transforming the regional growth model from the extensive paradigm to productivity-driven development. But in an evolving global economy amid FinTech innovation, developing a range of options makes strategic sense.

Despite important advances, the legacy of the past weighs heavy, partly because hydrocarbons and infrastructure will remain concomitants of the development journey for years to come. But there is also a growing need to reduce to heavy reliance of economic diversification on state-linked capital. Similarly, there are far too few specialized productive activities that compete on more than just cost. The incentives to invest in reputation building, quality, and effective differentiation through brands remain relatively rare despite some impressive success stories.[94] But, on the other hand, the Gulf countries have shown a growing appetite for evolutionary progress, devising ways of making assets on the ground work better through policy adaptation.

Notes

1 Niblock, *The Political Economy*, p. 41.
2 Graz, *The Turbulent Gulf*, p. 134.
3 Economy and Levi, *By All Means Necessary*, p. 24.
4 Nuttall, *Shipping and Development in Dubai*, pp. 41–44, 47.
5 Economy and Levi, *By All Means Necessary*, p. 24.
6 Khamis *et al.*, *Impact of the Global Financial Crisis*, p. 8.
7 Davidson, *Dubai*, p. 106.
8 Graz, *The Turbulent Gulf*, p. 187.
9 Field, *The Merchants*, pp. 60–61.
10 Graz, *The Turbulent Gulf*, p. 186.
11 Nuttall, *Shipping and Development in Dubai*, p. 45.
12 Nuttall, *Shipping and Development in Dubai*, pp. 79, 123.
13 Mogielnicki, *A Political Economy of Free Zones*, p. 2.
14 Brook, *A History of Future Cities*, pp. 5–6.
15 https://www.dubaiplan2021.ae/dsp-2015-2/
16 Davidson, *The United Arab Emirates*, p. 230.
17 Quoted in: Davidson, *The United Arab Emirates*, p. 230.
18 Brook, *A History of Future Cities*, p. 355.
19 Fazal, *The Urban Development in Dubai*, p. 11; Mayo *et al.*, "Sheikh Mohammed," p. 13.
20 Matein Khalid, "Dubai's Innovative Model of Development," *Khaleej Times*, 30 March 2007.
21 Brook, *A History of Future Cities*, p. 362.
22 Brook, *A History of Future Cities*, p. 354.
23 Brook, *A History of Future Cities*, p. 367.
24 Brook, *A History of Future Cities*, p. 353.
25 Brook, *A History of Future Cities*, p. 370.
26 de Boer *et al.*, *The Coming Oil Windfall.*
27 Niblock, *The Political Economy*, p. 174.
28 Khamis *et al.*, *Impact of the Global Financial Crisis*, p. 7; Niblock, *The Political Economy*, p. 179.
29 Khamis *et al.*, *Impact of the Global Financial Crisis*, p. 4.
30 Khamis *et al.*, *Impact of the Global Financial Crisis*, pp. 7, 10.
31 IMF, *United Arab Emirates: 2008 Article IV*, p. 13.
32 IMF, *United Arab Emirates: 2006 Article IV*, p. 15.
33 IMF (2014), *United Arab Emirates: Selected Issues*, p. 5.
34 IMF (2011), *United Arab Emirates: Selected Issues*, p. 20.
35 IMF, *United Arab Emirates: 2009 Article IV*, p. 14; Woertz, "Repercussions of Dubai's Debt Crisis," p. 139.
36 Niblock, *The Political Economy*, p. 188.
37 Ed James, "The MEED View of the GCC Construction Market," https://www.slideshare.net/meeddubai1/the-meed-view-of-the-gcc-construction-market-2010.

38 Hanieh, *Capitalism and Class*, pp. 112–113.
39 Khamis *et al.*, *Impact of the Global Financial Crisis*, p. 4; AlShehabi, "Rootless Hubs," pp. 105–108.
40 Dargin, *The Dolphin Project*, p. 13.
41 Khamis *et al.*, *Impact of the Global Financial Crisis*, p. 4.
42 Khamis *et al.*, *Impact of the Global Financial Crisis*, p. 10.
43 Saif, *The Oil Boom*, p. 15.1
44 Khalili, *Sinews of War and Trade*, p. 116.
45 Khalili, *Sinews of War and Trade*, p. 117.
46 Shayah and Qifeng, "Development of Free Zones in the United Arab Emirates," pp. 290–291; Mayo *et al.*, "Sheikh Mohammed," p. 7; Christopher Gunson, "Case Study: The Dubai Free Zones," Second Meeting of the Working Group on Investment Zones in Iraq, Session 2: Attracting Investment Zone Users, Pillsbury Winthrop Shaw Pittman LLP; https://www.oecd.org/mena/49226268.pdf.
47 Saif, *The Oil Boom*, p. 13.
48 Saif, *The Oil Boom*, p. 14; Aissaoui, "Saudi Arabia's Economic Diversification" p. 84; https://www.oecd.org/mena/competitiveness/38906206.pdf.
49 https://www.meed.com/ceer-joins-lucid-at-king-abdullah-economic-city; https://www.meed.com/firms-prepare-jizan-industrial-city-consultancy-bids.
50 Khalili, *Sinews of War and Trade*, p. 119.
51 Hertog, "Public Industry," pp. 130–131.
52 IMF, *Trade and Foreign Investment*, p. 4.
53 IMF, *Trade and Foreign Investment*, p. 9.
54 IMF, *Trade and Foreign Investment*, p. 5.
55 Hanieh, *Money, Markets, and Monarchies*, pp. 53, 57.
56 Alshakhanbeh, "GCC Integration with International Trade Mechanisms," pp. 123–129.
57 IMF, *Trade and Foreign Investment*, p. 16.
58 Khamis *et al.*, *Impact of the Global Financial Crisis*, p. 7; IMF, *United Arab Emirates: 2007 Article IV*, p. 11.
59 IMF, *Middle East and Central Asia Regional Economic Outlook*, May 2008, p. 8.
60 IMF, *United Arab Emirates: 2007 Article IV*, p. 11.
61 https://centreforaviation.com/analysis/airline-leader/middle-east-aviation-outlook-2020-growth-to-resume-modestly-504783.
62 Saudi Arabia Ministry of Hajj and Umrah.
63 IMF (2014), *United Arab Emirates: Selected Issues*, p. 3.
64 IMF (2014), *United Arab Emirates: Selected Issues*, p. 10.
65 Mayo *et al.*, "Sheikh Mohammed," p. 8.
66 Callen *et al.*, *Economic Diversification*, pp. 23–24.
67 Mayo *et al.*, "Sheikh Mohammed," pp. 7, 9–10.
68 Khamis *et al.*, *Impact of the Global Financial Crisis*, p. 16.
69 Khamis *et al.*, *Impact of the Global Financial Crisis*, p. 23.
70 IMF, *United Arab Emirates: 2011 Article IV*, p. 11.
71 IMF, *United Arab Emirates: 2009 Article IV*, p. 11; Mayo *et al.*, "Sheikh Mohammed," p. 14; Woertz, "Repercussions of Dubai's Debt Crisis," pp. 140–141.
72 Khamis *et al.*, *Impact of the Global Financial Crisis*, pp. 32–33.
73 Saif, *The Oil Boom*, p. 10.
74 Osama, *The Dilemma of Development*, p. 22.
75 Saif, *The Oil Boom*, p. 7.
76 Saif, *The Oil Boom*, pp. 15–16.
77 IMF (2014), *United Arab Emirates: Selected Issues*, p. 8.
78 IMF (2014), *United Arab Emirates: Selected Issues*, p. 5.
79 IMF (2014), *United Arab Emirates: Selected Issues*, p. 5.
80 Shochat, *The Gulf Cooperation Council*, pp. 11–12.
81 Khamis *et al.*, *Impact of the Global Financial Crisis*, p. 7.
82 IMF, *Trade and Foreign Investment*, p. 4.

83 Callen *et al.*, *Economic Diversification*, pp. 11–12.
84 IMF, *Trade and Foreign Investment*, p. 10.
85 IMF, *Trade and Foreign Investment*, p. 6.
86 IMF, *Trade and Foreign Investment*, p. 6; Shehabi, "Slowing the Pump?," p. 11.
87 Khamis *et al.*, *Impact of the Global Financial Crisis*, p. 7.
88 https://www.dhl.com/content/dam/dhl/global/core/documents/pdf/g0-en-gci-2019-update-complete-study.pdf; https://www.dhl.com/content/dam/dhl/global/dhl-spotlight/documents/pdf/spotlight-g04-global-connectedness-index-2020.pdf.
89 IMF, *Trade and Foreign Investment*, p. 16.
90 IMF, *Trade and Foreign Investment*, pp. 20–21, 27.
91 IMF, *Trade and Foreign Investment*, p. 3.
92 IMF, *Trade and Foreign Investment*, p. 3.
93 IMF, *Trade and Foreign Investment*, p. 24.
94 Wilson, *Economic Development*, pp. 128–138.

References

Brook, Daniel (2013), *A History of Future Cities*, New York: W.W. Norton.

Dargin, Justin (2008), *The Dolphin Project: The Development of a Gulf Gas Initiative*, NG 22, Oxford Institute for Energy Studies, January 2008.

Davidson, Christopher M. (2005), *The United Arab Emirates: A Study in Survival*, Boulder, Colo.: Lynne Rienner Publishers.

——— (2008), *Dubai: The Vulnerability of Success*, New York: Columbia University Press.

Economy, Elizabeth C. and Michael Levi (2014), *By All Means Necessary: How China's Resource Quest Is Changing the World*, Oxford: Oxford University Press.

Fazal, Fatema (2008), *The Urban Development in Dubai: A Descriptive Analysis*, Masters thesis, Department of Economics, Uppsala University.

Field, Michael (1984), *The Merchants: Big Business Families of Arabia*, London: John Murray Publishers.

Graz, Liesl (1993), *The Turbulent Gulf: People, Politics and Power*, London: I.B. Tauris.

Hanieh, Adam (2011), *Capitalism and Class in the Gulf Arab States*, New York: Palgrave Macmillan.

International Monetary Fund (2006), *United Arab Emirates: 2006 Article IV Consultation—Staff Report; Staff Statement; Public Information Notice on the Executive Board Discussion; and Statement by the Executive Director for the United Arab Emirates*, IMF Country Report, No. 06/257, Washington, D.C.: International Monetary Fund, July 2006.

——— (2007), *United Arab Emirates: 2007 Article IV Consultation—Staff Report; Staff Statement; Public Information Notice on the Executive Board Discussion; and Statement by the Executive Director for the United Arab Emirates*, IMF Country Report, No. 07/347, Washington, D.C.: International Monetary Fund, October 2007.

——— (2009), *United Arab Emirates: 2008 Article IV Consultation—Staff Report; Staff Statement; and Public Information Notice on the Executive Board Discussion*, IMF Country Report, No. 09/124, Washington, D.C.: International Monetary Fund, April 2009.

——— (2010), *United Arab Emirates: 2009 Article IV Consultation—Staff Report; Public Information Notice; and Statement by the Executive Director for the United Arab Emirates*, IMF Country Report, No. 10/42, Washington, D.C.: International Monetary Fund, February 2010.

——— (2011), *United Arab Emirates: 2011 Article IV Consultation—Staff Report; Staff Supplement; Public Information Notice on the Executive Board Discussion*, IMF Country Report, No. 11/111, Washington, D.C.: International Monetary Fund, May 2011.

——— (2011), *United Arab Emirates: Selected Issues and Statistical Appendix*, IMF Country Report, No. 11/112, Washington, D.C.: International Monetary Fund, May 2011.

——— (2014), *United Arab Emirates: Selected Issues*, IMF Country Report, No. 14/188, Washington, D.C.: International Monetary Fund, July 2014.

——— (2018), *Trade and Foreign Investment – Keys to Diversification and Growth in the GCC*, Gulf Cooperation Council/IMF Policy Paper, Washington, D.C.: International Monetary Fund.

Khalaf, Abdulhadi, Omar AlShehabi, and Adam Hanieh, eds. (2015), *Transit States: Labour, Migration and Citizenship in the Gulf*, London: PlutoPress.

Khalili, Laleh (2020), *Sinews of War and Trade: Shipping and Capitalism in the Arabian Peninsula*, London: Verso Books.

Khamis, May, Abdelhak Senhadji, Maher Hasan, Francis Kumah, Anantakrishnan Prasad, and Gabriel Sensenbrenner (2010), *Impact of the Global Financial Crisis on the Gulf Cooperation Council Countries and Challenges Ahead*, Washington, DC: Middle East and Central Asia Department, International Monetary Fund.

Mayo, Anthony J., Nitin Nohria, Umaimah Mendhro, and Johnathan Cromwell (2010), "Sheikh Mohammed and the Making of 'Dubai, Inc.,'" Harvard Business School Case Study 9–410–063, Rev.: 26 August 2010.

Mogielnicki, Robert (2021), *A Political Economy of Free Zones in Gulf Arab States (International Political Economy Series)*, London: Palgrave Macmillan.

Niblock, Tim with Monica Malik (2007), *The Political Economy of Saudi Arabia*, Abingdon: Routledge.

Nuttall, Keith (2021), *Shipping and Development in Dubai: Infrastructure, Innovation and Institutions in the Gulf*, London: I.B. Tauris.

Saif, Ibrahim (2009), *The Oil Boom in the GCC Countries, 2002–2008: Old Challenges, Changing Dynamics*, Carnegie Papers 15, Washington, D.C.: Carnegie Endowment for International Peace.

Shayah, M. Hazem and Yang Qifeng (2015), "Development of Free Zones in the United Arab Emirates," *International Review of Research in Emerging Markets and the Global Economy*, vol. 1, no. 2, pp. 286–294.

AlShehabi, Omar (2015), "Rootless Hubs: Migration, Urban Commodification and the 'Right to the City' in the GCC," in: Khalaf *et al.*, *op. cit.*, pp. 101–131.

Shochat, Sharon (2008), *The Gulf Cooperation Council Economies: Diversification and Reform: An Introduction*, London: London School of Economics, Kuwait Programme on Development, Governance and Globalisation in the Gulf States.

Wilson, Rodney, with Abdullah Al-Salamah, Monica Malik, and Ahmed Al-Rajhi (2004), *Economic Development in Saudi Arabia*, London: RoutledgeCurzon.

Woertz, Eckart, ed. (2012), *GCC Financial Markets: The World's New Money Centers (The Gulf Region: Economic Development and Diversification*, vol. 3), Berlin: Gerlach Press.

——— (2012), "Repercussions of Dubai's Debt Crisis," in: Woertz, *op. cit.*, pp. 137–164.

7 All together now?

Regional collaboration in the Arabian Gulf builds on millennia-long tribal and trading ties. The small size of the Gulf emirates always made external relations critically important. Uniting different parts of the peninsula was central to King Abdulaziz's vision for the Saudi kingdom. In 1954, following the death of the Imam, Sultan Said bin Taimur managed to re-establish Al Busaid authority over all of Oman "for the first time in a hundred years." Safeguarding this unity was Sultan Qaboos' key objective after he took power in 1970 amid a conflict with the Dhofar rebels.[1]

The broader Middle East region saw largely ineffective attempts to pursue economic integration under the aegis of the Arab League starting in the 1950s. But the issue suddenly moved to center stage when, in 1966, Britain decided that it could no longer afford to uphold its treaty relationships with the Gulf emirates. Despite rapid oil-fueled development, the Gulf emirates were heavily reliant on British administrative and security support. After 1971, these newcomers in the league of fully independent countries faced daunting challenges, squeezed as they were between far larger regional hegemons.

Regional collaboration in the Gulf has been shaped by two countervailing influences. On the one hand, the Gulf countries share a geography, history, and a culture. Their modest resident populations suggest considerable synergies from collaboration. On the other hand, however, the Gulf economies have very similar economic profiles and competitiveness drivers. This not only risks limiting the potential benefits achievable from integration – it has also served as a source of tactical thinking and competitive tension, repeatedly trumping designs for coordination.

A plan for regional collaboration

The post–World War II era witnessed the emergence of a novel phenomenon in international politics – the creation of blocks that were not primarily military or political in nature. They echoed the customs unions established in the 19th century, notably the German *Zollverein* of 1834, but even such ventures had been typically underpinned by a political agenda. While postwar alliance building linked to security concerns in a world torn asunder by great power rivalry, the painful legacy of the 1930s had underscored the criticality of economic prosperity as a guarantor of security. Such considerations had motivated John Maynard Keynes when he cautioned against

DOI: 10.4324/9781003373353-7

unduly punitive treatment of Germany after the Great War.[2] It took the Great Depression and another global conflagration to prove Keynes right.

An explicit repudiation of isolationism became a key driver of integration in post–World War II Western Europe.[3] Following an initial impetus from the US Marshall Aid program, in 1952 the European Coal and Steel Community was seen as "the first step in the federation of Europe."[4] The 1957 Treaty of Rome created the European Economic Community (EEC). Initially a group of six states committed to progressive integration, the European project in time came to span most of the continent. The progress of the EEC was underpinned by the conviction that development through trade would cement the unity of Western Europe and build a buffer against the Soviets, who controlled the landmass east of the Elbe. The Soviets themselves sought to emulate the model through the Council of Mutual Economic Assistance (COMECON, SEV), set up in 1949.

At its inception in 1961, the Association of Southeast Asia (ASA) brought together the Philippines, the Federation of Malaysia, and Thailand, partly to contain the expansionist ambitions of communist China. By 1967, this entity morphed into the Association of Southeast Asian Nations (ASEAN), which added Singapore and Indonesia to its membership. The goal of the new alliance was to accelerate economic growth, social progress, and cultural development while promoting regional peace and collaboration in other ways. Similar blocks emerged during the wave of decolonization in the 1960s, sometimes to create a link between former colonies and their erstwhile masters. But they also provided a framework for reaping economies of scale among countries with small and fragile domestic markets.

The momentum toward regional blocks coincided with international efforts to reduce barriers to trade and foster economic integration, notably under the auspices of the General Agreement on Tariffs and Trade (GATT), which was initially signed in 1947. The broader Bretton Woods system sought to stimulate global commerce by reducing exchange rate uncertainty by linking all currencies to the dollar standard.[5] The average tariff imposed by the leading GATT members stood at 22 percent in 1947 but progressively declined to just 5 percent at the conclusion of the Uruguay Round in 1999.[6] Global trade volumes expanded more than 40-fold between 1950 and 2020, while their value rose 274 times.[7]

Regional blocks have often pursued integration along two axes: deepening and geographic expansion. Thus, the EU started out as a framework for facilitating trade among economies with complementary resource endowments and needs. With time, it expanded into a full customs union and eventually a single market underpinned by the free movement of all factors of production. Further integration has been achieved through progressive regulatory harmonization and the creation of the European Monetary Union. Concurrent with its institutional and regulatory evolution, the EU expanded from its original core of six founding members to a community of 28 countries until the departure of the UK in 2020. Similarly, ASEAN is now made up of ten countries able to present themselves as a block to rival their gigantic neighbors China and India.

The idea of regional integration also gained currency in the Middle East. The League of Arab States, established in Cairo in March 1945, initially brought together six countries, including Saudi Arabia, to "draw closer the relations between member states and co-ordinate collaboration between them, to safeguard their independence and sovereignty, and to consider in a general way the affairs and interests of the Arab countries."[8] With time, the league's membership has risen to 22 and its constituent organizations include the Council of Arab Economic Unity, which as early as 1957 published the Joint Arab Economic Action Charter.[9] However, the pan-Arab integration ambitions have been complicated by recurrent disputes among members, partly reflecting a wide diversity in political systems and levels of economic development. Moreover, decision making reflects "the reluctance of Arab leaders to transfer any sovereignty to supranational bodies."[10] Joint decisions "bind only those [governments] that accept them."

The Greater Arab Free Trade Area (GAFTA) agreement was established in 1997 by 14 member states in line with the 1981 Agreement to Facilitate and Develop Trade among Arab Countries. Launched in January 1998, the agreement foresaw the lifting of manufacturing tariffs by 2005 and of agricultural tariffs by 2008. Following annual customs duty reductions of 10 percent, GAFTA was due to free 95 percent of regional products of duties by 2008, albeit with provisions for exemptions and suspensions. In 2009, the League agreed to institute an Arab Customs Union by January 2015, another goal that failed to be met.[11] Despite plans to tackle them, non-tariff barriers of different kinds abound, and trade costs are typically twice as high in the region as in the EU countries. Even as tariffs have come down, "the major barrier[s] to trade ... today are transport costs and weaknesses in trade facilitation."[12]

Economic integration has made limited progress despite pronounced income differentials that should in principle create opportunities for intra-industry trade: "MENA trade agreements have done little to promote trade."[13] Most Arab countries have more extensive ties with their non-Arab partners than with each other. But even more generally, a "typical MENA country exports less than half, and as little as one quarter of its potential."[14] Integration has also been held back by a small product market and a narrow manufacturing base. In the GCC, job creation for nationals has sometimes trumped broader perspectives, a bias strengthened by the dominance of state-controlled enterprises. During the Saudi wheat program, "the incentives provided by the Saudi government ensured that it was more advantageous for landowners to import labor to tend wheat fields in Saudi Arabia than it was to import Egyptian wheat, even though Saudi Arabian wheat cost five times the world market price to produce and that wheat was sold domestically for less than the world price for much of the period."[15]

While merchandise trade is the primary driver of integration in most parts of the world, in the Middle East, "labor flows, and the remittances of capital associated with migration have been the most important feature of regional integration."[16] Cross-border labor movements reflect sharp differences in population and financial resources. Historically, Egyptian, Jordanian, and Yemeni workers flocked to the Gulf countries, whereas their home countries failed to become significant exporters, whether of manufactured goods or food, because they "adopted inward-oriented import substitution policies that discouraged the production of tradable goods."[17] Remittances from migrant labor have consistently exceeded the value of regional merchandise trade and official capital flows. In 2006, "workers' remittances were over US$15 billion in 2006, much larger than net FDI flows and net official flows. Remittances exceed 15 percent of GDP in Jordan and Lebanon."[18] This happened despite substantial Gulf capital flows into the broader Middle East – some 42.5 percent of greenfield FDI in 2003–2015 as well as 45 percent of the over $20bn spent by European, GCC, and North American investors on mergers and acquisitions (M&A) in 2010–2015.[19] But it continues to be the case that "without efforts to solidify regional economic ties on the basis of efficiency and mutual self-interest, the integration that results from labor migration will remain an anomaly in an otherwise fragmented region."[20]

The Organisation of the Islamic Conference, known since 2011 as the Organisation of Islamic Cooperation, has also sought to foster Middle Eastern economic development and integration through various initiatives. Originally established in 1969, it now boasts 57 members. It has a number of subsidiary and affiliated entities dealing with economic issues, notably the Islamic Development Bank (IsDB) established in 1973.

Exploring options

The idea of Gulf integration has long antecedents. By seeking to regularize relations among the coastal sheikhdoms, the treaties with Britain created a basis for more structured coordination even as periodic conflicts remained a fact of life. These included disagreements between the Nejd and Kuwait about their border, ultimately settled by the Uqair Treaty in 1922. Qatar and Abu Dhabi had an open conflict as a result of raids by the Manasir in 1876–1891. Bahrain and Qatar faced off repeatedly over the Hawar Islands. Even the decision by the political resident to award them to Bahrain in 1939 was subsequently questioned, most recently in 1986.[21] In 2001, the International Court of Justice finally ruled in favor of Bahrain. The Buraimi Oasis was a persistent source of contention, not least because of its assumed oil wealth. The Wahhabis had controlled the region for parts of the 19th century. Oil exploration plans in Abu Dhabi revived the dispute. In 1952, Saudi Arabia sent troops to the area, a move countered by the British and Omanis, who secured the area in 1955, dividing its between Abu Dhabi and Oman. Under the 1974 Riyadh Treaty, Saudi Arabia relinquished its claims to Buraimi in return for the UAE surrendering the 25-km Khour al Adeed coastal strip between the UAE and Qatar. Skirmishes were common on the Trucial Coast, where Abu Dhabi and Dubai clashed swords as recently as the 1940s. As the Qawasim holdings fragmented, the British formally acknowledged Ra's al Khaimah as independent in 1921, followed by Kalba in 1936 (reincorporated into Sharjah in 1951) and Fujairah in 1952. Disputes among the northern emirates persisted past independence, sometimes because of expectations of oil finds. Oman and Ra's al Khaimah clashed over the Musandam Peninsula as recently as 1989.[22]

The British deliberately sought to encourage collaboration among the Gulf territories under their influence, and even formal unification was mooted at times. The British residency recorded meetings among the Trucial sheikhs as early as 1905. In the 1930s, a formal proposal was made for a ten-member association of the regional emirates from Kuwait to the Trucial coast. The ambitious project called for:

- the establishment of a council in which each emirate would field a representative;
- the establishment of an assembly to propose regulations and ratify draft legislation;
- the unification of the judiciary and legislative systems;
- the creation of a common nationality, with the abolition of the necessity of passports for travel between the member emirates;
- the establishment of a unified education system, with a central administrative headquarters in Bahrain; and
- the creation of a unified postal service.[23]

These designs were undone by the onset of World War II before they had a chance to be developed further. But similar ideas resurfaced after the war. In 1945, "two prominent Lebanese newspapers ... proposed an 'Arab federation of the Gulf' in which Britain would play no role and in which the city of Manama in Bahrain would serve as the capital, directing a common foreign policy, abolishing all passport restrictions, and forming a High Council for all of the constituent emirates."[24] In 1964, Sayed Nofal, Deputy Secretary General of the Arab League, presented a similar proposal to the rulers of Abu Dhabi, Dubai, and Sharjah.[25]

Indian independence in 1947 effectively removed the historical driver of the British presence in the Gulf. By the late 1940s, rumors were circulating of plans to create a unified state composed of the Gulf principalities. However, in a statement of exceptional foresight, in 1950 Political Resident Sir Rupert Hay observed that "while we might try to work towards a federation of the Trucial Coast Shaikhdoms ... I do not think a federation of all the Gulf Shaikhdoms will be practicable for a very long time to come."[26] By contrast, Hay did advocate the creation of a Gulf Council that would pursue coordination in areas such as education, health care, and postal services. In practice, however, discussions among British policymakers were far from unanimous, and not even particularly structured. In the meantime, in 1958, Sharjah actually concluded a common market agreement with Fujairah, to which Umm al Qaiwain and Ajman were expected to be invited later. There was an apparent plan to seek Arab League approval for the grouping.[27]

Such endeavors were by no means unique to the Gulf: "From the second half of the nineteenth century, amalgamating contiguous territories had become a standard feature of British imperial policy whether in Canada, Australia, or South Africa."[28] However, a new realism had begun to curb this enthusiasm following a checkered track record outside of the European-settled dominions. The Federation of South Arabia, established in 1962, brought together 17 Yemeni principalities and other jurisdictions, including the crown colony of Aden. However, it was dismantled a mere five years later. Partly in recognition of this débâcle, in 1972, ambassador to Abu Dhabi C.J. Treadwell admitted that "federations have not proved to be durable and the British have earned themselves a dismal reputation recently as their architects."[29]

Ideas around cooperation nonetheless persisted. The small size of the coastal emirates raised questions about political viability, economic sustainability, and external security. Two of the regional "superpowers" had territorial claims on them – Iraq on Kuwait and Iran on Bahrain as well as a number of islands off the Trucial Coast. Security considerations moved up the agenda at a time when both the rising tide of pan-Arab nationalism and aggressive Soviet expansionism were recognized as real threats. The establishment of the People's Democratic Republic of Yemen in 1967 brought a direct Soviet presence to the Arabian peninsula. Economic considerations were no less important. These included the need to secure the supply of oil along with the importance of shoring up the sterling area at a time of chronic economic challenges for the UK.

The creation of the Trucial States Council of Rulers in 1952 marked a concrete step toward structured collaboration. It brought together the rulers of Abu Dhabi, Dubai, Sharjah, Ajman, Umm al Qaiwain, Ras al Khaimah, and Fujairah some 30 times between 1952 and 1968.[30] The entity was chaired by the British political agent in Sharjah until 1965, but the chairmanship subsequently rotated among the local rulers. A committee staffed by two representatives from each emirate prepared policy proposals for the council. However, the formal powers of the grouping were minimal, since it "had no written constitution and no executive and policy making powers but was merely consultative and advisory."[31] While little was achieved in terms of formal integration, the council proved instrumental in giving the rulers "a voice in British-sponsored development schemes and ... a framework for co-operation and consultation."[32] The issues discussed were far-ranging and included "the prohibition of the sale of slaves; the issue of traffic regulations; domestic slavery; travel documents; nationality laws; anti-locust measures; the reincorporation of the independent state of Kalba with Sharjah; and above all development."[33]

Trucial collaboration became increasingly structured with time. A proposal by Abu Dhabi to create a fund made up of 4 percent of the oil revenues of any member sheikhdom that produced crude was accepted but never implemented. A British-administered Trucial Development Fund covered the costs of the council. Sheikh Zayed, keen to project his power beyond Abu Dhabi, "already in 1966 ... donated relatively large sums to the Trucial States Development Fund."[34] Saudi contributions began to be received in the mid-1960s following a British deal with King Faisal.[35] The Trucial Development Office took on the task of implementing the 1955 and 1960 five-year development plans. Concrete achievements included the establishment of agricultural and fisheries services, educational support through schools and scholarships, administrative training, the development of health services, the establishment of a public works department, and progress in the area of law enforcement and judicial institutions.[36]

This progress triggered occasional proposals for expanding the geographic remit of such initiatives. Sir William Luce, who served as the British political resident in the Gulf in 1960–1966, "tried to promote a cooperative arrangement between the nine protected states and Saudi Arabia based on what he saw as their fundamentally shared interests and their common hostility to Nasserism."[37] There were even suggestions that the Saudi riyal be adopted as a Gulf-wide currency, while expectations mounted that Saudi Arabia would step in as the regional security guarantor to fill the vacuum created by the departing British. In 1967, Political Resident Sir Robert Crawford maintained that there was "no alternative to putting our money on Saudi Arabia in the long-term as the state best able to provide the support which the Gulf States will need if they cannot count on us."[38]

Saudi Arabia was by no means a passive observer in these plans. King Faisal engaged in the broader Gulf region, sponsoring, among other things, a regional meeting in Dubai in 1965 that was attended by Deputy Leaders from Bahrain, Qatar, and Abu Dhabi. The conference produced an ambitious policy agenda: "In addition to concurring on the need to co-operate in the interests of improving standards of living and maintaining the peace in the area, the Shaikhs also approved the creation of Gulf currency to replace the Indian rupee, including the establishment of an Arabian Gulf Currency Board."[39] It was agreed to arrange similar gatherings going forward, and the subsequent signing of the Arabian Gulf Currency Agreement was described by Sheikh Shakhbut of Abu Dhabi as a "turning point in the history of the Gulf."[40] However, a British proposal for permanent committees was not approved, nor was Sir William "Luce's suggestion that the three oil-producing states contribute to the Trucial States Development Fund on the basis of fixed percentages of their annual oil revenues."[41] Luce attributed the lack of progress to external political realities:

> *There was a general feeling at the meeting that it was still too early to think in terms of such a league, the creation of which at this particular moment might have been regarded outside as being in direct opposition to the Arab League and might have become a focal point of attack by the latter on the Rulers as a group, with a consequent worsening of relations between them and the Arab League.*[42]

Disagreements also undermined the Gulf currency project. As a harbinger of future disputes, "[a]ttempts by the new Ruler of Abu Dhabi, Shaikh Zaid, to breathe life into the common currency project foundered on account of the rivalry between Bahrain and Qatar over the location of the prospective currency board's headquarters."[43] Sheikh Zayed proved much more sympathetic to the idea of a narrower union with the northern Trucial states but had to contend with British concerns that such a structure would be dominated by Abu Dhabi. Some collaboration was formalized through the 1965 creation of the Bahraini dinar, which was also adopted by Abu Dhabi, as well as the 1966 launch of the Qatar and Dubai riyal, which also circulated in the northern emirates.

With time, economic development considerations began to shape the Gulf integration agenda. A growing recognition of the highly uneven distribution of the regional hydrocarbons assets prompted the British to advocate intra-regional wealth redistribution as a way of boosting regional cohesion and security. Kuwait drew particular attention, as observed in 1961 by P. Cranston, who served as the economic counsellor to the political resident:

> *It may well be that the promise of substantial Kuwaiti financial contribution to future Arab economic development may be part of the price which Kuwait will have to pay in order to secure her future independence and to remove the current feeling of resentment, not wholly justified, that Kuwait is retaining her wealth and not sharing it with her neighbours.*[44]

Kuwait did indeed provide generous support, especially to the Trucial Coast, starting with harbor improvements in Dubai and funding for schools.[45] In 1953 the Kuwaiti government established the General Board of the South and Arab Gulf. The Kuwait Fund for Arab Economic Development was incorporated after independence in 1961, while the Gulf Permanent Assistance Committee was set up the following year with the explicit goal of supporting the states of the lower Gulf. The Kuwait Fund disbursed "some $145 million in development loans to seven Arab countries including Jordan, Lebanon, and Egypt"[46] in 1961–1966. Kuwait ultimately spent some 10 percent of its GDP on development assistance in the late 1960s and early 1970s.[47] However, the idea of Kuwait's magnanimity translating into a more formal role in driving regional integration was rebuffed by the other regional rulers. Development funds sprung up across the region in the 1970s.

Gulf cooperation was quickly catapulted to the forefront of the policy agenda when it became clear that the British presence in the region could no longer be taken for granted. By 1966, the economic challenges faced by the UK made it unrealistic and politically undesirable to continue the involvement in the Gulf. The decision to withdraw from the remaining bases "east of Suez" within four years was announced by Prime Minister Harold Wilson in January 1968. Despite offers by Gulf rulers to cover the cost of the British forces, Wilson's position was reaffirmed by his Conservative successor, Edward Heath, in March 1971. The special relationship with Britain finally came to an end in December 1971, marking the exit of a global power – however much in decline – that had guaranteed Gulf security for well over a century.

Filling the security vacuum presented a daunting challenge but also triggered some immediate countermeasures: "The first decisive step ... was taken by the rulers of Abu Dhabi and Dubai when they met on February 18, 1968 on the border between their two states, resolved their frontier difficulties, and declared their states united."[48] Joint responsibilities were to include foreign affairs, defense, social services, and immigration. The sheikhs invited other regional leaders to join their project. On 25 February 1968, the rulers of Bahrain, Qatar, and the Trucial emirates convened in

Dubai. Even the idea of involving Oman was mooted and persisted despite Sultan Qaboos' diplomatic refusal in October 1970. The new Supreme Council of Rulers meeting in Doha in the late summer even discussed the creation of permanent committees domiciled in different member states. In practice, progress in agreeing to the treaty terms was slow and encountered some external resistance. Bahrain and Qatar ultimately chose to opt for fully independent statehood. However, the UAE was established as a federation of the Trucial emirates. Even Ra's al Khaimah, having initially held out, joined the new formation two months later, in part because of dwindling optimism about discovering sizable oil resources.[49]

The transition of the Gulf emirates to full sovereignty instantaneously brought to the fore new risks and vulnerabilities. The day before the UAE declared independence, the Iranian navy seized the Tunb islands. Ra's al Khaimah had refused to negotiate on the status of the two islands whose residents were evacuated to the mainland. Iran also seized the island of Abu Musa but initially on more favorable terms to Sharjah, which "retained sovereignty over the island except for a part to be handed over to Iranian forces. In the event of oil being produced on the island, Shārjah and Iran would have equal shares of the revenue, but until Shārjah's own revenue from oil reached £3 million a year Iran was to give aid to Shārjah amounting to £1.5 million annually."[50] In Bahrain, Iranian claims prompted a UN-supervised referendum that settled the issue in favor of independent statehood.

There were some early attempts to formalize ties within the region. In 1971, Kuwait signed a series of bilateral agreements to formalize cooperation in economic and social affairs, first with the UAE in 1971 and then with Bahrain the following year, while others followed. These agreements brought concrete benefits such as customs duty exemptions, "the exchange of expertise, and the establishment of joint ventures."[51]

Independence and the oil boom

The 1970s boom instilled a growing sense of confidence in the newly sovereign Gulf states, but it did not dispel the long-standing concerns about the absorptive capacity. In keeping with ideas popular at the time, structured economic collaboration began to attract attention. For instance, William Demas had argued in 1965 that "economic regionalism may be an important means of [small] economies achieving a more self-sustaining pattern of growth."[52] Integration promised to deliver scale economies and curb harmful competition among countries with similar economic profiles.

The early economic diversification ventures in the 1970s were often undertaken in a national context and elicited skepticism about duplication of capacity. The regional drydock schemes were an early case in point. A pioneering venture in Bahrain was soon followed by another in Dubai that "by 1980 aim[ed] to provide one of the largest ship repair facilities in the world."[53] Similarly, the Aluminium Bahrain project was followed in 1975 by the launch of a $400mn smelter in Dubai. Yet in the depressed global economy of the 1970s, ALBA was already struggling to cover its costs despite running at capacity. Dubai also matched Qatar's Umm Said iron and steel complex with a similar 300,000 tn facility at Jebel Ali. Similarly aggressive capacity creation occurred in the cement industry and in fertilizer production. In a rush to drive local development, sheer logic often failed to carry the day as "the various countries are unwilling to forget past differences and plan their economies on a co-ordinated basis to avoid duplication."[54]

Gulf cooperation nonetheless gained attention as a way to enhance the impact of some planned development initiatives. Integration also offered an avenue for regional convergence by checking the dominance of Saudi Arabia while also opening up new opportunities for the less oil-rich Bahrain and Oman. Standing united promised to bolster the region's credibility vis-à-vis third parties, something that mattered in particular for ventures that could only reach the necessary scale by securing access to the global markets. Even amid the boom, the perceived urgency of diversification was growing: "Realization that the region has not yet nearly reached the threshold of sustained economic growth independent of oil revenue is … coupled with the realization that the necessary rate of sustained growth may be possible only within a framework of regional cooperation and economic integration."[55] The oil boom lent an impetus to Gulf cooperation by making it easier to finance joint ventures.

Sheikh Jaber Al Sabah of Kuwait in 1976 called for "the establishment of a Gulf Union, with the object of realizing cooperation in all economic, political, education and informational spheres, to serve the interests of the region."[56] Sultan Qaboos of Oman organized a conference on the initiative in Muscat later in the year. There were even broader designs for aligning economic planning efforts and a 1977 proposal to create a common market in the Gulf.[57]

Some concrete achievements materialized through joint enteprises but also cross-border programs in areas such as education, transportation, communications, and even industrial development. Early regional institutions included the Gulf Technical College, the Arabian States Education Bureau, and the Higher Education Council. The Gulf Organization for Industrial Consulting (GOIC) was established in 1976 to foster cooperation in petrochemical and other manufacturing ventures. The better-known pan-regional joint enterprises included Gulf Air, the United Arab Shipping Company, the Gulf Ports' Union, Gulf International Bank, and the Gulf News Agency. These were complemented by numerous bilateral initiatives; for instance, the Saudi–Kuwaiti and the Saudi–Bahraini cement companies.[58] The Gulf countries also cooperated within multilateral agencies and organizations such as OPEC and the Organization of Arab Petroleum Exporting Countries (OAPEC).

The oil plenty of the 1970s allowed the Gulf countries to assume an important role in supporting economic development in the broader Arab world. It was estimated that by 1980 net disbursements from Kuwait, Qatar, Saudi Arabia, and the UAE:

> *had reached some $8.3 billion before falling sharply to $4.4 billion in 1984. … [D]uring the period 1974–78, by far the largest share – just over two-thirds – was directed towards the three front-line states*

[Egypt, Syria, and Jordan], with another 17 percent to the rest of the Arab Middle East and another 3.6 percent to North Africa.[59]

Loans made by Saudi Arabia, Kuwait, Qatar, and the UAE to Iraq had reached $24bn by 1983. One estimate claimed that the GCC provided 13.5 percent of all global assistance between 1974 and 1994.[60] Remittances sent home by Arab workers in the Gulf represented another major fund flow, which a 1980 estimate put at "$3 billion going to Egypt, over $1 billion to the YAR, and about $0.5 billion to Jordan."[61] By 2006, remittances from the GCC to the rest of the Middle East–North Africa region reached $24.7bn, with Jordan, Lebanon, and Egypt particularly heavily dependent on them.[62] Moreover, significant quantities of goods were sent by expatriate workers to their home countries.

Joining forces

It took a decade into the full sovereignty of the Gulf emirates before a formal cooperation framework was established. The critical trigger, in an echo of multiple precedents around the world, was security. The Iranian Revolution of 1979 pushed six states of the Arabian Peninsula (other than the two Yemeni states) to formalize their collaboration under the auspices of a block that was eventually renamed the Cooperation Council for the Arab States of the Gulf. The events in Iran also unleashed a sequence of events that fundamentally reshaped the regional balance of power. Iran lost its pre-eminent role as the "regional policeman" that the US had assigned to it. The Iran–Iraq war, which erupted in September 1980, left the two largest regional countries embroiled in a debilitating conflict for the best part of a decade and eventually much weakened. By lifting the shadow of the traditional Gulf hegemons, these new realities made it possible and logical for the Gulf countries to come together as a formal group. But the shadow of the larger neighbors did not vanish. In July 1981 Iraq re-stated an old request to lease Bubiyan Island from Kuwait, an issue that had been dormant since 1977.[63]

The founding charter of the GCC was signed on 25 May 1981 in Abu Dhabi. The unified economic agreement was endorsed on 11 November 1981. The image of unity projected by the Gulf countries, along with the mounting oil windfall, cemented the credibility of the "Arabian alternative" to the previously dominant neighbors. In 1980, the Gulf region contained less than 1 percent of the world's oil wells but accounted for 42 percent of the world's proven crude oil reserves and 25 percent of the world's natural gas reserves. The oil reserves were deemed equivalent to 53 years of production.[64]

The key objective of the GCC Economic Agreement was to create a free trade area that eliminated all tariffs on regional products while imposing a unified tariff on imports from elsewhere. However, the signatories openly admitted that the ultimate ambition of a unified economic space was challenged by a number of factors, not least the physical environment of the region. The agreement stressed the strategic importance of linking the regional markets and centers of production by connecting all GCC transport networks, both overland and air. It noted that "the economic autarky of the area can be eliminated only as national infrastructures come to be joined and integrated within a common regional framework."[65]

The Economic Agreement called on the GCC members to coordinate their external commercial policies. It established the goal of a Gulf common market within which GCC citizens would enjoy free movement along with the right to work, own property, and inherit across the member states. A common legal framework was envisaged for trade and investment. The organization even articulated a plan to harmonize national development plans with a view to achieving fuller integration, specifically through a shared policy on oil and hydrocarbon-based industrialization. Joint projects were seen as a way of creating regional value chains. Importantly, the agreement called for the "coordination of manpower policies to prevent harmful competition for scarce labour."[66] Even the regional water infrastructure was to be unified. A common development aid policy was set out as the final objective. But despite lofty ambitions, the agreement endorsed "gradualism, so that cooperation is expected to proceed pragmatically and cumulatively. ... Furthermore, the Economic Agreement stipulates an important role for the private sector in the implementation and maintenance of economic interrelationships."[67] The GCC may have effectively adapted the European model of integration but most emphatically not the supranational governance.

The founders of the GCC embarked on their endeavor with a realistic assessment of the region's economic advantages and limitations. Economic diversification was recognized as a key strategic necessity and hydrocarbon-based manufacturing as the most logical opportunity for taking it forward: "Industrial processing ... often entails high degrees of utilization of capital and energy, which fits well with the resource endowments of the GCC region and with a desire to avoid increased dependence on an already scarce supply of labour. ... The diversification of exports is important, because the markets in which these products can be sold are more diversified geographically than those of crude oil and minerals."[68] While economies of scale required a degree of centralization, this was not seen as a zero-sum game: "When the processing of raw materials is carried to the fabricating or manufacturing stages, it may also encourage local production of products not related to the original raw materials. In this way forward and backward integration of the input–output structure of the economy lessen the GCC's dependence on crude oil and thus promote more generally the important objective of industrial diversification."[69] These themes have remained a constant element in the regional economic development plans ever since.

An uphill struggle

The GCC project collided with reality in a fiscal tailspin soon after its inception. An abrupt market downturn pushed the annual oil revenues of the block from some \$450bn in 1981 to \$50bn by 1986. As late as 1998, the aggregate had only recovered to \$60bn, while the hydrocarbon sector still generated an average 65 percent of GCC budget revenues. The seemingly unassailable growth driver of the boom years, the oil–government nexus, was now radiating austerity across the peninsula. The preoccupation of the Gulf governments with their mounting internal difficulties inevitably pushed regional integration ambitions down the list of priorities. In November 1986, the GCC Associate Secretary-General for Economic Affairs Abdullah al Kuwaiz made a prophetic statement about the implications of these realities:

> *In reflecting on what has been accomplished in the last five years, a great deal of ground has been covered in the economic area. In most cases the sailing has been smooth and welcomed by member states. However, as we continue going will get less smooth, as has been the case in all similar economic groupings. The GCC is not an exception. A slowing-down of integration therefore is expected and quite natural.*[70]

The funding for integration projects grew scarcer, while falling oil production dramatically limited the associated gas available to new manufacturing ventures. Plans for a regional gas grid were discussed but not actioned. The same fate befell a planned 1,700-km oil pipeline that would have bypassed the Straits of Hormuz choke point to a planned new oil export terminal and a refinery on the Omani coast. Even designs for a US-style strategic oil reserve remained on the drawing board.[71]

The initial ambitions for policy coordination quickly waned as the crisis narrowed the horizons of policymakers to local concerns. In early 1998, Saudi Arabia "raised customs duties from 7% to 12% ad [valorem] on most imports, while increasing tariffs from 10% to 20% on re-exports coming in the kingdom through Port Rashid in the UAE."[72] While contravening the plans for a unified external tariff, the proposal won approval as one of the limited number of significant additional sources of revenues seen as politically acceptable. Bahrain set out to protect domestic businesses through preferential treatment in procurement. Underscoring the tendency of fiscal considerations to trump the integration agenda, "the six ministers of industry proposed in June 1989 to regularize tariffs among member-states, the proposal ended up being rejected by the six finance ministers, who recommended that different products continue to be treated in different ways."[73] Saudi Arabia and the UAE deliberately increased tariffs in a bid to stimulate a rebound in their domestic manufacturing in the 1990s.

Calls for greater coordination in industrial development tended to fall on deaf ears. GOIC recommendations about pursuing economies of scale in the cement sector were flatly disregarded by Kuwait and the UAE, who instead focused on stimulating local economic activity. Despite similar arguments for iron and steel production, three new rolling mills were mothballed by the UAE as soon as they ceased to be profitable. Moreover, as the demand for aluminum began to increase, "Qatar, Saudi Arabia, and Umm al-Qaiwain in the UAE all announced plans to construct large-scale smelters, which would compete not only with one another, but also with existing aluminum plants in Bahrain and Dubai."[74]

The shifting regional balance of power was not without complications, as manifested by the 1990 Iraqi invasion of Kuwait. Kuwait had supported its northern neighbor during the war with Iran. But relations subsequently deteriorated when Kuwait refused to forgive an outstanding $65bn debt while also increasing its oil production by some 40 percent. The Rumaila oil field became a particular bone of contention, and Iraq formally complained to OPEC about illicit extraction by Kuwait. After a period of mounting tensions, Iraq annexed its neighbor in August 1990. The US-led Operation Desert Storm, launched in mid-January 1991, expelled the invaders by the end of February. But more than 1,000 Kuwaiti civilians lost their lives, and the economic impact was devastating. The retreating Iraqi army set many Kuwaiti oil wells on fire, and "[i]nfrastructure was severely damaged by both military means and government-sanctioned looting. Roads and ports were damaged, communications systems destroyed. Power outaged hampered the effectiveness of the desalination plants. Kuwait's industrial area in Shu'aibah was destroyed."[75]

The Kuwait crisis saw the other GCC states rally behind their beleaguered neighbor while also bearing a substantial share of the costs incurred by the Western armies.[76] A contemporary report by the Arab Monetary Fund put the financial burden on the Arab countries at $620bn. The costs of destruction to Kuwait were estimated at $160bn. The governments of Saudi Arabia, Kuwait, and the other Gulf emirates paid $84bn to the US, the UK, and France for military expenses. A further $51bn was provided primarily by Saudi Arabia and Kuwait for the logistical support required for some 600,000 US and other allied troops stationed in Saudi Arabia between August 1990 and March 1991. Saudi Arabia housed Kuwaiti civilians; 400,000–600,000 of the roughly 1mn Kuwaitis had left their home country by January.[77] The indirect costs to 21 Arab countries were estimated as a 1.2 percent drop in GDP in 1990 followed by a further 7 percent decline in 1991.

A 1992 US Congressional report reached similar conclusions. It put the financial toll of the war to the US at $61.1bn, some $36bn of which was said to have been covered by the Gulf states. Moreover, in March 1991, "GCC finance minister authorized the creation of a US$10 billion fund to support Arab and Islamic countries whose economies had been damaged as a result of the conflict."[78] Kuwait "used $15 billion of its more than $100 billion overseas assets to pay for the war and the immediate reconstruction."[79] Saudi Arabia, the UAE, Qatar, and Kuwait were leading contributors to the 24-country Gulf Crisis Financial Co-ordination Group, which agreed to provide $14bn in support to affected developing countries. These were massive commitments, and the 1990–1991 amalgamated Saudi budget posted a $42.8bn deficit, which was equivalent to 19.2 percent of GDP. It compared to $9.3bn in 1989 and was followed by shortfalls of $17.9bn and $17.1bn in 1992 and 1993, respectively. Only thereafter did the budget deficits once again fall below $10bn and thus back into the single digits in GDP terms.[80]

The closing years of the 20th century saw the GCC integration agenda largely stall even as the clouds of austerity began to disperse. The joint budget shortfall of the member states fell from 30 percent of GDP in 1991 below 10 percent in 1994 and to some 4 percent in 1996. But local aspirations increasingly trumped regionwide objectives. The rapid rise of Emirates and the Jebel Ali free zone seemed to demonstrate that development plans did not need to be explicitly regional in nature to gain traction.[81] In neither case did Dubai's small size seem to stand in the way of success that far transcended the entire Gulf region, thereby seemingly shaking one of the key arguments of the advocates of regional integration. On the other hand, however, much like Bahrain's offshore banking, in practice, Jebel Ali contributed substantially to the regional integration agenda. It became an ever more important link in regional value chains and a dominant distribution point for imports from other parts of the world.

The late 20th-century era of low oil prices was not completely devoid of achievements in the area of formal integration. The Gulf Investment Corporation, established in November 1982 to fund industrial projects, had $420mn of its $2.1bn capital paid up by April 1985. Having launched its operations in May 1984, it employed 110 people by the end of 1985. By 1987, it had made commitments in principle for more than 30 projects with an aggregate value of $750mn.[82] February 1984 saw the approval of a draft Common Agricultural Policy that called for coordination across the member states, not least in order to boost the food security of the block as a whole. A joint defense force, the Peninsula Shield, was formed the same year.[83] By May 1985, the GCC finance ministers agreed to form dedicated committees to study ways of protecting locally produced goods from competition.

There were recurrent calls for measures to ease the movement of goods between member states. Intra-GCC duties on animals, agricultural products, and regional manufactured goods were lifted in March 1983.[84] It was agreed to standardize prices and fees for telex, telephone, postal, and telegraph services, although implementation was as usual left to the discretion of the individual members. No progress materialized on a proposed railway linking Saudi Arabia, the UAE, Qatar, Oman, and Kuwait with Iraq, and ultimately even to Europe, for which a preliminary agreement had been reached in 1978. However, another study on the plan was commissioned in 1983. By contrast, a 1968 plan for a causeway between Saudi Arabia and Bahrain was implemented in 1981–1986 and has since then played an important role in tying the two economies closer together.[85] The Supreme Council meeting at Abu Dhabi in November 1986 approved measures to allow GCC investors to obtain loans from banks and industrial development funds throughout the block. It further endorsed proposals to permit Gulf citizens to engage in retail or wholesale trade on equal terms across the region. The November 1989 summit sanctioned an estimated $2bn regional gas grid to distribute gas from Qatar's North Field across the region. Policy disputes eventually challenged the project, but the Dolphin pipeline to the UAE and Oman was approved in 1999 and began operations in 2006.[86] The December 1994 GCC summit decided that GCC citizens could own and trade shares in all six states.

The Unified Economic Agreement had called for the establishment of a common Gulf currency, and agreement was reached on aligning the national currencies. Bahrain, Qatar, and the UAE all announced comparable fixed dollar peg regimes in 1978–1980. Oman adopted its current peg after a devaluation in 1986, and Saudi Arabia took a similar step. Kuwait deviated somewhat from the norm, announcing in February 1987 the creation of a currency grid akin to the European monetary system "as the first step towards a single currency."[87] In late 1991, the GCC ministers of commerce discussed ways of accelerating the steps toward a regional customs union, while the central bank governors announced that "they intended to issue a single currency by the year 1999."[88] Even Kuwait signaled that it would conform to the regional norm by pegging the dinar to the US dollar. But the change was only implemented in 2003, before being abandoned again within four years.

Even as integration initiatives moved in fits and starts, the practical impact of closer economic ties was gradually beginning to make itself felt. Cross-border business ventures grew in number from 263 in 1990 to 401 by 1997, at which point such businesses had total capital of $19.8bn. Joint ventures were established in virtually every sector, but the trade sector dominated with 167 companies.[89]

Catching a second wind

The early 21st-century boom injected new energy and enthusiasm into the economic development designs of the Gulf states as government oil revenues rebounded from $82bn in 1999 to $133.4bn in 2003. The combined oil export earnings reached $204bn in 2004. The GCC rose in global stature as its aggregate GDP, having stood at $350.7bn in 1980, reached $664.6bn by 2005 and $1.1trn in 2010. Reflecting the renewed sense of economic dynamism, in 2001 the GCC Supreme Council signed a revised economic agreement that established clear milestones for integration. Effectively acknowledging the delays to the original plans, the agreement vowed to create a customs union by January 2003, a common market by 2007, and a single currency by 2010. In practice, progress once again fell short of expectations. The third goal has proven far more elusive than originally hoped, partly due to the exceptional volatility of the global economy in the new millennium.

In 2001, the GCC members agreed on a mechanism to jointly share customs duties on imports to the block. Customs tariffs on foreign imports were unified in 2003, two years ahead of the original deadline. The customs union, formally signed into being in 2003, was implemented in 2005 and removed all restrictions on intra-regional trade. For goods of GCC origin, defined as having a minimum of 40 percent local value added or 51 percent of local investment, tariffs were waived altogether. The Gulf common market was declared in January 2008 and removed some important barriers to free movement of goods and services as well as to the mobility of national labor and capital. It permitted citizens to seek employment across the region, incorporate businesses, and establish residency in any member state.[90] However, the practical implementation of these grand designs was uneven, hampered by a multitude of non-tariff barriers, notably procedural challenges in cross-border transportation and inconsistencies in national regulatory standards and practices. Limitations on data sharing and communication technology continue to complicate regional trade. In some cases, national policy priorities – for instance, in employment – have curtailed labor mobility.

Despite the re-invigoration of the integration agenda, some of the original aspirations have been relegated in importance. With the oil windfall rushing in, the GCC countries showed themselves ready to pursue diversification and development in a primarily national context, notwithstanding risks of duplication. Old-fashioned beggar-thy-neighbor thinking undermined the effectiveness of some ventures. Moreover, the stunning successes of the "Dubai model" of diversification won a growing crowd of admirers ready to emulate elements of it. Past apprehensions proved easier to cast aside as ventures initially dismissed by critics as unrealistic subsequently went on to decisively confound the naysayers. But this ethos sowed future challenges by allowing "structural redundancy to proliferate and impede future integration."[91]

Ultimately, external circumstances once again conspired to challenge the onward march of integration. The onset of the global financial crisis in 2007–2008 delivered major disruptions in the financial sector as well as in real estate, which had been among the key growth engines of the Gulf economy during the boom. Immediate dislocations diverted the attention of policymakers from more strategic long-term designs. Moreover, the cascading problems the crisis unleashed in the EU drew scrutiny to potential pitfalls of integration. It revealed significant differences in the abilities of member states to respond to economic challenges and highlighted the de facto absence of shared financial institutions for managing such disruptions. Existential questions even began to be asked about the European single currency, which undermined the perceived political and economic appeal of the proposed Gulf monetary union in the eyes of many.

Another shock to the system came with a wave of socio-economic unrest that swept through the Middle East in 2011. This distracted from strategic endeavors but, on the other hand, also proved instrumental in cementing the broader sense of GCC exceptionalism and the value of unity. Protests in Bahrain and Oman were quickly followed by the announcement of $10bn development support packages for the each of two countries that were expected to be disbursed over a decade.[92] The Gulf countries mobilized their Peninsula Shield force during a state of emergency in Bahrain. But the GCC also seized the occasion to extend its reach beyond the Arabian Peninsula. In May 2011, the GCC invited Jordan and Morocco to join the organization, although little practical progress has followed to date, much as occurred with earlier designs for closer collaboration with Yemen.[93]

Dissenting voices

The practical implementation of the GCC integration agenda has been repeatedly challenged by differences of opinion. As suggested by Abdul Khaleq Abdulla, "The political and economic coming together of the six Arab Gulf states has been and will be ... an agonizing and protracted process with many breakdowns and few breakthroughs."[94] Of course, this reality is far from unique to the GCC, and most blocks have various mechanisms for accommodating such differences. For instance, the EU has found a way of progressing through multispeed integration while also forging ahead with its geographic expansion. At no point has the membership of the union fully coincided with the membership of key programs such as the eurozone or the Schengen area.

Some of the key integration projects of the GCC have become a source of discord, with the plans for a monetary union constituting a particular challenge. Oman withdrew from the project in 2007, citing its desire to ensure national control of fiscal policy, a move that reflected uncertainty about the country's ability to handle significant shocks within the constraints of a single currency. The UAE defected in 2009 with a move that was widely interpreted as a response to Abu Dhabi losing its bid to host the Gulf Monetary Council, while noting that it would reconsider if "the terms are different."[95] On the other hand, it was agreed by the members that the 2010 deadline for the single currency was not about to be met, which triggered a much more pragmatic approach to developing monetary policy coordination. The Gulf Monetary Council was established in March 2010 as a precursor for the regional central bank to lead on practical preparations. The Council has a permanent headquarters in Riyadh. The initial signatories of the agreement were Bahrain, Kuwait, Qatar, and Saudi Arabia.[96]

Recent years have also seen major political disputes among the regional countries. Following regional turmoil in 2011, Saudi Arabia unveiled a proposal to transform the GCC into a union, an initiative that Oman formally blocked in December 2013. The period of broader political tensions in the Middle East also left individual GCC countries with divergent perspectives on the way forward. In March 2014, Saudi Arabia, the UAE, and Bahrain withdrew their ambassadors from Doha in protest of Qatari support for the Muslim Brotherhood, which the three governments branded as a terrorist organization. The rupture also reflected longer-standing differences of opinion between Saudi Arabia and Qatar. The standoff was cleared by November 2014 but left simmering tensions, and a more serious crisis erupted in June 2017. Egypt, as well as some other Arab countries, joined Saudi Arabia, the UAE, and Bahrain in a renewed diplomatic standoff vis-à-vis Qatar. Not only did the group of nations sever their diplomatic ties with Doha but they also restricted Qatari-registered aircraft and sea vessels from entering their sovereign territory. The land crossing to Saudi Arabia was closed. The renewed confrontation followed claims that Qatar had not honored the 2014 agreement. The role of the Al Jazeera TV channel and Qatari relations with Iran were a particular focus. Kuwait and Oman chose to remain neutral in the dispute, and the former even made attempts to mediate between the two sides.[97]

The 2017 standoff was far more significant than its predecessors as the two sides showed readiness to resort to economic measures. Regular trade relations were severed, with significant implications for established supply chains. On the other hand, this demonstrated how important GCC integration had become at the practical level. Before the dispute, nearly 80 percent of Qatar's food needs had been met by shipments from the neighboring GCC countries. More generally, Jebel Ali had channeled over 85 percent of maritime cargo going to Qatar. In a challenge to these concrete achievements of Gulf integration, Qatar developed new sources of supply from Turkey and Iran. The countries involved in the standoff also repatriated their citizens from the opposing side. Despite these restrictions, Qatar continued to supply natural gas to the UAE and Oman through the Dolphin gas pipeline.

The post-2017 crisis had significant repercussions for other aspects of the Qatari government's aspirations. Qatar Airways, which has been a key plank of the country's diversification strategy, was forced to divert its flights outside of its neighbors' airspace. Its regional hub ambitions were challenged by the suspension of flights from three GCC countries. The possibility of withdrawing Qatar's right to host the 2022 FIFA World Cup was explored but, in the end, the original decision was honored. The crisis was finally settled in January 2021 when Kuwait and the US brokered a diplomatic solution. The blockade was lifted and borders reopened. The symbolic normalization of ties happened through the Al Ula' Statement signed on 2 January 2021 at a GCC summit attended by Qatar's Emir Tamim bin Hamad. The Al Ula' accord, which was also signed by Egypt, more generally sought to inject new energy into regional integration though 117 collaboration initiatives.[98]

Limits of integration

During the past four decades, GCC integration has moved forward at a very uneven pace. Moments of ambition and determination have been followed by swift progress. But these forward strides have alternated with periods when the integration agenda has drifted, eclipsed by national priorities. Much of it has reflected macro-economic volatility that determined the political and financial resources available for Gulf-wide ventures. But the institutional design of the GCC also explains much of this track record. In particular,

> *The GCC is not a supranational institution with independent legislative and judicial authority. The member states have not ceded sovereignty to the GCC. Policies, resolutions and other actions ... have the effect of law under the legal systems of the member states in accordance with their individual constitutional or other requirements.*[99]

There is no centralized driver of integration, as the Council lacks executive organs. The administrative resources of the GCC are modest and heavily focused on studies and analyses. With decision making decentralized, "key decisions emerge from opaque intergovernmental processes rather than from empowered regional institutions."[100] The responsibility for implementation tends to rest entirely at the national level. Noncompliance typically does not entail penalties, not even explicit "naming and shaming" of the kind the EU Commission has routinely engaged in: "there is an absence of GCC supranational political institutions powerful enough to enforce rules, with the exception of the Supreme Council, which is itself not designed to deal with day-to-day issues such as enforcing a single market."[101] As a result, "the GCC is structured to proceed spasmodically, essentially to allow each member nation the ability to remove itself from the process if it is does not agree."[102]

While the institutional architecture of the GCC may have slowed down integration, it has also accommodated a multiplicity of different types of intra-regional collaboration. These have sometimes deviated from the pan-regional agenda; for instance, through proactive initiatives to forge closer bilater relations. Among other things, Saudi Arabia and the UAE created a formal coordination council in May 2016 along with working committees involving some 350 civil servants. Kuwait and Bahrain have subsequently set up similar mechanisms with Saudi Arabia.

The initial designs to reap region-wide economies of scale met with limited success as "GCC countries compete with each other in sectors that might otherwise offer scope for regional initiatives, such as finance, transport, and downstream energy."[103] The desire to prioritize national interests and infrastructure assets has, for instance, held back the GCC Railway project, sometimes due to a desire to protect domestic legacy assets. These qualifications notwithstanding, the GCC has emerged as an economic space with a growing weight in the global economy. Its sustained investments in infrastructure and competitive regulation have earned it a reputation as an attractive crossroads at the heart of the Eurasian–African mega-continent. Its transportation and logistics prowess along with deepening commercial ties in multiple directions, potentially increasingly backed by financial innovation, positions it as a nimble hub that is able to pivot in different directions in the face of evolving realities. While little of this has been achieved with an explicitly regional agenda, the perception of the Arabian peninsula as a global player of growing importance is becoming established.

Various GCC institutions are driving standardization among member states while encouraging individuals and companies to think beyond their home markets. The GCC Secretariat has brought transparency to the workings of the block through a range of studies and reports. GCC-Stat is improving the availability and quality of statistical data region-wide. Among other pan-regional agencies are the Standardization and Meteorology Organization for GCC as well as the GCC Patent Office in Riyadh, the Technical Telecommunications Bureau in Bahrain, and the Regional Committee for Electrical Energy Systems registered in Qatar. A GCC Commercial Arbitration Centre has been operating since 1993.

Some formal integration initiatives have triggered an ongoing process of regulatory harmonization. The 2003 Customs Union Agreement was followed by a profound shift from decades of state-led import substitution policies that protected local production through a combination of tariffs, government investment, and subsidies. The average Most Favored Nation tariff rate dropped from 8.2 percent in 2000–2004 to 5.9 percent in 2006–2009.[104] Non-tariff barriers have been lowered through progressive harmonization and streamlining of customs procedures as well as common technical standards established for many products.

Good progress has materialized in equalizing rights of property ownership and movement of capital. GCC citizens can trade in equities region-wide, although trading procedures and costs vary. Increasing interaction is reshaping behavior and identity. The annual number of intra-regional visitors more than tripled, from 8mn in 2000 to 28mn in 2016, and has held fairly steady since then. The number of students studying in other GCC countries has hovered around the 40,000 mark for primary and secondary education and reached some 6,000 for tertiary education by 2019. The number of nationals working in a member state other than their own increased from 25,000 in 2005 to 33,000 in 2019. In 2019, 15,000 people were registered in the pension systems of another member state, a three-fold increase since 2008. In addition, 13,000 were registered for social insurance in 2019, up from 4,000 in 2008. It has become increasingly common for GCC citizens to acquire real estate in member states other than their own. Annual purchases rose from 2,000 in 2002 to 45,000 in 2019, reaching a cumulative total of 358,000 properties; 90.3 percent of all new purchases were in the UAE in 2019, while 18.8 percent of the buyers were Kuwaitis and 15.3 percent were Saudis.[105]

Increasing regional mobility is driving the growth of tourism, above all in the UAE. Similarly, visitors from Saudi Arabia "represented about 90 percent of Bahrain's total tourist arrivals in 2016 and 5 percent of its non-oil GDP."[106] The emergence of regional hubs for various services has driven regional interaction, a process led by Bahrain's rise as a financial center. It has become very common for foreign firms to establish representative offices, especially in Dubai, which has established itself as the leading regional cluster for especially foreign service providers. However, local content requirements are driving some renewed rivalry with, for instance, Saudi Arabia, which declared in January 2021 that international businesses will have to locate regional headquarters in the Kingdom to qualify for government procurement.[107]

Shared infrastructure has been recognized as a key integration driver since the inception of the GCC despite slow progress. Following the establishment of the GCC Interconnection Authority in 2001, the regional power exchange agreement was signed in 2009 with the target of "sharing capacity reserve and improving supply reliability."[108] Although similar usage patterns across the region limit its practical impact, the grid was accessed more than 150 times in 2016 and achieved savings of $150mn. A total of 734.4 GWh of power was traded. Hitherto mainly limited to a backup function, the grid could potentially create the basis for a regional power market, potentially one extending beyond the region. Connections are being developed to Egypt and Iraq, while Egypt is building a cable to Greece that could allow the Gulf to become a power exporter in time.[109] The introduction of renewable and nuclear power will create new opportunities to move toward a more regional energy market, even if long-term power purchase agreements remain a constraint for now. A GCC water grid was due to be completed by 2020 but has been delayed. The old Oman pipeline project found an alternative in Abu Dhabi's Habshan–Fujairah pipeline (ADCOP), which became operational in 2006 and could potentially connect more Gulf fields to the Arabian Sea coast. Integration is increasing in importance as the Gulf economies work to reduce their carbon footprint and ensure the optimal use of scarce resources.

All GCC states have now signed an open skies agreement liberalizing regional aviation. Some progress has also materialized toward the planned 2,117-km GCC Railway network, which was revived by a 2009 agreement. However, its projected budget of $250bn became a challenging prospect after the 2014 oil price correction. Several states suspended tendering in 2016 because of coordination problems, and the original 2018 deadline for completion was missed. Work by individual member states is progressing, albeit mainly reflecting and in abeyance to national needs and priorities.[110] An agreement was reached on the Saudi–Qatar and UAE–Oman rail links in 2022.[111]

Consistent tax treatment is a key goal of the Gulf Common Market. The fiscal landscape still presents a diversity of different – and divergent – levies and taxes. Coordination designs resurfaced during the post-2014 fiscal overhaul with a regional framework agreement on excise duties and the value-added tax endorsed in December 2015. Both were to be introduced at a standardized rate, set in the case of VAT at 5 percent. The practical implementation, as usual, was left to the national governments, which has resulted in significant differences. Saudi Arabia and the UAE made a head start in 2018. Bahrain undertook a phased implementation in 2019. Oman launched VAT in March 2021, but the remaining two member states are yet to begin. Differences exist in the scope of the tax and the policy on exemptions. Saudi Arabia tripled the rate of VAT as of July 2020. Bahrain, under its revised Fiscal Balance Program, doubled the rate in 2022.

After the signing of the US–Bahrain free trade agreement in 2005, GCC members agreed to coordinate all future external trade negotiations. The GCC is part of GAFTA, whose practical progress has been complicated by divergent regulations and infrastructure constraints.[112] Attempts by the GCC as a block to negotiate significant trade deals have tended to progress slowly and unevenly. Negotiations for a GCC–EU free trade treaty were originally launched in 1990 but have not concluded despite a 2017 agreement to establish a more structured dialogue. Post-Brexit Britain now views the GCC as a high-priority target for its future commercial relations. The China–GCC FTA talks were reported to be in "final stages" in late 2022. In practice, economic ties between individual GCC states and third countries have continued to develop on a bilateral basis. The 2022 Comprehensive Economic Partnership Agreement between the UAE and India is expected to eventually cut duties on almost 90 percent of bilateral merchandise trade. The UAE has agreed to similar deals with Turkey and Israel, and others are planned.[113]

Important intra-Gulf differences persist in areas such as public procurement, subsidies, and customs border controls. Policy implementation still typically happens with minimal regional coordination. Security concerns have at times introduced additional complications, as seen again during the COVID-19 pandemic. Domestic initiatives sometimes continue to challenge even past achievements. For instance, Saudi Arabia not only tripled VAT but also increased import duties on several categories of goods in 2020, followed by a decision to stop applying GCC treatment to the UAE free zones in 2021.[114]

Taking stock

While political traditions and institutions may explain much of the checkered track record of GCC integration, actual economic convergence is brought about by individuals, firms, and markets. The discussion around Gulf integration has focused on the policy inputs rather than economic outcomes, but integration is not merely the consequence of removing barriers to it. Remarkably little attention has been paid to date to the limited progress of de facto integration through private sector initiative, although the regional common market has created a reasonable basis for it. By contrast, in many other parts of the world, integration among neighboring countries has often made substantial headway even in the absence of a political push for it.

Despite low trade barriers, intra-GCC trade volumes are modest, seemingly stuck at around 10 percent of the region's total foreign trade, even as absolute values have increased from just $15bn in 2003 to $147bn in 2018. During the two decades leading up to 2003, this tally had "only" tripled in value. The weight of intra-GCC trade differs a great deal country to country. Saudi–Bahraini commercial ties have for decades been anchored in supply agreements between Saudi Aramco and the Bapco refinery. Saudi Arabia receives more than a quarter of Bahrain's non-oil exports. In 2014, the combined merchandise imports and exports between Bahrain and the rest of the GCC made up 56 percent of the Kingdom's GDP, up from 43 percent in 2005.[115]

Saudi Arabia's large manufacturing base makes it an important exporter to the rest of the Gulf – to the tune of "more than $12 billion in 2016, including transport equipment, machinery, electronics, and metals."[116] The rise of regional distribution hubs, above all Jebel Ali, has typically given the UAE a 30–40 percent share in intra-regional commerce, followed

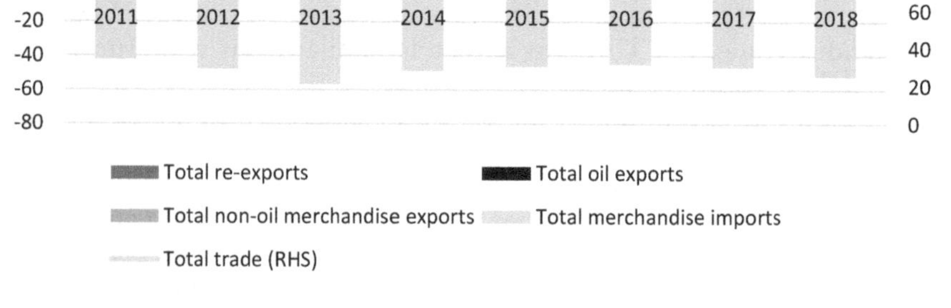

Figure 7.1 Value of intra-GCC trade flows, $ bn.

Source: GCC Secretariat, GCC-Stat, al-suq al-khalijiah al-mushtarakah fi duwal majlis al-ta'wun 2020, p. 24.

by Saudi Arabia and Oman. Re-exports in recent years have routinely accounted for around a third of the intra-regional export volume. But weak complementarities limit progress "due to similar economic structure and levels of economic development."[117] Regional value chains similarly remain underdeveloped.

Regional entrepreneurship has gained popularity. In December 2010 the Supreme Council allowed Gulf companies to set up branches in any member state "on an equal footing with national firms."[118] The cumulative number of commercial registrations issued to citizens of other GCC member states has increased from 14,000 in 2005 to 49,000 in 2019, some 80 percent of them in the UAE, largely reflecting the continued appeal of its free zones. The number of GCC banks operating regionally outside their home market increased from 14 in 2005 to 27 in 2019. Similarly,whereas in 2005 some 270,000 GCC citizens owned shares in companies domiciled in another GCC member state, this figure had almost doubled, to almost half a million, by 2011.[119]

Intra-regional cross-border investments in the GCC totaled less than $3.6bn in 1990–2003, but a subsequent wave of privatization and deregulation quickly changed this. Booz & Co. observed in 2011 that "intra-GCC M&A activity has been quite robust across all industry sectors, growing to $26.4 billion between 2000 and 2008."[120] Despite slower progress thereafter, intra-Gulf FDI has become systemically significant. The inward FDI stock of GCC origin in Saudi Arabia totaled more than $35bn in 2015 – some 10 percent on non-oil GDP. Kuwait and Saudi Arabia have routinely been the two leading sources of inward FDI in Bahrain. The total FDI stock from the rest of the region was equivalent to two-thirds of the inward FDI stocks in Bahrain and nearly 60 percent of non-oil GDP.[121]

Despite its geographic and cultural homogeneity, not to mention four decades of structured collaboration, the GCC to this day can claim relatively few truly pan-GCC brands or companies. In fact, foreign businesses from outside the region have been more likely to build a region-wide presence than local companies. The track record of these non-Gulf companies suggests that region-wide expansion is not meaningfully limited by purely regulatory factors. Sectors such as financial services, telecommunications, retail, hospitality, and property development have seen the largest number of cross-border deals in the Gulf. Some of the largest regional banks operate in multiple jurisdictions but almost never with a truly region-wide network. Rather, they remain domestically focused and typically have at best a small number of representative offices or branches elsewhere.[122] Banks with a truly pan-regional footprint are invariably international groups such as Citigroup, HSBC, Standard Chartered, and BNP Paribas. Several of them are present in most – if not all – Gulf economies No single GCC financial institution of scale can claim the same, although groups such as the National Bank of Kuwait, First Abu Dhabi Bank, Qatar National Bank, and al Baraka have established a significant presence within and beyond the region.

The same is true in telecommunications, where market liberalization has encouraged especially erstwhile national incumbents to look beyond their increasingly contested home markets. Both Saudi Telecommunications

Company (STC) and Etisalat (e&) of the UAE have expanded both through acquisition and organically. STC today has subsiaries in Bahrain and Kuwait. Etisalat operates in Saudi Arabia under the Mobily brand and is present in many other markets as well, mainly in Africa. Qatar's Ooredoo (formerly Qtel) has a presence in Kuwait and Oman. Zain is a relative newcomer that set out to challenge the incumbents in several Gulf markets. Established as the Mobile Telecommunications Company in Kuwait in 1983, Zain has expanded into nine other Middle Eastern markets, including Bahrain (2003) and Saudi Arabia (2008). The company's owners include Omantel. In hospitality, a handful of regional brands have emerged, among them the Rotana Hotels of Abu Dhabi and Dubai's Jumeirah. Retail businesses with a regional presence include Kuwait-based Alshaya Group, the Al-Futtaim Group, Majid al Futtaim Group, and LuLu Group International of the UAE, as well as Jashanmal. Dubai's Emaar Group, among others, has undertaken property developments across the region.[123]

The lack of greater cross-border expansion is likely due in no small part to the economic dynamics of the individual Gulf countries. Historically, robust growth was easily achieved thanks to a combination of demographic dynamism (including a growing expatriate workforce), high oil prices, increasing government spending, etc. The domestic market typically offered compelling growth prospects, which, in the eyes of many, reduced the perceived urgency and attractiveness of entering other markets that almost invariably entailed greater costs, regulatory complications, and even risks. The ownership structure of state-owned companies or family businesses strengthened the local bias in many cases.

The structure of the financial sector has also entailed complications: "[t]he financial systems in the GCC remain ... dominated by commercial banks, which limited the importance of cross-border equity flows."[124] An IMF assessment of financial market integration in 2010 found mixed evidence of actual market integration as measured by indicators such as interest rate convergence and the price dynamics of cross-listed stocks. Similarly, "international markets differentiate among GCC countries in assessing risks as evidenced by trends in credit default swaps (CDS) spreads."[125]

One area where progress has been limited is labor market integration, which truly reflects the realities of employment in the region. While GCC nationals can now work across borders, this is not true for the non-nationals who dominate private sector employment. Significant differences in regulations combine with limited cross-border mobility, although travel across the region has been liberalized. This market fragmentation is a source of inefficiency and cost. The general liberalization of residency regulations likely also heralds future progress in this area.

The way forward?

For decades, high-level GCC integration ambitions have been plagued by setbacks and delays. Political disputes have repeatedly complicated the way forward. Economic development plans are as a rule drafted in the national – sometimes even the subnational – context. The perceived solution to the majority of economic reform challenges in the eyes of most policymakers is national. Yet it is becoming increasingly obvious that the future well-being of the region stands to benefit a great deal from a more proactive focus on integration. Even after decades of rapid economic and population growth, the age-old arguments about limitations of scale have not lost their validity. The potential for building regional value chains is obvious, a process further facilitated by the growing range of opportunities created by the gradual onward march of economic diversification that is creating more opportunities for intra-industry trade. Specifically, "[s]maller GCC economies can become integrated into the supply chains of larger ones."[126] Intra-GCC and even broader Middle Eastern commerce may well come to attract more attention in a de-globalizing world. Nonetheless, the Gulf economies continue to fall far short of their potential in terms of intra-GCC non-oil goods exports. The gap was calculated by the IMF to be highest in Oman, Kuwait, and Qatar in 2015 – from 4 percent to more than 7 percent of non-oil GDP.[127]

Gulf integration looks likely to become increasingly market led. Slower trends in GDP growth and fiscal consolidation have pushed more Gulf businesses to think beyond their home markets. For most, Gulf neighbors remain the logical first ports of call. The regional market offers the comfort of shorter distances, familiar culture, and a degree of regulatory harmonization. The spectacular rise of e-commerce is changing consumer habits. Cross-border M&A activity has been minimal but is becoming easier now that fiscal reforms are contributing to more transparent accounting practices and allaying concerns about fair valuations. M&A has the potential to become its own driver of integration by casting light on practical challenges.

Technological progress can facilitate integration by permitting more efficient cross-border procedures and risk mitigation. It can potentially allow customs formalities to be moved to the external borders of the GCC – or at least of willing members – by allowing shared access to the relevant data. National regulatory ring-fencing and data protection remain challenges, but innovation is making it much easier to share information while respecting considerations about privacy and data protection.

There are signs of encouraging convergence between market-led integration and political ambitions, not least thanks to the growing stature and evolving focus of sovereign investors. The 2021 Saudi National Investment Strategy explicitly refers to "increasing regional integration." In October 2022, PIF confirmed plans to set up investment companies in Bahrain, Iraq, Jordan, Oman, and Sudan. Other GCC investors, including ADQ, AD Ports, and Qatar Energy, are eyeing new opportunities across the Middle East.[128] This posture promises to replace, or at least eclipse, the more established intra-regional aid flows with more productive investments. With more progress in privatization and PPPs, cross-border acquisitions are likely to grow in number. This is a welcome development, for:

> *It is not in the strategic interests of the GCC to retreat within itself, nor ... do sufficient financial resources exist for bailing out failing Arab*

> *regimes indefinitely. The only alternative is for a much smarter, strategic Gulf engagement with the rest of the MENA region, one that stimulates prospects for private sector growth and ultimately reduced dependence upon donor handouts and remittances.*[129]

There is an obvious opportunity to adopt a more pragmatic perspective on regional integration: "Regional cooperation may be best pursued on an à la carte, bottom-up, pragmatic basis – as opposed to relying on the type of trade agreements that have been the focal point to date in the region and largely failed to deliver."[130] This concept is little different from the EU practice of a "multispeed" Europe coupled with the commitment to subsidiarity. Different jurisdictions can take integration forward at their own pace, provided some basic minimum standards are observed by all. Initial holdouts could eventually follow suit as the value of certain initiatives is more conclusively demonstrated. Such an approach would also allow different national and political preferences to be accommodated without holding back others. This can also make the integration process more explicitly responsive to concrete needs. The evolution of the EU has involved on the pragmatic acceptance of different visions for integration and a growing focus on tackling concrete issues.

The process of integration can never be expected to be linear. The years since the global financial crisis have seen globalizing forces lose much of their forward momentum. Such factors are also likely to create periodic complications in the GCC, but they also have the potential to focus minds around more feasible regional solutions rather than – or potentially also as a complement to – global visions. Intra-regional integration might well prove an easier way to reap some of the benefits of globalization in a world of moving goalposts even as the balancing act between national needs and a regional vision will doubtless persist. The one-upmanship in pursuit of regional hubs or rankings has deep roots.

But it is clear that the Gulf economies are developing a sense of "togetherness," whether as a group of six or smaller sub-groupings. Growing inter-dependency and interaction is strengthening a *khaleeji* identity, partly reflecting increased intra-regional tourism. In a world characterized by multiple risks and uncertainties, the Gulf region stands out from the broader neighborhood, whose challenges serve as a constant reminder of its own achievements. Progress for Gulf integration also promises to pave the way for a more multifaceted engagement with the broader Middle East. While genuine trade integration within GAFTA has multiple historical, cultural, and institutional hurdles to overcome, using the organization "as an instrument of cooperation to agree to lower barriers to trade in services, labor and capital could generate significant potential gains, much larger than what can be realized with respect to trade in goods."[131] For the Gulf, this would entail new complementaties and a substantially larger market opportunity. By transcending outdated "zero-sum" considerations, it would also make the GCC less of an oasis by leveraging its capital for shared prosperity through regional complementarities and synergies.

Notes

1 Zahlan, *The Making of the Modern Gulf States*, pp. 111–114, 118.
2 Keynes, *The Economic Consequences*, p. 211.
3 Terborgh, "The Post-War Rise of World Trade," pp. 3–12.
4 https://european-union.europa.eu/principles-countries-history/history-eu/1945-59/schuman-declaration-may-1950_en.
5 Terborgh, "The Post-War Rise of World Trade."
6 Bown and Irwin, "The GATT's Starting Point," p. 21.
7 https://www.wto.org/english/res_e/statis_e/trade_evolution_e/evolution_trade_wto_e.htm.
8 Pact of the League of Arab States, March 22, 1945, https://avalon.law.yale.edu/20th_century/arableag.asp.
9 Hoekman and Sekkat, "Arab Economic Integration," p. 3.
10 Hoekman and Sekkat, "Arab Economic Integration," p. 2.
11 Hoekman, *Intra-Regional Trade*, p. 22; Hoekman and Sekkat, "Arab Economic Integration," p. 28.
12 Hoekman and Sekkat, "Arab Economic Integration," pp. 10, 33; Hoekman and Sekkat, "Arab Economic Integration," p. 22.
13 Hoekman, *Intra-Regional Trade*, p. 20.
14 Hoekman, *Intra-Regional Trade*, p. 1.
15 Shafik, "Labor Migration and Economic Integration," p. 293; Hoekman and Sekkat, "Arab Economic Integration," pp. 3–7.
16 Shafik, "Labor Migration and Economic Integration," p. 292; Hoekman, *Intra-Regional Trade*, p. 7.
17 Shafik, "Labor Migration and Economic Integration," p. 293.
18 Hoekman and Sekkat, "Arab Economic Integration," p. 13; Shafik, "Labor Migration and Economic Integration," p. 279; Hoekman, *Intra-Regional Trade*, p. 2.
19 Hanieh, *Money, Markets, and Monarchies*, p. 3.
20 Shafik, "Labor Migration and Economic Integration," p. 296.
21 Zahlan, *The Making of the Modern Gulf States*, pp. 140–141.
22 Zahlan, *The Making of the Modern Gulf States*, pp. 96, 98–99, 105, 121; Heard-Bey, *From the Trucial States*, pp. 35, 46, 118, 202–205; Anthony, *Arab States of the Lower Gulf*, pp. 115–117, 213–215; Davidson, *Dubai*, p. 275.
23 Quoted in: Davidson, *The United Arab Emirates*, p. 46.
24 Davidson, *Dubai*, p. 40.
25 Davidson, *Dubai*, p. 56.
26 Quoted in: Smith, *Britain's Revival*, p. 49.
27 Davidson, *Dubai*, p. 250.
28 Smith, *Britain's Revival*, p. 49.
29 Quoted in: Smith, *Britain's Revival*, p. 49.
30 Hawley, *The Trucial States*, pp. 176–178.
31 Hawley, *The Trucial States*, p. 177.
32 Smith, *Britain's Revival*, p. 50; Hawley, *The Trucial States*, p. 178.
33 Hawley, *The Trucial States*, p. 177.
34 Heard-Bey, "The United Arab Emirates," p. 132.
35 Davidson, *Dubai*, p. 58.
36 Fenelon, *The Trucial States*, pp. 46–50; Heard-Bey, *From the Trucial States*, pp. 319–332; Davidson, *The United Arab Emirates*, p. 43.
37 Legrenzi, *The GCC*, p. 12.
38 Quoted in: Smith, *Britain's Revival*, p. 69; Legrenzi, *The GCC*, pp. 24–25.
39 Smith, *Britain's Revival*, pp. 59–60.
40 Smith, *Britain's Revival*, p. 60.
41 Smith, *Britain's Revival*, p. 60.
42 Quoted in: Smith, *Britain's Revival*, p. 61.
43 Smith, *Britain's Revival*, p. 62.

44 Quoted in: Smith, *Britain's Revival*, p. 17.
45 Nuttall, *Shipping and Development in Dubai*, pp. 32–33.
46 Owen and Pamuk, *A History*, p. 222.
47 Owen and Pamuk, *A History*, pp. 222–223.
48 Heard-Bey, "The United Arab Emirates," p. 130.
49 Davidson, *Dubai*, pp. 61–63; Heard-Bey, "The United Arab Emirates," p. 130; Heard-Bey, *From the Trucial States*, pp. 358–370.
50 Heard-Bey, *From the Trucial States*, p. 366.
51 Zahlan, *The Making of the Modern Gulf States*, p. 136.
52 Demas, *The Economics of Development in Small Countries*, p. 38; Al-Kuwari, *Oil Revenues in the Gulf Emirates*, p. 176.
53 Wilson, *The Economies of the Middle East*, p. 80.
54 Wilson, *The Economies of the Middle East*, pp. 80–81.
55 Al Makhawi, *The Gulf Cooperation Council*, pp. 43–44.
56 Quoted in: Legrenzi, *The GCC*, p. 24.
57 Al Makhawi, *The Gulf Cooperation Council*, pp. 46–47.
58 Zahlan, *The Making of the Modern Gulf States*, p. 136; Al Makhawi, *The Gulf Cooperation Council*, pp. 45–46.
59 Owen and Pamuk, *A History*, p. 223.
60 Zahlan, *The Making of the Modern Gulf States*, p. 147; Burke and Bazoobandi, "The Gulf Takes Charge," pp. 36–39.
61 Owen and Pamuk, *A History*, p. 223.
62 Burke and Bazoobandi, "The Gulf Takes Charge," pp. 33–35.
63 Zahlan, *The Making of the Modern Gulf States*, p. 148.
64 Al Makhawi, *The Gulf Cooperation Council*, p. 42.
65 Al Makhawi, *The Gulf Cooperation Council*, p. 50.
66 Al Makhawi, *The Gulf Cooperation Council*, p. 45.
67 Al Makhawi, *The Gulf Cooperation Council*, p. 49.
68 Al Makhawi, *The Gulf Cooperation Council*, p. 51.
69 Al Makhawi, *The Gulf Cooperation Council*, p. 51.
70 Quoted in: Al Makhawi, *The Gulf Cooperation Council*, p. 71.
71 Al Makhawi, *The Gulf Cooperation Council*, p. 56.
72 Lawson, *Transformations of Regional Economic Governance*, p. 8.
73 Lawson, *Transformations of Regional Economic Governance*, p. 8.
74 Lawson, *Transformations of Regional Economic Governance*, p. 9.
75 Crystal, *Kuwait*, p. 156.
76 Niblock, *The Political Economy of Saudi Arabia*, pp. 103, 114–116.
77 Crystal, *Kuwait*, p. 156.
78 Lawson, *Transformations of Regional Economic Governance*, p. 9.
79 Crystal, *Kuwait*, p. 156.
80 Champion, *The Paradoxical Kingdom*, p. 148.
81 Nuttall, *Shipping and Development in Dubai*, pp. 86–88.
82 Zahlan, *The Making of the Modern Gulf States*, p. 139; Al Makhawi, *The Gulf Cooperation Council*, p. 61.
83 Dargin, *Desert Dreams*, p. 241.
84 Al Makhawi, *The Gulf Cooperation Council*, p. 64.
85 Al Makhawi, *The Gulf Cooperation Council*, p. 63; Dargin, *Desert Dreams*, p. 254.
86 Dargin, *The Dolphin Project*, pp. 1, 18–24.
87 Al Makhawi, *The Gulf Cooperation Council*, pp. 63–64.
88 Lawson, *Transformations of Regional Economic Governance*, p. 9.
89 Alasfoor, *The Gulf Cooperation Council*, p. 75.
90 Beblawi, "Gulf Industrialization," p. 190; Dargin, *Desert Dreams*, pp. 258–259.
91 Dargin, *Desert Dreams*, p. 258.
92 Dargin, *Desert Dreams*, p. 281.
93 Burke, "'One Blood and One Destiny'?," pp. 58–64.

94 Abdulla, "The Gulf Cooperation Council," p. 152.
95 Adomaitis, "UAE May Rejoin."
96 Lawson, *Transformations of Regional Economic Governance*, pp. 13–15; Dargin, *Desert Dreams*, pp. 274–275.
97 Hanieh, *Money, Markets, and Monarchies*, pp. 246–251.
98 Richard Thompson, "Al-Ula the First Step to Restoring GCC Unity," *MEED*, 6 January 2021.
99 Alasfoor, *The Gulf Cooperation Council*, p. 44.
100 World Bank, *Economic Integration*, p. 1.
101 Abdulghaffar et al., "The Malfunctioning," p. 54.
102 Dargin, *Desert Dreams*, p. 275.
103 World Bank, *Economic Integration*, p. 1.
104 World Bank, *Economic Integration*, p. 17.
105 Al-Ubaidly and Jones, *GCC Economic Integration*, pp. 12–14; GCC-Stat, *al-suq al-khalijiah al-mushtarakah fi duwal majlis al-ta'wun 2020*, pp. 9, 13, 17, 27, 37–40.
106 Adedeji *et al.*, "Saudi Arabia's Growth," p. 6; Shediac *et al.*, *Integrating, Not Integrated*, p. 4.
107 "Saudi Arabia Won't Work with Foreign Firms without Regional HQ from 2024," Reuters, 15 February 2021; Aziz El Yaakoubi, Marwa Rashad, and Davide Barbuscia, "Saudi Arabia Amends Import Rules from Gulf in Challenge to UAE," Reuters, 5 July 2021.
108 World Bank, *Middle East*, p. 1.
109 Al-Ubaidly and Jones, *GCC Economic Integration*, p. 11; World Bank, *Middle East*, p. 1.
110 Dargin, *Desert Dreams*, pp. 252–253.
111 Colin Foreman, "UAE Leads Regional Rail Resurgence," *MEED*, 13 October 2022.
112 Hoekman, *Intra-Regional Trade*, p. 10.
113 https://www.moec.gov.ae.
114 Aziz El Yaakoubi, Marwa Rashad, and Davide Barbuscia, "Saudi Arabia Amends Import Rules from Gulf in Challenge to UAE," Reuters, 5 July 2021.
115 Adedeji *et al.*, "Saudi Arabia's Growth," p. 5; Al-Ubaidly and Jones, *GCC Economic Integration*, p. 7.
116 Adedeji *et al.*, "Saudi Arabia's Growth," p. 5.
117 IMF, *Trade and Foreign Investment*, p. 9.
118 Lawson, *Transformations of Regional Economic Governance*, p. 16.
119 Al-Ubaidly and Jones, *GCC Economic Integration*, pp. 9–10, 16–17; Shediac *et al.*, *Integrating, Not Integrated*, p. 4; GCC-Stat, *al-suq al-khalijiah al-mushtarakah fi duwal majlis al-ta'wun 2020*, p. 22.
120 Shediac *et al.*, *Integrating, Not Integrated*, p. 16; Lawson, *Transformations of Regional Economic Governance*, p. 17.
121 Adedeji *et al.*, "Saudi Arabia's Growth," p. 6; GCC-Stat, *al-suq al-khalijiah al-mushtarakah fi duwal majlis al-ta'wun 2020*, p. 24.
122 GCC-Stat, *al-suq al-khalijiah al-mushtarakah fi duwal majlis al-ta'wun 2020*, pp. 21–22.
123 Hanieh, *Money, Markets, and Monarchies*, pp. 67–111, 143–145, 154–158, 165–171, 188–190.
124 Espinoza *et al.*, "Regional Financial Integration," p. 7.
125 Espinoza *et al.*, "Regional Financial Integration," pp. 4–6.
126 IMF, *Trade and Foreign Investment*, p. 23.
127 IMF, *Trade and Foreign Investment*, p. 23.
128 https://www.meed.com/saudi-arabia-pif-to-invest-5bn-in-bahrain; https://www.meed.com/riyadh-approves-pif-deal-for-egypt; https://www.meed.com/pif-to-invest-24bn-in-six-mena-countries.
129 Burke and Bazoobandi, "The Gulf Takes Charge," p. 44.
130 Hoekman, *Intra-Regional Trade*, p. 25.
131 Hoekman and Sekkat, "Arab Economic Integration," p. 35.

References

Abdulghaffar, Mahmood, Omar Al-Ubaydli, and Omar Mahmood (2013), "The Malfunctioning of the Gulf Cooperation Council Single Market: Features, Causes and Remedies," *Middle Eastern Finance and Economics*, No. 19, pp. 54–67.

Abdulla, Abdul Khaleq (1999), "The Gulf Cooperation Council: Nature, Origin, and Proces," in: Hudson, *op. cit.*, pp. 150–170.

Adedeji, Olumuyiwa S., Sohaid Shadid, and Ling Zhu (2018), "Saudi Arabia's Growth and Financial Spillovers to Other GCC Countries: An Empirical Analysis," IMF Working Paper, WP/18/278, Washington, DC: International Monetary Fund.

Adomaitis, Nerijus (2009), "UAE May Rejoin Monetary Union if Terms Change," *Arabian Business*, 23 May 2009, https://www.arabianbusiness.com/politics-economics/uae-may-rejoin-monetary-union-if-terms-change-18131.

Anthony, John Duke (1975), *Arab States of the Lower Gulf: People, Politics, Petroleum* (*The James Terry Duce Memorial Series*, vol. III), Washington, D.C.: The Middle East Institute.

Alasfoor, Reyadh (2007), *The Gulf Cooperation Council: Its Nature and Achievements, a Political Analysis of Regional Integration of the GCC States 1979–2004* (*Lund Political Studies 149*), Lund: Department of Political Science, Lund University.

Beblawi, Hazem (2010), "Gulf industrialization in perspective," in: Seznec and Kirk, *op. cit.*, pp. 185–197.

Bown, Chad P. and Douglas A. Irwin (2015), "The GATT's Starting Point: Tariff Levels circa 1947," NBER Working Paper Series, Working Paper 21782, Cambridge, Mass.: National Bureau of Economic Research.

Burke, Edward (2012), "'One Blood and One Destiny'?: Yemen and the Gulf," in: Youngs, *op. cit.*, pp. 45–72.

Burke, Edward and Sara Bazoobandi (2012), "The Gulf Takes Charge: The GCC in the MENA Region," in: Youngs, *op. cit.*, pp. 23–44.

Champion, Daryl (2005), *The Paradoxical Kingdom: Saudi Arabia and the Momentum of Reform*, New York, Columbia University Press.

Crystal, Jill (1992), *Kuwait: The Transformation of an Oil State*, Boulder, Colo.: Westview Press.

Dargin, Justin (2008), *The Dolphin Project: The Development of a Gulf Gas Initiative*, NG 22, Oxford Institute for Energy Studies, January 2008.

——— (2011), *Desert Dreams. The Quest for Arab Integration from the Arab Revolt to the Gulf Cooperation Council*, Dordrecht: Republic of Letters.

Davidson, Christopher M. (2005), *The United Arab Emirates: A Study in Survival*, Boulder, Colo.: Lynne Rienner Publishers.

——— (2008), *Dubai: The Vulnerability of Success*, New York: Columbia University Press.

Demas, William G. (1965), *The Economics of Development in Small Countries – With Special Reference to the Caribbean*, Montreal: McGill University Press.

Espinoza, Raphael, Ghada Fayad, and Ananthakrishnan Prasad (2013), *The Macroeconomics of the Arab States of the Gulf*, Oxford: Oxford University Press.

Fenelon, Kevin (1969), *The Trucial States: A Brief Economic Survey*, Beirut: Khayats.

GCC-Stat (2020), *al-suq al-khalijiah al-mushtarakah fi duwal majlis al-ta'wun 2020*, Muscat: al-markaz al-ihsa'ii li-duwal majlis al-ta'wun li-duwal al-khalij al-'arabiayah.

Hanieh, Adam (2018), *Money, Markets, and Monarchies: The Gulf Cooperation Council and the Political Economy of the Contemporary Middle East*, Cambridge: Cambridge University Press.

Hawley, Sir Donald (1971), *The Trucial States*, London: George Allen & Unwin.
Heard-Bey, Frauke (1982), *From Trucial States to United Arab Emirates*, London: Longman.
Hoekman, Bernard (2016), *Intra-Regional Trade: Potential Catalyst for Growth in the Middle East*, MEI Policy Paper 2016–1, Middle East Institute, Regional Cooperation Series, April 2016.
Hoekman, Bernard and Khalid Sekkat (2010), "Arab Economic Integration: The Missing Links," Working Paper, SciencesPo – Groupe d'Économie Mondiale, April 2010.
Hudson, Michael C., ed. (1998), *The Middle East Dilemma: The Politics and Economics of Arab Integration*, New York: Columbia University Press.
International Monetary Fund (2018), *Trade and Foreign Investment – Keys to Diversification and Growth in the GCC*, Gulf Cooperation Council/IMF Policy Paper, Washington, D.C.: International Monetary Fund.
Keynes, John Maynard (1919), *The Economic Consequences of the Peace*, London: Macmillan & Co. Ltd.
Al-Kuwari, Ali Khalifa (1978), *Oil Revenues in the Gulf Emirates: Patterns of Allocation and Impact on Economic Development*, Boulder, Colo.: Westview Press.
Lawson, Fred H. (2012), *Transformations of Regional Economic Governance in the Gulf Cooperation Council*, Occasional Paper No. 10, Georgetown University School of Foreign Service in Qatar, Center for International and Regional Studies, August 2012.
Legrenzi, Matteo (2011), *The GCC and the International Relations of the Gulf: Diplomacy, Security and Economic Coordination in a Changing Middle East*, London: I.B. Tauris.
Al Makhawi, Rashid A. (1990), *The Gulf Cooperation Council: A Study in Integration*, Thesis submitted for the degree of Doctor of Philosophy, International Studies Unit, University of Salford.
Niblock, Tim with Monica Malik (2007), *The Political Economy of Saudi Arabia*, Abingdon: Routledge.
Nuttall, Keith (2021), *Shipping and Development in Dubai: Infrastructure, Innovation and Institutions in the Gulf*, London: I.B. Tauris.
Owen, E. Roger and Şevket Pamuk (1999), *A History of Middle East Economies in the Twentieth Century*, Cambridge, Mass.: Harvard University Press.
Seznec, Jean-François and Mimi Kirk, eds. (2010), *Industrialization in the Gulf: A Socioeconomic Revolution*, London: Routledge.
Shafik, Nemat (1999), "Labor Migration and Economic Integration in the Middle East," in: Hudson, *op. cit.*, pp. 279–298.
Shediac, Richard, Parag Khanna, Taufiq Rahim, and Hatem A. Samman (2011), *Integrating, Not Integrated: A Scorecard of GCC Economic Integration* (Ideation Center Insight), Booz & Company.
Smith, Simon C. (2004), *Britain's Revival and Fall in the Gulf: Kuwait, Bahrain, Qatar, and the Trucial States, 1950–1971*, London: Routledge Curzon.
Terborgh, Andrew G. (2003), "The Post-War Rise of World Trade: Does the Bretton Woods System Deserve Credit?," Working Paper, No. 78/03, Department of Economic History, London School of Economics.
Al-Ubaydli, Omar and Erik Jones (2018), *GCC Economic Integration: Opportunities and Challenges*, Background Paper for Bahrain 2018 National Human Development Report, Manama: Derasat.
Wilson, Rodney (1979), *The Economies of the Middle East*, London: Macmillan.
World Bank (2010), *Economic Integration in the GCC*, Washington, D.C.: The World Bank.

Youngs, Richard, ed. (2012), *The GCC in the Global Economy* (*The Gulf Region: Economic Development and Diversification*, vol. 1), Berlin: Gerlach Press.
Zahlan, Rosemarie Said (1989), *The Making of the Modern Gulf States: Kuwait, Bahrain, Qatar, the United Arab Emirates and Oman*, London: Unwin Hyman.

8 The imperative of change

When then–Deputy Crown Prince Mohammed bin Salman unveiled Saudi Arabia's Vision 2030 on 25 April 2016, he magnetized not only his compatriots but also much of the global community. In the wake of a major oil price shock, he projected himself as a young, energetic Arab leader, determined to call things by their right names and transform the Saudi economy for a brighter future in the face of the ever accelerating pace of global economic change. What the rising star of Middle Eastern politics presented was nothing fundamentally new, but his exuberant determination represented a resolute shift in terms of dispensing with the traditional deference to political convention, consensus, and gradualism.

While policymaking in the Gulf has been evolving for years toward increasingly ambitious structural reform, it is now clear that a new chapter beckons in the regional development journey as the impetus of past growth drivers wanes. The oil–government nexus propelled the region's spectacular race to modernity. However, the expected oil market dynamics and regional demographic trends have diverged to a point where this model can no longer predictably or sustainably deliver the prosperity it once did.

The Great Arabian Infrastructure Boom marked an impressive fresh start after a drawn-out crisis. This second wave of diversification positioned the Arabian Gulf at the heart of the emerging global economic geography with remarkable speed, ever more effectively capitalizing on its exceptional locational advantages. The 2008 financial crisis delivered a moment of reckoning and cast doubt over the sustainability of the extensive growth paradigm that had relied almost exclusively on input accumulation. Nonetheless, aggressive stimulus spending by the Gulf governments permitted a swift normalization of activity until the renewed oil price correction of 2014–2015.

Just as oil price dynamics helped trigger and sustain the first two chapters of the Gulf region's modern economic transformation, they were instrumental in putting an end to them as well. The painful oil price crash of the 1980s underscored the strategic necessity of economic diversification. Similarly, the consecutive oil shocks of 2008, 2014, and 2020 revealed some of the drawbacks of a heavy reliance on infrastructure investment, which in the end proved little more of a magic formula than oil did. The tighter liquidity conditions during the crisis years not only curbed the availability of capital for grandiose investments but also markedly checked

DOI: 10.4324/9781003373353-8

demand growth. Construction as a growth engine echoed the dynamics of the oil economy to which it remained significantly linked. Due to its inherently cyclicality, real estate in some ways served to amplify economic fluctuations.

The infrastructure narrative in many areas came to be challenged by its inherent vulnerability to the law of diminishing returns. Amid the manic rush to build, it was sometimes easy to forget that the longer-term economic impact of infrastructure investment is determined by the effectiveness with which it is used to anchor different types of sustained economic activity. While achieving this during the early years of the boom was very easy, the rapidly growing stock of physical capital eventually resulted in lower utilization and returns. Many Gulf markets have had to grapple with significant oversupply challenges in residential and commercial real estate markets. The disruptions visited by COVID-19 and the growing preference for digital interaction further accentuated these mismatches in some sectors. Added to this, the long-standing problems of capacity duplication among and even within the Gulf economies, often justified by excessive optimism about future demand growth, remain a challenge. In the past, such projections benefited from less savory practices, such as tax evasion and money laundering, which subsequent regulatory initiatives have significantly curtailed. Last but not least, the market imbalances were in important ways also the result of the continued unevenness of the regional capital markets and the global problem of malinvestment at a time of ample liquidity and cheap capital. Regulatory and business practices continued to favor immovable assets even as economic growth markedly decelerated.

The transition of the Gulf region to a global hub of connectivity coincided with the ascendancy of an extensive growth model that involved the large-scale mobilization of capital into new areas concurrently with historically rapid population growth. Problematically, a substantial proportion of the influx of new residents was low-cost labor drawn to the region by the massive project spending and the labor-intensive activities it either directly entailed (construction) or enabled (retail, hospitality, etc.). The main shortcoming of this era of ebullient expansion was the total failure to make productivity an underpinning of the brisk forward momentum. Under the circumstances, the rate of GDP growth was almost entirely dependent on the ability of the economies to keep supplying new capital and labor: "Economic growth ... has mostly been achieved through increases in employment, whereas labor productivity growth, measured as an increase in output per worker, has been negative across the board. In fact, labor productivity declined by 2 percent per year on average from 2000 to 2018."[1] As observed by the IMF in 2014:

> *Investment and employment have been the main drivers of growth in the GCC. ... The growth of real investment in the GCC during this period was on par with other fast-growing emerging markets. ... On the other hand, TFP [total factor productivity] growth has generally been negative.*[2]

As impressive as strides made by the Gulf economies since the 1930s have been, it is now both obvious and widely accepted that the two waves of rapid, transformative development have matured to a point where their ability to sustain growth in line with past trends has been largely exhausted. The third chapter of the modern economic development journey of the Gulf states is still taking shape. It will inevitably integrate elements of the earlier chapters, but its success will be determined by which growth drivers independent of hydrocarbons and infrastructure are activated and enhanced.

The growth slowdown of the mid-2010s laid the foundation for change by reshaping the policy discourse, fiscal incentives, and popular attitudes. COVID-19 served to dramatically further underscore the urgency of an economic overhaul. It hit the region amid the post-2014 transition and further underscored the structural vulnerabilities that the old growth dynamics entailed. The next chapter of the Gulf development narrative looks certain to be one of a progressive shift away from natural resources and input accumulation as determinants of growth dynamics, even as the regional resource endowments and continued demographic dynamism will inevitably retain a prominent place among the Gulf countries' competitiveness drivers. However, the ability of the Gulf governments to meet the expectations of their citizenry will hinge above all on their ability to unleash the power of productivity as a contributor to growth. The potential in this regard is strikingly obvious given the dismal track record of recent decades. This entails substantial opportunities for improvement, including multiple "quick wins." The ultimate success of this paradigm shift will depend on firmly embedding far greater dynamism in the corporate sector and the broader economy alike. Business model overhauls and capital allocation are likely to be of comparable importance in charting the way forward, but neither will succeed unless the economic and business cultures of the region change in tandem. Success in this regard requires economic incentives that reward productivity.

Overcoming volatility

The development journey of the Gulf region has often been a bumpy ride, although bouts of rapid, transformative growth more than made up for the periodic reversals and slowdowns. The main reason for the recurrent volatility was an economic model that amplified the inherent cyclicality of the oil sector at its heart. Higher prices and production pushed up public spending and banking sector liquidity alike, often delivering double-digit annual growth rates during oil booms. As a result, good times saw increased capital mobilization and drew in more people to the region. By contrast, years of austerity tended to bring the development journey to a grinding, albeit temporary halt. The ability of the Gulf economies to influence oil output and prices was always limited by the realities of a global market. Periods of very high prices tended to bring their own challenges, whether through limited absorptive capacity or their adverse impact on global oil consumption. The extraordinary cycle seen in the 1970s and 1980s brought these realities home with painful clarity. Saudi Arabia saw its per capita income in 1981–1989 drop by an extraordinary 55 percent to $6,441, albeit from an exceptional base.[3]

The era of infrastructure-led growth came with similar complications. A spectacular, Chinese-style boom in 2003–2008 lifted the entire non-oil economy. Brisk growth in construction fueled manufacturing and trade as suppliers of key inputs. The real estate and financial services raced ahead, all the more after established mortgage products became more widely available. However, like oil, the infrastructure narrative was not just inherently cyclical but its fluctuations tended to reverberate with an amplified force across the broader economy given the multitude of linkages between construction and other sectors. The potential risks associated with this dependency grew over time as the scale of infrastructure investments expanded. The unusually sharp reversal of the boom after 2008 delivered considerable pain across large swathes of the Gulf economy. Project activity was dramatically culled and corporate profits dropped by an estimated 30 percent.[4] However, the regional governments responded though a robust countercyclical stimulus, which revived activity with remarkable speed, supported by a V-shaped recovery in the oil markets thanks to unprecedented global liquidity creation. For instance, Saudi Arabia unveiled a plan for $300bn of investment over five years – one of the largest stimulus package globally in relative terms.[5]

This macroeconomic rollercoaster ride often entailed inefficient utilization of productive resources. Good times gave rise to ambitious plans, some of which had to be suspended or abandoned when adversity hit. For decades, the ability of the regional governments to meaningfully dampen the impact of the oil cycle was limited because of a narrow fiscal policy toolkit and tended to involve disproportionately changes in public capital expenditure. The end result was a considerable waste of valuable capital. Overall, the growth trajectory of the GCC countries has been markedly more volatile in recent decades than that of less oil-reliant economies. Moreover, the economic ups and downs eroded trend growth: "From the late 1970's till the onset of the COVID pandemic, growth has averaged just 4 percent a year."[6]

Even as population growth and economic diversification have dramatically improved the absorptive capacity of the Gulf economies, palpable limitations remain in place. Real estate sales continue to be constrained by the size of the local population, as well as their purchasing power and access to credit. Improving access by foreign buyers on more flexible terms has helped alleviate this to some extent. But even this practice faces important constraints involving property prices, the available options for connectivity, and residency regulations. Moreover, the increasingly onerous international rules on money laundering, terrorism funding, and tax evasion, while boosting transparency, also entail ancillary costs and potential legal risks. Tourism has delivered an increasingly potent boost to the region's development but has had to find a way forward in a globally competitive marketplace. It has required its own infrastructure but also ongoing innovation to appeal to new demographics or to give previous visitors a reason to come back. Activity in this area was dramatically disrupted by

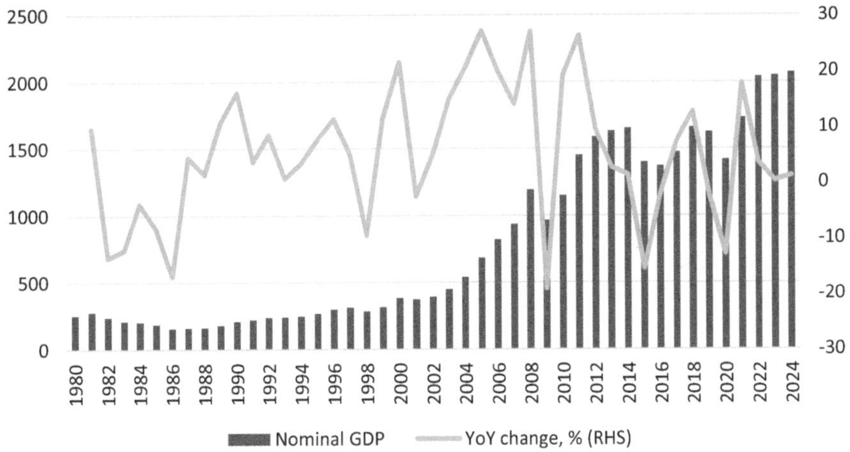

Figure 8.1 GCC nominal GDP ($ bn) and annual change (percent).
Source: World Bank.

the COVID-19 pandemic but has revived with surprising speed thanks to the effective handling of the pandemic by the regional governments.

A "new normal"

Few today expect the future dynamics of the global oil markets to generate wealth in the Gulf at a rate that would sustaimably exceed, let alone match, the regional population growth rates. Despite a gradual downtrend in fertility, the Gulf remains a highly demographically dynamic region by international standards. Population growth typically exceeds 2 percent a year even in the absence of immigration. Moreover, OPEC policy has prioritized oil price stability over market share, even if this position has seen periodic modifications; for example, in 2014–2015 as well as 2020. The organization has a long history of concerted interventions through periodic output cuts designed to stabilize oversupplied markets. This stance has tended to give way to output normalization when markets were deemed to be in balance or facing impending supply constraints. The leading GCC producers have typically found themselves at the forefront of such moves thanks to their significant spare capacity in the global context. Saudi Arabia has often deliberately overcompensated for market imbalances, as happened during COVID-19 when the Kingdom ensured a high level of overall discipline within the OPEC+ alliance.

OPEC's balancing act has become more challenging with the evolving realities of the international energy markets since the early 21st century. Some of the current drivers have lengthy antecedents. They reflect a long-standing structural downtrend in the global demand for oil that population and economic growth concealed for decades. The underlying decline is the result of several factors, including substantial improvements in energy efficiency along with the growing importance of alternative energy sources.

The costs of generating renewable energy have fallen sharply, with the cost of solar energy declining by 68–85 percent in 2010–2020, while wind energy halved. As a result, "solar and wind projects are now approximately 30 percent cheaper than the cheapest fossil fuel plants."[7]

These factors have, according to IMF estimates, subtracted an estimated 2.5 percent a year from global oil demand between 1971 and 2016, with a cumulative impact of more than 100mn b/d as of 2016.[8] This was almost exactly equal to the total global oil demand in 2019 –100.1mn b/d, which means that this stealthy energy transition has by now halved global oil consumption from where it would have stood in its absence. These transformative trends entail a realistic prospect of the long-running uptrend in oil consumption being irrevocably reversed in the foreseeable future, even if a number of uncertainties still continue to shroud the timing and exact nature of this inflection point. The IMF recently estimated that the peak of global oil demand would be reached around 2041 at approximately 115mn b/d, which would be followed by a gradual downtrend.[9] The International Energy Agency expects oil demand to peak in 2030, whereas OPEC forecast a peak demand of 109.3mn b/d in 2040 followed by a very measured decline. By contrast, in 2020 the global oil major BP went as far as to present scenarios suggesting that COVID-19 might trigger a permanent decline in oil use from the 2019 level.[10] While peak oil is likely drawing closer, shifting energy market realities are heavily influenced by government policies, which entail significant differences in the demand dynamics of individual countries, making it difficult to draw firm conclusions on a global scale.[11]

Just as the 1970s oil crisis ended the predominance of oil as the stationary fuel of choice, technological innovation and changing attitudes are now challenging its hitherto unquestioned supremacy in transportation. Electric and hybrid vehicles are gaining popularity, while researchers are developing ways of applying alterative energy sources to other types of transportation as well. Steady gains in energy efficiency mean that even if oil retains its preferred status in certain market segments, less of it will be required for a given purpose.[12] A glimpse into a less polluted world during the COVID-19 lockdowns as well as an increasingly strident climate debate seem to be shaping attitudes toward more conservation. The political risk factors underscored by the 2022 Russian invasion of Ukraine have served as a distraction from these issues but also seem to have strengthened the sense of purpose around reducing the reliance on imported hydrocarbons, especially in the European Union.

The accelerating rise of renewable energy has coincided with dramatic shifts in the global oil markets. New sources of oil have come online thanks to technological innovation that has dramatically cut costs and field development times alike. The spectacular rise of the shale oil industry in the US has been the most striking case in point. Following the innovative development of fracking during the first decade of the new millennium, this technology was scaled up with extraordinary speed. The subsequent shale boom ultimately restored the US to its one-time status as the world's largest oil producer. Having hovered at or just above the 5mn b/d mark for years, US crude output shot up to nearly 9.5mn b/d by mid-2015

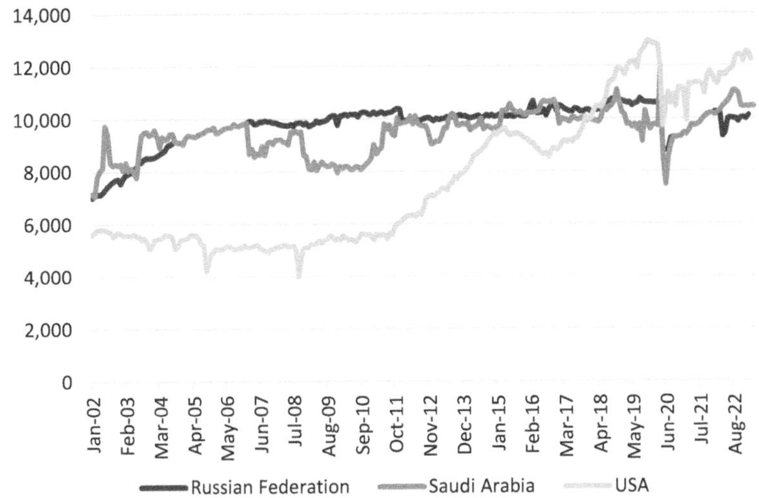

Figure 8.2 Crude output by the world's leading producers, '000 b/d.

Source: Joint Organisations Data Initiative.

and peaked at 13.1mn b/d in February 2020. The COVID-19 pandemic reversed this progress, delivering a trough of 9.7mn b/d just months later, in May 2020. The aggregate output reached some 10.9mn b/d by mid-2021 but ultimately recovered to an annual average of 11.2mn b/d. It is expected to increase to 11.9mn b/d in 2022 and to 12.8mn b/d in 2023, thereby surpassing the previous record.[13]

The North American shale producers operate according to a very different dynamic than established oil companies. Until some recent consolidation, they tended to be relatively small, privately owned, and heavily leveraged, with every incentive to embrace new opportunities and pursue cost savings where possible. Substantial productivity gains were achieved during the 2014–2015 oil price reversals. Moreover, the shale companies focus on an incremental growth model. Whereas a typical Saudi well produces some 6,000 b/d, the US average is only 10.6 b/d. This makes the shale sector extremely nimble; production can be turned on and off much more quickly and cheaply than conventional oil drilling. This agility entails fast responsiveness to price variations.[14]

The post-2014 oil market volatility, further amplified by the COVID-19 pandemic, pushed the US shale producers to a new stage in their evolution. The exceptional market volatility disrupted the sector through company closures and reduced capacity. Moreover, investors in the shale sector have become much more emphatic about financial performance rather than growth, and the heavily debt-reliant, aggressive pursuit of growth seems to have given way to a more measured approach.[15] While the shale market will doubtless mature further and achieve greater consolidation, its ownership looks set to remain private and its considerations more short-term focused than those of the large OPEC producers. Despite its triumphs in recent years, the shale sector faces potential challenges in the years ahead.

Fracking is controversial, potentially all the more as environmental considerations increase in salience. The financial attractiveness of the sector will suffer from the changing global discourse and increased cost of capital, at least in the near term. The supportiveness of the federal government is far from a foregone conclusion. This, along with similar developments in other producer nations, will likely open up new growth opportunities for GCC oil even in a declining oil market. Their scale, low operating costs, and established infrastructure position the Gulf oil companies well to compete even in a declining market. Moreover, the role of the Gulf producers as guarantors of market stability may well increase in the years ahead, as suggested by the tight demand–supply in the wake of COVID, further exacerbated by questions about access to Russian oil.[16] In recognition of this, the regional economies are investing in increasing their capacity, with Saudi Arabia planning to ramp up its total by more than 1mn b/d to 13.2–13.4mn b/d by early 2027. ADNOC is planning investments of $127bn in 2022–2027 to raise capacity to 5mn b/d. The Kuwait Petroleum Corporation has announced a capacity target of 4.75mn b/d by 2040. The consequence may well be years when oil will once again serve as an important growth driver in the Gulf, but its ability to do so on a sustained basis is likely history.

The recent volatility of the oil market has been mirrored by the fiscal position of the Gulf governments. The multitude of ongoing public revenue diversification efforts across the region has not yet fundamentally challenged the overriding fiscal dependence on hydrocarbons revenues. With the exception of Kuwait's substantial investment income, the UAE has so far made the most progress in reducing its dependency on oil income, but even there, non-oil income is still estimated at less than 20 percent of all general government revenue.[17] These realities have also tended to make fiscal policy reform pro-cyclical. Major oil price corrections have typically

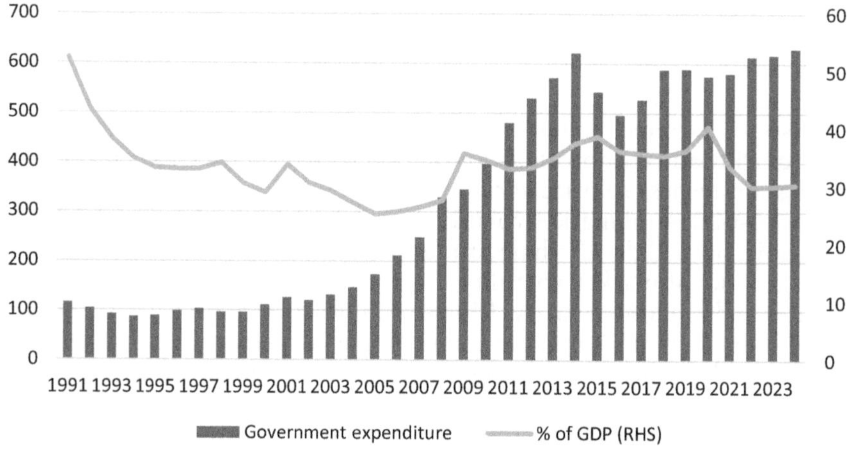

Figure 8.3 GCC aggregate general government expenditure, $ bn.

Source: World Bank.

been followed by efforts to overhaul the fiscal model, while periods of plenty have also coexisted with structural reforms and spending cuts.

While fiscal reform may have somewhat diminished in urgency after the initial achievements and the post-COVID oil price rally, the commitment to gradually diversifying the fiscal model while building stronger buffers now appears firm. In time this should further reduce the disruptive impact of oil market volatility. Countries such as Saudi Arabia and Oman have recently led the way in reforming their budgeting processes in a further bid to make fiscal policy less reactive and cyclical. There is a greater willingness to neutralize the impact of price swings with, for instance, the Saudi government announcing in May 2022 that the oil windfalls created by the Ukraine conflict would be used to bolster the holdings of the Public Investment Fund and the National Development Fund.[18] More problematic, oil market risks have likely increased following the pandemic and the East European war. This may entail additional challenges for in fiscal policymaking is likely, which should further strengthen the sense of purpose around structural reform.

The Great Arabian Infrastructure Boom is also showing signs of fraying on the edges. The growth contribution of infrastructure investments has been diminishing for some time. This looks likely to continue even as funding becomes less reliant on government revenues. After a long period of substantial capital mobilization in physical infrastructure, even just matching the absolute increments of preceding years will translate into steadily decelerating growth rates. But beyond this, there are growing signs of market imbalances after a period of historically subdued demand growth and disruptive technological change. In particular, recent years have witnessed a rapid buildup of capacity in sectors such as retail trade and hospitality, not to mention residential real estate. Weaker demand dynamics have tended to erode profit margins and led to labor shedding by companies,

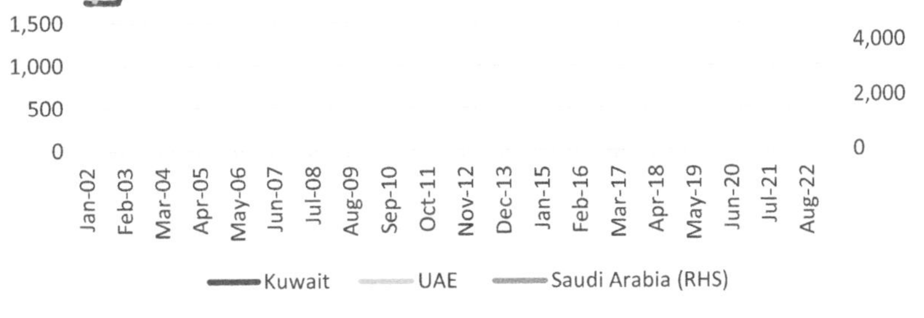

Figure 8.4 Monthly oil output of GCC OPEC members, '000 b/d.

Source: Joint Organisations Data Initiative, OPEC.

a process accelerated by the dislocations caused by the COVID-19 pandemic. Imbalances in some segments of the residential real estate markets have resulted in drawn-out price corrections in several cities. This has been particularly striking in the UAE, mirroring the brisk supply growth prior to the reversal. Added complications have come from fiscal reforms that have pushed up utility costs and helped reveal the relative lack of energy efficiency in much of the regional real estate stock. Only in 2021 did the market finally show tentative signs of stabilizing, partly thanks to the delayed Expo 2020. A pronounced post-crisis rebound has been in evidence after high vaccination coverage permitted more or less full normalization of economic activity by the second half of 2021. A fairly broad-based recovery materialized in 2022 and was also observed in cities such as Riyadh as well as Doha, partly thanks to the 2022 FIFA World Cup.

Steps taken to further stimulate mortgage lending have breathed new life into the market, most notably in Saudi Arabia. In parts of the region, renewed immigration can support price dynamics, at least for now. Even as the Gulf real property market is showing signs of plateauing or returning to growth, there is significant geographic variation and differences among market segments. This is not least because the pandemic significantly disrupted the expatriate labor markets with one estimate suggesting that the regional population declined by 4 percent in 2020.[19] Globally, the COVID-19 crisis was estimated to threaten up to 15 percent of jobs.[20]

The regional property market imbalances have been eroding the returns on investment in the infrastructure space for several years. This has depressed the overall growth impetus of capital mobilization and reflects the continued challenges the Gulf financial sector faces in channeling capital into new activities that might more effectively push the diversification agenda forward. Recent estimates by the IMF have revealed the

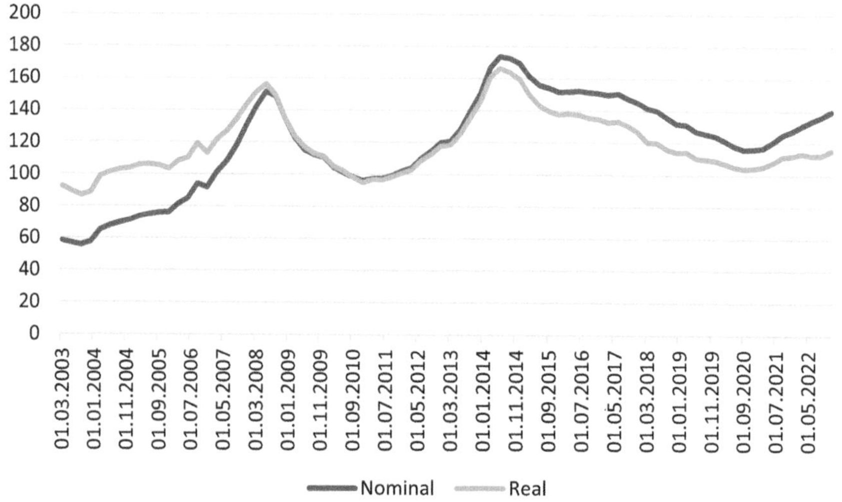

Figure 8.5 UAE property price index (2010 = 100).

Source: Bank for International Settlements.

significant erosion of positive multiplier effects from public infrastructure investments.[21]

These circumstances brought a new sense of realism to the Gulf infrastructure projects market, notably during the post-2014 slowdown. Having peaked at more than $160bn in 2006, the GCC-wide project award tally declined steadily to just over $120bn in 2012. While a subsequent rebound pushed the annual totals to around $180bn in 2014–2015, they soon relapsed below $100bn. The pandemic constituted another major trial by presenting execution risks while also raising questions about the assumptions underpinning project design. In time-honored fashion, cutting capital expenditure became a standard government response to the fiscal pressures. But the banking system, having been mobilized to support economic continuity, was also less well equipped to fund projects on this scale, except in the area of residential mortgages, which has seen brisk growth.

More encouraging, the challenges around capital mobilization have stimulated innovation, especially in terms of funding mechanisms. There is a growing interest in public–private partnerships as well as project financing, especially by Asian credit export agencies and similar institutions. Across the region, sovereign funding vehicles have stepped in to assume a greater role in mobilizing capital locally. The Saudi PIF has been particularly active in this regard and is expected to take over many of traditional government-funded projects as well as others while also developing new funding models. Across the region, leading sovereign funds have been developing ways of monetizing their existing assets to channel more capital into new ventures, whether at home or abroad. Policymaking around investment is becoming more strategic and holistic, as reflected, for instance, by Saudi Arabia's National Investment Strategy.

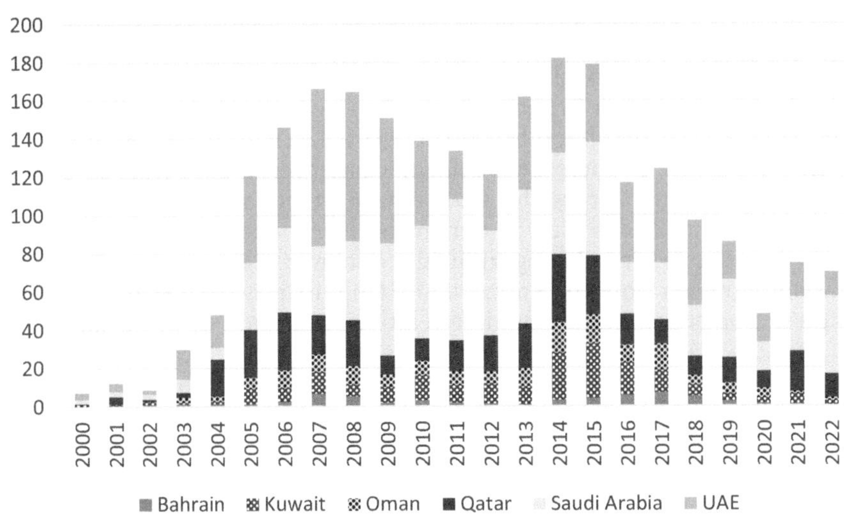

Figure 8.6 Project awards in the GCC countries, $ bn.

Source: MEED Projects.

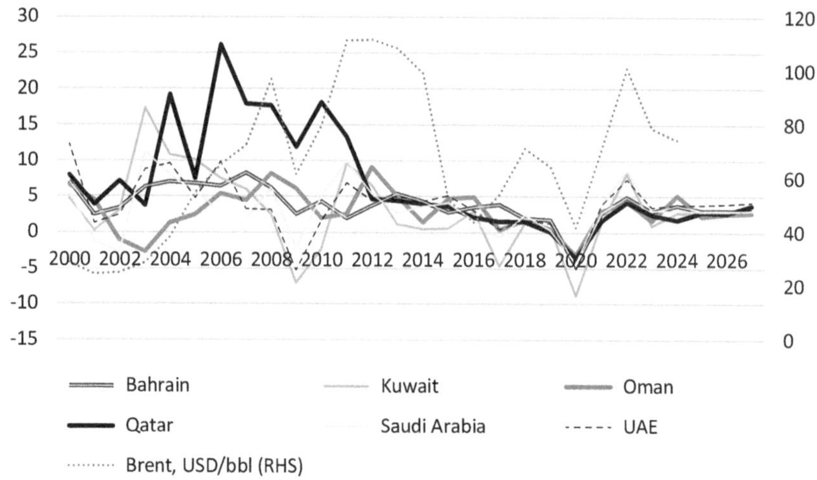

Figure 8.7 Real growth rates of the GCC countries since 2000, percent.
Source: International Monetary Fund, US Energy Information Authority.

The economic realities of recent years have brought the GDP growth rate trend in the GCC well below the early 21st-century levels. Growth dynamics in the oil sector may well receive at least a temporary impetus from renewed attempts to boost capacity and the Gulf producers' critical role as swing producers. However, it is less obvious that the downtrend in non-oil growth has been sustainably reversed beyond the robust rebound from the pandemic. Fiscal consolidation measures are depressing disposable incomes and thus curbing discretionary spending. The concomitant squeeze on company profits margins will adversely affect investment, although it should also stimulate attempts to boost the efficiency of capital allocation. While a benign oil price environment, especially in 2022, has brought considerable refief, this effect is likely to prove temporary.

The end result of these developments has been a convergence of real GDP growth rates across the Gulf region at historically modest levels of 2–3 percent. These growth dynamics, if left unattended, will pose a thorny challenge for a demographically dynamic region even in the event that immigration slows down markedly from its pre-2015 norm. The risk of these trends persisting would be relative stagnation in living standards at a time when the region is nearing its demographic peak. This underscores the importance and urgency of a policy overhaul that substantially strengthens productivity as a growth driver and brings about a more inclusive growth model.

Envisioning a different future

The idea of a structural transformation has been a pillar of policy discussions in the Gulf for a long time. It was at the heart of the earliest diversification initiatives that sought to balance out the dominant oil–government nexus. In recent years, the transformation debate has become increasingly vocal and ambitious. In a sign of things to come, the future King Abdullah of Saudi Arabia told a GCC summit as early as 1998: "We must all get used to a different way of life which does not stand on total dependence on the state."[22]

Success in this regard necessitates transformative, multidimensional diversification. While growing amounts of capital have flowed into the non-oil economy, progress in diversification has remained strongly linked to oil output and price variations. During downturns, a contracting oil sector created the impression of advances in diversification. But the gains were often largely washed away by positive oil market reversals. Moreover, the fundamental interdependency between oil windfalls and investments in other parts of the economy proved very difficult to shake off.

The past two decades have seen increasingly structured efforts to shape the discourse and policies around economic change. The rise of a new global policy ethos in the spirit of the Washington Consensus coincided with a shift toward increasingly strategic and holistic structural reform in the Gulf during the early 21st century. Ambitious visions were adopted by one GCC government after the other. Oman made a head start by releasing its Oman Vision 2020 as early as 1995 while the Bahrain Economic Vision 2030 and Qatar National Vision 2030 were both adopted around the peak of the pre-crisis cycle in 2008. The Kuwait Vision 2035 and UAE Vision 2021 followed two years later. The most recent, and best known, in this succession of policy manifestos was the Saudi Vision 2030 adopted in 2016 in the face of fundamentally different economic realities. More recently, the Oman Vision 2040, the New Kuwait, and the UAE Vision 2031 have updated earlier plans.

These documents have served as powerful communication tools and proved increasingly effective in reframing policy debates and popular expectations. This became particularly obvious in Saudi Arabia where the vision was unveiled at a time of obvious need and leveraged to create a new sense of urgency and purpose around reform. However, implementation has seldom proved straightforward. The earlier visions coincided with an oil boom when concrete economic pressures for change were muted by a tidal wave of liquidity. The global financial crisis challenged the perceived relevance of the earlier aspirations by making some targets seem altogether unrealistic. Exceptional economic volatility left policymaking in an increasingly reactive posture as the immediate emergency inevitably constrained the resources available for longer-term strategic ventures. In general, while the visions articulated a sense of direction, there was often less clarity on the implementation mechanisms. Moreover, it was sometimes unclear how these were integrated with the regular government working documents, budgets, etc.

The structure of the GCC visions tends to follow a fairly similar format. Beyond the inevitable emphasis of productivity-driven diversification, they all reflect a desire to achieve inclusive development. Logically, a credible alternative to the old oil-era social contracts must bring meaningful benefits to all through new opportunities for economic participation. Similarly, all of the visions exude a determination to restructure the public sector with a view to achieving more efficient service delivery and better value for money. Such an overhaul is essential for incentivizing Gulf nationals to pursue opportunities in the private sector. While downsizing and otherwise rationalizing the government bureaucracy are essential, digitalization now seems to offer particularly compelling potential, not least thanks to its ability to potentially transform delivery mechanisms and even broader business models. Moreover, the various ongoing efforts to redraw the demarcation line between the private and the public sectors are likely to be a central component of the way forward. In recent years, regulatory liberalization has permitted private sector competition to government service provision. The growing scope of mandatory health insurance coverage has further supported this trend.

Privatization represents the most logical means of redrawing the line between the public and the private sectors. However, implementation has never been straightforward. Even after a period of concentrated activity around the turn of the millennium, most state-owned enterprises in the Gulf have seen at best partial privatizations through the sale of small minority stakes as governments have been keen to safeguard important non-oil revenus sources. But even the qualified progress to date has boosted governance and transparency, motivating former SOEs to operate more and more like their private sector counterparts while opening up new opportunities for market-based capital raising. Starting in 2021, a growing number of regional sovereign funds turned to partial privatizations again as a way of monetizing key assets to raise capital for new investments. These partial privatizations soon gave rise to one the most impressive IPO booms in the region's history. The change proved particularly impressive on the Saudi, Abu Dhabi, and Dubai markets.[23] Practices such as mutualization are also under consideration as a way of restructuring certain government functions through private provision. Farming out certain functions to the private sector similarly remains an underutilized opportunity to date.

Public–private partnerships have increased in importance since the turn of the century and have received a new lease on life in recent years. However, they continue to be primarily motivated by fiscal constraints rather than the strategic goal of resizing the government. The application of PPP structures has been uneven both geographically and across sectors. At one end, independent power and water projects have become well established and seen their remit expand from conventional gas-powered stations to renewable energy projects. Somewhat more problematic, the use of long-term power purchase agreements has delayed the evolution of the regional power markets. PPP structures have also been successfully applied to sewerage treatment as well as social and affordable housing. Saudi Arabia has applied such partnerships in the transportation sector, starting with the Prince Mohammed bin Abdulaziz International Airport of Madinah in 2012. But many project types still lack well-established, scalable models, although there is an evident interest in innovation. Bahrain is working to apply the PPP approach to the planned King Hamad causeway to Saudi Arabia as well as a national light rail project. Saudi Arabia is also undertaking public transport schemes in several cities, including Jeddah, on a PPP basis. Regional governments are also seeking to leverage partnerships with the private sector in areas such as education and health care with, for instance, school construction projects undertaken by private companies.

Interest in PPPs dramatically increased amid the fiscal pressures created by COVID-19. In recent years, Kuwait, Abu Dhabi, Oman, and Qatar have adopted formal PPP laws, but working enabling regulatory frameworks exist region-wide. Saudi Arabia introduced a new General Tenders and Procurement Law in November 2019.[24] Saudi Arabia's National Centre for Privatisation & PPP now has a pipeline of over 100 projects following a five-fold increase over three years. Structured properly, such project delivery mechanisms can become a way of ensuring economic continuity, boosting competition, and sustainably downsizing the public sector. But project design and governance are critically important for ensuring transparency and cost-effectiveness. Establishing stronger standards and practices more generally will matter a great deal from the project and investment continuity perspective. The IMF recently estimated that as much as a third of global infrastructure spending is wasted through inefficiency. The situation in the Middle East was found to be in line with the global norm.[25]

The visions have been followed by a growing number of other medium-term strategy documents. While these have tended to be more thematically focused, they serve a similar purpose in terms of laying out a clear direction with high-level objectives. They are also, much like the visions, used for public communication and messaging around economic policy. Anecdotal as the evidence largely is, it appears that this new approach for engaging the public sector and the population, as well as target groups such as foreign investors, is proving fairly effective. Awareness of key policy objectives is increasingly widespread, which has likely helped win public acceptance for even more potentially more controversial reforms such as fiscal consolidation. From the perspective of external investors, the visions and strategies can help communicate a sense of policy cohesion and continuity while also boosting the standards of transparency around policymaking.

The implementation of Saudi Vision 2030 engendered a growing toolkit of programs and strategies, a trend that has been to varying degrees mirrored region-wide. In June 2016, the Royal Council of Ministers approved a National Transformation Program (NTP) as the implementation document for the Vision until 2020. Twelve Vision Realization Programs (VRPs) were unveiled in April 2017, ranging from the National Industrial Development and Logistics Program to a Fiscal Balance Program, as well as a revamped NTP. The VRPs are reviewed, updated, and adapted on an ongoing basis. In connection with with these programs, the authorities have adopted several strategies focusing on individual sectors, sub-sectors, or regions of the country. The National Investment Strategy (NIS) unveiled in late 2021 is among the best-known such documents. It set out to "drive investment in the Kingdom by enhancing the business environment, increasing investment attractiveness and competitiveness, instigating key regulatory and legislative measures."[26] The NIS aspires to make the Kingdom one of the top 15 economies global by mobilizing more than SAR12trn, or over $3.3trn, by 2030. The strategy revolves heavily around economic diversification that encompasses the digital and green economies while seeking to increase private sector participation in the economy to 65 percent. Above all, the plan is about achieving sustainable improvements in the Kingdom's competitiveness.

In late 2021, Bahrain adopted an Economic Recovery Plan to drive its post-COVID recovery while enhancing the thematic structure around the government's medium-term development goals. The plan was composed of 27 programs, including the updated Fiscal Balance Program and a $30bn pipeline of major investment projects. More detailed strategies were developed for individual priority sectors.

The Operation 300bn project unveiled by the UAE in early 2022 is a ten-year national industrial strategy that seeks to boost the sector's GDP contribution from AED133bn to AED300bn by 2031. The strategy prioritizes industries making use of advanced technologies and Fourth Industrial Revolution applications as well as sustainable development. The volume of spending on R&D in the industrial sector is set to rise from 1.3 percent to almost 2 percent of GDP by 2031.[27]

Fiscal triggers

Despite being repeatedly tested by the vagaries of the oil markets, the Gulf growth model proved remarkably resistant to change. During the lean 1980s and 1990s, the oil–government nexus retreated but did not regroup. Reforms somewhat curbed the excesses of the boom years, but change was far from transformative. A comparable narrative unfolded following the onset of the global financial crisis, partly because again the challenges of determining the depth and duration of the downturn complicated the policy efforts to balance the appropriate response between short-term crisis management and longer-term structural reforms. But the posture of the Gulf governments also mirrored a global push for countercyclical stimulus.

The momentous decision in late November 2014 of the OPEC producers to abandon their erstwhile oil production ceilings amid the rise of shale oil proved a more potent trigger for change. The ensuing global oil glut soon brought prices down to historic lows. Motivated as the OPEC move was by protecting market share, the dynamics of the US oil cluster confounded expectations. The highly leveraged shale producers focused their efforts on generating cash flow, which, amid sharply lower prices, had to involve further pushing up output even if this in turn exacerbated the glut. But the US shale cluster also achieved impressive productivity gains, which frustrated the OPEC efforts to reconfigure the markets in favor of the traditional low-cost producers. On 20 January 2016, the Brent benchmark recorded a cyclical low of $26.01 per barrel, a fraction of its 19 June 2014 high of $115.19. In late 2016, OPEC established the "OPEC+" alliance with a number of other large producers (not least Russia), which went on to successfully rebalance the market through output controls, implicitly accepting that the "new kids on the block" were there to stay.

Painful as the rollercoaster ride of oil prices proved, the OPEC stance coincided with a new determination among the Gulf producers to tackle their long-standing dependence on oil as the primary guarantor of prosperity. It also reflected an acceptance that the most rational economic plans would struggle to deliver results in the absence of concrete economic incentives. Saudi Arabia's Vision 2030 was the most salient embodiment of this new ethos. Even as it was widely questioned, the new document promised a long-overdue shift away from outdated growth models. Unveiled just over a year after the price collapse, the Vision embodied an ambitious plan to reshape the Saudi economy through structured diversification.

Many of the ambitious NTP targets went far beyond what had previously been thought acceptable in the conservative atmosphere of the Kingdom. Among other things, the government set out to proactively develop the tourism and entertainment sectors. The newly established General Authority for Entertainment has organized a growing number of public events and concerts. The once cumbersome visa regulations have been overhauled to align with an ambitious tourism strategy. Plans are afoot for new resorts as well as a large sports, culture, and entertainment complex near Riyadh. The Vision has also reshaped Saudi society by deliberately empowering women in new ways. Strict gender segregation has been removed in many areas. Perhaps the most symbolic manifestation of this new ethos was the 2018 lifting of the long-standing ban on women driving in order improve their mobility and ability to participate in the labor force.

The fiscal consolidation undertaken by the GCC governments is significantly reshaping the regional economies by reconditioning the economic behavior of individuals and companies through new incentives. Among the key tenets of this shift has been a substantial scaling back of universal subsidies on items ranging from foodstuffs to utilities and hydrocarbons. Notably, the significant repricing of power and water has dramatically altered the cost base facing private sector companies. But by putting a price on waste, the reforms have also encouraged conservation and dramatically amplified interest alternative energy. Welfare provision is becoming more focused on areas of genuine need in a departure from the universal generosity of yesteryear.

Revenue diversification has begun to shift government fiscal models away from the long-standing practice of near-total oil-based funding to a more diversified revenue base with an increasingly strong link to the non-oil economy. Beyond unveiling VAT and excise duties in most of the region, governments have taken important steps to achieve fuller cost recovery for public services. The removal or reduction of many universal subsidies is a further element in this fiscal re-engineering. Despite gradual implementation and considerable cross-country variation, it is clear that past certainties about government service provision at next to no cost are now over. This is beginning to have profound implications for the regional corporate sector and popular expectations alike.

The emerging fiscal realities are beginning to have far broader economic implications, something that Adam Hanieh referred to as the "market creating" effect of fiscal policy.[28] This is a profound, multidimensional process. At the most basic level, by activating the economic incentives embodied in the basic forces of demand and supply, it is driving more informed decisions and more efficient allocation of resources. But these are also "essential to the actual *making* of new markets."[29] Market-based pricing enables the private provision or privatization of activities that in the past were previously undertaken by the state. By changing the relative pricing of different commodities and services, it is creating concrete economic incentives for production that previously lacked a financial rationale. A case in point is the repricing of hydrocarbons, which has helped eliminate their previously compelling cost advantage over renewable energy. Going forward, these developments should allow Gulf governments to retreat more and more from their traditional role as providers to that of regulators.

In keeping with the ambitions of creating a more efficient government, the Gulf authorities have taken steps to overhaul the structure of the public sector, reduce waste, and cut inefficient expenditures. The adoption of new technologies, notably digitization, is boosting efficiency. Given the historically critical dominance of the payroll in government spending, there have also been initiatives to encourage early retirement or transfers to the private sector. In some cases, the reduction or elimination of various financial benefits is reducing the relative attractiveness of government careers as compared to private sector employment.[30]

Saudi ambitions have engendered a great deal of admiration but also considerable criticism, often colored by politically tinted commentary. Many targets have been dismissed as unrealistic or overly grandiose in view of their unprecedented scale. Moreover, some landmark goals of the Vision have proven harder to implement than expected; for instance, the flagship sale of a 5 percent stake in Saudi Aramco. Ultimately, Aramco announced the listing of 1.5 percent of its stock on Saudi Exchange. The company raised $25.6bn, having received subscriptions worth $119bn. Traded since December 2019, Aramco was initially valued at $1.88trn. The IPO paved the way for much more market-based capital raising through *sukuk* and sales of stakes in subsidiaries. But it is also evident that many of the strategies are to a large extent about staking out a direction, drawing a line in the sand. This does not preclude, and may often deliberately invite, creative thinking and adaptiveness around implementation. Success is ultimately likely to be determined not just by effective project implementation but also by ongoing agility to ensure efficiency and impact in the face of an uncertain global context.

A bolt out of the blue…

Soon after the 2014–2015 oil price correction, the COVID-19 pandemic dealt a further massive blow to old assumptions. Anyone seeking validation of the structural reform agenda of the years leading up to the public health calamity found it in the pandemic. Its direct impact was amplified by renewed sharp disruptions to the global energy markets as global mobility plummeted. In February 2020 the International Energy Agency estimated that the global oil demand could relapse to 2011 levels.

Having cut its collective production by 2.1mn b/d by January 2020, the OPEC+ alliance initially struggled to agree on an appropriate policy response. Russia resisted the 5 March decision by the OPEC summit to cut production by a further 1.5mn b/d in the wake of a sharp fall in Chinese imports. The failure to agree prompted Saudi Arabia and its partners to raise crude extraction, much as they had in 2014. Amid precipitously falling consumption, this triggered an unusually aggressive price correction. The Brent benchmark price plummeted by 30 percent on 8 March alone as Saudi Arabia offered discounts to many of its customers. The Kingdom also announced plans to increase production from 9.7mn b/d to 12.3mn b/d, further deepening the plunge. A 17-year low was reached on 18 March when Brent was trading at $24.72 per barrel, something that in real, inflation-adjusted terms took prices back to 2001 levels.[31] The end result of this sharp market imbalance was an extraordinary 65 percent quarter-on-quarter price decline during the first three months of the year.

In contrast to the 2014–2016 price reversal, the COVID plunge proved short-lived. Unusually, even the US participated in the discussions around corrective interventions, having seen its shale industry pushed to the verge of an existential crisis. It was estimated that only 16 US shale producers could operate profitably with prices at $35 per barrel. In anticipation of a policy reversal, an oil price rebound began in early April, with Brent rising to $32 per barrel on 3 April. A formal agreement between Saudi Arabia and Russia followed on 9 April on a collective output reduction of 10mn b/d.

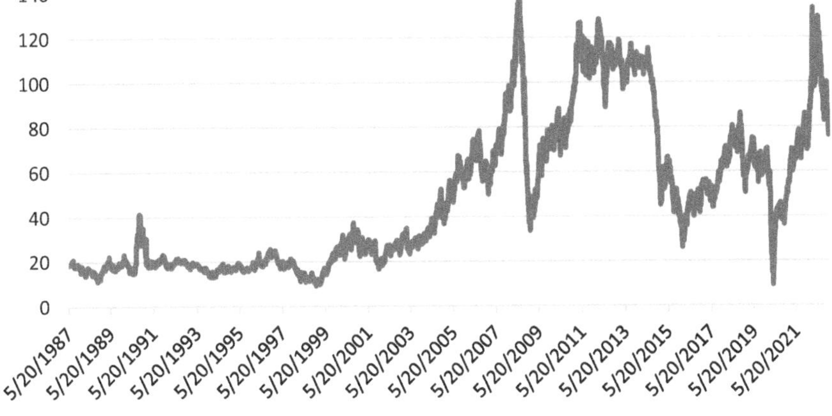

Figure 8.8 Brent spot price, $/barrel.

Source: Thomson Reuters.

Nonetheless, the legacy of overproduction and extreme uncertainty about the demand outlook continued to buffet the market, especially in North America, where limited storage capacity constituted an additional problem. The market gyrations reached a particularly dramatic point on 20 April when the WTI crude contract for May delivery turned negative, reaching an unprecedented –$37 per barrel. The Brent benchmark hit a low of $18 per barrel. Thereafter, fairly steady normalization ensued, with Brent rebounding to an average of $40.91 in September and to just under $50 per barrel in December. Nonetheless, the overall 2020 average of $41.96 fell far short of the 2019 figure of $64.36 per barrel. Thereafter, a combination of unusually aggressive monetary stimulus along with a demand recovery fueled Brent above the $70 mark by June 2021, eventually averaging $70.86 during the year as a whole.

Another shock followed in early 2022 when Russia's decision to dramatically escalate the long-brewing crisis in Ukraine suddenly pushed up risk premiums. Contrary to widespread expectations, the Western governments proved quick to introduce sanctions, while many traders began to shun Russian oil, raising major uncertainties about supply. The Brent price briefly hit $139.13 on 6 March. Since that point, however, prices have trended down, albeit with recurrent volatility. This has reflected the military stalemate in Ukraine but also a dramatic policy reversal by Western central banks in the face of four-decade inflationary highs. The global cost of living crisis was triggered by significant supply chain and labor market disruptions during the pandemic, further amplified by the Ukrainian conflict, which curbed the availability of many foodstuffs and pushed up energy costs. The dramatic monetary tightening has sharply reduced the positive liquidity impact on prices but also curtailed economic activity, with growing fears of a recession in many countries.

These vagaries of the oil price have delivered multiple challenges in the Gulf. While the pandemic necessitated increased public spending, the dwindling oil revenues dramatically compromised government revenues. The costly emergency and stimulus measures sharply widened the fiscal gap just as the Gulf countries had begun to make headway with their fiscal overhauls. Nonetheless, governments across the region chose to maintain a high degree of fiscal discipline, combining emergency interventions with further tightening in other areas. This need for fiscal rigor was particularly acute in Bahrain and Oman, which faced the greatest vulnerabilities. Both countries adopted new fiscal strategies in 2021, Bahrain by recalibrating its pre-crisis Fiscal Balance Program and Oman by establishing a new fiscal roadmap with IMF technical support. But most of the region still has fiscal breakeven prices that are higher than the current (and expected) oil prices.

While the exceptional oil windfall of 2022 removed some of the urgency around fiscal reform, the Gulf governments have generally maintained their focus and indicated that most of the additional income will be channeled into strategic ventures outside of government budgets. Moreover, what goes up, comes down. While the Gulf governments are working to entrench their competitiveness in the rapidly evolving global energy

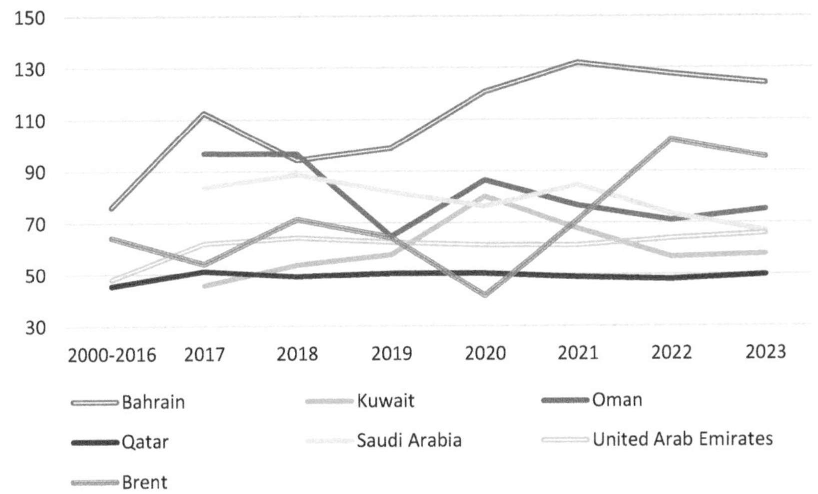

Figure 8.9 Estimated fiscal breakeven oil prices in the GCC, $/barrel.

Source: International Monetary Fund, Regional Economic Outlook, Statistical Appendix, Table 6.

markets, the extraordinary volatility of the early 21st-century global economy has underscored the risks and costs of complacency. Building resilience is accepted as a strategic priority. Despite the undoubted challenges it will continue to deliver, this new posture is likely to prove a cloud with a silver lining. The removal of subsidies has opened up new business opportunities by creating a sustainable basis for profitable operations for private companies in areas where price distortions previously made it impossible. In the case of food, for instance, this has brought in new importers as well as local producers and opened up opportunities for stretching value chains. Power generation is increasingly driven by economically independent companies, and private capital is increasingly engaged in the growing provision of renewable energy. Sharp cost declines in recent years are driving a wave of new investments, whether through solar farms or through distributed projects. Apart from the reduced reliance on governments, the end result is conservation of resources, reduced emissions, and a more productive economy.

Shaking up the corporate sector

As the Gulf region has repeatedly discovered, political ambition alone is not enough to reshape an economy. The roots of the regional resistance to structural change are microeconomic, social, and cultural. Obvious as the high-level causes of the recent growth deceleration are, the microfoundations of the problem have received remarkably little attention. This is an important oversight, since roughly half of all observed productivity growth in economies globally is due to improvements within firms thanks to innovation, new technology adoption, and better management.[32] The weakness of these drivers is at the heart of the underdevelopment of the Gulf private sector.

It is unrealistic to expect that the GCC countries' productivity problem can be solved at the macro level, merely by shifting resources between sectors. The disappointing track record in productivity reflects a lack of dynamism at the level of individual companies. Even as the idea of business formation has gained popularity, most new companies in recent years have been characterized by static or even negative productivity. While, for instance, Dubai saw 9 percent annual growth in SME numbers between 2008 and 2017, a large proportion of the new companies simply replicated established business concepts.[33]

The extraordinary longevity of the old rentier culture remains a major constraint on the economic dynamism of the region. Capital has continued to flow disproportionately into low-productivity activities, and most businesses have shown a relatively static modus operandi, with minimal growth, diversification, or innovation. The long-standing practices of universal subsidies and easy access to cheap labor historically bear much of the blame. In the past, the lack of stringent regulation in areas such as pollution, building maintenance, etc., further contributed to low costs. While some of these practices were originally driven by infant industry considerations, they quickly became entrenched and widespread, covering "[e]verything from date production to fishing ... making new ventures risk-free and highly profitable."[34] Such realities created next to no incentives for companies to prepare for unexpected changes.

With some simplification, the Gulf corporate sector can be divided into three partially overlapping main categories. The top tier consists of large corporations, typically established with sovereign capital. These tend to be companies in the energy sector, utilities, some financial service providers, major manufacturers, transportation businesses, and large infrastructure operators. Following partial privatizations and regulatory reform, many erstwhile SOEs have been made dramatic strides in governance, becoming dynamic, growth-oriented businesses. They have shaken off their one-time dependency on government funding and successfully raised capital in the equity and bond/*sukuk* markets. These businesses are usually capable of quickly adapting to changing economic conditions. Some of them, notably in hydrocarbons and manufacturing, have grown far beyond the region. For instance, Saudi Aramco's stated ambition is to establish itself as the world premier refiner and petrochemicals producer.[35] QatarEnergy is pursuing an international diversification strategy.

At the opposite end of the spectrum is a multitude of micro and small businesses, predominantly small trading ventures, restaurants and cafes, basic service providers, or subcontractors to larger construction businesses.[36] The numerical dominance of SMEs in the Gulf matches the international norm. They make up over 98 percent of all business establishments – 99 percent in Saudi Arabia, 98.4 percent in Bahrain, and 99.2 percent in Dubai, according to recent data. In this "bazaar economy," subsidized inputs and low-cost expatriate labor historically allowed companies to break even at a minimal scale. For instance, in Saudi Arabia, a remarkable 88 percent of the 950,000 SMEs were micro enterprises with one to five employees in

2017. Their share still stood at 81.3 percent in mid-2022. Only in Dubai had this proportion declined to as low as 61 percent.[37] Whereas SMEs generate some 70 percent of all jobs in the advanced OECD economies, their small average size in the Gulf means that this share seldom exceeds 50 percent. The GDP contribution of SMEs in the advanced economies stands in the 50–60 percent range, but in the GCC it tends to lag below a third, although Dubai recently reached a regional high of 46.4 percent. In Europe, non-financial SMEs generated some 57 percent of GDP in 2017 while accounting for 52 percent of all new jobs during the decade leading up to 2017.[38] Service businesses made up 48 percent of Dubai's SMEs in 2017, followed by 47 percent in trading but only 5 percent in manufacturing.[39] In Bahrain, trade, at 32 percent, is the largest single category.

The realities of SMEs are broadly comparable across the Gulf: a highly fragmented market with a predominantly domestic focus and systematic reliance on low-cost expatriate labor. In Saudi Arabia, SMEs employed roughly a million Saudi citizens in 2017 – some 32 percent of the economically actively national population – but expatriate employees numbered 3.76mn. The SME contribution to the Kingdom's non-oil GDP was estimated at 21 percent, a share that the Vision 2030 is hoping to boost to 35 percent.[40] Bahraini SMEs provided 53 percent of private sector employment in early 2020, but only 10.9 percent of their workforce were Bahraini nationals. Their GDP contribution has in recent years been on the order of just under 30 percent.[41] In Dubai, SMEs employ 51 percent of the total workforce, but this is likely to rise as the gross value-added contribution of medium-sized businesses increased from 17 percent in 2008 to 28 percent in 2017. Their labor productivity now equals 0.9 times the average for large companies and 0.8 times the EU average.[42] But digitization and human capital development lag well behind international benchmarks. The proportion of SMEs providing formal training is 1.8 times below the EU and Singapore and the gap has been growing.[43]

The third pillar of the Gulf corporate sector is made of up family businesses, a phenomenon with deep roots: "More than in any other area of the world, in the Gulf, business is viewed as a way to enhance a family's social standing rather than as an impersonal, wealth-generating, market-driven activity."[44] This diverse category includes some of the most dynamic business groups in the region[45] but also conventional SMEs. Some estimates suggest that 90 percent of the private sector in Saudi Arabia and the UAE are family businesses, while "98 percent of all commercial activities in the region are family-run."[46] Such companies are estimated to account for 30–60 percent of the regional GDP and as much as 80 percent of its labor force. But frustratingly little formal data exist. A 1990 estimate put the weight of family firms at a quarter of Oman's GDP and 70 percent of Bahrain's GDP, with the rest of the region within this range.[47] In 2005 the Dubai Chamber of Commerce & Industry classified 54 percent of its members as family businesses; 68 percent of them were active in trading and 10 percent in construction. A 2011 study for Bahrain found that 52 percent of local family firms were active in real estate and construction and 35 percent in retail and consumer products.[48]

In the absence of standardized definitions, the main common thread is the genesis of Gulf family businesses; their founders tend to be "restless entrepreneurs," motivated by a desire to seize profitable opportunities but often less interested in the scale and institutionalization of the business. Historically, expansion often rested on powerful political and financial alliances as well as limited competition.[49] The line between the founding family and their business is often blurred, with negative implications for transparency and governance. Management is seldom fully professional or structured. Performance may be further challenged by various loyalties, to brands, technologies, locations, etc., but also to traditions.[50]

While many Gulf family businesses began as trading firms, they have frequently expanded to other activities in a quest to generate income for expanding families; an estimated 18 percent annual growth is needed just to preserve wealth across generations. Yet expansion is often unstructured, driven by tactical rather than strategic considerations, with little medium-term planning.[51] Many businesses are not conventional profit maximizers, and there is "a lack of emphasis on financial analysis and productivity in firms across the Gulf."[52] Business management is often personalized, and "many family businesses are weighed down by a slow decision making process resulting from conflicting emotional/traditional attachments, fear of family conflict, or slowness of the senior generations."[53] Company development can be compromised by excessive profit distribution and a reluctance to erode control by tapping external capital. Behavior can be opportunistic as firms enter new business lines to enhance their image, to sideline competitors, or even to find career opportunities for family members. Conversely, many firms hang on to unprofitable ventures for reasons of prestige or history.[54] Specialization is rare: a 2019 survey concluded that 59 percent of family businesses operate in multiple sectors. Another assessment found 48 percent active in five or more sectors. Control is often fragmented, with the Shari'ah inheritance rules entailing dilution within a generation or two. Despite regulatory innovation around trust structures, many businesses are poorly prepared for generational transitions. Most family firms are less than 60 years old, with one estimate putting their average age at 23 years. Core family-owned businesses seem to underperform their peers.[55]

Gulf businesses are unevenly distributed in terms of size, and the region lacks a German-style *Mittelstand* of medium-sized businesses, reflecting the failure of most SMEs to scale up. Companies still typically have only one founder, a tradition that is carrying over to start-up entrepreneurship, where it reduces the range of skills and networks brought to bear. But it also means that management decisions are unlikely to be questioned on an ongoing basis. Practices such as employee share ownership or even corporate pension schemes remain rare, leaving staff without a stake in the success of their employer. Many, especially junior employees, are easily lured away. The main source of business continuity is the founder him- or herself. Legal structures such as joint-stock companies, partnerships, or co-operatives remain relatively rare despite some recent progress.[56]

The traditional labor market dynamics encouraged a heavy reliance on low-cost expatriate labor with minimal investment in labor-saving technology. Companies were often able to capture significant economic rents, or margins, without having to invest in productivity. This, along with limited financing options, channeled entrepreneurial activity into areas where inputs were cheap while outputs commanded market prices. Such realities gave rise to a static culture while limiting the perceived need to acquire or develop managerial capacity. Businesses typically had little compelling reason to focus on growth, organization, or innovation. While some did so voluntarily, the lack of urgency contrasted with the cost of such investments. Short-term cyclical variations could typically be handled through changes in the headcount, while brisk population growth along with steadily increasing government expenditure delivered strong revenue gains. The fragmented business landscape further held back investments as most companies lacked the scale to think more dynamically about growth and development.

With the recent fiscal overhauls across the GCC, the habits of the past are becoming increasingly outdated. Fiscal consolidation is reducing input price distortions. Slower immigration has weakened demand growth, particularly during COVID-19. Sectors such as retail have been challenged by technological disruptions such as e-commerce. Intensifying competition has forced many businesses to compete on price, with the consequence of margin erosion, often to a point where many companies are only able to survive through deliberate cost minimization. More ambitious change is often difficult even as some champions have emerged and even been listed on regional stock markets. But all too often, growth and control remain conflicting ambitions, as evident as it is that regional (family) businesses "will have to become much more performance-driven if they are going to survive in the long-term."[57]

Despite numerous short-term challenges, the ongoing economic overhaul is also creating many of the necessary conditions for transitioning to a productivity-led growth model. Challenges penalize complacency. Productivity is often the result of tax and regulatory pressures, mounting labor costs (sometimes driven by trade unions), and intense competition, among other things. Such an environment favors the survival of the fittest and punishes a lack of agility. These dynamics are likely to grow in importance in the Gulf. There will be a far greater premium on governance and management, as well as on strategic thinking.

Increased attention to overhauling business models is critical to boosting productivity. COVID-19 amplified pressures to do so by disrupting business as usual by pushing up the costs of complacency but also increased awareness of what change could look like. Nonetheless, change is likely to be gradual. Because of the long shadow of rentierism, most regional companies lack the cultural agility and internal resources to quickly adapt to new circumstances. Declining margins along with limited funding options erode the appetite for changes that require up-front investments. But the historical neglect of productivity also means that most regional companies face numerous immediate opportunities for better cost management and revenue gains. In terms of transitioning to a productivity-led sustainability model, such companies can benefit from numerous "low-hanging fruit."

Global trends are also opening up new opportunities for the Gulf corporate sector to contemplate – and prepare itself for – a different kind of future at a faster pace than would have been realistic in the past. Rapid and increasingly transformative technological progress is dramatically increasing the availability and versatility of solutions that constitute an increasingly compelling alternative to the systemic dependence of regional private businesses on low-cost labor. For example, cloud computing allows companies to cater to their IT needs through flexible service contracts while embodying ongoing improvements in technology as well as strict security standards. Its scalability allows companies to align IT spending with evolving needs without substantial fixed costs. Digitalization can allow for better value chain integration and process optimization.

With domestic growth opportunities less abundant, many Gulf companies are receptive to new ideas. They are leveraging technology for better marketing, brand building, and new distribution channels. Attitudes toward human capital development are changing as technology adoption reduces the erstwhile labor bias, while governments encourage private sector job creation for nationals. There is a renewed push for skill development, especially in growth areas such as technology, whether through further education or proactive interventions to address emerging needs in area such as coding. Having cost-effective, even subsidized access to training programs can help smaller companies boost productivity, a task made easier by the rise of online options. A growing range of efficient digital solutions exists for sourcing and developing talent. From the impact perspective, however, it is important that training be provided on a clear needs basis and subjected to ongoing evaluation.

Going forward, the successful creation of the entrepreneurial ecosystem is likely to require ongoing adaptation while ensuring effective cross-fertilization among the different initiatives. Appropriate funding models, awareness building, and access to talent will be essential for building up momentum and eventually ensuring timely exits. Some regional stock exchanges have set up dedicated platforms for growth companies. However, near-term progress is likely to be much more closely dependent on activating effective crowdfunding solutions and engaging regional investors. Exits will create new sources of entrepreneurial capital and mentors.

Investing in innovation

Innovative capacity is an important driver of economic competitiveness. Most indicators of innovation in the GCC make for depressing reading. The funding channeled into research and development remains minuscule in comparison to the West. The higher education sector is heavily teaching focused, and there are few substantial private institutions – such as foundations – that undertake or sponsor research on a significant scale. Most innovation globally is undertaken by private companies amid pressures created by a competitive marketplace along with regulatory and fiscal factors, etc. Such considerations have historically been relatively muted in the GCC and effectively limited the incentives to innovate.

But things are changing. The amount of capital channeled into research capacity in the Gulf has grown markedly in recent years. Saudi Arabia's King Abdullah University of Science and Technology was established in 2009 in Tuwal on the Red Sea Coast as a private research institution with a $10bn endowment donated by King Abdullah. The first class included 400 students from more than 60 countries, and the university has maintained an explicitly international flavor ever since. English is the language of instruction, and KAUST is the only co-educational university campus in the Kingdom. All students are fully funded. KAUST research applies science and technology to problems of human need, social advancement, and economic development. It offers master of science and PhD degrees and operates interdisciplinary research teams in three academic divisions: Biological and Environmental Science and Engineering; Computer, Electrical, and Mathematical Science and Engineering; and Physical Science and Engineering. In 2013, KAUST was ranked as having one of the 500 fastest growing research and citation records in the world. In 2016 the Nature Index Rising Stars ranked the institution 19th globally among the fastest rising universities for high-quality research. The university has a 2.7mn sq m Research and Technology Park and hosts 11 research centers, including the Clean Combustion Research Center (2014) and the Saudi Aramco Research Center, set up in 2019. Logically, some centers have a very local or national focus; for example, the Red Sea Research Centre and the Water Desalination and Reuse Centre.

The King Abdullah Petroleum Studies and Research Center (KAPSARC) was established by the government in Riyadh in 2007. It is an international research hub focusing on energy economics and sustainability. KAPSARC was ranked 13th out of 60 global energy and resource policy think tanks by the University of Pennsylvania Think Tank and Civil Societies Program. Abu Dhabi's clear energy hub, Masdar City, is home to the Mohamed bin Zayed University of Artificial Intelligence, founded in 2019 as a graduate-level research institution.

Perhaps the best-known case of collaboration with foreign institutions is the Education City outside of Doha. Championed by Qatar Foundation for Education, Science, and Community Development, this is a 14 sq m facility located in Al Rayyan City. Launched in 1997 with the Virginia Commonwealth University, the city was officially inaugurated in 2003. It now houses branch campuses of six US universities as well as one each from the UK and France. The participating institutions include Weill Cornell Medicine–Qatar (2001), Texas A&M University at Qatar (2003), Carnegie Mellon University in Qatar (2004), Georgetown University in Qatar (2005), Northwestern University in Qatar (2008), HEC Paris (2010), UCL Qatar (2010), and Hamad bin Khalifa University (2010). The city also includes research centers such as Qatar Science & Technology Park, Qatar National Research Fund, and Sidra Medical and Research Centre.

Corporate innovation is also receiving increased attention, whether in-house research and development or collaboration with academic institutions. Such initiatives tend to be led by the largest corporations. For instance, Aramco and SABIC have launched ambitious projects such as a plan to produce petrochemicals from oil. Similarly, the financial sector is taking a strong interest in technological innovation. Bahrain's FinTech Bay counts a number of established banks in its clientele. This reflects a growing interest on the part of the sector incumbents to coopt new ideas to protect their own competitiveness.

While innovative thinking is gathering momentum, structured collaboration between academia and industry in the Gulf has been relatively limited to date. This reflects the traditional separation of the two sectors. Regional business has either underinvested in innovation or purchased solutions from consultants. The public educational establishment has traditionally faced significant regulatory restrictions on its ability to engage in commercial research or business activities. Private universities typically seek to earn their income primarily through teaching and lack the scale, ambition, or even resources to engage in commercial research.

Financial market development is likely to be another important driver of innovation, whether through new funding mechanisms for innovative start-ups or deeper bond and equity markets enabling the growth of established businesses. The regional venture capital and private equity industries went through a rocky inception around the time of the global economic crisis but are again regrouping. Several government funds support innovation, with, for instance, the Saudi PIF partnering with Japan's SoftBank in 2017 to create the Softbank Vision Fund, which was intended to be the world's largest private equity fund, with a capital of up to $100bn.[58] Investors also include large multinationals such as Apple, Qualcomm, and Foxconn, as well as the UAE's Mubadala.

Openness is likely to be critical as a driver of innovation. The world's leading innovation hubs are inherently cosmopolitan in outlook as well as their makeup. The US shows a strong correlation between the average income of cities and the percentage of foreign-born residents. Importing qualified talent is likely to be the fastest way for the GCC of building credibility as an environment conducive of innovation. This can help build momentum before more intractable issues are tackled or substantial investments are made. Positioning the Gulf – or parts of it – as an attractive platform for innovative activities can capitalize on the strides it has made in regulation and connective infrastructure at the heart of the Old World. Efforts, notably in the UAE, to proactively encourage the creation of cosmopolitan creative industry and start-up clusters have developed some traction and reflect the lack of appropriate enabling conditions in large parts of the world, not least the broader Middle East region. But they also serve as another reflection of the enduring appeal of GCC capital to innovators seeking to commercialize and scale their ideas. By meeting global standards of excellence in this area, the Gulf region can position itself as a serious contender far beyond its scale.

Making change work for all

As necessary and pressing as the economic paradigm shift in the Gulf is, it comes with multiple uncertainties. The transition from a model of universal distribution after generations of government largesse and dependency heralds a shift from a distributive to a productive economic order. This shift is needed to counter of the schlerotic dynamic inefficiency of the oil–government nexus. Despite the impressive benefits it delivered in its day, this model did little to incentivize productive behavior and often directly encouraged waste on a large scale. Moreover, it became increasingly costly as the regional population expanded.

The Great Arabian Infrastructure Boom gave rise to powerful new mechanisms for generating wealth from non-oil sources. But its impact was far less universal, as observed by Daryl Champion, commenting on the lean years of the late 20th century and the subsequent economic reforms:

> *While the average Saudi citizen is becoming poorer, a new generation of corporate Saudis is already beginning to take advantage of the processes of deregulation and privatisation that are slowly being initiated in the kingdom. Saudi Arabia is set to follow the global trend of increasing inequalities of wealth distribution; as the distributive-welfare state is reined in, and as the Saudi economy becomes more integrated into the emerging global economy, the gap between the haves and the have-nots in the kingdom will increase.*[59]

Regional governments have sought to boost inclusion through mechanisms such as large-scale public privatizations of state-owned enterprises along with a growing recognition of the power of real estate ownership to generate financial security. The old practices of sovereign grants, free land plots, and heavily subsidized housing have increasingly given way to market-based delivery mechanisms.

Despite differences in their socio-economic impact, these new tools of wealth generation had an important communality with the oil–government nexus. They, too, revolved primarily around tapping rents, whether thanks to the influx of new residents into the region, the divestment of state assets, or opportunities for sponsoring foreign residents, businesses, and projects. But it is clear that rents alone will not deliver sustained prosperity on the desired scale. For the emerging post-oil order to succeed, it has to build on increased economic participation and productivity. Quality diversification can reduce the reliance on rents while creating the basis for new economic opportunities. Productivity growth is ultimately the sole guarantee of sustained increases in living standards.

For the paradigm shift to succeed, the Gulf must change the way productive resources – labor and capital – are developed and allocated. The old default option of rentierist public sector employment must yield to more dynamic private economic activities. This expanding private sector must support the government treasuries and ensure a sustainable current account position but, above all, deliver quality employment in sufficient numbers. This necessitates not just technical economic re-engineering but also a profoud change in culture. The state must become not a generous benefactor but an enabler of opportunities that ultimately build on a market-friendly, efficient regulatory framework and diverse, developed financial markets.

As clear as the conceptual case for change is, policy changes themselves are likely to prove far simpler and faster than the cultural reconditioning of the behavior of individuals and businesses. As observed by Monte Palmer *et al.* in 1984 with reference to Saudi Arabia:

> *... prevailing behavior patterns ... pose a serious obstacle to the government's efforts to break the rentier pattern. If most of the population remains psychologically aloof from the productive sector of the economy, no amount of capital expenditure will produce a diversified indigenous economy capable of sustaining itself at anything approaching current consumption levels without massive infusions of oil rents.*[60]

This view holds true even as important generational differences are appearing. The idea of entrepreneurship has gained considerable popularity, but much of it remains "rentierist" or "opportunistic," only seldom underpinned by a clear business plan and a formal governance structure. There is a disproportionate focus on low-productivity "me too" entrepreneurship in areas with minimal barriers to entry. Many of the preferred sectors have become increasingly congested, while they are also often being disrupted by technological change. As a result of the "double whammy" delivered by the fiscal overhaul and the COVID-19 pandemic, not to mention technological disruption, Schumpeterian creative destruction has played out with almost unprecedented force. Renting businesses for expatriate operators is common despite attempts to combat it through inspections and penalties. It also persists in countries where the liberalization of foreign ownership regulations should have obviated the need for it, something that reflects both a lack of awareness and the fact that many, especially lower income expatriates, lack the financial resources required for even modest start-up costs.

The fiscal overhaul is reshaping the Arabian welfare state. Combining a deregulated market economy with generous welfare provision is difficult and likely to become more so as the Gulf demographic transition gathers momentum and dependency ratios grow. Such realities have manifested themselves even in the most traditionally egalitarian of market economies. Yet both socio-cultural factors and economic logic will likely put a continuing premium on an inclusive growth agenda. Achieving this is not just – indeed, not even primarily – about reforming the traditional Arabian welfare state toward greater focus and efficiency. Rather, truly inclusive growth is above all about shared participation in generating wealth. Quite apart from the near-term fiscal and growth challenges, the ongoing demographic transition now makes increased economic participation by nationals critically important. In view of these trends and the sustainability challenges of the regional social insurance funds, the current generation of *khalijis* will have to generate most of the wealth needed for their prosperity today and in retirement. As a result, the productivity and inclusion agendas in the Gulf region are effectively aligned.

Economic participation is likely to increase as government largesse dwindles. For instance, in December 2017 the Saudi government introduced its Citizen's Account Program, which provides monthly cash payments designed to ensure an acceptable basic income for poorer citizens. The support available is determined by the size and composition of a family, the age of dependents, and family income. Such an approach will allow for greater differentiation and selectivity going forward. Nonetheless, it is important not just to reduce waste in the system but also to ensure that appropriate incentives for limiting welfare dependency are embedded. The system should not disincentivize but should encourage a transition to productive economic participation where possible.

Effective inclusion requires profound changes in the labor market and private sector growth dynamics. The Gulf economies will have to curb their systemic reliance on low-cost labor in favor of labor-saving technology. The speed of change will likely hinge on a relative repricing of the two factors of production. COVID-19 delivered important changes as technology became a critical lifeline to many businesses. For the first time in the modern history of the Gulf region, private businesses dramatically boosted their investments in technology simultaneously with an exodus of expatriate laborers. It is still unclear to what extent this has resulted in enduring business model overhauls, but at least the traditional default assumptions have been challenged, and cost-effective technology solutions are available even to the smallest SMEs. By reshaping business models, this shift promises to create new opportunities for more skilled employees that are more likely to appeal to nationals.

The dynamics of the Gulf labor markets and the long-standing cultural attitudes associated with them have also have been disrupted by the pandemic. By making traditional full-time employment at a given physical location more difficult, whether because of social distancing or cost pressures, the pandemic made businesses and individuals more receptive to alternative arrangements. The increase in remote work is boosting broader labor market flexibility and the receptiveness to it. This is a process that deserves to be supported further by less rigid regulations around working hours and conditions. Along with the rise of the so-called gig economy, this can become a powerful force for inclusion. It can lower the threshold – perceived or real – to new entrants to the workplace. This is particularly true for women, who are historically less economically active but now face new opportunities that can liberate them from the traditional binary choice between family and career. These trends can also reduce the reliance of companies on costly physical infrastructure. Reduced commuting naturally also delivers environmental and lifestyle benefits.

Notes

1 The Conference Board, *Prioritizing Productivity*, p. 3.
2 IMF, *Labor Market Reforms – Update*, p. 22.
3 Champion, *The Paradoxical Kingdom*, p. 210.
4 Khamis *et al.*, *Impact of the Global Financial Crisis*, p. 27.
5 Abdelbaki, "Assessing the Impact of the Global Financial Crisis," pp. 143–144.
6 World Bank, "Green Growth Opportunities," p. 24.
7 World Bank, "Green Growth Opportunities," p. 26.
8 Mirzoev *et al.*, *The Future of Oil*, pp. 2, 9.
9 Mirzoev *et al.*, *The Future of Oil*, p. 10; Fattouh and Sen, "Economic Diversification," p. 22.
10 BP, *Energy Outlook*, 2020 edition.

11 Fattouh and Sen, "Economic Diversification," p. 22.
12 Howell, *Empires in Collision*, p. 285; Arezki, "Oil-Producing Countries," p. 26.
13 https://www.eia.gov/outlooks/steo/.
14 Arezki, "Oil-Producing Countries," p. 26; Seznec, *Saudi Energy Changes*, p. 2.
15 Robert Rapier, "What Is Holding Back U.S. Oil Production?," *Forbes*, 11 March 2022, https://www.forbes.com/sites/rrapier/2022/03/11/what-is-holding-back-us-oil-production/?sh=352136c96b6f; Deloitte, *The Great Compression*.
16 Krane, "Gulf Energy Set to Win."
17 IMF, *United Arab Emirates: 2021 Article IV*, p. 8.
18 Andrew England and Samer Al-Atrush, "Saudi Arabia to Use Oil Windfall to Bolster Sovereign Fund," *Financial Times*, 25 May 2022, https://www.ft.com/content/d48d61a2-d1c1-4c4d-8e3c-332c954deeea
19 S&P Global Ratings, "Expatriate Exodus," p. 3; Oxford Economics, "GCC Expat Exodus – From a Trickle to a Deluge," Research Briefing – Africa and the Middle East, 22 May 2020.
20 *OECD Employment Outlook 2020.*
21 Fouejieu *et al.*, "Fiscal Adjustment," p. 16.
22 Quoted in: Champion, *The Paradoxical Kingdom*, p. 211.
23 Jarmo T. Kotilaine, "Kingdom Writes a New Chapter in the Gulf IPO Story," *Arab News*, 2 December 2021, https://www.arabnews.com/node/1979246.
24 Aguinaldo, "Riyadh Refocuses PPP Plans," meed.com, 31 July 2020.
25 Schwartz *et al.*, *Well Spent.*
26 https://investsaudi.sa/en/news/HRH-Crown-Prince-Launches-the-National-Investment-Strategy.
27 Gillian Duncan, "UAE Projects of the 50: The First 13 Are Announced," *The National*, 6 September 2021; Georgia Tolley and Rory Reynolds, "UAE Projects of the 50: Plan to Get 75,000 Emiratis into the Private Sector," *The National*, 12 September 202x1.
28 Hanieh, *Money, Markets, and Monarchies*, p. 227.
29 Hanieh, *Money, Markets, and Monarchies*, p. 226.
30 Hanieh, *Money, Markets, and Monarchies*, pp. 223–225.
31 IMF, *Regional Economic Outlook – Middle East and Central Asia*, p. 2.
32 Cusolito and Maloney, *Productivity Revisited*, p. 27.
33 Government of Dubai, Dubai SME, *The State of Small & Medium Enterprises (SMEs) in Dubai*, 2019, p. 20.
34 Chaudhry, *The Price of Wealth*, p. 151.
35 Hertog, "In the Spotlight," p. 44; Krane, "Climate Strategy," p. 48.
36 National Commercial Bank, *GCC Economic Review*, October 2011, pp. 16, 18; Government of Dubai, Dubai SME, *The State of Small & Medium Enterprises (SMEs) in Dubai*, 2019, p. 20.
37 Saudi General Authority for Statistics; Jadwa Investment, *SMEs and Vision 2030: Smaller Units for a Larger Economy*, March 2019; Monsha'at, *Masdar al-monsha'at al-saghira wa al-mutwassata, Taqrir "monsha'at" – al-rub' al-thani li-'aam 2022*, p. 12; Government of Dubai, Dubai SME, *The State of Small & Medium Enterprises (SMEs) in Dubai*, 2019, pp. 20, 24, 85, 92.
38 National Commercial Bank, *GCC Economic Review*, October 2011, pp. 16, 18.
39 Government of Dubai, Dubai SME, *The State of Small & Medium Enterprises (SMEs) in Dubai*, 2019, p. 20.
40 Saudi General Authority for Statistics; Jadwa Investment, *SMEs and Vision 2030: Smaller Units for a Larger Economy*, March 2019.
41 Bahrain Ministry of Industry, Commerce and Tourism; Bahrain Economic Development Board, "Building an Entrepreneurial Economy."
42 Mohammed Bin Rashid Al Maktoum Global Initiatives, Dubai SME, *SME Definition and Statistics 2018*, http://sme.ae/StudiesAndResearchDocument/SME-Definition-and-Statistics-2018.pdf; Government of Dubai, Dubai SME, *The State of Small & Medium Enterprises (SMEs) in Dubai*, 2019, pp. 20, 24, 85, 92.

43 Government of Dubai, *The State of Small & Medium Enterprises (SMEs) in Dubai*, 2019, pp. 43, 67.
44 Davis *et al.*, "Challenges Facing Family Companies," p. 217.
45 Hanieh, *Money, Markets, and Monarchies*, pp. 63–111.
46 BFBA, *Assessment of Family Business Enterprises*, p. 13.
47 Darwish *et al.*, "Family Businesses in GCC," pp. 1–2; Al-Barghouthi, "Passing the Torch," p. 279; Davis *et al.*, "Challenges Facing Family Companies," p. 218.
48 Rettab *et al.*, "Family Businesses in Dubai," pp. 17, 22; Hussain, *Corporate Governance in Family Owned Businesses*, p. 32; Darwish *et al.*, "Family Businesses in GCC," p. 9.
49 *PwC Middle East Family Business Survey 2019*, p. 15; Saddi *et al.*, *GCC Family Businesses*, pp. 5–7.
50 BFBA, *Assessment of Family Business Enterprises*, p. 57.
51 Saddi *et al.*, *GCC Family Businesses*, pp. 2, 10, 12; Davis *et al.*, "Challenges Facing Family Companies," p. 227; *PwC Middle East Family Business Survey 2019*, pp. 10, 13.
52 BFBA, *Assessment of Family Business Enterprises*, pp. 18, 23–24.
53 BFBA, *Assessment of Family Business Enterprises*, p. 42.
54 Saddi *et al.*, *GCC Family Businesses*, p. 7; Davis *et al.*, "Challenges Facing Family Companies," pp. 227–228.
55 Saddi *et al.*, *GCC Family Businesses*, p. 7; Davis *et al.*, "Challenges Facing Family Companies," pp. 227–228; Darwish *et al.*, "Family Businesses in GCC," p. 2; Al-Barghouthi, "Passing the Torch," p. 279; Jaffari, *Performance of Manufacturing SMEs*, pp. 226–230, 266.
56 BFBA, *Assessment of Family Business Enterprises*, pp. 32–35.
57 BFBA, *Assessment of Family Business Enterprises*, pp. 15, 17.
58 Hanieh, *Money, Markets, and Monarchies*, p. 1.
59 Champion, *The Paradoxical Kingdom*, p. 313.
60 Quoted in: Champion, *The Paradoxical Kingdom*, p. 202.

References

Abdelbaki, Hisham H. (2010), "Assessing the Impact of the Global Financial Crisis on GCC Countries," *Journal of Business & Economics Research*, vol. 8, no. 2, pp. 139–151.

Arezki, Rabah (2019), "Oil-Producing Countries in the Middle East and Africa Must Focus on How to Transform Their Economies," *Forum: A Quarterly Journal for Debating Energy Issues and Policies*, vol. 118 (June), pp. 25–27.

Bahrain Economic Development Board (2015), "Building an Entrepreneurial Economy: Taking Stock of the Track Record to Date," White Paper, Manama: Economic Development Board, February 2015.

Bahrain Family Business Association (2010), *Assessment of Family Business Enterprises in the Kingdom of Bahrain*, Manama.

Al-Barghouthi, Samar J. (2016), "Passing the Torch, Family Business Succession: Case Study, Bahrain," *International Journal of Business and Management Studies*, vol. 5, no. 1, pp. 279–294.

Champion, Daryl (2005), *The Paradoxical Kingdom: Saudi Arabia and the Momentum of Reform*, New York: Columbia University Press.

The Conference Board (2019), *Pioritizing Productivity in the Gulf Region: A Path toward Sustained Growth through Smart Diversification*, Kuwait City: Gulf Center for Economics and Business Research.

Cusolito, Ana Paula and William F. Maloney (2018), *Productivity Revisited: Shifting Paradigms in Analysis and Policy*, Washington, D.C.: World Bank Group.

Darwish, Saad, Anjali Gomes, and Venus Bunagan (2020), "Family Businesses (FBs) in Gulf Cooperation Council (GCC): Review and Strategic Insights," *Academy of Strategic Management Journal*, vol. 19, no. 3, pp. 1–13.

Davis, John A., Elye L. Pitts, and Keely Cormier (2000), "Challenges Facing Family Companies in the Gulf Region," *Family Business Review*, vol. 13, no. 3 (September), pp. 217–238.

Fattouh, Bassam and Anupama Sen (2019), "Economic Diversification by Arab Oil Exporters in the Context of Peak Oil and the Energy Transitions," *Forum: A Quarterly Journal for Debating Energy Issues and Policies*, vol. 118 (June), pp. 22–25.

Fouejieu, Armand, Sergio Rodriguez, and Sohaib Shahid (2018), "Fiscal Adjustment in the Gulf Countries: Less Costly than Previously Thought," IMF Working Paper, WP/18/133, Washington, D.C.: International Monetary Fund.

Government of Dubai, Dubai SME (2019), *The State of Small & Medium Enterprises (SMEs) in Dubai.*

Hanieh, Adam (2018), *Money, Markets, and Monarchies: The Gulf Cooperation Council and the Political Economy of the Contemporary Middle East*, Cambridge: Cambridge University Press.

Howell, David (2016), *Empires in Collision: The Green versus Black Struggle for our Energy Future*, London: Gilgamesh Publishing.

Hussain, Saleh (2017), *Corporate Governance in Family Owned Businesses: Importance of Constitution and Governance*, Manama: Saleh Hussain.

International Monetary Fund (2014), *Labor Market Reforms to Boost Employment and Productivity in the GCC – An Update*, Gulf Cooperation Council/IMF Policy Paper, Annual Meeting of Ministers of Finance and Central Bank Governors, 25 October 2014, Kuwait City, Kuwait, Washington, D.C.: International Monetary Fund.

——— (2022), *Regional Economic Outlook – Middle East and Central Asia: Mounting Challenges, Decisive Times*, Washington, D.C.: International Monetary Fund.

——— (2022), *United Arab Emirates: 2021 Article IV Consultation—Press Release; and Staff Report*, IMF Country Report, No. 22/50, February 2022, Washington, D.C.: International Monetary Fund.

Jaffari, Akbar (2020), *Performance of Manufacturing SMEs in Fluctuating Economy*, 2nd edition, Manama: JAFCON Consultants for Productivity Improvement.

Khamis, May, Abdelhak Senhadji, Maher Hasan, Francis Kumah, Anantakrishnan Prasad, and Gabriel Sensenbrenner (2010), *Impact of the Global Financial Crisis on the Gulf Cooperation Council Countries and Challenges Ahead*, Washington, D.C.: Middle East and Central Asia Department, International Monetary Fund.

Krane, Jim (2021), "Gulf Energy Set to Win in Climate Action," Near East Policy Forum, https://nepf.org.au/index.php/gulf-energy-set-to-win-in-climate-action.

Mirzoev, Tokhir, Ling Zhu, Yang Yang, Andrea Pescatori, and Akito Matsumoto (2020), *The Future of Oil and Fiscal Sustainability in the GCC Region*, Washington, D.C.: Middle East and Central Asia Department Research Department, International Monetary Fund.

Rettab, Belaid, Tarek Abu Fakhr, and Marietta P. Morada (2005), "Family Businesses in Dubai: Definition, Structure & Performance," Working Paper, Dubai: Data Management and Business Research Department, Dubai Chamber of Commerce & Industry.

Saddi, Joe, Per-Ola Karlsson, Ahmed Youssed, and Karim Abdallah (2009), *GCC Family Businesses Face New Challenges* (Perspective), Booz & Company.

Schwartz, Gerd, Manal Fouad, Torben Hansen, and Geneviève Verdier, eds. (2020), *Well Spent: How Strong Infrastructure Governance Can End Waste in Public Infrastructure*, Washington, D.C.: International Monetary Fund.

Seznec, Jean-François (2016), *Saudi Energy Changes: The End of the Rentier State*, Washington, D.C.: Atlantic Council: Global Energy Center.

World Bank (2022), "Green Growth Opportunities in the GCC," *Gulf Economic Update*, Washington, D.C.: The World Bank, Fall 2022.

9 Navigating choppy waters

Today, GCC citizens and policymakers alike are envisioning a future where their prosperity revolves around the ingenuity of people, openness to the world, and, above all, productivity. The GCC is on the world map like never before. But many questions still cloud the future trajectory of the Gulf economy, whose evolution to date has seen many dramatic reversals of fortune. The steady forward march of diversification notwithstanding, oil remains critical for the economic well-being of the region. However, the future of fossil fuels is shrouded in uncertainty due to profound changes in technology, consumer preferences, investor attitudes, and the politics of environmental sustainability. The International Energy Agency announced in May 2021 that achieving net zero carbon emissions by 2050 would mean "no new oil and gas fields approved for development ..., and no new coal mines or mine extensions"[1] beyond ones committed as of 2021. The share of hydrocarbons in the global energy mix would "fall from almost four-fifths of total energy supply today to slightly over one-fifth by 2050."[2]

Whereas the GCC has established itself as a haven of stability and prosperity, much of the neighborhood around it remains saddled with thorny challenges. The early 21st-century promise of brisk development has faded into history as the problems facing the Arab world have grown in magnitude and complexity. The long-standing rivalry between the Gulf Arabs and Iran has ebbed and flowed over the centuries, and full normalization still appears remote despite some encouraging signs in 2023. Yemen presents a host of long-standing issues, and GCC forces have been involved in an open military conflict in the country since late 2014. The Houthi rebels have launched several missiles on Saudi Arabia and even the UAE during the conflict. Iraq has struggled to achieve enduring stability following the US-led invasion in 2003. Recent developments in Afghanistan are of broader regional concern. Terrorist actions by non-state actors constitute another potential risk.

The prosperity of the GCC remains critically linked to its openness. The Gulf economies require secure access to the global markets on reasonable terms given their exceptional trade dependency. Yet exclusionary nationalism is once again rearing its ugly head around the world, while the COVID-19 recovery has strengthened preferences for localizing value chains, potentially challenging the strategic value of intermediaries. The escalating conflict in Eastern Europe since 2022, and the Western sanctions it triggered, entails the possibility of a Cold War–style bifurcation of the global economy.

DOI: 10.4324/9781003373353-9

Black swans are here to stay

The world is an unpredictable place, where the once unquestioned pillars of the Cold War order and the "end of history" mirage of the late 20th century have given way to endemic volatility. The post–Cold War *Pax Americana* seems to be morphing into a much more multipolar and less stable world order. The GCC, because of its exceptional openness, small population, and narrow domestic resource base, is particularly vulnerable to the various risks that this entails. In general, the threats of particular importance for shaping the Gulf region's way forward are (i) risks to global financial and macroeconomic stability, (ii) political risk, (iii) climate change, and (iv) public health risks.

The young 21st century has already delivered an extraordinary economic roller-coaster ride. Months into the new millennium, the "irrational exuberance" of the late 1990s was tested when, after a five-year, 400 percent rally, the Nasdaq stock market crashed, putting an unceremonious end to the so-called dot-com bubble. The 9/11 attacks in 2001 palpably revealed new fault lines in a world reshaped by decades of progressive integration and apparent cultural convergence. Exceptional monetary loosening nonetheless pushed financial markets to unprecedented highs until they were dealt a massive blow by the financial crisis of 2007–2008. A downturn in the US subprime mortgage market triggered a chain reaction that shook the global financial system to its core and led to the most painful economic downturn since the Great Depression of the 1930s. A succession of crises followed, with, for instance, the eurozone rocked by fiscal vulnerabilities in several member states, most notably Greece.

These events shook up a global economic order built on decades of concerted financial liberalization and deepening integration, reflected in rapidly growing cross-border goods and capital flows.[3] The crisis revealed that, quite apart from delivering "great moderation," this was a system with profound vulnerabilities. The shock to it triggered unprecedented economic policy interventions, both by governments, which in many cases found themselves taking on losses incurred by private businesses but also by central banks. Aggressive monetary stimulus not only re-stabilized the global financial system but also drove unprecedented liquidity creation. A major overhaul of financial regulation, best embodied by Basel III, ensued. However, while the regulation of the formal banking sector has been tightened, other types of institutions and structures subject to less supervision have been growing.[4]

After initial financial consolidation, the lower cost of credit eventually increased its availability well beyond the pre-crisis levels, particularly markedly in emerging economies. Importantly, this increase began from an already high base, and non-financial sector debt worldwide rose from 138 to 152 percent of the global GDP during the 2010s. This trend was further amplified by the policies adopted in response to COVID-19 as policy permissiveness was justified by the common view that the post-global financial crisis recovery had been held back by an unduly speedy withdrawal of stimulus measures.[5] However, the emergence of unexpectedly strong inflationary pressures in response to supply chain disruptions and labor market changes in 2021, further amplified by the 2022 Ukraine crisis, resulted in a sharp policy reversal. A retreat from the era of ample liquidity may finally beckon. More problematic, after an unusually protracted period of loose monetary conditions, many debtors are extremely sensitive to even small increases in interest rates. Aggressive tightening under the circumstances might prove very disruptive.

While central bank interventions may have proven effective in managing the financial market vulnerabilities of recent years, their longer-term effectiveness remains in doubt. Even as ultra-loose monetary policy has given rise to protracted financial market rallies, the years of loose liquidity led to growing concerns about "malinvestment," something that the poor productivity track record of the global economy would seem to confirm. Global labor productivity growth decelerated from a peak of 2.8 percent in 2007 to a low of 1.4 percent in 2016, remaining below 2 percent in 2017–2018. Emerging markets saw productivity gains decelerate even more sharply, from 6.6 percent in 2007 to 3.1 percent in 2015, "the steepest, longest, and most synchronized [fall] in the recent decades."[6]

These new economic realities have had far-reaching socio-political repercussions. The massive stimulus to asset prices has deepened income and wealth inequality as economic disruptions and the productivity slowdown have simultaneously eroded access to and income from employment. The ability of the governments to offer social benefits has been challenged by more precarious fiscal realities. Leverage has also entailed a wealth transfer between generations at a time when the demographic trends in much of the Western world are leaving welfare provision increasingly dependent on a dwindling working-age population. This decade of economic underperformance has left an enduring socio-political legacy of discontent emanating from dashed expectations and uneven access to opportunities, whose impact has at times been amplified by global issues such as migration and refugees. Many countries have seen slower growth concentrate minds around distributional issues, contributing to the rise of populist pressures and political instability. Some of these shifts have had global implications; for instance, through events such as Brexit and the 2016 election of Donald Trump. The Middle East was rocked in 2011 by the Arab Spring, which many attribute at least in part to perceptions of unfair distribution of the benefits delivered by the early 21st-century emerging markets boom.

Political risk has become a household word in recent decades. It has spawned a whole industry of analysts but also gained recognition as an important factor shaping economic dynamics. It has repeatedly delivered significant bouts of instability to individual countries and even globally. Political risk considerations are of particular interest in the Gulf as they have profoundly reshaped the political and economic realities of the regions flanking the Arabian Peninsula. Iran is a particularly salient case in point. After years of strained relations, the West set out to normalize relations with Tehran through the 2015 Joint Comprehensive Plan of Action, which lifted economic sanctions in return for Iranian commitments to reduce its stocks of enriched uranium and gas centrifuges. However, the Trump administration withdrew from the deal in May 2018. The Biden administration showed interest in reviving the setup, but progress has been complicated by Iran's internal politics and external relations. The relative isolation of Iran has had mixed implications for the GCC. As occurred so often in the past, the weakness of a historic rival has doubtless boosted the Gulf countries' appeal as international hubs. It has marginalized a potential challenger in the oil market by limiting exports but also production capacity following years of underinvestment. However, these challenges have also served to contain opportunities in the near abroad of the Gulf countries. Any renewed settlement or normalization would create some competition in the Middle East region but would probably also permit the GCC to capitalize even more on its infrastructure and other advantages. The Gulf economies would likely be instrumental in facilitating increased interaction between Iran and the rest of the world, as Dubai, in particular, has done for years.[7] Properly managed, regional *détente* could also significantly reduce the external political risk perceptions of the GCC.

Potential risks exist even further afield. The future of China is of particular strategic interest for the GCC. The spectacular rise of the People's Republic as a global economic power has been one of the main external factors shaping the development of the Gulf in the early 21st century. China's extraordinary development trajectory made it the world's leading source of incremental demand for commodities ranging from oil to metals and various manufacturing outputs. Many of the heavy industrial projects in the Gulf region, whose viability had at times been in doubt, were among the key beneficiaries of China's rise. Its growing wealth made the People's Republic an increasingly important source of imports, investors, and visitors for the Gulf region. For instance, Dubai's ambitions to establish itself as a global tourism hub received a major boost from the ever more mobile and prosperous Chinese middle class, who have been flocking to the city. By now, the UAE is home to some 200,000 Chinese residents. With the growing international footprint of Chinese companies and the government's One Belt One Road ambitions, China's ties with the GCC have dramatically grown in depth and diversity in recent years.[8]

China's prosperity matters a great deal for the GCC. This is the case indirectly, given the country's economic weight and criticality for global growth. But the rapid expansion in interactions between the two geographies also entails a significant direct impact. China's future outlook is potentially clouded by its heavy reliance on leverage as well as its challenging demographics. Optimists point to centralized policymaking and the strong commitment of the authorities to ensuring socio-economic stability. Pessimists highlight the mounting indebtedness along with weakening structural growth drivers, as highlighted by the recent turbulence in the large real estate sector. The decades-long one-child policy has continued to cast a long shadow even after it was formally jettisoned in 2015. Investors are growing anxious about a more interventionist state. Even with the apparent readiness to resort to renewed stimulus measures, the trend rate of growth looks likely to remain on a downward trajectory, further complicated by COVID-related challenges in 2022. Slower growth in China might be countered to an extent by the more robust growth dynamics in some of its southern neighbors. However, even these economies are also influenced by the performance of China.

Political risk clearly has a domestic and regional dimension as well. While the history of the GCC countries is one of exceptional continuity by international standards, much has been written over the years about disputes in and among these countries. The regional governments have responded to such challenges in a variety of ways that have, importantly, included institutional and constitutional reforms. Kuwait in particular but also Bahrain now have fairly powerful parliaments, and national representative and consultative mechanisms exist across the region. For instance, the Consultative (Shura) Council of Saudi Arabia has a total membership of 150 representatives, including women. Policymaking in the region has become increasingly transparent and technocratic along with more vociferous policy debates, not least thanks to the rise of social media. In practice, the regional political system has found ways of combining commitment to tradition and continuity with evolutionary adaptation to change. But this will remain an ongoing balancing act going forward.

Dealing with the specter of protectionism

The just under three decades leading up to the global financial crisis were characterized by a global wave of economic liberalization and integration. The GCC countries took on key aspects of the Washington Consensus in many of the strategic choices made during this period. But since the global financial crisis, global public opinion has generally been drifting away from the economic liberalism of yesteryear. This reverse momentum has been neither fast, uniform, nor altogether continuous, but it is clear that the erstwhile broad-based consensus around market-led development and global integration is fraying. Moreover, its importance as a driver of economic prosperity has weakened. It now seems reasonable to assume that this relative retreat from globalization may endure for an extended period, all the more because the COVID-related disruptions have highlighted risks associated with global value chains. The growing tensions between the West and China, along with the Ukraine conflict, have further fueled the popularity of ideas such as near-shoring while raising the prospect of more formal fragmentation into rival blocks.

Part of the dimished appeal of the late 20th- to early 21st-century wave of market deregulation doubtless comes from its dwindling ability to unleash significant new growth drivers, reflecting the law of diminishing returns. The returns to reform may appear even less compelling in net terms, since liberalization has given rise to many risks as well, not least financial market volatility. There is also growing political sensitivity to the uneven distribution of the benefits delivered by globalization. It is thus possible that we are now facing another reversal of the historic pendulum movements between liberalism and control.

Not only has the consensus around trade liberalization been fraying over the past decade but the concept of globalization itself now enjoys a less central place in international economic policy debates than it used to. The commitment to upholding the international economic order has eroded in tandem with the perceived political payoffs from doing so. International platforms such as G7 have seen modest progress on meaningful policy reforms, while even the degree of consensus around some of the previously unassailable key priorities has eroded. In many countries, policy interventions focusing on protecting jobs and living standards command increased appeal even if the economic logic underpinning them is often flawed. A more contested policy debate has created an environment where more and more key planks of the early 21st-century economic thinking are now up for discussion. Politically divisive issues such as seemingly uncontrolled immigration, whether following EU enlargement, in connection with the Syrian refugee crisis, or the northward migration from Central America, have further fueled popular skepticism about globalization. This economic success formula of the past is increasingly frequently presented as a source of vulnerabilities that are not easy to manage.

The longer-term consequences of these changing political winds are difficult to predict. Many of the forces unleashed by the global financial crisis and COVID-19 are neither linear nor continuous as the old contends with the new in multiple ways. However, what seems beyond dispute is that many elements of this post–Cold War global economic order are no longer uncontested. Attempts to question free trade, whether through initiatives such as Brexit or the US–China trade disputes, are a growing concern for businesses and a source of uncertainty and risk. The renewed focus on the role of the state along with mounting expectations in this regard, as seen, for instance, during the pandemic, often results in a more national focus for policy debates. Job concerns and global risk perceptions have fueled an increased interest in localizing business activities in an attempt to reduce perceived vulnerabilities of globalization.

These realities matter for the GCC countries because of their exceptional openness, which, moreover, constitutes a central strategic focus of their diversification plans. Openness allows the regional economies to scale by transcending their domestic constraints, which, even after decades of rapid, transformative development, remain acute. The population of the region has increased some 25-fold over the past century but at around 60mn remains relatively modest in international comparison. This contains the domestic and regional market size. While economic diversification is adding to local productive activities, the Gulf in many ways remains more a region of brokers and traders than one of producers. The local natural resource base is exceptional but narrow, heavily dominated by hydrocarbons. By contrast, openness as a source of economic development is something that the Gulf economies are in a position to meaningfully influence through policy, regulation, and infrastructure development. It is becoming ever more central to the future economic plans and ambitions of the region.

Development strategies across the Gulf region prioritize export growth, increased foreign direct investment, tourism, and the attraction of qualified talent. Policy innovations during the COVID-19 pandemic have revolved heavily around attracting new capital and skilled residents to the region. Recent strategic initiatives such as Saudi Arabia's National Industrial Development and Logistics Program and the UAE's Operation 300bn reflect a renewed interest in making export-oriented manufacturing a stronger growth and diversification driver. Technology and communications investments also figure prominently in the policy toolkit. Tourism development in particular has been able to capitalize on the region's effective handling of the COVID-19 pandemic, giving Gulf businesses and governments an opportunity to consolidate their reputations for safety and reliability.[9] Safeguarding, entrenching, and, where appropriate, adapting this posture of openness are essential since a failure – or even a loss of momentum – in this regard would jeopardize key non-oil growth drivers. But these ambitions entail a potential vulnerability; the region depends on the future of globalization and openness worldwide. For instance, less trade and lower growth by countries such as China would entail slower growth in global energy demand. It would also have adverse effects on the pricing of many of the manufacturing products that the Gulf countries have prioritized in their efforts to diversify exports.

In practice, reversing globalization is easier said than done. Even the political payoffs from it may be greater on the rhetorical level than through any actual policy redesign or implementation. The forces of globalization may be a useful scapegoat for politicians, but attempts to counter them will entail a direct assault on a potent driver of global economic well-being of recent decades. Moreover, the sensitivity of financial markets to protectionist rhetoric, let alone concrete measures, may well serve as a powerful bulwark in the way of significant de-globalization. Such factors may ultimately also help check populist impulses. After all, following the reforms of the recent decdes, the wealth of key demographic groups in the leading Western economies critically depends on the state of the financial markets throught market-based pension and insurance schemes as well as homeownership. But there is little doubt that the parameters of debate have shifted. Global economic integration looks unlikely to regain its stature as a leading growth driver any time soon.

Whatever the future of globalization may be, the GCC countries need not be passive spectators as events unfold. Offense is often the best defense. Their achievements and forward-looking strategic posture have turned the regional countries into increasingly confident and weighty players in the evolving global debate. One of the transformative successes of the early 21st century has been the ability of the Gulf countries – and many regional businesses – to diversify and deepen their external relations. As the pole of demand growth in the hydrocarbons markets shifted east, the ties with the rising Asian consumers gained importance and received much more attention. The growing stature of China as an oil and gas market is a case in point. Having exceeded 70 percent of Oman's crude export since 2014, China's share reached almost 90 percent in the spring of 2021. China's share of Saudi oil exports rose to one-third from just 13.6 percent in 2014, making the Kingdom China's leading supplier. China claimed 10.8 percent of Kuwaiti oil exports in 2014 but 23 percent in 2018.[10] Geographic and demographic realities will almost certainly further cement the economic ties between the GCC and Asia, as well as – with time – Africa. Whatever the future of multilateralism, the GCC countries can proactively deepen these newer dimensions of their external relations by negotiating trade agreements and other treaties that reduce the risks and costs associated with trade and investment.

The GCC is likely to best protect its strategic interests when it can position itself as a trusted intermediary and facilitator in multiple directions, effectively diversifying its external economic relations, ideally on the basis of strategic neutrality. The evolution of Gulf foreign policy in recent years has positioned the region well for a multipolar world order. While deeper ties with India and China entail attractive opportunities, these are potentially highly asymmetric relationships, given the size of these two economies. In the 19th and early 20th centuries, the GCC became an annex to the much larger Indian market. This time, it can hope to be a much more equal partner, but sustainable success must build on significant reciprocal dependencies and benefits. The same is like to be true for the One Belt One Road initiative championed by China. Even compelling potential opportunities should not become exclusionary. Building a broader, multidirectional network will limit significant dependencies and the risks these may entail. It will also permit more agility in response to evolving circumstances.

However great the dependence of the GCC countries on openness is, the region itself is not a stranger to protectionist pressures. There is an established historical pattern between fast growth and a laissez-faire political posture going hand in hand. Similarly, regulatory reforms have always been a key component of the policy response to slower growth. Diversification has tended to rise on the list of political priorities whenever the oil–government nexus has threatened to run out of steam. More problematic, such steps have tended to coincide with a more politically contested environment. Slower growth has typically shifted attention to distributional issues, such as company ownership rules, labor market regulations, and provisions about residency. Debates around corporate ownership have threatened the strategic ambitions of enabling foreign capital to capitalize on the locational (and other) advantages of the region. In the labor markets, the attention has tended to focus on how to protect national employment at a time of slower public sector job creation. Such attitudes have mirrored long-standing regulatory differences between nationals and non-nationals but also the fact that the Gulf countries, despite their long-standing openness, are most emphatically not melting pots.[11]

While these concerns are understandable, they must be appropriately managed in view of the development opportunities facing the Gulf economies. Short-term political expediency must not undermine longer-term strategic priorities and needs. Access to foreign capital and talent will be critical for long-term prosperity of the Gulf, something that all of the regional governments now appear to recognize. The value of capital often comes from the technology, know-how, connections, and innovative spirit it is coupled with. Talented individuals tend to bring their own networks, which translates into more visitors and access to different sources of capital and knowledge. The logical solution for balancing the conflicting aspirations of openness and domestic interests is simple. The region will have to find a way of shifting from quantity to quality. The Gulf can afford to be more selective than it has been, but this puts the onus on its ability to attract higher-quality capital, whether human or corporate. In the domestic context, it is important to establish a shared understanding of where the long-term needs of the region lie. In the external setting, potential investors and residents must be assured that somewhat more conditional openness is all the firmer and therefore more secure and reassuring than before.

Prospering in a troubled neighborhood

The Middle East and North Africa region enjoys a firmly established but dubious reputation as a troubled part of the world. This unfortunate state of affairs has been underpinned by endemic conflicts such as the decades-long Palestinian–Israeli standoff and the aggressive regional ambitions of Iran, notably since the 1979 revolution. While the Middle East has experienced recurrent moments of optimism and brisk growth, its longer-term economic performance has been relatively weak, not to mention volatile, in global comparison. Several countries have undergone bouts of serious political instability, and not a single decade since World War II has passed without an open military conflict in some part of the Middle East. The structural vulnerabilities of the Arab world were powerfully laid bare after the early 21st-century emerging markets rally succumbed to the global financial crisis and its after-tremors in 2011. Three regional economies – Libya, Syria, and Yemen – have been embroiled in persistent and bloody internal strife since then. Iraq has struggled to achieve political stability and restore its economic health. Lebanon has been beset by sectarian tensions and a deepening economic crisis. Even Egypt, the most populous nation in the region, experienced an unusual period of chronic political discord in the aftermath of 2011 and had to contend with major macroeconomic challenges even thereafter. Both Algeria and Sudan witnessed a renewed spike in internal political tensions in 2019, followed by Tunisia in 2021. Sudan saw open conflict in 2023. The realities have left the GCC uncomfortably squeezed between neighbors beset by exceptionally thorny challenges.

Many of the political and security challenges in the Middle East are underpinned by problematic social realities. The 2003 *Arab Human Development Report* commented on "the existence of deeply rooted shortcomings that stand as obstacles to building human development."[12] Decades of economic underperformance have entailed perpetual challenges in educating and gainfully employing successive generations of the region's young, rapidly growing population. The demographic dividend promised by this human capital has frequently turned into its opposite, further burdening fragile economies with unproductive resources. In many parts of the Middle East, these social dynamics have combined with acute resource constraints that have manifested themselves in pressing problems such as constrained access to water or fragile food security. Water, always scarce, is emerging with seeming inevitability as an existential source of strife in parts of the Arab world following decades of rapid demand growth and poor resource governance. Yemen is now billed as the first country in the world that will likely run out of water as "current annual use of water at 3.5 m^3 exceeds renewable resources by 1.4 billion m^3."[13]

These challenges have made parts of the Middle Eastern population responsive to political radicalization. The descent of many countries into a vicious cycle of economic underperformance and recurrent socio-political instability has proven difficult to escape from because of the persistent failure to develop stronger institutions and governance. This has deterred foreign investment, which under different conditions could have helped alleviate some of these pressures. If anything, the current demographic trends may well make the problem more acute going forward, as "60 percent of the population have not yet reached the age of 30."[14]

Today, the GCC stands out in the broader Middle East region as never before as a block characterized by exceptional prosperity (even by global standards), high levels of human development, and a track record of political continuity. Prosperous, stable, and highly integrated in the global economy, it is almost as if this group of six countries had transcended the troubles of the broader Arab world. The economic resilience of the Gulf countries contrasts increasingly sharply with the chronic underperformance and endemic challenges of many of their regional neighbors.[15] The Gulf economies have been able to capitalize on this divergence by establishing a reputation as havens of stability that draw talent and capital from their troubled neighbors and beyond. They have successfully positioned themselves as globally significant hubs for travel, trade, and investment. The ability of other Middle Eastern economies to meaningfully challenge this Gulf exceptionalism any time soon appears minimal. In some ways, therefore, the misfortune of the broader neighborhood has spelled opportunity for the GCC. Arguably the only near-neighbor that has managed to credibly match some of the Gulf countries' achievements is Turkey.

Amid this deepening divergence in economic fortunes between the GCC and the rest of the Middle East, the foreseeable potential for any meaningful convergence appears remote. Economic relations within the region have remained narrow and fairly lopsided. While the arrival of contract workers and businessmen from other parts of the region may have benefited the Gulf, it has also entailed a costly brain drain for these neighboring countries. While doubtless helping to diffuse social pressures in the broader Middle East, it has also engendered some less healthy dependencies between the Gulf and the surrounding economies. The expectations of greater regional engagement and intra-regional travel in the pre-2008 period were challenged by the subsequent economic and political volatility and further exacerbated by the dislocations brought on by COVID-19.

This striking contrast between the GCC and the broader Middle East entails a potentially risky balancing act for the Gulf countries. Containing a problem does not eliminate it. Moreover, Gulf exceptionalism has entailed substantial costs. While the vicissitudes of the broader neighborhood may have reduced competition while drawing talent and capital, they have also circumscribed opportunities. The crescent of countries from Somalia to Pakistan, with which the GCC shares a land or sea border, has a substantial combined population well in excess of half a billion people. The GCC visions, in an echo of the trading past of the region, have invariably commented on the potential of the GCC to position itself as a hub for a very significant geography. But doing this has not been easy, as the inner leaves of the "onion of opportunity" surrounding the Gulf have been mired in economic underperformance and socio-political strife. Instead of allowing the GCC to capitalize on its wealth of capital to serve as an attractive gateway to larger, much more populous nearby markets, the near-neighborhood has increasingly become a risk to be managed. Financial aid from the GCC has at times been important for securing a degree of macroeconomic stability in some Arab countries. Such support is not necessarily cheap or effective. It can engender moral hazards, potentially reducing the incentives for the recipients of aid to wean themselves off such support. Encouragingly, these realities are gaining renewed attention and once again focusing minds around regional engagement and integration. Increasingly, the Gulf governments are seeking ways to engage through investments rather than traditional aid. Ventures such as Neom have an explicitly regional dimension.[16] However, success will necessitate productive investment, progress beyond the traditional predilection for financial sector and telecommunications equity, along with capital mobilization around "real estate, tourism, and American-style shopping malls."[17] While the way forward may not be simple, it is the only way to move beyond a situation where the region continues to be "held together more by cultural affinity than economic expediency."[18]

Sweet are the uses of adversity

The persistent challenges of their near abroad may have played at least an indirect role in prompting GCC governments and businesses to look further afield. This has also reflected the evolution of the global growth dynamics as well as profound shifts in the hydrocarbons markets. The end result has been growing multidimensionality of the Gulf region's external economic relations. Ties with the Indian subcontinent are particularly noteworthy in terms of their historic overhaul. With India emerging as a weighty force on the world stage, the traditional exchange of Middle Eastern oil for Indian low-cost labor and foodstuffs is morphing into a multidimensional trade and investment partnership. But even amid this diversification, India's growing hunger for energy is set to remain a key anchor for the foreseeable future. The Gulf, led by Saudi Arabia, is historically the main source of India's oil imports.[19] The relationship between the UAE and India is particularly close and builds on long antecedents in areas such as gold trade. It reflects the strategic role of Dubai as a regional logistics and tourism hub. The UAE was India's second-largest export destination in 2017, a trade that after centuries still consists heavily of pearls, diamonds, and precious metals. Strikingly, the UAE was also India's second-largest source of imports. Indian exports to the UAE totaled $28b, while $22.1bn was traded in the opposite direction.[20] In February 2022 the two countries signed a Comprehensive Economic Partnership Agreement that is expected to boost annual bilateral non-oil trade from $60bn to $100bn within three to five years. The deal also covers services, investments, and intellectual property and involves a commitment by the UAE to create 140,000 highly skilled jobs by 2030.

China has also been rapidly building up its presence in the Gulf region. Kuwait was the first Gulf country to establish diplomatic relations with Beijing in 1971, but Saudi Arabia only did so in 1990. The Gulf features in the Belt and Road initiative unveiled in 2015, not least thanks to its logistics prowess, above all the "infrastructural readiness of the UAE to enable and support the flow of Chinese goods across both the immediate and wide region and other ... markets like Africa."[21] The UAE intermediates some 60 percent of China's European and African trade. Reflecting these realities, in 2016, China signed a Comprehensive Strategic Partnership with Saudi Arabia, followed by the UAE in 2018. Future ambitions clearly extend much further, with Beijing explicitly prioritizing an "'1 + 2 + 3 cooperation pattern' with the Gulf where '1' represents energy as a core interest; '2' infrastructure construction, as well as trade and investment; and '3' nuclear energy, satellites, and new energy sources."[22]

The rapid expansion in relations has made China the leading trade partner and investor in the GCC. Bilateral trade, having stood at less than \$10bn in 2000, had reached \$165bn by 2013. The value of Saudi–Chinese bilateral trade stood at \$65.2bn in 2020 and \$87.3bn in 2021. The over \$50.9bn of Saudi exports to China in 2021 made up some 18.4 percent of the Kingdom's aggregate exports. The Sino–Gulf relationship rests on strong fundamentals and shared interests, as almost 30 percent of China's oil imports in 2018, some 2.9mn barrels per day, came from the GCC. Natural gas is similarly of growing importance and, pre-COVID, Qatar was on track to supply nearly 30 percent of China's LNG imports by 2023. In the case of Oman, trade with China generated 44 percent of total export revenues in 2017. Significant progress also has been made in facilitating trade finance and renminbi-based trading, with currency swap agreements in place with the UAE and Qatar.[23]

Chinese companies have established a growing presence in the Arabian peninsula, with an estimated 4,000 companies in the UAE alone, many of them engaged infrastructure projects. The Chinese telecommunications giant Huawei played a key role building the regional 5G mobile networks. Salient projects undertaken by Chinese companies have included the Haramain railway for pilgrims visiting Makkah and Madinah as well as large-scale power and housing projects. Within a remarkably short period of time: "The scope of China's interests in the Gulf has grown ... from a narrow focus on the hydrocarbons trade to wide-ranging investments in energy, industry, finance, transport, communications, and other technology."[24]

Chinese FDI into the GCC rose sharply from \$2bn in 2001 to \$60bn in 2008 and totaled more than \$62bn between 2005 and 2017. The value of Chinese FDI to Saudi Arabia totaled \$2.32bn in 2013–2021, while the aggregate value of contracts and investments in 2005–2021 reached \$43.5bn.[25] China is eying a direct foothold in the Gulf region through the China–Pakistan economic corridor and the massive investments in the Gwadar port where Saudi Arabia is planning to develop a \$10bn refinery and petrochemicals complex. China has been a key driver of Oman's Duqm special economic zone project, although progress has been slow. China is also gradually building up a portfolio of direct investments in GCC assets, including 49 percent of the Oman Electricity Transmission Company since 2019 and a similar share of ACWA Power's renewable energy arm.[26]

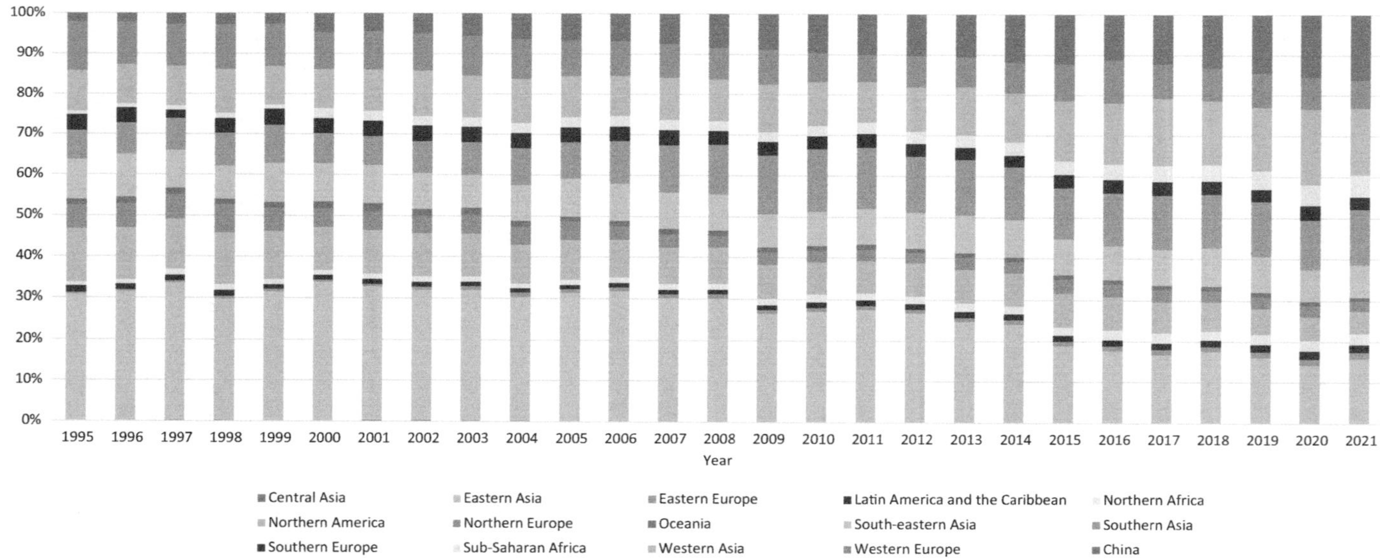

Figure 9.1 The geographic composition of the GCC countries' foreign merchandise trade. (N.B. The "East Asia" totals exclude China, which is presented separately.)

Source: United Nations Conference on Trade and Development, https://unctadstat.unctad.org/wds/ReportFolders/reportFolders.aspx?sCS_ChosenLang=en.

Turkey has gained much popularity as a travel and investment destination for Gulf citizens and residents, even if political relations between the two sides have recently proven much less straightforward, not least because of sometimes conflicting regional ambitions. This has hampered the progress of a partnership that offers exceptional economic complementarity.[27] However, by 2022, there were clear indications that the two sides were ready to move toward normalizing their ties after years of tension. The Gulf countries are also working to reactivate their centuries-old ties with Africa, a process that accelerated during the global financial crisis. Africa holds considerable appeal because of its proximity, demographic dynamism, and ability to enhance the Gulf region's food security, which up to now has relied heavily on North Africa, above all Egypt, and the Levant.[28] Progress in ties offers new opportunities to make better use of GCC infrastructure to facilitate trade and travel between the two large continents that flank them. But the GCC is also working to develop African infrastructure for better connectivity and integration. For instance, the UAE "invested an estimated $11 billion in capital in Africa in 2016, overtaking Saudi Arabia to become the largest GCC investor and the second largest in the world after China."[29] Trade volumes have been expanding, with, for instance, UAE goods imports from Africa averaging some $5bn a year in 2010–2015 before shooting up to $23.9bn in 2016.[30] Stronger ties have also emerged in the northern direction, with both the Central Asian and trans-Caucasian economies but also with Russia, which has been a leading strategic partner of OPEC in recent years.

The end result of these trends has been a dramatic geographic diversification of the GCC foreign trade and investment patters, a process that looks set to continue. The deepening ties with the world's most rapidly growing economies are a logical way to develop new export and investment opportunities while building resilience in an uncertain world. By establishing a broad portfolio of partner markets, the GCC has increased the effective demand facing its expanding logistics infrastructure while probably also ensuring that this demand will prove more resilient. For instance, during the global financial crisis, growth dynamics in the Gulf proved less vulnerable to the weakness of the advanced economies of the West as they were in a position to benefit from the faster growth of Asia and even Africa. The increasingly diverse network of external relations allows the Gulf countries to pivot on a global scale in response to evolving economies realities. This flexibility proved important amid the changes to global energy trade dynamics in 2022. This growing global network constitutes an important insurance policy in the face of the stronger protectionist tendencies observed in many countries. To the extent that globalization as a force does lose momentum, bilateral economic relation are likely to grow in relative importance. The wider the range of such "special relationships," the better for the future growth of the Gulf. However, sustainable success looks likely to require more effort to safeguard strategic neutrality and protect key interests in a potentially more polarized world.

Facing the prospect of climate change

Even as the topic remains politically divisive, it is by now widely accepted that the climate worldwide is indeed changing. While the climate has never been static, the pace of change appears to be accelerating. We are seeing evidence of rising average temperatures and an increasing frequency of extreme weather phenomena. The UN International Panel on Climate Change (IPCC) has for some time focused attention of the Middle East as one of the regions likely to be most affected by climate change in the decades ahead. Moreover, it is becoming abundantly clear that climate change is not only a major threat to the region but also a factor reshaping global public opinion and policy in ways that can have profound consequences for the Gulf.

The 2021 IPCC report on climate change was billed as "a code red for humanity,"[31] with the Paris target of a 1.5°C average temperature rise from pre-industrial levels perilously close to proving unattainable as potentially irreversible changes unfold for the global climate. In 2019, atmospheric concentrations of carbon dioxide were found to be higher than in at least 2mn years, while surface temperatures since 1970 have risen faster than during any other 50-year period in at least two millennia. Many of these trends are felt with particular force in the GCC: "The annual average temperature has seen an increase of 1.3°C ... since the turn of the millennium. ... [P]recipitation averaged 6.7mm annually compared to 16 mm for MENAP and 94 mm for the world over the period of 1991–2020."[32] It is now becoming increasingly likely that the Paris target will be missed in the absence of significant technological and policy innovations, whether increased carbon withdrawals or solar geoengineering. In both cases, important questions pertain to the potential cost. This will put a growing premium of adaptation and risk mitigation.

The Middle East exhibits multiple vulnerabilities in the face of the prospect of a warmer planet. The region is home to some 5 percent of the world's population but only approximately 1 percent of its renewable freshwater resources. Freshwater availability has fallen by some 75 percent since the 1950s and is expected to decline by a further 40 percent or more by 2030. Virtually the entire region is classified as "water stressed," which entails per capita freshwater availability of less than 1000 cu m per annum. The GCC countries rank in the global top-10 in their likelihood of suffering from water stress by 2040. This has obvious implications for food security as well, since agriculture has been the main consumer of freshwater resources in most of the region (some 85 percent in Oman, Saudi Arabia, and the UAE)[33] despite a heavy import dependency, typically on the order of 90 percent. These realities also mean that disruptions in international food trade, which risk becoming more frequent due to climate change, could entail daunting challenges for the GCC.

The Arabian Peninsula is characterized by an exceptionally harsh climate and significant environmental vulnerabilities. Its geography outside the peripheral mountains is mainly composed of low-altitude plains. Much of the population is concentrated in low-lying coastal areas, in many cases boosted by land reclamation. These regions are highly likely to be affected by rising sea levels but also the expected rise in the frequency of extreme weather phenomena, such as coastal flood risks and extreme rainfall. The 2009 floods in Jeddah are estimated to have resulted in losses of $1.36bn.[34] Some climate models now project a 0.5 meter rise in sea levels by the end of the century. The Gulf is also exceptionally sensitive to rising temperatures, not least because these would result in extreme heat waves beyond the ability of human beings to endure, as well as recurrent droughts. On current projections, average temperatures in the Gulf could rise by 1.8°C by 2040 and by as much as 3.6°C by 2070. Combined with reduced precipitation, these developments would risk exacerbating desertification. The World Bank estimates that "water scarcity related to climate change might lead to 6 percent to 14 percent reductions in annual GDP growth in the region."[35] The long-standing challenge of dwindling groundwater reserves is likely to become even more acute. Nonetheless, political turmoil in parts of the Middle East is "a major impediment to collective action, and this makes the situation even more dangerous since climate change will affect all."[36] While the threats posed by these risks to the GCC may be mitigated by factors such as the widespread use of water desalination, the broader regional context is far from irrelevant. The growing challenges can produce contagion effects or trigger waves of migration.

While climate change entails potentially significant risks in its own right, the evolving policy responses to it are likely to grow in importance as well. The GCC region has a significant carbon footprint directly and indirectly because of its heavy reliance on hydrocarbons as a source of wealth and driver of economic activity. Efforts to combat global warming will inevitably have a global dimension. Polluters, or enablers of pollution, will face mounting risks because of a hostile public opinion, changing investor behavior, and fiscal measures designed to penalize or disincentivize pollution. Such developments can serve as a stimulus for increased investment in activities and technologies that seek to counter pollution and use energy more efficiently, a process that is already underway. But they can also, depending on their speed and nature, turn into a major, potentially even existential, challenge for some GCC businesses.

The new climate challenges are attracting increasing attention in the Gulf, with the regional governments unveiling plans and strategies to counter climate change or to mitigate its impact. Regional governments have published National Adaptation Plans in connection with the 2015 Paris Agreement. Oman has approved a National Strategy for Adaptation and Mitigation 2020–2040, while Saudi Arabia has adopted a Circular Carbon Economy National Progra. The UAE is implementing a National Climate Change Plan 2017–2050.[37] The UAE, Saudi Arabia, and Bahrain have all committed to net zero targets by 2050–2060. Encouragingly, these steps are also beginning to gain recognition as a substantial economic opportunity, with the World Bank recently suggesting that they could offer an effective way of counteracting the region's long-standing productivity crisis, among other things.[38]

Whither oil … and gas?

Even as the dependence of the individual GCC economies on hydrocarbons varies markedly, oil and gas invariably loom large among their known natural resource endowments. Three issues are particularly important for charting the future trajectory of the region. Firstly, how substantial are the Gulf hydrocarbons deposits? Secondly, to what extent will the regional economies continue to be able to extract economic value from these endowments? Thirdly, how much will the successful monetization of the hydrocarbons endowments matter for the future prosperity of the Gulf? While conclusive answers elude us today, certain aspects already appear relatively clear.

The GCC is home to exceptional hydrocarbons endowments whose full scale is not known to this day because of incomplete geological mapping. Heavily subsidized domestic gas prices for years severely disincentivized systematic exploration even as rapid demand growth left most of the region with a growing demand–supply imbalance.[39] More structured exploration efforts and the progressive removal of subsidies have enabled significant discoveries in recent years. Bahrain, long deemed to be in the twilight of its oil era, announced what promises to be its largest ever oil find in 2018. Moreover, innovation in oil extraction has dramatically pushed up recovery rates from existing fields, while a growing range of unconventional oil deposits have become economically viable. Enhanced recovery techniques and other innovations have, for instance, allowed Oman to markedly boost its oil and gas production in recent years. It can thus be expected that a growing proportion of the GCC hydrocarbons assets will become technically recoverable in the future.

The Gulf countries enjoy many advantages as hydrocarbons producers. In 2021, the GCC countries accounted for nearly 30 percent of the global proven oil reserves, and their share of the global total for natural gas exceeded 20 percent. Both indicators are of global significance and suggest that the GCC will play a critical role in the hydrocarbons markets for as long as oil and gas remain part of the global energy mix or can be used for other value generating activities.

Table 9.1 GCC proven hydrocarbons reserves, 2021

Country	*Proven oil reserves, billions of barrels, 2021*	*Proven gas reserves, trillion cubic meters, 2021*
Bahrain	0.2	2.9
Kuwait	102	63
Oman	5.4	23
Qatar	25	843
Saudi Arabia	259	333
United Arab Emirates	98	215
World	1,662	7,257*

*2021 global total unavailable. The reported 2020 global total 7,257 tcf.

Source: US Energy Information Administration, https://www.eia.gov/international/data/world.

The GCC share of global reserves far exceeds its current proportion of hydrocarbons extraction. This means that the region is well positioned to increase its weight in the oil and gas markets going forward. The remaining life span of the proven reserves at current rates of production is typically measured in decades.[40] Saudi Arabia is expected to be able to sustain its current rate of oil extraction for up to 70 years. While there is a credible prospect of boosting reserves further, a rapid energy transition could potentially threaten the region with substantial stranded assets. In the event that the Paris goals do indeed become the global policy anchor, an estimated third of oil, half of gas, and 80 percent of coal reserves could be left in the ground forever.[41] The issue of future-proofing the hydrocarbons assets is thus of the utmost strategic importance.

Gas – often billed as an ideal transition fuel – is likely to be of particular importance as the world works to wean itself off more polluting fossil fuels. Substantial investments into boosting gas production capacity are underway, and indeed often being ramped up, across the Gulf region.[42] Qatar in 2020 extracted 5 percent of the global total and supplied a fifth of all LNG.[43] It is currently working to dramatically expand its capacity further. In 2022, QatarEnergy announced agreements with five international oil majors to develop its $29bn North Field East project, which is designed to boost total extraction capacity from 77mn to 110mn tn by 2026. Partnership selection is also underway for the North Field South LNG expansion project, which should take aggregate capacity to 126mn tn/y by the end of the decade. Some transformative discoveries have materialized also elsewhere in the region, an example being the Khazzan–Makarem tight gas field developed by BP in Oman. Discovered in 2000, it began production in 2017.[44] Saudi Arabia unveiled an initiative to develop new sources as early as 1998 and has made important discoveries, starting with the Karan non-associated gas offshore field in 2006. The giant Jafurah unconventional gas field announced in 2021 is estimated to have 200trn cu ft of gas and could make Saudi Arabia the world's third largest natural gas producer by 2030.[45]

Whatever the future of hydrocarbons, the Gulf countries are well positioned to compete even during what is now widely expected to be the (probably very drawn-out) twilight era for oil and gas. The Gulf oil deposits offer some of the lowest costs of extraction globally. Even after decades of progressive depletion, the region boasts a number of large active fields with relatively simple geological structures and high productivity. The cost of oil extracted by the five largest Middle East exporters – Saudi Arabia, Iraq, Iran, Kuwait, and the UAE – was estimated at less than $10 per barrel in 2017. By contrast, most shale fields in the US require at least $35 per barrel to break even, while even conventional fields face costs that are at least double the Gulf norm. Gulf oil producers also boast other competitive advantages. Saudi Arabia only emits some 3.5 g of CO_2 equivalent per megajoule (MJ) of oil extracted. This compares to more than 20 g CO_2/MJ in Algeria and Venezuela at the other end of the spectrum. Other parts of the oil value chain are highly cost-competitive, while the flaring of associated gas has been successfully curbed.[46]

The circular carbon economy model represents another important initiative. Announced by Saudi Arabia in late 2019, the initiative is designed to incorporate a number of climate mitigation options at all stages of the carbon cycle. This approach is underpinned by the assumption that the world economy will remain dependent on hydrocarbons for a long time even as the energy transition continues to make headway: "Rather than focusing solely on reducing or avoiding the amount of carbon that enters the system, the circular carbon economy recognizes the need for a range of carbon mitigation options."[47] Structured around the "four R's" of "Reduce, Reuse, Recycle, and Remove," the policy prioritizes initiatives such as energy efficiency, a shift toward less polluting energy sources, the use of carbon as an input in industrial processes, and chemical/geological storage of carbon, among other things.

These steps should help shield the Gulf producers from the vagaries of the global oil markets even after aggregate oil consumption begins to shrink. The modes of development of the regional hydrocarbons assets are also evolving, with significant steps taken in recent years to facilitate access by foreign companies and investors. Apart from reducing the investment burden on the Gulf energy companies, many foreign players can expect to find a more attractive operating environment in the Arabian Peninsula than in countries with more complex geographic or political realities. This is likely to be the case even amid a growing dependency on costlier enhanced recovery techniques and more challenging geological formations. The fact that North America has been able to revive its oil sector through technological innovation suggests that the Gulf countries can adopt similar innovations with lower initial costs. Moreover, the location of any new finds in the Gulf is typically likely to be in the geographic vicinity of older fields, which should allow producers to capitalize on existing infrastructure.

The ongoing progress with natural gas exploration and development also matters in the domestic context in view of its critical role in power generation and manufacturing. Improving access to gas is supporting the growing interest in innovative industrial ventures. It also promises important sustainability benefits in countries such as Kuwait and Saudi Arabia, which will be able to reduce their heavy reliance on fuel oil in power generation, thereby reducing their carbon footprint.[48] Developing the regional gas deposits also makes sense from the export perspective inasmuch as any serious progress toward emission reductions hinges on more and more countries substituting gas for more heavily polluting energy sources such as coal. The widespread boycotts of Russian energy in 2022 are further contributing to this process.

The progressive elimination of hydrocarbons subsidies in the Gulf is driving efficiency gains in domestic energy use, reducing waste, and enhancing the returns on investment. In time, this should reduce the need to import energy, such as LNG. Moreover, by reducing the cost distortions vis-à-vis other types of energy, the more market-based prices of hydrocarbons have triggered a rapidly growing interest in renewables, which is further reducing the future reliance of power generation on hydrocarbons.

Although the supply outlook for the Gulf hydrocarbons cluster seems relatively benign, developments on the demand side are potentially more challenging. Despite continued challenges in efforts to meet the Paris emissions target, the idea of countering climate change is continuing to shape attitudes around energy consumption and framing policy discussions. The August 2021 UNIPCC climate change report reflected an acute sence of urgency about countering a process that was depicted as spinning out of control, with potentially irreversible consequences.[49] Growing popular, political, and even corporate backing now seems to be coalescing to deliver a growing sense of purpose behind efforts to counter global warming. For instance, the EU is adopting ambitious measures in a bid to achieve carbon neutrality by 2035, with many member states committed to phasing out fossil fuel–powered cars within a decade or two. Environmental considerations are pushing more and more institutional investors away from hydrocarbons assets, which risks making oil field development projects more expensive to fund in the future. A growing number of international oil majors are rebranding themselves as generic energy companies and working to create more diverse portfolios of energy assets.

The growth of alternative energy sources has eroded the traditional appeal of hydrocarbons thanks to their improving cost-effectiveness.[50] While wind met only some 2.5 percent and solar barely 1 percent of the global power demand in 2016, some projections now suggest that the share of renewables could rise to 14 percent by 2040. Overall, the share of renewables in global energy has risen by more than 70 percent since 2000, "by just over 23 million barrels of oil equivalent per day (Mboe/d) to roughly 56 Mboe/d in 2021."[51] Since 2010, the annual demand growth rates for renewables have consistently exceeded those for oil and gas, at 3.3 percent vs. 1.4 and 2 percent, respectively. Solar and wind have achieved 7 percent annual growth.[52]

Even as faster change now almost certainly beckons, it is important to remember that energy transitions are never instantaneous: "Since the rise of oil and gas, no individual energy source has been able to win a dominant market share – and no major energy source has been fully eliminated."[53] In 2015, oil accounted for 33 percent of primary energy consumption globally, while the share of natural gas was 24 percent. Both are likely to retain an important place in the global energy mix for an extended period due to incumbent advantages and the configuration of existing infrastructure.[54] This would translate into a continued structural need for more oil to be extracted and more capital to be invested in development in order to avoid demand–supply imbalances.

Such expectations shaped most projections about the global energy markets until recently. For instance, in 2018, the IEA forecast 25 percent growth in global energy demand by 2040. While the share of renewables in the global energy mix was projected (on baseline assumptions) to grow from 25 percent to 40 percent, hydrocarbons were still thought to account for a large share of the pie and continue to register absolute increases in demand. Gas was expected to establish itself as the second most important energy source globally after coal. Oil demand was set for continuous growth. Only strict compliance with current climate change targets could lead to oil demand peaking around 2030 but would still keep it an important part of the global energy mix for decades to come.

The debate is evolving, however, and even recent assumptions are being questioned with growing frequency, even if the possibility of a drawn-out standoff between Russia and the West has created new uncertainties. In May 2021 the IEA announced that meeting the Paris goal of zero net carbon emissions by 2050 would require investments in low-carbon technologies to rise from around $2bn a year at present to $5bn, which was estimated to add some 0.4 percent annually to global GDP growth. Under this scenario, global coal consumption would fall by 90 percent and oil consumption by 75 percent by 2050. Natural gas consumption would halve. Two-thirds of all energy in 2050 would have to come from renewable sources such as wind, solar, bioenergy, geothermal, and hydro energy.[55] Reaching that outcome would require these challenger energy sources to meet a lion's share of incremental energy demand. However, the political will to push for this speed and magnitude of change on a global scale is in some doubt, not least amid the post-COVID cost of living crisis. Important questions also pertain to feasibility, as highlighted by recent gas market pressures and potential challenges in meeting the growing demand for rare earth metals, especially should it result in a growing dependency on China. Nuclear power appears to have traction as a more established energy source that would contribute to the emissions reduction goals.

While these profound structural shifts entail downside risks for the global oil industry, the implications for the GCC are far from unambiguous. In a shrinking oil market, the competitiveness of individual producers will grow in importance. Moreover, the evolving investment realities may well favor the Gulf producers that have access to capital locally and from their key consumers in Asia. This could well enable the Gulf to increase its share even in a shrinking hydrocarbons market. It would also give oil an important role in the regional economies for many decades to come.[56] However, a significantly weaker demand outlook for oil may also prompt producers to boost their output for fear of their reserves becoming worthless, a phenomenon known as the "green paradox." Lower prices could then become a tool for securing oil's share in the global energy mix but also for defending market share.[57] But even if the Gulf producers can remain competitive in a lower-price environment, declining prices would necessitate a significant fiscal overhaul beyond what has already been achieved. At present, the regional economies across the board need oil prices of at least $50 per barrel to balance their budgets.

Potential opportunities also exist in terms of repositioning oil for a different future. Exporting crude to fuel combustion engines has never been the only way of generating economic value from it, as suggested by Luciani: "the sensible approach to diversification is not *away* from oil but *leveraging the availability* of oil and gas. The opportunity for GCC countries to find a rewarding role in the context of globalization is using what they have – oil and gas – to develop industrial and, progressively, technological capabilities in areas where they enjoy an initial comparative advantage."[58] Saudi Arabia has been investing in new ways of extracting value out of its crude reserves locally for decades. Industrial products now amount to about 43 percent of the oil sales.[59] In 2022, Saudi Arabia presented plans to allocate more than a third of its current oil output – some 4mn b/d – to chemical production by 2030 in a bid to squeeze more value from its barrels as the world shifts toward a low-carbon economy. Aramco estimates that, even under a net zero scenario, petrochemicals could still account for more than half of total global oil demand by 2050. Chemical industry innovation is likely to deliver increasingly sustainable materials while reducing costs. Eventually, Saudi Arabia expects to sell all of its crude output as oil products or petrochemicals.

While the development of the Gulf petrochemical industry outside of Qatar has been held back by gas constraints, several initiatives are underway to develop petrochemicals production from oil as an input. Oil can, in principle, become an important driver of diversification if hydrocarbons-related value chains are stretched out to create products whose prices are no longer significantly linked to international crude prices.[60] Becoming more reliant on such value addition can serve not only as a way to accommodate climate change concerns but also as a way to future-proof oil: "Conversion of unburned crude oil and natural gas into chemical products may be Saudi Aramco's most promising climate hedge. ... As in the manufacture of lubricants, the carbon from oil and gas is sequstered in the finished product – rather than released upon combustion."[61] It is also an ambition that tallies with the region's broader strategic thrust as future competitiveness and growth in a dynamic sector is likely to require substantial investments and human capital development and research. Moreover, producing innovative petrochemical products in a region with the space and infrastructure for carbon capture and storage promises to be a key competitive advantage.[62]

Such future hedges are likely to grow in importance, but their longer-term sustainability must be based on realistic energy prices and utilization. Moreover, the conversation around manufacturing and hydrocarbons-based products will continue to evolve, potentially in unpredictable ways, as has been seen, for instance, with the global debate about plastics production and use.[63] Export ambitions have to be reconciled with international trade regulations. Industrial investments can trigger anti-dumping action, as they have in the past, if Gulf producers are seen to enjoy unfair competitive advantages. Such considerations will probably increase in importance as pressure grows on polluters globally to compensate for their carbon footprint through sustainable investments. But change is unlikely to be linear or uniform. The dynamics observed in the advanced economies of the West may not be matched by the emerging markets.

The economic dependence of the Gulf region on oil and gas remains very heavy even after decades of strategically anchored diversification. A significant paradigm shift looks unlikely in the foreseeable future, as the Gulf economies are continuing to make substantial investments in hydrocarbons exploration and development. Even as the oil–government nexus no longer towers over the regional economy with the unchallenged supremacy it once enjoyed, its influence on other sectors remains profound.

More encouraging, economic diversification appears to have reached a critical mass in many "new" areas. Parts of the regional economy are now primarily driven by demographic, connectivity, and regulatory factors that are no longer directly linked to the oil sector dynamics. The region's role as a transportation hub looks virtually certain to grow further thanks to new infrastructure investments and capacity addition. Some Gulf economies have made impressive progress in positioning themselves as internationally attractive platforms for investments in various new activities. The prospect of a significantly more diversified portfolio of growth drivers in the years ahead is looking more real than ever. As an important reflection of the new realities, a significant proportion of the regional hydrocarbons sector investments are no longer happening within the GCC but represent increasingly ambitious attempts on the part of the regional oil and petrochemicals companies to build a global footprint, including more secure markets for their products.

The invisible enemies

Even after recurrent bouts of exceptional uncertainty in the early 21st century, the world proved ill-prepared for the the sudden, massive shock that the onset of the COVID-19 pandemic delivered in late 2019–early 2020. Within weeks the accelerating spread of the disease, and especially the myriad of restrictions adopted to slow down its transmission, pushed the global economy into an unprecedented maelstrom of financial market turbulence and economic contraction. The pandemic revealed the lack of preparedness of governments and corporations alike for a crisis for which few had any relevant experience. Assumptions about the likely course of the public health calamity diverged widely, which was reflected in a lack of coordination in policy responses by individual governments. Moreover, as the pandemic spread, policies also evolved. Some countries sought to ensure a high degree of economic continuity while relying on recommendations instead of compulsion while channeling resources into areas of greatest vulnerability. However, the conventional wisdom came to prioritize strict lockdowns as authorities set out to stall the virus by limiting gatherings and mobility. But this approach exacted an enormous economic toll. Moreover, each move to relax the lockdowns created false expectations of normality that led to renewed spikes, amplified by the appearance of new, more easily transmissible variants of the virus. More than two years down the line, economic activity in China was still significantly hampered by the government's strict zero-COVID policy until a policy refocusing in late 2022, at least initially with the consequence of increased transmission – an uncomfortable reminder that the COVID story is not yet over.

While devastating, the COVID-19 shock was not altogether unprecedented. A century earlier, the infamous Spanish flu infected approximately a third of the world's population, with the consequence of up to 100mn fatalities over a two-year period (1918–1920). In the postwar decades, the Asian flu of 1957–1958 and the Hong Kong flu of 1968–1969 jointly claimed at least 2mn lives, potentially multiples of this. There have been more than 250 biological disasters since 1960, which have collectively exacted a death toll of over 10mn. While such episodes have grown in frequency, the vast majority of them have been localized or not very severe.[64]

The only public health crisis to have been declared a global pandemic in recent decades was HIV/AIDS, first identified in 1981, which has up to now caused an estimated 32mn deaths.

The young 21st century has seen several harbingers of COVID-19. The years 2002–2004 witnessed a global SARS (severe acute respiratory syndrome) outbreak, similarly caused by a coronavirus whose origins were eventually traced back to horseshoe bats in Yunnan province of China. By June 2003, 8,422 cases had been reported in 26 countries, with a fatality rate of 11 percent. The years 2009–2010 saw an H1N1 influenza epidemic, commonly known as swine flu, triggered by the same pathogen as the Spanish flu. It may have infected as much as a fifth of the world's population, with an estimated 150,000–575,000 deaths. March 2013 witnessed the H7N9 avian influenza, widely branded as bird flu. The cumulative total of cases stood at 1,622 as of October 2017, with 619 deaths. But limited human-to-human transmission contained the epidemic to China and Southeast Asia. A largely localized coronavirus outbreak took place in the Arabian Peninsula in 2012, followed by a further flare-up in Saudi Arabia in 2018. The Middle East respiratory syndrome (MERS), sometimes colloquially referred to as "camel flu" because of the typical transmission channel, bore many similarities to SARS, but person-to-person transmission was rare outside of hospitals. Some 2,500 cases have been reported to date in 26 countries, with an estimated fatality rate of 35 percent. These pandemics played an important role in boosting the institutional, regulatory, and cultural readiness of certain countries – including the Gulf States – to deal with public health emergencies. But it is widely agreed that such preparedness will be needed again, even if the medical research community confounded expectations with the speedy development of the COVID-19 vaccines and the drug design innovations it gave rise to. Epidemics are often held up as one of the many consequences of climate change.[65]

Learning to live with risk

As the Gulf economies reposition for the post-COVID-19 era, the imperatives to build resilience and boost growth dovetail. Diversified economies with strong businesses and public institutions will be better positioned to weather unanticipated shocks while delivering higher living standards. During the pandemic, the Gulf governments showed admirable capacity to mobilize the necessary resources to mitigate risks.[66] Testing and tracing were scaled up swiftly, and the region led the way globally in vaccinating the population. These decisions allowed a high degree of normalization in economic activity, even if periodic restrictions could not be avoided altogether. The regional health care system almost invariably faced up to the COVID-19 caseload without major strain.[67] Economic activity benefited from a strong, well-regulated banking system and a pragmatic policy of proactively managing risks while targeting direct support to counter the most significant disruptions. The Gulf region's strengths amid the pandemic reflected a strong institutional capacity in several areas. There is an obvious opportunity to further boost and expand these good qualities to build defenses for future challenges: "Well-designed and enforced policies and regulations concerning the prudent management of financial institutions, construction, and environmental protection can help reduce the likelihood and impact of adverse shocks."[68]

Of course, success in short-term crisis management does not automatically translate into longer-term strength. The focus of policymakers must now shift to sustainability. The region must continue to reduce its fiscal reliance on oil revenues while pursuing opportunities to create employment that can sustainably engage the growing young population.[69] While this transformation cannot be instantaneous, change of this magnitude is not unprecedented. Scandinavia saw a thriving entrepreneurial culture spring up from the early 1990s crisis created by a sclerotic welfare state and swift financial liberalization. Eastern Europe and the former Soviet Union have seen several successful market economies sprout from the ruins of communist central planning. Many emerging economies around the world have been able to rise from endemic poverty to rapid growth, not least the so-called Asian Tigers.

The metrics of success will also change. The way forward is less about "quick wins" and more about working more effectively and consistently at all levels. The value of data and analysis will grow dramatically as the regional economies seek to recalibrate their policymaking toward greater effectiveness. Decisions will have to be subjected to impact analysis and – perhaps most important – to ongoing evaluation. Even as the to-do list for Gulf governments and corporations commands growing support, the way forward is not always obvious in a world of endemic uncertainty. The ability to tweak and adapt without losing sight of the overriding objectives is essential. Agility as a guarantor of competitiveness will matter across the board.

Change comes with particular challenges in countries with a history of consensual decision making and a culture that values stability and continuity. But it should not be forgotten that the Gulf has adapted to major challenges before, and multiple indications suggest its ability to do is growing stronger. The larger companies are thinking strategically, with more and more instances of consolidation and overseas expansion. Lower down the ladder, start-up entrepreneurship is establishing itself with remarkable speed, shifting the ambitions of entrepreneurs beyond the traditional focus on retail, hospitality, and contracting. The economic culture – and behavior – of companies and individuals alike is beginning to change. The long tradition of continuity, whether in business models or policymaking, is being shaken up as people increasingly embrace a more dynamic, forward-looking mindset. COVID-19 has – out of necessity – offered concrete examples of what that change could look like while also delivering substantial payoffs to adaptability.[70]

With change the new norm, sustained effort and focus are required to successfully put the Gulf economies on a faster growth trajectory. As significant as the dramatic shift in fiscal policy since 2014 is, it is far from sufficient to fundamentally reduce the regional economies' vulnerability to oil price fluctuations. Weeks before COVID-19 was recognized as a global pandemic, the IMF raised eyebrows in the Gulf by claiming that a failure to push fiscal consolidation further could deplete the region's financial wealth within 15 years.[71] By delivering a major exogenous shock and necessitating

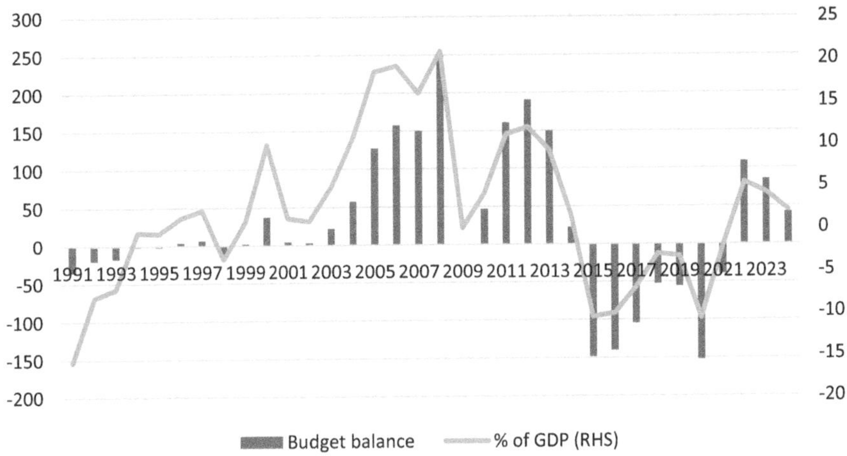

Figure 9.2 GCC aggregate general government fiscal balance, $ bn.
Source: World Bank.

large-scale emergency and stimulus spending, COVID-19 further underscored the urgency of continued reform, with the IMF stating: "Long-term fiscal sustainability in the GCC requires the average non-oil primary fiscal deficit to decline from the present level of 44 percent of non-oil GDP to mid-single digits by 2060."[72]

While resilience during the pandemic along with the subsequent strong recovery has significantly improved the situation, further structural fiscal overhaul is needed to build longer-term resilience. This will curb the trend economic growth contribution of the oil–government nexus going forward. As a result, the private sector will have to do much more to pick up the slack, not least by activating new mechanisms for allocating capital. There is much evidence to suggest that this pending shift from public spending in fact represents a logical reallocation of resources. The economic impact of government expenditure has declined in recent years, with its historical role as a driver of non-oil growth seemingly breaking down more than a decade ago, according to IMF estimates.[73] While a one percentage point increase in government spending increased non-oil GDP growth by 1.4 percentage points in 1990–2007, this figure more than halved to 0.6 during 2008–2016. This trend seems to be linked above all to a growing reliance on imports, which do little to stimulate the local economy; regional goods imports rose from 55 percent of non-oil GDP in 1990–2016 to nearly 80 percent in 2008–2016. Remittances and foreign travel have also grown. The lower efficiency of public investment along with supply-side bottlenecks and other implementation constraints may also help explain the weaker relationship between spending growth and non-oil GDP growth.[74] The ongoing initiatives around local capacity and better alignment between infrastructure investment and productive capacity should bring some relief. But they will not obviate the need for a greater productivity focus.

The danger of muddling through

The case for an economic overhaul in the Gulf is widely understood. The economic challenges of recent years have profoundly reshaped policymaking. The idea of a holistic fiscal overhaul now commands fairly widespread acquiescence among the regional population. Despite intra-regional variance in policy, the direction of travel is broadly similar everywhere. The new fiscal realities represent a formal departure from the distributive rentier state. This comes with multiple benefits. The increasingly market-based pricing of inputs is incentivizing more efficient resource allocation. Companies seeking to protect their margins are being pushed to focus on productivity. Government policy is tackling the trend growth slowdown through supply-side reforms designed to facilitate company formation as well as to attract foreign capital and talent. Labor market reforms are incentivizing technology adoption and creating pressures to scale up. Governments are setting up new mechanisms for investment, whether through sovereign wealth funds or other entities, helping circumvent structural limitations of the financial sector. These new realities are extremely important for conditioning corporate behavior. Productivity cannot be driven by political ambition alone. Rather, it is underpinned by rational economic responses to circumstances and incentives that penalize inefficiency. More and more companies are focusing on more rational resource use, looking for ways to tap new markets while better managing their cost base. Old business models are being questioned like never before.[75]

COVID-19 further accelerated the process of change by challenging conventional default assumptions, incentivizing the provision of more cost-effective solutions, and increasing risk awareness. By forcing companies to adopt with their customers and suppliers, the pandemic pushed even low-productivity businesses to embrace technology. This period of economic disruption was the first time in the modern history of the Gulf region that private businesses invested incrementally more in technology than in the traditional default option of cheap expatriate labor. The strategic significance of this shift, if it can be sustained, is profound and very much in line with the regional development visions.[76]

While the unusually resolute policy response to the COVID-19 crisis boosted market confidence and avoided some economic scarring, it will be important to strike a realistic balance between short-term relief and policy postures that can be sustained in the longer term.[77] Despite the relief provided by the oil price rally in 2021–2022, a strong commitment to fiscal stability around a clearly articulated policy framework remains essential. Similarly, it is important to build adequate buffers for renewed oil price downturns.

While there are profound structural shifts in GCC corporate and broader economic culture, change is never easy. Achieving the desired economic paradigm shift in the Gulf transition is as much an art as it is a science. Delivering on the ambitions for a more productivity-led growth paradigm necessitates further changes in business models, governance, and cultural attitudes. Yet the ability of individuals and companies to adapt is variable, and delays tend to entail costs. There is an obvious risk of settling for solutions that are just barely sufficient or letting perceived short-term needs compromise the longer-term strategic goals. Moreover, the inevitability of a drawn-out transition raises risks of reform fatigue.

The consequence of muddling through would almost certainly be a further gradual deceleration in the trend rate of economic growth in the region. It would hold back living standards while also limiting the ability of the GCC states to properly future-proof their economies. Potential challenges range from adequate job creation to securing future pensions. But they may also come to involve the ability to make more substantial investments to protect people's well-being in more fundamental ways. The Gulf will potentially require large-scale capitalization mobilization to secure adequate fresh water, to ensure food security, and to protect against changing climate.

Challenging though it is, the change agenda is far from impossible. Even amid inevitable vulnerability to exogenous shocks, the Gulf countries have substantial resources to draw on to mitigate risks and build resilience. The key balancing act in the years ahead will involve managing flexibility in macro-economic policymaking with the structural re-engineering of the regional economies. Sustainable change is unlikely to prove fast or altogether linear. The Gulf governments have consistently recognized the need for an appropriate degree of give and take. But it is critical to ensure that any temporary relaxation in the transformation agenda does not erode the sense of purpose behind the strategic ambitions.

Many skeptics will point out that the key policy aspirations – above all the broad concept of diversification – have been part of the regional policy toolkit since the 1960s. Even as economic diversification has continued to make headway, it remains lopsided. Most notable, effective "diversification into human capital is missing."[78] From the perspective of the Gulf nationals, for decades generous public sector employment concealed the otherwise pernicious effects of a private sector productivity crisis on living standards. Key planks of the oil–government nexus continue to exert a profound influence on the behavior of companies and individuals alike. While Saudi Vision 2030 is relatively fresh, several other regional visions were developed a decade or longer ago. Despite forward strides, many of the structural vulnerabilities have persisted. Why should this time be any different? This may well be where we find the silver lining of the painful pandemic and the broader challenges presented by an uncertain world. COVID served as an important stress test for the regional economy. Necessity is once again showing itself to be the mother of all invention. While some, especially smaller, businesses have struggled to rise to the occasion, many others have sought new solutions and in turn inspired others to do the same. Customers have changed their habits. Attitudes appear to be evolving in ways that may well prove lasting. Digital communication, home delivery, and other aspects of the "new normal" are increasingly seen as more convenient and cost-effective than the pre-pandemic norm. Perhaps most important, this ordeal – and others – has inculcated the importance of considering and preparing for risks. Thinking ahead with a strategic perspective marks a major shift of the opportunistic rentierism of yesteryear.

Notes

1 IEA, *Net Zero by 2050*, p. 21.
2 IEA, *Net Zero by 2050*, p. 18.
3 Sherman, *A Short History of Financial Deregulation*.
4 IMF, *Global Financial Stability Report*, pp. 56, 73.
5 Barajas *et al.*, "Loose Financial Conditions," pp. 3, 5.
6 Dieppe, *Global Productivity*, pp. i.6–i.7.
7 Burke and Bazoobandi, "The Gulf Takes Charge," p. 33.
8 Emirates NBD, "UAE–China: A Global Trade Axis," *Trade*, 17 October 2021.
9 World Bank, "COVID-19 Pandemic," pp. 48–53.
10 Mogielnicki, "How China Is Quietly Expanding."
11 al-Sharekh and Freer, *Tribalism and Political Power*.
12 UNDP/AFESD, *Arab Human Development Report*, p. 18.
13 Lackner, *Yemen in Crisis*, p. 218.
14 UNDP, *Arab Human Development Report 2016*, p. 22.
15 UNDP, *Arab Human Development Report 2016*, pp. 24–26.
16 Mogielnicki, *A Political Economy of Free Zones*, p. 107.
17 Burke and Bazoobandi, "The Gulf Takes Charge," pp. 30–31.
18 Burke and Bazoobandi, "The Gulf Takes Charge," p. 25.
19 Mogielnicki, "New Opportunities and High Stakes," p. 5.
20 Mogielnicki, "New Opportunities and High Stakes," p. 7.
21 Emirates NBD, "UAE–China: A Global Trade Axis," *Trade*, 17 October 2021; Fulton, *Strangers to Strategic Partners*, p. 3; Holden and Zaamout, *A New Great Power Engages*, p. 4.
22 Lons *et al.*, "China's Great Game," pp. 11–12.
23 Fulton, "Domestic Politics as Fuel," pp. 5–6, 9; Fulton, *Strangers to Strategic Partners*, pp. 12–13.
24 Lons *et al.*, "China's Great Game," pp. 26–27; Fulton, "Domestic Politics as Fuel," p. 9; Fulton, *Strangers to Strategic Partners*, p. 2.
25 Al-Tamimi, "Saudi Arabia's Once Marginal Relationship with China," p. 76.
26 Fulton, "Domestic Politics as Fuel," p. 7; Mogielnicki, "New Opportunities and High Stakes," p. 5; Mogielnicki, "How China Is Quietly Expanding."
27 Talbot, "Turkey–GCC Relations;" Al-Atiqi *et al., Turkey–GCC Relations*.
28 Hanieh, *Money, Markets, and Monarchies*, pp. 130–143.
29 Todman, "The Gulf Scramble for Africa."
30 Todman, "The Gulf Scramble for Africa."
31 https://press.un.org/en/2021/sgsm20847.doc.htm.
32 IMF, *Economic Prospects and Policy Challenges – 2021*, p. 17.
33 IMF, *Economic Prospects and Policy Challenges – 2021*, p. 17.
34 World Bank, *Water for Prosperity and Development*, p. 16.
35 World Bank, *Water for Prosperity and Development*, p. 16.
36 Osama Al-Sharif, "Climate Change Is the Region's Ultimate Enemy," *Arab News*, 10 August 2021, https://www.arabnews.com/node/1908991.
37 IMF, *Economic Prospects and Policy Challenges – 2021*, p. 17.
38 World Bank, "Green Growth Opportunities."
39 Fattouh and Stern, "Conclusion," pp. 531–532.
40 El-Katiri, "Energy Sustainability in the Gulf States," pp. 25–27.
41 Arezki, "Oil-Producing Countries," p. 26; IEA, *Net Zero by 2050*, p. 18.
42 Rania El Gamal, "Analysis: UAE's Oil Expansion Gives It New Weight within OPEC," Reuters, 3 December 2020, https://www.reuters.com/article/us-oil-opec-emirates-adnoc-analysis-idUSKBN28D1PM.
43 Mosis, *Navigating the Energy Transition*, p. 9.
44 Ledesma, "Natural Gas in Oman," p. 396; bp.com.
45 Fattouh and Stern, "Conclusion," p. 531; Fattouh, "The Saudi Gas Sector," pp. 219–221; https://oxfordbusinessgroup.com/analysis/tap-new-gas-development-poised-increase-capacity-and-help-meet-growing-demand-around-world.

46 Fattouh and Sen, "Economic Diversification," p. 23; Krane, "Climate Action versus Inaction," p. 133.
47 Williams, "Achieving Climate Goals," pp. 4–5.
48 Fattouh, "The Saudi Gas Sector," p. 211; Alami, "Natural Gas in Bahrain and Kuwait," p. 508.
49 https://www.ipcc.ch/report/sixth-assessment-report-cycle.
50 World Bank, "Green Growth Opportunities," p. 26.
51 Seznec and Mosis, *The Energy Transition in the Gulf*, p. 8.
52 Seznec and Mosis, *The Energy Transition in the Gulf*, p. 8.
53 Fattouh *et al.*, "The Rise of Renewables," p. 52; Howell, *Empires in Collision*, p. 285.
54 Fattouh and Sen, "Economic Diversification," p. 23.
55 Fattouh *et al.*, "The Rise of Renewables," p. 46.
56 Fattouh and Sen, "Economic Diversification," p. 23; Krane, "Climate Strategy," p. 47.
57 Krane, "Climate Action versus Inaction," p. 134; Krane, "Beyond 12.5," pp. 542, 545; Fattouh *et al.*, "The Rise of Renewables," p. 55; Kimmeridge, "Charting a Path to Net Zero Emissions."
58 Luciani, "GCC Refining and Petrochemical Sectors," p. 184.
59 Seznec, *Saudi Energy Changes*, p. 14.
60 Fattouh and Sen, "Economic Diversification," p. 23.
61 Krane, "Climate Strategy," p. 47.
62 Luciani, "GCC Refining and Petrochemical Sectors," pp. 210–212.
63 Carbon Tracker Initiative, *The Future's Not in Plastics*; Kimmeridge, "Charting a Path to Net Zero Emissions."
64 Dieppe, *Global Productivity*, p. 111.
65 Kotilaine, *Trials of Resilience*, pp. 12–13.
66 IMF, *Economic Prospects and Policy Challenges – 2021*, p. 8.
67 World Bank, "COVID-19 Pandemic," pp. 13–16.
68 Dieppe, *Global Productivity*, p. i.13.
69 Luciani, "Unsustainable: But Why?," pp. 6–7.
70 Hertog, *The Private Sector and Reform*, pp. 51–52.
71 Mirzoev *et al.*, *The Future of Oil*, p. 2.
72 Mirzoev *et al.*, *The Future of Oil*, p. 2.
73 Fouejieu *et al.*, "Fiscal Adjustment in the Gulf Countries," pp. 8–9.
74 Fouejieu *et al.*, "Fiscal Adjustment in the Gulf Countries," pp. 8–9, 11.
75 Luciani, "GCC Refining and Petrochemical Sectors," pp. 187, 197–205.
76 Kotilaine, *Trials of Resilience*, pp. 68–72, 94–95.
77 IMF, *Middle East and Central Asia – Regional Economic Outlook July 2020 Update*, p. 8.
78 Beutel, "Conceptual Problems," p. 68.

References

Alami, Randa (2011), "Natural Gas in Bahrain and Kuwait," in: Fattouh and Stern, *op. cit.*, pp. 486–518.

Arezki, Rabah (2019), "Oil-Producing Countries in the Middle East and Africa Must Focus on How to Transform Their Economies," *Forum: A Quarterly Journal for Debating Energy Issues and Policies*, vol. 118 (June), pp. 25–27.

Al-Atiqi, Suliman, Emre Caliskan, Catherine Long, and Behar Sadriu (2015), *Turkey–GCC Relations: Trends and Outlook*, Istanbul: Uluslararasi ışbırlığı platformu (International Cooperation Platform).

Barajas, Adolfo, Woon Gyu Choi, Ken Zhi Gan, Pierre Guérin, Samuel Mann, Manchun Wang, and Yizhi Xu (2021), "Loose Financial Conditions, Rising Leverage, and Risks to Macro-Financial Stability," IMF Working Paper, WP/21/222. Washington, D.C.: International Monetary Fund.

Beutel, Jörg (2012), "Conceptual Problems of Measuring Economic Diversficiation, as Applied to the GCC Economies," in: Luciani, *op. cit.*, pp. 29–70.
Burke, Edward and Sara Bazoobandi (2012), "The Gulf Takes Charge: The GCC in the MENA Region," in: Youngs, *op. cit.*, pp. 23–44.
Carbon Tracker Initiative (2020), *The Future's Not in Plastics: Why Plastics Demand Won't Rescue the Oil Sector*, London, September 2020.
Dieppe, Alistair, ed. (2020), *Global Productivity: Trends, Drivers, and Policies*, Advance Edition, Washington, D.C.: World Bank Group.
El-Katiri, Laura (2013), "Energy Sustainability in the Gulf States: The Why and the How," *MEP*, No. 4, Oxford Institute of Energy Studies, March 2013.
Fattouh, Bassam (2011), "The Saudi Gas Sector and Its Role in Industrialisation," in: Fattouh and Stern, *op. cit.*, pp. 196–234.
Fattouh, Bassam, Rahmatallah Poudineh, and Rob West (2019), "The Rise of Renewables and Energy Transition: What Adaptation Strategy Exists for Oil Companies and Oil-Exporting Countries," *Energy Transitions*, vol. 3, no. 1–2, pp. 45–48.
Fattouh, Bassam and Anupama Sen (2019), "Economic Diversification by Arab Oil Exporters in the Context of Peak Oil and the Energy Transitions," *Forum: A Quarterly Journal for Debating Energy Issues and Policies*, vol. 118 (June), pp. 22–25.
Fattouh, Bassam and Jonathan Stern, eds. (2011), *Natural Gas Markets in the Middle East and North Africa*, Oxford: Oxford Institute for Energy Studies.
——— (2011), "Conclusion," in: Fattouh and Stern, *op. cit.*, pp. 531–554.
Fouejieu, Armand, Sergio Rodriguez, and Sohaib Shahid (2018), "Fiscal Adjustment in the Gulf Countries: Less Costly than Previously Thought," IMF Working Paper, WP/18/133, Washington, D.C.: International Monetary Fund.
Fulton, Jonathan (2019), "Domestic Politics as Fuel for China's Maritime Silk Road Initiative: The Case of the Gulf Monarchies," *Journal of Contemporary China*, https://doi.org/10.1080/10670564.2019.1637566.
——— (2020), *Strangers to Strategic Partners: Thirty Years of Sino–Saudi Relations*, Washington, D.C.: Atlantic Council, August 2020.
Gunter, Jacob and Helena Legarda, eds. (2022), *Beyond Blocks: Global Views on China and U.S.–China Relations*, *MERICS Papers on China*, No. 11, Mercator Institute for China Studies, August 2022.
Hertog, Steffen (2013), *The Private Sector and Reform in the Gulf Cooperation Council*, LSE Kuwait Programme Paper Series, No. 30, London: LSE Kuwait Programme, The London School of Economics and Political Science.
Houlden, Gordon and Noureddin M. Zaamout (2019), *A New Great Power Engages with the Middle East China's Middle East Balancing Approach*, Alberta: China Institute, University of Alberta, January 2019.
Howell, David (2016), *Empires in Collision: The Green versus Black Struggle for our Energy Future*, London: Gilgamesh Publishing.
International Energy Agency (2021), *Net Zero by 2050: A Roadmap for the Global Energy Sector*, Paris: International Energy Agency.
International Monetary Fund (2018), *Global Financial Stability Report: A Decade after the Global Financial Crisis: Are We Safer?*, Washington, D.C.: International Monetary Fund, October 2018.
——— (2021), *Economic Prospects and Policy Challenges for the GCC Countries – 2021*, Washington, D.C.: International Monetary Fund.
Kimmeridge (2020), "Charting a Path to Net Zero Emissions for Oil & Gas Production," Environmental Paper, New York.
Kotilaine, Jarmo T. (2021), *Trials of Resilience: How Covid-19 Is Driving Economic Change in the Arab Gulf*, London: Gilgamesh Publishing.

Krane, Jim (2017), "Beyond 12.5: The Implications of an Increase in Saudi Crude Oil Production Capacity," *Energy Policy*, vol. 110, no. C, pp. 542–547.

——— (2018), *Climate Strategy for Producer Countries: The Case of Saudi Arabia*, Working Paper, Houston, Tex.: Rice University's Baker Institute for Public Policy.

——— (2020), "Climate Action versus Inaction: Balancing the Costs for Gulf Energy Exporters," *British Journal of Middle Eastern Studies*, vol. 47, no. 1, pp. 117–135.

Lackner, Helen (2017), *Yemen in Crisis: Autocracy, Neo-Liberalism and the Disintegration of a State*, London: Saqi Books.

Ledesma, David (2011), "Natural Gas in Oman," in: Fattouh and Stern, *op. cit.*, pp. 386–428.

Lons, Camille, Jonathan Fulton, Degang Sun, and Naser Al-Tamimi (2019), "China's Great Game in the Middle East," European Council on Foreign Relations Policy Brief, October 2019.

Luciani, Giacomo (2012), "GCC Refining and Petrochemical Sectors in Global Perspective," in: Luciani, *op. cit.*, pp. 183–212.

———, ed. (2012), *Resources Blessed: Diversification and the Gulf Development Model*, Berlin: Gerlach Press.

——— (2019), "Unsustainable: But Why?," *Forum: A Quarterly Journal for Debating Energy Issues and Policies*, vol. 118 (June), pp. 5–8.

Mirzoev, Tokhir, Ling Zhu, Yang Yang, Andrea Pescatori, and Akito Matsumoto (2020), *The Future of Oil and Fiscal Sustainability in the GCC Region*, Washington, D.C.: Middle East and Central Asia Department Research Department, International Monetary Fund.

Mogielnicki, Robert (2019), "New Opportunities and High Stakes for Gulf–South Asia Relations," *The AGSIW Gulf Rising Series*, Issue Paper, No. 4, Washington, D.C.: The Arab Gulf States Institute in Washington.

——— (2020), "How China Is Quietly Expanding Its Economic Influence in the Gulf," *World Politics Review*, 21 July 2020.

Mosis, Samer Joseph (2020), *Navigating the Energy Transition: How Gulf NOCs Can Weigh in on the Climate Crisis*, Washington, D.C.: Gulf International Forum.

Seznec, Jean-François (2016), *Saudi Energy Changes: The End of the Rentier State*, Washington, D.C.: Global Energy Center, Atlantic Council.

Seznec, Jean-François and Samer Mosis (2021), *The Energy Transition in the Arab Gulf: From Vision to Reality*, Washington, D.C.: Global Energy Center, Atlantic Council.

al-Sharekh, Alanoud and Courtney Freer (2021), *Tribalism and Political Power in the Gulf: State-Building and National Identity in Kuwait, Qatar and the UAE*, London: I.B. Tauris.

Sherman, Matthew (2009), *A Short History of Financial Deregulation in the United States*, Washington, D.C.: Center for Economic and Policy Research, July 2009.

Talbot, Valeria (2013), "Turkey–GCC Relations in Transforming Middle East," *ISPI Analysis*, No. 178, June 2013.

al-Tamimi, Naser (2022), "Saudi Arabia's Once Marginal Relationship with China Has Grown into a Comprehensive Strategic Partnership," in: Gunter and Legarda, *op. cit.*, pp. 73–82.

Todman, Will (2018), "The Gulf Scramble for Africa: GCC States' Foreign Policy Laboratory," CSIS Briefs, Washington, D.C.: Center for Strategic & International Studies, 20 November 2018.

United Nations Development Programme (2016), *Arab Human Development Report 2016: Youth and the Prospects for Human Development in a Changing Reality*, New York: Regional Bureau for Arab States, United Nations Development Programme.

United Nations Development Programme, Arab Fund for Economic and Social Development (2003), *Arab Human Development Report 2003: Building a Knowledge Society*, New York: Regional Bureau for Arab States, United Nations Development Programme.

Williams, Eric (2019), "Achieving Climate Goals by Closing the Loop in a Circular Carbon Economy," *Instant Insight*, KS – 2010-II10, Riyadh: King Abdullah Petroleum Studies and Research Center, 6 November 2019.

World Bank (2017), *Water for Prosperity and Development: Risks and Opportunities for the Gulf Cooperation Council Countries*, Washington, D.C.: World Bank Group, December 2017.

——— (2021), "COVID-19 Pandemic and the Road to Diversification," *Gulf Economic Update*, No. 6, Washington, D.C.: World Bank Group, August 2021.

——— (2022), "Green Growth Opportunities in the GCC," *Gulf Economic Update*, Washington, D.C.: The World Bank, Fall 2022.

Youngs, Richard, ed. (2012), *The GCC in the Global Economy* (*The Gulf Region: Economic Development and Diversification*, vol. 1), Berlin: Gerlach Press.

10 Charting the way forward

The 20th century proved the most transformative era in the often tumultuous history of the Arabian Peninsula. Within a couple of generations, one of the poorest regions in the world became one of the wealthiest, with living standards and financial wealth topping the global league tables. This also reconfigured the regional context as the nouveau riche peninsula increasingly outshone the adjacent landmass from Egypt to Iran. While oil accounts for much of this divergence, it cannot be the sole explanatory factor. The Gulf has gone through severe challenges during the hydrocarbons era, just as much as its neighbors – many of which also boast substantial hydrocarbons endowments – have experienced moments of hope and reform. But on balance, the Gulf has tended to emerge stronger from its ordeals, while others have tended to stagnate or even regressed. The Gulf has become the greatest economic success story of the modern Arab world, having once possessed some of the poorest initial conditions for achieving this. In the words of Rami Khouri, the Gulf has "transformed itself in just decades from a largely barren backwater to a dynamic engine of Arab economic investment, efficient planning and execution, orderliness and modernity."[1]

The 21st century promises to transform Arabia even more profoundly than the previous century. The traditional growth drivers in the region have weakened amid the ongoing global energy transition. But hydrocarbons will retain a place in the global energy mix: "Over the coming decade, the global middle class will increase by more than one billion people, economic growth will be skewed toward hydrocarbon-intensive industries across the developing world, and a lag in the rate of penetration of new technologies will exist."[2] The Gulf is well positioned to cater to this demand at less cost and environmental impact than many others. But it will likely have to do so with much more innovation and versatility than before.

The various vision statements unveiled by the Gulf governments have consistently underscored the importance of redefining the role of the government in the economy. But it is no less imperative to sever the persistent link of diversification to the oil–government nexus: "Over the past two decades, household income growth and public investment have allowed the GCC countries to diversify GDP composition away from hydrocarbons."[3] For a genuine paradigm shift, the Gulf private sector must "move from living off the sale of imports and import substitution activities and feeding off government contracts to taking the initiative in diversification efforts."[4]

DOI: 10.4324/9781003373353-10

But for private investors step to the plate, the Gulf governments must step back and proactively redefine their traditional remit of responsibilities.

While the proverbial handwriting may be on the wall for the oil-driven development model, the alternatives to it remain far from clear. The early 21st century has repeatedly shown how the volatile oil market dynamics still set the tone for the broader Gulf economy. The reordering of the economic paradigm will almost certainly be gradual, potentially uneven, and discontinuous. The extensive growth model of the Great Arabian Infrastructure Boom days will hold appeal to many thanks to its track record of seemingly simple effectiveness. But it now comes with risks and complications, not least that of de-globalization, however relative.[5] Economic growth that is achieved by simply expanding the local population with a blind focus on numbers will deliver short-term growth bumps but will make it difficult to sustainably boost living standards. Such an approach risks perpetuating labor-intensive practices and hence ultimately deterring investments in more productive technologies and innovative business models. Using redistributive measures to compensate for the shortcomings of this model – for instance, through targeted wealth transfers to nationals – comes with its own risks. For welfare provision to be sustainable, it has to be targeted and, where possible, designed to minimize long-term dependencies. For the vast majority of GCC inhabitants, nationals or not, work and entrepreneurship must become the road to economic security and well-being.

At least in the short term, the fiscal overhaul that all of the regional economies have been pursuing since 2015 is testing the profitability of the traditional practice of input accumulation. A more market-based system of pricing utilities is pushing up the ancillary costs of expatriate labor as basic necessities command a higher price. Quite apart from repricing labor relative to other inputs, this is also causing some laborers to vote with their feet as their take-home pay is squeezed. Gulf governments are further accelerating the process through measures to foster national employment. COVID-19 sped up the shift by triggering an expatriate exodus while also concentrating minds on technology.[6]

The new economic realities underscore the urgency of "better," more impactful and sustainable diversification that is dynamic, not just a static transfer or resources from the oil to the non-oil economy. The most popular non-oil activities of the recent past are weighed down by challenges amplified by the pandemic. Traditional physical real estate is becoming costlier to build, although, over time, smarter buildings and better regulations can establish a more sustainable foundation for renewed expansion. Slower population growth – whether through declining average family sizes or less immigration – will entail more muted demand dynamics following years of brisk supply growth, even if this is to an extent muted by new ideas around openness.

Profound challenges also loom for the trade sector, which has continued to see substantial bricks-and-mortar investments, whereas the region has lagged in e-commerce. The Gulf retail cluster is now likely to be squeezed on two sides. Firstly, the expected demographic dynamics, likely coupled with slower growth in disposable incomes (at least past the 2021–2022 oil windfall), will almost certainly upend many demand projections.

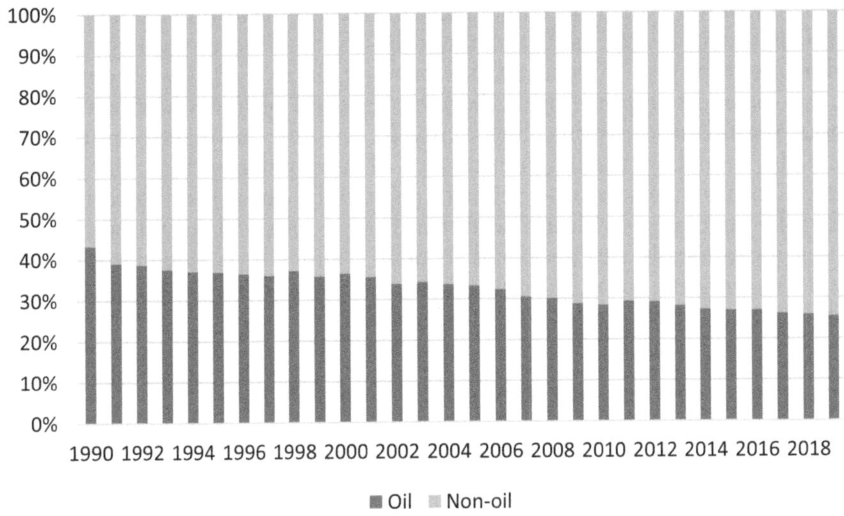

Figure 10.1 GCC aggregate real GDP composition.

Source: World Bank.

Businesses are being forced to compete on pricing, with the consequence of eroding margins. But the strategic posture of the sector is also long overdue for a rethink. Physical premises may have to be scaled back or repurposed as more capital flows into e-commerce. A reconfiguration of the business landscape is likely, which probably entails significant challenges for many SMEs.

The future of international travel and tourism remains somewhat uncertain, partly because of the many structural challenges facing the global economy. During the pandemic, Gulf destinations, led by Dubai, normalized conditions with remarkable speed, while Saudi Arabia redoubled efforts to move forward its ambitious tourism strategy backed up by $1trn of investments. Evolving attitudes and policies around climate change may push up the costs and even challenge the popularity of travel. The tourism sector itself is undergoing changes, and the emphasis will likely have to shift from conventional hotel and resort offerings more to attractions, events, and experiences. Resorts will also face opportunities for redevelopment toward more eco-friendly and health and wellness offerings. Gulf economies have channeled massive amounts of capital into airport development in recent years, with a new wave of initiatives being unveiled such as the King Salman International Airport in Riyadh.[7] Even as some assumptions may have to be revisited, the Gulf carriers also look well positioned to further cement their global competitive standing, even as ambitious new entrants such as Riyadh Air and NEOM Airline look set to join their number.

With time, these evolving realities should begin to stimulate more productive and profitable ways of mobilizing capital, shifting the focus from the favorite sectors of yesteryear in favor of other asset classes. But the efficiency of the transition will depend in part on the ability of the financial services sector, as well as financial regulators, to respond with appropriate solutions. Many of the disruptions brought on by COVID-19 entail particular business opportunities. Forcing regional businesses to get serious about digitalization is enabling many to tap new business opportunities globally. Similarly, the heightened risk of supply disruptions has brought increased attention to food security. Not only can self-reliance in many areas be increased without compromising ecological sustainability but doing more locally can also lead to new avenues for value chain capture by developing the local food processing industry. Better risk management solutions promise opportunities for insurers.[8]

Creating a culture of change in a world in flux

The prospect of a profound economic paradigm shift is not new to the Gulf region. Henry Azzam's description of an economy confronting systemic change over three decades ago, sounds almost eerily prophetic today: "The Gulf countries are at the threshold of a new economic era characterized by reduced dependence on oil revenues, diversification of the economic structure, rationalization of public expenditures, wider involvement of the private sector, enhancement of local skills and products and greater emphasis [on] regional co-operation."[9] Written at a time of crisis, Azzam perceived opportunity in the challenges that beset the region after the ebullient 1970s. The expected transformation never truly materialized, and the oil-fueled exuberance of the new millennium eventually reduced the perceived sense of urgency. The region bought a three-decade respite by kicking the can down the road. But the underlying structural challenges did not disappear.

There is reason to believe that Azzam's prophesy might prove "second time valid." The overriding priority must be to deliver a development model that is sustainable on multiple levels – in terms of economic development but also socially and environmentally. But for the Gulf region, this pursuit of true sustainability will come at the cost of the economic certainties of the past. A world where much of a family's consumption bundle is one way or another underwritten or subsidized by the state is receding to memory with the ongoing fiscal reforms. The idea that companies can operate for decades without meaningfully reviewing their business models has been undermined by slower growth and recurrent exogenous shocks. As change becomes the norm, it is essential to be able to embrace and manage it directly instead of the reactive, discontinuous posture that past public largesse made possible. Rising to this challenge requires building resilience, or the capacity to anticipate, understand, and manage uncertainty in ways that allow its costs to be mitigated while opportunities are maximized. Unleashing the free market by ensuring the efficient pricing of inputs and outputs in transparent exchange, limiting the distorted incentives and arbitrage opportunities of the past, will lend a key impetus to this process.

As the Gulf economies set out to break free from the shackles of the past, they have to do so in an increasingly competitive and volatile global environment. Success in any field has become a game of continuously moving goalposts given evolving social attitudes and political risk but also the unprecedented speed of technological change thanks to "exponential advances in a suite of enabling technologies ranging from computing power to data storage, to the scale and performance of the Internet. These advances are creating tipping points – moments at which technologies such as robotics, artificial intelligence (AI), biology, nanotechnology and 3D printing cross a threshold and trigger sudden and significant change."[10] Even if these processes will not continue unchecked, the prospect of a fundamentally different future – for instance, widespread application of AI – now seems tantalizingly within reach. Some futurist visions foresee robots integrated in much of human activity within a couple of decades. This is a logical transformation for the Gulf to embrace, even to try to lead on, given its financial wealth and (relative) population scarcity. But technology is also likely to be a powerful enabler of the necessary shift from static business models and reactive culture to something inherently dynamic. Building skills and capacity in this area is likely to become an important driver of innovation.

As the Gulf region weighs options for its future, unleashing the potential of the available competitiveness drivers must be a key consideration. At least with the exception of energy, these have shown remarkable continuity over the centuries. The most enduring advantage is geography, even if it is potentially vulnerable to climate change. The quality of human capital and regulations are two factors that Gulf policymakers can directly influence. With the rise of digitalization and green economy opportunities, among many other emerging areas, talent will command a growing premium. Not only is human ingenuity the one factor of production not subject to diminishing returns but it is also needed to localize activities that allow the region to more fully capitalize on its impressive connectivity advantages. The Gulf countries' demographic realities will dictate a two-pronged strategy. Firstly, much more will have to be done to boost the local education system and access to quality training. There is a pressing need to generate market-relevant skills on a growing scale while creating more globally competitive research capacity that fuel ideas generation and and commercialization locally. But the limited population base underscores the importance of boosting the economic contribution of foreign labor more effectively than before. A productive GCC will have to successfully compete in the global race for brains while weaning itself off its systemic dependency on low-cost manual labor.

Regulatory reform will play an important role in ensuring the attractiveness of the Gulf as an investment destination. Regulations must be efficient, transparent, and easily enforceable at a reasonable cost. The use of free zones as a magnet for productive resources is a tried and tested approach. While their track record is far from uniform, there are several impressive success stories to demonstrate the enduring arbitrage opportunity that quality regulation represents. But national regulations are also being overhauled with growing determination. Recent initiatives have focused heavily on company formation, financial sector development, and the scaling back of foreign ownership and residency regulations.[11]

Regulatory reform is instrumental for driving the necessary economic paradigm shift by creating the appropriate incentives for it. The region must learn to live through productive work, not resource endowments and a generous state. The regional population must become economically active on a scale that compares to the global norm. More locals must find their way into higher-productivity activities to reduce reliance on the public sector as the default of employer, something that now entails substantial costs: "Except for Oman, Qatar and the UAE, [public sector] wage bills stand above 10 percent of total GDP."[12]

Economic governance must support free markets while protecting against abuse and distortions, an issue of particular importance with respect to competition law, especially in the smaller Gulf economies. Further fostering regional integration can be a key enabler of this process. The IMF recently found that a globally competitive business environment provides more than 40 percent of all productivity gains. Bureaucratic red tape and corruption must be combated as they are a source of cost, delays, and uncertainty. Government downsizing and reconfiguration must be used to achieve more cost-effective service delivery. The payoffs to reform are substantial, with the IMF estimating that matching international standards in the three main reform areas of competition, human capital, and financial market development could raise potential GDP growth by 1.5 percentage points.[13]

The dwindling economic returns to input accumulation in the Gulf point to an inescapable conclusion: only through productivity can the region achieve sustainable increases in living standards. Productivity is also a precondition for a less resource-intensive mode of production. The ongoing fiscal reforms are pushing up the cost of waste, while the environmental impact of pollution is drawing growing attention worldwide. Attitudes are rapidly changing in favor of more sustainable modes of production and a reduced reliance on depletable resources. Hence, the reputational and financial implications of business as usual are mounting, a process that may further accelerate.

The growing focus on sustainability vindicates the Gulf countries' diversification aspirations but also raises the bar in terms of desired outcomes. In contrast to the oil–government nexus and the Great Arabian Infrastructure Boom, the productivity conundrum has no quick fix. This mirrors the multifaceted nature of the problem but also the reality that many of the necessary corrective measures will not yield immediate results.[14] First of all, more resources must be channeled into activities where they can be expected to generate value. The closed sector of the economy today achieves its margins almost exclusively through a heavy reliance on low-cost labor. Regulatory reform, financial market development, and government support are needed to shift more capital into genuinely productive activities, especially ones with the potential for future growth, whether through technology or scalability.

The heavy legacy of the Dutch disease–like consumerism that supported low-productivity service sector businesses entails substantial opportunities for better resource allocation and utilization. The Gulf governments have created dedicated funding vehicles for activities ranging from manufacturing to start-up entrepreneurship. But sustainable progress depends on the regional financial sector assuming a much more proactive posture. For instance, SME finance still remains a challenge by global standards, although government support programs, credit bureaus, moveable collateral registries, and FinTech solutions are beginning to make headway.[15] Crowdfunding mechanisms are attracting growing attention and, despite some teething issues, can become an effective tool for grassroots funding for ventures that might struggle with conventional banks. FinTech permits more efficient collection and utilization of information for better decisions.

The corporate sector must be a central element of the economic overhaul as it is impossible to build a strong economy without dynamic businesses.[16] In large swathes of the non-oil economy, the distorted input price environment of yesteryear permitted extreme fragmentation with minimal barriers to entry in many sectors. With the minimum efficient scale now increasing, collaboration and consolidation are presenting themselves as compelling options. The old corporate culture of personalized entrepreneurship and inefficient corporate valuation mechanisms remain important hurdles. However, new challenges are testing old attitudes, while fiscal diversification is improving accounting practices and laying the foundation for private capital markets. These changes are likely to push more businesses toward ongoing dynamism.

Making existing businesses work better is an important investment opportunity.[17] The COVID-19 crisis provided ample evidence of the transformative impact of technology on business models. Small, low-productivity businesses in sectors such as retail and basic services were disproportionately hit. This was to an extent the result of restrictions on mobility, but it also reflected low margins and an inability to adapt to the new realities through a digital presence and alternative distribution mechanisms. The growing availability of flexible, cost-effective technology solutions allowed many companies to reduce their reliance on labor or physical real estate. Many larger regional businesses are looking at consolidation as a way of streamlining their operations. The cultural and economic readiness of smaller business for this is much less, but encouraging businesses to explore collaboration is likely to pay off in time.

As Gulf businesses seek to streamline costs, solutions that are available on a flexible basis without the need for substantial up-front investments will be particularly important. Cloud- or SaaS-driven digitalization can help businesses cater to their needs through flexible service contracts. Business process outsourcing is gaining ground in areas such as accounting and auditing, legal advice, security, and human resources. Mature solutions are available for energy efficiency and renewables through energy service company arrangements that require no up-front investments. They allow customers to achieve immediate savings, initially on a shared basis through power purchasing contracts that permit the service providers to recoup their investment. Apart from savings, such solutions offer increased certainty about future costs. Flexibility and cost are likely to determine to what extent these solutions can provide an enduring alternative to rentier-style cost minimization.

The traditional notions of entrepreneurship are long overdue for an overhaul. The strategic appeal of start-ups comes precisely from the antithesis that they represent to these exhausted practices. Start-ups tend to address real economic problems instead of merely emulating business concepts. They frequently bring together several founders, thus combining skills, experience, network, and funding sources. These novel ventures tend to be productive instead of serving as intermediaries for goods sourced elsewhere. They are outward focused, growth oriented, and scalable. Their relative capital intensity often makes them highly productive. Despite a significant probability of failure, such ventures also promise substantial payoffs when successful. This underscores the importance of fostering success but also of simplifying and, above all, de-criminalizing business failure. Properly leveraging technology can help the Gulf leapfrog the more organic development experienced by other geographies. The start-up model can also set a helpful example for the broader SME sector. More institutionalized companies will be better able to grow through acquisitions and mergers, not just organically. The Gulf region has begun to see a growing number of start-ups graduate into multi-million-dollar ventures, which should help further popularize the idea.[18]

A more productive private sector matters not just for the overall economic growth dynamics but also for the labor market. Increased technology adoption should begin to reduce the long-standing labor bias of Gulf businesses while also creating new opportunities for more skilled employees. This will be to the benefit of sustainable employment of citizens and should also draw new businesses and talent to the Gulf. Similarly, the increase in remote work is boosting labor market flexibility, which can be supported further by less strict regulations around working hours as an alternative to the old norm of full-time employment.

Making the most of regional assets

The regional resource base will inevitably shape the development journey of the Gulf countries in important ways. Limited though the range of known natural resources is, the globally significant hydrocarbons plenty promises substantial opportunities even amid the global energy transition. Not utilizing these endowments is not a realistic near-term option, and natural gas now seems to have gained ground as a preferred transition fuel. For instance, well before the COVID-19 pandemic, ADNOC unveiled plans to boost natural gas production "by the mid-2020s to cover the Emirates' gas supply deficit and make it a net exporter of natural gas."[19]

The global energy transition also promises new opportunities for the Gulf. In a shrinking hydrocarbons market, the cost competitiveness of the regional endowments will be a compelling advantage.[20] By contrast, the regulatory environment and political backdrop in other producer countries look likely to become increasingly challenging. As investor tolerance of carbon emissions diminishes, "energy exporters will increasingly compete based on the carbon intensity of their exports."[21] Saudi crude production generates an average of 4.6 grams of carbon dioxide equivalent per megajoule, compared to an average of 11 grams in the US.[22] Innovation around the circular carbon economy is further entrenching these advantages. For instance, Qatar is integrating carbon capture and storage in the North Field expansion, increasingly marketing itself on its ability to "control and account for carbon emissions across its entire value chain."[23] This will matter in a market where carbon accreditation will allow cargoes to trade at a premium.

The evolving investment climate will favor technologies that minimize pollution and utilize hydrocarbons in novel ways. The Gulf region is making immense strides in capturing more of the oil and gas value chain with fewer emissions than ever before. Saudi Aramco's acquisition of SABIC is creating a diverse energy and chemical giant with an international footprint. The flagship venture for transforming oil directly into chemicals marks an important step toward future-proofing oil. A $20bn Yanbu-based project will convert 400,000 b/d of crude into some 9mn tn of chemicals per year and promises to boost the efficiency of hydrocarbons use by 15–50 percent. SABIC's 2007 $11.6bn acquisition of GE Plastics came with research and production facilities in 35 countries, and the company now operates 123 joint ventures globally.[24]

The Gulf countries are well positioned in the area of carbon capture. Aramco's Hawiyah gas plant captures some 800,000 tn of carbon annually, which is piped 85 km and pumped into the Uthmaniyah oil field, where it also enhances oil recovery. Similarly, CO_2 emitted by power generation, desalination, and heavy industry can be injected into oil fields or converted into chemicals. Such linkages can benefit from the region's "vast underground storage potential in old oil fields and access to substantial local capital."[25] Aramco and ADNOC combined are estimated to have some 1.6mn tn per annum of carbon capture capacity – roughly 4 percent of the global total. At least a further 4.2mn tn per annum is reportedly at advanced planning stages in Qatar and the UAE.[26] However, amid a polarized global debate, ensuring concrete progress through ongoing innovation is likely to prove of growing reputational importance.

The Gulf region's status as an energy producer no longer needs to depend on fossil fuels alone. Arabia possesses massive untapped potential in the area of renewable energy thanks to its combination of generous solar radiation and vast empty spaces: "Close to 60% of the GCC's surface area is found to have excellent suitability for solar PV deployment, and developing just 1% of this area could create almost 470 gigawatts (GW) of additional power-generation capacity."[27] While renewables have attracted interest for some time, until recently, concrete progress was held back by the generous hydrocarbons subsidies. Interest was initially driven by a desire to curb rapidly rising domestic hydrocarbons consumption to free up volumes for export. Ventures such as Masdar City reflected a desire to create future capacity in research and power generation. But it took the fiscal reforms since 2015, along with considerable progress in the economics of solar power, for the calculus to truly shift in favor of renewables.

All of the GCC governments have set formal targets for renewable energy adoption in recent years. Under its Vision 2030, Saudi Arabia set a goal of increasing the share of solar energy to 30 percent of power generation. This compared to only 0.1 percent at the time, whereas 56.9 percent came from natural gas and 40.3 percent from oil. In 2018, the clean energy target was set at 57.8 GW, which compared to an actual total of only 397 MW at the end of 2020. Saudi Arabia is currently home to some 16 percent of the GCC region's solar capacity, whereas the UAE's share stands at 68 percent and Kuwait's at 9 percent. The UAE's Energy Strategy 2050 set out to increase the contribution of clean energy from 25 to 50 percent by the middle of the century while pledging $600bn of investment in renewables. Abu Dhabi's Barakah nuclear plant began production in 2020. Following the completion of all four reactors, the facility is expected to meet up to a quarter of the country's power demand. The UAE also boasts 2.3 GW of operational solar capacity and a pipeline of almost 4 GW.[28]

The Gulf region has in recent years broken one renewable energy record after the other. A 2021 project in Saudi Arabia's Sudair region achieved a tariff of $0.0104/kWh, outdoing the $0.0135/kWh December 2020 winning bid for Abu Dhabi's Al Dhafra PV project.[29] But ambitions are continuing to mount. In January 2021 the Saudi government announced a 50 percent target for the share of renewables in energy use by 2030. In October 2021 the UAE became the first Middle East country to set a net zero carbon emissions target for 2050. Waste-to-energy along with better waste management through recycling remain largely untapped opportunities.

The advantages of embracing a greener future go far beyond environmental benefits. The World Bank estimates that a strategic focus on green growth would "reverse trends in [total factor productivity] enabling the region to grow at between 7–10 percent annually,"[30] a near-doubling of the historical norm. But taking advantage of the energy transition must be seen as a strategic investment, the benefits of which "will accrue to countries that can quickly position themselves through appropriate policy frameworks, investment funds, partnerships with the private sector and academia, and create changes in societies' values and practices."[31] These are logical opportunities for the Gulf countries in view of their potential to contribute to long-term strategic objectives around productivity, job creation, financial sector development, and multidimensional economic diversification. Among other things, timely progress toward the renewable energy targets would create an estimated 135,000 direct jobs a year.[32] With power generation accounting for three-quarters of CO_2 emissions in the Gulf, facilitating a shift to renewables and energy efficiency stands out as a particularly compelling opportunity now that their cost has declined below that of hydrocarbons. The emerging grid connections to the Levant, Egypt, and even Europe promise, potentially even India, to open up avenues for clean energy exports, while the dramatically falling costs of power storage are increasing flexibility at home. By powering a growing range of activities, cost-effective renewables can potentially future-proof, and perhaps even enhance, the cost advantage hitherto provided by low-cost hydrocarbons in many areas. They will also permit new ways of extracting value out of hydrocarbons.

Hydrogen has emerged as another area of rapidly growing interest for the GCC. The global demand for hydrogen increased fourfold to 75–85mn metric tn between 1975 and 2018. Nearly two-thirds of this was linked to ammonia production for fertilizers and a quarter for lowering the sulfur content of diesel. Hydrogen has several desirable characteristics, not least its storage potential and exceptional energy density, which permits 2.6 times the energy production of a comparable amount of natural gas. Its only by-product when used to generate energy through a fuel cell is water.[33] More problematic, most hydrogen production to date has come from burning fossil fuels, although the sector is evolving in fundamental ways. Clean hydrogen production is possible by using carbon capture and storage to collect the CO_2 by-product of conventional hydrogen production. Alternatively, renewable energy can power electrolysis to break up water molecules for green hydrogen. The potential of hydrogen for de-carbonization is gaining recognition as some activities will be difficult to electrify without it. New applications in heat, power, and transportation, along with evolving attitudes and regulations, are expected to boost hydrogen demand globally to 580mn metric tn by 2050.[34] Some 350 projects are underway worldwide to develop green hydrogen production and distribution, as well as industrial plants using hydrogen.[35] Through increased scale, the levelized cost of hydrogen is expected to fall by 30–50 percent by 2030.

The Dubai Electricity and Water Authority and Siemens are developing an industrial-scale green hydrogen pilot project, and the government has launched the UAE Hydrogen Technical Committee. Abu Dhabi has announced its Hydrogen Alliance involving ADNOC. The most ambitious regional venture is planned in Neom, with projected 4 GW of renewable power generation capacity. The output will be converted into green ammonia for export. A landmark $5bn solar-powered green hydrogen venture was signed with Air Products and ACWA Power in July 2021.[36] The project is expected to supply 650 tn of carbon-free hydrogen daily while saving 3mn tn of CO_2 annually. Oman unveiled the Hyport Duqm Green Hydrogen Project in December 2020, while Sohar has ambitions to become the first green hydrogen generation hub in the region.[37]

The GCC is well positioned for global leadership in hydrogen production thanks to cost-effective renewable energy, estimated by the IEA at $1.5–2 per kilogram in the long run. Local funding sources and the strategic location are additional advantages. The GCC has "geological conditions that could allow the development of large-scale underground storage facilities in rock formations which could serve a buffer for varying seasonal demand."[38] Regions such as Europe may struggle to build desired capacity, and EU hydrogen imports could reached 100mn metric tn by 2050, while East Asia could demand as much as 85mn metric tn of ammonia. The GCC's own hydrogen demand may increase from some 5.5mn metric tn to 25–50mn by 2050 because of manufacturing growth as well as transportation and energy needs. Ramping up renewables generation in line with their 2030 targets could allowe the GCC to produce 50–70mn metric tn by 2050, whereas a more aggressive goal of 80–100mn metric tn would entail annual revenues of $70–200bn. This would require renewables capacity of 700–1,000 GW and annual investments of $16–60bn – 30–40 percent of it for renewable energy. A proactive approach to developing the hydrogen economy and localizing value chains could create 400,000–900,000 direct and indirect jobs in the GCC by 2050.[39] Apart from a strategic focus, success will require an appropriate enabling environment through investment in hydrogen valleys that can offer synergies and economies of scale and develop know-how and R&D capacity. Hydrogen can well prove a powerful future hedge that can benefit and safeguard the GCC energy cluster on multiple levels.[40]

Other natural resources are also attracting attention. Ma'aden was established for the purpose of exploiting Saudi Arabia's mineral wealth in 1997 and has since evolved into a globally significant mining conglomerate extracting bauxite, phosphate, gold, copper, and a growing range of other industrial minerals. Local resources, with some 5mn metric tn of bauxite production in recent years, have allowed it to establish a pioneering integrated aluminum complex.[41] But progress in GCC mining has not always been straightforward. For instance, Oman revived the ancient copper mines near Sohar to feed a nearby smelter. However, "the supply of copper ore was exploited in ten years and the smelter managed to limp on only by importing copper ingots."[42] Saudi Arabia is thought to possess substantial future development potential in mining, with the government estimating that only 7–8 percent of the Kingdom's mineral deposits have been extracted, while untapped finds are value at about $1.3trn. Much of the peninsula has not been systematically explored, and the Saudi authorities are encouraging prospecting through a new Mining Investment Law. The Kingdom is planning to auction new licenses for gold, copper, and zinc, among others, in a bid to triple the mining sector's GDP contribution to $64bn while doubling employment to 470,000 by 2030.[43]

Food production has historically suffered from exceptionally acute natural constraints. However, the introduction of new farming techniques has opened up opportunities for the Gulf to boost local production without compromising scarce resources. Hydroponic farming and comparable innovations have revived agriculture in parts of Arabia. Similarly, efforts to develop fish farming are enabling a transition to a more sustainable exploitation of the indigenous seafood stocks depleted by overfishing even if climate change constitutes a risk. Substantial growth has been achieved with shrimp and fish species such as the European sea bass and the European sea bream. Oman, where fishing remains an important source of livelihood, has been granting new licenses for several years, and the UAE has seen multiple investments in high-value seafood production such as sturgeon caviar and salmon. Saudi Arabia is working to increase its seafood production from roughly 100,000 to 600,000 metric tn over the current decade, with the government unveiling plans in 2019 to invest $347mn in aquaculture. The GCC possesses considerable potential as a seafood exporter. The government of Oman is planning to boost production to as much as 22,000 tn, with a market value of $900mn and 11,000 employment opportunities, by 2040. Several governments have worked to establish a favorable investment regime with various incentives.[44]

The Gulf countries possess exceptional financial wealth, which entails enviable opportunities for capital mobilization for impact.[45] Despite impressive progress, there is a continuing need to further diversify and deepen the regional capital markets. Constrained access to capital remains one of the principal complaints of entrepreneurs and innovators across the peninsula. At the moment, physical infrastructure – notably real estate –

remains much easier to invest in than venture capital or private equity. There is a pressing need for product diversification and the development of markets. The evolution of the fiscal system is an important driver of this process. But the region must also continue to leverage its capital to build bridges to other markets and development opportunities.

The growing popularity of innovative start-up entrepreneurship is driving change. Reaching a point where meaningful success stories are generated on a regular basis should have broader positive implications for the GCC business culture. They will attract more capital into entrepreneurial ventures, help popularize new asset classes, and – through successful exits – help create a new class of investors and mentors with a different outlook on capital allocation than their more established peers. The COVID-19 pandemic delivered concrete evidence of the economic potential of innovative, technology-based solutions while leading more investors to question some of the more conventional investment propositions. Even amid some reversal to pre-pandemic behaviors, much of the change looks likely to endure. The champions of the new economy will also motivate more established businesses to look for new ideas. The growing interest by incumbent financial institutions in the rise of FinTech is a case in point. Companies such as Aramco have shown effective leadership in this area.

The most important resource in the Gulf is the local human capital through which and for which the economic transition has to take place. Human capital in the Gulf is young by global standards and better educated than ever before. Putting this talent at the heart of the economic paradigm shift need not – indeed, must not – be an exclusionary endeavor. The ability to attract and retain global talent is becoming an ever more important aspect of economic competitiveness and remains a necessity in view of the Gulf region's limited population base. But it is essential to give indigenous talent a real stake in the construction of the region's future and the benefits this engenders. Local talent must be channeled into productive activities that can deliver acceptable compensation but also remain competitive in the face of an evolving competitive landscape. Doing this right requires real, market-based economic incentives. The region should not relinquish its competitive advantages in areas such as low-cost energy. But excessive subsidies will distort resource allocation, generate waste, and – ultimately – undermine productivity. Moreover, the process of entering the labor market and changing jobs must become much easier and more flexible. Economic participation today is too low. Progress is partly conditional on unleashing the transformative potential of part-time, flexi-time, and remote work. Technology allows new modes of economic participation with a potentially global remit.

Location, location, location ...

As the Gulf economies set out to shape a different future, echoes of the pre-oil era abound, not only because of the ultimately diminishing reliance on hydrocarbons but also due to the changing global balance of economic power. The economic potential of the Arabian peninsula is on the rise because its age-old trade partners in South Asia and Africa now count among some of the world's most dynamic emerging economies. Taken together, the two vast continents are home to 5.6bn people, over three-quarters of the global total. As the West ages, this proportion is set to grow further, while brisk economic development is driving the rise of a middle class with an interest in traveling and investing outside of their home countries. For growing companies in nearby regions, the GCC can offer an attractive, accessible, but different – and therefore potentially complementary – alternative. For instance, the GCC has successfully established a compelling value proposition in an increasingly centralized global logistics market where the top seven shipping lines controlled around three-quarters of all container ships in 2020.[46] Their operations were focused on large distribution hubs competing on scale, infrastructure, and efficiency. This is a game that Dubai had excelled in, while the Omani open sea ports are emerging as potential future hubs.

The Gulf countries have made remarkable strides positioning themselves for these new economic realities. There is an obvious need for insurance policies, with new threats coming from regional political risk and climate change. While the regional context will necessitate an evolving mix of containment and engagement, it is quite possible that a more positive scenario will emerge over time. For instance, the China–Pakistan corridor has the potential to develop into a real bridge between the Gulf and the Middle Kingdom. While the risks of climate change may prove particularly thorny, the Gulf economies are becoming more active participants in the debates on climate policy while investing more aggressively in climate adaptation and potentially even emerging areas areas such as carbon withdrawal.

The GCC is well positioned to capitalize on its locational advantages in an interconnected world of flows. Its track record as a preferred intermediary between the hitherto dominant North Atlantic world and the rapidly rising Indian Ocean economic space is already well established, further enhanced by the perception of the GCC as a relative haven of stability amid many more troubled countries. Several cities within the Gulf region are now considered internationally attractive locations to live in and hence attract people and businesses from all over the world.

The GCC is emerging as a platform with high potential for location-agnostic activities that target other geographies. The potential catchment area is immense, with much of the Old World within easy reach. The locational advantage is further boosted by a competitive regulatory and institutional environment accessible at a competitive cost. However, location as an opportunity can only be fully unleashed through an explicit commitment to openness. To date, key elements of the Gulf countries' generally exceptional openness have been selective — for example, labor imports, the use of free zones, etc. – although some of these arrangements were conceived as temporary. By leveraging its assets to attract globally competitive talent, the Gulf can further boost its chances of outcompeting its regional rivals in terms of quality, productivity, and innovation.

In order to future-proof its advantages, the GCC will have to develop deeper partnerships with other geographies. China's Belt and Road initiative is an important case in point, but so are bilateral trade treaties. For historical reasons, ties with Europe and the US are well developed.

A long-standing relationship exists with the Indian sub-continent, although it has been skewed toward low-value activities to date. In most other cases outside the broader Middle East, relations tend to be more recent and narrow. Further integration will have to involve increased interaction. The recent inroads in making parts of Arabia a popular tourist destination along with increasingly versatile opportunities for real estate investment are important steps in the right direction.

Successful differentiation has the potential to turn the GCC into a magnet in other ways as well. Tourism is a fairly well-established aspect of this strategy. Continued success will have to involve the further development of local tourism assets along with innovative marketing. The initial achievements of Dubai as a shopping destination have given way to a more diverse offering, most recently with a slew of world-class theme parks. Oman has established itself as an authentic leisure destination with a flavor of the region's past and culture. Saudi Arabia, besides further developing pilgrimage to the two holy mosques, is crafting a diverse offering drawing on its geography, historical assets, and new developments. Bahrain is working to capitalize on its unique island identity and exceptional history. But despite all of this, Arabia's past, as well as its natural assets, remain relatively unknown in the global context. Moreover, there is little tourism that targets more than one regional destination at a time.

Through an appropriate strategic focus and investment in quality, the GCC can replicate some of the long-standing successes of other "magnet" countries such as Switzerland, Monaco, the UK, Singapore, etc. The Gulf is working to establish increasingly competitive offerings in areas such as health care, education, and asset management. Successful recent initiatives to seize these emerging growth opportunities include ventures such as the Dubai Healthcare City and the Abu Dhabi Global Market. There has been substantial investment in educational institutions, albeit primarily in response to local demand. As the US, the UK, and many other countries have shown, investments in education can become a potent tool for attracting talent. For instance, the UAE has managed to position itself as a dynamic hub of educational tourism, with 39 higher education institutions as of 2017, including 24 foreign branch campuses from 12 countries. It has also adapted its regulatory framework with a view to retaining some of the talent that comes to its university campuses.The number of international degree students rose from 48,653 in 2011 to 77,463 in 2016. The American University of Sharjah now claims to be the most international university in the world, with 84 percent international students. The UAE's "inbound mobility ratio of 48.6 percent … dwarfs that of all major destinations."[47] However, the country remains heavily dependent on he Indian market, which provided 17 percent of the total in 2016, followed by Syria, Jordan, Egypt, Oman, and Pakistan.

Linked to education is the growing need for local innovation and research capacity. R&D is emerging as a diversification driver of growing importance while stimulating increased local value creation. Much needs to be done to upgrade the regional academic institutions from teaching establishments to R&D hubs. The same is true for the corporate sector, which must also build deeper ties with academia. R&D represents a key plank of a broader innovation agenda that can attract creative talent, skills, and investors. Success is conditional on matching the track record of other innovation hubs that are inherently international in nature. Supported by appropriate infrastructure and regulatory investments, a growing network of international partnership in this area can accelerate progress. While change will not be instantaneous, the Gulf is increasingly well positioned to establish itself as an attractive complement to its neighbors, offering superior standards to those who can afford it but also credible solutions lower down the value chain.

Despite the compelling advantages offered by the location of the GCC region, being able to transcend the geographic context may well prove an even more attractive opportunity in the long run. In today's digital global economy, much economic activity is not significantly location specific. Creative, tech-based entrepreneurship can be carried on virtually anywhere as digital technology provides the bridge to inputs and end markets alike. Such businesses tend to gravitate toward environments that provide regulatory flexibility and connectivity along with strong digital infrastructure. Conversely, however, these "global nomads" may prove fickle friends if their expectations are not met. But success is attainable, not least thanks to the deep pools of private and public capital across the Gulf. The ability to succeed as a platform is critically linked to willingness to compete at the highest levels, subject to the most rigorous standards. Despite its multiple impressive achievements, the GCC still tends to fall short of global leaders in rankings such as *Doing Business* or the *Global Competitiveness Report*. Much more work is needed to build credibile reputations. For instance, "Saudi Arabia used to be regarded as an open economy though in many respects a closed society."[48]

The platform par excellence opportunity need not be embraced by the entire Gulf region, especially if regional integration continues to make headway. Positioning parts of the GCC in this way can put the entire Gulf region on the global start-up map and create broader region-wide synergies. Such an outcome would be very much in line with the kind of gateway or hub function that Bahrain and Dubai in particular have played in the past. The free zones have been the frontier of change and are also beginning to drive change in the rest of the economy. But Dubai, for instance, has in many areas been able to move beyond the "magic bullets" culture to a model of ongoing adaptation, making this ongoing dynamism an important competitive advantage: "Dubai's policy has been to continue to widen the base and increase the scale of activity, focussed on the free-zone cities, in more sophisticated industries, to make Dubai indispensable both to business and international institutions."[49]

Mega-projects 2.0

Even as innovation through free zones appears to maturing, the Gulf penchant for big announcements and mega-projects is far from over. Many aspects of the current Saudi development agenda mirror this practice of redrawing the map through high-profile projects. The amounts of capital expected to be mobilized behind these ventures are unprecedented, with an annual investment target of SAR2trn by 2030, estimated at 30 percent of GDP. The importance assigned to ambitious mega-projects reflects the historic role given to infrastructure as a development driver. But this is now coupled with a more holistic perspective designed to ensure greater impact and productivity. The most ambitious single venture is Neom, which, as a smart city and an innovation hub, is effectively designed to constitute "a vision of what a New Future might look like."[50] The new foundation is expected to operate outside of the existing government framework with its own legal system and judiciary. All energy needs are to be met through renewables, while robots will perform key functions in areas ranging from security and logistics. A stand-alone development away from the main population centers of the Kingdom, Neom is a bid to create a new regional growth hub but also a platform for creative experimentation. Neom's progress has been challenged by an unusually volatile global economic backdrop that has also created a stronger sense of purpose around trailblazing designs and new kinds of funding mechanisms. Effective project management remains critical, but the Gulf region has by now built considerable capacity and experience in infrastructure development.

The renewed focus on sustainable diversification has spawned several other mega-projects with a potentially transformative impact on the Kingdom's future as they set out to boost the quality of life for residents and draw in more tourists. Neom will be coupled with ventures such as The Line, the Oxagon floating industrial city, the Red Sea Project, and the Amaala luxury destination with its own airport. The Trojena project seeks to develop mountain tourism, among other things providing the first outdoor skiing site in the region. The Diriyah Gate project seeks to make the ancient capital the "cultural and heritage capital" of the country. A plan to more than triple the country's rail network by additional 8,000 km of new track will boost connectivity. The National Renewable Energy Program sets out to create 58.7 GW of capacity.[51]

In parallel with the heavy focus on infrastructure, the Saudi government intends to dramatically increase the country's population, potentially to 50–60mn by 2030, half of them non-Saudis. The ambitious Riyadh Strategy 2030 expects the capital's population to double from 7.5mn to 15–20mn by 2030, with the goal of making it one of the top ten city economies in the world that can draw more than 40mn visitors a year. In the longer run, the population could reach 25mn. The plan also involves planting 7.5mn trees to cover 9.1 percent of the city's surface, including the 16 sq km King Salman Park, in a bid to reduce temperatures and dust levels. Neom is expected to accommodate 1.5mn people upon completion in 2030 and some 9mn in 2045.[52] While these plans are ambitious, they are also transformative. Significant progess toward realizing them will create fundmentally new facts on the ground.

Similar plans are afoot region-wide. Notably, the UAE marked its 50th anniversary by unveiling an ambitious "Projects of the 50" agenda. While the plan is heavily focused on an infrastructure buildup, like the Saudi program, it combines extensive development initiatives with a broader strategic perspective. More funding is allocated to business creation in priority sectors to drive productivity-led economic diversification that fosters technology adoption and innovation. By prioritizing productive activities, the projects also seeks to boost Emirati exports to key markets globally. The strategy focuses heavily on boosting national employment in the private sector by setting a minimum target of 10 percent of Emirate employees

– some 75,000 jobs – in private companies within five years. The authorities are facilitating investments in local businesses and projects while also fostering the creation of local value chains through in-country initiatives.[53]

The Gulf countries' determination to build a more sustainable future couples with the long-standing predilection for greenfield over brownfield ventures. Their scale is often no less about reshaping attitudes and building reputations than it is about economics. In many cases, projects compete on capacity and flexibility rather than short-term profitability of asset utilization. In a volatile world, this inevitably involves risks. Fears of "white elephants" in the Gulf go back to Dubai's early diversification ambitions, and concerns about capacity duplication have been present for decades. Yet in some ways, the old concept of "build it and they will come" appears surprisingly vibrant, even adaptable, after multiple economic cycles, provided it is accompanied by real commitment and effective governance.

Did Dubai encourage a "culture of gambling" by betting on projects that were seen as speculative but ultimately winning big? Has this tradition of bold risk-taking dispensed with the perceived need to properly prepare? The tradition of using demographic dynamism and diversification to justify new investments has sometimes delivered miscalculations and poor capital mobilization. However, as an idea, it retains considerable power, not least if the Gulf countries are indeed ready to make immigration a growth driver while further redoubling efforts to boost tourism. For instance, the Saudi Aviation Strategy calls for tripling annual passenger traffic to 330mn by 2030, boosting the number of destinations to 250 from 99 at present, and establishing a new flag carrier. These ambitions are backed by $100bn in investments.

But the Gulf track records also suggests that boldness can pay off in other ways. The region has repeatedly shown itself capable of mobilizing substantial capital behind structural changes previously, or on a scale, unmatched by others. Jebel Ali's early success as a scalable trailblazer of multimodal shipping is a case in point. The substantial amounts of capital available for potentially risky but also transformative investments can allow the Gulf countries to make bets that can at a minimum generate interest and put the region on the radar of new groups of investors and visitors. The increased focus on quality of life – a key plank of the Saudi vision, for instance – can allow projects to deliver substantial intangible benefits almost irrespective of their financial returns. Building "for the future" at its best represents a pre-commitment that creates structure and appropriate incentives around other policies and practices so as to enhance the changes of success. Even when success initially proves elusive, the regional economies have shown themselves increasingly adept at tweaking their approach to enhance performance. Such creative experimentation can also help the Gulf emerge as an innovative hub that, by attracting new residents and capital to the region, can potentially improve the financial calculus around some of the initially less successful ventures.

Regulating for prosperity

Regulation has gained widespread recognition as a strategic development tool in the Gulf region. Early examples for leveraging it for a transformative impact came from Bahrain: the Mina Salman port free trade zone in 1962 and the offshore banking regulations in the 1970s. The exempt companies regulations were used to attract foreign businesses.[54] Proactive regulatory reform as an enabler of growth began to attract renewed attention with the establishment of the Saudi industrial cities of Jubail and Yanbu, as well as Dubai's Jebel Ali free zone.[55]

By establishing a more conducive framework for private businesses, regulatory reform can reduce the heavy reliance on public capital expenditure as the driver of non-oil development. While substantial progress has been achieved in terms of streamlining and overhauling corporate law in the GCC, the situation is far from uniform across the region. Some sectors and geographic areas match best-in-class regulations, while many others continue to be governed by outdated legacy legislation or an uneven patchwork of rules. Much of the region operates with a mixed legacy of different legal cultures and traditions, ranging from Shariah jurisprudence to Egyptian legal traditions (often entrenched by expatriate legal professionals) and English common law. Moreover, many rigidities still exist. As a rule, registered businesses are required to have a unique physical address even if shared offices have gained popularity. Permitting even greater flexibility for many activities makes sense from the perspective of reducing barriers to genuine entrepreneurship, as reflected by Bahrain's "virtual corporate registrations." Similarly, insolvency regulations often remain a challenge. While important reforms have been implemented in recent years, the new practices are not necessarily well established. Very often, winding down a business remains a slow, costly, and potentially punitive process. This also highlights the fact that judicial reform has been making relatively slow progress outside the free zones. Court cases tend to drag on, sometimes for years. There is limited specialization among courts, although the introduction of mediation and arbitration institutions has brought some relief. Regulation in many cases remains overly prescriptive, while development in some areas is hampered by the absence of appropriate enabling regulation.

Quite apart from the letter of the law itself, regulatory and administrative processes often leave much to be desired. With multiple regulators, there is sometimes insufficient attention to integrating and aligning rules and processes. This can give rise to bottlenecks even amid a generally friendly regulatory landscape. Administrative practices can be similarly uneven and even inconsistent. Moreover, there are significant differences in practices around drafting regulations, which can compromise quality and impact. The readiness of some institutions to engage in frequent tweaking and amendments creates the impression of moving goalposts and results in additional costs. Much more can be done to establish proper practices for industry hearings and appropriate independent reviews. Good regulatory practices make regulators accessible and responsive, as demonstrated by some of the free zones, which have successfully established much of their appeal on the quality of regulation and enforcement.

Some Gulf economies have sought to circumvent the limitations of their legal systems through selective modernization. Instead of trying to overhaul their regulations and practices across the board, they have created "oases of opportunity" through regulatory or jurisdictional differentiation. Bespoke regulations have been drafted for many economic clusters, often for the purpose of proactively enabling their development, while the GCC region is currently home to some 60 free zones.[56] Many of them have served as potent magnets for international capital and talent but also as effective instruments of modernization and diversification. By creating controlled conditions for change, they have allowed most established business activity to continue undisturbed. This may have allowed the reform agendas to be less contested by distributional challenges on the part of incumbent businesses. Free zones have also served as an instrument of rent generation, especially in economies with less plentiful hydrocarbons endowments.[57] Sandbox arrangements have been introduced, for instance, by the Central Bank of Bahrain for FinTech. Abu Dhabi, through its Two-Four54 zone, has pioneered creative industries and arts. Free zones have also been used to support the energy transition, starting notably with Masdar City, originally established with the ambition of becoming the region's first carbon neutral urban center. "Selective modernization" holds continuing appeal because it can circumvent regulatory, cultural, and institutional constraints of the "old economy" without immediately necessitating a holistic and potentially controversial overhaul of institutions and practices that have existed for generations.

There have been growing calls, not least by the IMF, for Gulf policymakers to dismantle the legal differentiation between the free zones and their mainstream jurisdictions. Some regional governments have taken successful concepts from free zones and adopted them in their national legislation. Recent reforms in the UAE have focused on attracting foreign talent and capital through reforms of the federal or emirate-level jurisdictions. This is potentially creating a situation where "new economic reforms … threaten to diminish many of the traditional business incentives associated with free zones in the Gulf."[58] Nonetheless, there seems to be a strong political commitment to continue with the practice of jurisdictional fragmentation for now. Dubai's 50-year charter, presented in January 2019, explicitly speaks of "the creation of a geo-economic map within the emirate as a precursor for increasing special economic zones."[59] Besides physical zones, Dubai has launched a Virtual Commercial City program to encourage virtual company registration by entrepreneurs from all over the world. Special zones also figure heavily in the future plans of Saudi Arabia and Oman. The Saudi National Investment Strategy indicates that the free zones will be dedicates to "high-priority sectors" for which they will offer competitive regulation.[60]

While selective modernization looks set to persist for the foreseeable future, the free zones can claim other benefits that may endure even amid regulatory convergence. For instance, the practice of using dedicated zones as magnets for particular types of companies and talent may well prove more effective than a less targeted approach. In effect, they could continue to play a role "as a branding or even super-branding strategy."[61] The free zones are effective instruments of awareness and reputation building. Apart from assurances of continuity, they offer at least the perception of simplicity and predictability by combining well-defined regulations with purpose-built infrastructure, something that many businesses are willing to pay a premium for. This may prove a particular growth opportunity at a time when fiscal consolidation and labor market reforms reshape the main national jurisdictions. Whether there is the readiness to reposition the zones as tax havens is less clear, but this remains an obvious potential opportunity. Free zones can also be used as targeted tool for developing clusters, particular geographic regions, or relations with other countries.

Taking the regulatory frameworks and culture of these ad hoc platforms national is no simple undertaking in view of the challenges associated with many of the legacy legal practices and institutions. Doing so requires not just a one-off overhaul but an inevitable evolutionary cultural shift, likely over many years. It is also important to recognize that regulatory reform cannot be pursued in isolation from other considerations. Economic opportunities, however compelling, are not necessarily aligned with political, social, or cultural realities. The ability to embrace aggressive regulatory innovation will likely vary between countries and will, in some cases, be checked by competing policy agendas and/or significant vested interests.

The GCC economic strategies and regulatory practices will have to balance two important opportunities. On the one hand, the region will have to do more to enhance the productive potential of its local resources through appropriate enabling regulation. On the other, there is an exceptional opportunity to capitalize on flows passing through the Gulf and activities localized by outsiders in the region. In this regard, regulations will serve as an enabler and guarantor of access on predictable terms. But the two axes of change are unlikely to happily coexist without careful policy design. For instance, success as an inter-continential hub may reduce the urgency of extracting value out of regional resources, potentially turning some of them into stranded assets. Similarly, unconditional openness risks delivering local unemployment or creating a population of unproductive rentiers, neither of which builds resilience for the future. Conversely, however, attempts to unduly limit the ability to capitalize on the region's location would challenge one of its most compelling development opportunities. Merely prioritizing local employment or entrepreneurship would risk imposing a degree of autarky on a region that has always thrived on openness, thereby leaving the Gulf far short of realizing its potential. Regulation will have to play a key role in managing the balancing act between these two extremes.

The UAE is widely viewed as the most salient example of a Gulf economy placing its bets on an explicit commitment to openness. While Abu Dhabi can boast ample hydrocarbons reserves, other resources are in limited supply and the native population base historically modest. In the UAE and Qatar, the decision to leverage the locational advantage was a logical response to extremely limited local populations, which otherwise would have constrained the economic potential of a purely resource-based strategy – or, worse, it would have risked creating the prospect of super-rentierism. By embracing a dual approach, the countries could expand the local market and build a stronger foundation for economic diversification. The two countries now have the lowest proportion in the region of citizens in their resident populations. For instance, in 2013, the UAE resident population of 9.2mn included only 1.4mn Emirati citizens. On the other hand, the UAE economy expanded nearly 231 times between the formation of the Federation in 1971 and 2013.

Saudi Arabia represents the opposite end of the spectrum, making up nearly 60 percent of the GCC population and with the lowest percentage of non-citizen residents. Economically activating and educating Saudi nationals must therefore be overriding priorities. Nonetheless, the Saudi private sector has matched the regional norm of systemic dependency on expatriate labor for decades. A progressive departure from past rentierist practices is a key prerequisite for sustainably employing increasing numbers of nationals in the private sector. Better salaries are needed to attract and retain Saudis, while competitive salaries necessitate productivity. The ongoing efforts to develop parts of the country – notably the new economic cities and Neom – on the basis of more liberal regulations are laying the foundation for an explicitly dual-track strategy. But Saudi Arabia is also committed to continuing to overhaul its national regulations. Indeed, the Vision 2030 commits Saudi Arabia to become one of the top ten economies in the Global Competitiveness Index of the World Economic Forum. The 2019 edition ranked the Kingdom 36th globally.[62]

Where there is a will …

Future-proofing the Gulf countries' prosperity remains a work in progress after decades of proactive diversification. Some still argue that the region owes its progress more to luck than to strategy. The serendipitous discovery of oil allowed it to transcend endemic underdevelopment. The malaise of the late 20th century was overcome thanks to a commodity market rally driven by the rise of the emerging markets, above all China. Following the global financial crisis, creative monetary policy globally reignited these dynamics, even if they were to an extent countered by technological innovation, energy efficiency, and the energy transition. In the meantime, many of the region's structural challenges in terms of productivity, labor markets, and innovation have proven painfully persistent. As noted by J.E. Peterson in 2009, "the obstacles today remain eerily similar to those of forty years ago."[63]

It is important to recognize, however, that, extreme as the economic vagaries of the recent decades have been, the Gulf has invariably emerged stronger from them. While the early 21st-century commodities boom helped transform the economic fortunes of the region, it alone cannot explain the depth and breadth of the changes that ensued. Much of the exceptional windfall in 2003–2008 was channeled to restoring macroeconomic health and building savings. The mobilization of private capital benefited from initiatives ranging from privatization to FDI promotion. Important strides have been made in regulatory reform and financial market development alike.

There is a palpable determination among GCC policymakers to build resilience and reduce vulnerabilities. The GCC management of the COVID-19 pandemic gained global recognition. Government revenue diversification is reducing the cyclicality of fiscal policy but also eliminating price distortions, thereby giving rise to more complete and efficient markets. Encouragingly, neither the COVID-19 response nor the management of the post-COVID oil boom has led to meaningful erosion of the commitment to fiscal discipline and long-term strategic development goals. While sovereign issuance is recognized as an enabler of fixed income markets, there is little tolerance of large public debt burdens.[64] In a global economy addicted to leverage, positioning the Gulf through macroeconomic prudence represents a reputational and a competitive advantage. Much evidence suggests that indebtedness increases vulnerability to economic shocks but also depresses investment and innovation, which risks turning short-term crises into an enduring break on growth.

Despite the many impressive forward strides, the speed of refashioning the Gulf economies will almost certainly have to accelerate to deliver on the promise of sustained prosperity. Success is contingent on a credible long-term strategic vision and persistence in implementation. Appropriate flexibility in the face of evolving circumstances is essential, but so is ongoing evaluation of the track record and a willingness to act on the lessons learned. Every forward stride changes the success formula as some areas of achievement pass the point of diminishing returns while new opportunities arise.

Whatever the future may bring, this economic remodeling will have to prioritize a number of structural factors. Encouragingly, these are all now recognized as important planks of policy. Firstly, the drawn-out departure from the critical role of the oil–government nexus must be taken forward past the point of no return. Realizing the ambition of making economic development truly private sector led can only succeed if the public sector is simultaneously proactively repositioned for a more supporting role. The GCC governments are making progress in transitioning from rentier-distributors and default employers of nationals to more dynamic, transparent, and lean organizations. New technologies are being applied to public sector service provision, which is reducing labor intensity. The key challenge going forward is to ensure that this government repurposing becomes a strategic and transformative process, not just an exercise in reactive – and potentially temporary – downsizing in response to fiscal pressures. Technology adoption should not be just a recipe for incremental productivity gains but an opportunity to overhaul the operating model of the public sector on an ongoing basis. To ensure appropriate discipline around this, rules-based fiscal policy is needed to ensure that hydrocarbons windfalls are increasingly neutralized and saved for the future, not used to re-inflate the government. Reapportioning the governments to mirror the non-oil sector dynamics is a logical formula for sustainability. The reality of a leaner public sector should not preclude an opportunity to lead by example. The Gulf governments can be repositioned as efficient, business-friendly regulators relying on advanced technology and disseminating accurate information while providing cost-effective services. This efficiency must extend to communication, the drafting of regulations, and dispute resolution.

For the public sector to assume a supporting posture, the private sector much be ready and able to lead. Above all, this necessitates a regulatory framework that works for businesses while also ensuring a level playing field. The important strides made in regulatory reform should coalesce to a holistic vision that makes business formation, growth, and closure as simple and cost-effective as prudently possibly while encouraging robust governance and transparency. By earning a reputation for excellence in regulation, the region will have succeeded in making enabling regulation a true growth driver. Concurrent with this, the financial sector must live up to its core economic function of efficiently allocating capital across the economy. For this to happen, assets and businesses must be investible with appropriate legal structures and valuation mechanisms. But above all, capital must be available at reasonable cost and on fair terms for productive activities. This necessitates continued product diversification and more efficient markets. FinTech is now opening up new avenues to connect capital with its users through innovations such as crowdsourcing and tokenization. But even the conventional capital markets can do much more to serve the regional private sector.

Many of the opportunities for public sector modernization also apply to the private sector. Technology adoption remains critical for boosting productivity and overhauling business models. A productive private sector will have to break free from the "Gulf paradox" whereby a capital-rich and population-poor region became ever more labor intensive. The decades-long race to the bottom made possible and profitable by easy access to low-cost unskilled labor is incompatible with the regional aspirations of a knowledge-based, innovative economy. The long-standing default attitudes linked to rentierist cost minimization must go since they are antithetical to productivity and a deterrent to innovation. While low-cost labor exists in every economy, it cannot be the default option for businesses if the private sector is to truly drive economic activity. The process of reviewing the relative pricing factors of production for greater efficiency must continue.

Scale has emerged as an issue of growing importance for the Gulf private sector. While economic and fiscal realities have pushed up the minimum efficient scale of companies, popular assumptions about low-cost businesses in retail and hospitality hold enduring appeal. For many, such companies remain a way of generating some extra income rather than establishing corporate ventures dedicated to pursuing growth and profits. But it is obvious that economies of scale can be substantial in many sectors, all the more because of technological disruption. Reaping these benefits is an important precondition for boosting productivity, the scale and quality of private sector employment, as well as innovation. There is a need to culturally popularize alternatives to the traditional default assumption of one-man – or, increasingly, one-woman – business formation. But it is also becoming increasingly important to encourage legal structures that are flexible while fostering the development of private capital markets that can enable more economically efficient decisions. A one-man business should not become a one-way road.

At the macro level, the Gulf economies must build their future prosperity on the available competitiveness drivers while safeguarding and further developing them on a continuous basis. As the region transforms its natural resources into financial capital, it must make sure that the process does not erode national wealth but ideally enhances it further – an important consideration for intergenerational fairness.[65] This has several implications. Firstly, the ongoing fiscal re-engineering is needed to reduce the reliance of recurrent public expenditure on oil and gas revenues. Part of the way forward will come from better cost recovery from public sector service provision and the adoption of more insurance-based solutions. Part of it involves reducing the reliance on governments by encouraging private provision. But there is also a unique and compelling emerging opportunity to embrace the ongoing energy transition to harness renewable energy to generate recurrent income, whether through power or hydrogen exports or by enabling other activities.

Protecting financial wealth also entails judicious investments, whether in domestic diversification opportunities or in strategic global opportunities. But it is important to make sure that domestic investments do not crowd out private capital and have appropriate governance, since very often "state-managed diversification efforts and development activities are slow, inefficient, and biased in one way or another."[66] The continued importance of sovereign and semi-sovereign capital means that efforts to leverage it for development purposes risk turning into systemic dependencies in the absence of proactive countermeasures. Once successful ventures mature, they should be handed over to the private sector and the proceeds reinvested, a process that some of the regional sovereign investors have been leading on in recent years. The evolving policy toolkit around new kinds of partnerships with private capital can become a way of ensuring economic continuity, boosting competition, and reinventing government. International investments should, where possible, be used for additional domestic value creation to extend the remit of returns from the financial to the socio-economic. The ongoing initiatives around electric vehicle manufacturing in Saudi Arabia are an encouraging case in point.

As widespread as the recognition of the benefits of openness is across the Gulf, it cannot be taken for granted. Domestic social and political pressures must be managed to avoid casting doubt on the ability of foreigners to reside and do business in the region. The implications of protectionist pressures elsewhere must be proactively mitigated where possible as they otherwise risk jeopardizing access to the global markets and pushing up the costs of trading. The strategic value of openness must be embedded in domestic policy discussions. Proactive commercial diplomacy is critical for deepening ties to trade partners and minimizing barriers on trade and investment in ways that cannot be easily reversed.[67]

For openness to be a sustainable formula for sucess, it is important to demonstrate that it can deliver meaningful benefits to all relevant stakeholders. Foreign capital and trade must generate quality employment, know-how, and opportunity in the Gulf. A commitment to openness must be harnessed as a guarantor of excellence in infrastructure, regulation, and living conditions by creating the right incentives for prioritizing the quality of life more generally. Even as openness need not be unconditional, it should be explicitly rules-based and effectively enforced while recognizing and respecting the traditions and culture of the Gulf. Such an approach has worked in a number of countries that are prized for their excellence in regulation and known for their prosperity but also viewed as desirable places to live and do business in.

The openness agenda in the Gulf is evolving in important ways in the direction of a strategically anchored immigration policy. Such reforms have grown ever more ambitions as governments have abandoned the one-size-fits-all rules of yesteryear in a bid to more explicitly prioritize skills, experience, and capital. This is partly driven by a desire to retain qualified individuals, something that, for instance, prompted the Qatari authorities to offer foreign professionals long-term residency when a diplomatic dispute with its neigbors triggered an exodus of residents. Saudi Arabia presented the idea of a five-year "green card" in connection with its Vision 2030. Some Gulf economies have made special visas available to investors and entrepreneurs, with the UAE explicitly targeting professional competence and high-net-worth individuals. A 2021 landmark decision made the Emirati citizenship available to exceptionally qualified professionals.[68] Traditionally, GCC legislation tended to allow for naturalization only subject to stringent conditions and with considerable discretion. Under UAE law, a person can ordinarily apply for citizenship after a minimum residency period of 20 years, provided he has no criminal convictions and is proficient in Arabic. In 2019, Oman announced a policy of naturalization following 20 years of residency in the Sultanate. In November 2021, even Saudi Arabia approved a similar scheme.[69] Even as residency policies are changing, it is unrealistic to expect the process to be uniform. Some countries can maintain more restrictive policies while benefiting from the liberalism of their neighbors, provided travel and trade within the region remain easy and free.

There is much debate within the Gulf and beyond about the sustainability of the massive investments made in physical infrastructure. However, quality infrastructure remains a key precondition for transcending the constraints of the home market in a population-poor region. It is also a key differentiating factor, especially vis-à-vis countries that share some of the same locational advantages. In relative terms, such connectivity is far more critical for prosperity in the GCC than for countries with larger populations and more diversified economies. Infrastructure represents an opportunity for the Gulf region – through astute capital mobilization – to safeguard and further enhance its competitive edge. Most physical infrastructure investments are made for decades or even longer. Once in place, they tend to anchor and direct flows, creating facts on the ground that are difficult for others to challenge when strategically safeguarded and developed further.

But the Gulf must "diversify" its diversification policies away from their strong real estate bias, embracing a more strategic posture to replace the "build it and they will come" paradigm. More attention must be given to understanding the needs and expectations on the demand side but, above all, to enhancing the utilization of infrastructure assets through proper alignment with the broader economic strategies. While infrastructure development can almost always be a growth driver in the short run, it can only do this sustainably if it is effectively mobilized to enable other activities. Failing this, market imbalances risk eroding not only asset values but also economic value creation as companies in overcrowded markets see their profits decline. Under the circumstances, a potential growth driver/enabler becomes its opposite.

More can be done to enhance the returns to physical infrastructure investments in the Gulf. Regulation has an important role to play. New developments must incorporate smart infrastructure and design for sustainable value. They must meet appropriate energy efficiency specifications and utilize renewable energy and cost-effective scalable technologies such as district cooling. Similarly, urban planning – the spacing of buildings and the provision of green areas – is needed to ensure that cities can absorb extreme weather events such as heavy rainfall and flooding. Building maintenance standards have to safeguard value. There are obvious opportunities to encourage the smart redevelopment of existing infrastructure; for instance, by rejuvenating older inner cities, which are often delapidated and relegated to dormitories for expatriate laborers. Yet, they offer opportunities to rediscover the past, strengthen the local identity, and offer new experiences to visitors. It is also important to establish an efficient marketplace for physical infrastructure, underpinned by transparency and proper valuation mechanisms. Apart from muting cyclicality and reducing waste, efficient markets will create incentives to upgrade underperforming assets.

The road to realizing the goals of Saudi Vision 2030 and similar ambitions region-wide will be fundamentally different from the earlier chapters of the Gulf development narrative. The two first waves of modern development – the oil–government nexus and the Great Arabian Infrastructure Boom – both delivered very tangible results with remarkable speed. The first propelled the Gulf countries from poverty to prosperity, and the second reshaped the regional cityscapes and integrated Arabia in the global economy as a connective hub par excellence. Cities were transformed and massive infrastructure investments reshaped countries and wove Arabia into an increasingly integrated global economy. This was an era of extensive growth, rapid accumulation of productive resources, and often impressive advances in living standards.

The current economic transition cannot lead to an abrupt departure from past trends. The Gulf remains a demographically dynamic part of the world, surrounded by populous regions with which it is building deeper ties. Economic diversification will channel capital into new areas, while impressive infrastructure projects are continuing to make headway region-wide. Even as strategic priorities shift, the Gulf is continuing to court global fame, now increasingly with ventures such as record-breaking solar farms and new, sustainable communities. Greenfield ventures such as Neom hold continuing appeal because they offer a way to transcend the constraints of the "old economy." An integral aspect of agility is the ability to explore new ventures whose viability can only be established through a trial run.

But building a sustainable future is not about magic bulllets. Productivity as a growth driver is unlikely to generate a multitude of the kinds of headline-grabbing manifestations of progress the Gulf has grown accustomed to. Rather, it is about working more effectively and consistently at all levels. The goal is to enable people to learn better, encourage high levels of productive economic participation and create stronger and, above all, more dynamic businesses. The way forward has to be multipronged, balanced, and strategically anchored in the region's economic assets and realities. Agility as a guarantor of competitiveness will matter across the board in a world of endemic uncertainty.

It is too soon to accurately discern the parameters of future success in the Gulf, but a firm commitment to openness and excellence in regulation will have to unequivocally constitute its central foundation. There is little reason to believe that the Gulf region could not carve out an important niche as a preferred hub for all manner of flows at the heart of the Old World, as well as an attractive complement to the populous economies that flank Arabia. Apart from cementing and further developing its status as a hub, the Gulf faces obvious opportunities to project its prosperity and success to facilitate a broader transformation in the adjacent geographies as well. In 2012, Richard Youngs commented on the Gulf as "a forgotten emerging power" in the emerging global order.[70] Whether the region today is on the cusp of greatness remains to be seen. But it looks unlikely that the oversight of early 21st-century commentators will be repeated in conversation about its place in the global economic order. The forward-looking focus of today, backed up by growing confidence and global recognition, reflects a determination to position the region for a role as a dynamic nave of the global economy. While there is much unfinished business, the Gulf todays possesses not just the vision but also the means through an increasingly versatile toolkit to build a future that is about much more than energy and infrastructure and, indeed, to build the foundation for sustainable prosperity.

Notes

1 Quoted in: Burke and Bazoobandi, "The Gulf Takes Charge," p. 23.
2 Mosis, *Navigating the Energy Transition*, p. 4.
3 World Bank, "COVID-19 Pandemic," p. 42.
4 Peterson, "Life after Oil," pp. 11–12.
5 Wilson, *Economic Development*, p. 2.
6 S&P Global Ratings, "Expat Exodus"; National Bank of Kuwait, "Kuwait: Population Increased in 1H22, though Still Well below Pre-Covid Peak," *Population and Labor*, 26 October 2022.
7 meed.com.
8 Kotilaine, *Trials of Resilience*, pp. 169–172.
9 Azzam, *The Gulf Economies*, p. 33.
10 Butler, "Tomorrow's World," p. 33.
11 World Bank, "COVID-19 Pandemic," pp. 42–47.
12 IMF, *Economic Prospects and Policy Challenges*, p. 19.
13 Mitra *et al.*, *Avoiding the New Mediocre*, pp. xi, 9–10, 16.
14 Dieppe, *Global Productivity*, p. i.20.
15 IMF, *Economic Prospects and Policy Challenges*, pp. 25–27.
16 Cusolito and Maloney, *Productivity Revisited*, p. 27; Dieppe, *Global Productivity*, pp. i.6, i.20.
17 Dieppe, *Global Productivity*, p. 115.
18 magnitt.com.

19 Mosis, *Navigating the Energy Transition*, p. 9.
20 S&P Global Ratings, "GCC Low-Cost Producers May Be Better Placed."
21 Seznec and Mosis, *The Energy Transition in the Arab Gulf*, p. 10.
22 Mosis, *Navigating the Energy Transition*, p. 7.
23 Mosis, *Navigating the Energy Transition*, p. 9.
24 Seznec and Mosis, *The Energy Transition in the Arab Gulf*, p. 16; Seznec, "The Saudi Aramco–SABIC Merger," pp. 2–4.
25 Seznec and Mosis, *The Energy Transition in the Arab Gulf*, pp. 15–16, 23.
26 Mosis, *Navigating the Energy Transition*, p. 12.
27 IRENA, *Renewable Energy Market Analysis*, 2016, p. 13.
28 Seznec and Mosis, *The Energy Transition in the Arab Gulf*, pp. 19–21.
29 Seznec and Mosis, *The Energy Transition in the Arab Gulf*, p. 11.
30 World Bank, "Green Growth Opportunities," p. 24.
31 World Bank, "Green Growth Opportunities," p. 25.
32 World Bank, "Green Growth Opportunities," p. 33.
33 "A Very Big Balancing Act," *The Economist*, 9–15 October 2021, p. 20.
34 MENA Hydrogen Alliance & Roland Berger, *The Potential for Green Hydrogen*, pp. 10–11.
35 "A Very Big Balancing Act," *The Economist*, October 9th–15th, 2021, p. 19.
36 Mosis, *Navigating the Energy Transition*, p. 13; Seznec and Mosis, *The Energy Transition in the Arab Gulf*, p. 15.
37 MENA Hydrogen Alliance & Roland Berger, *The Potential for Green Hydrogen*, p. 18.
38 MENA Hydrogen Alliance & Roland Berger, *The Potential for Green Hydrogen*, p. 7.
39 MENA Hydrogen Alliance & Roland Berger, *The Potential for Green Hydrogen*, pp. 12–16, 23.
40 Seznec and Mosis, *The Energy Transition in the Arab Gulf*, p. 15.
41 Ma'aden, *Global Ambitions with Resilient Sustainability: Ma'aden Annual Report 2020*, pp. 78, 82, 87.
42 Peterson, "Life after Oil, p. 15.
43 "Saudi Arabia to Auction Mining Lincenses in 2022," https://www.arabnews.com/node/1878706/business-economy.
44 https://www.seafoodsource.com/news/aquaculture/new-hatchery-boosts-saudi-arabia-s-ambitious-seafood-plan.
45 Woertz, "Gulf Sovereign Wealth Funds," pp. 233–236.
46 Nuttall, *Shipping and Development in Dubai*, p. 47.
47 Kamal and Trines, "Education in the United Arab Emirates."
48 Wilson, *Economic Development*, p. 2.
49 Nuttall, *Shipping and Development in Dubai*, p. 83.
50 Quoted in: Mogielnicki, *A Political Economy of Free Zones*, p. 229.
51 Ian Oxborrow, "Saudi Megaprojects 2022: From The Line at Neom to the Red Sea Project," *The National*, 17 August 2022; Marian Nihal, "Saudi National Day: Eight Mega-Projects Shaping the Kingdom's Future," *The National*, 21 September 2022.
52 "Crown Prince Expects Saudi Arabia's Population to Reach 50–60 Million by 2030," *argaam*, 26 July 2022; David Kane, "Saudi Crown Prince Unveils Plan to Make Riyadh One of World's 10 Largest City Economies," *Arab News*, 29 January 2021; "Saudi Crown Prince Reviews Riyadh Strategy 2030," *TradeArabia*, 27 December 2021.
53 https://u.ae/en/about-the-uae/initiatives-of-the-next-50/projects-of-the-50.
54 Mogielnicki, *A Political Economy of Free Zones*, pp. 109–111.
55 Akinci and Crittle, *Special Economic Zones*, p. 43.
56 Mogielnicki, *A Political Economy of Free Zones*, pp. 244–249.
57 Mogielnicki, *A Political Economy of Free Zones*, pp. 235–237.
58 Mogielnicki, *A Political Economy of Free Zones*, p. 227.
59 Mogielnicki, *A Political Economy of Free Zones*, p. 228.
60 https://www.bloomberg.com/news/articles/2021-10-11/saudi-arabia-plans-to-create-special-economic-zones-to-raise-fdi.

61 Peterson, "Life after Oil," p. 9.
62 WEF, *The Global Competitiveness Report 2019*, p. xiii.
63 Peterson, "Life after Oil," p. 1.
64 IMF, *Middle East and Central Asia – Regional Economic Outlook July 2020 Update*, p. 8.
65 Heal, "Are Oil Producers Rich?"
66 Peterson, "Life after Oil," p. 2.
67 Jarmo T. Kotilaine, "Gulf Nations' Great Recalibration," *Arab News*, 23 October 2022.
68 https://u.ae/en/information-and-services/passports-and-traveling/emirati-nationality.
69 https://www.arabnews.com/node/1966146/saudi-arabia.
70 Youngs, "The Gulf in the New World Order," p. 5.

References

Akinci, Gokhan and James Crittle (2008), *Special Economic Zones: Performance, Lessons Learned, and Implications for Zone Development*, Washington, D.C.: The World Bank Group.

Azzam, Henry T. (1988), *The Gulf Economies in Transition*, London: Macmillan Press.

Burke, Edward and Sara Bazoobandi (2012), "The Gulf Takes Charge: The GCC in the MENA Region," in: Youngs, *op. cit.*, pp. 23–44.

Butler, Declan (2016), "Tomorrow's World," *Nature*, vol. 530 (25 February), pp. 398–401.

Cusolito, Ana Paula and William F. Maloney (2018), *Productivity Revisited: Shifting Paradigms in Analysis and Policy*, Washington, D.C.: World Bank Group.

Dieppe, Alistair, ed. (2020), *Global Productivity: Trends, Drivers, and Policies*, Advance Edition, Washington, D.C.: World Bank Group.

Heal, Geoffrey (2007), "Are Oil Producers Rich?," in: Humphreys *et al.*, *op. cit.*, pp. 155–173.

Humphreys, Macartan, Jeffrey Sachs, and Joseph E. Stiglitz, eds. (2007), *Escaping the Resource Curse*, New York: Columbia University Press.

International Monetary Fund (2020), *Economic Prospects and Policy Challenges for the GCC Countries*, Gulf Cooperation Council/IMF Policy Paper, Annual Meeting of Ministers of Finance and Central Bank Governors, 25 October 2020, Virtual Meeting, Washington, D.C.: International Monetary Fund.

——— (2020), *Regional Economic Outlook July 2020 Update: Middle East and Central Asia*, Washington, D.C.: International Monetary Fund.

International Renewable Energy Agency (2016), *Renewable Energy Market Analysis: The GCC Region*, Abu Dhabi: International Renewable Energy Agency.

——— (2019), *Renewable Energy Market Analysis: GCC 2019*, Abu Dhabi: International Renewable Energy Agency.

Kamal, Kevin and Stefan Trines (2018), "Education in the United Arab Emirates," *World Education News & Reviews*, 10 August 2018, https://wenr.wes.org/2018/08/education-in-the-united-arab-emirates.

Kotilaine, Jarmo T. (2021), *Trials of Resilience: How Covid-19 Is Driving Economic Change in the Arab Gulf*, London: Gilgamesh Publishing.

MENA Hydrogen Alliance & Roland Berger (2021), *The Potential for Green Hydrogen in the GCC Region*, May 2021.

Mitra, Pritha, Amr Hosny, Gohar Minasyan, Mark Fischer, and Gohar Abajyan (2016), *Avoiding the New Mediocre: Raising Long-Term Growth in the Middle East and Central Asia*, Washington, D.C.: Middle East and Central Asia Department, International Monetary Fund.

Mogielnicki, Robert (2021), *A Political Economy of Free Zones in Gulf Arab States (International Political Economy Series)*, London: Palgrave Macmillan.

Mosis, Samer Joseph (2020), *Navigating the Energy Transition: How Gulf NOCs Can Weigh in on the Climate Crisis*, Washington, D.C.: Gulf International Forum.

National Bank of Kuwait (2022), "Kuwait: Population Increased in 1H22, though Still Well below Pre-Covid Peak," *Population and Labor*.

Nuttall, Keith (2021), *Shipping and Development in Dubai: Infrastructure, Innovation and Institutions in the Gulf*, London: I.B. Tauris.

Peterson, John E. (2009), "Life after Oil: Economic Alternatives for the Arab Gulf States," *Mediterranean Quarterly*, vol. 20, no. 3, pp. 1–18.

S&P Global Ratings (2021), "Credit FAQ: GCC Low-Cost Producers May Be Better Placed than Most Oil and Gas Majors as the Energy Transition Heats Up," Comments, 27 September 2021.

Seznec, Jean-François (2020), "The Saudi Aramco–SABIC Merger: How Acquiring SABIC Fits into Aramco's Long-Term Diversification Strategy," Issue Brief, Washington, D.C.: Atlantic Council: Global Energy Center, January 2020.

Seznec, Jean-François and Samer Mosis (2021), *The Energy Transition in the Arab Gulf: From Vision to Reality*, Washington, D.C.: Atlantic Council: Global Energy Center.

Wilson, Rodney with Abdullah Al-Salamah, Monica Malik, and Ahmed Al-Rajhi (2004), *Economic Development in Saudi Arabia*, London: RoutledgeCurzon.

Woertz, Eckart, ed. (2012), *GCC Financial Markets: The World's New Money Centers (The Gulf Region: Economic Development and Diversification*, vol. 3), Berlin: Gerlach Press.

——— (2012), "Gulf Sovereign Wealth Funds in International Comparison," in: Woertz, *op. cit.*, pp. 229–254.

World Bank (2021), "COVID-19 Pandemic and the Road to Diversification," *Gulf Economic Update*, No. 6, August 2021, Washington, D.C.: World Bank Group.

Youngs, Richard, ed. (2012), *The GCC in the Global Economy (The Gulf Region: Economic Development and Diversification*, vol. 1), Berlin: Gerlach Press.

——— (2012), "The Gulf in the New World Order," in Youngs, *op. cit.*, pp. 5–22.

Index